Batsford Chess Library

The Complete Benoni

LEV PSAKHIS

Translated by Sarah J. Young

An **Owl** Book
Henry **H**olt and Company
New **Y**ork

D0920306

Henry Holt and Company, Inc.
Publishers since 1866
115 West 18th Street
New York, New York 10011

Henry Holt® is a registered
trademark of Henry Holt and Company, Inc.

First published in the United States in 1995 by
Henry Holt and Company, Inc.
Originally published in Great Britain in 1995 by
B. T. Batsford Ltd.

Library of Congress Catalog Card Number: 94-72763
ISBN 0-8050-3904-X (An Owl Book: pbk.)

First American Edition—1995

Printed in the United Kingdom
All first editions are printed on acid-free paper.∞

10 9 8 7 6 5 4 3 2 1

Contents

Symbols

+	Check
++	Double check
#	Checkmate
$\pm$ ($\mp$)	Slight advantage to White (Black)
$\pm$ ($\mp$)	Clear advantage to White (Black)
+– (–+)	Winning advantage to White (Black)
Δ	Intending
=	Level position
∞	Unclear position
!	Good move
?	Bad move
!!	Outstanding move
??	Blunder
!?	Interesting move
?!	Dubious move
Ch	Championship
Cht	Team championship
tt	Team tournament
jr	Junior Event
wom	Women's event
rpd	Rapidplay
Wch	World Championship
Z	Zonal
IZ	Interzonal
Ct	Candidates
OL	Olympiad
Corr	Postal game
(D)	Diagram follows

Introduction

Winning with Black is no easy matter, especially in this day of high level technique. Against 1 e4 there are options such as the Sicilian Defence, but what is it possible to do against 1 d4?

I faced this problem before the critical game with Yuri Balashov in the penultimate round of the 1980 Soviet Championship. I was fighting for the Soviet title and it seemed to me that my Queen's Indian Defence would bring a draw at best, and perhaps only after a difficult defence. I eventually decided to play the Modern Benoni and the rest, as they say, was history.

Despite its risky reputation, I can say that after 15 years' experience with this defence, it is certainly no worse than any other and has a definite plus in that it does not allow White an easy life. My own results have been exceptional: from over 60 games I scored 70 percent, losing only four games. Amongst my opponents were the likes of Gligorić, Khalifman, Polugaevsky, Beliavsky and Tukmakov, and those few defeats could not be blamed on my positions from the opening. For rating enthusiasts, my career Benoni performance comes out at 2635, which with Black is quite a success.

Recently White has favoured Taimanov's plan of 7 f4 and 8 ♗b5+ (Chapter 8), against which I had not had the youthful enthusiasm to defend for some five years. These days I only play the Benoni after 1 d4 ♘f6 2 c4 e6 3 ♘f3 and now 3...c5, which cuts out this and other worrying plans. Of course most players are now using the plan of ♗d3 and h3 (Chapter 11), which has caused Black some trouble. But there are signs that the teeth are being drawn from this system, after which the Benoni may be set for a full-scale comeback.

I hope that after reading this book you will be inspired to march into battle and fight to the death, in the style of Mikhail Tal and the other Benoni specialists. This is definitely not an opening for cowards. As the ancient Spartans' wives used to say, as they marched to war with their shields in hand: "Either with it or upon it."

Lev Psakhis
Hertzliya 1994

1 A60: Rare Moves

1	d4	♞f6
2	c4	c5
3	d5	e6

There are three principal ideas in this chapter:

A) Lines without early ♞c3.
B) 4 ♞c3: Early deviations.
C) The 'Snake' Benoni (...♝d6).

Firstly we should mention that White cannot to achieve an advantage with 4 dxe6 fxe6 5 g3 (or 5 ♝g5 d5 6 e4 h6 7 ♝xf6 ♛xf6 8 exd5 exd5 9 cxd5 ♝d6 with compensation) 5...♞c6 6 ♝g2 d5 7 ♞h3 d4 8 ♞f4 ♝d6 9 ♞d3 h6 10 e4 e5 Mochalov-Tseshkovsky, Minsk 1982.

A) Lines without early ♞c3

4 g3

After 4 ♞f3 exd5 5 cxd5 *(D)* White has a few ideas to try to benefit from delaying developing the knight to c3, for example:

a) For 5...♝d6, see C.

b) White has an advantage after 5...g6 6 e4!? ♞xe4?! (for 6...d6!? see 5...d6) 7 ♝d3 ♞d6 8 0-0 ♝e7 9 ♝h6 f6 10 ♞c3 ♚f7 11 h4 ♞a6 12 ♛d2, Murey-Grünfeld, Jerusalem 1986.

c) White has a pleasant game after 5...b5 6 ♛c2 (6 d6!?) 6...♝b7 7 e4 ♛e7 8 ♞bd2 ♝xd5 9 ♝xb5 ♝xe4 10 ♞xe4 ♛xe4+ 11 ♛xe4+ ♞xe4 12 0-0 ♞d6 13 ♝a4 ♝e7 14 ♜e1, Polugaevsky-Beliavsky, Las Palmas 1974.

d) 5...d6 6 e4 (for 6 ♞c3 see 4 ♞c3) 6...g6 7 ♝d3 (for 7 ♞c3!? see A70) 7...♝g7 8 0-0 0-0 9 h3 (or 9 ♜e1 ♜e8 10 ♞bd2 ♝g4 11 h3 ♝xf3 12 ♞xf3 ♞bd7 13 ♝f4 ♛b6 14 ♞d2 ♞h5 15 ♞c4 ♛d8 16 ♝h2 ♞e5 = Murey-Grünfeld, Beersheba 1985) and now Black has two reasonable methods:

d1) 9...c4 10 ♝c2 ♞a6 (10...b5!? 11 a3 a5 12 ♞c3 ♝a6 13 ♞d4 b4 14 ♞cb5 ♞bd7 ∞ Razuvaev-Wahls, Berlin 1987) 11 ♞c3 ♝d7 12 ♝f4 ♞e8 13 a3 ♞c5 14 ♜e1 b5 15 e5 dxe5 16 ♝xe5 ♝xe5 17 ♞xe5 ♞d6 = Lisik-Dukhov, Russian Cht 1992.

d2) 9...b5 10 ♜e1 and now Black should play 10...c4 11 ♝c2 (or 11 ♝f1 ♜e8 12 a4 b4 13 ♝xc4 ♞xe4 14 a5 ♝a6 15 ♛c2 ♞c5 16 ♜xe8+ ♛xe8 17 ♞bd2 ♞bd7 = P.Cramling-Winants, Brussels tt 1987) 11...♞a6

12 ♘c3 ♗d7 13 a4 b4 14 ♘b5 ♗xb5 15 axb5 ♘c5 with mutual chances in Van der Wiel-Winants, Dutch Cht 1987. Instead the error 10...♗d7?! dooms Black to a difficult defence after 11 a4! bxa4 (11...c4 12 ♗f1!) 12 ♗f4 ♗e8 13 ♘c3 a5 14 ♘d2 ♘h5 15 ♗h2 ± Zsu.Polgar-Romanishin, Biel 1987.

4   ...   exd5
5 cxd5

This position often arises from the Catalan move-order 1 d4 ♘f6 2 c4 e6 3 g3 c5 4 d5 exd5 5 cxd5.

5   ...   b5 (D)

This move gives the game an original character. Alternatives:

a) 5...d6 6 ♗g2 g6 7 e4 (7 ♘c3!? ♗g7 8 ♘f3 0-0 merely transposes to A62) 7...♗g7 looks reasonable: 8 ♘e2 0-0 9 0-0 ♖e8 10 ♘ec3 b5!? 11 ♘xb5 (11 e5!?) 11...♘xe4 12 ♖e1 a6 13 ♘5c3 ♘xc3 14 ♖xe8+ ♕xe8 15 ♘xc3 ♘d7 with equality; Volzhin-Tunik, Katowice 1992.

b) If however Black plays 5...g6 6 ♗g2 ♗g7 7 ♘c3 0-0, then the correct move is probably 8 ♘f3 when 8...b5 (for 8...d6!? see A62) 9 ♘xb5 ♕a5+ 10 ♘c3 ♘e4 11 ♗d2 ♘xd2 12 ♘xd2 d6 13 0-0 ♘d7 14 ♘de4 ♖b8 15 ♕c2 ± Kakhiani-G.Kuzmin, Helsinki 1992, favours White. Instead the ambitious 8 d6 creates no problems for Black, for example 8...♘c6 9 ♘h3 (or 9 ♘f3 ♖b8 10 ♗e3 b6 11 0-0 ♗b7 12 ♕d2 ♘a5 13 ♗g5 ♕e8 14 ♖ad1 ♘e4 ∓ Poluliakhov-Arkhipov, Moscow 1992) 9...b6 10 0-0 ♗b7 11 e4 ♘e8 12 ♗g5 f6 13 ♗e3 ♕b8 14 ♘b5 ♔h8 15 ♘f4

♘e5 with a complicated game; Savchenko-G.Kuzmin, St. Petersburg 1992.

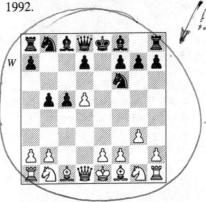

6 ♗g2

Black has no problems after:

a) 6 e4 ♘xe4 7 ♕e2 ♕e7 8 ♗g2 ♘d6 9 ♗e3 b4 10 ♗xc5 ♕xe2+ 11 ♘xe2 ♘a6 12 ♗d4 ♘f5 = Sosonko-F.Olafsson, Wijk aan Zee 1977.

b) 6 a4 b4 7 f3 g6 8 e4 ♗g7 9 ♘d2 0-0 10 ♘c4 d6 11 ♗f4 ♗a6! 12 ♕d2 (unfortunately 12 ♗xd6 doesn't work because of 12...♗xc4 13 ♗xf8 ♗xf1 14 ♗xg7 ♗g2 15 ♗xf6 ♕xf6 16 ♖b1 ♗xh1 17 ♔f2 ♘d7 18 ♘h3 ♖e8 with a big advantage to Black – Ftačnik) 12...♗xc4 13 ♗xc4 ♕e7 14 ♖c1 ♘h5 15 ♗g5 f6 16 ♗e3 f5, Korchnoi-Timman, Tilburg 1987.

6   ...   d6
7 b4!?

This is the only move which lays any claim to an advantage. White has also tried:

a) 7 a4 b4 8 ♘d2 (Black quickly gained an advantage in Beim-Dautov, Berlin 1991, after 8 ♘h3?! g6 9 0-0 ♗g7 10 ♘d2 ♘bd7 11 e4 ♗a6

12 Rel 0-0 13 f4 Re8 14 ᐃf2 c4! with initiative) 8...g6 9 ᐃc4 (Black need not fear 9 ᐃgf3 ♗a6 10 ♕c2 ♗g7 11 ᐃc4 0-0 12 0-0 Re8 13 ᐃe1 ♗xc4 14 ♕xc4 ᐃbd7 15 a5 ♕e7 16 ᐃd3 ᐃe5 = Ragozin-Botvinnik, Sverdlovsk 1943) 9...♗a6 10 ♕d3 ♗g7 11 ♕e3+ ♔f8 12 ♕f4 ♗xc4 13 ♕xc4 ᐃbd7 14 a5! ᐃe8 = Henley-Seirawan, Indonesia 1983.

b) 7 ᐃf3 g6 (7...♗e7 8 ᐃfd2 0-0 9 a4 b4 10 ᐃc4 ♗a6 11 ᐃbd2 ᐃbd7 12 b3 ᐃb6 = Vanheste-Timman, Dutch Cht 1987, is not bad either) 8 ᐃfd2 (or 8 0-0 ♗g7 9 a4 b4 10 ᐃbd2 ♗a6 11 ♕c2 ᐃbd7 12 Re1 0-0 13 e4 ᐃg4! with the initiative to Black in Kouatly-Stean, Lucerne OL 1982) 8...ᐃbd7 9 ᐃc3 a6 10 a4 b4 11 ᐃce4 a5 12 ♕b3 ♗e7 13 ᐃc4 ᐃxe4 14 ♗xe4 ᐃb6 = Portisch-Korchnoi, Lucerne OL 1982.

c) 7 e4 ♗b7 (7...g6 8 ♕e2!? gives Black extra possibilities, for example 8...ᐃbd7 9 f4!? ♗g7 10 e5 0-0 11 exf6 Re8 12 fxg7 Rxe2+ 13 ᐃxe2 ♕e7 14 ♔f2 ᐃf6 15 Re1 ♗b7 16 ᐃa3! ± Plaskett-Groszpeter, Thessaloniki OL 1984) 8 ᐃf3 (or 8 a4 b4 9 ᐃd2 g6 10 a5 ♗a6! 11 ♗f1 ♗g7 12 ♕a4+ ♕d7 = Davies-Onishchuk, Budapest 1993) 8...g6 (after 8...ᐃxe4 9 0-0 ᐃf6 10 ♕e2+ ♕e7 11 ♕xb5+ ♕d7 12 ᐃc3 ᐃxd5 13 ᐃd4! cxd4 14 ♕xd7+ ᐃxd7 15 ᐃxd5 ♗xd5 16 ♗xd5 Rb8 17 b3 White has more than enough compensation for the pawn – Ulybin) 9 0-0 ♗g7 10 e5 dxe5 11 ᐃxe5 0-0 12 ᐃc6 ♕b6 13 ᐃe7+ ♔h8 14 ᐃc3 ᐃbd7 and Black had no cause for

alarm in the game Ulybin-Izeta, Mesa 1993.

d) 7 a3 a5 8 ᐃc3 ♕b6 9 ᐃf3 ♗e7 10 0-0 0-0 11 e4 ᐃbd7 12 Re1 ♗a6 13 ♗f4 (13 e5 dxe5 14 ᐃxe5 ᐃxe5 15 Rxe5 Rfe8 16 ♗g5 h6 = Larsen-Tal, Bled Ct (3) 1965) 13...ᐃg4! = Larsen-Tal, Bled Ct (7) 1965.

7 ...   ᐃa6 (D)

White has an easy and pleasant game if Black accepts the pawn sacrifice, for example 7...cxb4 8 a3 bxa3 (8...b3 9 ♕xb3 a6 10 a4 bxa4 11 ♕xa4+ ᐃbd7 12 ᐃf3 ♗e7 13 ᐃd4 0-0 14 ᐃc6 ♕e8 15 ♗e3 ± Alburt-I.Ivanov, New York 1983) 9 ᐃxa3 ♕d7 (9...g6 10 ᐃxb5 ♗g7 11 ᐃf3 0-0 12 ᐃfd4 ♗b7 13 ᐃc3 ᐃbd7 14 0-0 ᐃb6 15 e4 ± Agzamov-Chernin, Riga 1985) 10 ♕b3 ᐃa6 11 ♕xb5 Rb8 12 ♕xd7+ ♗xd7 13 ᐃc2 ᐃc5 14 Rxa7 ♗e7 (14...Rb1 15 Ra8+! ♔e7 16 Ra1) 15 ᐃf3 ᐃxd5 16 ᐃfd4 ᐃc3 17 ᐃc6 ± Sosonko-Adorjan, Wijk aan Zee 1984.

	W	

8	bxc5	ᐃxc5
9	ᐃf3	g6
10	ᐃd4	♗g7
11	0-0	a6

12 ♘c6

12 ♘c3 0-0 13 ♘c6 ♕c7 14 ♗e3 ♗b7 15 ♗d4 ♖fe8 16 a4! ± Kasparov-Korchnoi, London Ct (11) 1983, is not bad either.

12 ... ♕d7
13 ♘c3 0-0

Now White should play 14 ♗e3!? ± instead of 14 a4?! ♘fe4 15 ♘xe4 ♘xe4 16 ♗f4 ♘c3 with an unclear game in Gelfand-Chernin, Dortmund 1990.

B) 4 ♘c3: Early deviations

4 ♘c3 exd5
5 cxd5 (D)

The other capture, 5 ♘xd5, is not dangerous for Black, for example 5...♘xd5 6 ♕xd5 ♘c6 7 ♘f3 d6 8 e4 ♗e6 9 ♕d1 ♗e7 10 ♗d3 0-0 11 0-0 a6 12 ♗f4 ♗f6 = S.Nikolić-Rogers, Moscow GMA 1989.

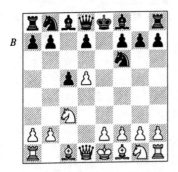

B

5 ... g6

5...d6 will generally lead us into the main lines given later in this book. After 6 ♘f3 (6 h4?! a6 7 a4 g6 8 ♘h3 ♗g7 9 ♘f4 0-0 10 h5 ♘bd7 11 hxg6 fxg6 12 f3 ♘e5 13 ♔f2 c4!

∓ Gurgenidze-Rashkovsky, USSR 1976, and 6 g3 g6 7 h4?! ♗g7 8 ♘h3 a6 9 ♘f4 h6 10 ♗g2 0-0 11 ♗d2 b5 12 ♕c1 b4 13 ♘d1 ♘bd7 ∓ S.Nikolić-Sax, Smederevska Palanka 1982, don't deserve much attention) 6...g6 we find ourselves within the framework of A61, whilst 6...♗e7 7 g3 (or 7 e4 0-0 8 ♗e2 ♘bd7 9 0-0 a6 10 a4 b6 11 ♗f4 ♗b7 12 ♘d2 ♖e8 13 ♗g3 ♗f8 14 f4 ± Bilek-Korchnoi, Hamburg 1965) 7...0-0 8 ♗g2 ♖e8 9 0-0 ♗f8 10 ♗f4 (White also has an advantage after 10 ♘d2 ♘a6 11 ♘c4 ♖b8 12 a4 ♘b4 13 e4 b6 14 ♗f4 ♗a6 15 b3 g6 16 ♖e1 Chernin-Murey, Paris 1989) 10...♘a6 11 ♖e1 h6 12 e4 g5 13 ♗d2 g4 14 ♘h4 c4 15 ♕c1! ♔h7 16 ♕b1!? ♔g8 17 ♗f1 ± A.Kuzmin-Murey, Moscow 1989 is of very little interest from the theoretical point of view.

6 ♘f3 ♗g7

This attempt to omit ...d6 is very risky.

7 d6!?

7 ♗g5 h6 8 ♗h4 ♕a5 9 ♘d2 0-0 10 e3 ♕b4 11 ♗g3 ♘h5 12 ♕c2 ± also looks reasonable, and similarly 7 e4 0-0 8 ♗g5 (if 8 ♗e2 then the correct move would be 8...d6!? – see A74 – whilst 8...b5 9 e5 ♘g4 10 ♗f4 ♖e8 11 ♘xb5 ♘xe5 12 ♘xe5 ♗xe5 13 ♗xe5 ♖xe5 14 0-0 d6 15 ♖e1 a6 16 ♘a3 ♖a7 17 ♘c4 gave White a small but stable advantage in Burger-D.Gurevich, Reykjavik 1982) 8...♖e8 (8...h6 9 ♗h4 ♖e8 10 ♗d3!?, but not 10 ♗e2?! g5 11 ♗g3 ♘xe4 12 ♘xe4 ♖xe4 13 0-0 d6 14 ♗d3

罩b4 15 b3 f5! ∓ Polajzer-Djurić, Ljubljana 1981) 9 ♗d3 h6 10 ♗e3 d6 11 0-0 a6 12 a4 ♘g4 13 ♗f4 ♕f6 14 ♗g3 ♘d7 15 ♗e2 ♕e7 16 ♘d2 ± Kožul-T.Horvath, Frankfurt 1990.

| **7** | **...** | **0-0** |
| **8** | **e4** | **罩e8** |

Or 8...♘c6 9 ♗c4 b5 10 ♘xb5 ♘xe4 11 0-0 ♗b7 12 罩e1 ± Alburt-Kudrin, USA 1984.

| **9** | **♗c4** | **b5** |

9...♘xe4 10 ♗xf7+! ♔xf7 11 ♕d5+ ♔f8 12 ♘xe4.

10	**♗d5**	**♘c6**
11	**0-0**	**b4**
12	**♘b5**	**♗a6**
13	**♘c7**	**♗xf1**
14	**♔xf1**	**罩c8**
15	**♗xc6**	**dxc6**
16	**♘xe8**	**♕xe8**
17	**e5**	

White wields the initiative; Vaganian-Suba, Kecskemet 1979.

C) The Snake Benoni

1 d4 ♘f6 2 c4 c5 3 d5 e6

| **4** | **♘c3** | |

After 4 ♘f3 exd5 5 cxd5 ♗d6 White should generally continue with 6 ♘c3, transposing to the main line. Another possibility is 6 g3 0-0 7 ♗g2 ♗e7 8 0-0 d6 9 ♘fd2 a6 10 a4 ♘bd7 11 ♘c4 ♘b6 12 b3 罩e8 13 ♘c3 罩b8 14 h3 ♗d7 15 ♗f4 with a minimal advantage; Chuchelov-Kalinichev, Bundesliga 1993.

| **4** | **...** | **exd5** |
| **5** | **cxd5** | **♗d6** (D) |

This strange-looking move is characteristic of the Snake Benoni.

| **6** | **♘f3** | |

White must be careful, e.g. 6 e4 0-0 7 f4?! ♘xe4! 8 ♘xe4 罩e8 9 ♕e2 ♗f8 10 g4 (10 f5 ♕h4+) 10...d6 11 f5 ♗xf5 12 gxf5 ♕h4+ 13 ♔d1 罩xe4 and Black gets a dangerous attack; Hebden-Hector, Nantes 1987.

Another option for White is 6 g3. Then Black may try:

a) 6...♗c7?! 7 d6 ♗a5 8 ♗g2 0-0 9 ♘h3 ♘c6 10 0-0 罩e8 11 ♘d5 罩e6 12 ♘g5! favours White; Knaak-Hector, Kecskemet 1987.

b) In Nesis-Mojzić, Corr 1992, White gained a winning attack after his opponent's mistake: 6...a6 7 ♗g2 0-0 8 ♘f3 b5 9 ♗g5 ♕e7?! (9...罩e8!?) 10 ♘h4! c4 11 0-0 罩e8 12 ♘f5 ♕f8 13 ♗xf6 gxf6 14 ♘e4 ♗e5 15 e3! +-.

c) 6...0-0 7 ♗g2 罩e8 (7...a6 8 a4 ♗c7 9 d6 ♗a5 10 ♘h3! ♘c6 11 0-0 罩e8 12 ♘f4 ♗xc3 13 bxc3 b6 14 a5! b5 15 ♗e3 ♗b7 16 ♗xc6 ♗xc6 17 ♗xc5 ± Tabatadze-Zaichik, USSR 1988) 8 e3 ♗c7 9 ♘ge2 d6 10 0-0 a6 11 a3 ♘bd7 12 h3 b5 13 b4 ♗b6 14 bxc5 ♗xc5 15 ♘d4 ♗b7 = Sakaev-Catalan, Doha 1993.

| **6** | **...** | **0-0** |

6...♗c7 *(D)* is another possible move-order:

a) White has a slight advantage after 7 e4 d6 8 ♗e2 0-0 9 ♗g5 ♖e8 10 0-0 ♘bd7 11 ♘d2 a6 12 a4 ♘f8 13 f4 h6 14 ♗h4 ♘g6 15 ♗g3 ♗a5 16 ♗f3 I.Ivanov-Allan, Chicago 1989.

b) 7 g3 d6 8 ♗g2 a6 9 a4 ♘bd7 10 0-0 ♘f8 11 ♘d2 ♘g6 12 ♘c4 ♗d7 13 ♗g5 also suffices for an edge; Marin-Hauchard, Bucharest 1993.

c) Black makes great gains in the event of 7 ♗g5 d6 8 e3 a6 9 ♘d2 h6 10 ♗h4 ♘bd7 11 ♗e2 ♘e5 12 0-0 ♘g6 13 ♗g3 0-0 14 a4 ♖e8 15 ♕c2 h5!? 16 h3 ♗a5 ∞ M.Gurevich-Hodgson, Tallinn 1987.

d) 7 ♘d2 (not so effective here) 7...d6 8 ♘c4 a6 9 a4 ♘bd7 10 ♗g5 0-0 11 e4 (11 e3!?) 11...♖e8 12 ♗d3 ♖b8 13 ♘e3 h6 14 ♗h4 ♘e5 15 0-0 ♗d7 16 ♗c2 ♘g6 17 ♗g3 b5 18 axb5 axb5 with equality; Portisch-Benjamin, Szirak IZ 1987.

e) 7 d6 (the most principled move) 7...♗a5 8 ♗g5 ♕b6 9 ♗xf6 ♕xb2 10 ♗xg7 ♗xc3+ 11 ♗xc3

♕xc3+ 12 ♘d2 b6 13 ♖c1 ♕d4!? (very likely stronger than 13...♕g7 14 h4! ♗b7 15 ♖h3 ♘c6 16 ♖e3+ ♔f8 17 g3 ♖e8 18 ♖xe8+ ♔xe8 19 ♗g2 ± Lalić-Hodgson, Sochi 1987) 14 e3 ♕xd6 15 ♕f3 ♘c6 16 ♗c4 with the initiative to White in a complicated game; Eslon-Jacobs, Seville 1986.

7 g3

Black has no problems after the passive continuation 7 e3 a6 8 a4 ♖e8 9 ♗e2 ♗c7 10 ♘d2 d6 11 e4 ♘bd7 12 0-0 ♘e5 13 h3 ♗d7 14 ♕c2 ♖b8 15 f4 ♘g6 Vladimirov-Gorbatov, Leningrad 1991.

7 ♗g5 is significantly more dangerous, for example 7...♖e8 (or 7...a6 8 a4 ♗c7 9 ♘d2 d6 10 e4 ♖e8 11 ♗e2 ♘bd7 12 0-0 h6 13 ♗h4 ♘e5 14 f4 ± Danner-Schüssler, Vienna 1986) 8 e3 h6 9 ♗h4 a6 (9...♕e7 10 ♗c4 b6 11 ♕d3 a6 12 a4 g5 13 ♗g3 ♔g7 14 ♗xd6 ♕xd6 15 0-0 ± Lukacs-Fernandes, Almada 1988, brings Black no relief) 10 a4 g5 (or 10...♗c7 11 ♗d3 d6 12 0-0 ♘bd7 13 ♖e1 ♗a5 14 e4 ♕b6 15 ♕c2 ♘h5 16 ♘d2 ♘e5 17 ♘c4 ♘xc4 18 ♗xc4 with a small advantage for White in Dussol-Forintos, Val Maubuee 1988) 11 ♗g3 ♗xg3 12 hxg3 ♔g7 13 d6! with the initiative to White.

7 ...   ♗c7

Weakening the queenside with 7...a6 8 a4!? only plays into White's hands, for example 8...♗c7 9 d6! ♗a5 and now:

a) 10 ♘d2 b5 (10...♖e8 11 ♗g2 ♘c6 12 0-0 ♖b8 13 ♘de4 ♗xc3 14

♘xc3 b5 15 axb5 axb5 16 ♗g5 ±
Beliavsky-Peresipkin, Kiev 1978)
11 ♗g2 ♘c6 12 0-0 ♖b8 13 ♘de4
♘xe4 14 ♘xe4 c4 15 axb5 axb5 16
♕d5 is good for White; Vaiser-Grün-
berg, Tallinn 1987.

b) 10 ♗g2 is not bad: 10...♘c6
(10...♘e4 is better for White: 11 0-0
♘xc3 12 bxc3 ♗xc3 13 ♗g5 ♗f6 14
♕d5 ♘c6 15 ♕xc5 b6 16 ♕f5 ♗xg5
17 ♘xg5 Simić-Aleksić, Yugoslavia
1987, with an overwhelming advantage) 11 0-0 ♖e8 12 ♘h4!? ♗xc3 13
bxc3 ♘e4 14 ♕d3 c4! 15 ♕xc4 b5
16 ♕d3 ♘c5 17 ♕c2 ♘xa4 18 ♘f5
with initiative, Cebalo-Bellón, Biel
1987.

After 7...♖e8 8 ♗g2 ♗f8 9 0-0 d6
we find ourselves in the middle of
the variation 5...d6 6 ♘f3 ♗e7 7 g3
(see the note to Black's 5th move in
B).

8	♗g2	d6
9	0-0	a6
10	a4	♖e8
11	b3!? (D)	

Black has no problems after 11 h3
♘bd7 12 ♗f4 ♘f8 13 ♕c2 ♗d7 14
e4 b5 15 axb5 axb5 16 ♖xa8 ♕xa8
17 ♗g5 ♗d8 18 ♖e1 ♘g6 = Ulybin-
Hauchard, Oakham 1992.

11 ♘d2 ♘bd7 is less effective:

a) Black equalizes with no problems after 12 h3 ♖b8 13 ♖b1 b5!?
(13...♕e7?! 14 ♕c2 ♘e5 15 b3 ♗d7
16 ♗b2 h5 17 f4 ± Tukmakov-Or-
tega, Sochi 1987), when 14 axb5

axb5 15 b4 cxb4 16 ♖xb4 is not very
good on account of 16...♗a5.

b) White also has no success after
12 ♘c4 ♘e5 (the line 12...♖b8!? 13
♗f4 ♘f8 also deserves attention) 13
♘xe5 ♖xe5 14 h3 ♖b8 15 ♗f4 ♖e8
16 b3 ♗f5 17 ♖c1 ♗a5 = Grigorian-
Ortega, Erevan 1986.

c) 12 b3 ♖b8 13 e4 ♘f8 14 h3
♘g6 15 ♗b2 ♗a5 16 f4 b5 17 axb5
axb5 with a complicated game; Dol-
matov-Hodgson, Moscow 1987.

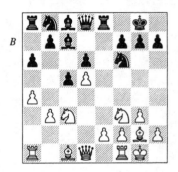

| 11 | ... | ♗a5 |

Or 11...♘bd7!? 12 ♗b2 ♖b8 13
♘d2 ♘e5 14 h3 ♗d7 15 f4 ♘g6 16
e4 b5 17 axb5 axb5 18 e5! dxe5 19 f5
with initiative; Vokac-Danner, Prague 1986.

12	♗b2	♗g4
13	h3	♗h5
14	g4	♗g6
15	♘d2	

with a slight advantage for White;
Razuvaev-Steinbacher, Bundesliga
1991.

2 6 ♘f3: Introduction (A61)

1	d4	♘f6
2	c4	c5
3	d5	e6
4	♘c3	exd5
5	cxd5	d6
6	♘f3	g6 *(D)*

One of the most important positions in the Modern Benoni, from which perhaps the main variation of the opening begins. Now 7 g3 is examined under A62-A64, and 7 e4 leads us to A70-79, whilst within the bounds of this chapter White can continue:

A) 7 h3
B) 7 ♘d2 (Knight's Tour)
C) 7 ♗f4
D) 7 ♗g5

The first often leads into the fashionable lines of A70, but Black may wish to avoid this transposition.

The second can also be transpositional, but in the lines considered here, the knight completes its journey to c4; the so-called Knight's Tour Variation. Currently, this does not seem a problem for Black, provided he knows precisely what he is doing.

The third is a poisonous little move, which aims to cause Black inconvenience over the d6-pawn.

The final line considered in this chapter is one of White's many lines in which the bishop comes to g5. Black must either cope with the pin on his knight, or else advance his kingside pawns.

A)   7 h3!?

7   ...   a6
For 7...♗g7 8 e4 0-0 9 ♗d3 see A70.

8   a4   ♕e7
9   ♗g5 *(D)*

The most testing. White may instead choose:

a) 9 g3 ♗g7 10 ♗g2 (10 ♘d2!?) 10...♘e4! 11 ♘xe4 ♕xe4 12 ♘d2 ♕e7 13 ♘c4 ♘d7 14 ♗f4 ♘e5 = Atalik-Ionescu, Mangalia 1992.

b) 9 ♘d2 ♘bd7 10 e4 (or 10 ♘c4 ♘e5 11 ♘b6 ♖b8 12 ♗g5 {12 e4 ♗g7 13 ♗e2 0-0 14 0-0 ♘ed7 15 ♘xc8 ♖fxc8 16 ♗f4 c4 = Shabtai-Lev, Tel Aviv 1992, is not dangerous for Black} 12...h6 13 ♗f4 ♗g7 14 e3

♗f5 15 ♗e2 0-0 16 0-0 ♘fd7 with equality; Salgado Allaria-Ionescu, Bucharest 1993) 10...♗g7 11 ♗e2 0-0 12 0-0 ♖b8! (more precise than 12...♖e8?! 13 f4 ♖b8 14 ♖e1! Garcia-Magerramov, Nîmes 1991) 13 ♖e1 ♘e8, Magerramov.

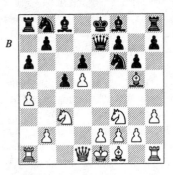

9 ...   h6
10 ♗h4

10 ♗f4 also leads to an equal game: 10...♘bd7 11 ♘d2 ♘e5 12 e4 ♗g7 13 ♗e2 0-0 14 ♗e3 g5 15 g3 ♘h7 16 h4 g4 17 0-0 f5 = Dukhov-Magerramov, Russian Cht 1992 and 10 ♗xf6 ♕xf6 11 ♘d2 ♘d7 12 e3 ♕e7 13 ♘c4 ♘e5 14 ♘b6 (or 14 ♘xe5 ♕xe5 15 ♗d3 ♗g7 16 0-0 0-0 ∓ Züger-Gavrikov, Suhr 1991) 14...♖b8 15 a5 ♗g7 16 ♕a4+ ♘d7 with equality.

10 ...   ♗g7

Black had an interesting game in J.Horvath-Suba, Debrecen 1992: 10...g5 11 ♗g3 ♘h5 12 ♗h2 ♗g7 13 e3 ♘f4!? 14 ♕c2 ♘d7 15 ♘d2 ♘g6 16 ♘ce4 ± , which unfortunately did not lead to equality.

11 e3   ♘bd7
12 ♗e2   0-0

13 0-0   ♘e5
14 ♘d2

14 ♘xe5 ♕xe5 15 ♗g3 ♕e7 =.

14 ...   g5
15 ♗g3   ♗f5!?

Giving better chances for a good game than 15...♘e8 16 ♕c2! (16 a5 f5 17 ♗h2 ♖b8 18 ♘a4 ♗d7 19 ♘b6 ♗b5 = Stohl-Maus, Bundesliga 1991) 16....f5 17 f4 ± Stohl, or 15...♖e8 16 ♖e1 ♖b8 17 a5 ♗f5 18 e4 ♗g6 19 ♖a4! ♘fd7 20 ♕c2 again with a small advantage in Karpov-de Firmian, Biel 1990.

16 a5

16 e4 ♗h7.

16 ...   ♖ae8
17 ♖e1   ♕c7 =

Garcia Ilundain-Spraggett, Candas 1992.

B) Knight's Tour Variation

7 ♘d2   ♗g7

This is generally considered the soundest move for Black. Others:

a) 7...♘bd7 8 e4!? (Black has no problems after 8 ♘c4 ♘b6 9 ♘e3 ♗g7 10 a4 ♗d7 11 g3 {or 11 a5 ♘c8 12 ♘c4 ♕e7 13 ♗g5 h6 14 ♗h4 0-0 15 e3 ♖b8 =} 11...0-0 12 ♗g2 ♖b8 with approximate equality, Copeland-Thomas, British Ch (Swansea) 1987) 8...♗g7 9 ♗e2 (for 9 ♘c4 ♘b6 10 ♘e3 see A70) 9...0-0 10 0-0 ♖e8 and we have transposed to A77.

b) 7...♘a6?! gives White too much freedom, for example 8 ♘c4 ♘c7 9 e4! b5 10 ♘a5 a6 11 ♗g5 ♗g7 12 ♕f3 ♗d7 13 e5! dxe5 14 ♘b7 ♕e7 15 d6 +− Sadler-Stratil,

Oakham 1988. This is not forced, but it is revealing enough.

c) Nor do I like 7...a6, which weakens the queenside too soon. White can continue 8 a4 ♗g7 (after 8...♘bd7 White's simplest solution is to transpose after inserting the moves ...a6 and a4 to the not disadvantageous Four Pawns Attack: 9 e4!? ♗g7 10 ♗e2 0-0 11 0-0 ♖e8 12 f4, especially as 9 ♘c4 ♘b6 10 ♘a3 ♗d7 11 ♗g5 h6 12 ♗f4 ♘h5 13 ♗d2 ♗g7 14 e4 0-0 15 ♗e2 ♘f6 16 0-0 ♘xa4! 17 ♘xa4 b5 18 ♘c3 b4 creates no problems for Black; Benjamin-Zaichik, Philadelphia 1990) 9 ♘c4 0-0 10 ♗f4 (10 ♗g5!? ♖e8 11 ♕d2 Lebredo-Gil. Garcia, Bayamo 1983) 10...♘e8 11 ♕d2! Vaganian-Haïk, Marseilles 1987. In view of the d6-pawn and the b6-square it is very difficult for Black to develop his pieces on the queenside.

8 ♘c4   0-0 *(D)*

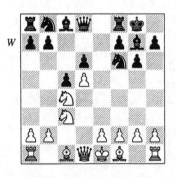

White faces a choice: he can either put pressure on d6, or pin the knight, viz.

B1) 9 ♗f4
B2) 9 ♗g5

B1) 9   ♗f4

Black can defend the pawn with 9...♘e8, as was played in the good old days, or sacrifice it in exchange for a couple of tempi. The latter plan can be executed in several different ways:

9 ...   ♘e8

We shall take this as our main line, since there is the largest body of theory on it. This is not to imply it is better then the more aggressive alternatives. Here is what happens when Black decides to sacrifice the pawn:

a) 9...♖e8?! 10 ♘xd6 ♘h5 11 ♘xe8 ♗xc3+ 12 bxc3 ♘xf4 13 ♕a4! g5 14 e3 ♘g6 15 ♗b5 a6 16 d6 ± I.Zaitsev-Lenchukov, Kirov 1974.

b) 9...♘h5!? 10 ♗xd6 ♖e8 11 a4 ♘d7 12 ♗g3 (12 ♘b5!?) 12...♘b6 13 ♘xb6 ♕xb6 14 ♕d2 f5 with sufficient compensation in Lin Ta-Liu Wenze, China 1987.

c) 9...b6!? 10 ♗xd6 ♖e8 11 ♗g3 ♘e4 12 ♘xe4 ♖xe4 13 e3 b5 14 ♘d6 (or 14 ♘d2!? ♖b4 15 b3 c4!? 16 ♖c1 c3 with sharp play; Meduna-Nunn, Biel 1982) 14...♖b4 15 ♗e2!? (15 ♗xb5 is interesting: 15...♗f8 16 ♗c6 ♗a6! 17 ♕d2! {but not 17 ♗xa8? ♖xb2 18 ♕a4 ♕f6 −+ Donner-Planinc, Wijk aan Zee 1973} 17...♘xc6 18 dxc6 ♕f6 19 ♕c3 ♕e6 20 ♖d1 is unclear − Kapengut) 15...♗xb2! (White has a big advantage after 15...♖xb2?! 16 0-0 ♘a6 17 ♗xb5 ♘b4 18 ♘xc8 ♖xc8 19 d6 ±) 16 0-0 c4 with chances for both sides.

d) 9...♘a6!? 10 e3 (10 ♕d2? only

places the queen under attack from 10...b5! 11 ♘xd6 {11 ♘xb5 ♘e4} 11...b4 12 ♘ce4 ♘xe4 13 ♘xe4 f5 14 ♗g5 ♕b6 15 ♘g3 c4 ∓ Dauebuler-Kindermann, Bad Wörishofen 1989, and an unclear game arises after 10 ♗xd6 ♖e8 11 e3 {11 ♗g3 ♘b4!} 11...♘e4 12 ♘xe4 ♖xe4 13 ♗g3 b5 14 ♘d6 ♖b4 ∞) 10...♘e8 and now:

d1) Surprisingly enough, the d6-pawn is again unassailable, and White cannot organize himself after 11 ♘e4? b5 12 ♘cxd6 ♘xd6 13 ♘xd6 ♗xb2.

d2) 11 ♘b5?! ♗d7 12 ♘bxd6 b5 13 ♘xe8 ♗xe8 14 ♘e5 ♘b4 ∓.

d3) I also like Black's position after 11 ♕d2 f5 12 ♘b5 (12 h4 ♘ac7 13 a4 b6 14 ♗e2 transposes to 'd4') 12...g5 13 ♗xd6 ♘xd6 14 ♘cxd6 f4 15 ♘xc8 fxe3 16 fxe3 ♕xc8 17 0-0-0 c4! with a good game in return for the pawn; A.Petrosian-Ermenkov, Riga 1981.

d4) 11 ♗e2 f5 12 h4 ♘ac7 13 a4 b6 14 ♕d2 (14 ♕b3 ♖b8 15 ♘b5 ♘xb5 16 axb5 ♖b7 17 ♖d1 h6 = Brisenko-Kapengut, Yaroslavl 1979) 14...♗a6 15 ♖d1 (15 ♗g5 ♕d7 16 0-0 ♘f6 ∓ Nascimiento-Renet, Lucerne tt 1985) 15...♘xc4 16 ♗xc4 Dydyshko-Kapengut, Minsk 1980, and 16...a6! would have given approximately equal chances.

10 ♕d2 (D)

Considered to be the most exact, as Black has no particular difficulties after 10 e3 g5! 11 ♗g3 f5 12 ♕d2 (or 12 f4 ♕e7 13 a4 gxf4 14 ♗xf4 ♘d7 15 ♗e2 ♘e5 16 0-0 ♘xc4 17 ♗xc4

♘f6 is equal, *ECO*) 12...♗xc3!? (the line 12...♕e7 13 ♗e2 ♘d7 = is also possible) 13 bxc3 b5 14 ♘b2 ♕e7 15 f3 ♘c7 16 a4 ♗b7 with mutual chances, especially as 10 ♘b5?! ♗d7 11 ♘bxd6 b5 12 ♘xe8 ♗xe8 13 ♘e5 ♕d6 14 ♘d3 ♕xd5 gives him a clear-cut advantage.

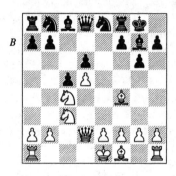

10 ...   b6

There are plenty of other moves:

a) 10...♘d7?! (an unsuccessful pawn sacrifice) 11 ♘xd6 ♘e5 12 ♗xe5 ♗xe5 13 ♘c4 ± (Hartston).

b) 10...f5 11 g3 ♕e7 12 ♗g2 ♘d7 13 0-0 ♘e5 14 ♘xe5 ♗xe5 15 ♗h6 ♗g7 16 ♗g5 ♗f6 17 h4 ♘g7 18 ♖fe1 ± Anikaev-Chiburdanidze, Minsk 1983.

c) 10...♗xc3!? is an absurd-looking move, but it is not easy for White to gain an advantage:

c1) 11 ♕xc3, which I believe has not been seen in recent practice, would be interesting to try again; one may continue 11...b5 12 ♘d2 f5 (12...b4?! 13 ♕c2 ♕e7 14 h4!? ♘g7 15 e4 f5 16 ♗g5 ♕e5 17 0-0-0 fxe4 18 ♘c4 ± Boleslavsky) 13 h4 ♕f6 14 ♕g3!? with a small advantage.

c2) 11 bxc3 b5 12 ♘b2 (after the absurd 12 ♘a3?! Black seizes the initiative with 12...a6 13 ♗h6 ♘g7 14 h4 ♖e8 15 ♗xg7 ♔xg7 16 h5 ♖a7! ∓ Giustolisi-Tal, Rome tt 1957) 12...♘d7 (Black cannot equalize after 12...a5 13 e4 ♕e7 14 ♗d3 b4 15 0-0 ♘d7 16 ♘c4 ♗a6 17 ♖fe1 ♗xc4 18 ♗xc4 ♘e5 19 ♗f1 ± Borisenko-Tal, Riga 1955, or 12...f5 13 e3 g5 14 ♗g3 ♕e7 15 ♗e2 ♘f6 16 f3 ♘bd7 17 0-0 ♖b8 18 a4 a6 19 axb5 axb5 20 ♖a7 ± Seirawan-D.Gurevich, Hollywood 1985) 13 g3 (Black has an excellent game after 13 e4 c4! 14 ♗e2 ♘c5) 13...♗b7 14 ♗g2 f5 15 0-0 (15 a4!? a6 16 c4 is not bad) 15...c4!? (or 15...♕e7 16 a4 a6 17 c4 ±) 16 ♗g5!? ♕c7 17 ♘d1! ♘b6 18 ♘e3 ♘f6 19 ♕d4 ♘fd7 20 ♖fd1 ±.

11 a4 *(D)*

The pawn on d6 is unassailable: 11 ♘b5 ♗a6 12 a4 (12 ♘bxd6? ♘xd6 13 ♘xd6 g5! 14 ♗g3 f5 −+) 12...♗xb5 13 axb5 ♘d7! 14 e3 (14 ♘xd6 ♘df6 15 ♘xe8 ♖xe8 with enough compensation for the pawn) 14...♘e5 15 ♗xe5 ♗xe5 16 ♘xe5 dxe5 17 ♗e2 ♘d6 18 ♕c3 ♖e8 = Sliwa-Suetin, Polanica Zdroj 1957.

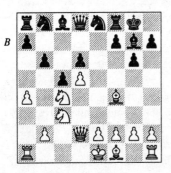

11 ... ♗a6

11...♘a6?! 12 e4 ♕e7 13 ♗e2 ♘b4 14 0-0 ♗a6 15 ♖ae1 ♖d8 16 ♔h1 ♘c7 17 ♗g5 ♗f6 18 ♗xf6 ♕xf6 19 ♖d1! ♕g7 20 f4 and White's advantage was obvious in Agzamov-Gavrikov, Erevan 1982.

12 e3

12 e4?! ♕e7 13 ♕e3 ♘d7 14 ♗d3 ♗d4 15 ♕e2 ♗xc4 16 ♗xc4 ♘c7 =.

12 ... ♗xc4

Or 12...f5 13 h4! ♗xc4 14 ♗xc4 a6 15 ♕e2! ♘f6 16 ♗d3 ± Kapengut.

13 ♗xc4 a6

White preserves his advantage after 13...♘d7 14 0-0 ♘e5 15 ♗e2 f5 16 e4 a6 17 ♗g3 (17 exf5 gxf5 18 ♗g3 ♕d7 19 f4 ♘g6 = Donner-Spassky, Leiden 1970 is not as convincing) 17...♕d7 18 f4 ±.

14 0-0 ♘d7
15 ♕e2!

It's not worth White hurrying to push the e-pawn: 15 e4 ♕e7 16 ♖ae1 ♘c7 17 ♗h6 Ghitescu-Suetin, Sochi 1979, and after 17...♗xh6 18 ♕xh6 b5! 19 axb5 ♘e5 20 b3 ♘xb5 21 ♘xb5 axb5 22 ♗xb5 ♖fb8 Black has enough compensation for the pawn.

15 ... f5
16 ♗g3 ♕c8
17 ♖fc1 ♘e5
18 ♖ab1 ♘c7
19 b4

White has an advantage – Ciocaltea.

B2)
9 ♗g5 *(D)*

This move, which provokes weaknesses in Black's kingside pawn

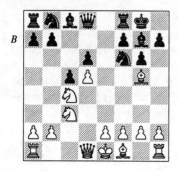

structure, has recently enjoyed more popularity than 9 ♗f4, although play often develops along the same lines.

9 ...   h6 (D)

This is the most popular continuation at the moment, but there are a number of reasonable alternatives for Black:

a) 9...♖e8 10 e3 (10 ♘b5?! h6 11 ♗f4 ♘h5 12 ♗xd6 a6 13 ♘c7 ♖e4 14 e3 ♖a7 ∓) 10...a6 (10...b6?! 11 ♘b5 ♗a6 12 ♘cxd6 ♖e5 13 ♗f4 ♖xd5 14 ♕f3 ♘c6 15 ♗c4 ±) 11 a4 ♕c7 12 ♗f4 ♗f8 13 a5 ♘bd7 14 ♘a4 and White's position is noticeably the more active.

b) 9...♕d7!? 10 a4 (10 ♗xf6 ♗xf6 11 ♘e4 ♗g7!) 10...♘a6!? 11 e3 ♘b4 12 ♗e2 ♕f5 13 ♗xf6 ♕xf6 14 0-0 ♕e7 and Black could look with hope into the future in Popov-Romanishin, Stara Pazova 1988.

c) 9...♕e7 and White can now make use of the pin on the knight by means of 10 ♕d2 or quietly continue his development with 10 e3:

c1) 10 ♕d2 b6 (not 10...♘bd7?! 11 ♕f4! h6 12 ♗xh6 ♗xh6 13 ♕xh6 ♘e5 14 e3 ♗f5 15 ♖d1 ± Ftačnik-

P.Cramling, Biel 1984) 11 ♕f4 and Black has a reasonable choice between the lines 11...♗a6!? 12 ♘xd6 (12 ♕xd6!?) 12...h6 13 ♗xf6 ♗xf6 14 ♘de4 ♗g7 15 e3 f5 16 ♘d2 g5 17 ♕a4 ♗xf1 18 ♖xf1 ♘d7 with compensation; Evdokimov-Suba, Stiges 1992, and 11...♖d8 12 ♘e4 (if 12 0-0-0 then 12...♗a6 13 e4 ♗xc4 14 ♗xc4 a6 15 ♕h4 ♘bd7 16 ♖he1 ♕f8 17 ♔b1 b5 18 ♗f1 h6 19 ♗c1 ♘b6 with an entirely decent game, Portisch-T.Horvath, Hungarian Ch 1984) 12...♕xe4 13 ♕xe4 ♘xe4 14 ♗xd8 b5 15 f3 bxc4 16 fxe4 ♗xb2 17 ♖b1 c3 with compensation, Yusupov.

c2) 10 e3 and now:

c21) 10...b6 is not bad, for example 11 a4 ♗a6 12 ♗e2 (Black gets a good game after both 12 ♘b5 ♗xb5 13 axb5 ♘bd7 14 ♗e2 ♘e5 15 ♘a3 ♘ed7 = Muse-Wahls, Bundesliga 1986, and 12 ♖c1 ♘bd7 13 b3 ♗b7 14 ♗e2 ♘e5 15 0-0 h6 16 ♗h4 ♖ad8 17 ♔h1 ♗c8 18 ♕d2 ♖fe8 Portisch-de Firmian, Tunis IZ 1985) 12...h6 13 ♗h4 g5 14 ♗g3 ♗xc4 15 ♗xc4 ♘e4 16 ♘xe4 ♕xe4 17 ♕b3 was Yusupov-Christiansen, Mexico 1980, and now 17...♕e7 = would have equalized according to Yusupov.

c22) 10...♘bd7!? 11 ♗e2 (again, winning a pawn does not give White any advantage: 11 ♘b5?! ♘e5 12 ♘bxd6 ♖d8 13 ♘xc8 ♖axc8 14 d6 ♕e6 with compensation. Black also equalizes after 11 a4 ♘e5 12 ♘a3 h6 13 ♗h4 g5 14 ♗g3 ♘fd7 15 ♗e2 f5 = Dlugy-Klinger, Sharjah jr 1985)

11...♘e5 12 ♘xe5 (or 12 ♘d2 h6 13 ♗h4 g5 14 ♗g3 ♘h7 15 0-0 f5 with a good game in Inkiov-Palkovi, Stara Zagora Z 1990) 12...♕xe5 13 ♗f4 ♕e7 14 0-0 ♗f5 15 ♖c1 a6 16 a4 ♖fb8 17 h3 ♗d7 = Gulko-Wahls, Groningen 1990.

d) 9...b6!? 10 a4 ♗a6 11 ♘b5 ♗xb5 12 axb5 ♘bd7!? 13 ♘xd6 h6 14 ♗h4 ♘e5 15 ♘e4 g5 16 ♘xf6+ ♕xf6 17 ♗g3 ♘c4 (Kapengut) with strong play for Black.

e) 9...♘a6 10 e3 ♘c7 11 a4 b6 12 ♗e2 ♗a6 13 0-0 h6 14 ♗h4 ♕d7 15 ♖b1 ♖fe8 16 b3 ♘h7!? 17 ♖c1 ♘g5 = Atlas-Hoeksema, Dieren 1989.

Of course, the last two variations need practical tests.

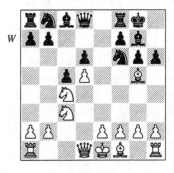

10 ♗h4 *(D)*

After 10 ♗f4:

a) Just as he can after 9 ♗f4, Black is quite able to continue 10...b6, e.g 11 ♗xd6 ♖e8 12 ♗g3 (12 e3 ♗a6 13 ♗g3 ♘h5 14 a4 f5! with compensation; Nenashev-Semeniuk, Riga 1988) 12...♘e4 13 ♘xe4 ♖xe4 14 e3 b5 (14....♗a6?! favours White: 15 ♕c2! ♕xd5 16 ♖d1 ♕e6 17 ♖d8+ ♔h7 18 ♘d2!

♗xf1 19 ♖xf1 ♖b4 20 b3 with advantage – Cabrilo) 15 ♘d2 (15 ♘d6 ♖b4 16 ♗e2 ♗xb2 17 0-0 c4 gives Black an attack) 15...♖b4 16 b3 c4! (16...♖xa1? is significantly weaker, e.g. 17 ♕xa1 ♕xd5 18 a3 ♖g4 {or 18...♖xb3 19 ♘xb3 ♕xb3 20 ♗e2 ±} 19 ♗e2 ♘c6 20 ♗f3 ♕e6 21 ♗xg4 ♕xg4 22 0-0 ♗b7 23 f3 ± T.Petrosian-Nunn, Hastings 1977, or 16...♕a5?! 17 ♗e2 ♗b7 18 0-0 ♗xa1 19 ♕xa1 ♗xd5 20 a3 ♖a4 21 bxa4 ♕xd2 22 ♗xb5 +–) 17 bxc4 (but not 17 a3?! ♖xb3 18 ♗e2 ♖b2 19 0-0 c3 20 ♘f3 ♗f5 ∓ Chandler-Denman, Brighton 1979) 17...bxc4 18 ♗xc4 ♗xa1 19 ♕xa1 ♖xc4 20 ♘xc4 ♕xd5 21 ♕d4 ♗e6 = Nunn.

b) 10...♘bd7!? is also interesting: 11 ♗xd6 ♖e8 12 e3 (12 ♗g3 ♘e4 13 ♘xe4 ♖xe4 14 e3 ♘b6 15 ♖c1 ♘xc4 16 ♖xc4 ♖xc4 17 ♗xc4 b5! ∓ Foisor-Ilijin, Romania 1979) 12...♘e4 13 ♘xe4 ♖xe4 14 ♖c1 b5 15 ♘d2 ♖b4 16 b3 ♕a5 17 ♕c2 ♗b7 with compensation; Andruet-Armas, Wijk aan Zee 1989.

c) 10...♘e8 11 ♕c1 g5 12 ♗d2 ♘c7 (or 12...f5 13 h4 f4 14 hxg5 hxg5 15 e3 ♗f5 16 exf4 ♕e7+ Ftačnik-Podzielny, Trnava 1984, and after 17 ♔d1! White's chances are clearly better) 13 a4 ♘ba6 14 h4 f6 15 e4 ♘b4 16 ♗e2 ♕e7 17 0-0 ♗d7 with an unclear position; Portisch-Spassky, Turin 1982.

d) 10...♘a6!? and now:

d1) Complications which are good for Black arise after 11 ♕d2 b5! 12 ♘xb5 ♘e4 13 ♕c1 (13 ♕c2 ♗f5 14 ♕a4 ♘b4 15 f3 a6 ∓)

13...♘b4 14 f3 Kaplun-Kapengut, Rostov 1980, and 14...♗d7! 15 a4 a6 ∓ would have given Black an advantage – Kapengut.

d2) 11 ♗xd6 ♖e8 is dubious for White:

d21) 12 ♗g3 ♘b4! 13 e3 (or 13 ♘d6 ♗f5! 14 ♘xf5 {14 ♘xe8? ♘c2+ 15 ♔d2 ♘xd5 16 ♘d6 ♘xc3 17 bxc3 ♗xc3+! 18 ♔xc3 ♕a5+ and Black wins} 14...gxf5 15 e3 f4! 16 ♗xf4 ♘fxd5 ∓) 13...♗f5 14 ♖c1 ♘e4 15 ♘xe4 ♗xe4 16 a3 ♘xd5 with a slight plus for Black; Petran-Barczay, Hungary 1980.

d22) 12 e3 ♘e4 13 ♘xe4 ♖xe4 14 ♗g3 b5 (14...♗g4?! 15 f3 b5 16 ♕d2!) 15 ♘d6 ♖b4 16 ♗e2 ♗xb2 17 0-0 c4 with chances for both sides.

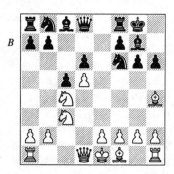

10 ...   **♕d7!?**

After 10...♘a6 11 e3 ♘c7 12 a4 b6 13 ♗e2 ♗a6 14 0-0 White holds the initiative after both 14...♗xc4 15 ♗xc4 a6 16 h3! ♕d7 17 ♕d3 ♘h7 18 f4! f5 19 e4 Ehlvest-Bellón, Logroño 1991, and 14...♕d7 15 b3 ♖fe8 16 ♕d3 ♖ab8 17 ♗g3 ♗xc4 18 bxc4 ♘a6 19 ♖a3 ♘b4 20 ♕b1 with

a slight plus for White; Danner-Moskalenko, Dornbirn 1989.

It would be interesting to test 10...b6 11 e3 ♗a6 12 a4 ♕e7, for example 13 ♕c2 ♘bd7 14 ♗e2 ♗xc4 15 ♗xc4 g5 16 ♗g3 ♘h5 17 ♕f5!? ♘xg3 18 hxg3 ♗xc3+!? 19 bxc3 ♕e5 (Kapengut) with a reasonable game for Black.

11 ♗g3

Black has no problems after 11 a4 ♕g4 12 ♗xf6 ♕xc4 13 ♗xg7 ♔xg7 14 a5! ♗d7 15 e3 ♕b4 16 ♕d2 ♘a6 = Makarychev.

11	**...**	**b5!**
12	**♘xd6**	**b4**
13	**♘a4**	

Or 13 ♘ce4 ♘xe4 14 ♘xe4 ♗xb2 15 ♖b1 ♗g7 16 ♖c1 ♗b7 17 ♖xc5 ♘a6.

13	**...**	**♘h5**
14	**♘e4**	

The following variation holds no fears for Black: 14 ♘xc5 ♕c7 15 ♘ce4 ♘xg3 16 hxg3 ♗xb2 17 ♖b1 ♗c3+ 18 ♘xc3 bxc3 19 ♘b5 ♕a5 20 ♕c2 ♗f5.

14	**...**	**c4!**
15	**e3**	**♘xg3**
16	**hxg3**	**♕e7**

and Black had sufficient compensation for the pawn in Gulko-Romanishin, Biel 1987.

One might remark that Black can successfully deal with the difficulties of the variation with 7 ♘d2.

C) 7 ♗f4 *(D)*

This move initiates a system which has proved very dangerous for Black.

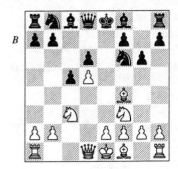

An attack on d6, linked with a distant check from a4, brings some discomfort into Black's position and demands exact defence.

Now 7...♘h5 favours White: 8 ♗g5 ♗e7 9 ♗h6 ♘d7 10 ♕d2 ♘df6 11 h3 ♘g8 12 ♗e3 a6 13 g4 ♘hf6 14 a4 ♘d7 15 ♗f4 ± Gaprindashvili-Rajković, Tbilisi 1987; and 7...b6? is even worse: 8 e4 ♗g7 9 ♗b5+ ♗d7 (9...♔f8) 10 ♗xd6 ♗xb5 11 ♘xb5 ♘xe4 12 ♘c7+ ♔d7 13 ♗f4 +– Lev-Karp, Tel-Aviv 1990.

This leaves two moves worth considering in depth:

C1) 7...a6
C2) 7...♗g7

C1)   7 ...   a6
      8 a4

Instead:

a) 8 e4!? b5 transposes to A65.

b) 8 ♘e4 ♘xe4 9 ♕a4+ ♘d7 10 ♕xe4+ ♗e7!? 11 ♗xd6 ♘f6 12 ♗xe7 ♕xe7 13 ♕xe7+ ♔xe7 14 ♖c1 (14 0-0-0 ♘e4) 14...b6 15 ♘e5 ♘xd5 16 g3 ♗e6 and Black wields the initiative; Dreev-Ivanchuk, Lvov 1987.

c) 8 ♘d2 is often used by the Armenian players:

c1) 8...♗g7?! cannot be recommended for Black: 9 ♘c4 0-0 10 a4 ♘e8 11 ♕d2 ♘d7 12 ♘xd6 ♘xd6 13 ♗xd6 ♖e8 14 e3 ± Vaganian-Haïk, Marseilles 1987.

c2) White also has a small plus after 8...♘h5 9 ♕a4+! ♕d7 (or 9...b5?! 10 ♘xb5 axb5 11 ♕xa8 ♕b6 12 ♗g3 ♗g7 13 ♕a3 0-0 14 e3 ± A.Petrosian-Cebalo, Sarajevo 1986) 10 ♕e4+ ♗e7 11 ♗h6! b5 12 ♕c2 and at this point Black should try 12...♗f8!?, which is stronger than 12...f5 13 e4! ± A.Petrosian.

c3) 8...b5 9 a4 ♘h5 (Fauland-Wahls, Aosta 1988, continued with the interesting 9...b4 10 ♘ce4 ♘h5 11 ♗g5 f6 12 ♗h4 g5 13 e3 ♘g7 14 ♕f3 ♗e7 15 ♗g3 f5 16 ♘xc5 g4 17 ♕f4 dxc5 18 ♕e5 ♔f8 19 d6 ♗f6 with wild complications) 10 ♗e3 b4 (10...f5 is not enough because of 11 g4! fxg4 12 axb5 ♘d7 13 ♘c4 ♘b6 14 ♗g5! ♕c7 15 bxa6 ♘xc4 16 ♕a4+ ♔f7 17 ♕xc4 ♗g7 18 e3 with an advantage, A.Petrosian-Foisor, Moscow 1987) 11 ♘ce4 ♘d7!? (again if 11...f5 then 12 g4! fxg4 13 ♘c4 ♗f5 14 ♗g5 ♕c7 15 ♕d3 {or 15 ♕d2 ♔f7 16 ♗g2 ♘d7 17 ♘g3 h6 18 ♗f4 ♘df6 with mutual chances in Lputian-Wahls, Altensteig 1989} 15...h6 16 ♕e3 ♔f7 17 ♗f4 ♘xf4 18 ♕xf4 with strong pressure in Dementiev-Minasian, Erevan 1983) 12 ♘c4 ♘df6 13 ♘xf6+ ♘xf6 14 g3 a5! 15 ♗g2 ♗a6 16 ♕c2 ♗g7 17 ♗f4 ♗xc4 18 ♕xc4 0-0 with an equal position; A.Petrosian-Guseinov, Azov 1991.

      8 ...   ♗g7

With 8...♕e7 (D) Black is trying to hinder the move e4:

a) The problems facing Black are simplified after 9 g3 ♘bd7 10 h3 (10 ♗g2 ♗g7 11 0-0 ♘g4!) 10...♖b8 11 a5 ♗g7 12 ♗g2 0-0 13 0-0 ♘h5 14 ♗g5 f6 15 ♗d2 f5 16 ♕c1 ♘e5 17 ♘xe5 ♕xe5 = Röder-Gavrikov, Vienna 1990.

b) 9 e3 ♗g4 10 ♗e2 ♗xf3 11 ♗xf3 ♘bd7 12 0-0 ♗g7 13 ♕c2 0-0 14 ♗e2 ♘e8 15 e4 ♘c7 = Vyzhmanavin-Ivanchuk, Lvov 1987.

c) Black also achieves a decent game in the event of 9 ♘d2 ♘h5 10 ♗e3 f5 11 ♘c4 ♘d7 12 ♕d2 ♘e5 13 ♘b6 ♖b8 14 ♗g5 ♘d3+! 15 ♕xd3 ♕xg5 16 g3 ♗g7 17 ♗g2 0-0 = Lputian-Pigusov, Irkutsk 1986.

d) 9 h3!? (White does not wish to see his opponent's bishop on g4 and in the meantime will keep his bishop on the important h2-b8 diagonal) 9...♘bd7 10 e3 (or 10 ♘d2 ♘e5 11 ♗xe5!? ♕xe5 12 ♘c4 ♕e7 13 ♕d2 h5! 14 ♕f4 ♗f5 15 e3 ♖d8 16 ♗e2 ♘e4 17 0-0 ♗h6 18 ♕h2 ♗g7 = Browne-D.Gurevich, Los Angeles 1987) 10...♗g7 11 ♗e2 0-0 12 0-0

♖b8 13 ♗h2 ♘e8 14 ♖e1 ♘c7 15 e4 b5 16 axb5 ♘xb5 17 ♘xb5 axb5 18 ♖a7 and White wields the initiative, Gurgenidze-Gorelov, Volgodonsk 1981.

9 e3

9 e4!? 0-0 10 ♘d2 leads to A70, whilst both 9 h3!? and 9 g3!? deserve attention.

9 ...   0-0 (D)

9...♗g4 doesn't look too bad either, as 10 ♕b3 (10 ♗e2 0-0 leads to 9...0-0) is not dangerous because of 10...♗xf3 11 gxf3 ♕c7 12 ♗xd6 ♕xd6 13 ♕xb7 ♘fd7 14 a5 (14 ♕xa8 ♕b6!) 14...0-0 15 ♕xa8 ♗xc3+! 16 bxc3 ♕f6 17 ♖c1 ♕xf3 18 ♖g1 ♘e5 19 ♗e2 ♕e4 and Black had a strong attack in Gunawan-Hulak, Sarajevo 1988.

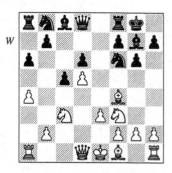

10 h3

Black has no problems after 10 ♗e2 ♗g4 11 0-0 ♕e7 12 ♕b3 ♕c7 13 h3 ♗xf3 14 ♗xf3 ♘bd7 15 ♖fe1 ♖fe8 16 e4 ♖ab8 = Gunawan-Wedberg, Thessaloniki OL 1988.

10 ...   ♘h5

10...♕e7 is also quite possible, for example 11 ♘d2 ♘h5 12 ♗h2 f5 13 ♘c4 (13 ♗e2 deserves attention: 13...f4 14 0-0! fxe3 15 fxe3 ♕xe3+ 16 ♔h1 ♘g3+ 17 ♗xg3 ♕xg3 18 ♖xf8+ ♗xf8 19 ♘ce4 ♕h4 20 ♕b3 ♘d7 21 ♗g4 with compensation in Gunawan-Kovacević, Vrnjacka Banja 1988) 13...f4 14 ♗e2 fxe3 15 ♗xh5 ♖xf2 16 ♗g3 ♖xg2 17 ♕f3 ♖xb2! with unclear complications in Raičević-Wojtkiewicz, Athens 1992.

11   ♗h2

11 ♗g5!?.

11   ...   f5

12   ♕d2

Or 12 ♗e2 f4 13 e4 ♘d7 14 0-0 ♔h8 15 ♔h1 ♖b8 =.

12	...	♗h6
13	♗d3	f4
14	0-0	♘d7
15	♖ae1	♖b8!
16	♕c2	♔g7

With equality; Genov-Pigusov, Berlin 1992.

C2)   7   ...   ♗g7

8   ♕a4+

This is significantly more dangerous for Black than 8 e3 0-0 9 h3:

a) 9...♘a6 10 ♗c4 (10 ♗e2 ♘c7 11 0-0 ♖e8 12 a4 a6 13 ♕b3 ♖b8 14 a5 ♘e4 = Gurgenidze-Zaichik, Tbilisi 1991) 10...♘c7 11 a4 b6 12 0-0 ♖e8 13 ♖e1 ♗f5 14 g4!? ♗c8 15 e4 with a small advantage to White, Lerner-Agzamov, Tashkent 1983.

b) 9...♘e8 10 ♗e2 ♘d7 11 0-0 ♘e5 12 ♗xe5 dxe5 13 ♘d2 f5 14 ♕b3 ♘d6 was equal in Tal-Spassky, Leningrad 1954.

It is difficult to assess correctly

the unlikely complications which occurred in A.Petrosian-Psakhis, Erevan 1988, after 8 ♘d2 ♘h5 (8...0-0!? is quieter) 9 ♕a4+ ♔f8 (the only move; 9...♗d7 is bad because of 10 ♕e4+ ♕e7 11 ♗xd6 +−) 10 ♗e3 a6 11 ♕b3 b5 12 a4 f5!? 13 g4! c4! (13...f4 14 ♗xc5!) 14 ♕b4 f4 15 ♗c5!? dxc5 16 ♕xc5+ ♔f7 17 gxh5 ♗f5! with an interesting game.

8   ...   ♗d7

Black cannot obtain a comfortable game with 8...♘bd7? 9 ♗xd6 ♕b6 10 ♘b5 a6 11 e3 axb5 12 ♕xa8 ♕xd6 13 ♕xc8+ ♔e7 14 ♕xb7 +− Benjamin-Kraidman, Jerusalem 1986.

White has a distinct advantage after 8...♔f8 9 e4 ♘h5 (or 9...a6 10 ♗e2 ♗g4 11 0-0 ♘e8 12 ♗g5 ♕d7 13 ♕c2 ♗xf3 14 ♗xf3 ♕c7 15 ♖fe1 ♘d7 16 ♗e2 ± Grigorian-Sandler, Belgorod 1989) 10 ♗g5 ♕b6 11 ♕c2 h6 12 ♗e3 ♔g8 13 ♗d3 ±.

9   ♕b3   b5!? (D)

A critical position for the fate of the variation. The bold pawn move enjoys incomparably greater popularity than the passive 9...♗c8 10 e4 0-0 11 ♗e2 a6 12 a4 ♕e7 13 ♘d2 ♘bd7 14 0-0 ♘e8 15 ♖fe1 with a small but obvious advantage to White; Nestorović-Nenadović, Belgrade GMA 1988.

You also see 9...♕c7, after which you may continue 10 h3!? (10 e4 0-0 relates to A70 whilst 10 ♘d2 leads to a complicated game: 10...♘h5 11 ♗g5 h6 12 ♗h4 g5 13 ♗g3 ♘xg3 14 hxg3 a6 15 a4 ♗f5 16 ♘c4 ♘d7 17 a5 0-0 18 ♘a4 ♖ae8 Sturua-Eolian, Erevan 1982) 10...0-0 11 e3 ♘a6 12

♘d2 ♖ab8 (or 12...♖fd8 13 ♖c1 ♖ab8 14 a4 ♘b4 15 ♗e2 a6 16 0-0 b5?! 17 axb5 axb5 18 ♘ce4! ♘xe4 19 ♘xe4 ♗f5 20 ♘xc5! with advantage; A.Petrosian-Gutierrez, Tunja 1987) 13 a4 ♘b4 14 ♘c4 ♘e8 15 ♖d1 with a minimal advantage; Velichko-Peresipkin, USSR 1984.

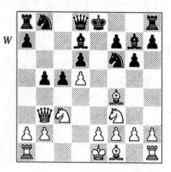

Now White must chose between two continuations of approximately equal value:

C21) 10 ♗xd6
C22) 10 ♘xb5

Instead 10 e3?! creates no problems for Black: 10...c4 11 ♕a3 0-0 12 ♘d4 ♕b6 13 ♕xd6 b4 (13...♕a5 is not as convincing: 14 ♕c7 ♕b4 15 ♖b1 ♘xd5 16 a3 ♗xd4 17 axb4 ♗xc3+ 18 bxc3 ♘xc7 19 ♗xc7 ± Hertneck-Wittmann, Badenweiler 1990) 14 ♘d1 ♖c8 15 ♖c1 ♕a5 16 ♗xc4 b3+ and now the initiative belongs to Black; Gaprindashvili-Winants, Brussels tt 1987.

C21) 10 ♗xd6   ♕b6
It would also be interesting to test 10...c4 11 ♕d1 ♕b6 12 ♗e5 b4 13

♗d4 bxc3!? 14 ♗xb6 axb6, as seen in Cholushkina-Prudnikova, USSR 1991.

11 ♗e5
It is obvious that 11 ♗g3 0-0 12 e3 c4 13 ♕d1 b4 14 ♘b1 ♗b5 15 a4 ♗a6 16 ♗e5 ♘bd7, Litinskaya-Levitina, Tskhaltubo Ct 1988, favours Black.

11 ...   0-0
12 e3   c4
Precisely this pawn! 12...b4 is bad: 13 ♘b1 ♗b5 14 ♗xb5 ♕xb5 15 ♘c3! ♕a6 16 ♗xf6 ♕xf6 17 ♘e4 with a big advantage; Khenkin-Jaulin, Paris 1991.

13 ♕d1 (D)

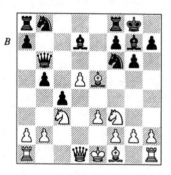

13 ...   ♘a6!
The most precise move. White is assisted by:

a) 13...♖d8?! 14 a3 ♘a6 15 ♗e2 ♘c5 16 ♕d4 ♗f5 17 0-0 ± Timman-Winants, Brussels 1986.

b) 13...b4?! 14 ♘b1 ♗b5 15 ♘bd2 ♖c8 (nor can Black settle after 15...♘bd7 16 ♗d4 ♕c7 17 ♗xc4 ♗xc4 18 ♖c1 ♘b6 19 ♗xb6 with a big advantage for White) 16 ♖c1 c3 (16...♘bd7?! loses: 17 ♗xc4 ♘xe5

18 ♘xe5 ♗xc4 19 ♘dxc4 ♕a6 20 0-0 +− Yakovich-Zelčić, Belgorod 1991) 17 bxc3 ♗xf1 18 ♔xf1 bxc3 19 ♗xc3 ♕b5+ 20 ♔g1 ♕xd5 21 ♗xf6 ♖xc1 22 ♕xc1 ♗xf6 23 g3 ♘d7 24 ♔g2 ♖b8 25 ♕c4 and Black faces a tough battle for the draw in Yrjölä-Winants, Dubai OL 1986.

14 ♕d4
The weakness of b3 becomes clear in the variation 14 a3 ♘c5 15 ♕d4 ♗f5 16 ♖d1 ♗c2! 17 ♖d2 ♗f5 and White must play 18 ♖d1 =, but not 18 g4?! ♗e4! 19 ♘xe4 ♘cxe4 20 ♕xb6 axb6 21 ♖c2 ♘xg4 ∓ Van der Sterren-Winants, Budel Z 1987.

14 ...   ♖fc8!
14...♘b4?! turns out to be a lone shot, for example 15 ♖c1 ♗f5 16 ♕xb6 axb6 17 a3 ♘c2+ 18 ♔d2 b4 19 axb4 ♘xb4 20 ♗xc4 ♖fd8 21 ♔e2 ±.

15	♖c1	b4
16	♘d1	♕xd4
17	♘xd4	♘xd5
18	♗xg7	♔xg7
19	♗xc4	

Black has a good game for the pawn after 19 ♖xc4 ♘c5 20 ♗e2 ♖ab8 21 0-0 a5.

19 ...   ♘b6!
Again Black has sufficient compensation for the pawn; Aleksandria-Shabalov, USSR 1989.

C22) 10 ♘xb5   ♗xb5!?
White has a clear advantage after 10...♕a5+ 11 ♘c3 ♘e4 12 ♗d2!? (12 ♘d2 ♘xc3 13 bxc3 ♗a4 14 ♕a3 ♗xc3 15 ♖c1 ♗b4 16 ♕b2 0-0 17 a3 ♗xd2+ 18 ♕xd2 Bellón-Ochoa,

Matalascañas 1986 is not bad either) 12...♘xd2 13 ♘xd2 0-0 14 ♘c4 ♕c7 15 e3 ♘a6 16 ♗e2 ♖ab8 17 ♕c2 ♗f5 18 e4 ♗c8 19 a3 ± Zsu. Polgar-Renet, Paris m 1987.

The little-researched 10...0-0!? deserves attention, for example 11 ♘c3 (or 11 ♘xd6 ♘a6 12 e4 ♖b8 13 ♕d1 ♖xb2 14 ♗d3 ♕a5+ 15 ♗d2 ♕a3 with a complex game; Nasybulin-Ulybin, Pavlodar 1987) 11...♘a6 12 ♗xd6 ♖e8 13 e3 ♘e4! 14 ♗xa6 ♘xd6 15 ♕a3 ♖b8 16 0-0 ♕b6 and here Black has sufficient compensation for the pawn; Ružele-Gelfand, Kramatorsk 1989.

11	♕xb5+	♘bd7
12	♗xd6 (D)	

Or 12 ♕d3 0-0 and 13 e4? ♘xe4 is bad.

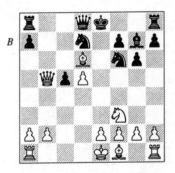

12	...	♘e4
13	♗e5	0-0
14	♗xg7	♔xg7
15	♕a4	♖b8
16	♕xe4	♕a5+
17	♘d2!	

In the first game with 10...♗xb5, Zsu.Polgar-Illescas, Bilbao 1987, White suffered a crushing defeat after 17 ♔d1? ♖xb2 18 e3 ♘f6 19 ♕e5 ♕a4+ 20 ♔e1 ♕b4+ 21 ♔d1 ♖e8 −+.

| 17 | ... | ♖xb2 |
| 18 | ♖d1 | ♘f6!? |

Nor can White rely on an advantage after 18...♖fb8 19 ♕f4! (19 e3? ♖xd2! 20 ♖xd2 ♖b2 21 ♕d3 ♘e5 and wins) 19...♖xa2!? (White managed to defend himself in Ivanchuk-Norwood, Arnhem jr 1987, after 19...♘f6 20 e4 ♖e8 21 ♗d3 ♘xd5 22 ♕g5! ♘c3 23 ♘c4! ♘xe4+ 24 ♘xa5 ♘xg5+ 25 ♔f1 ♘e4 26 ♘c4! ♖xf2+ 27 ♔g1 ♖xa2 28 ♖e1 ±, but 19...♖8b4 20 e4 ♖d4 deserves attention) 20 e4 ♖bb2 and, in view of the fact that 21 ♗c4?! is not very good because of 21...♖xd2! 22 ♖xd2 ♖a1+, one should prefer Black's position.

19   ♕c4

White must be very careful, as 19 ♕e5? loses; 19...♖xa2 20 e3 ♖e8 21 ♕f4 ♖xd2 22 ♖xd2 ♘e4 −+ Barlov-Zelčić, Biel 1991.

19	...	♖xa2
20	e3	♖b8
21	♗d3	

Or 21 ♗e2 ♖bb2 22 0-0 ♖xd2 23 ♖xd2 ♕xd2, Khenkin-Arkhipov, Moscow 1989.

| 21 | ... | ♖bb2 |
| 22 | 0-0 | |

22 ♕c1? is not advisable for White: 22...♘xd5 23 ♗c4 ♖xd2! 24 ♕xd2 ♖xd2 25 ♖xd2 ♕a1+ 26 ♖d1 ♕c3+ −+.

22	...	♖xd2
23	d6!	♘d7
24	♕b5	♕c3
25	♗c4	♖ab2
26	♕xd7	♕xc4

with a small advantage to Black, Gaprindashvili-Bellón, Biel 1988.

D) 7 ♗g5 h6

Matters turn out worse for Black if he fails to disturb the dark-squared bishop, for example 7...♗g7 8 e3 0-0 9 ♘d2 (D) and now:

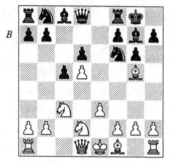

a) White's chances are much preferable after 9...b6 10 ♗c4!? ♘bd7 11 0-0 h6 (or 11...♕e7 12 a4 ♖b8 13 ♗e2 ♖e8 14 ♔h1 h6 15 ♗h4 g5 16 ♗g3 ♘e5 17 h3 ± Psakhis-Barczay, Dortmund 1982) 12 ♗h4 a6 13 a4 ♘e5 14 ♗e2 ♕c7 15 ♖c1 ♖b8 16 h3 with a small but tangible advantage to White in Psakhis-Karlsson, Dortmund 1982.

b) 9...♘a6 10 e4 ♖e8 11 ♗e2 ♘c7 12 a4 a6 13 0-0 ♖b8 14 a5 ♗d7 15 f4 ♘b5 16 ♗d3 ± Psakhis-Suba, Las Palmas 1982.

c) 9...a6 10 a4 ♘bd7 11 ♗e2 ♖e8 12 0-0 ♖b8 (or 12...♕c7 13 ♖c1!? b6 14 e4 h6 15 ♗h4 g5 16 ♗g3 ♘e5 17 h3 ± intending f4 and kingside play)

13 h3! ♕c7 14 ♔h1 h6 15 ♗f4 g5 16 ♗g3! (16 ♗h2 ♘e5 17 f4 gxf4 18 exf4 ♘g6 19 f5 ♘h4! Tukmakov) 16...♘e5 17 f4 gxf4 18 exf4 ♘g6 19 f5 ♘e5 20 ♘de4 ♘xe4 21 ♘xe4 with an obvious plus for White; Tukmakov-Larsen, Las Palmas 1978.

8 ♗h4

After the illogical 8 ♗f4 Black quickly seizes the initiative: 8...♘h5 9 ♗g3 ♗g7 10 ♘d2 ♘xg3 11 hxg3 ♘d7 12 e3 0-0 13 ♗e2 ♘e5 14 a4 b6 15 ♕c2 ♕e7 16 0-0 h5! Filip-Rajković, Smederevska Palanka 1978.

8 ...   g5

I think this is a very precise move. The dark-squared bishop is an important piece and its destruction might be decisive in weakening the pawn structure. You also see 8...♗g7 *(D)*:

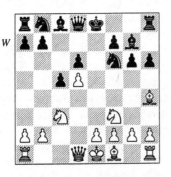

a) 9 e4!?, leading us to A71.

b) 9 ♘d2 g5 (it's not worth weakening the queenside with 9...a6?! 10 a4 g5 11 ♗g3 ♘h5 12 ♘c4 ♘xg3 13 hxg3 ♗f5 14 e3 0-0 15 ♗d3 ♗xd3 16 ♕xd3 ± Vasiliev-Blekhtsin, Liepaja 1974; White also has an advantage after 9...♕e7 10 e4 ♘bd7 11

♗e2 g5 12 ♗g3 ♘e5 13 0-0 ♗d7 14 a4 ± Horvath-Garcia Palermo, Oakham 1986) 10 ♗g3 ♘h5 11 ♕a4+ ♔f8 12 e3 (or 12 e4 ♘xg3 13 hxg3 a6 14 ♗e2 ♘d7 15 ♕c2 ♘e5 16 0-0 h5 ∞ Popov-Kluger, Sofia 1962) and now:

b1) 12...a6 13 ♕c2 b5 14 a4 b4 15 ♘ce4!? ♗f5 (or 15...♘xg3 16 ♘xg3) 16 ♗d3 ♘xg3 17 hxg3 ♘d7 18 0-0 ± Cebalo-J.Horvath, Zenica 1987.

b2) 12...♘xg3 13 hxg3 ♘d7 14 ♕c2 ♘e5 15 ♗e2 a6 16 a4 h5!? (significantly stronger than 16...g4?! 17 ♖h5! ♖b8 18 a5 ± Spasov-Arnandov, Bulgaria 1972) 17 a5 (17 ♖xh5 ♖xh5 18 ♗xh5 g4 and big problems with the bishop suddenly appear for White) 17...g4 = Uhlmann-Espig, Raach 1969.

c) 9 e3 0-0 (for 9...g5 10 ♗g3 ♘h5, see 8...g5, and Black also has a reasonable game after 9...a6 10 a4 ♗g4!? 11 ♕c2 ♗xf3 12 gxf3 ♘bd7 13 a5 0-0 14 f4 b5 15 axb6 ♕xb6 = Hartston-Bronstein, Tallinn 1979, as well as after the rarely played 9...♕b6!? 10 ♖b1 ♗g4 11 ♗e2 ♗xf3 12 ♗xf3 0-0 13 0-0 ♘bd7 14 ♗g3 ♖fc8 = Yuferov-Magerramov, USSR 1978) 10 ♘d2 and now:

c1) 10...a6 11 a4 ♘bd7 12 ♗e2 ♕e7 (12...♖e8 does not equalize, for example 13 0-0 ♕c7 14 e4 ♖b8 15 f4 c4 16 ♔h1 b5 17 axb5 axb5 18 e5! dxe5 19 fxe5 with advantage; Csabolcsi-Armas, French Cht 1993) 13 0-0 ♖b8 14 ♕c2 ♖d8 15 h3 ±.

c2) 10...♘bd7 11 ♗e2 ♕e7 (or 11...♘e5 12 ♘de4!? ♕e7 13 0-0 a6

14 a4 ♖e8 15 a5 with a small advantage, but after 15...♗f5? Black loses quickly: 16 ♘xf6+ ♗xf6 17 ♗xf6 ♛xf6 18 f4! ♘d7 19 g4 ♗e4 20 ♖a4! +− Lechtynsky-Bönsch, Halle 1981) 12 0-0 g5 13 ♗g3 ♘e5!? 14 a4 ♗f5 15 e4 ♗d7 and White should have played the simple 16 h3!? instead of 16 ♖e1?! ♖fe8 17 ♘f1 h5! 18 f3 h4 19 ♗f2 ♘h5 after which Black seized the initiative in Bjork-Romanishin, Stockholm tt 1986.

c3) 10...♘a6 11 ♘c4 (Black can achieve a satisfactory game with exact play after 11 ♗c4 ♘c7 12 0-0 a6 {or 12...♖e8 13 a4 ♖b8 14 e4 g5 15 ♗g3 a6 16 a5 b5 17 axb6 ♖xb6 18 ♗d3! ♘b5 19 ♘c4 ± T.Georgadze-Dorfman, Erevan Z 1982} 13 a4 ♖b8 14 a5 b5 15 axb6 ♖xb6 was unclear in D.Gurevich-Wedberg, Helsinki 1983) 11...♖e8 (White is a little better after 11...♘c7 12 a4 b6 13 ♗e2 ♗a6 14 ♘a3!? ♗xe2 15 ♛xe2 g5 {15...♛d7!?} 16 ♗g3 ♘cxd5 17 ♘xd5 ♘xd5, Cebalo-Franco, Lucerne 1989, and White should have continued 18 ♘c4! ±) 12 ♗e2 ♘c7 13 a4 b6 14 0-0 ♗a6 15 ♛b3 ♛e7 16 ♖fd1 ♗xc4 Tukmakov-Lechtynsky, Vilnius 1978, and I think that after 17 ♛xc4 White's position is the more promising.

9 ♗g3   ♘h5 (D)
10 e3

10 e4 ♘xg3 11 fxg3 (11 hxg3 ♗g7 12 ♛c2 a6 13 a4 ♘d7 14 ♘d2 ♘e5 quickly leads to an equal line of A71) 11...♗g7 12 ♛a4+ ♘d7 13 ♗e2 0-0 14 0-0 ♛e7 15 ♛c2 ♘e5 and it was already difficult for White

to equalize in the game Peev-Gochev, Sofia 1981.

After the dubious 10 ♛a4+?! Black gets a wonderful game from both 10...♗d7!? 11 ♛e4+ ♛e7 12 ♗xd6 ♛xe4 13 ♘xe4 f5 14 ♗xb8 ♖xb8 15 ♘c3 b5 Geller-Suetin, Moscow 1960, and from the probably even stronger 10...♘d7 11 ♛e4+ ♛e7 12 ♗xd6 ♛xe4 13 ♘xe4 f5 14 ♗xf8 fxe4 15 ♗xh6 ♖xh6 16 ♘xg5 e3! ∓ Shadursky-Suetin, Vladimir 1962.

Finally, 10 ♘d2 ♘xg3 11 hxg3:

a) We have already seen many times that Black's activity on the queenside rarely pays him any kind of dividends, and this position is no exception: 11...a6 12 e3 b5?! 13 a4 b4 14 ♘ce4 g4 15 ♘c4 f5 16 ♘ed2 ± Piket-Riemersma, Dutch Cht 1987.

b) Black played better in Agdestein-Ljubojević, Wijk aan Zee 1988: 11...♘d7 12 ♘c4 ♘b6 13 e3 a6 14 a4 ♗g7 15 ♛d2 ♘xc4 16 ♗xc4 ♗d7 17 a5 and after the simple 17...b5 18 axb6 ♛xb6 his chances would have been no worse

c) 11...♗g7 12 ♘c4 0-0 (12...a6?! 13 a4 0-0 14 ♘e4!? ♘d7 15 ♘exd6

♘b6 16 a5 ♘xc4 17 ♘xc4 ♗d7 18 ♖a2 ± Agdestein-Cebalo, Taxco IZ 1985) 13 e3 and we find ourselves in the variation with 10 e3.

Returning to the position after 10 e3 *(D)*:

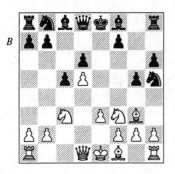

10 ...   ♘xg3

If he wishes, Black can also play 10...♗g7, as he need not fear checks on either b5 or a4; indeed his king is quite comfortably positioned on f8:

a) 11 ♕a4+ ♗d7 12 ♕b3 ♘xg3 13 hxg3 ♕c7 14 ♘d2 0-0 15 ♗e2 ♘a6 16 0-0 ♖ab8 ∓ Zurakhov-Zhidkov, Kiev 1971.

b) 11 ♗d3 0-0 12 ♕c2 (or 12 ♘d2 ♘xg3 13 hxg3 ♘d7 14 ♘c4 ♘b6 15 ♘xb6 ♕xb6 16 ♕c2 ♗d7 17 ♖b1 f5 = Antoshin-Psakhis, Sochi 1979) 12...f5 13 ♗e2 ♘a6 14 ♘d2 ♘xg3 15 hxg3 ♕e7 = Malaniuk-Van der Werf, Groningen 1990.

c) 11 ♗b5+ and now:

c1) There's no point in Black exchanging bishops with 11...♗d7? 12 ♗xd7+ ♘xd7 (12...♕xd7 13 ♘e5!) 13 ♗xd6 ♕b6 14 ♘e4 f5 15 ♘fd2 g4 16 ♕a4! fxe4 17 ♕xe4+ ± Szilagyi-Sergian, Hungary 1977.

c2) 11...♔e7?! is equally unsatisfactory, for example 12 ♗d3 ♘xg3 13 hxg3 ♗g4 14 ♕c2 a6 15 ♘d2 b5 16 a4 b4 17 ♘cb1 ♖e8 18 ♘c4 ♔f8 19 ♘bd2 ± Knežević-Rogulj, Smederevska Palanka 1977.

c3) 11...♔f8 with the branch:

c31) 12 ♗e2 ♘xg3 13 hxg3 ♘d7 (13...f5? 14 ♘d2 ♘d7 15 ♕c2 ♘e5 16 f4! gxf4 17 exf4 ± Lerner-Ionescu, Moscow 1987) 14 ♕c2 ♕e7 15 ♖b1 ♘e5 16 ♘xe5 ♕xe5 17 g4 ♗d7 18 a4 h5! 19 gxh5 g4 and Black already has better prospects; Spasov-Hort, Slanchev Briag 1974.

c32) Black also has an excellent game after 12 ♕c2 a6 13 ♗d3 ♘xg3 14 fxg3 b5 15 0-0 ♖a7! 16 ♖f2 ♘d7 17 a4 b4 18 ♘e4 ♘b6 19 ♖af1 a5!? ∓ Borges-Gavrikov, Tallinn 1989.

c33) 12 ♗d3 ♘xg3 13 hxg3 (13 fxg3 ♕e7 14 0-0!? ♘d7 15 ♗f5 ♘f6 16 ♘d2 a6 17 ♕f3 ♔g8 18 ♗xc8 ♖xc8 19 ♖f2 ♖e8 20 ♖af1 h5 = Yusupov-Gavrikov, Frunze 1981, is interesting, but not sufficient for an advantage) 13...♘d7 14 ♕c2 ♕e7 15 ♗f5 (castling too soon gives Black an object for attack: 15 0-0?! h5! 16 ♗f5 g4 17 ♘d2 h4 with initiative) 15...♖b8 16 a4 a6 17 a5 ♕f6 18 ♘d2 h5 = Antoshin-Psakhis, Moscow 1981.

11 hxg3   ♗g7
12 ♗d3!?

Other moves:

a) Again the check is superfluous: 12 ♕a4+?! ♘d7 13 ♕e4+ ♕e7 14 ♘d2 and Black has a good game after both 14...♘f6!? 15 ♕xe7+ (15 ♕a4+ ♗d7 16 ♗b5 a6 =) 15...♔xe7 with equality, and 14...♘e5 15 ♗b5+ ♔f8 16 ♘c4 ♖b8! 17 ♘xe5 ♗xe5 18 ♗d3 f5 with an edge for Black; Gil-Dolmatov, Barcelona 1983.

b) After 12 ♗b5+, the reply 12...♔f8 again seems best, whilst after 12...♗d7 13 a4 0-0 14 ♕d3! f5 15 ♘d2 a6 16 ♗xd7 ♘xd7 17 f4 White's position was preferable in Mi.Tseitlin-O'Shaughnessy, Hastings 1992.

c) 12 ♘d2 *(D)* enjoys notably more popularity, although in my opinion Black can achieve equality in various ways:

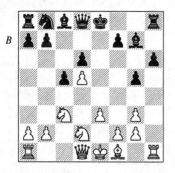

c1) 12...0-0 13 ♘c4 ♕e7 (the alternative 13...♘a6!? deserves attention, for example 14 ♘b5?! ♗d7 15 a4 ♗xb5 16 axb5 ♘b4 17 ♗e2 f5 = or 14 ♗e2 ♘c7 15 a4 b6 16 e4 ♕e7 17 ♕d2 ♗d7 18 e5!? ♗xe5 19 ♘xe5 ♕xe5 20 ♖xh6 ♕g7 with an unclear game; Agdestein-D.Gurevich, Jerusalem 1986) and now:

c11) 14 ♗e2 ♖d8 15 0-0 ♘d7 16 a4 ♘e5 17 ♘xe5 ♗xe5 (17...♕xe5 18 a5! ♖b8 19 ♖a2 ♗d7, Botvinnik-Tal, Moscow Wch 1960, and White could have played 20 ♗b5!? with a

small advantage) 18 ♕c2 f5 with a level position.

c12) Black has no problems after 14 ♕c2 f5 15 ♗e2 (greed is punished: 15 ♘b5 ♖f6! 16 ♘cxd6? ♗d7 17 ♕b3 ♖xd6 18 ♘xd6 ♕xd6 19 ♕xb7 ♕b6 20 ♗a6 {20 ♕xa8 ♕xb2 −+} 20...♕a5+! 21 ♔d1 ♗a4+ −+ Piket-Wahls, Adelaide jr Wch 1988) 15...♗d7 16 a4 ♘a6 17 0-0 ♘b4 = Smejkal-Ftačnik, Prague 1989.

c13) 14 ♗d3 ♘d7 (Black has a good alternative in 14...♘a6!? 15 ♖c1 ♘c7 16 a4 ♗d7 17 ♘e4 ♘xd5 18 ♘exd6 ♘b6!? = Bonin-D.Gurevich, Boston 1988) 15 0-0 (Black need not fear 15 ♘e4 ♘e5 16 ♘exd6 ♗g4! 17 ♗e2 ♘xc4 18 ♘xc4 ♗xe2 19 ♕xe2 ♕e4 20 0-0 ♕xd5 = Bonin-Psakhis, rapid 1989) 15...♘e5 16 ♘xe5 ♕xe5 17 ♖e1 ♗d7 18 ♖b1 g4 = Germek-Tal, Bled 1961.

c2) 12...a6 13 a4 ♘d7 14 ♘ce4!? (or 14 ♗e2 ♘e5!? {14...b6 15 g4!?} 15 f4!? {in K.Grigorian-Kasparov, Baku 1980, Black easily achieved equality after 15 g4 0-0 16 0-0 f5 =} 15...♘d7 16 ♕c2 ♕e7 17 ♘c4 ♘f6 18 a5 ♗d7 19 e4 with pressure on Black's position; Kraidman-Greenfeld, Israeli Ch 1986) 14...♘f6 15 ♘xf6+ ♕xf6 16 ♘c4 ♖b8 17 a5 ♗d7 18 ♖a2 ♗b5 19 ♘b6 ± Bagirov-Beliavsky, Vitebsk 1970.

c3) 12...♘d7 13 ♕c2 (in the event of 13 ♘c4 complete equality can be achieved by both 13...♘e5 14 ♘xe5 ♗xe5 15 ♕c2 a6 16 a4 ♗g7 17 ♗d3 ♕e7 18 a5 0-0 Bagirov-Savon, Moscow 1973 and 13...♘b6 14 ♘xb6 ♕xb6 15 ♗b5+ ♔f8 16 ♕c2

♕d8 17 ♗d3 ♕f6 18 f4 ♕e7 19
♔f2 ♗d7 Naivelt-Moiseev, Voronezh 1981) 13...♘e5 (13...♕e7 is
also interesting, for example 14 a4
♘e5 15 ♗b5+ ♔f8 16 a5 h5! 17 a6
h4 18 gxh4 gxh4 with good counterplay; Karpov-Gavrikov, rapid 1988)
14 ♗b5+ ♗d7 (14...♔f8!?) 15 a4 a6
(or 15...0-0 16 ♗e2 ♕e7 17 ♖a3 f5 =
Geller-Malaniuk, Moscow 1983) 16
♗xd7+ ♕xd7 17 a5 0-0 18 0-0 ♕c7
19 ♖a4 b5 with an equal position;
Mi.Tseitlin-Kaidanov, Cheliabinsk
1980.

12   ...   ♘d7

Black experiences no problems
after 12...0-0!? 13 ♕c2 f5 (more
interesting than 13...♘d7 14 ♖b1
♕e7 15 ♗h7+! ♔h8 16 ♗f5 ♘e5 17
♗xc8 ♖axc8 18 ♕f5! ♘xf3+ 19
gxf3 ± Yuferov-Sarbai, Minsk 1978)
14 ♘d2 ♘a6 15 ♘c4 (15 a3!?)
15...♘b4 16 ♕d2 ♘xd3+ (it is also
possible to wait with this exchange:
16...a6!? 17 a4 b6) 17 ♕xd3 a6 18 a4
b6 = Lerner-Dolmatov, Kislovodsk
1982.

13   ♕c2 (D)

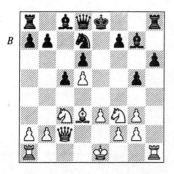

13   ...   ♕e7

In Tal-Tatai, Las Palmas 1975, after 13...♘f6 14 ♘d2 0-0 15 ♘c4
♕e7 16 a4 ♗d7 17 0-0 ♖ab8 18 ♖fe1
b6 White could have gained an advantage if he had played 19 ♗f5!.

Black may also try 13...a6 14 a4
♖b8 (alternatively, 14...♕e7 15 ♗f5
♘e5 {15...♘f6?! 16 a5 ♗xf5 17
♕xf5 ♖b8 18 ♘d2 0-0 19 ♘c4 is
less successful; Groszpeter-Stajčić,
Caissa KFT 1993} 16 a5!? ♗xf5 17
♕xf5 ♘d7 {Black has a dangerous
position after 17...♘xf3+ 18 gxf3
♕d7 19 ♕xd7+ ♔xd7 20 ♘a4!} 18
♘d2 b5 19 axb6 ♘xb6 20 g4 ±
Groszpeter-Kindermann, Budapest
1985) 15 0-0 (but not 15 ♗f5?! because of 15...b5 16 axb5 axb5 17
♖a7 ♕b6 18 ♖a2 b4 and Black already has the initiative; Yusupov-
Hulak, Toluca IZ 1982) 15...0-0 16
♖ab1 and now 16...♕e7!? should be
compared with the main line, whilst
after 16...♕c7?! White has an easy
and pleasant game: 17 ♖fc1 ♖e8 18
b4 cxb4 19 ♖xb4 ♘c5 20 ♗h7+
♔h8 21 ♘d4 ♗d7 22 ♗f5 ± Furman-Tal, Tallinn 1971.

14   a4 (D)

After 14 0-0?! h5 15 ♗f5 g4 16
♘h4 (16 ♘d2!?) 16...♗f6 17 ♘e4
♗xh4 18 gxh4 ♘e5 Black seizes the
initiative – Kapengut.

He also has no problems after 14
♘d2 ♘e5 15 ♗f5 ♗xf5 16 ♕xf5
♕d7!? (but not 16...c4?! 17 ♔e2! 0-0
{17...♕d7!?} 18 ♘ce4 b5 19 ♖xh6!
+– Psakhis-Gavrikov, Erevan 1982)
17 ♘ce4 ♔e7!.

14   ...   a6

15   ♖b1

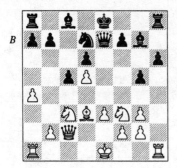

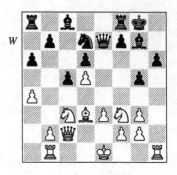

Again it's not worth White's while hurrying into castling: 15 0-0?! h5! 16 ♗f5 g4 17 ♘d2 ♘e5 (17...h4!? 18 ♘e2 ♘e5) 18 ♗xc8 ♖xc8 19 f4 gxf3 20 ♘xf3 ♘xf3+ 21 ♖xf3 ♖c7 = Balashov-Kapengut, Baku 1972.

Also possible: 15 ♗f5 b6!? (more circumspect than 15...♘e5?! 16 a5 ♗xf5 17 ♕xf5 ♕d7 18 ♕c2 0-0-0 19 ♘xe5 ♗xe5 20 ♘a4 ♔b8 21 ♘b6 ♕e7 22 g4 with an edge for White; Tukmakov-Agzamov, Erevan Z 1982) 16 ♘d2 ♖b8 and Black has a reasonable game.

15	...	0-0 *(D)*
16	0-0	♘e5!?
17	♘xe5	♕xe5
18	a5	♖b8
19	♖a1	b5
20	axb6	♖xb6 =

Hartston-Nunn, London 1981.

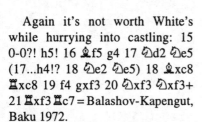

3 Fianchetto System: Introduction (A62)

1 d4 ♘f6 2 c4 c5 3 d5 e6 4 ♘c3 exd5 5 cxd5 d6

6	♘f3	g6
7	g3	♗g7
8	♗g2	0-0
9	0-0 (D)	

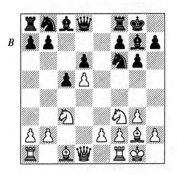

_B_

The system in which the bishop is developed to g2 occupies a very important place in the Modern Benoni, and this variation has particular importance as it can be reached by other move orders from the King's Indian Defence. It is hardly the most dangerous system for Black. However, it is especially difficult for Black to achieve an active game, which, strictly speaking, is the aim of those brave souls who play the Modern Benoni. We shall examine concrete variations as events develop.

Occasionally White tries 9 ♘d2, when there can follow 9...a6 10 a4 ♘bd7 11 ♘c4 (for 11 0-0 see A63) 11...♘b6 12 ♘a3 ♗d7 13 ♗d2 ♘xa4! 14 ♘xa4 b5 15 ♘c3 b4 = Krasenkov-Tolnai, Budapest 1989.

On the ninth move Black has a fairly large choice of continuations, which we divide up as follows:

A) Rare moves
B) 9...♖e8
C) 9...a6 10 a4 ♖e8
D) 9...♘a6

A) Rare moves

9	...	♗g4

Or:

a) 9...b6 (too slow, and besides the bishop on a6 has practically no function) 10 ♖e1 ♖e8 11 ♗f4 a6 12 e4 ♘g4 (12...b5 13 e5! is risky) 13 a4 ♖a7 14 h3 ♘e5 15 ♗xe5 ♗xe5 16 ♘xe5 dxe5 17 ♕b3 ± Zaitsev-Rashkovsky, Sochi 1976.

b) 9...♗d7 10 ♗f4 ♕e7 11 ♖e1 ♘a6 12 h3 ♖fe8 13 e4 ♘h5 14 ♗g5 ♕f8 15 g4 h6 16 ♗d2 ♘f6 17 ♗f4 with a small advantage to White; Urban-Anastasian, Debrecen 1992.

c) 9...♕e7 10 ♖e1 ♘bd7 11 h3 ♘e4 (or 11...♖b8 12 a4 ♘e4 13 ♖a3!? ♘df6 14 ♘d2 ♘g5 15 ♔h2

± Razuvaev-Nikoloff, Saint John 1988) 12 ♘xe4 ♕xe4 13 ♗f4 ♕e7 14 ♕d2 Birnboim-Lobron, Biel 1982, and even after the improvement 14...♘e5!? 15 ♘xe5 ♗xe5 16 ♗xe5 ♕xe5 17 e4 White's position is preferable.

10 ♘d2

10 h3 is not dangerous for Black: 10...♗xf3 11 ♗xf3 (or 11 exf3 a6 12 a4 ♘bd7 13 f4 c4 =) 11...♕d7!? (more interesting than the traditional 11...a6 12 a4 ♘bd7 13 ♖b1 ♕c7 14 ♗d2 ♖ab8 15 ♗g2 ♖fe8 16 ♕c2 b5 17 axb5 axb5 18 b4 ±) 12 ♔h2 b5 13 a3 ♕b7 14 ♗f4 ♘e8 15 e4 ♘d7 = Verat-Tatai, Cannes 1992. Black also has a decent game after 10 ♗f4 ♘h5 11 ♗g5 ♕d7 12 ♕b3 ♘a6.

10 ...   ♕d7
11 a4

Or 11 ♕b3 ♘a6 12 ♖d1 ♖ab8 13 f3 ♗h3 14 ♗xh3 ♕xh3 = Furman-Taimanov, USSR 1961.

11 ...	**♗h3**
12 ♘c4	**♗xg2**
13 ♔xg2	**♕e7**
14 f3	**♘bd7**
15 ♗f4	**♘e8**
16 ♕d2	

with a small advantage for White; Makarov-Gufeld, Podolsk 1992.

B) 9...♖e8 *(D)*

10 ♗f4

Without doubt the most popular move, but not for certain the best. White also has various other continuations, some of which offer hope of an adavantage:

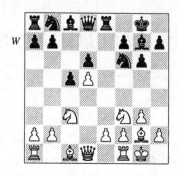

a) Black has an easy game after 10 a4?! ♘e4 11 ♘xe4 ♖xe4 12 ♗g5 ♕f8 13 ♘d2 ♖b4 14 ♖a2 h6 15 ♗e3 ♘d7 16 ♕c1 b6 = Jukić-Shabalov, Geneva 1992.

b) Chances for both sides arise after 10 ♖e1 ♘e4!? (White develops an initiative without any problems after the sluggish 10...b6?! 11 h3 a6 12 e4 ♖a7 13 e5 dxe5 14 ♖xe5 ♖ae7 15 ♗f4 ♘bd7 16 ♖xe7 ♖xe7 17 ♗c7! ± Sosonko-Ljubojević, Reggio Emilia 1985) 11 ♘xe4 ♖xe4 12 ♗g5 ♕f8 13 ♘d2 ♖g4 14 ♗f4 g5 15 ♗e3 ♗xb2 16 ♖b1 ♖b4 ∞ Razuvaev-Chiburdanidze, Tashkent 1980.

c) Black has several ways to strive for a satisfactory game after 10 ♘d2, e.g. 10...♘g4!? (10...a6!? 11 a4 ♘bd7 reaches A64] and 10...♘a6 11 ♘c4 ♘c7 transposes to variation D32; 10...b6 doesn't look too bad either, and after the rough variation 11 ♘c4 ♗a6 12 ♕a4 ♗xc4 13 ♕xc4 a6 14 a4 b5! 15 ♕b3 b4 Almeida-Gonzalez, Barcelona tt 1993, Black has nothing to complain about in the result of the opening) 11 ♘de4 a6 12 ♗g5 f6 13 ♗f4 ♘e5 14 a4 ♘f7 15 ♘d2 g5 16 ♗e3 ♘d7 17 ♘c4 ♘de5 with an equal position; Kharitonov-Agzamov, Sevastopol 1986.

d) On the other hand, 10 h3!? deserves attention: 10...♘e4 11 ♘xe4 ♖xe4 12 ♗g5 ♕c7 13 ♘d2 ♖e8 14 ♗f4!? (after 14 ♘e4, Black is able to execute a rabid exchange sacrifice: 14...♖xe4! 15 ♗xe4 ♗xh3 16 ♗g2 ♗xg2 17 ♔xg2 ♗xb2 18 ♖b1 ♗g7 19 ♕a4 ♘d7 ∓ G.Kuzmin-Tal, Riga IZ 1979) 14...♘d7 15 ♘c4 ♘e5 16 ♘xe5 ♗xe5 17 ♗xe5 ♖xe5 18 e4 ♗d7 19 ♕d2 ± G.Kuzmin-Bouaziz, Riga IZ 1979.

Returning to the position after 10 ♗f4 *(D)*:

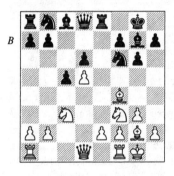

10 ... ♘a6

Of course, this position can be reached by a different move order – 9...♘a6 10 ♗f4 ♖e8. In practice Black has also tried:

a) 10...♗g4 11 ♕b3 b6 12 h3 ♗xf3 13 ♗xf3 ♗f8 14 a4 ♘bd7 15 e4 ± Adorjan-Perenyi, Hungary tt 1987.

b) 10...b6 11 ♘g5 (or 11 h3!?) 11...♘a6 12 ♘ge4 ♘xe4 13 ♘xe4 ♗f8 14 ♕d2 ♘c7 15 ♗g5 ♗e7 = Sosonko-Andersson, Tilburg 1977.

c) 10...♘e4 11 ♘xe4 ♖xe4 12 ♘d2 ♖xf4 (an interesting idea was used in Alburt-Peters, USA Ch 1981: 12...♖b4 13 a3 ♖xf4!? 14 gxf4 ♗xb2 15 ♖a2 ♗g7 16 e4 ♘a6 17 ♖e1 b5 18 e5 ♗f5 with sufficient compensation; with a cunning manoeuvre Black caught his opponent's rook occupying a passive position) 13 gxf4 ♗xb2 14 ♖b1 ♗g7 15 ♘f3 (15 ♘c4 b6) 15...♘d7 with compensation; Dam-Norwood, Groningen 1988.

d) 10...♘h5 11 ♗g5:

d1) Black has a reasonable game after 11...♕d7 12 a4 (12 e4 b5 13 ♖e1 b4 14 ♘a4 ♘a6 15 h3 ♗b7 16 a3 ♘f6 = Sosonko-Smyslov, Tilburg 1977) 12...♘a6 13 ♖e1 b6 14 e4 ♘b4 15 ♗f1 ♗a6 16 ♗xa6 ♘xa6 17 ♘d2 h6 18 ♗e3 ♘c7 = Peicheva-Maus, Copenhagen 1990.

d2) 11...♕b6:

d21) 12 ♕d2 ♘a6!? (White's position is more active after 12...♘d7 13 h3 a6 14 ♖ac1 ♘e5 15 g4 ♘f6 16 ♘xe5 ♖xe5 17 b3 ♗d7 18 ♔h1 ♖f8 19 f4 ♖ee8 20 e4 Sosonko-Timman, Tilburg 1979, or 12...♗g4 13 ♘h4! {13 h3 ♗xf3 14 ♗xf3 ♘f6 15 e4 ♘bd7 16 ♗g2 a6 = Ligterink-Psakhis, Plovdiv 1983} 13...♗c8?! 14 e4 ♘d7 15 ♘f3 a6 16 ♖ac1 ♘e5 17 ♘xe5 ♗xe5 18 f4 ♗d4+ 19 ♔h1 with an edge for White; Ligterink-Kudrin, Wijk aan Zee 1985) 13 h3 f6 14 ♗e3 f5 15 ♖ab1 ♗d7 16 ♗h6 ♗h8 = I.Ivanov-Kapengut, USSR 1977.

d22) 12 ♕c1!? (possibly better than the line above) 12...♘d7 (the eternal choice of where to develop the knight, d7 or a6; this time it is better to decide in favour of d7 – 12...♘a6?! 13 ♗h6 ♗h8 14 ♘d2! ♘c7 15 ♗f3 ♘f6 16 ♘c4 ♕a6 17 ♕f4, with a big advantage to White in Alburt-D.Gurevich, USA 1985) 13 a4 (or 13 ♗h6 ♗h8 14 h3 a6 15 g4 ♘hf6 16 ♘d2 ♕c7 17 f4 b5 18 f5 ♗b7 19 e4 ♘e5 ∞ Alburt-Kudrin, Hastings 1983) 13...c4 14 ♗e3 ♘c5 15 ♘d2 ♖xe3! (the only move, for example 15...♕b4?! 16 ♗xc5! ♕xc5 17 ♘ce4) 16 fxe3 ♕b4 17 ♘a2 ♕xb2 18 ♘xc4 ♕xa1 19 ♕a3 (19 ♕xa1 ♗xa1 20 ♖xa1 ♘xa4) 19...♕xf1+ 20 ♔xf1 ♗f8 21 e4 f6 Birnboim-Grünfeld, Munich Z 1987. I suspect that White's chances could be better, but proving this will not be easy.

11 ♖e1 *(D)*

White is promised little by 11 ♘b5 ♗f8 12 ♖e1 ♘c7 13 ♘xc7 ♕xc7 14 ♖c1 a5! 15 b3 ♗d7 = Kaidanov-Romanishin, Groningen PCA 1993, or 11 ♘d2 ♘h5 12 ♗e3 ♘c7 13 a4 b6 14 ♘c4 ♗a6 15 ♕b3 ♕d7 and the position is balanced; Kapelan-Davies, Vršac 1989.

Interesting possibilities arise for both sides after 11 h3 ♘c7 12 a4 ♘e4 (or 12...b6 13 ♖e1 ♘e4 14 ♘xe4 ♖xe4 15 ♘d2 ♖xf4 16 gxf4 ♕h4 17 e3 and in this unclear position the players agreed a draw in Fedorowicz-D.Gurevich, New York 1988) 13 ♘xe4 ♖xe4 14 ♘d2 ♖b4 15 b3 b5!? (it is also difficult to assess the position after 15...♖xf4!? 16 gxf4 ♗xa1 17 ♕xa1 ♕h4 18 ♕c3 ♕xf4 19 e3 ♕h4 20 e4 ♕f4 21 b4!

Savchenko-Romanishin, Simferopol 1988) 16 ♖a2 a5 17 ♕c1 ♗a6 18 ♘e4 ♘e8 19 axb5 ♗xb5 20 ♕c2 c4 and Black's chances are definitely no worse; Razuvaev-Romanishin, Palma GMA 1989.

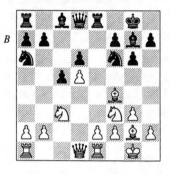

11 ... ♗g4

a) If 11...♘c7 then 12 e4 ♘h5 (or 12...♗g4 13 h3 ♗xf3 14 ♗xf3 ♕d7 15 e5! {15 a4 h6 16 ♗g2 ♘h5 17 ♗e3 b5 18 axb5 ♘xb5 19 ♕a4 a6 = Barbero-Frias, Wijk aan Zee 1991} 15...dxe5 16 ♗xe5 ♖ad8 17 ♕b3! ±) 13 ♗g5 f6 14 ♗d2 b5 15 h3 ♗f8 16 a3 a5 17 b4! Lahav-Grünfeld, Tel Aviv 1988, leads to a clear advantage for White.

b) 11...♘h5 is also in White's favour; 12 ♗g5 ♕d7 13 e4!? (or 13 ♕d2 b5 14 ♗h6 ♗h8 15 ♘g5 b4 16 ♘d1 ♘c7 17 a3 ± Sosonko-Ligterink, Hilversum 1986) 13...b5 14 ♗f1 ♘c7 15 e5 dxe5 16 d6 b4 17 ♘a4 ♘e6 18 ♗c4 Scheeren-Ligterink, Hilversum 1984.

c) 11...♘e4 deserves a great deal of attention: 12 ♘xe4 ♖xe4 13 ♘d2 ♖d4 (13...♖xf4!?) 14 a3 ♖xf4 15 gxf4 ♗xb2 16 ♖a2 ♗g7 17 e4 b5 18

11. Nd2 - Nc4 - NxNe5

e5 ♗f5 gave rise to interesting play in Gleizerov-Moskalenko, Alushta 1993.

12 h3

12 ♘d2!? may promise more, but after 12 e4?! ♘d7! 13 ♕b3 (13 ♗xd6 ♕b6) 13...♗xf3 14 ♗xf3 ♘e5 15 ♗e2 ♖b8 Hausner-Razuvaev, Bundesliga 1991, White is the only one who may face problems.

12 **...**	**♗xf3**
13 ♗xf3	**♕d7**
14 e4	**♖ad8**

14...c4!?.

15 ♔g2	**c4**
16 ♗e3	**♘b4**

16...b6!?.

17 ♗xa7	**♘d3**
18 ♖e2	**b5**

with chances for both sides; Adorjan-Romanishin, Debrecen 1990.

C) 9...a6

10 a4	**♖e8** (D)

10...♘bd7!? leads to A63.

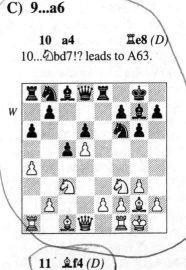

11 ♗f4 (D)

A logical move; White impedes the development of the knight to d7,

and, depending on the situation, can either increase the pressure on the d6 pawn, or try to organize a breakthrough in the centre by advancing the e-pawn. We shall look at the possible events after other continuations:

a) 11 ♗g5 h6 12 ♗xf6 ♗xf6 13 ♘d2 ♘d7 14 ♘ce4 ♗e7 15 ♘c4 ♘b6 16 ♘xb6 ♕xb6 17 ♕d2 ♔h7 was level in G.Kuzmin-Moldobaev, Frunze 1987. Exchanging the bishop limits White's possibilities.

b) 11 ♕c2 ♕c7 12 e4 ♘bd7 13 ♗f4 ♖b8 14 ♖fe1 h6 15 h3 g5 16 ♗d2 ♘f8 17 a5 ♘g6 18 ♘a4 ± G.Kuzmin-Aseev, Tashkent 1984.

c) 11 h3 ♘e4 12 ♘xe4 (12 ♖a3 ♘d7 13 ♘xe4 ♖xe4 14 ♘d2 ♖e8 15 ♘c4 ♘e5 = Hübner-Tal, Montreal 1979) 12...♖xe4 13 ♘d2!? (or 13 ♗g5 ♕c7 {13...♕f8 14 ♘d2 ♖b4 15 ♖a2 ♘d7 16 b3 b5 17 axb5 ♖xb5 18 ♘c4 ± G.Kuzmin-Sideif Zade, Tashkent 1980} 14 ♕d2 ♖b4 15 ♖a2 ♘d7 16 b3 ♖b8 17 a5 b5 18 axb6 ♘xb6 19 ♕c2 a5 = Sosonko-Galego, Novi Sad OL 1990) 13...♖b4 14 ♖a2 b5 15 axb5 ♘d7 16 ♕c2 with a small advantage to White.

d) 11 ♖e1 ♘e4 12 ♘xe4 ♖xe4 13 ♕c2!? (13 ♗g5 ♕c7 14 ♘d2 ♖b4 15 ♘e4 ♘d7 = and immoderate optimism led White to failure in Iskov-Karlsson, Esbjerg 1981: 16 ♗e7? ♖xe4! 17 ♗xe4 f6 18 ♗g2 ♘e5) 13...♖e8 14 e4 ♘d7 15 ♗f4 ♕c7 16 ♖ad1 ♖b8 17 b4 and White's pressure is very unpleasant; Manor-Levitt, Tel Aviv 1989,

11 **...**	**♘e4**

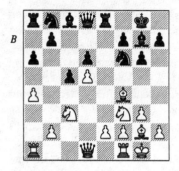

By exchanging the knight, Black activates his rook and uncovers an attack on the b2-pawn, which is temporarily undefended. Others:

a) 11...h6 and now:

a1) 12 ♖e1 is not convincing: 12...g5 (12...♗f5 is better for White: 13 ♕b3 ♘e4 {13...♕c7!?} 14 ♘xe4 ♖xe4 15 ♕xb7 ♘d7 16 ♗xd6 ♖b4 17 ♕c7! ± Gulko-Zakharov, Moscow 1976) 13 ♗c1 ♘bd7 14 ♕c2 ♖b8 15 ♖b1 b5 16 axb5 axb5 17 b4 cxb4! 18 ♖xb4 ♕a5 19 ♕b1 ♘c5 was unclear in Kharitonov-Mi.Tseitlin, Sochi 1981.

a2) 12 ♕c1 g5 13 ♗d2 ♘bd7 14 h4 g4 15 ♘e1 ♔h7 16 ♘c2 ♘e5 17 ♘e3 ♖b8 18 b4!? (18 ♖b1 b5 19 axb5 axb5 20 b4 ± Gleizerov-Ulybin, Kursk 1987, is also not that bad) 18...b5 (18...cxb4 19 ♕b1+) 19 axb5 axb5 20 ♕c2+ ♔g8 21 ♖fb1 with advantage for White; P.Nikolić-Kindermann, Plovdiv 1983.

b) 11...b6 12 ♖e1 (12 ♖c1 ♖a7 13 ♘d2 ♘h5 14 ♗e3 f5 15 ♘c4 ♗b7 ∞ Vaulin-Kovalev, Katowice 1990) 12...♖a7 13 e4 and Black does not succeed in equalizing after either 13...h6 14 ♕d2 ♖ae7 (14...g5 15

♗xd6! ♕xd6 16 e5) 15 e5 ± Kaidanov-Ashley, New York 1992, or 13...♖ae7 14 ♘d2 ♘g4 15 ♘c4 ♗d4 16 ♖f1 ♘e5 17 ♘xe5 ♗xe5 18 ♗g5 f6 19 ♗e3 ± Kaidanov-Vazquez, Andorra 1991.

c) 11...♕c7 12 ♖c1 (12 ♕c1 ♗g4 13 ♖e1 ♗xf3 14 ♗xf3 ♘bd7 15 b3 ♖ab8 16 ♕a3 ♘g4 = Hulak-Åkesson, Berlin 1988 does not create any problems for Black) 12...♘bd7 13 b4! ♘h5 14 ♗d2 ♖b8 15 ♖e1 b5 16 axb5 axb5 17 e4 and White preserves his traditional advantage; Manor-Ward, Oakham 1990.

d) 11...♗f5 12 ♘h4 ♗c8 13 ♕d2 ♕e7 14 h3 ♖f8 15 g4 ♘bd7 16 ♘f3 ♘e4 17 ♘xe4 ♖xe4 18 e3 ♖b4 19 ♖a2 ± Christiansen-Sax, Moscow IZ 1982.

e) 11...♗g4 12 ♕d2 ♗xf3 13 ♗xf3 ♕c7 14 ♖fc1! ♘bd7 15 b4 ♘e5 16 ♗xe5 ♖xe5 17 bxc5 ♕xc5 18 ♖ab1 and again White's position is slightly better; Sosonko-Smejkal, Biel IZ 1976.

f) 11...♘h5!? 12 ♗g5 f6 (Black's chances for an attacking game diminish after the dark-squared bishop is swapped; 12...♗f6 13 ♗xf6 ♘xf6 14 ♘d2 ♘bd7 15 a5 ♖b8 16 h3 ♕e7 17 ♕c2 h5 18 e3 ± Dautov-Brauner, Baden-Baden 1990; White's chances are also better after 12...♕b6 13 ♕d2 ♘d7 14 a5 ♕c7 15 ♖fc1 ♖b8 16 b4! b5 17 axb6 ♕xb6 18 bxc5 ♘xc5 19 ♖ab1 ♘b3 20 ♕d1 ± Hausner-Damljanović, Trnava 1982) 13 ♗e3 f5 14 ♕d2 ♘d7 15 ♗g5 ♕c7 16 ♖fe1 ♘df6 with equality; Parker-Levitt, Dublin 1991.

12 ♘xe4

Or 12 ♖a3 ♗g4 13 h3 ♗xf3 14 ♗xf3 ♘f6 15 ♕c2 ♕c7 16 ♘b1 ♘bd7 17 b4 b5! = Kaminsky-Korchnoi, Sverdlovsk 1957.

12 ... ♖xe4
13 ♘d2 ♖b4 (D)

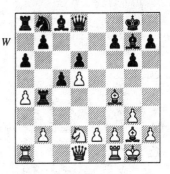

The premature standard exchange sacrifice 13...♖xf4 14 gxf4 ♗xb2 15 ♖b1 ♗g7 16 ♘c4 b5 17 axb5 axb5 18 ♖xb5 ♗a6 19 ♖a5 gave White a big advantage in Hulak-Bonin, New York 1989.

14 ♖a2!?

14 e4!? leads to an interesting game: 14...♖xb2 (14...♗xb2!?) 15 ♘c4 ♖b4 16 ♖c1 ♗d7 17 ♘xd6 ♗xa4 18 ♕f3 with initiative; Hofmann-Izeta, Benasque 1993.

14 ♘e4 also deserves attention: 14...h6 15 ♖a2! (more exact than 15 ♗d2 ♖xb2 16 ♕c1 ♖xd2! 17 ♕xd2 f5 18 ♘c3 ♕a5 19 ♖ac1 b5 with an excellent game for Black; Savon-Tal, USSR 1970) 15...♗h3!? (Black is left with just his pawn weaknesses after 15...f5 16 ♘c3 ♕f6 17 e4 ♘d7 18 exf5 gxf5 19 ♗d2 ± Adorjan-Marin, Szirak IZ 1987) 16

♗xh3 ♖xe4 17 a5 ♕c7 18 ♕c2 Adorjan-Armas, Bundesliga 1990, and now 18...♖d4!? 19 ♗g2 b5 leads to an unclear game.

14 ... ♕e7

The difficulties Black faces are well illustrated in the following variation: 14...g5 (or 14...♗xb2 15 ♕c2 ♗g7 16 ♘c4 ♕f6 17 ♘xd6 ♖xf4 18 ♘xc8 ♘d7 19 ♘e7+!? ♕xe7 20 gxf4 ± Rechlis-Plaskett, Netanya 1987) 15 ♗e3 f5 16 ♘f3 h6 17 ♕c1 ♕f6 18 h4! gxh4 (18...g4 19 ♘d2 ±) 19 ♘xh4 b5 20 axb5 ♖xb5 21 ♗h3 with an advantage to White; Sosonko-Hulak, Indonesia 1982.

15 b3 ♗e5
16 ♗xe5 ♕xe5
17 ♘c4 ♕e7
18 e4 ♘d7
19 f4 ♘b6!?

± Gleizerov-V.Gurevich, Uzhgorod 1988.

D) 9...♘a6 (D)

We shall now examine three possibilities in detail:

D1) 10 h3
D2) 10 ♗f4
D3) 10 ♘d2

A better place than c4 will not be found for the knight, and with line D3 he will quickly make for there. It is a good plan, but naturally not the only one. Another good plan is linked with an attempted breakthrough in the centre, principally considered in D1 and D2.

Let us briefly examine other possibilities:

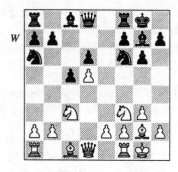

W

a) 10 a4 b6 (10...♞c7!? is not bad either; White's position is more promising after 10...♖e8 11 ♞d2 ♞b4 {or 11...♞d7 12 h3 ♞b4 13 ♞de4!? ♞f6 14 ♗g5 ♗f5 15 g4 ♗xe4 16 ♞xe4 h6 17 ♗xf6 ♗xf6 18 ♞xf6+ ♛xf6 19 ♛d2 Baquero-Garcia, Medellin 1987} 12 ♞c4 b6 13 ♗f4 ♗f8 14 ♛d2 ♗a6 15 b3 ± Hulak-Norwood, Toronto 1989) 11 ♗f4 ♞b4 12 ♛d2 ♖e8 13 ♗h6 ♗h8 14 ♗g5 ♛d7 15 ♖fe1 ♗a6 = Chiburdanidze-Winants, Brussels tt 1987.

b) 10 e4 ♗g4!? (after 10...♖e8 11 ♞d2 ♞c7 12 a4 b6 13 ♖e1 ♞g4! 14 ♞f3 ♞e5 15 ♞xe5 ♗xe5 16 h4, as in the game Moskalenko-Ehlvest, Helsinki 1992, Black could have had a promising position by continuing 16...f5!? 17 h5 ♛f6) 11 h3 ♗xf3 12 ♗xf3 ♞d7 13 ♗g2 c4 14 ♗e3 ♞ac5 with equality; Ghitescu-Ionescu, Timisoara 1987.

c) 10 ♖e1 ♖e8 11 ♞d2!? (11 ♗g5 ♛b6 12 ♛c2 ♞b4 13 ♛d2 ♗d7 is equal; Chernin-Lautier, Wijk aan Zee 1991) 11...♞c7 (11...♞d7!?) 12 ♞c4 ♞g4 (it is difficult to recommend 12...b5?! because of 13 ♞xd6! ♛xd6 14 ♗f4 ♛b6 15 d6 ♞e6 16

♗xa8 ♞xf4 17 gxf4 ♖d8 18 e3 ♖xd6 19 ♛e2 with advantage; Antić-Barlov, Yugoslav Ch 1991) 13 ♗f4 ♞e5 14 ♗xe5 ♗xe5 15 ♞xe5 ♖xe5 16 e4. White's position is somewhat preferable.

D1)   10 h3 (D)
A useful move, restricting Black's knight and bishop, and preparing to advance the e-pawn.

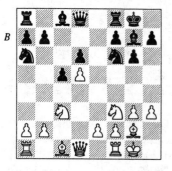

B

10   ...   ♖e8 (D)
Temporarily hindering the opposition's plans. Also possible:

a) 10...♗d7 and now:

a1) Complex variations arise after 11 e4 ♖e8 (11...♛c8 is imprecise: 12 ♗f4! {12 ♔h2 ♖e8 13 ♖e1 c4 14 e5 dxe5 15 ♞xe5 ♗f5 =} 12...♗xh3 13 ♗xd6 ♗xg2 14 ♔xg2 ♖e8 15 ♖e1 ♛d7 16 e5 ♞g4 17 ♞e4 ♖ad8 18 ♖c1 b6 19 e6! with a big advantage; Alburt-D.Gurevich, USA Ch 1989) 12 ♖e1 b5 13 e5 dxe5 14 ♖xe5 (or 14 ♞xe5 b4 15 ♞b1 ♞h5 16 ♞c6 ♗xc6 17 dxc6 ♗d4 18 ♖xe8+ ♛xe8, with the initiative to Black; Birnboim-Blees, Tel Aviv 1988) 14...b4 15 ♞e2 ♞e4 16 ♖xe8+ ♛xe8 17

♘f4 ♖d8 18 a3! ± Urban-Panczyk, Poland 1992.

a2) 11 ♗f4 also gives good chances for an advantage: 11...♖e8 12 ♘d2 (12 ♗xd6 ♗xh3) 12...♗f8 (12...♘h5 13 ♗xd6 ♗xh3 14 ♗xh3 ♕xd6 15 ♘c4 ♕d8 16 ♕b3 ♕g5 17 ♗g2 ♘b4, Kozlov-Agrest, USSR 1988, is interesting) 13 e4 b5 14 ♖e1 c4 15 a4! ♘c5 16 axb5 ♘d3 17 ♘xc4! ♘xe1 18 ♕xe1 ♕c7 19 ♕f1 ♘h5 20 ♗e3, with plenty of compensation for the exchange; Korchnoi-Honfi, Baden-Baden 1981.

a3) 11 a4!? ♘b4 (11...♖e8!? 12 ♖e1 is examined in the notes to 10...♖e8) 12 ♘d2 ♘e8 13 ♘c4 ♕e7 14 e4 ♖d8 15 ♖e1 b6 16 ♗f4 g5 17 ♗e3 h6 18 ♕d2 ± Birnboim-Gallagher, Tel Aviv 1988.

b) 10...♖b8 11 e4 ♖e8 12 ♖e1 b5 (more precise than 12...c4 13 e5! dxe5 14 ♘xe5 ♘b4 15 a3 ♖xe5 16 ♖xe5 ♘d3 17 ♖e2 b5 18 ♗e3 ± Schüssler-Shirazi, New York 1986) 13 e5 b4! 14 ♘a4 ♘d7 15 exd6 ♖xe1+ 16 ♕xe1 ♗b7 17 ♕d1 ♘e5 18 ♗f4 ♕xd6 19 ♕e2 ♖e8 with a double-edged game; Sosonko-Sygulski, Rotterdam tt 1987.

c) 10...♘c7 allows White to develop a steady initiative:

c1) 11 a4 b6 12 e4 ♘d7 13 ♗f4 ♕e7 14 ♖e1 f6 15 ♕d2 ♗a6 16 h4 ♘e5 17 ♘xe5 fxe5 18 ♗g5 ♗f6 19 ♗e3 ♗c8 20 ♘b1! followed by transferring the knight to c4; Goldin-Bjerring, Cappelle la Grande 1992.

c2) 11 e4 ♘d7 (or 11...b5 12 e5! ♘fe8 13 ♗f4 ♗b7 14 exd6 ♘xd6 15 ♘e5 ♖e8 16 ♘c6 ♕d7 17 ♖c1 ♗a6

18 b4! c4 19 ♗xd6 ♕xd6 20 ♘e4 ± Stern-Barlov, Baden-Baden 1991) 12 ♗f4 (in the classic encounter Korchnoi-Tal, Erevan 1962, White was successful by another means: 12 ♖e1 ♘e8 13 ♗g5 f6 14 ♗e3 ♖b8 15 a4 a6 16 ♗f1 ♕e7 17 ♘d2 ♘c7 18 f4 b5 19 e5! dxe5 20 ♘de4 ±) 12...♕e7 13 ♖e1 f6 14 a4 (14 ♘h2 ♖b8 15 ♗e3 b5 16 f4 b4 17 ♘a4 ♘b5 18 ♖c1 ± Korchnoi-Tringov, Lucerne OL 1982, is not bad either) 14...♘e5 15 ♘xe5 fxe5 16 ♗e3 b6 17 ♖b1 ♘a6 18 ♘a2 ♗d7 19 ♗f1 ♘c7 20 b4 with advantage to White; Razuvaev-Romero, Palma 1991.

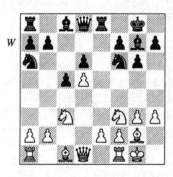

11 ♖e1

11 ♗f4 is examined in the notes to the variation 9...♖e8 10 ♗f4 ♘a6 11 h3.

It is possible to transfer the knight to c4 right now, but it seems to me that including the moves 10 h3 ♖e8 then works to Black's advantage, for example 11 ♘d2!? ♘c7 and now:

a) After 12 ♘c4?! Black can exploit the position of the pawn on h3: 12....b5! 13 ♘xd6 ♕xd6 14 ♗f4 ♕b6! (14...♕d7? 15 d6) 15 d6 ♘e6

16 &xa8 ♘xf4 17 gxf4 &xh3 18
&f3 &xf1 19 ♔xf1 ♖d8 with an advantage to Black, Kaidanov-Foisor,
Moscow 1987.

b) 12 a4 b6 13 ♖e1 ♕e7!? (or
13...&a6 14 e4 ♘d7 15 ♘f3! ♘e5
16 ♘xe5 &xe5 17 &e3 &g7 18
♕d2 ± Goldin-Emms, Cappelle la
Grande 1992) 14 ♕c2 (White has
nothing realistic after 14 ♖b1 &a6
15 ♘de4 ♘d7 16 &g5 f6 17 &f4
♘e5 = Razuvaev-Wedberg, Reykjavik 1990, or 14 ♘c4 &a6 15 ♘a3
&b7 16 ♖b1 ♖ab8 17 &f4 ♘h5, as
in the game Ivanov-Emms, Gausdal
1993) 14...&a6 15 ♖d1 (but not 15
e4? ♘fxd5!) 15...♘d7 = Razuvaev-
Stempin, Paris 1990.

11 ... &d7

Black cannot obtain equality after the automatic 11...♘e4 12 ♘xe4
♖xe4 13 ♘d2 (his problems are simpler after 13 &g5 ♕f8 14 ♕c1
♖b4!? 15 b3 ♖e4 16 ♘d2 {16 ♖b1
&f5} 16...♖e8 17 ♘e4 f5 18 ♘c3
&d7 = Alburt-Wedberg, New York
1988) 13...♖e8 14 a4 ♘b4 (14...♘c7!?
15 ♘c4 ½-½ Razuvaev-Suba, Moscow 1986) 15 ♘c4 b6 16 &f4 &f8
17 ♕b3 &a6 18 &d2 &g7 19 e3 ±
Csom-D.Gurevich, Beersheba 1986.

	12 a4	♘e4
	13 ♘xe4	♖xe4
	14 ♘d2	♖b4
	15 ♖a2	b5!?
	16 axb5	♘c7
	17 b3	♘xb5
	18 &b2	&xb2
	19 ♖xb2	a5

with equality; Razuvaev-Lautier,
Sochi 1989.

D2) 10 &f4   ♘c7

After 10...♖e8 the most precise reply
is probably 11 ♖e1!?, which is considered under 9...♖e8, whilst after
11 ♖c1 Black's chances to equalize
aren't too bad: 11...♘h5 12 &g5 ♕d7
13 a3 b5 14 b4 &b7! = Urban-Chu-
chelov, Cappelle la Grande 1993.

11 a4

Or 11 e4 &g4 12 ♕d2 &xf3 13
&xf3 ♘fe8 14 a3 ♕d7 15 ♖ab1 a5!?
with equality; Vanheste-Ligterink,
Hilversum 1990.

11 ...   ♖e8 (D)

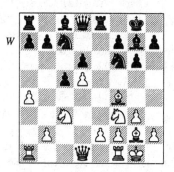

11...b6?! is too sluggish: 12 e4
&g4 (12...♘h5 13 &g5 f6 14 &e3 f5
15 &g5! &f6 16 &h6 ♖e8 17 exf5
&xf5 18 h3 ±) 13 h3 &xf3 14 &xf3
♘fe8 15 ♕d2 a6 16 &g2 ♖b8 17
&g5! ± Dautov-Grünberg, Bad Lau-
terberg 1991.

12 ♘d2

Dautov's recommends 12 ♖e1!?
♘e4 13 ♘xe4 ♖xe4 14 ♖a2 ♖b4 15
b3. This line, which gives White an
edge, deserves attention.

	12 ...	♘h5
	13 &e3	b6
	14 ♖c1	

Only White will have problems after 14 ♘c4 ♗a6 15 ♘a3 ♕d7 16 ♕c2 ♖e7 17 ♖fe1 ♖ae8 18 ♗f3 ♘f6 19 ♗f4 h6, Birnboim-Suba, Beer Sheva 1986.

14 ...   ♖xe3!?

The exchange sacrifice is very tempting, all the more so as the alternative 14...♗a6 15 ♖e1 f5 16 ♘f1 ♕f6 17 ♕d2 b5 18 b4! c4 19 a5 gives White a good game; Draško-Marin, Tallinn 1989.

15 fxe3   ♗h6

Black has enough compensation.

D3)   10 ♘d2   ♘c7

Now the knight can continue its tour to c4 immediately, while a judicious alternative is 11 a4, guaranteeing the knight a place on c4. Thus we have the following split:

D31) 11 a4
D32) 11 ♘c4

D31) 11 a4

The game might develop in the following fashion:

11 ...   b6 (D)

11...♖e8 12 ♘c4 a6 13 ♗f4 ♗f8 14 a5 ± is too passive.

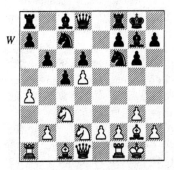

12 ♖b1

Probably the most promising move – White removes the rook from the g7 bishop's sphere of influence, and so he will always have the possibility of supporting the knight on c4 with a pawn. Others:

a) Black is fine after 12 ♘c4?! ♗a6 13 ♕b3 ♕d7!? (13...♗xc4 is also quite sufficient: 14 ♕xc4 a6 15 e4 {15 ♖b1 ♘d7 16 b4 b5 17 axb5 axb5 18 ♕d3 c4 19 ♕c2 ♘b6 ∓} 15...♖b8 {or 15...♘d7 16 ♕e2 ♖b8 17 ♗f4 ♘e5 18 ♖ab1 b5 19 axb5 axb5 20 b4 c4 ∓ Van Parreren-Gheorghiu, Brocco 1991} 16 f4 b5 and Black seized the initiative in Schmidt-T.Horvath, Budapest 1993) 14 ♗f4 ♘h5 15 ♗d2 f5 and Black had a brilliant position in Borges-Vera, Matanzas 1992.

b) 12 h3 is just as inoffensive: 12...♗a6 13 ♖e1 ♘d7 (13...♖e8 14 ♘de4 ♘xe4 15 ♘xe4 ♕d7 16 ♗g5!? ♖xe4 17 ♗xe4 ♗xb2 18 ♖a2 ♗c3 19 ♗d2 ♗d4 with compensation; Dao Thien Hai-Ionescu, Novi Sad OL 1990) 14 ♖b1 f5 15 f4 ♖e8 16 ♘f3 ♘f6 and Black's position is again more promising; Saeed-Gheorghiu, Novi Sad OL 1990.

12 ...   ♖e8

Black does not manage to equalize after 12...♘d7 13 ♕c2 ♗a6 14 b4 cxb4 15 ♖xb4 ♘c5 16 ♗b2 ♕e7 17 ♘f3 ♗b7 18 ♖d1 ± Psakhis-Gheorghiu, Novi Sad OL 1990, or 12...♘fe8 13 ♕c2 ♘a6 14 ♘a2 ♗d7 15 ♘c4 b5 16 axb5 ♗xb5 17 ♗d2 ♖c8 18 b3 ♘f6 19 ♖fe1 ± P.Nikolić-Nogueiras, Havana (3) 1987, but

12...♘g4!? deserves attention, for example 13 h3 ♘h6 14 ♘de4 ♘e8 15 ♗f4 f6 16 ♕c1 ♘f7 17 ♗d2 h6 18 f4 f5 19 ♘f2 ♗a6 = Gutman-Brunner, Bad Wörishofen 1989.

13   ♖e1

Alburt used an interesting idea: 13 b4!? cxb4 14 ♖xb4 ♗b7 15 ♘b3 ♖c8 16 ♖h4! h5 17 ♗g5, thereby gaining an advantage, in Alburt-Sax, Hastings 1983.

13   ...   ♗a6

In Brenninkmeijer-Blees, Dutch Ch 1990, the many steps of the knight's dance turned out only to give White the upper hand: 13...♘g4 14 h3 ♘e5 15 f4 ♘d7 16 ♘c4 ♘f6 17 ♗d2 ♗a6 18 b3 ±.

At the same time Black has achieved good results after 13...♕e7, for example 14 h3 ♗a6 15 ♕c2 (or 15 ♘de4 ♘xe4 16 ♘xe4 f5 17 ♗g5 ♕f8 = Davies-Suba, London 1989) 15...♗b7! (15...c4?! is significantly weaker: 16 ♖d1 ♖ac8 17 e4 ♘d7 18 ♘a2! ♘e5 19 ♘b4 ♗b7 20 f4 with a clear advantage to White; Hulak-Ionescu, Kastel Stari 1988) 16 ♕b3 ♖ab8 = Ionescu.

14   b4

After 14 b3 b5 (14...♘g4 15 ♗b2 ♕e7 16 ♘f1 ♘e5 = Dzhandzhgava-Khalifman, Simferopol 1988, is not a bad alternative) 15 axb5 ♘xb5 16 ♗b2 ♘g4 17 ♘xb5 ♗xb2 18 ♖xb2 ♕f6 19 ♗f3 ♗xb5 (19...♕xb2 20 ♘c4!) 20 ♖a2 h5 Black has no problems; Grün-D.Gurevich, Belgrade 1988.

14   ...   cxb4
15   ♖xb4   ♘d7

16   ♘b5   ♘c5

16...♗xb5?! 17 axb5 ♘c5 18 ♗b2 a5 19 bxa6 ♘7xa6 20 ♖b5 ♕d7 21 ♖xb6 ♘a4 22 ♖xd6! ♕xd6 23 ♗xg7 ♔xg7 24 ♕xa4 and Black faced a tough defence in Grün-Ionescu, Berlin 1988.

17   ♗b2   ♗xb2
18   ♖xb2   ♕d7 =

D32) 11   ♘c4 (D)

11   ...   ♘fe8 (D)

Of course one doesn't really want to remove the knight from the centre, but on the other hand the d6 pawn is now reliably defended and the way is open for the f-pawn. This is what else has happened in practice:

a) 11...♖e8 12 ♗f4 ♗f8. Now 13 a4 guarantees White a stable advantage and hinders Black's activity, which may arise after 13 e4?! b5 14 ♘xd6? ♖xd6 15 e5 ♗xe5 16 d6 ♖b8 17 ♗c6 ♗d7 18 ♗xe5 ♖xe5 19 dxc7 ♕xc7 20 ♗xd7 ♕xd7; Verat-Csom, Budapest tt 1987.

b) 11...b6 12 ♘xd6! ♕xd6 (the lesser of two evils, as White has a big advantage after 12...♗a6?! 13 ♕a4!

♕xd6 14 ♗f4 ♕d7 15 ♕xd7 ♘xd7 16 ♗xc7 ♖ac8 17 d6 ± Scherbakov-Nunn, Pardubice 1992) 13 ♗f4 ♕d7 14 d6 ♘e6 15 ♗xa8 ♘xf4 16 gxf4 ♕g4+ 17 ♗g2 and now, rather than 17...♗b7?! 18 e4 ♕xf4 19 ♕f3! ♕e5 (19...♕xd6 20 e5!) 20 ♕g3 +−, Black should continue 17...♕xf4!?, when White's chances are better, but Black is not deprived of counter-play.

c) 11...♖b8 12 ♗f4 ♘ce8 13 a4 ♘h5 14 ♗d2 f5 15 ♖e1 f4 16 ♗f3 fxg3 17 hxg3 b6 18 ♘e4 ± Gleiz-erov-Czerniak, Wisla 1992.

d) 11...♘h5 12 a4 b6 (or 12...f5 13 ♗f3 ♘f6 {13...f4 is too optimis-tic: 14 ♘e4! fxg3 15 hxg3 ♗h3 16 ♖e1 ♘e8 17 ♘g5 was promising for White in Sosonko-Blees, Nether-lands tt 1993} 14 ♗f4 with unpleas-ant pressure) 13 ♗d2 ♗a6 14 b3 f5 15 ♕c2.

e) 11...b5 (a move which was for many years considered to be a mis-take, although it is not that simple) 12 ♘xd6! ♕xd6 13 ♗f4 ♕d7 (bet-ter than retreating the queen to b6, for example 13...♕b6 14 d6 ♘e6 {14...♖d8 15 dxc7! ♖xd1 16 ♖fxd1 ♗b7 17 ♗xb7 ♕xb7 18 ♖d8+ ♘e8 19 ♖ad1 ♗d4 20 ♖b8 ♕c6 21 ♘d5 +− is terrible} 15 ♗xa8 ♘xf4 16 gxf4 ♗h3 17 ♗g2 ♗xg2 18 ♔xg2 ♖d8 19 e3 ±) 14 d6 ♘e6 15 ♗xa8 ♘xf4 16 gxf4 ♕g4+ (16...b4 17 ♘e4 ♘xe4 18 ♗xe4 ♕g4+ 19 ♗g2 ♗b7 20 e4 ♕xf4 21 ♕c1 ♕g4 22 h3 ♕h5 23 a3! ± P.Nikolić-Pliester, Lugano 1986) 17 ♗g2 ♕xf4!? (a better chance than 17...♗b7 18 e4

♕xf4 19 ♕f3 ♕e5 20 ♕g3 ±) 18 ♕c1 ♕xd6 19 ♘xb5 ♕e5 20 ♕c3 (20 ♘c3!?) 20...♕xe2 21 ♘xa7 ♗e6 22 ♕xc5 ♘d7! gave Black rea-sonable chances for a draw in Uly-bin-Tunik, Russian Cht 1992.

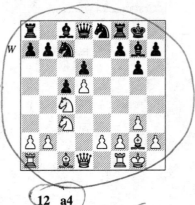

12 a4

12 a3?! is too passive after 12...b6 13 ♕c2 ♗a6 14 ♘a2 (14 ♘d1!?) 14...♗xc4 15 ♕xc4 b5 16 ♕c2 a5! ∓ Djurić-Suba, New York 1987.

Wild complications follow 12 ♗f4 b5 13 ♘a5 b4 14 ♘e4 ♗xb2 15 ♘c6 ♕d7 16 ♖b1 ♗g7 17 ♘xc5! dxc5 18 d6 ♘e6 19 ♘e7+ ♔h8 20 ♗c6 (20 ♗xa8 is no less interesting: 20...♘xf4 21 ♘xc8 ♕xc8 22 ♗f3 ♘h3+ 23 ♔g2 ♘f6 24 d7 ♘xd7 25 ♔xh3 ♘e5+ with compensation) 20...♕d8 21 ♗xa8 ♘xf4 22 gxf4 ♗h3 23 ♗g2 ♗xg2 24 ♔xg2 ♘xd6 with an unclear position; Alburt-D.Gurevich, New York 1986.

12 ... b6
13 ♕c2

This is not the only move:

a) In Youngworth-Shamkovich, Lone Pine 1978, Black quickly seized the initiative after 13 ♕b3

♗a6 14 ♘b5?! ♕d7 15 ♗f4 ♘xb5 16 axb5 ♕xb5 17 ♕xb5 ♗xb5 18 ♘xd6 ♗xe2 19 ♖fe1 ♘xd6 20 ♗xd6 ♖fe8 21 ♗c7 ♗b5! ∓.

b) Black's problems are considerably more difficult after 13 ♗d2!? (D), for example:

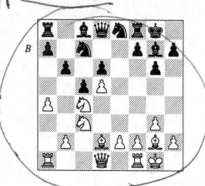

b1) 13...♖b8 14 ♕c1 (the line 14 ♘b5 ♘xb5 15 axb5 ♘c7 16 ♖xa7 ♘xb5 17 ♖a2 ♕c7 is equal; Tal-Mnatsakanian, Moscow tt 1959) 14...♗a6 15 b3 ♕d7 usually leads to a transposition to 13...♕d7.

b2) 13...♕d7 14 ♕c1 ♗a6 15 b3 ♘f6 (15...♖b8 16 ♖a2 ♗c8 17 ♗f4 a6 18 ♖d1 f5 19 e4 ± Kuligowski-Shamkovich, New York 1981) 16 h3 ♖ab8 17 ♖e1 with a small advantage; Lahav-Blees, Tel Aviv 1988.

c) It has become very popular to employ 13 ♕d2!?, introduced into tournament practice by Sosonko. One may continue 13...♖b8 (or 13...f5 14 b3 ♕d7 15 ♗b2 ♗b7 16 ♖ab1 ♘f6 17 ♗a1 ♗a6 18 ♖fd1 ♘g4 19 e3 ♘e5 ∞ Arkell-Quinn, British Ch 1992) 14 ♖b1 ♗a6 (the move 14...♗d7 is more passive: 15 b3 a6 16 ♘e4! ♗f5 17 ♘e3 ♗xe4 18

♗xe4 b5 19 ♗b2 ♘f6 20 ♗g2 ♕d7 21 b4! ± L.Hansen-Sax, Polanica Zdroj 1993) 15 b3 ♕d7 (the prematurely active 15...b5?! 16 ♘a5 ♕d7 17 ♘c6 ♖b7 18 axb5 ♘xb5 19 ♘xb5 ♖xb5 20 ♕a2 ♖b6 Sosonko-Lautier, European Club Cup 1991, can lead Black into difficulties after 21 b4!) 16 ♗b2 f5 with chances for both sides.

13 ... f5 (D)

White has transferred the knight to a strong position and is more active. It is not easy for Black to equalize, no matter what he plays at this point:

a) 13...♗a6 14 b3 f5 15 ♗b2 ♘f6 (15...♕d7 16 ♖fe1 f4 17 ♘e4! ♖d8 18 ♖ad1 ♗xb2 19 ♕xb2 ♕e7 20 ♕c1 ± Hulak-Damljanović, Belgrade GMA 1988) 16 ♖fe1 ♕d7 17 e4 fxe4 18 ♘xe4 ♘xe4 19 ♗xe4 ♗xb2 20 ♕xb2 with a small advantage; Galliamova-Psakhis, Groningen 1993.

b) 13...♘a6 14 b3 ♘b4 15 ♕d2 a6 16 ♗b2 ♖b8 17 ♘a2! ♗xb2 18 ♕xb2 ♘xa2 19 ♖xa2 ♕d7 20 ♖e1! f5 is Adorjan-Speelman, Lucerne 1989, and after 21 e4! White's position is the more active.

c) 13...♖b8 14 ♗f4 (14 ♖b1 ♗d7 15 b3 a6 16 ♘e4 ♗f5 17 ♘e3 ♗xe4 18 ♗xe4 b5 = L.Hansen-Sax, Polanica Zdroj 1993) 14...♕e7 15 ♖fe1 a6 16 ♕d2 b5 17 ♘a5 ♗d7 18 axb5 axb5 19 ♘c6 ♗xc6 20 dxc6 b4 21 ♘d5 and White is again better; Gleizerov-Budnikov, Voronezh 1988.

d) 13...♕e7!? 14 b3 (or 14 e4!?) 14...♗f5!? 15 e4 ♗xe4 16 ♗xe4

♗xc3 17 ♕xc3 ♕xe4 18 ♗h6 ♘xd5 19 ♕b2 ♕f3 20 ♖fd1 ♘df6 led to complications in the game Saeed-Agdestein, Taxco IZ 1985.

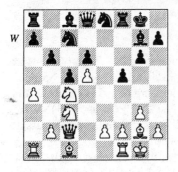

14 ♗d2

Black equalizes without problems after 14 ♖b1 ♗a6 15 ♘a2 (15 b3 b5 16 axb5 ♘xb5 17 ♘xb5 ♗xb5 is also equal) 15...♕d7 16 ♖d1 ♗xc4! 17 ♕xc4 a6 = Draško-Suba, New York 1988, and it is no wonder, as the white knight has chosen too passive a role. Nor did Black experience any difficulties in Arkell-Suba, London 1991: 14 e3 ♗b7 15 ♖d1 ♘f6 16 ♖b1 ♔h8 17 b3 ♕d7 18 ♗b2 ♖ad8 19 ♖d2 ♕f7 =.

14	...	♗b7
15	♖ad1	♕d7
16	♗f4	♖d8
17	♖fe1	♕f7
18	♕d2	♗a6
19	b3	♗b7
20	♘b1!?	♗d4
21	e3	♗g7
22	h4	

White has an edge; Scherbakov-Emms, Hastings Challengers 1993. Given the permanent weakness on d6, it is difficult for Black to activate his pieces, and White can slowly increase the pressure.

4 Fianchetto with ...♘bd7: Introduction (A63)

1 d4 ♘f6 2 c4 c5 3 d5 e6 4 ♘c3 exd5 5 cxd5 d6

6	♘f3	g6
7	g3	♗g7
8	♗g2	0-0
9	0-0	a6

In the overwhelming majority of cases, Black combines ...♘bd7 with the moves 9...a6 10 a4, but occasionally he tries to make do without them, viz. 9...♘bd7 *(D)* and now:

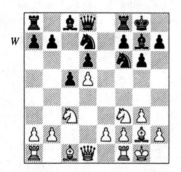

a) Black has no problems after 10 h3 a6 11 ♗f4 ♕e7 12 e4 ♘h5 13 ♗g5 ♗f6 14 ♗h6 ♘g7 (14...♖e8!?) 15 ♖e1 b5 = Vaganian-Sax, Rotterdam 1989.

b) In the event of 10 a4 it is best for him to settle on the fundamental variation 10...a6, as White will easily achieve a small plus after 10...♘e8 11 ♗g5 (11 e4 ♘e5 12 ♘xe5 ♗xe5

13 ♗h6 ♘g7 14 ♕d2 b6 15 ♔h1 ♗a6 16 ♖fe1 ♖e8 = Sliwa-Spassky, Gothenburg IZ 1955) 11...f6 12 ♗f4 ♕e7 13 ♖e1 b6 14 h4 ♘e5 15 ♘xe5 fxe5 16 ♗g5 ± Kuligowski-Spassky, Bundesliga 1987.

c) 10 ♗f4 is played quite often, but Black usually manages to equalize: 10...♕e7 (10...♘e8 is not bad either: 11 ♕d2 a6 12 ♖ab1 {12 a4!?} 12...b5 13 b4 cxb4 14 ♖xb4 ♘b6 15 ♘d4 ♘c4 = P.Nikolić-Shamkovich, Esbjerg 1982) and now:

c1) 11 ♕c2 a6 12 e4 ♘g4 13 ♖ad1 b5 (13...♘de5!? is equal) 14 ♗g5 Bönsch-T.Horvath, Lvov 1984, and now 14...♗f6!? would have equalized.

c2) 11 h3 leads to a similar result: 11...h6 12 ♖e1 g5 13 ♗d2 ♘b6!? 14 e4 ♘c4 15 ♗c1 ♘d7 16 ♗f1 ♘ce5 = Poluliakhov-Ruban, Anapa 1991.

c3) Black also has no cause for complaint at the outcome of the opening after 11 e4 ♘g4 (11...a6 12 ♖e1 ♘g4 13 ♗g5 ♕e8 14 e5!? ♘dxe5!? 15 ♘xe5 ♘xe5 16 f4 ♘g4! 17 ♖xe8 ♖xe8 18 ♘e2 ♘e3 with wild complications in Ligterink-Nunn, Marbella Z 1982) 12 ♕d2 ♘ge5 13 ♗h6 ♘xf3+ 14 ♗xf3 ♘e5 with equality; Christiansen-Nunn, Hastings 1979.

c4) 11 ♖b1 ♘g4 12 ♕d2 ♘de5 13 b4 b6 14 ♘xe5 ♘xe5 15 ♗h6 ♗xh6 16 ♕xh6 f5 = P.Nikolić-Sax, Niksić 1983.

d) 10 ♘d2 and now Black should place his rook on the e-file since it is not easy to equalize by other methods:

d1) 10...♘h5 11 ♘c4 (11 ♘de4 ♘df6 12 ♗g5 h6 13 ♗xf6+ ♗xf6 14 ♗d2 ♖e8 15 h3 ♗f5 16 ♕c1 h5 = Djurić-de Firmian, New York 1986, is inoffensive) 11...♘e5 12 ♘xe5 ♗xe5 13 ♗h6 ♖e8 14 ♕d2 ♖b8 15 a4 a6 16 ♖ab1 b5 17 axb5 axb5 18 b4 ± Akopian-de Firmian, Moscow GMA 1990.

d2) White also has the initiative after 10...♕e7 11 a4 (or 11 ♖e1 ♘e8 12 e3 ♘c7 13 a4 ♘a6 14 f4 ♘b4 15 ♘c4 ♘b6 = Korchnoi-Kaplan, Hastings 1975; Black also has quite a decent position after 11 h3 b6 {11...♘h5!? 12 ♔h2 f5 13 f4 ♘df6 =} 12 a4 ♗a6 13 ♖e1 ♘e8 14 ♘b5 ♗xb5 15 axb5 ♘c7 16 ♕b3 ♘f6 17 ♘b1 ♖fb8 18 ♘c3 a6 = Donner-T.Petrosian, Gothenburg Z 1955) 11...♘h5 (11...a6!? leads to the line with 9...a6) 12 e4 ♘e5 13 ♕e2 f5 14 f4 ♘g4 15 ♘c4 fxe4 16 ♘xe4 ♗d4+ 17 ♔h1 with a small advantage for White; Hort-Nunn, Hastings 1975.

d3) 10...♖e8 11 h3 (everything is in order for Black after 11 ♘c4 ♘b6 12 ♘xb6 ♕xb6 13 ♕c2 ♗d7 14 ♖b1 ♕c7 15 a4 a6 16 ♗d2 ♖ac8 = Goldin-Romanishin, USSR 1986, and after 11 a4 Black is perhaps better reacting with the standard 11...a6, as 11...♘e5 leads to a game which

favours White, for example 12 h3 g5?! 13 ♘de4! ♘xe4 14 ♘xe4 h6 15 f4 gxf4 16 gxf4 ♘g6 17 f5 ± Uhlmann-Larsen, Beverwijk 1961) 11...♘h5 (11...♘b6 12 a4 ♗d7 13 a5 ♘c8 14 ♘c4 ♕c7 15 e4 b5 16 axb6 ♘xb6 17 ♘a3 ± Capablanca-Marshall, New York 1927) 12 ♘de4 ♘df6 13 g4 ♘xe4 14 ♘xe4 f5!? 15 ♘xd6 ♕xd6 16 gxh5 f4 17 hxg6 hxg6 with chances for both sides; Akopian-Shabalov, Minsk 1990.

10 a4 ♘bd7 (D)

In this position, which is critical for the 7 g3 variation, White has a wide choice of continuations which allow him to aspire (not always successfully) to gaining an advantage out of the opening. He must try to play on the queenside, where Black has weaknesses after 9...a6. He must create pressure on the d6 pawn which he can attack with the knight on c4 and the bishop on f4, and play in the centre of the board, where he already has a pawn more, but in none of these plans does Black remain an extra, and he can expect an active game.

The main lines here are:
A) 11 e4
B) 11 ♘d2
C) 11 ♗f4

Here are the less popular alternatives:

a) 11 ♕c2 ♖b8 12 a5 b5 13 axb6 ♘xb6 14 ♘d2 ♘fd7 15 ♘b3 ♘c4! 16 ♘e4 ♖b4 = Rohde-D.Gurevich, New York 1985.

b) 11 ♖a2 ♘g4!? 12 h3 ♘ge5 13 ♘d2 f5 14 f4 ♘f7 15 ♘c4 ♘b6 16 ♘xb6 ♕xb6 17 a5 ♕c7 with equality; Kharitonov-Psakhis, Sevastopol 1986.

c) 11 ♖e1 ♖b8 (or 11...♕c7 12 ♘d2 ♖b8 13 a5 b5 14 axb6 ♘xb6 15 ♖a2 ♘fd7 16 ♕c2 c4 = Alburt-Hjartarson, Philadelphia 1986) 12 ♗f1!? (Black has no problems after 12 ♗f4 ♘e8 13 e4 b5 14 axb5 axb5 15 e5 dxe5 16 ♘xe5 ♘xe5 17 ♗xe5 ♗xe5 18 ♖xe5 ♘d6 = Csom-Pinter, Hungarian Ch 1981, or in the event of 12 a5 b5 13 axb6 ♖xb6 14 ♗f1 ♖e8 15 ♘d2 ♖b4 Kouatly-Lautier, Marseilles 1988) 12...♘g4 13 ♘d2 b5 (13...f5 looks quite tempting: 14 h3 ♘xf2!? 15 ♔xf2 f4 16 ♘f3 fxg3+ 17 ♔xg3 ♘e5 with a massive initiative for the sacrificed piece) 14 axb5 axb5 15 e3! b4 16 ♘b5 ♘df6 17 h3 Ligterink-Szalanczy, European Club Cup 1987, and the game is promising for White, but complicated after 17...♘e5!? 18 f4 ♘ed7 19 e4 (Ligterink).

d) 11 ♖b1 ♖e8 (in Korchnoi-Kapengut, USSR 1969, Black also equalized after 11...♖b8 12 ♖e1 {12

b4!?} 12...♕c7 13 ♗d2 ♘g4! 14 ♕c2 c4 15 b4 cxb3 16 ♕xb3 ♘c5 =) 12 b4 ♕c7 (12...♘g4 13 ♕b3 cxb4 14 ♕xb4 ♘c5 15 ♗g5 ♗xc3 16 ♕xc3 ♘e4 17 ♕c1 ♘xg5 18 ♕xg5 ♕xg5 19 ♘xg5 ♖xe2 20 ♖b6 will not gladden Black, despite the extra pawn; Alburt-Sigurjonsson, Reykjavik 1984) 13 ♗d2 ♘b6 14 ♘g5 ♗f5 15 bxc5 ♕xc5 16 ♖c1 ♘c4 with an unclear game; P.Nikolić-Velimirović, Yugoslav Ch 1983.

e) 11 h3 *(D)* often transposes to other lines:

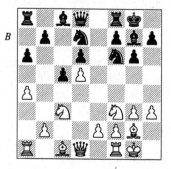

e1) 11...♖b8 doesn't look bad, for example 12 ♗f4 (12 a5 b5 13 axb6 ♘xb6 14 ♘d2 ♖e8 leads us to A64) 12...♘e8 (12...♕e7!? will be examined under 11 ♗f4 ♕e7) 13 ♕d2!? b5 14 axb5 axb5 15 ♘e4 ♕b6 (15...♘df6 16 ♘xc5! ♘c7 17 ♘d3) 16 ♖fe1 b4 17 ♕c2 Kaidanov-Ermenkov, Calcutta 1988, and now 17...♗a6 ∞ deserves attention – Kaidanov.

e2) White did not succeed in obtaining an advantage in Khalifman-Arnason, Groningen 1990 after 11...h6 12 ♖b1 ♕c7 13 ♗f4 ♖e8 14

♕c2 ♖b8 15 ♖fc1 b5 16 axb5 axb5 17 b4 cxb4 18 ♖xb4 ♘h5, with mutual chances.

e3) 11...♖e8 12 ♖e1 (12 ♘d2 leads to A64) 12...♘e4 13 ♘xe4 ♖xe4 14 ♕c2!? (14 ♗g5 ♕e8 15 ♖a2 h6 16 ♗f4 ♕e7 17 b3 g5 18 ♗c1 c4 19 bxc4 ♖xc4 20 ♘d2 ♖c7 21 ♗b2 ♘e5 led to a complex game in Razuvaev-Romanishin, Novi Sad 1982) 14...♖e8 (or 14...♕e7 15 ♗d2 ♘f6 16 ♘h4 ♗d7 17 ♗c3 ♖e8 18 ♗xe4 ♘xe4 19 ♗xg7 ♔xg7 20 ♖a3 ♕g5 and Black's compensation for the exchange is perhaps not quite sufficient for equality; Razuvaev-Tal, Moscow 1983) 15 ♗f4 ♕c7 16 ♘d2 ♘e5 17 b4 c4 18 ♖a3 ♗f5 19 e4 ♗d7 20 ♗xe5 ♗xe5 21 ♕xc4 ♖ac8 22 ♗f1 ♕b6 and a strong dark-squared bishop allows Black to look to the future with optimism; Smejkal-Grünberg, Prague 1989.

A) 11 e4 (D)

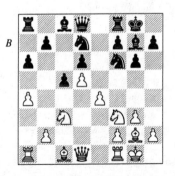

Now Black has a choice of two rook moves:

A1) 11...♖b8
A2) 11...♖e8

A1) 11 ... ♖b8
12 ♖e1

A prophylactic move; White frees f1 for the bishop and prepares for Black's active play on the queenside. 12 a5 does not create big problems for Black, for example 12...♖e8 13 ♖e1 b5 14 axb6 ♖xb6 15 ♗f1 ♖b4! 16 ♕c2 a5 = Winants-Pigusov, Dordrecht 1987.

12 ... b5 (D)

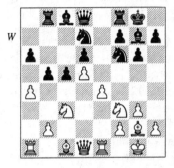

12...♘g4 is good for White: 13 ♘h4 ♘ge5 14 ♗f1 (14 f4 ♘c4 15 ♗f1 ♘a5 16 ♘f3 ♖e8 17 ♗e3, Scheeren-Stoica, Thessaloniki OL 1984, is less clear, e.g. 17...♗xc3!? 18 bxc3 ♖xe4 is interesting) 14...c4 15 f4 ♘d3 16 ♗xd3 cxd3 17 ♗e3 b5 18 axb5 axb5 19 ♕xd3 b4 20 ♘a4 ♖e8 21 ♘f3 ± Sosonko-Cebalo, Reggio Emilia 1985.

12...♕e7?! also favours White: 13 ♗f1 ♖e8 14 h3 ♘h5 15 g4 ♘hf6 16 ♗f4 h5 17 e5! dxe5 18 ♘xe5 Sosonko-Nunn, London 1980.

There is perhaps only one conclusion to be drawn from these two variations – don't play the Modern Benoni against Sosonko!

13 axb5   axb5
14 ♗f1

Or 14 ♗f4 ♘e8 15 e5 dxe5 16 ♘xe5 ♘xe5 17 ♗xe5 ♗xe5 18 ♖xe5 ♘d6 =.

14 ...   ♘g4!?

14...b4 also doesn't look too bad; 15 ♘b5 ♖b6!? (White has strong pressure after 15...♘e8/ 16 ♘a7! ♗b7 17 ♘c6 ♗xc6 18 dxc6 ♘e5 19 ♘xe5 ♗xe5 20 ♗c4 ♘c7 21 ♖a7 ± Sax) 16 ♗f4 ♘e8 17 ♕c2 ♗b7 18 ♖a7 (White can run into difficulties after the overly active 18 ♘a7?! h6 19 ♗b5 g5 20 ♗e3 ♘c7 21 ♗c6 ♗a6! 22 ♗a4 ♗b5! 23 ♗xb5 ♘xb5, as in Ree-Sax, Amsterdam 1983) 18...♕b8 19 ♖ea1 h6 with an unclear game, Sosonko-de Firmian, Tunis IZ 1985.

15 ♘d2

After some complications, Black achieves equality in the event of 15 ♘xb5 ♘de5! 16 h3 ♘xf3+ 17 ♕xf3 ♘e5 18 ♕e2 (not 18 ♕d1 ♗xh3!) 18...♖xb5 19 ♕xb5 ♘f3+ 20 ♔h1 ♘xe1 21 ♕e2 ♖e8 22 ♕xe1 f5 23 ♖a8 ♖xe4 = Scheeren-Van der Wiel, Hilversum 1986.

15 ...   ♘de5
16 h3

Or 16 ♘xb5 ♕b6 17 ♘c4 ♘xc4 18 ♗xc4 ♘e5 19 ♗e2 f5 with compensation.

16 ...   b4
17 ♘b5   c4!
18 ♘xc4   ♘xc4
19 ♗xc4   ♘e5
20 ♗f1   ♗xh3
21 ♗xh3   ♖xb5 =

Alburt-Sax, Subotica IZ 1987.

A2) 11 ...   ♖e8
12 ♖e1   c4!? (D)

The passive 12...♕c7 favours White; 13 ♗f1 ♘e5 (13...♘g4!?) 14 ♘xe5 ♖xe5 15 ♗f4 ♖e8 16 e5 dxe5 17 d6 ♕c6 18 ♗xe5 ± Sosonko-Rechlis, Jerusalem 1986.

12...♘g4 has less clear-cut consequences, for example 13 ♘h4!? ♘f8!? (this move looks unattractive, but it is stronger than 13...♘ge5 14 f4 ♘c4 15 ♘f3 ♖b8 16 ♕c2 ♕a5 {16...b5 17 axb5 axb5 18 ♘xb5!} 17 ♖a2! which is slightly better for White; Ligterink-Short, Plovdiv Echt 1983) 14 h3 ♘e5 15 f4 ♘c4 16 ♗f1 ♘a5 17 ♘f3 c4!? 18 ♗e3 ♗xc3 19 bxc3 ♖xe4 with an unclear game; Ligterink-Franco, Amsterdam 1983.

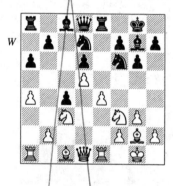

13 h3

13 ♗f1 leads to a double-edged position after 13...♕c7!? (better than 13...♘c5 14 ♘d2 ♕c7 {14...♘d3 15 ♗xd3 cxd3 16 ♘c4 ♗h3 17 ♕xd3 ± Ligterink-Lobron, Wijk aan Zee 1985} 15 ♗xc4 ♗h3 16 ♗f1 ♗xf1 17 ♔xf1 ♖ac8 18 ♖e3 ♕d7 19 ♔g2 ♘g4 20 ♖e2 and White's chances are preferable; Alburt-de Firmian,

USA Ch 1985) 14 ♕e2 ♘c5 15
♕xc4 ♗g4 16 ♘d2 (if 16 ♗g2 then
16...♘fd7 17 ♗f4 ♘b6! with the
idea of 18 ♕f1 ♗xc3 19 bxc3 ♘xe4
with excellent compensation for the
pawn; Piket-Winants, Wijk aan Zee
1987).

Black gains a slight advantage after 13 ♕e2 ♘c5! 14 ♕xc4 b5 15
axb5 (15 ♕f1 b4) 15...axb5 16 ♕xc5
dxc5 17 ♖xa8 b4 (Ligterink).

13 ...   ♘c5

13...♕c7 14 ♕e2 ♘c5 15 ♕xc4
♗d7 Zihani-Franco, Lugano 1989,
is insufficient because of 16 a5!?.

14 ♘d2   ♘d3
15 ♖e2   ♕c7
16 a5   ♗d7
17 ♘a4   ♗b5
18 ♘b6   ♖ad8
19 ♖a3   ♕c5 =

Brenninkmeijer-de Firmian, Lugano 1989.

B) 11 ♘d2 ♖b8 *(D)*

The other possibilities are:

a) 11...♖e8 – see A64.

b) 11...♘h5!? 12 ♘ce4!? (Black
has no reason to worry after 12 ♘c4

♘e5 13 ♘e3 ♖b8 14 a5 b5 15 axb6
♖xb6 16 h3 ♖b4 = Youngworth-de
Firmian, Lone Pine 1981) 12...♘df6
13 ♘xf6+ ♕xf6 (probably more ac-
curate than 13...♗xf6 14 ♘c4 ♗d4
15 e3 ♗g7 16 e4 ♖e8 17 ♗d2 ♖b8
18 a5 f5 19 exf5 ♗xf5 20 ♖a3 ±
P.Nikolić-de Firmian, Wijk aan Zee
1986) 14 ♘c4 ♖b8 15 ♘b6 (15 a5
♗d7) 15...♕d8 16 ♕b3 ♖e8 17 ♖e1
♘f6 18 ♗f4 ♘h5 19 ♗d2 ♘f6 with
equality; Reefschläger-Kindermann,
Bundesliga 1984.

c) 11...♕c7 12 ♕b3!? (standard
play is not dangerous for Black: 12
♘c4 ♘b6 13 ♘a3 ♗d7 14 a5 {or 14
h3 ♖fe8 15 ♕e2 ♖ac8 16 a5 ♘a8 17
♘c4 b5 18 axb6 ♘xb6 = Podlesnik-
Danner, Ptuj 1989} 14...♘c8 15 ♘c4
♗b5 16 ♕b3 ♗xc4 17 ♕xc4 b5 18
axb6 ♘xb6 19 ♕h4 ♖fb8 = Arkell-
Yudasin, Leningrad 1989; you also
see 12 h3 c4 13 a5 b5 14 axb6 ♘xb6
15 ♘f3 ♗b7 16 ♘d4 ♖fe8 17 e4
♘fd7 18 ♗e3 ♘c5 = Birnboim-Dan-
ner, Lucerne OL 1982) and now instead of the unsuccessful 12...♘e8?!
13 ♘c4 ♖b8 14 ♗f4 b5?! 15 axb5
♘e5 (or 15...axb5 16 ♘xb5 ♕b7 17
♖a5 +−) 16 ♗xe5 ♗xe5 17 b6 +−
Ivanchuk-Yudasin, Riga Ct 1991,
Black should play 12...♘e5!? 13 h3
♘h5 with counter-chances.

d) 11...♘e8 12 ♘c4 (Black has
an easy game after 12 e4 ♖b8 13
♕e2 ♘c7 14 a5 b5 15 axb6 ♘xb6 16
f4 ♖e8 = Hinčić-Velimirović, Arand-
jelovac 1993, but 12 h3 deserves
attention, for example 12...♖b8 13
♘e4 ♘b6 {or 13...♘e5 14 ♘a3 f5 15
f4 ♘f7 16 ♘c4 ♗d7 17 a5 ♘c7 18

♖e1 ♖e8 19 ♗d2 ♗b5 20 ♘b6) 14
♘e3 ♗d7 15 ♖e1 ♘c8 16 a5 ♘a7 17
♗d2 ♘b5 18 ♘c4 ♘d4 19 e3 with a
small plus) 12...♘b6 13 ♘xb6!?
(promising more than 13 ♘a3 ♗d7
14 a5 ♘c8 15 ♘c4 ♗b5 16 ♕b3
♗xc4 17 ♕xc4 b5 18 axb6 ♘xb6 19
♕d3 ♘c7 = Shapiro-Browne, USA
Ch 1988) 13...♕xb6 14 ♗d2 ♕c7 15
♖b1 ♗d7 16 ♕c1 b5 17 axb5 axb5
18 b4 c4 19 ♗h6 ± Rohde-Browne,
San Francisco 1987.

e) 11...♕e7 12 h3 (the classic
game Gligorić-Petrosian, Zurich Ct
1953 continued 12 ♘c4 ♘e5 13
♘xe5 ♕xe5 14 a5 ♖e8 15 ♗f4 ♕e7
16 ♕b3 ♘d7 17 ♖fe1 ♘e5 18 ♘a4
♗d7 19 ♘b6 ♖ad8 20 ♗d2 ♗b5 21
♗c3 ±) 12...♖b8 13 ♘c4 ♘e5 14
♘b6 ♘fd7 (14...♘ed7!?) 15 ♘xc8
♖fxc8 16 a5 b5 17 axb6 ♖xb6 18
♕c2 ♘f8 19 ♘a4 ♖bb8 20 ♖a2 and
White preserved his opening advantage in Stempin-Psakhis, Paris 1990.

12 ♘c4   ♘e8 (D)

13   ♕b3!?
The Israeli International Master
Birnboim plays this move fre-
quently and successfully, and it is

most likely the strongest in the position. Others:

a) 13 a5 ♘e5 14 ♘b6 ♘c7 (or
14...♘d7!? 15 ♘xc8 ♖xc8 16 ♗d2
♘c7 17 ♕a4 ♖b8 18 ♖ab1 b5 19
axb6 ♘xb6 = Melnikov-Ulybin,
Kursk 1987) 15 h3 (White has no advantage after either 15 ♕b3 ♗d7 16
h3 ♗b5 17 ♔h2 ♖e8 18 ♗e3 ♘d7 19
♘c4 ♗xc4 20 ♕xc4 b6 = Kraidman-
Pein, Tel Aviv 1989, or 15 ♘e4 ♗f5
16 ♗g5 f6 17 ♗d2 ♗xe4 18 ♗xe4 f5
19 ♗g2 ♘d7 20 ♘c4 ♘e5 = Smys-
lov-Pachman, Amsterdam OL 1954,
and the dubious 15 f4?! gives Black
the initiative after 15...♘g4 16 e3
♖e8 17 ♖e1 ♗b5! 18 ♘xb5 axb5 ∓)
15...f5 (15...♘b5 16 ♖a2 h5 17
♘e4!? ♗f5 18 ♘d2 ♘c8 19 ♘dc4 ±
Scherbakov-Ruban, Voronezh 1988)
16 f4 ♘d7! 17 ♘xc8!? ♕xc8 18 e4
♘b5 Ross-Farago, Oberwart 1987,
and according to Farago White
should have continued 19 exf5! gxf5
20 ♘xb5 axb5 21 ♕e2 c4 22 ♕e6+
♔h8 23 ♕xd6 ♕c5+ 24 ♕xc5
♘xc5, although Black has good
compensation for the pawn.

b) 13 ♗f4 ♘b6 14 ♘a3 ♗d7 15
a5 ♘c8 16 ♘c4 ♗b5 17 ♕b3 ♘c7!?
(17...♗xc4 18 ♕xc4 ♕d7 19 e4 ♘c7
20 ♖fe1 ♖e8 21 ♕f1 b5 = Maiwald-
Ree, Ostend 1991, is not bad either)
18 ♖fe1 ♗xc4 19 ♕xc4 b5 20 axb6
♖xb6 21 ♖a2 ♖b4 22 ♕d3 ♘b6 =
Reefschläger-Sax, Lugano 1986.

c) 13 ♗d2 ♘e5 14 ♘xe5 ♗xe5
15 ♗h6 ♘g7 16 ♕d2 ♖e8 (or 16...b5
17 axb5 axb5 18 f4 ♗f6 19 ♘e4 ♗e7
20 b4 ±) 17 ♗g5 f6 18 ♗f4 ♗xf4 19
♕xf4 f5 20 b4 ± Gutman-Grünfeld,

Beersheba 1982. White's chances are somewhat preferable.

> **13 ...   ♘e5**

Black cannot manage to equalize after 13...♕e7 either, for example 14 a5 ♘e5 15 ♘b6 ♘c7 16 e4 ♗d7 17 f4 ♘g4 (after 17...♘d3 18 ♗e3 is strong, with the idea of 18...f5 19 ♖ad1 fxe4 20 ♘xe4 ♗f5 21 ♕xd3 ♖be8 22 ♗xc5! and White is clearly better) 18 e5! dxe5 19 h3 exf4 20 ♗xf4 ♘e5 21 ♘e4 with a clear advantage to White; Birnboim-Rohde, Beersheba 1987.

> **14 ♘b6   f5**

Or 14...♗f5 15 a5 ♘c7 16 h3 g5 17 ♗d2 g4 18 hxg4!? ♘xg4 19 ♕a4 h5 20 ♗f3 ♗d4 21 e3 ♗g7 22 ♔g2 ± Birnboim-L.Bronstein, Lucerne OL 1982.

> **15 ♗d2   ♗d7**
> **16 f4   ♘g4**
> **17 ♖fe1   ♗b5!**
> **18 a5   ♘c7**
> **19 h3   ♘f6**
> **20 e4**

White has the better game. Birnboim-Bischoff, Munich Z 1987.

C) 11 ♗f4 *(D)*

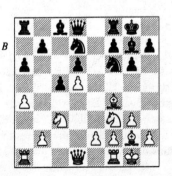

These days this is the most popular move. Black usually defends the pawn with his queen, as the passive 11...♘e8 12 ♕d2 ♘b6 13 ♗h6 ♘c4 14 ♕c1 ♘a5 15 ♗xg7 ♘xg7 16 ♖b1 ♗g4 17 b4 cxb4 18 ♖xb4 is better for White; Adorjan-Mascariñas, Bacolod 1991.

Thus the material divides quite naturally:

C1) 11...♕c7
C2) 11...♕e7

C1) 11 ...   ♕c7
12 h3

A useful prophylactic move, preventing Black from transferring his knight from f6 via g4 to e5. There are other approaches:

a) Nikolić frequently uses 12 ♖c1, but without great success, as Black gets a good game after both 12...♖e8 13 b4 ♘h5 14 ♗g5 h6 15 ♗e3 (15 ♗d2!?) 15...♖xe3!? 16 fxe3 cxb4 17 ♘e4 ♕b6 18 ♘d4 a5 19 ♕c2 f5 ∞ P.Nikolić-Hjartarson, Linares 1988, and the immediate knight move to h5: 12...♘h5 13 ♗g5 h6 14 ♗d2 ♕b6 15 ♕c2 f5 = P.Nikolić-Yudasin, Tilburg 1993.

b) Black had no problems in P.Nikolić-Marin, Thessaloniki OL 1988, after 12 a5 ♖e8 13 ♘a4 h6 (13...♘e4 14 ♘d2 ♘xd2 15 ♗xd2 ♘e5 16 ♗c3 ±) 14 ♕d3 g5 15 ♗d2 ♘e4 16 ♗e1 ♖b8 17 ♖c1 ♘df6 18 ♘d2 ♘xd2 19 ♗xd2 ♗d7 =.

c) Major, unclear complications arose in Polugaevsky-Vaiser, Sochi 1981 after 12 e4 ♖e8 13 ♕c2 ♖b8 14 a5 ♘h5 15 ♗e3 b5 16 axb6 ♘xb6 17

h3 h6 18 g4 ♘f6 19 ♘d2 ♕e7 20
♖ae1 a5!? ∞.

d) 12 ♕d2 is possible: 12...♖e8
13 ♖fc1 c4 14 ♘d4 (14 ♗h6!? ♗h8
15 ♕f4 deserves attention) 14...♘c5
15 ♖a3 ♗d7 16 a5 b5 17 axb6 ♕xb6
with equality; Bonin-Zaichik, New
York 1990.

12 ...   ♖e8 (D)

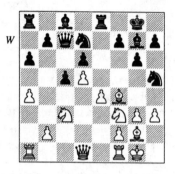

13 ♖e1

Another plan linked with 13 ♖c1
attempts to exploit the opposition of
the rook and queen; this may continue 13...♖b8 (or 13...♘h5 14 ♗d2
♕d8 15 g4!? ♘hf6 16 ♗f4 ♕e7 17
e4! ± Dzhandzhgava-Moldobaev,
Pavlodar 1987) 14 b4!? (14 ♕d3?! is
significantly weaker: 14...c4 15 ♕d1
♘h5 16 ♗d2 ♘c5 17 ♘a2 b5 18
axb5 axb5 and Black seized the initiative in I.Sokolov-Ki.Georgiev,
Reggio Emilia 1988) 14...♘h5 15
♗d2 cxb4!? 16 ♘e4 ♘c5 17 ♘xc5
dxc5 18 ♗xb4 b6 19 a5 ♕e7 20
♗d2!? (White fell into a typical trap
in Csom-Kindermann, Dortmund
1983: 20 ♗a3? ♘xg3! 21 fxg3
♕e3+ 22 ♔h2 ♕xa3 23 axb6 ♖xb6
∓) 20...♕xe2 21 ♕xe2 ♖xe2 22 axb6

♖xb6 23 ♖xc5 with a small advantage to White (Kindermann).

13 ...   ♖b8

13...♘h5!? deserves attention: 14
♗d2 ♖b8!? (14...c4 is worse: 15 b4
cxb3 16 ♕xb3 ♘c5 17 ♕b4 ♘f6 18
♖ac1 ♕d8 19 a5 ± Razuvaev-Ben-
jamin, Paris 1989) 15 a5 b5 16 axb6
♘xb6 17 g4 ♘f6 18 e4 ♘c4 19 ♗c1
♘d7 with a good game for Black;
Brückner-Wahls, Bundesliga 1986.

14 e4

Chances are approximately equal
after 14 a5 b5 15 axb6 ♘xb6!, which
is more precise than 15...♖xb6 16
♘d2!? ♖b4 (16...♘h5!?) 17 ♘a2!
♖b8 18 ♘c4 ♗f8 19 ♘c3 ♘h5 20
♗d2 ♘e5 21 ♘a5 ± G.Kuzmin-
R.Rodriguez, Riga IZ 1979.

14 ...   ♘h5 (D)

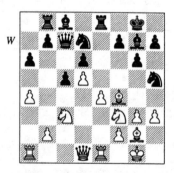

15 ♗e3

15 ♗d2 b5 16 axb5 axb5 17 g4
♘hf6 18 ♗f1 c4! 19 b4 cxb3 20
♕xb3 ♘c5 21 ♕b4 ♘a6 22 ♘xb5
♘xb4 23 ♘xc7 ♖xe4, Christiansen-
Mestel, Lucerne OL 1982, leads to
an interesting game with chances for
both sides.

15 ...   b5

White has an advantage after both 15...♘hf6 16 ♘d2 b5 17 axb5 axb5 18 ♗f1 b4 19 ♘b5 ♕b6 20 ♗f4, and 15...c4 16 a5 b5 17 axb6 ♖xb6 (17...♘xb6!?) 18 g4 ♘hf6 19 ♗xb6 ♘xb6 20 ♕c2 ♘fd7 21 ♘a4 ± Razuvaev-Semkov, Sochi 1982.

16 axb5   axb5
17 ♗f1!   ♕b6

But not 17...b4?! 18 ♘b5 ♕b6 (18...♖xb5 19 ♗xb5 ♖xe4 20 ♕c2 ±) 19 ♘d2! ♘e5 20 ♘a7 ♗d7 21 g4 ♘f6 22 g5 (stronger than 22 f4 ♘exg4! 23 hxg4 ♘xe4 24 ♘c6 ♗xc6 25 ♖a6 ♕c7 26 ♖xc6 ♕d8 27 ♘c4 ♕h4 28 ♗g2 ♖a8 with complications in Razuvaev-Panchenko, Minsk 1985) 22...♘h5 23 f4 ♖a8 (the only move for Black) 24 fxe5 ♖xa7 25 ♘c4 ♕b8 26 ♖xa7 ♕xa7 27 ♘xd6 ♖xe5 28 ♕f3 ± Hernandez-Vilela, Cuba 1993.

18 ♘d2

Black has no problems after 18 ♗xb5 ♗xc3 19 ♖xd7 ♗xd7 20 bxc3 ♖xe4 =, or 18 ♘xb5 ♖xe4 19 ♘d2 ♖b4.

18	...	♗a6
19	♖a2	♖a8
20	♕a1	♕b7
21	♖a5	c4
22	♘a2	♕c7
23	♘c3	♕b7

with equality in Razuvaev-Arnason, Jurmala 1987.

C2)   11 ...   ♕e7 (D)
12 h3!?

We have already seen the use of this strong prophylactic move many times. Other approaches:

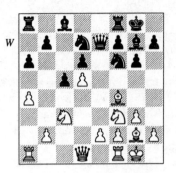

a) 12 ♖e1 h6 (White obtained a small advantage in Hort-Langeweg, Amsterdam 1983, after 12...♘g4 13 ♕b3 ♖b8 14 ♗g5 f6 15 ♗d2 b6 16 h3 ♘h6 17 ♕c2 ♘f7 18 b3 b5 19 axb5 axb5 20 e4 ±) 13 e4 ♘g4 14 a5 ♘ge5 15 ♘a4 ♘xf3+ 16 ♗xf3 ♘e5 17 ♘b6 ♖b8 18 ♗g2 ♗d7 = Borges-Ruban, Santa Clara 1991.

b) 12 a5 and now:

b1) 12...♖b8 13 ♘a4 (alternatively, 13 h3 h6 14 e4 g5 15 ♗c1 {15 ♗e3!?} 15...b5 16 axb6 ♘xb6 17 ♖e1 ♘fd7 18 ♗f1 ♘e5 19 ♘xe5 ♕xe5 20 ♗e3 ♘d7 ± Savchenko-V.Gurevich, Kherson 1989) 13...b5 14 axb6 ♘xb6 15 e4 ♘fd7 16 ♘xb6 ♖xb6 17 ♘d2 P.Nikolić-Tal, Reykjavik 1988, and even after the improvement 17...g5!? 18 ♗e3 ♘e5 19 ♗xg5!? ♕xg5 20 f4 ♕h6 21 fxe5 ♗xe5 22 ♘c4 ♗d4+ 23 ♔h1 White preserves an edge (P.Nikolić).

b2) Nor does Black manage to equalize after 12...b5 13 axb6 ♘xb6 (13...♖b8 favours White: 14 e4! ♖xb6 15 ♘d2 ♘e8 16 ♘c4 ± P.Nikolić-Cebalo, Brezovica 1988) 14 e4 ♘g4 15 h3 ♘e5 16 ♘xe5 ♗xe5 (retaining more chances than 16...dxe5

17 ♗e3 ♘c4 18 ♗c1 ± P.Nikolić-Barlov, Zagreb IZ 1987) 17 ♗xe5 ±.

b3) 12...♘g4!? 13 ♘a4 (13 ♗g5 does not lead to success: 13...f6 14 ♗d2 b5 15 axb6 ♘xb6 16 h3 ♘h6 17 b4 cxb4 18 ♘a4 ♘xa4 19 ♖xa4 a5! 20 ♗xb4 ♗a6! with an equal position; Gleizerov-Shestoperov, Budapest 1990) 13...♖b8 14 h3 (14 ♖c1?! h6 15 ♗d2 b5 16 axb6 ♘xb6 with an edge for Black; Manor-Wahls, Bern Z 1990) 14...♘ge5 15 ♘xe5 ♘xe5 16 ♘b6 ♗d7 =.

c) 12 ♕d2 ♘g4 13 h3 (a complex game which is sufficiently good for Black follows 13 ♖ab1 ♘de5 14 b4 b6 15 bxc5 bxc5 16 h3 ♘xf3+ 17 exf3 ♘e5 18 ♖be1 ♕c7 19 ♗xe5 ♗xe5 20 ♖xe5!? dxe5 21 f4 ♖b8 22 d6 ♕a5 23 fxe5 ♗e6 with an attack, Korchnoi-Hulak, Wijk aan Zee 1983; nor does he have any problems after 13 ♖ac1?! ♖b8 14 h3 ♘ge5 15 ♘xe5 ♘xe5 16 ♘e4 ♗f5 17 b4 ♗xe4 18 ♗xe4 c4 ∓ Cech-Hort, Biel 1992) 13...♘ge5 14 ♘xe5 ♘xe5 15 a5 ♗d7 (15...♖b8 16 ♘a4 ±) 16 ♖fb1 Smyslov-Grooten, Tilburg 1992, and after 16...♖fb8!? 17 ♗h6 ♗h8 Black could have looked to the future with optimism.

d) 12 ♕c2 ♘h5 (after 12...h6 13 ♖ab1 ♖e8 14 ♖fe1 g5 15 ♗d2 ♘b6 16 ♕b3! ♘bd7 17 a5 ♖b8 18 ♕a2 b5 19 axb6 ♖xb6 20 ♘a4 ♖b8 21 e4 White's position is preferable; Razuvaev-Ruban, Sochi 1989) 13 ♗g5 f6 14 ♗d2 f5.

e) 12 e4 ♘g4!? (12...♖b8 is not bad for Black either: 13 ♖e1 {13 h3!? takes us to 12 h3} 13...♘g4! 14

♘d2 ♘de5! 15 ♘f1 {or 15 h3 g5! 16 ♗xe5 ♘xe5 17 ♕e2 ♗d7 18 ♘f1 c4 ∓ Scheeren-Langeweg, Leeuwarden 1980} 15...♘c4 16 ♕e2 b5 17 h3 ♘ge5 and Black seizes the initiative; Smyslov-Portisch, Hungary 1978) 13 ♗g5 f6 14 ♗d2 ♘de5 15 ♘xe5 ♘xe5 = 16 f4?! ♘c4 17 ♗c1 f5 ∓ Bönsch-Ehlvest, Tallinn 1983.

Now we return to the position after 12 h3 *(D)*:

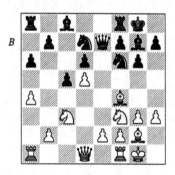

12   ...   ♖b8 *(D)*

The most natural, preparing an active game on the queenside, but it is far from being the only move. Also used:

a) 12...♖e8 13 e4 (nor is it easy for Black to equalize after 13 ♖e1 ♘h5 {13...♕f8 14 e4 ♘h5 15 ♗d2 ♘e5 16 ♘xe5 ♗xe5 17 ♔h2 ♗d7 18 f4 ♗d4!? Gleizerov-Magerramov, Pavlodar 1987, and now 19 g4!? ± deserved attention} 14 ♗g5 ♗f6 {or 14...f6 15 ♗d2 f5 16 e4} 15 ♗xf6 ♕xf6 16 ♘d2 ♕e7 17 ♘c4 ♘e5 18 ♘b6 with an edge) 13...♘h5 14 ♗g5 ♕f8 15 ♖e1 ♖b8 16 g4 ♘hf6 17 ♗f4 b5 (or 17...♘e5 18 ♘xe5 dxe5 19 ♗e3 ♕d6 20 ♕d3 b6 21 ♗f1 h5

22 f3 ± Lobron-Wahls, Dortmund 1990) 18 axb5 axb5 19 e5! ± Draško-Cebalo, Budvar 1986.

b) 12...h6!? and now:

b1) Black has no problems whatsoever after 13 ♖e1 ♖b8 (Black is also fine after 13...♘h5 14 ♗c1 ♖b8 15 e4 b5 16 axb5 axb5 17 ♗f1 b4 18 ♘b5 ♘e5 19 ♖a7 ♖b7 Vanheste-Arnason, Belgrade 1988) 14 e4 (14 ♖b1 b5 15 axb5 axb5 16 b4 ♘h5 17 ♗d2 allows the standard combination 17...♘xg3! 18 ♘xb5 {18 fxg3 ♗xc3} 18...♖xb5 19 fxg3 cxb4 20 ♗xb4 ♗a6 with advantage to Black; Csom-Sax, Hungarian Ch 1986) 14...g5 15 ♗e3 b5 16 axb5 axb5 ∞ Vanheste-Farago, Graz 1987.

b2) 13 ♕c1!? deserves consideration, e.g. 13...♔h7 (13...g5!?) 14 e4 g5 15 ♗d2 ♖b8 16 ♖b1 ♖e8 (16...b5 17 axb5 axb5 18 b4 ±) 17 ♖e1 ♕f8 18 ♕c2 and White exerts unpleasant pressure; Scherbakov-Palkovi, European Club Cup 1993.

b3) 13 e4 ♘h7 (White gained an advantage in Alburt-Fedorov, New York 1992, after 13...g5 14 ♗e3 {14 ♗d2 ♘h7 15 ♕c2 ♖e8 16 ♖ae1 ♕d8 = Adorjan-Portisch, New York 1987} 14...♖b8 {14...♘h7!?} 15 a5 b5 16 axb6 ♖xb6 17 ♕c2 ♘e8 18 ♘d2 ♖b4 19 ♘b3 ♘e5 20 ♘a5 ±) 14 ♕d2 g5 15 ♗e3 ♘b6!? 16 ♕d1 (or 16 b3 f5) 16...♘c4 17 ♗c1 f5 18 exf5 ♗xf5 = G.Kuzmin-Velimirović, Palma GMA 1989.

c) 12...♘h5!? 13 ♗g5 f6 14 ♗d2 f5 15 ♕b3 (returning to g5 does not work in White's favour: 15 ♗g5 ♘hf6 16 ♖b1 h6 17 ♗d2 ♘e4 18

♘xe4 fxe4 19 ♘e1 ♘e5 ∓ Ulybin-Hall, Oakham 1992) 15...♘e5 16 ♘xe5 ♗xe5 17 f4 ♗g7 18 ♔h2 ♘f6 19 ♖ae1 ♕f7 = Browne-D.Gurevich, USA Ch 1987.

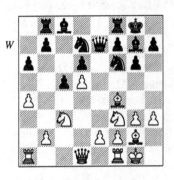

13 ♖b1

Instead:

a) 13 a5 has also been tried, but Black can equalize by 13...b5 (more interesting than 13...♘h5 14 ♗g5 f6 15 ♗d2 f5 16 ♖e1 ♘e5 17 ♘xe5 ♗xe5 18 e3 b5 19 axb6 ♖xb6 20 ♘a4 ♖b8 21 ♕c2 with some advantage; Savchenko-Ragozin, Leningrad 1989) 14 axb6 ♘xb6 15 e4 ♘fd7 16 ♖c1 ♘c4 17 b3 ♘ce5 18 ♘xe5 ♘xe5 19 ♗e3 c4 = Bönsch-Grünfeld, Hertzliya 1993.

b) 13 e4 gives Black significantly more problems:

b1) If 13...♘e8 14 ♖e1!? (14 ♕d2 b5 15 axb5 axb5 16 ♖a7 b4 17 ♘a4 ♖b7 18 ♖xb7 ♗xb7 = Bartels-Dizdarević, Berlin 1988) 14...b5 15 axb5 axb5, then after 16 ♕e2 we have reached a position examined in line 'b3'.

b2) 13...♘h5 14 ♗g5 ♗f6 15 ♗xf6 ♕xf6 16 ♕d2 b5 17 axb5 axb5

18 b4! cxb4 19 ♘e2 b3 20 g4 ♘g7 21 ♘ed4 Draško-Cebalo, Sarajevo 1986, is not sufficient for equality either.

b3) 13...b5 14 axb5 (the immediate 14 ♖e1 is interesting, for example 14...b4 {14...♘e8!?} 15 e5! bxc3 16 exf6 ♕xf6 17 ♗g5 c2 18 ♕xc2 ♕xb2 19 ♕xb2 ♗xb2 20 ♖ab1 ♖b4 21 ♗e7 ± Zaitsev-Abramović, Moscow 1982) 14...axb5 15 ♖e1 (15 ♖a7 is not frightening: 15...♘h5 16 ♗g5 ♗f6 17 ♗xf6 ♕xf6 18 ♖e1 ♖e8 ∞ Vanheste-Grooten, Dieren 1988) 15...♘e8!? (15...b4 16 e5!) 16 ♕e2 ♖b6! (the only move) 17 ♘xb5 ♗a6 18 ♖xa6! ♖xa6 19 ♘bd4 ♘b8! 20 ♘c6 ♖xc6 21 dxc6 ♘xc6 22 ♖d1!? (22 e5 ♘xe5 23 ♘xe5 dxe5 24 ♗xe5 ♘c7! 25 ♗xg7 ♕xe2 26 ♖xe2 ♔xg7 = led to a quick draw in Razuvaev-Psakhis, Irkutsk 1986) 22...♘d4!? (a more exact move than 22...♘e5 23 ♘xe5 dxe5 24 ♗e3 ♘c7 25 ♖c1 ♘e6 26 ♕b5! ± Draško-Renet, Vrnjačka Banja 1987) 23 ♘xd4 ♗xd4 24 ♗h6 (by using a tactical peculiarity of the position, Black gets a good game after 24 b4 ♘c7 25 b5 ♖b8 26 ♖b1 ♘d5! =) 24...♗g7 25 ♗e3 ♘c7 26 ♕d3 ♗xb2 27 ♕xd6 ♕xd6 28 ♖xd6 ♘e6 29 ♗f1, Draško, and the assessment of the position lies somewhere between ± and =.

13 ...   ♘h5

White makes no particular gains after 13...♖e8 14 ♖e1 ♘h5 15 ♗g5

♕f8 16 e4 b5 17 axb5 axb5 18 g4 ♘hf6 = Hausner-Cebalo, Banja Luka 1981, and he preserves a minimal advantage after 13...h6 14 e4! (but not 14 b4?! ♘h5 15 ♕c1 {15 ♗d2? ♘xg3! 16 fxg3 ♗xc3} 15...♘xf4 16 gxf4 ♖e8 = Goldin-Yedidia, New York 1993) 14...♘h5 (14...b5 15 axb5 axb5 16 b4) 15 ♗d2 ♘e5 16 ♘xe5 ♕xe5 17 f4 ♕e7 18 ♔h2 b5 19 axb5 axb5 20 b4 ± Dautov-Matthias, Lippstadt 1991.

14 ♗g5   f6

Exchanging dark-squared bishops eases White's problems: 14...♗f6 15 ♗xf6! ♘hxf6!? (or 15...♕xf6 16 ♕d2 ♖e8 17 b4 b6 18 ♖fe1 ♖b7 19 bxc5 bxc5 20 a5 ± Khalifman-Petran, Berlin 1989) 16 ♖e1 with a small advantage.

15 ♗d2   f5
16 ♕c1

16 b4? cxb4 17 ♖xb4 is bad because of 17...♘xg3! (17...♘c5? 18 ♘d4 ♗d7 Tukmakov-Ulybin, Simferopol 1988) 18 fxg3 ♗xc3. We have already seen this combination more than once.

Black also has an excellent game after 16 ♗g5 ♕e8 17 ♕d2 ♘e5 =, when 18 ♗h6?! ♗xh6 19 ♕xh6 f4 gives him the initiative.

16 ...   ♘hf6
17 b4   cxb4
18 ♖xb4   ♘c5
19 ♘d4   ♗d7

with equality in Obukhov-Cherniak, Smolensk 1991.

5 Fianchetto: Main Line (A64)

1 d4 ♘f6 2 c4 c5 3 d5 e6 4 ♘c3 exd5 5 cxd5 d6 6 ♘f3 g6 7 g3 ♗g7 8 ♗g2 0-0

	9	0-0	a6
	10	a4	♘bd7
	11	♘d2	♖e8 (D)

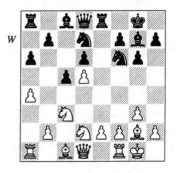

Now 12 h3 is the most frequently played and most promising move. 12 ♘c4 is also a popular move, and so the chapter is structured as follows:

A) 12 ♘c4

B) 12 h3

Other continuations are not as dangerous for Black, although they do have their advocates:

a) 12 ♖e1 ♖b8 13 ♘c4 ♘e5 (13...♘b6!?) 14 ♘xe5 ♖xe5 15 a5 ♖e8 (or 15...b5 16 axb6 ♖xb6 17 e4 ♖e8 18 h3 ♘d7 = Jokić-Liu Wenze, Belgrade 1988) 16 ♗f4 b5 17 axb6 ♖xb6 18 ♖a2 ♘g4 = Grigorian-Polugaevsky, Leningrad 1974.

b) 12 ♖b1 ♖b8 13 b4 b5 14 axb5 axb5 15 ♗b2 (Black was able to seize the initiative after 15 bxc5?! b4 16 ♘ce4 ♘xc5 17 ♘xc5 dxc5 ∓ Vaganian-Tseshkovsky, Leningrad 1974) 15...♘e5 16 ♗a1 ♗d7 17 h3 ♘h5 18 ♘ce4 ♗f5 ∞ Smyslov-Ivanović, Bugojno 1984.

c) 12 a5 b5 13 axb6 ♘xb6 14 ♘b3 ♘c4! (stronger than the old 14...♕c7 15 ♘a5 ♗d7 16 h3 {16 ♕c2 ♘g4 17 h3 ♘e5 18 b3 c4 = Granda-Wedberg, New York 1988} 16...♗b5 17 ♗e3 ♘fd7 18 ♕b3 with a small advantage to White; Euwe-Kotov, Zurich Ct 1953) 15 ♖a4 ♘b6 (15...♘e5 16 ♘a5 ♗d7 17 ♖a2 ♕c7 18 h3 ±) 16 ♖a2 ♘c4 17 ♕d3 (the best solution was probably 17 ♖a4!? with equality) 17...♖b8! 18 ♘d2 (obviously neither 18 ♘a1 ♘e5 19 ♕d1 ♘h5 ∓ L.Grigorian-Kapengut, USSR 1970, nor 18 ♕xc4 ♖b4 gives White anything) 18...♘xd2 19 ♗xd2 ♘g4 with equality; Mascariñas-Franco, Medina del Campo 1982.

d) 12 ♕b3 and now:

d1) 12...♘e5 is premature, and leads Black into unpleasantness: 13 f4 c4 (the only move – 13...♘eg4 14 ♘c4) 14 ♕a2 (but not 14 ♕b4? a5 15 ♕a3 ♕b6+ 16 ♔h1 ♘eg4; similarly White cannot organize himself after 14 ♘xc4 ♘xc4 15 ♕xc4

♛b6+ 16 ♔h1 ♘g4 17 ♘d1 ♗d7 18 h3 ♖ac8 19 ♕d3 ♘f6 20 ♗e3 ♕b4 21 ♗d2 ♕c4 with compensation) 14...♕b6+ 15 ♔h1 ♘eg4 16 ♘xc4 ♕c5 (16...♘f2+? 17 ♖xf2 ♕xf2 18 ♗e3 ♖xe3 19 ♖f1 and Black loses his queen) 17 ♗d2 ♘h5 18 e3 ♗f5 19 b4 ♕c7 20 ♖ac1! with the better game for White; Rogozenko-Giurumia, Bucharest 1992.

d2) 12...♖b8!? 13 ♘c4 ♘e5 14 ♘b6 ♘fd7 (Black also has a reasonable game after 14...♘ed7 15 ♘xc8 ♕xc8 16 a5 b5 17 axb6 ♖xb6 18 ♕a4 Johansen-Rogers, Sydney 1991, and 18...♕b7!? 19 ♖a2 ♖a8 would have led to equality, Stohl; 14...♘h5 15 a5 f5 16 ♖a4 ♗d7 17 ♘xd7 ♕xd7 18 ♕c2 ♖f8 = Karklins-Grigorian, Leningrad 1990, is also possible) 15 ♘xc8 ♕xc8 16 h3 (or 16 a5 b5 17 axb6 ♖xb6 18 ♕c2 c4, again with an equal position) 16...b5! 17 axb5 axb5 18 ♖a5 (Black has a mighty game after 18 ♘xb5 c4 19 ♕b4 ♖b6 20 ♕a5 ♕b7 21 ♘c3 ♘c5) 18...b4 19 ♘e4 ♕c7 ∓ Sakaev-Anastasian, Frunze 1989.

e) 12 e4 *(D)* gives Black a pleasant choice:

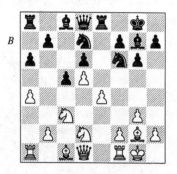

e1) 12...♖b8 13 ♘c4 ♘e5 (the alternative 13...♘b6 also deserves attention: 14 ♘a3 ♘a8 15 ♖e1 ♘c7 16 ♗f1 b5! 17 axb5 axb5 18 ♘axb5 ♘xb5 19 ♗xb5 ♗d7 with compensation) 14 ♘xe5 ♖xe5 15 f4 ♖e8 16 a5 (16 e5?! favours Black: 16...dxe5 17 fxe5 ♘d7 18 e6 fxe6 19 dxe6 ♗d4+! 20 ♔h1 ♘e5 ∓) 16...b5 17 axb6 ♕xb6 and Black's position is probably preferable already; Sommerfeld-Martin, Corr 1983.

e2) Black has no reason to complain at the result of the opening after 12...♕c7!? either, e.g. 13 ♘c4! (13 ♕e2?! is weaker: 13...♘b6! 14 ♕d3 ♘g4 15 h3 ♘e5 16 ♕c2 c4 17 ♘d1 a5! with a better game; Hort-Timman, Montreal 1979) 13...♘e5 (not 13...♖b8?! 14 ♗f4 ♗f8 15 a5 b5 16 axb6 ♘xb6 17 ♘a5 ± Letić-Dunhaupt, Corr 1983) 14 ♘xe5 ♖xe5 with an unclear game.

f) 12 ♖a2 ♖b8 (12...h5 13 ♘c4 ♘e5 14 ♘xe5 ♖xe5 15 ♗f4 ♖e8 16 a5 b5 17 axb6 ♕xb6 18 ♕a4 ♗d7 19 ♕a5 ♖eb8 = is also sufficient; Hertneck-Kindermann, Munich Z 1987) 13 a5 (or 13 ♘c4 ♘e5 14 b3 b5 15 axb5 axb5 16 ♘a5 b4 17 ♘b1 ♗d7 was a little better for Black; Trufanov-Moiseev, Kemerovo 1991) 13...b5 (Black held the balance in Roos-Dokhoian, Bonn 1993, after 13...♕e7 14 ♕c2 ♘h5 15 ♘c4 ♘e5 16 ♘xe5 ♗xe5 17 ♘a4 ♗g7 18 ♖e1 ♗d7 19 ♘b6 ♗b5 =) 14 axb6 ♘xb6 15 b3 with two interesting ideas for Black:

f1) 15...♘h5!? 16 ♗b2 f5 (better than 16...♘a8?! 17 ♘c4 ♘c7 18

公a5 奠d7 19 豐d2 公f6 20 罝d1 豐e7 21 e4 公b5 22 公xb5 axb5 23 罝e1 ± Suba-Foisor, Romania 1983) 17 e3 公f6 18 奠a1 豐e7 19 罝e1 公g4 = Dautov-Oll, Kiev 1984.

f2) 15...h5!? 16 公f3 奠b7 17 奠g5 豐d7 with counter-chances; Shapiro-Fedorowicz, Somerset 1986.

A) 12 公c4 公b6

After instead 12...公e5 *(D)*:

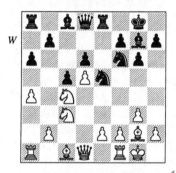

a) It's difficult for White to rely on having an advantage after 13 公a3 公h5 14 罝b1!? (matters are even simpler for Black after 14 h3 f5 15 含h2 {15 e4 b5! 16 axb5 axb5 17 公cxb5 fxe4 18 奠xe4 罝xh3 干} 15...b5!? 16 f4 {16 axb5!?} 16...b4 17 fxe5 奠xe5 18 奠f4 bxa3 19 罝xa3 奠xf4 20 gxf4 豐h4 with an advantage to Black; Sideif Zade-Pavlenko, USSR 1984, or 14 e3 f5 15 奠d2 奠d7 16 豐e2 罝b8 17 罝ab1 公f7 18 奠f3 f4! 19 奠xh5 fxe3 20 奠xg6 hxg6 21 奠xe3 奠h3 with more than enough compensation for the pawn; Unzicker-Hübner, Bad Kissingen 1980) 14...奠f5!? 15 e4 奠d7 (15...奠g4 16 f3 奠d7 17 g4

公f6 18 h3 c4 19 奠e3 ±) 16 b4 cxb4 17 罝xb4 豐a5 18 公a2 b5 with approximately equal chances; Marin-Sax, Odorheiu Secuiesc 1993.

b) 13 公xe5 罝xe5 14 奠f4 (Khalifman-Shabalov, USSR 1986, continued in interesting fashion: 14 豐c2 罝h5!? 15 h4 罝e5 {the Moor has done its job and can retire} 16 罝b1 罝e8 17 b4 cxb4 18 罝xb4 奠g4 19 e3 罝c8 20 奠b2 罝c7 with an unclear game) 14...罝e8 15 豐c2 公h5 16 奠d2 罝b8 (16...f5 17 e3 奠d7 18 a5 b5 19 axb6 豐xb6 20 罝a2 公f6 21 罝fa1 ± Ribli-Hertneck, Dortmund 1986, or 16...f5 17 e4 奠d7 18 罝ab1 罝c8 19 b4 cxb4 20 罝xb4 ± Goldin-Bagaturov, USSR 1986) 17 罝ab1 (17 a5!?) 17...b5 18 axb5 axb5 19 b4 c4 20 罝a1 豐e7 21 罝fe1 f5 22 罝a5 奠d7 23 奠f3 公f6 = Kharitonov-Psakhis, Irkutsk 1983.

13 公a3

The only move which gives Black problems; he can equalize after 13 公xb6 豐xb6 14 a5 豐c7 15 豐c2 罝b8 16 e4 Krasenkov-Sher, Moscow 1990, by playing 16...b5!? 17 axb6 罝xb6 ∞; his task is even simpler after 13 公d2 奠d7 14 豐b3 罝b8 15 罝e1 豐c7 16 a5 公c8 17 公c4 b5 18 axb6 公xb6 = Inkiov-Gheorghiu, Baile Herculane 1982, or 13 公e3 公g4!? 14 豐b3 罝b8 15 h3 公xe3 16 奠xe3-公d7 = Romani-Tal, Rome tt 1957.

13 ...　　　　奠d7 *(D)*

13...奠f5 is interesting, but not sufficient for equality: 14 a5 (things turned out rather better for Black in Kaidanov-Moskalenko, Lvov 1985:

14 f3 ♗d7 15 e4 ♘c8 16 ♗d2 ♖b8 17 ♖b1 b5 18 axb5 ♗xb5! 19 ♘axb5 axb5 20 b4 ♘d7 21 ♔h1 ♕c7 =) 14...♘c8 15 ♘c4 b5 16 axb6 ♘xb6 17 ♘a5 ♗e4 18 ♘xe4 ♘xe4 19 ♕d3 ♘f6 20 ♖a2 ♕c7 21 b3 with a clear advantage to White; Ilić-Kudrin, Bor 1984.

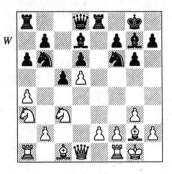

14 a5!?

White quite often tries to avoid altering the queenside pawn structure:

a) 14 ♖e1 ♕c7 (14...♘xa4!?) 15 h3 ♘xa4 16 ♘xa4 b5 17 ♘xc5 ♕xc5 18 ♕d3 b4 = Carlhammar-Isaacs, St.Martin 1991.

b) 14 h3 ♘xa4!? (we have already seen similar combinations, typical of this variation, more than once. Black brought it about in another fashion in the following game: 14...♕c7 15 ♗f4 ♘h5!? 16 ♗d2 ♘xa4! 17 ♘xa4 b5 18 g4 ♘f6 19 ♘c3 b4 20 ♕c2 bxa3 21 ♖xa3 ♗b5=Chianets-Pukshansky, USSR 1978) 15 ♘xa4 b5 16 ♘c3 b4 17 ♗d2 bxc3 18 ♗xc3 ♘e4 19 ♗xg7 ♔xg7 20 ♕c2 f5 = Akopian-Zelčić, Belgrade GMA 1988.

c) 14 ♗d2 ♖b8 (or 14...♘xa4!? 15 ♘xa4 b5 16 ♘c3 b4 17 ♘c4 bxc3 18 ♗xc3 ♗b5 19 b3 ♘g4 20 ♗xg7 ♔xg7 21 e4 {21 h3 ♘e5 22 ♘a5 h5 23 ♖e1 ♕f6 24 ♕d2 h4 = Arkell-Yudasin, Oviedo 1992} 21...♘e5 22 ♘xe5 ♖xe5 23 ♖e1 ± Lalić-Sax, Sarajevo 1985) 15 ♖e1 h5! 16 ♖b1 ♘xa4 17 ♘xa4 b5 18 ♗f4 (or 18 ♘c3 b4 19 ♘c4 bxc3 20 ♗xc3 ♗f5) 18...bxa4 19 ♗xd6 ♖b3 20 ♗xc5 ♗f5 with compensation; Neverov-Magerramov, Baku 1986.

d) 14 ♕b3?! ♘xa4!? 15 ♘xa4 b5 16 ♘c3 b4 17 ♘c4 bxc3 18 ♘xd6 ♖b8 19 ♕a3 cxb2 20 ♗xb2 ♖xe2 with an advantage to White; Kunsztowicz-Lau, Bundesliga 1983.

e) 14 ♕c2!? ♖b8 15 ♗d2 (or 15 a5 ♘c8 16 ♘c4 ♗b5 17 ♕b3 ♗xc4 18 ♕xc4 Vladimirov-Psakhis, Tashkent 1978, and Black would have equalized after 18...b5!? 19 axb6 ♘xb6) 15...♕c7 (the temporary sacrifice on a4 is not so good now: 15...♘xa4 16 ♘xa4 b5 17 ♘c3 b4 18 ♘c4 bxc3 19 ♗xc3 ±) 16 h3 ♘c8 17 ♖ab1 b5 18 axb5 ♗xb5!? 19 ♘axb5 axb5 20 b4 ♘e7 21 ♖fc1 ♘f5 22 e3 c4 23 ♖a1 and White has a small advantage; Kharitonov-Arbakov, USSR 1983.

14	...	♘c8
15	♘c4	♗b5
16	♕b3	♗xc4
17	♕xc4	b5

More exact than 17...♘d7 18 e4! b5 19 axb6 ♘cxb6 20 ♕e2 c4 21 ♗e3 ♕c7 22 ♘a4! ± Ermeni-Arsović, Yugoslav Ch 1991.

18	axb6	♘xb6

19 ♕h4 ♘fd7!
20 ♗g5
20 ♕xd8 ♖exd8 21 ♖a2 ♖db8 22 ♖d1 a5!? =.
20 ... ♕b8 =
Piankov-Psakhis, Irkutsk 1977.

B) 12 h3 ♖b8

Others:

a) 12...h6 is rarely used, but deserves attention: 13 ♖e1 (13 e4!? ♖b8 14 ♘c4 ♘e5 15 ♘a3) 13...♖b8 14 a5 b5 15 axb6 ♘xb6 16 e4 Hulak-Barlov, Pucarevo 1987, and Barlov gives 16...♕c7! 17 ♘a4 ♘xa4 18 ♖xa4 ♘d7 19 b3 ♘b6 =.

b) 12...♘h5 *(D)* is more popular, but recently White has managed to find the key:

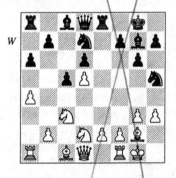

b1) White has no hint of an advantage after 13 e4 ♘e5 14 ♕c2 f5 15 exf5 gxf5 16 ♕d1 ♘f6 17 ♘f3 ♘g6 = Youngworth-Arnason, Lone Pine 1981.

b2) 13 ♘de4 ♘df6! 14 ♘xf6+ ♘xf6 15 ♗f4 ♖b8 16 ♕d3 ♕e7 17 e4 ♘h5 18 ♗d2 ♕e5! = Osnos-Tal, Alma-Ata 1968; White has nothing.

b3) Black also need not fear 13 ♔h2 f5 14 e4 (or 14 ♘c4 ♘e5 15 ♘xe5 ♗xe5 16 e3 ♖b8 17 ♕d3 ♗d7 18 a5 ♕h4!? with initiative; Timoshchenko-Kindermann, Baden-Baden 1985) 14...f4! (14...♘e5 15 exf5 ♗xf5 16 g4 ♘xg4+ 17 hxg4 ♕h4+ 18 ♔g1 ♗xg4 19 ♘f3 ♕f6 20 ♖a3! is tempting, but insufficient) 15 g4 ♘hf6 16 ♘c4 ♘xg4+! 17 ♕xg4 (or 17 hxg4 ♘e5 18 ♘xe5 ♗xe5 19 ♕f3 ♕h4+ 20 ♕h3 f3+ 21 ♔g1 ♕xh3 22 ♗xh3 h5 ∓) 17...♘e5 18 ♕e2 ♘xc4 19 ♕xc4 ♕h4 20 ♕d3 ♗e5 and Black has a strong attack; Todorović-Šahović, Zemun 1983.

b4) 13 ♘ce4!? ♘df6 14 ♘xf6+ ♘xf6 (not 14...♗xf6?! 15 ♘c4 ♖b8 16 a5 ♗e7 17 b4 cxb4 18 ♗d2 ♗f6 19 ♖b1 ± Birnboim-Maus, Netanya 1987) 15 ♘c4 ♗f5 Nogueiras-Cifuentes, Buenos Aires 1991, and White could have increased his small advantage after 16 a5!? ♗e4 17 ♗g5.

Returning to the position after 12...♖b8:

13 ♘c4

Wild complications arose in the game Lalić-Kovačević, Osijek 1984: 13 ♖b1 ♘h5 14 ♘de4 ♘df6 15 g4 ♘xe4 16 ♘xe4 f5!? 17 ♘xc5 fxg4 18 ♘e6 ♗xe6 19 dxe6 gxh3 20 ♗xh3 ♕h4; the consequences were unclear.

Black has no particular problems in the line 13 a5 b5 14 axb6 ♘xb6 15 ♕c2 ♕c7 (or 15...c4 16 ♖d1 ♕c7 17 g4, Vyzhmanavin-Chekhov, Sverdlovsk 1987, and now 17...♘fd7 = looks reasonable, as does 15...♘fd7 16 b3 ♖xe2 17 ♘xe2 ♗xa1 18 ♘e4

♕f8 19 ♘2c3 ♝xc3 20 ♕xc3 ♘xd5 21 ♕d2 ♝b7 22 ♝b2 with sufficient compensation for the sacrificed material, but it is not clear whether White has more than equality; Tal-Hjartarson, Moscow 1990) 16 e4 ♘fd7 17 ♘d1 c4!? 18 ♘e3 ♘e5 = V.Alterman-Yudasin, Haifa 1993.

Now Black has to make a principled choice between:

B1) 13...♘b6, leading to a complex positional struggle, and

B2) 13...♘e5, after which it is practically impossible to escape wild complications.

Instead, the passive 13...♕c7?! allows White to gain an advantage easily: 14 ♝f4 ♝f8 15 a5 b5 16 axb6 ♘xb6 17 ♘a5 ♘bd7 18 b3 ± N.Nikolić-Ademi, Kladovo 1990.

B1)   13   ...   ♘b6 (D)

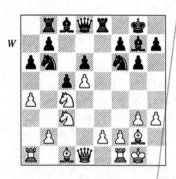

14   ♘a3

Black has no hint of a problem after 14 ♘e3 ♘fd7 (he also gets quite an adequate game after 14...♝d7 15 ♝d2 ♘h5 {in this opening you must not play passively; 15...♖e7?! 16 ♕c2 ♕e8 17 ♖fe1 ♖d8 18 a5 ♘c8 19

♘c4 ♝b5 20 b3 ± Marović-Ljubojević, Zagreb 1975} 16 a5 ♘a8 17 ♔h2 f5 18 f4 ♝b5 19 ♝f3 ♘f6 = Spasov-Rajković, Trstenik 1978) 15 a5 ♘a8 16 ♘c4 ♘e5 17 ♘xe5 ♝xe5 18 ♕d3 b5 19 axb6 ♘xb6 = Pachman-Mecking, Manila IZ 1976.

His problems are also quite simple after 14 ♕b3 ♘xc4 15 ♕xc4 ♘d7 16 f4 f5 17 e4 ♝d4+ 18 ♔h2 ♘f6 ∓ Hertneck-Gheorghiu, Lugano 1984.

14   ...   ♝d7

The provocative 14...♝f5 only aids White's plan: 15 g4!? ♝d7 16 ♝f4 ♘c8 17 ♕d3 ♖e7 18 ♘c4 ♝e8 19 ♕g3 ♖d7 20 a5 ± Van der Sterren-Short, Amsterdam 1983.

15   e4

Also seen:

a) 15 ♝f4?! ♘h5! (15...♘c8?! 16 ♘c4 ♕c7 17 a5 ♘h5 18 ♝d2 ♝b5 = Buslaev-Tal, Tbilisi 1956) 16 ♝xd6 ♝xc3 17 ♝xb8 ♝xb2 18 ♝a7 (18 g4 ♕xb8 19 gxh5 ♘xa4 20 ♖a2 ♘c3 21 ♕b3 ♘xe2+ 22 ♔h1 ♝g7 23 hxg6 hxg6 −+ as in Hort-Marović, Banja Luka 1976, does not ease White's situation) 18...♘xa4! (greed is punished: 18...♝xa1? 19 ♝xb6 ♕xb6 20 ♕xa1 ♖xe2 21 ♖b1 ♕c7 22 ♘c4 with more than enough compensation for the pawn; Gheorghiu-Ljubojević, Manila 1974) and now White should anticipate a troublesome time.

b) 15 a5 ♘c8 16 ♘c4 (D) and now:

b1) 16...♕c7 is not convincing: 17 ♝d2!? (17 ♖e1 ♝b5 18 ♕b3 ♝xc4 19 ♕xc4 ♘d7 20 ♕h4 b6 21

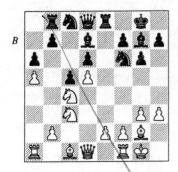

axb6 ♖xb6 22 ♖a4 ♘e7 = Averbakh-Korchnoi, Leningrad 1960) 17...b5 18 axb6 ♘xb6 19 ♘a5 ♗b5 20 b3! (a more precise move than 20 ♖e1 ♘fd7 21 ♕b3 ♘e5 22 ♘xb5 axb5 23 ♘c6 ♘bc4 with equality; Tal-Andersson, Biel IZ 1976) 20...♖a8 21 ♖e1 V.Kovačević-Andersson, Titovo Užice 1978; Black is deprived of counterplay and White can gradually increase the pressure on his position.

b2) 16...♗b5 17 ♕b3 ♗xc4 18 ♕xc4 ♘d7 19 ♖a3 (19 ♕d3 ♘e5 20 ♕c2 ♘a7 21 ♖d1 ♘b5 = Liberzon-Yusupov, Lone Pine 1981, is also not dangerous for Black) 19...♘e5 (or 19...♘e7!? 20 ♕a2 ♘f5 21 e3 ♘e5 22 ♖d1 ♕c7 23 ♖a4 ♖ec8 24 ♔h2 h5 = Rubinetti-Gheorghiu, Buenos Aires 1979) 20 ♕a2 ♘a7 21 f4 ♘d7 22 ♕c4 ♕c8 23 e4 b5 24 axb6 ♖xb6 with equality; V.Kovačević-Ilić, Yugoslavia 1980.

c) 15 ♕c2 ♘xa4! (in the game Timoshchenko-Quinteros, Baden-Baden 1985, Black postponed this combination for a move and still equalized: 15...♕c7 16 ♗d2 ♘xa4!? 17 ♘xa4 b5 18 ♘c3 b4 19 ♘c4 bxc3 20 ♗xc3 ♗b5 21 b3 ♕e7 22 ♖fe1

♘d7 =) 16 ♘xa4 b5 17 ♘c3 (17 ♘xc5 dxc5 18 e4 b4 19 ♘c4 b3! 20 ♕d3 ♖b4 21 ♗d2 ♖xc4 22 ♕xc4 ♗b5 with a complex game – Magerramov) 17...b4 18 ♗d2 (Black is even better after 18 ♘c4?! bxc3 19 bxc3 ♗b5 20 ♘e3 ♘d7 ∓ Godzaev-Magerramov, USSR 1987) 18...bxc3 19 ♗xc3 =.

d) 15 ♖e1 ♕c7!? (the most reliable; Black cannot settle after either 15...♘xa4 16 ♘xa4 b5 17 ♗f4!? ♕c7 18 ♘xc5 ♕xc5 19 ♖c1 ±, or 15...♘c8 16 ♕d3 ♕c7 17 ♗d2 ♘a7 18 ♘c4 ♘c8 19 a5 once again with advantage to White; Hübner-Wockenfuss, Bundesliga 1984) 16 e4 ♘xa4 17 ♘xa4 b5 18 ♘c5 ♕xc5 19 ♗e3 ♕c8! 20 ♖c1 ♕b7 21 ♗d4 ♖bc8 22 b4 ♖xc1 23 ♕xc1 ♖c8 = Akopian-Yudasin, Lvov Z 1990.

Now we return to the position after 15 e4 *(D)*:

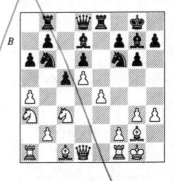

15 ... ♕c7

With correct play the following simply leads to a transposition: 15...♘c8 16 ♕d3 ♕c7 (Black does not get enough compensation for the pawn after 16...b5?! 17 axb5 axb5 18 ♘axb5 ♗xb5 19 ♘xb5 ♘d7 20 ♘c3 ♘e5 21 ♕c2 ♕b6 22 ♖a3 ± Ljubojević-Barlov, Vršac 1982, nor does he equalize in the event of 16...♕e7 17 a5 ♘a7 18 ♗d2 ♘b5 19 ♘c4 ♘xc3 20 ♗xc3; Birnboim-Lobron, Randers Z 1982) and White's best chances lie in returning to the main variation with 17 ♗e3 ♘a7, as examined under 15...♕c7. The reason is that both 17 ♖b1?! c4! 18 ♕c2 (18 ♕xc4 ♕xc4 19 ♘xc4 b5 20 axb5 axb5 21 ♘a5 b4 is a little better for Black) 18...b5 19 axb5 axb5 20 b4 cxb3! 21 ♕xb3 b4 22 ♕c4 ♕xc4 23 ♘xc4 ♘a7 ∓ Ljubojević-Hulak, Yugoslavia 1981, and 17 ♗d2 b5!? 18 axb5 c4! 19 ♕xc4 ♕xc4 20 ♘xc4 axb5 21 ♘a5 b4 22 ♘e2 ♘xe4 23 ♗xb4 ♗xb2 Reefschläger-Brunner, Bundesliga 1986, are more than satisfactory for Black;

16 ♗e3 *(D)*

Again it is not to White's advantage to play 18 ♖e1 ♘c8 17 ♕d3 ♘a7 18 ♖b1 b5 19 axb5 axb5 20 b4 cxb4 21 ♖xb4 ♕c5 22 ♘c2 ♘g4!? 23 ♘d1 ♘e5 and Black seized the initiative in Stern-J.Horvath, Budapest 1991.

16 ... ♘c8

An interesting idea, doubtless worthy of further investigation, was used in Osnos-Moskalenko, Lvov 1984: 16...♘xa4!? 17 ♘xa4 ♘xe4 18 ♘c2 b5 19 ♘c3 ♘xc3 20 bxc3 ♗xc3 21 ♖xa6 b4 22 ♗f4! ♖b6 23 ♖xb6 ♕xb6 with compensation for the knight.

17 ♕d3 b5!?

a) 17...c4 promises nothing good for Black: 18 ♘xc4 b5 19 ♘d2 bxa4 20 ♕xa6 ♘g4 21 hxg4 ♗xc3 22 ♖fc1 (22 bxc3 ♗b5) 22...♕a5 23 ♕xa5 ♗xa5 24 ♘c4 with a clear advantage for White, Hulak-Gobet; Reggio Emilia 1983.

b) 17...♘a7 deserves attention, although White most probably preserves the better chances, for example 18 ♖fc1 b5 19 b4 c4 and now:

b1) Black has no problems in the event of 20 ♕f1 bxa4!? 21 ♘xc4 ♖xb4 (21...♘b5 is also interesting: 22 ♘xa4 ♘xe4 23 ♗xe4 ♗xa1 24 ♘d2 ♗c3 25 ♕d3 {or 25 ♔h2 ♗xd2 26 ♖xc7 ♘xc7 27 ♗xd2 ♖xe4 28 ♕a1 ♘e8} ∓ Glek-Belinkov, corr. 1986} 25...♖bc8 26 ♘b6 {26 ♘b1? is simply bad: 26...♖xe4 27 ♕xe4 ♗f5 28 ♕f3 ♗xb1 29 ♖xb1 ♗d4 ∓} 26...f5! 27 ♘xc8 {Ginting-Lukov, Thessaloniki OL 1988} and after 27...fxe4!? 28 ♘xe4 ♖xc8 29 ♘xc3 ♗xc3 30 ♗d2 a draw is already not far off) 22 ♘xd6 (another interesting possibility for White: 22 ♘a2!? ♖b7 23 e5 dxe5 24 d6 ♕b8 25 ♗xb7 ♕xb7 26 ♘a5 ♕a8 with compensation) 22...♕xd6 23 ♗xa7 ♘xe4 24 ♘xe4 ♖bxe4 25 ♗c5 ♕xd5 26

♗xe4 ♕xe4 with an excellent game for Black; Quinteros-Kir.Georgiev, Thessaloniki OL 1984, and 20 ♕e2 bxa4! 21 ♘xc4 ♘b5 22 ♘xb5 ♗xb5 23 e5 dxe5 24 ♕a2 ♗f8 ∓ Korchnoi-Franco, Lucerne OL 1982 also leads to a pleasant result.

b2) 20 ♕d2!? (the only move that preserves hopes of an advantage) 20...bxa4 21 ♘xc4! ♕xc4 22 ♗xa7 ♖bc8 23 e5! and White had the initiative in Birnboim-Grünfeld, Israel Ch 1986.

18	axb5	c4
19	♕xc4	♕xc4
20	♘xc4	axb5
21	♘d2	b4
22	♘d1	♗b5
23	♖e1	♗d3
24	f3	♘d7
25	♗f1	♗c2

with good compensation for the pawn; Quinteros-Gheorghiu, Novi Sad OL 1982.

B2) | 13 | ... | ♘e5 |
|----|------|-----|
| 14 | ♘a3 | ♘h5 (D) |

In reply to 14...♕c7, White's best retort of all is 15 ♖e1 (things get complicated after 15 f4?! ♘ed7 16 e4 {or 16 ♗d2 c4!? 17 ♖c1 b5 18 axb5 axb5 and definitely not 19 b4? because of 19...♕a7+} 16...c4! 17 ♗e3 ♘h5 18 ♗f2 ♘c5, the result being not unadvantageous for Black) 15...c4 16 ♗e3 ♘h5 17 a5 f5 18 ♗b6 ♕e7 19 f4 ♘d7 20 ♗f2 b5 21 axb6 ♘xb6 22 e4 ± Hübner-Torre, Leningrad IZ 1973.

The move 14...♗d7!? deserves further study, for example 15 f4 ♘h5

16 fxe5 (16 ♔h2 b5!) 16...♗xe5 17 g4!? (or 17 ♘e4 f5 18 ♘g5 ♘xg3 Ginting-Antonio, Thessaloniki OL 1988, and even after the improvement 19 ♖f2!? b5 20 axb5 axb5 21 ♘e6 ♕h4 one cannot give this position a comprehensive assessment) 17...♘g3 18 ♖f2 (18 ♘c4?! is fatal: 18...♗xc3 19 bxc3 ♗xg4! 20 ♕d3 {20 hxg4 ♘xe2+ 21 ♔h2 ♕h4+ 22 ♗h3 ♕g3+} 20...♘xe2+ 21 ♔h1 ♘xc1 −+ Saeed-Norwood, London 1985) 18...b5 19 axb5 axb5 20 ♘c2 b4 21 ♘b1 and White's chances are preferable.

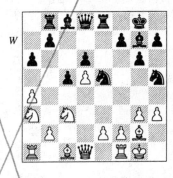

15 e4

The strongest and most principled move. White frees e2 for the queen and threatens to hinder his opponent significantly with a headlong pawn advance on the kingside. Less powerful alternatives:

a) 15 g4?! ♕h4! (15...♗xg4?! 16 hxg4 ♕h4 17 gxh5 ♘g4 18 ♗f4 ♗e5 19 ♕d3 ♗xf4 20 ♕h3 +−) 16 ♘e4 (White must be at his most careful; 16 gxh5? ♗xh3 17 ♗xh3 ♕xh3 18 ♗f4 ♘f3+! 19 exf3 ♖e5! −+) 16...h6 17 gxh5 (or 17 f3 f5 18

♘xd6 fxg4 19 ♘xe8 gxh3 – Tseshkovsky) 17...♗xh3 18 ♘g3 ♘g4 19 ♗f4 ♗d4! with the most powerful of attacks; Kakageldiev-Tseshkovsky, USSR 1978.

b) 15 f4?! ♘xg3!? (15...♘d7 16 ♔h2 f5 17 ♖e1 ♘hf6 18 ♘c4 ♘b6 = is not bad either) 16 fxe5 ♗xe5! (instead of the text move Kapengut suggests 16...♘xf1 17 ♕xf1 b5!? 18 axb5 axb5 19 ♘axb5 ♗xe5 20 ♖a7 ♖b7 21 ♖xb7 ♗xb7 22 ♗f4 ♗a6 ∓) 17 ♘c4 ♗xc3 18 bxc3 b5 19 axb5 axb5 20 ♘e3 ♘xf1 21 ♘xf1 ♕h4 ∓ Donner-Ree, Amsterdam 1979.

c) 15 e3 f5 16 ♖b1 ♗d7 17 b4 cxb4 18 ♖xb4 ♕a5 19 ♘a2 b5! 20 ♗d2 ♕c7 21 axb5 axb5 = Osnos-Stein, Tbilisi 1966.

d) 15 ♗d2 f5 16 e3 (16 ♖b1 f4!? 17 ♗xf4 ♘xf4 18 gxf4 ♕h4!? Kapengut) 16...♗d7 =.

e) 15 ♔h2 f5 (the overly active 15...g5?! draws Black into difficulties: 16 ♘c2 g4 17 ♘e3 f5 18 hxg4 fxg4 19 ♘e4 b5 20 ♖h1! h6 21 axb5 ♖xb5 22 ♕c2 ♖f8 23 ♔g1 with advantage; Szabo-Christiansen, Hastings 1981) 16 f4 (Black would seize the initiative after the cautious 16 ♗d2 ♗d7 17 ♖b1 b5 18 axb5 axb5 19 b4 ♕e7 20 ♖e1 f4!) 16...♘f7 (16...b5 17 axb5 axb5 18 ♘axb5 ♘f7 19 ♘a7 ♖b6 20 ♘xc8 ♕xc8 is also interesting, Schmidt-Rohrbach, Bundesliga 1987) 17 e3 ♗d7 18 ♕d3 ♘f6 =.

15 ...   ♗d7!?

Black did not arrive at this cunning move, introduced into practice by Nunn, straight away, but only after experiencing failures in other continuations. Let us examine them:

a) 15...c4?! 16 ♗e3 ♕c7 17 a5! ♕xa5 18 ♘xc4 ♕c7 19 ♘xe5 ♗xe5 20 ♕d2 ♗d7 21 ♘e2 with advantage; Marović-Soos, Rome 1982.

b) 15...f5 16 exf5 ♗xf5 17 g4 ♗xg4!? (White easily repulses the attack after 17...♘xg4?! 18 hxg4 ♕h4 19 gxf5 ♗e5 20 ♖e1 ♕h2+ 21 ♔f1 ♗d4 22 ♖xe8+ ♖xe8 23 ♕g8 ♖f8 24 ♕h3 +−) 18 hxg4 ♕h4 19 gxh5 ♖f8 20 h6! (a brilliant move, as the pawn on h6 will greatly assist White's plans; 20 ♗g5? is significantly weaker in view of 20...♕xg5 21 ♘e4 ♕h4 22 ♕b3 ♖f4 with a strong attack; Kharlamov-Dvoirys, Cheliabinsk 1980) 20...♗h8 *(D)* and now:

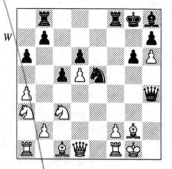

b1) 21 ♘e4?! ♘g4 22 ♕xg4 ♕xg4 23 ♘c4 (or 23 ♘c2 ♖f3! 24 ♘g5 ♖f5 25 f4 ♕e2 26 ♖f2 ♕d1+ 27 ♔h2 ♖xg5!) 23...b5! (but not 23...♖be8? 24 ♘cxd6 ♖e5 25 ♖a3 ♖xd5 26 ♖g3) 24 axb5 axb5 25 ♘cxd6 ♖b6! (25...♗e5!? leads to an unclear game: 26 ♗e3 {26 ♖a7?

♕h4 27 ♖g7+ ♔h8 28 f4 ♗d4+ 29 ♖f2 ♕xh6 –+ Akopov-K.Grigorian, USSR 1977} 26...♕h4 27 f4 ♖xf4 28 ♗xf4 ♗xf4 29 ♖xf4 ♕xf4) 26 ♗e3 ♗e5 27 ♖a7 ♖xd6! 28 ♘xd6 ♗xd6 29 ♖g7+ ♔h8 30 ♖a1 ♕h4 and Black has an obvious advantage, Kivlan-Petkevich, Riga 1974.

b2) 21 ♘c4! (a beautiful move) 21...♘g4 (the variation becomes practically forced, and it is difficult for either side to diverge; both 21...♕xc4? 22 ♘e4 and 21...♘xc4 22 ♕d3! are bad) 22 ♕xg4! ♕xg4 23 ♘xd6 ♗e5 (Black's situation is improved by neither 23...b5 24 axb5 axb5 25 ♘dxb5 ♗e5 26 ♖a4 ♕h5 27 f4 ± V.Kovačević, nor 23...♗d4 24 ♘ce4 ♖f3 25 ♖a3! ♖bf8 26 ♖xf3 ♖xf3 27 ♖e1 ±) 24 ♘de4 (Black's problems are eased in the event of 24 ♘ce4 ♕h4 25 f4 ♗d4+ 26 ♘f2 g5) 24...♖f5 (24...♖f3?! 25 ♘g5! ♖bf8 26 ♘xf3 ♖xf3 27 ♖e1 and White wins; V.Kovačević-Nemeth, Karlovac 1979; and 24...b5 is also bad in view of 25 axb5 axb5 26 d6! ♖f3 27 ♖e1 ♖bf8 28 ♘d5 +–) 25 ♗e3 ♖bf8 26 f4! (it's still not too late to fall into a trap: 26 ♗xc5? ♖h5 27 f3 ♖h1+! 28 ♔xh1 ♕h4+ mating) 26...♗d4 (26...♖xf4 is not enough: 27 ♗xf4 ♗d4+ 28 ♘f2 ♕xf4 29 ♘ce4 ♖f5 30 ♖a3 and all the white pieces meanwhile go to their monarch's aid) 27 ♖ae1 ♖xf4 28 ♖xf4 ♕xf4 29 ♗xd4 cxd4 30 ♘d1 ♕xh6 31 d6 g5 32 ♘df2 with an obvious advantage to White (analysis by Kapengut).

c) 15...♖f8 (D) and now:

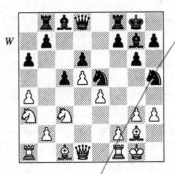

c1) 16 ♖e1?! leads to unpleasant consequences for White: 16...f5 (perhaps 16...♗d7 17 ♗f1 f5 18 exf5 ♗xf5 with initiative, is no less powerful, but 19 f4?! ♘xg3 20 fxe5 ♘xf1 21 ♖xf1 ♕h4 –+ led White to catastrophe in Scholseth-Andonov, Saint John 1988) 17 exf5 ♗xf5 18 ♖xe5?! ♗xe5 19 g4 b5! 20 axb5 axb5 21 ♘axb5 (or 21 ♘e2?! ♗xg4! 22 hxg4 ♕h4 23 ♗e3 ♗h2+ 24 ♔f1 ♖xf2+! 25 ♗xf2 ♖f8 and Black wins; V.Kovačević-Horvath, Yugoslavia 1980) 21...♗d7 22 ♘xd6 ♗xd6 23 ♘e4 ♗f4 24 gxh5 ♕h4 and Black's attack can scarcely be repulsed.

c2) 16 g4 ♕h4! 17 gxh5 ♗xh3 18 h6 ♗h8 19 ♕e2 (19 ♘e2?! is weaker because of 19...f5 20 exf5 ♖xf5 21 ♘g3 ♖bf8! 22 ♘xf5 ♖xf5 ∓ Scheeren-Timman, Holland 1980) 19...f5 20 ♘c2 ♖be8 with sufficient compensation.

c3) 16 ♔h2 is without a doubt the best move:

c31) 16...♗d7!? is interesting, but probably insufficient: 17 ♕e2 ♕e8 (or 17...b5 18 axb5 axb5 19 ♘axb5 ♗xb5 20 ♘xb5 ♕d7 21 ♘c3 c4 22 g4 ♘f6 23 f4 ♘d3 24 e5 dxe5 25 f5 with advantage; Birnboim-Kunze, Lugano 1989) 18 g4! (Black is fine after 18 a5 f5 19 f4 ♘f7 ∞) 18...b5 19 axb5 f5 (19...axb5 20 gxh5 b4 21 f4 bxc3 22 bxc3 and the knight is trapped) 20 exf5 gxf5 21 gxh5 f4 22 f3 axb5 23 h6! ♗xh6 24 ♘e4 b4 25 ♘c4 ♘xc4 26 ♕xc4 ♗b5 27 ♕c2 ± Kapetanović-Martić, Corr 1986.

c32) 16...f5 17 f4 b5!? (when you take off the head, don't mourn the loss of the hair; White has a clear advantage in a quiet position after 17...fxe4 18 ♘xe4!? ♘f7 19 ♘c4 ♘f6 20 a5 ♘xe4 21 ♗xe4 ♗d7 22 ♖a2 ♗b5 23 b3 Ki.Georgiev-Alexakis, Corfu 1991) 18 axb5 (but not 18 fxe5 because of 18...♘xg3! 19 ♔xg3 ♗xe5+ 20 ♔f2 ♕h4+ 21 ♔g1 ♕g3 22 ♖f3 ♕h2+ with an attack for Black: Birnboim-Arnason, Randers Z 1982) 18...axb5 19 ♘axb5 fxe4 with another division:

c321) 20 ♘a7!? leads to unclear complications, e.g. 20...♗d7!? (if 20...♘f3+ then 21 ♗xf3 exf3 22 ♘c6 ♕d7 23 f5! ♖b7 24 g4 leads to an advantage for White, whilst 20...e3 21 ♕e2 ♘xg3 22 ♔xg3 g5! 23 f5! ♗xf5 24 ♕xe3 deserves a great deal of attention, and now instead of 24...♕d7?! 25 ♘c6 ♖be8 26 ♕xg5 h6 27 ♕h5 ♗g6 28 ♖xf8+ ♖xf8 29 ♕e2 with a winning position for White, Alburt-Olafsson, Reykjavik 1982, Black should have continued 24...♘c4!? with an unclear game) 21 fxe5 ♘xg3 22 ♖xf8+ ♕xf8 23 ♘c6 ♗xc6 24 dxc6 ♗xe5

25 ♕d5+ ♔h8 26 ♕xe5+! dxe5 27 ♔xg3 – analysis by Timman.

c322) 20 ♗xe4 ♗d7 21 ♕e2 ♕b6 22 ♘a3 ♖be8. Now Korchnoi-Kasparov, Lucerne OL 1982, is a good illustration of Black's tactical possibilities: 23 ♗d2? ♕xb2! 24 fxe5 ♗xe5 25 ♘c4 ♘xg3 26 ♖xf8+ ♖xf8 27 ♕e1 ♘xe4+ 28 ♔g2 ♕c2 29 ♘xe5 ♖f2+ 30 ♕xf2 ♘xf2 31 ♖a2 ♕f5 32 ♘xd7 ♘d3! ∓. However, after 23 ♕g2!, Kasparov simply evaluates the position as better for White.

Now we return to the position after 15...♗d7 *(D)*:

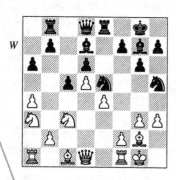

16   a5!?

Practically forced; only White will have problems after 16 g4 b5 17 axb5 axb5 18 ♘c2 (nor can White organise his position after 18 ♘axb5 ♗xb5 19 ♘xb5 ♖xb5 20 gxh5 ♕h4 21 hxg6 hxg6 ∓) 18...b4 19 ♘e2 ♕h4!? 20 ♘e3 f5 with an attack, or 16 f4?! ♘xg3 17 fxe5 ♗xe5 18 ♘c4 ♗d4+ 19 ♔h2 ♘xf1+ 20 ♕xf1 b5! 21 ♘xd6 ♗e5+ 22 ♗f4 ♕f6 23 ♘xe8 ♕xf4+ ∓ Kuligowski-Levitt, Bundesliga 1987.

16	...	♕xa5
17	g4	♘f6 *(D)*

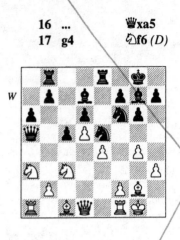

18 g5

Wild complications with unclear consequences arise after the further moves 18 f4 ♘exg4!? 19 hxg4 ♘xg4 (19...♗xg4!?) 20 ♗f3 h5 21 f5! ♕d8 22 ♗xg4 ♕h4! 23 ♘c2 ♕g3+ 24 ♔h1 ♗e5 25 ♕e2 hxg4 26 ♕g2

♕h4+ 27 ♔g1 g3 28 ♘e3 b5 Vaulin-Obukhov, USSR 1988.

18	...	♘h5
19	f4	♘c4
20	♘xc4!	♕xa1
21	♘xd6	♗d4+
22	♔h2	♖e7

Stronger than 22...♗xc3 23 bxc3 ♕xc3 24 ♖f3 ♕d4 25 ♖d3 ♕a4 26 ♕d2! ♕b4 27 ♕e3 c4 28 ♗a3 ♕a4 29 ♖c3 ± Heinbuch-Klinger, Bunde 1985.

23	♕f3	b5
24	e5	b4

and the mutual balancing act on a tightrope continues; Hulak-Nunn, Toluca IZ 1982.

In resumé, one may note that both 13...♘b6 and 13...♘e5 have equal rights to existence.

6 6 e4: Introduction (A65)

1 d4 ♞f6 2 c4 c5 3 d5 e6 4 ♞c3 exd5 5 cxd5 d6

    6 e4   **g6** *(D)*

I can honestly say that I can't imagine how you can play the Modern Benoni without the bishop on g7, but nevertheless you do see 6...♝e7 and then: 7 ♞f3 (7 ♝d3 0-0 8 ♞ge2 ♞a6 9 0-0 ♞b4 10 ♝b1 ♜e8 11 ♞g3 ♝f8 12 ♝g5 h6 13 ♝f4 ± Khalafov-Osnos, Moscow 1979) 7...0-0 8 ♝e2 ♞a6 9 ♞d2 ♞e8 10 ♞c4 ♜b8 11 a4 ± Manni-Gustafsson, Helsinki 1992.

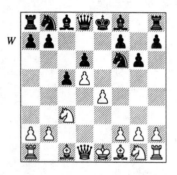

Now after 7 ♞f3 we arrive in the so-called Classical System (A70-A79), after 7 f4 the Four Pawns Attack arises (A66-A69), but in this chapter (A65) White usually employs one of three moves:

    A) 7 ♝f4
    B) 7 ♝d3
    C) 7 f3

Before discussing these continuations in detail, a few words about two continuations which aren't very popular:

a) Quite rarely White plays 7 g3 and then 7...♝g7 8 ♝g2 0-0 9 ♞ge2 a6 (or 9...♜e8 10 0-0 {10 a4!? ±} 10...b5 11 ♞xb5 ♞xe4 12 ♝xe4 ♜xe4 13 ♞ec3 ♜e8 14 ♝f4 ♝f8 15 ♕d2 a6 16 ♞a3 ♞d7 ∞ Murey-Quinteros, New York 1983) 10 a4 ♞bd7 11 0-0 ♜e8 12 h3 (12 ♜b1 c4!? 13 b3 ♞c5 14 bxc4 ♞fxe4 15 ♞xe4 ♞xe4 16 ♝a3 ♕c7 is also possible, with at least an equal game; Genov-Dzhandzhgava, Antwerp 1992) 12...♜b8 13 a5 (13 g4 leads to an unclear game: 13...b5 14 axb5 axb5 15 ♞g3 ♞e5 16 g5 ♞fd7 17 f4 ♞c4 Antoshin-Korchnoi, Riga 1970) 13...b5 (after 13...♞e5?! 14 f4 ♞ed7 15 g4 the initiative is safely in White's hands; Keres-Hromadka, Prague 1937) 14 axb6 ♕xb6 = *ECO*.

b) Black has no problems after 7 ♝b5+, e.g. 7...♞bd7 8 ♝f4 (for 8 ♞f3!? ♝g7 see A70) 8...♞h5 9 ♝e3 ♝g7 10 g4 ♞hf6 11 g5 ♞h5 12 ♝e2 0-0 13 ♝xh5 gxh5 14 ♕xh5 ♕a5 with an excellent game for the pawn.

A) 7 ♝f4 a6

I cannot recommend 7...♞h5 8 ♝e3 ♝g7 9 ♝e2 ♞f6 10 ♞f3 0-0 11

♘d2 a6 12 a4 ♘bd7 13 0-0 ♖e8 14 ♕c2 ± Forintos-Szalanczy, Hungary 1981.

After 7...♗g7 we very frequently transpose to other systems, for example:

a) 8 ♕a4+ ♗d7 (the overly extravagant 8...♚e7?! leads Black into great difficulties: 9 ♘f3 ♖e8 10 ♗b5 ♘bd7 11 0-0 a6 12 ♖fe1 ♘b6 13 ♕b3! {stronger than 13 e5!? dxe5 14 ♕a3 ♚f8 15 ♗xe8 exf4 16 ♕xc5+ ♚g8 17 ♗a4 ♘xa4 18 ♘xa4 ♘xd5 with only a small advantage for White; Korchnoi-Ljubojević, Bath 1973} 13...axb5 14 ♘xb5 ± Tal) 9 ♕b3 ♕c7 10 ♘f3 leads to A61.

b) 8 ♗b5+ ♗d7 9 ♗e2 ♕e7 (a better square for the queen than c7, for example 9...♕c7 10 ♘f3 0-0 11 0-0 a6 12 e5! dxe5 13 ♘xe5 ♕d8 14 ♗f3 ♗b5 15 ♖e1 ± Geller-Suetin, Leningrad 1960) 10 ♘f3 (or 10 ♕b3 b5! =) 10...0-0 11 0-0 ♗g4 12 ♘d2 ♗xe2 13 ♕xe2 ♘h5 14 ♗e3 ♘d7 leads to A72.

c) 8 ♘f3 relates to A70.

8 ♘f3   b5

Other moves do not guarantee Black an easy life:

a) White preserves a small advantage after 8...♗g4 9 ♕a4+ (Black has no problems after 9 ♗e2 b5!? {stronger than 9...♘bd7 10 0-0 ♘h5 11 ♗g5 ♗e7 12 ♗h6 ♗f8 13 ♗g5 ♗e7 14 ♗e3 0-0 15 ♘d2 ♗xe2 16 ♕xe2 b5 17 a4 b4 18 ♘d1 ± Tarjan-Kudrin, USA Ch 1983} 10 e5 ♗xf3 11 ♗xf3 dxe5 12 ♗xe5 ♗d6 13 ♗xf6 ♕xf6 = Bellón-Hulak, Indonesia 1982) 9...♘bd7 10 ♘d2 b5 11

♕c2 and Black does not achieve equality after either 11...♘b6 12 h3 ♗d7 13 a4 bxa4 14 ♘c4 ♕b8 15 ♘xb6 ♕xb6 16 ♘xa4 ♕b8 17 ♗c4 ♗g7 18 0-0 ± Mohr-Lobron, Bundesliga 1987, or 11...♘h5 12 ♗e3 ♘b6 13 a4!? b4 14 ♘cb1 ♗g7 15 a5 ♘c8 16 ♘c4 ±.

b) The risky 8...♕e7 can bring huge complications, for example 9 ♗e2 ♘bd7 10 0-0 b5 (or 10...♗g7 11 ♘d2 0-0 12 ♘c4 ♘xe4 13 ♘xe4 ♕xe4 14 ♗xd6 ♖e8 15 ♖e1 b5 16 ♗f3 ♕xe1+ 17 ♕xe1 ♖xe1+ 18 ♖xe1 ♗d4 {but not 18...bxc4 19 ♖e8+ ♗f8 20 ♗xf8 ♘xf8 21 d6 ♖b8 22 d7} 19 ♖e8+ ♚g7 20 ♘a5 with an initiative; Braga-Manor, London 1987) 11 ♗xb5!? axb5 12 ♘xb5 ♕d8 13 ♗xd6!? (13 e5 ♘h5! 14 exd6 f6 15 ♗d2 ♚f7 Komarov-Agapov, USSR 1987, is unclear) 13...♗xd6 14 ♘xd6+ ♚f8 15 ♘xc8 ♖xc8 16 e5 and White has strong pressure.

c) It is not easy for Black to equalize after 8...♗g7 9 ♕a4+!? *(D)*:

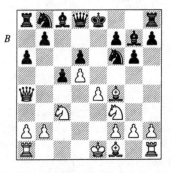

c1) 9...♚f8 10 ♗e2 ♕e7 11 0-0 ♘bd7 12 ♘d2!? (12 ♖fe1 doesn't look as convincing due to 12...♘g4! 13 ♕b3 h5 14 a4 ♗f6 15 a5 g5! 16 ♗d2 ♘de5 = Zlatiliov-Fedorov, Pazardzhik 1988) 12...♘e5 13 ♗g3 g5 14 f4 with initiative – Kapengut.

c2) 9...♘fd7 leads to approximately the same result: 10 ♕c2 ♕e7 11 a4 0-0 12 ♗e2 ♖e8 13 0-0 ♘f8 14 ♖fe1 ♘bd7 15 a5 ± Dydyshko-Kapengut, Minsk 1978.

c3) 9...♘bd7? is a serious error: 10 ♗xd6 ♕b6 11 ♘b5! axb5 12 ♕xa8 ♕xd6 13 ♕xc8+ ♔e7 14 ♕xb7 ♘xe4 15 ♗xb5 +–.

c4) 9...♗d7 10 ♕b3 (D) (Black's problems are simpler after 10 ♕c2 ♕e7!? {10...♗g4 11 ♘d2 ♘h5 12 ♗e3 0-0 13 h3 ♗c8 14 g4! ♘f6 15 a4 ± Korchnoi-Cebalo, Titograd 1984} 11 a4 0-0 12 ♗e2 ♗g4 =).

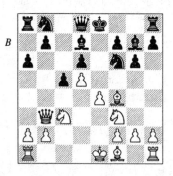

Now:

c41) 10...♗c8?! 11 a4 0-0 12 ♗e2 ♘h5 13 ♗g5 f6 14 ♗e3 f5 15 exf5 gxf5 16 ♘g5! ± Tarjan-Agzamov, Vršac 1983.

c42) 10...♗g4? 11 ♕xb7! ♗xf3 12 ♕xa8 (but not 12 gxf3?! ♘h5 13 ♗g3 ♘xg3 14 hxg3 ♘d7 15 ♗h3 ♘e5 16 f4 ♘f3+ 17 ♔f1 0-0 with

compensation; Forintos-Szalanczy, Hungary 1983) 12...♘xe4 13 ♖c1! and now:

c421) 13...♗d4 14 ♖c2! ♘xc3 (14...♘xf2 15 ♖xf2 ♗xf2+ 16 ♔xf2 ♗g4 17 ♗b5+! axb5 18 ♖e1+ ♔f8 19 ♗h6+ ♔g8 20 ♕e7! +– Zsu.Polgar-Hardicsay, Hungary tt 1984) 15 gxf3! ♘xa2 16 ♗c4 ♘b4 17 ♖e2+ ♔f8 18 ♗h6+ ♗g7 19 ♗g5 ±.

c422) 13...♘xc3 14 bxc3 ♗e4 15 f3 ♗f5 16 g4 g5 17 ♗xg5 ♕xg5 18 ♕xb8+ ♔e7 19 ♕c7+ ♗d7 20 ♖c2 and White can already take heart as he has a big advantage – Zsu.Polgar.

c43) 10...b5 11 ♗xd6 b4 and now:

c431) 12 ♘a4?! is rather dubious for White: 12...♘xe4 13 ♕e3 (13 ♗xc5?! ♘xc5 14 ♘xc5 ♕e7+ 15 ♕e3 ♗xb2) 13...♗xa4 14 ♕xe4+ ♔d7 and now neither 15 ♘e5+?! ♔c8 16 ♘xf7 (16 ♗xc5 ♗xe5 17 ♖c1 ♗xb2 18 ♗b6+ ♗xc1 19 ♕c4+ ♔d7 20 ♗xd8 ♖e8+ 21 ♗e2 ♔xd8 22 0-0 ♗d2 ∓) 16...♖e8!, nor 15 ♗e5 ♖e8 16 b3 (Krasenkov-Shabalov, Tashkent 1987) 16...♕e7! 17 0-0-0 ♗xe5 18 ♘xe5+ ♕xe5 ♕xe5 ♖xe5 20 bxa4 ♗d6 (Shabalov) can solve White's problems.

c432) Huge complications which are not unfavourable for White follow 12 e5 bxc3 13 exf6 cxb2 (probably more exact than 13...♗xf6 14 bxc3 ♗f5 15 ♗xc5!? ♗d7 16 ♗b4 a5 17 ♗d6 a4 18 ♕b4 ♕a5 19 ♖c1 ♔d8 20 ♗b5 ♖e8+ 21 ♔d2 ♕b6 22 ♘d4 ± Flear-Lamoureux, Belfort 1988) 14 ♕xb2 (but not 14 ♕e3+ ♗e6 15 ♖b1 ♗xf6 16 ♗e5 ♕xd5! 17

♗xf6 ♕f5 18 ♗d3 ♕xf6 19 ♗e4 ♖a7 20 ♕xc5 ♖e7 ±) 14...♗xf6 15 ♗e5 ♕e7 (White also preserves his advantage after 15...♗xe5 16 ♕xe5+ ♕e7 17 0-0-0 ♕xe5 18 ♘xe5 0-0 19 ♗c4 ♗b5 20 ♖he1 ± Flear-Stefansson, Hastings 1987) 16 d6 (promising more than 16 0-0-0 ♗xe5 17 ♕xe5 ♕xe5 18 ♘xe5 ♗a4 19 ♖d2 ♘d7 = Sosonko-Lobron, Bad Kissingen 1981) 16...♗xe5 17 ♘xe5 ♕f6 18 0-0-0 0-0 19 g3 with a small advantage.

c433) 12 ♘d1!? ♘xe4 13 ♕e3 ♗f5 14 ♗xc5 ♕a5!? (or 14...♕xd5 15 ♖c1 ♘d7 16 ♗xb4 ♕b7 17 ♗a3 ♗f8 18 ♗xf8 ♔xf8 19 ♕d4 Moiseev-Efimov, Ulan Ude 1988) 15 ♗d4 b3+ 16 ♘c3 0-0 17 ♗xg7 ♔xg7 18 ♕d4+ with a clear advantage to White.

c44) 10...♕c7 11 e5! (in Korchnoi-Suba, Beersheba 1988, an unsuccessful combination led White to defeat: 11 ♗xd6?! ♕xd6 12 ♕xb7 0-0 13 e5 ♗c8!! 14 ♕xa8 ♕b6 15 ♗xa6 ♗xa6 16 0-0-0 ♘g4 and now Black is clearly better) 11...♘h5 (11...dxe5?! 12 ♗xe5 ♕c8 13 ♘e4 ♘xe4 14 ♗xg7 ♖g8 15 ♗h6 ± Fedorowicz-Seret, Cannes 1987) 12 exd6 ♕a5 (or 12...♕c8 13 ♗e3 0-0 14 a4 ♗g4 15 ♗e2 ♘d7 16 0-0 ♘e5 17 ♕d1 ♘xf3+ 18 ♗xf3 ♗xf3 19 ♕xf3 ♖d8 20 ♘e4 ± Fedorowicz-Hjartarson, Reykjavik 1986) 13 ♗d2 ♕b4 14 ♗e2!? 0-0 15 0-0 ♖e8 16 ♖fe1 a5 17 ♕c2 with an obvious advantage for White; Ginsburg-Roos, Toronto 1984.

c45) 10...♕e7 (D) and now:

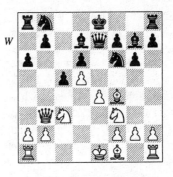

c451) Matters are relatively simple for Black after 11 ♕xb7 ♘xe4 12 ♘xe4 (12 0-0-0 is dangerous for White: 12...♗xc3! 13 bxc3 ♕f6 14 ♗d2 0-0 15 ♕xa8 ♘xc3 16 ♖e1 ♗f5 with an attack – Suba) 12...♕xe4+ 13 ♗e3 ♕b4+ 14 ♕xb4 cxb4 15 ♘d4 0-0 16 ♗c4 a5 17 0-0 ♘a6 18 b3 ♘c5 = Eingorn-Psakhis, USSR Ch (Riga) 1985.

c452) Black also has no problems after 11 e5 dxe5 12 ♗xe5 0-0 13 ♗e2 ♗g4 14 d6 ♕e6 15 ♕xe6 ♗xe6 16 ♘g5 ♗d7 17 0-0 ♘c6 with an equal position; Timman-Romanishin, Brussels 1986.

c453) 11 ♗e2 (this quiet move presents Black with the biggest problems) 11...b5 12 0-0. Now there is a further branching-out:

c4531) Who would envy Black after 12...b4?! 13 e5! dxe5 14 ♗xe5 bxc3 15 ♕b7?

c4532) 12...0-0 13 e5! dxe5 14 ♘xe5 ♗f5 (14...c4 15 ♕d1 b4 16 d6! ♕e6 17 ♗xc4 ♕f5 18 ♘e2 ♘h5 19 g4 ♕e4 20 ♗d5 +– Tarjan-D.Gurevich, USA Ch 1984) 15 ♗f3 c4 16 ♕d1 ± Khalifman-Psakhis, Sverdlovsk 1987.

c4533) 12...♗g4!? (the least of the various evils) 13 e5 dxe5 14 ♘xe5 (stronger than 14 ♗xe5?! 0-0 15 ♖fe1 ♘bd7 16 ♗g3 c4 17 ♕d1 ♕c5 and Black seized the initiative in the game Pekarek-Romanishin, Tbilisi 1986) 14...c4 15 ♕c2 ♗xe2 16 d6 ♕b7 17 ♕xe2 0-0 18 h3 ♘bd7 19 ♘xd7 ♘xd7 20 ♖fe1 with a small advantage.

Now we return to the position after 8...b5 (D) in the main line:

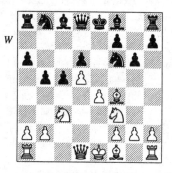

9 ♕e2!? (D)

White has a large enough choice of continuations, but none of them except the text move aspire to an advantage, for example:

a) 9 ♗d3 ♗g4 10 h3 ♗xf3 11 ♕xf3 ♗g7 12 0-0 0-0 13 ♖fe1 (or 13 e5 dxe5 14 ♗xe5 ♘bd7 =) 13...♘e8 14 a4 b4 15 ♘d1 ♘d7 16 ♕e2 a5 17 ♗c4 ♖a7 = Legky-Levin, Nikolaev 1987.

b) 9 ♕c2 ♗g7 10 a4!? b4 11 ♘d1 0-0 12 ♗e2 ♕e7 13 ♘d2 ♖e8 with equality; Kalantarian-Moldobaev, USSR 1988

c) 9 ♘d2 ♗g7 10 ♗e2 0-0 11 0-0 ♘e8 12 ♗g3 f5 13 exf5 ♗xf5 14 ♗g4 ♘d7 = Safin-Gelfand, Kramatorsk 1989, is just as inoffensive.

c) 9 e5, which is not dangerous for Black either, enjoys a great deal of popularity. A possible continuation: 9...dxe5 10 ♘xe5 (or 10 ♗xe5 ♗g7 11 g3 0-0 12 ♗g2 ♗b7 13 0-0 ♘xd5 14 ♘e4 ♘e3!? 15 ♕xd8 ♖xd8 Zaichik-Lukin, Sochi 1980, and White should have played 16 ♘xc5! with equality) 10...♗d6 (10...♗g7!? is not bad either, for example 11 ♗e2 0-0 12 ♗f3 g5!? 13 ♗g3 g4 14 ♘xg4 ♘xg4 15 ♗xg4 ♗xg4 16 ♕xg4 f5 17 ♕f4 b4 18 ♘e2 ♕xd5 19 0-0 ♘c6 and Black wields the initiative) 11 ♗e2 0-0 12 0-0 ♖e8 (12...b4 is less successful: 13 ♘c6! ♕c7 14 ♗xd6 ♕xd6 15 ♘a4 ♘bd7 16 ♗f3 ♗b7 17 ♕b3 ± Schüssler-T.Petrosian, Tallinn 1983) 13 ♘c6 ♘xc6 14 ♗xd6 ♕xd6 (14...♘d4!? 15 ♗xc5 ♘xe2+ 16 ♘xe2 ♕xd5 is also sufficient for equality) 15 dxc6 ♕xd1 16 ♗xd1 ♗e6 17 ♗f3 ♖ac8 with an equal position; Yusupov-Sax, Linares 1983.

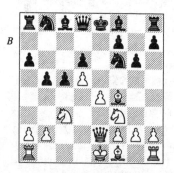

After 9 ♕e2 Black has two principal choices:

A1) 9...♗e7
A2) 9...♘h5

Firstly, here are the other options:
a) 9...♗g7? 10 ♗xd6 ♕xd6 11 e5 ♕e7 12 d6 ♕e6 13 ♘g5 ♕g4 14 f3! ♕xg5 15 exf6+ ♔f8 16 ♕e7+ ♔g8 17 ♕e8+ ♗f8 18 ♕xc8 is winning for White – Agdestein.

b) 9...b4? 10 e5.

c) 9...♕e7? 10 ♗xd6 ♕xd6 11 e5 ♕e7 12 exf6 ±.

d) 9...♖a7 looks a bit strange, but it may not be that bad. After 10 e5 Black may try:

d1) 10...♖e7 is interesting: 11 ♗e3 (11 ♗g5 ♗g7 12 ♘e4? ♘xe4 13 ♗xe7 ♕a5+) 11...dxe5 (Black loses immediately after the careless 11...♘g4? 12 ♘e4 dxe5 13 d6 ♖d7 14 ♗g5 f6 15 ♘xf6+! ♘xf6 16 ♘xe5 +– Kuuksmaa-Salceanu, Corr 1978) 12 ♗xc5 e4! 13 ♗xe7 ♗xe7 14 ♘d2 0-0 15 0-0-0 ♗f5 with some compensation for the exchange.

d2) 10...dxe5 11 ♗xe5 (if White wishes, he can be content with a small advantage with the safe continuation 11 0-0-0 ♗d6 12 ♗g5 h6 13 ♗xf6 ♕xf6 14 ♘e4 ♕e7 15 ♘xd6+ ♕xd6 16 ♕xe5+ ♕xe5 17 ♘xe5 0-0 18 ♗d3) 11...♖e7 12 d6 ♖e6 (12...♕xd6 13 ♗xd6 ♖xe2+ 14 ♗xe2 ♗xd6 15 0-0 ♗b7 16 a4 b4 17 ♘b1 ♘c6 18 ♘bd2 ± Zlatilov-Palkovi, Andorra 1991 is not sufficient for equality) 13 ♘g5 ♗g7! 14 ♘xe6 ♗xe6 15 ♕f3 0-0 16 ♗e2 ♖e8 17 0-0 ♘bd7 and again Black has compensation for the exchange, but it is not definitely sufficient.

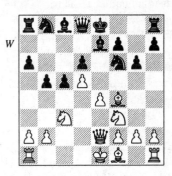

This clumsy-looking move presents White with the greatest problems in his quest for an advantage.

10 ♕c2

White's searches have also led him in the following directions:

a) 10 ♗h6?! ♘g4 11 ♕d2 b4.

b) 10 0-0-0 0-0 (10...♘h5 is also not bad: 11 ♗h6 ♗g4 12 e5 ♗xf3 13 ♕xf3 ♗g5+ 14 ♗xg5 ♕xg5+ 15 ♔b1, and now not 15...♕xe5 due to 16 ♗xb5+! ♔f8 17 ♗c6 ♖a7 18 ♖he1 ♕f5+ 19 ♘e4 with an advantage to White, Benjamin-D.Gurevich, USA 1985, but instead 15...0-0 16 exd6 ♘d7 with an unclear game) 11 e5 ♘g4! 12 ♘e4 dxe5 13 ♘xe5 ♘xe5 14 ♗xe5 ♘d7 15 ♗f4 ♖e8 16 ♕c2 ♘f6 is equal; Alburt-D.Gurevich, USA 1986.

c) 10 e5 dxe5 11 ♗xe5 ♘bd7 12 0-0-0 (White is already in difficulties after 12 ♗g3 0-0 13 d6 ♖e8! 14 dxe7 ♖xe7 15 ♘e5 b4!) 12...♘xe5 13 ♘xe5 ♕d6 14 ♘c6 ♗d7 (14...♔f8 also deserves attention, since 15 ♘xe7?! ♕xe7 16 ♕xe7+ ♔xe7 17 d6+ ♔d7 is not dangerous for Black, whilst 15 g3 ♗b7 16 ♗g2 ♖e8 leads to an equal game) 15 a4 (or 15 ♘e4 ♘xe4 16 ♕xe4 ♔f8 = Tarjan-de Firmian, USA 1984) 15...b4 16 ♘e4 ♘xe4 17 ♕xe4 ♔f8 18 ♘xe7 ♕xe7 19 ♕f4 ♔g7 20 b3 ♗f5 with mutual chances; Lputian-Khuzman, Sverdlovsk 1987.

10 ...   0-0
11 ♗e2

Black has a good game after 11 a4 b4 12 ♘d1 b3! 13 ♕c4 ♘bd7 14 ♖a3 ♖b8 15 ♖xb3 ♖xb3 16 ♕xb3 ♘xe4 Flear-Renet, Hastings 1987.

11 ...   ♖e8

Another possibility is 11...♗g4 12 0-0 ♖e8 13 h3 ♗xf3 14 ♗xf3 ♘bd7 15 a4 ♕b6 16 b3 ♗f8 17 axb5 axb5 18 ♖xa8 ♖xa8 19 ♗e2, Fedorowicz-Renet, Cannes 1987, and now 19...♖a5! would have led to equality.

12 ♘d2   ♗f8
13 0-0   ♘bd7
14 ♖fe1   ♖b8
15 b3   ♘e5
16 a4   b4
17 ♘d1   ♘h5!?
18 ♗xh5   gxh5
19 ♘b2   ♘g6

with an interesting and unclear game; Flear-Schulte, Oakham 1988.

A2) 9 ...   ♘h5
10 ♗g5   ♗e7

I don't think that 10...f6 eases Black's task; 11 ♗e3 ♗e7 (or 11...♘d7 12 g4 ♘g7 13 h4! ♘b6 14 ♘d2 h5 15 gxh5 ♘xh5 16 ♖g1 ♔f7 17 f4 ± Petursson-Portisch, Reykjavik 1988) 12 ♘d2 0-0 13 g4 ♘g7

14 f4 b4 15 ♘d1 f5 16 exf5 ♗h4+ 17 ♗f2 ♖e8 18 ♘e3 gxf5 19 h3 ♘d7 20 ♗g2 ± Schroer-Sax, Montreal 1986.

11 ♗h6 (D)

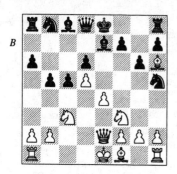

11 ...   ♗f8

a) 11...b4 gives White extra possibilities, for example 12 ♘d1 ♗f8 13 ♗xf8 ♔xf8 14 ♘d2 ♔g7 15 ♘e3 ♖e8 16 g3 a5 17 ♗g2 ♗a6 18 ♘dc4 ± McCambridge-Lobron, Dortmund 1982.

b) White also has an advantage after 11...f6 12 ♘d2!? ♔f7 13 g4 ♘g7 14 ♗g2 ♖e8 15 0-0 ♗f8 16 f4 ♘f5!? (16...♔g8 17 h3 ♗b7 18 ♕f2 ±) 17 gxf5 ♗xh6 18 fxg6+ hxg6 19 e5! with a strong attack; Gershkovich-Kozin, USSR 1989.

c) Nor does Black get any relief from 11...♗g4 12 e5!? (stronger than 12 a4 b4 13 ♘d1 ♘d7 14 ♘e3 ♘e5!? 15 ♘xg4 ♘xg4 16 ♗c1 ♗f6 17 g3 Agdestein-Grünfeld, Jerusalem 1986, and now 17...♕c7!? 18 ♗h3 ♘e5 19 ♘xe5 ♗xe5 would have led to equality) 12...b4 (but not 12...♗xf3 13 gxf3 ♗g5? 14 exd6+ ♔d7 15 ♗h3+ f5 16 ♕e6#) 13 ♘e4 dxe5 14 d6 ♗f8 15 ♘xc5 ♕xd6 16 ♘e4 ♕e7 17 ♗e3! ♘d7 18 ♖d1 and here Black's position is very difficult to defend; Flear-Martin, Hastings 1987.

12 ♕e3 *(D)*

Or 12 ♗xf8 ♔xf8 13 ♕e3 ♔g7 14 ♗e2 ♖e8 15 ♘d2 ♘f6 =.

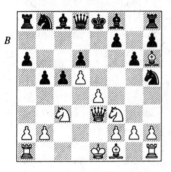

12 ... ♗xh6

The position is extremely dangerous for Black after 12...♘f6 13 ♗g5! ♗g7 (or 13...h6 14 ♗h4 g5 15 ♗g3 ♘h5 16 e5!) 14 e5 dxe5 15 ♕xe5+ ♔f8 (15...♕e7 16 ♕xe7+ ♔xe7 17 0-0-0 ±) 16 0-0-0 h6 17 ♗h4 g5 18 ♗g3 ♘bd7 19 ♕d6+ ♔g8 20 ♘e5, Christiansen, whilst 12...b4 13 ♘d1 ♘f6 14 ♗xf8 ♔xf8 15 ♕h6+ ♔g8 16 ♗d3 ♘g4 17 ♕f4 ♔g7 18 0-0 f6 19 ♘e3 leads to a clear advantage for White in a quiet position; Tarjan-Fedorowicz, USA Ch 1984.

13 ♕xh6 b4

Black may also try 13...♘d7 and then 14 a4 (it would also be interesting to test 14 g3!? ♘df6 15 ♗g2 b4 16 ♘d1 ♘xe4 17 0-0 ♘ef6 18 a3 with initiative, Agdestein, whilst 14 ♗e2 ♕f6 15 0-0 ♕f4 16 ♘g5 ♘df6

17 g3 ♕d2 18 ♗xh5 ♘xh5 19 e5 ♗f5 20 exd6 ♕xb2 21 ♖ae1+ ♔d7 led to wild complications in Benjamin-Grünfeld, New York 1985) 14...b4 15 ♘d1 ♘df6 16 ♗d3 ♗g4 17 ♘g1!? (quite an unusual variation; the heroic white queen is trapped after 17 ♘d2?? ♗xd1 18 ♖xd1 ♘g4 –+) 17...♗xd1 18 ♖xd1 ♕e7 19 ♘f3 with a small but tangible advantage; Agdestein-Arnason, Oslo 1984.

14 ♘d1 ♗g4!?

Alternatively, 14...♕f6 15 ♘d2 ♖a7!? (15...♗d7 cannot sort Black out: 16 a4! ♔d8 17 g3 ♗g4 18 ♘e3 ♗f3 19 e5! dxe5 20 ♘xf3 ♕xf3 21 ♗g2 ♕f6 22 d6 ± Yusupov-Dolmatov, Minsk 1987) 16 ♗c4 ♖e7 17 0-0 ♘d7 with a satisfactory position.

15	**♘d2**	**♗xd1**
16	**♖xd1**	**♕f6**
17	**♘c4**	**♘d7**
18	**♗e2**	**♘f4**
19	**♗f3**	**♘e5**
20	**♘xe5**	**♕xe5**
21	**0-0**	**c4**
22	**♖d2**	**♖c8**

with an unclear game; Lputian-Magerramov, Uzhgorod 1988.

B) 7 ♗d3

An interesting system begins with this move. White will place the knight on e2 to keep the path open for the f-pawn. White's initiative on the kingside can then become very dangerous. To neutralize these threats Black must play precisely and cold-bloodedly.

7 ...   ♗g7
8 ♘ge2   0-0
9 0-0 (D)

Occasionally White postpones castling, but this doesn't bring him any particular dividends. For example 9 ♘g3 a6 10 a4 ♘g4!? 11 h3 ♘e5 12 ♗e2 ♕h4 =, or 9 ♗g5 a6 10 a4 ♘bd7 11 ♘g3 h6 12 ♗f4 ♖e8 13 0-0 ♘e5 14 ♗e2 ♗d7 15 h3 g5 = Yusupov-Kasparov, USSR tt 1980.

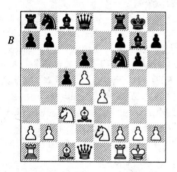

Two moves deserve close attention here:

B1) 9...♘a6
B2) 9...a6

A simple list of the moves Black has used in place of these two moves would take up at least two columns. We shall only look at the most widely used:

a) 9...♕b6?! (an absurd square for the queen) 10 ♔h1 ♖e8 11 f3 ♘bd7 12 ♖b1 a6 13 a4 ♖b8 14 ♘a2!? with an excellent game; Miles-Fries Nielsen, Esbjerg 1986.

b) 9...♘e8 (too passive a move, which gives White too much freedom for action) 10 ♗e3 ♘d7 (or 10...b6 11 ♕d2 ♗a6 12 ♗g5! ♕d7 13 f4 ♘c7 14 f5! ♗e5 15 ♗h6 ♖e8 16 ♖f3 ± Nenashev-Blodshtein, Tashkent 1992) 11 f4 a6 12 a3!? (12 a4 b6 13 ♖b1 ♕e7 14 ♗f2 ♘df6 15 h3 b5 16 axb5 axb5 17 b4! ± is not bad either) 12...b6 (12...b5 13 b4) 13 ♕d2 ♖a7 14 ♖ae1 ♘c7 15 a4! ♖a7 16 ♘g3 ♕c7 17 ♕e2 ± Kasparov-Yurtaev, Moscow 1977.

c) 9...♘g4 10 h3 (Black manages to equalize after 10 ♗f4 ♘a6 11 ♕d2 ♘e5 12 ♗c2 ♘c4 13 ♕c1 Nb4 14 ♗b1 ♘e5 15 ♕d1 ♕a5 = Miles-Perenyi, Porz 1986) 10...♘e5 11 ♗c2 ♘a6 and now:

c1) 12 f4 can be met by:

c11) 12...♘c4 13 b3 (Black is not endangered by 13 ♔h1 b5 14 b3 ♘b6 15 ♗b2 ♘c7 with a roughly equal game; Arduman-Ghinda, Komotini 1993) 13...♘a5 14 a3 (14 ♗e3 b5! 15 e5 dxe5 16 ♘xb5 exf4 17 ♗xf4 ♕b6! 18 ♘bc3 c4+ leads to an unclear position; Vilela-Andres, Havana 1987) 14...b5 15 ♖b1 b4 16 ♘a2!? bxa3 17 ♗xa3 ♖b8 18 ♔h2 ♗d7 19 ♘g3 with a small advantage to White; Serper-Nenashev, Novosibirsk 1989.

c12) 12...♘d7!? 13 ♗e3 ♘c7 14 a4 a6 15 ♘c1 ♖e8 16 ♗f2 ♖b8 17 ♘b3!? b6 18 ♕f3 ♗b7 19 ♖ad1 and White has the more active position; Arkhipov-Tsarev, USSR 1988.

c2) 12 a3! (a good precautionary move, limiting the opposition's pieces) 12...♖b8 13 f4 ♘c4 14 ♗d3 ♘xb2!? (14...b5 15 ♘xb5! ±) 15 ♗xb2 c4 16 ♗xc4 ♕b6+ 17 ♔h1 ♕xb2 and now both 18 e5!? ♕b6

(18...dxe5?? 19 ♘a4 +−) 19 e6 and 18 ♗xa6 ♗xc3 19 ♘xc3 ♕xc3 20 ♗d3 Knaak-Schneider, Stara Zagora Z 1990, lead to an advantage for Black.

d) 9...b6 *(D)* and now White has played:

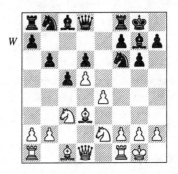

d1) 10 ♘g3 ♘g4!? (10...♗a6!? is not bad either: 11 ♗xa6 ♘xa6 12 f4 c4! 13 ♗e3 ♘c5 14 ♗d4 ♖e8 =) 11 h3 (White lost unexpectedly quickly in Flear-Velimirović, Zenica 1987 after 11 a4? ♕h4 12 h3 ♘xf2! 13 ♔xf2 ♗d4+ 14 ♔f3 h5! 15 ♘f5 gxf5 16 exf5 ♘d7 17 ♕e1 ♘e5+) 11...♘e5 12 ♗e2 ♗a6 13 f4 ♘c4 14 ♕a4 ♘a5 with chances for both sides.

d2) 10 f4?! ♖e8 11 ♘g3 ♘g4 12 ♘ce2 (12 ♕f3 ♗d4+ 13 ♔h1 ♘xh2 −+) 12...c4! with an excellent game.

d3) 10 ♖b1 ♗a6 11 ♗xa6 ♘xa6 12 a3 ♖e8 13 f3 ♘c7 14 ♗g5 ♕d7 15 b4 ♖ab8 16 ♕d2 ± Rivas-Bellon, Torremolinos 1983.

d4) 10 h3 ♗a6 11 ♗g5 (or 11 ♘g3 ♗xd3 12 ♕xd3 a6 13 a4 ♘bd7 14 f4 ♕c7 15 ♕c4 ♖fe8 with an equal position; Chekhov-Gdanski,

Warsaw 1990) and Black can now equalize:

d41) 11...♗xd3 12 ♕xd3 ♘bd7 13 f4 a6 14 a4 ♕c7 15 b3 (15 ♔h1 ♖fe8 16 ♘g3 h6 17 ♗xf6 ♘xf6 18 ♖ad1 c4 = G.Garcia-Quinteros, Linares 1981) 15...♖fe8 16 ♕c4 ♕b7 is level.

d42) 11...♕c7!? 12 ♔h1 ♗xd3 13 ♕xd3 c4 14 ♕d2 ♘bd7 15 f4 b5! = Haik-Hulak, Saint Maxime 1982.

d5) 10 a4!?:

d51) In the event of 10...♗a6 White is well prepared: 11 ♘b5! ♗xb5 (or 11...♘bd7 12 ♘ec3 ♕e7 13 ♖e1 ♘e5 14 ♗e2 ♘e8 15 f4 ♘d7 16 ♗f3 ± Knaak-Suetin, Sochi 1980) 12 axb5 ♘bd7 (12...c4 only creates weaknesses in Black's position: 13 ♗c2 ♖e8 14 ♘c3 ♕c7 15 ♖a4 ♘bd7 16 h3 ♖ec8 17 ♗e3 ♖ab8 18 ♕a1 ♖b7 19 ♕a2 ± Seirawan-Andrijević, Lugano 1988) 13 ♘c3 ♖e8 14 ♖a4 ♕e7 15 ♗d2 h5 16 ♗e2 ± Knaak-Bönsch, E.Germany 1980.

d52) 10...♘a6 11 h3 (11 ♗g5 deserves attention, e.g. 11...♘b4 12 ♗c4 a6 13 ♕d2 ♕e8 14 ♘g3 ♘g4 15 ♗e2! f6 16 ♗f4 ♘e5 17 ♗e3! ♗d7 18 f4 ♘f7 19 f5! with a distinct plus for White; Seirawan-Fedorowicz, USA Ch 1987) 11...♘b4 12 ♗b1 ♖e8 (12...♗a6!? 13 ♗g5 ♕d7 is possibly stronger) 13 ♗g5 h6 14 ♗h4! (a significant improvement in comparison with 14 ♗e3 ♗a6 15 ♕d2 ♔h7 16 ♖e1 ♖e7 17 f4 ♕d7 18 a5 ♕b7! 19 ♗f2 ♖ae8 = Knaak-Dolmatov, E.Germany tt 1981) 14...♗a6 15 f4 ♕d7 16 ♗xf6! ♗xf6 17 e5 dxe5 18 f5 and Black faces a hard defence; Knaak-Tseshkovsky, Telex 1982.

d6) 10 ♗g5!? *(D)* is strong:

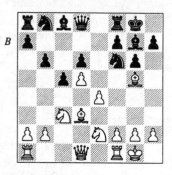

d61) 10...h6 only weakens the kingside, for example 11 ♗h4 (11 ♗f4 is less dangerous for Black: 11...♗a6 12 a4 {or 12 ♘g3 ♗xd3 13 ♕xd3 a6 14 ♖ae1 ♘g4 15 h3 ♘e5 16 ♗xe5 dxe5!? 17 a4 ♘c6! = Kasparov-Ghitescu, Malta OL 1980} 12...♖e8 13 h3 ♕e7 14 ♘g3 c4!? 15 ♗c2 ♘bd7 16 ♕d2 ♕f8 17 ♗e3 ♘c5 18 f3 ♘fd7 is equal; Beyen-Tal, Skopje OL 1972, but the alternative 11 ♗xf6!? deserves attention, for example 11...♕xf6 12 f4 ♗a6 13 e5 dxe5 14 ♘e4 ♕h4 15 f5 with an attack; Marin-Pares, Roses 1992) 11...♗a6 12 f4 ♗xd3 13 ♕xd3 ♘bd7 14 a4 a6 15 ♔h1 ♕c7 16 ♗xf6!? ♗xf6 17 e5 dxe5 18 f5 and Black is not to be envied.

d62) 10...♗a6 11 f4!? (Black's problems are simplified after 11 ♗xa6 ♘xa6 12 f3 h6 13 ♗h4 ♕d7 14 ♕d3 ♘c7 with equality; Vilela-Yap, Havana 1985) 11...♗xd3 12 ♕xd3 ♘bd7 13 ♔h1 a6 14 a4 ♕c7 15 ♖ad1 ♖fe8 16 ♘g3 c4 17 ♕f3

and here White's position is more active.

e) 9...♖e8. White can continue thus:

e1) 10 f4?! c4! 11 ♗c2 ♘g4! 12 ♘d4 ♕b6 13 ♘ce2 ♘a6 14 h3 ♘f6 with an advantage to Black.

e2) 10 h3 a6 (10...♗d7!? also deserves attention: 11 ♗g5 ♕c7 12 ♕d2 c4 13 ♗c2 b5 14 a3 ♘a6 15 ♘g3 b4 16 axb4 ♘xb4 17 ♗b1 ♖eb8! 18 ♔h2 ♘d3 19 ♖a2 ♘c5 = Spassky-Ljubojević, Manila IZ 1976) 11 a4 ♘bd7 is examined in B2.

e3) 10 ♘g3 ♗d7 (after 10...♘g4 11 h3 ♘e5 12 ♗e2 a6 13 a4 ♕h4 14 ♗e3 h6 15 ♕e1 ♘ed7 16 ♕d2 White's chances are preferable; Vogel-Magomedov, Berlin 1992) 11 h3 ♕c7 12 ♕e2!? h5 13 ♖e1 ♘a6! 14 ♗e3, Marin-Danailov, Manresa 1990, which should have continued 14...♖ac8 15 ♖ad1 c4 16 ♗c2 b5 17 a3 ♘c5 18 ♗d4 a5 =.

e4) 10 ♔h1!? c4 11 ♗c2 ♘a6 12 ♗g5 h6 13 ♗e3 ♗d7 14 ♕d2 b5 15 a3 ♘c5 16 f3 h5 17 ♘d4 with a small advantage; Ribli-Gheorghiu, Riga IZ 1979.

e5) 10 f3!? is a good reply to the rook move; White safely defends the e4 pawn and prepares for active operations on the queenside: 10...b6 (White has the more pleasant position after 10...a6 11 a4 ♘bd7 12 ♔h1 ♕c7 13 ♖b1 ♖b8 14 b4) 11 ♖b1 ♗a6 12 b4 ♗xd3 13 ♕xd3 ♘bd7 14 ♗f4 ♘e5 15 ♗xe5 ♖xe5 16 bxc5 bxc5 17 ♕a6! ± Spraggett-Suetin, Vienna 1990.

B1) **9** **...** **♘a6** *(D)*

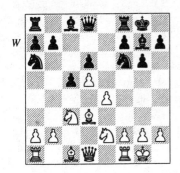

10 h3

a) 10 ♗g5 h6 (more precise than 10...♗d7 11 ♕d2 ♖c8 12 ♖ae1 c4 13 ♗c2 ♖e8 14 h3 b5 15 a3 ♘c5 16 ♘g3 a5 17 ♘d1! ± Chekhov-Cvitan, Warsaw 1990) 11 ♗f4 (White might prefer 11 ♗h4, for example 11...g5 12 ♗g3 ♘h5 13 ♕d2 ♘c7 14 a4 a6 15 f4 gxf4 16 ♗xf4 ♘xf4 17 ♘xf4 ♗e5 18 ♖f3 ♘e8 gives chances for both sides) 11...♗g4! 12 ♖c1 ♘c7 =, but after 13 ♘g3?! ♘xh2! 14 ♗xd6 ♕xd6 15 ♔xh2 b5! 16 b3 h5 Black seizes the initiative; Olafsson-Gelfand, New York 1989.

b) 10 a3 ♖e8 11 h3 c4! 12 ♗c2 ♘c5 13 ♘g3 h5 14 ♗g5 ♕b6 15 ♖b1 ♘h7 16 ♗e3 h4 =.

c) 10 f4?! ♕b6 11 ♔h1 ♖e8 12 ♘g3 ♗g4 13 ♕d2 ♗d7 14 h3 ♖ac8 15 ♕e2 h5 ∓ Ershov-Kagan, Corr 1980.

d) 10 ♘g3 ♘g4!? 11 h3 ♘e5 12 ♗e2!? (12 f4 ♘xd3 13 ♕xd3 ♘b4 =) 12...♕h4 13 ♗e3 f5 14 exf5 ♗xf5 15 ♘xf5 gxf5 16 f4 ♘g6 with a reasonable position for Black.

e) 10 f3 and now:

e1) 10...♗d7 11 ♗g5 (in Khalifman-Smirin, Sverdlovsk 1987, Black equalized after 11 a3 ♖b8 12 ♖b1 ♕a5 13 ♔h1 b5 14 ♗d2 c4 15 ♗c2 ♕c7 16 ♗f4 ♖fe8 17 ♘d4 ♘c5) 11...♖c8 12 ♗c4! ♘c7 13 a4 a6 14 a5 h6 (White also has a more promising position after 14...♘b5 15 ♕d3 ♘d4 16 ♖fc1 ± Miles-Vasiukov, Reykjavik 1980) 15 ♗e3 ♗b5 16 b3 ♘d7 17 ♕d2 ♔h7 18 f4 b6 19 ♘g3 ± Rivas-Suba, Spain 1980.

e2) 10...♘c7 11 ♗g5 a6 12 a4 ♖b8 13 ♕d2 b5 14 axb5 axb5 15 b4!? ♘a6 (15...cxb4 16 ♘a2) 16 ♘a2 ♖e8 17 ♖ab1 ± Grünberg-Ki.Georgiev, Varna 1982.

10 **...** **♖e8!?** *(D)*

After White has played h3, the rook move looks even better. After other moves White usually seizes the initiative, for example:

a) 10...♘c7 11 a4:

a1) 11...b6 12 ♗g5 h6 (White has an advantage after both 12...a6 13 f4 ♖e8 14 ♕e1 h6 15 ♗h4 ♕d7 16 ♖d1 ♗b7 17 ♗xf6! ♗xf6 18 e5 dxe5 19 f5 g5 20 ♘e4 ± Knaak-Meduna, Halle 1978, and 12...♕d7 13 f4 ♗b7 14 ♖b1 h6 15 ♗h4 ♖ac8 16 ♗c4 ♖fe8 17 ♘g3 a6 18 ♗xf6 ♗xf6 19 e5 dxe5 20 f5 ♔g7 21 d6 ± Sideif Zade-Mi.Tseitlin, USSR 1981) 13 ♗h4 ♗a6 14 f4 ♕d7 15 ♗xa6 ♘xa6 16 e5 dxe5 17 fxe5 ♘h7 18 ♗f6! ♗xf6 19 exf6 ♕d6 20 ♕d2 ♘xf6 21 ♕xh6 ± Bašagić-Barlov, Yugoslavia Ch 1984.

a2) 11...a6 12 ♗g5! (Black has an excellent game after 12 ♘g3 ♖b8 13 ♗f4 {13 f4?! b5! 14 axb5 axb5 15

♕f3 b4 16 ♘d1 ♘b5 17 ♗xb5 ♖xb5 18 ♘e3 ♘d7 ∓} 13...b5 14 axb5 axb5 15 ♕d2 ♖e8 16 b4!? cxb4 17 ♘a2 ♘fxd5! 18 exd5 ♘xd5 19 ♗g5 ♕a5 Grigore-Istratescu, Bucharest 1992) 12...♖b8 13 f4 ♕e8 14 ♗c2! h6 15 ♗xf6 ♗xf6 16 e5! dxe5 17 f5 ± Knaak-Anastasian, Erevan 1988.

b) White also has an active position after 10...♗d7 11 ♗f4!? (or 11 a4 ♖c8 12 ♗g5 c4 13 ♗c2 ♘c5 14 ♕d2 ♖e8 15 ♘g3 a6 16 ♕f4! ± Knaak-Sznapik, E.Germany-Poland 1982) 11...♘e8 12 ♕d2 ♖b8 13 ♗g5 f6 14 ♗e3 ♘b4 15 ♗b1 b5 16 f4 ♗h6 17 a3 ♘a6 18 ♗d3 ± Zaitsev-Rashkovsky, Sochi 1976.

c) 10...♖b8, deserves attention, for example 11 a3 ♖e8 12 ♘g3 ♘c7 13 ♗d2 b5 14 b4 ♘d7 15 f4 a5! with a complex game; Tunik-Ibragimov, Budapest 1992.

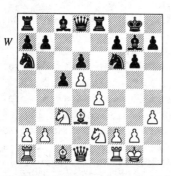

11   ♘g3

Thrusting the bishop forward is no longer dangerous: 11 ♗g5 h6 12 ♗h4 c4! 13 ♗c2 ♘c5 14 f3 ♗d7 15 ♗f2 ♘h5 16 ♗d4 ♗e5 17 b4 cxb3 18 axb3 a5 = Haïk-Kasparov, Evry sim 1989.

11   ...   ♘c7

It is not easy for White to gain an advantage after 11...♖b8, for example 12 a4 (12 f4 c4!? 13 ♗xc4 b5! – Kapengut) 12...♘b4 13 ♗b1 (13 ♗c4 ♘d7!? 14 f4 ♕h4 =) 13...a6 14 f4 b5 15 axb5 axb5 16 ♕f3 ♗b7 = Aaron-Stein, Stockholm IZ 1962.

12   a4

Or 12 ♗f4 a6 13 a4 ♖b8 14 a5 b5 15 axb6 ♖xb6 16 ♘a4 ♖b7 17 ♖b1 ♘b5 = Ivkov-Najdorf, Havana 1966.

12 ♗g5 deserves attention, for example 12...h6 13 ♗f4 a6 14 ♕d2 ♔h7 15 a3 ♘b5 (15...b5 16 b4 ±) 16 ♘xb5 axb5 17 ♖ae1 ± Kasparov-Morgulev, USSR 1979.

12   ...   b6

White has a small advantage after 12...♗d7 13 ♗g5 h6 14 ♗f4 ♕e7 15 ♕d2 ♕f8 16 ♖ae1 ♘h7 17 ♗e3 ± Sadler-Prasad, London 1987.

13   ♖e1   ♗a6
14   f4!?

Black's position is already preferable after 14 ♘b5?! ♗xb5 15 axb5 ♘d7 16 f4 a6! 17 bxa6 b5 18 e5 c4 19 ♗e4 ♘xa6 Knaak-Pokojowczyk, E.Germany-Poland 1980.

14   ...   ♗xd3
15   ♕xd3   a6
16   ♖d1   ♘d7
17   e5   dxe5
18   f5

with sufficient play for the pawn; Markauss-Zaermann, Corr 1987.

B2)   9   ...   a6
10   a4   ♘bd7 *(D)*

a) If 10...b6, White gains control of the initiative very simply: 11 h3

♘bd7 12 ♘g3 ♕c7 13 ♗e3 c4 14 ♗c2 ♖b8 15 f4 ♘c5 16 e5! ♘e8 17 ♕d2 with strong pressure.

b) The position is also better for White after 10...♘g4 11 h3 (11 ♗f4!? ♘e5 12 ♗c2 ♘bd7 13 b3 c4 14 b4 a5 15 ♖b1 ♖e8 16 ♕d2 axb4 17 ♖xb4 ♖a6 18 f3 ± Miles-Lobron, Lucerne tt 1985) 11...♘e5 12 ♗c2 ♘bd7 13 ♖b1 (Black has good counterplay after 13 b3?! c4! 14 b4 a5! 15 ♖b1 axb4 16 ♖xb4 ♘c5 17 ♗e3 ♘ed3 Chekhov-Tseshkovsky, Vilnius 1980) 13...♘c4 14 b3 ♘a5 15 ♗e3 ♖b8 16 f4 ♕c7 17 e5! b5 18 axb5 axb5 19 ♘e4 dxe5 20 f5 f6 21 ♘2g3 ± Ghitescu-Giurezu, Skopje 1988.

c) 10...♕c7 usually leads to the main variation after a transposition of moves, but sometimes the game can follow an original route, for example 11 b3 (11 h3 ♘bd7 leads to 10...♘bd7) 11...♘bd7 12 ♔h1 ♖e8 13 f3 ♖b8 14 a5 b5 15 axb6 ♘xb6!? (15...♖xb6 16 ♗d2 ♘e5 17 ♗c2 ± Miles-Grünfeld, Riga IZ 1979) 16 ♗c2 ♘fd7 =.

d) 10...♖e8 gives White a choice between the safe 11 f3!? ± and 11 ♘g3 ♘g4!? 12 h3 ♘e5 13 ♗e2 ♕h4 14 ♕e1 c4 15 f4 ♘d3 16 ♗xd3 cxd3 17 ♕e3 ♗xh3! Sideif Zade-Dumitrache, Baku 1988, when the game should be a draw after 18 gxh3 ♗d4! 19 ♕xd4 ♕xg3+ 20 ♔h1 ♕xh3+.

11 h3

Others:

a) Black has various ways to achieve a good game after 11 ♗g5, for example:

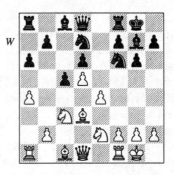

a1) 11...♖e8 12 ♕d2 ♕c7 13 ♔h1 ♖b8 14 ♖ac1 c4 15 ♗c2 b5 16 axb5 axb5 17 f3 b4 18 ♘d1 ♘c5 with a double-edged position; Razuvaev-Psakhis, Vilnius 1980.

a2) 11...♕c7 12 ♔h1 (12 b3 ♘e5 13 ♗c2 ♖b8 14 a5 b5 15 axb6 ♕xb6 16 h3 a5! = Meulders-Grünfeld, Amsterdam 1982) 12...♖b8!? 13 ♖c1 ♘e5 14 f4 ♘xd3 15 ♕xd3 b5 16 axb5 axb5 and Black is close to capturing the initiative; Hartston-Nunn, London 1981.

b) 11 f4 cannot be recommended because of 11...c4!? 12 ♗xc4 ♘g4 when Black holds the initiative.

c) Black is also well in order after 11 ♘g3 ♕c7 12 ♖e1 (or 12 ♕e2 ♖e8 13 f4 ♘b6!? {but not 13...c4?! 14 ♗xc4 ♘c5 15 e5! dxe5 16 f5 e4 17 ♗g5 ♕e5 18 ♗f4 ± Bilek-Stein, Amsterdam IZ 1964} 14 f5 c4 15 ♗b1 ♘bxd5 with a sharp game) 12...c4 13 ♗f1 ♖b8 14 a5 ♖e8 15 ♗e3 h5!? 16 f3 h4 17 ♘h1 b5 18 axb6 ♘xb6 19 ♘f2 ♘bd7 = Campos-Rivas, Leon 1989.

d) White preserves good chances for a small advantage after the quiet 11 f3, for example:

d1) 11...♖e8 12 a5 ♘h5 13 g4! ♘hf6 14 ♘g3 h6 15 ♗f4 ♘e5 16 ♗e2 b5 17 axb6 ♕xb6 18 ♕d2 ± Miles-Kestler, Baden-Baden 1981.

d2) 11...♖b8 12 ♗e3 ♖e8 13 ♕d2 ♘e5 14 ♖fb1 ♘xd3 15 ♕xd3 ♘d7 16 b4 with a slight plus for White; Renet-Haïk, Clichy 1986.

d3) 11...♕c7 12 a5 ♘e5 (another idea is 12...b5!?) 13 ♗b1 ♗d7 14 ♕b3 ♖ab8 15 f4 c4 16 ♕d1 ♘eg4 17 ♔h1 b5 18 axb6 ♕xb6 19 ♕e1 ± Granda-Barlov, Zagreb IZ 1987.

11   ...   ♕c7 (D)

After 11...♖e8:

a) 12 ♘g3:

a1) 12...♖b8 13 a5 (or 13 f4!?) 13...h5 14 ♖e1!? (14 ♗g5 b5 15 axb6 ♕xb6 16 ♖a2 ♘e5 17 ♗e2 ♘h7 18 ♗e3 h4 = Pinter-Kasparov, French League 1993) 14...h4 15 ♘f1 ♘h7 16 ♘e3 ± Pinter.

a2) 12...h5!? is interesting, e.g. 13 f4 h4 14 ♘h1 c4 15 ♗c2 ♘c5 16 ♘f2 ♘h5 = Arkhipov-A.Kuzmin, Moscow 1989.

b) 12 ♗e3 leads to a complicated game: 12...♘e5 13 ♗c2 ♖b8 14 ♕b1 ♘h5 15 f4 ♘c4 16 ♗c1 ♕h4 with an attack; Olafsson-Minasian, Moscow 1989.

c) White has recently successfully used 12 ♗g5!? ♖b8 (or 12...h6 13 ♗e3 ♘e5 14 ♗c2 ♖b8 15 ♕c1 h5 16 ♗g5 c4 17 ♕f4 b5 18 axb5 axb5 19 ♘d4 with an obvious advantage; Korchnoi-Kamsky, Biel IZ 1993) 13 ♔h1 h6 14 ♗h4 ♘e5 15 f4!? ♘xd3 16 ♕xd3 ♗d7 17 e5 dxe5 18 fxe5 ♖xe5 19 ♗g3 ± Goldin-Pigusov, Novosibirsk 1993.

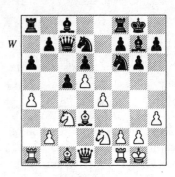

12   f4 (D)

Wild complications arose in Zakharov-Psakhis, Volgograd 1977, after 12 ♔h1 ♖e8 13 f4 c4 14 ♗c2 ♘c5 (14...♖b8!?) 15 ♘g3 ♖b8 16 e5! dxe5 17 fxe5 ♘fd7 18 d6 ♕c6 19 ♘h5! b5!! 20 axb5 axb5 21 ♘xg7 ♗b7.

Black must also play with precision after 12 ♘g3:

a) 12...♖e8, trying to hold back the opponent's onslaught in the centre, is not so effective. 13 f4 c4 14 ♗c2 and now:

a1) 14...♘c5 15 ♕f3 (15 ♔h1 is less clear: 15...h5 16 e5! dxe5 17 f5 ♘d3! 18 fxg6 fxg6 19 ♖xd3 cxd3 20 ♗g5! e4 21 d6 ♕xd6 22 ♗xf6 ♕xg3 23 ♕b3+ ♗e6 24 ♖xb7 Poluliakhov-Hever, Budapest 1992, and now 24...♗h6! 25 ♘xe4 ♕b8 26 ♕c6 ♕c8 27 ♕d6 ♕d7 would have given White a small advantage) 15...♘fd7 16 ♗e3 b5 17 axb5 ♖b8 18 ♕f2 axb5 19 e5! dxe5 (19...b4 20 ♘ce4 ♘xe4 21 ♘xe4 dxe5 22 f5 ♘f8 23 f6 ± Gheorghiu-Quinteros, Lone Pine 1980) 20 f5 ♗b7 21 ♖ad1 ♗a8 22 ♘ce4 and White's initiative is not easy to contain; at least Tal did not manage to do so in Penrose-Tal, Leipzig OL 1960.

a2) 14...♖b8 15 ♕f3 b5 16 axb5 axb5 17 ♗e3 b4 18 ♖a7 ♕d8 19 ♘a4!? and White's position is preferable.

b) 12...♖b8!? (giving the impression of preparing for counterplay on the queenside is most important) 13 ♕e2 (or 13 ♗e3 c4 14 ♗c2 ♘c5 15 f4 ♘fd7 16 ♗d4 ♗xd4+ 17 ♕xd4 b5 18 axb5 axb5 19 ♖ae1 f6! = Tourneur-Kovačević, Paris Ch 1992) 13...♖e8 14 ♗e3!? h5!? 15 f4 h4 16 ♘h1 ♘h5 with mutual chances.

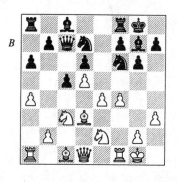

12 ...   ♖b8
13 ♗e3

Black has a reasonable game after 13 ♘g3 c4 14 ♗c2 b5 15 axb5 axb5 16 ♗e3 b4 (it is simple for White to act in the event of 16...♘c5, for example 17 e5! ♘e8 {or 17...♘fd7?! 18 e6! fxe6 19 dxe6 ♘f6 20 f5 b4 21 ♘d5 Ghitescu-Marasescu, Romania 1983} 18 ♔h1 b4 19 ♘a4 ±) 17 ♘ce2 (Black's house is also in order after 17 ♖a7 ♕d8 18 ♘a4 ♖b5 19 b3 c3 20 ♘e2 ♖a5 21 ♖xa5 ♕xa5 22 ♘d4 ♖e8 ∞ Bertok-Portisch,

Stockholm IZ 1962) 17...♘c5 18 ♘d4 ♗b7 19 ♕f3 Gess-Danner, Reggio Emilia 1980, and by continuing 19...b3!? 20 ♗b1 ♘fd7 Black would have obtained equality.

13 ...   ♖e8
14 ♘g3   c4

Not 14...♘xe4?! 15 ♗xe4 f5 because of 16 ♗xf5 ♖xe3 17 ♗e6+ ♔h8 18 ♖f3 ♖xf3 19 ♕xf3 ± Knaak-Rajković, Novi Sad 1979.

15 ♗c2   ♘c5

Black should not hurry with 15...b5?! due to 16 axb5 axb5 17 ♖a7 ♕d8 18 ♕d2 ♘c5? 19 ♗xc5 dxc5 20 e5 ♘d7 21 d6 and White wins; Knaak-Berend, Thessaloniki OL 1988.

16 ♗d4

Or 16 ♕f3 b5 (16...♘fd7?! 17 ♕f2 b5 18 axb5 axb5 19 e5) 17 axb5 axb5 18 e5 dxe5 19 fxe5 ♖xe5 20 ♗d4 ♖g5! and a position arises which is also possible after 16 ♗d4 with a transposition of moves.

16 ...   b5
17 axb5   axb5
18 f5!?

This apparently promises White more than the popular 18 e5, after which one may continue 18...dxe5 19 fxe5 ♖xe5! 20 ♕f3 and now Black can play:

a) 20...♖g5 21 ♘ge2! (but not 21 ♘ge4 ♘cxe4 22 ♗xe4 ♘g4! 23 d6 ♗xd4+ 24 ♔h1 ♕xd6 25 ♕xf7+ ♔h8 −+ Timman-Ljubojević, Amsterdam 1975, or 21 ♗xf6? ♖xg3 22 d6 ♕xd6 −+) 21...♘h5!? (21...♗f5 is also not bad: 22 ♕e3 ♗h6 23 ♕e5! ♕xe5 24 ♗xe5 ♗xc2!? 25 ♗xb8

♘xd5 with enough compensation in the game Pähtz-Goldberg, E.German Ch 1986) 22 ♗xg7 ♔xg7 (22...♖xg7?! 23 d6 ♕b7 24 d7! ♕xd7 25 ♕f4 +−) 23 d6 ♕xd6 24 ♕xf7+ ♔h6 25 ♖ad1, Knaak-Enders, E.Germany 1982, and now 25...♕c6! was possible.

b) 20...b4 21 ♗xe5 ♕xe5 22 ♖ae1 ♕d4+ 23 ♔h1 ♗xh3! (not 23...bxc3? 24 ♖e8+) 24 ♘ce2 ♕xb2 with an advantage to Black; Kasparov-Rachels, New York sim 1988.

18	...	♖f8
19	♕c1	b4
20	♗xf6	♗xf6
21	e5	♗xe5
22	f6	♗xf6
23	♖xf6	bxc3
24	♕h6	

It is very possible that 9...a6 presents White with too many attacking chances, and Black must deny him their use, for example with 9...♘a6!?.

C) 7 f3

The system linked with this move is going through a period of renewal at the moment, and anybody who is going to include the Modern Benoni in their opening repertoire must study carefully the variations which arise. You must give particular importance to the positions which can easily be reached from the Sämisch variation of the King's Indian Defence.

7	...	♗g7 (D)

Now there are three principal options for White:

C1) 8 ♘ge2, delaying the development of the bishop;
C2) 8 ♗e3;
C3) 8 ♗g5, the main line.

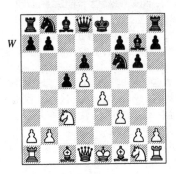

C1)

	8	♘ge2	0-0
	9	♘g3	a6

You also come across:

a) 9...h5 10 ♗e2 (alternatively, 10 ♗g5 ♕b6 11 ♕d2 ♘h7 12 ♗e3 ♘d7 13 ♘ge2 ♘e5 14 ♘f4 a6 15 ♗e2 ♕a5 16 0-0 b5 = Gulko-Spraggett, Hastings 1989) 10...♘bd7 (or 10...h4 11 ♘f1 ♘h5 12 g4!) 11 ♗g5 ♕a5 (11...a6!? 12 a4 ♕c7 deserves attention) 12 ♕d2 a6 13 0-0! b5 14 a4 b4 15 ♘d1 c4 16 ♖c1! c3 17 bxc3 b3 18 ♘b2 with advantage; Spassky-J.Polgar, Budapest 1993.

b) After 9...♘a6 10 ♗e2 ♘c7, both 11 0-0 ♖b8 12 ♗f4!? ♖e8 13 ♕d2 b5 14 ♔h1 h5 15 ♗g5 ♕d7 16 ♖ae1 b4 17 ♘d1, as in Christiansen-Nunn, Munich 1991, and 11 ♗g5 b5 12 ♕d2 ♗a6 13 a3! ♕e8 14 0-0 ♘d7 15 ♗h6, as in Gavrikov-Barlov, Oviedo 1992, guarantee White a small advantage.

c) 9...♗d7 10 ♗e2 h5 11 ♗g5 ♕e8 (11...♕b6!?) 12 ♕d2 (more

precise than 12 0-0 ♘h7 13 ♗e3 b5 14 ♕d2 h4 15 ♘h1 ♘a6 = Chernin-Stangl, Altensteig 1991) 12...♘h7 13 ♗h6, Chernin, and again White's chances are better.

10 a4   h5

10...b6 is too passive, and White has no problems in developing an initiative: 11 ♗e2 ♖a7 12 ♗g5 h6 13 ♗e3 ♖e7 14 ♕d2 ♔h7 15 0-0 ♖fe8 16 ♖ab1 ± Gavrikov-Schauwecker, Swiss Ch 1993.

11 ♗e2

In Gulko-Chiong, Bern 1992, Black equalized after 11 ♗g5 ♕a5 12 ♗e2 ♘h7 13 ♗d2 ♕d8 14 ♗e3 ♘d7 15 0-0 ♘e5 16 ♕d2 h4 17 ♘h1 f5 18 ♘f2 b6 19 ♖ab1 a5!? 20 f4 ♘f7 21 ♖be1 ♖a7.

11 ...   ♘bd7

11...h4 12 ♘f1 ♘h5 13 g4! gives White the initiative.

12 ♗g5

After 12 0-0 a good reply is 12...h4 13 ♘h1 ♘h5 14 ♗e3 ♗d4!? 15 ♗xd4 cxd4 16 ♕xd4 ♕g5 17 ♖ad1 f5 with enough compensation; Spassky-J.Polgar, Budapest 1993.

12 ...   ♕c7

13 ♕d2   ♘h7

Or 13...c4 14 0-0 ♖b8 15 ♗h6 h4 16 ♘h1 b5 17 axb5 axb5 18 ♘f2 b4 with equality; Christiansen-Fedorowicz, San Francisco 1991.

14 ♗h6   ♕d8

15 ♗xg7   ♔xg7

16 0-0   ♖b8

17 ♖ab1   ♕a5

18 ♖fd1   ♕b4 =

Akhsharumova-Xie Jun, Malaysia 1990.

C2)   8 ♗e3   0-0 *(D)*

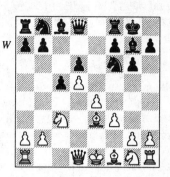

9 ♕d2

9 ♘ge2 leads to a very interesting game: 9...a6 10 a4 ♘bd7 11 ♘g3 ♘e5 (11...h5!?; 11...♖e8 12 ♗e2 ♕c7 13 0-0 ♖b8 14 ♕d2 ♕a5 15 ♕c2 ♘e5 16 h3 ♕b4 17 ♘a2 ♕a5 18 b4 cxb4 19 ♖ab1 ♗d7 20 ♖xb4 ± M.Gurevich-Tal, Jurmala 1985) 12 ♗e2 ♗d7 (or 12...♖e8 13 0-0 h5 14 ♘h1 ♘h7 15 ♘f2 f5 16 ♕d2 g5 17 exf5 ♗xf5 18 ♖ae1 ♘f7 19 ♘ce4 h4 20 b4 ± Gavrikov-Yurtaev, USSR 1983) and now:

a) Both sides have rich tactical possibilities after 13 f4!? ♘eg4 14 ♗d2 h5 15 h3 ♘h6 (or the overly wild 15...h4!? 16 hxg4 hxg3 17 e5 dxe5 18 fxe5 ♖e8! 19 ♗f4 {19 exf6 ♕xf6 ∓} 19...b5! 20 axb5 ♗xb5 with an attack; Portisch-J.Polgar, Biel IZ 1993) 16 e5 (16 0-0 ♖e8 17 ♗f3 ♘fg4!? 18 ♘ce2 f5 with initiative for Black; Topalov-Romero, Mesa 1992) 16...♘h7 17 0-0 ♖e8 18 ♘ge4 ♘f5, with chances for both sides, according to Hazai.

b) Incidentally, 13 h3!? deserves a great deal of attention.

c) 13 0-0 b5 and now:

c1) 14 h3 ♖b8 15 b3 (Black need not fear 15 ♖f2 ♘e8 16 ♕d2 ♘c4 17 ♗xc4 bxc4 18 ♔h2 f5 19 exf5 ♗xf5 20 ♘xf5 ♖xf5 21 g4 ♖f7 22 ♖c1 ♘f6 23 ♗g5 ♕f8 Vyzhmanavin-Hebden, Cappelle la Grande 1992) 15...♘e8 16 ♖c1 ♕h4 17 ♘h1 bxa4 18 bxa4 ♖b4 with equality; Gallagher-Nunn, London Lloyds Bank 1990.

c2) Black has no problems after 14 ♕d2 bxa4 15 ♘xa4 ♗b5 16 ♖fc1 ♖b8 17 ♖c2 ♘e8 = Züger-Chiong, Switzerland 1992.

c3) Black has more than enough play for the pawn in the event of 14 axb5 axb5 15 ♖xa8 ♕xa8 16 ♗xb5 ♗xb5! (16...♖b8 17 ♗xd7 ♘fxd7 18 ♕c2 ♕a6 Spraggett-Hazai, Szirak 1986, is also reasonable) 17 ♘xb5 ♕a6 18 ♘c3 (18 ♘a3 ♖b8 19 ♕c2 ♘xd5! 20 exd5 ♖xb2 ∓) 18...♖b8 19 ♕c2 ♕d3 20 ♕f2 ♘c4 Nikolaev-Belov, Podolsk 1991.

9 ...   a6

Other moves:

a) 9...b6 10 a4 ♘a6 11 ♘h3 ♘b4 12 ♘f2 ♖e8 13 ♗e2 ♗a6 14 ♗xa6 ♘xa6 15 0-0 ♘b4 16 ♗g5 ± Serebrianik-Hebden, Vrnjačka Banja 1991.

b) 9...♘a6 is interesting but almost never seen in practice. White should probably continue 10 ♘ge2 (10 ♗xa6 bxa6 promises hardly anything, and now 11 ♗h6? is unsatisfactory: 11...♘xe4 12 ♘xe4 ♕h4+ 13 g3 ♕xh6 14 ♕xh6 ♗xh6 15 ♘xd6 ♖d8 16 ♘e4 ♗g7 17 d6 ♗b7 ∓ Christofer-Tolnai, Novi Sad OL 1990) 10...♘c7 11 ♘g3 ♖b8 and

White should play 12 a4!?, but not 12 e5?! ♘fe8 13 exd6 ♘xd6 14 ♗xc5 ♖e8+ 15 ♔f2 ♕h4! when Black has the initiative; Kern-Honfi, Corr 1985.

c) 9...♖e8 is possible, for example 10 ♘ge2 (10 h4?! is too optimistic: 10...a6 11 ♗h6 ♗xh6 12 ♕xh6 b5 13 ♘ge2 ♘bd7 14 ♘f4 ♘e5 15 ♗e2 c4 16 h5 ♖a7 ∓ Kakageldiev-Gufeld, USSR 1982) 10...♘bd7 (or 10...♘a6!? 11 ♘g3 ♘c7 12 ♗e2 ♖b8 13 a4 a6 14 0-0 b5 15 axb5 axb5 16 ♗h6 b4 with equality; Damljanović-Ivanović, Kladovo 1990) 11 ♘g3 a6 (11...h5!?) 12 ♗e2 b5 13 a4 bxa4 14 0-0 ♘b6 15 ♗g5 ♗d7 16 ♔h1 ♕e7 17 ♗d3 and White has the initiative; Dydyshko-Ryskin, Katowice 1993.

10   a4 *(D)*

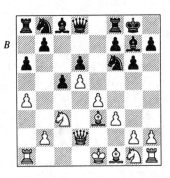

10 ...   ♖e8

10...♘bd7 allows 11 ♘h3, moving the knight later to f2. 11...♘e5 is then possible (things turned out better for White from the opening of Alterman-Fishbein, Beersheba 1991, after 11...♕a5 12 ♖a3 c4 13 ♘f2 ♘e5 14 ♗e2 ♕c7 15 0-0 b6 16 ♖c1

♖b8 17 b4 cxb3 18 ♖xb3 with initiative, but it is worth looking at 11...♖b8 12 ♘f2 ♘e8 13 ♗e2 ♘c7 14 a5 b5 15 axb6 ♘xb6, Raičević-Hulak, Niš 1985, and it is not easy for White to gain an advantage) 12 ♘f2 ♖b8 (or 12...♗d7 13 ♗e2 b5 14 axb5 axb5 15 ♖xa8 ♕xa8 16 ♘xb5 ♗xb5 17 ♗xb5 ♖b8 18 ♗e2 ♘fd7 19 ♘d1 ♕a4 20 ♕c1 ± Seirawan-Sax, Biel IZ 1985) 13 ♗e2 ♕d7 14 0-0 b5 15 axb5 axb5 16 b3 b4 17 ♘a4 ♕c7 18 ♘b2 and I prefer White's position; Cebalo-Veličković, Vršac 1981.

11 ♘ge2

11 ♗e2 h5!? leads us to 8 ♗g5, and 11 a5 presents Black with no danger, for example 11...b5 12 axb6 ♕xb6 13 ♗d3 ♘bd7 14 ♘h3 ♘e5 15 ♘f2 ♘xd3+ 16 ♘xd3 a5 17 0-0 ♗a6 ∓ Kraidman-Har Zvi, Tel Aviv 1991.

11	**...**	**♘bd7**
12	**♘d1**	**♘e5**
13	**♘ec3**	**♗d7**

White has a small advantage after 13...♕a5 14 ♗e2!? (14 ♖a3 ♘fd7!? 15 ♗e2 f5 16 0-0 ♘b6 17 b3 fxe4 and Black has already seized the initiative; Serebrianik-Hebden, Israel 1992) 14...b5 15 0-0 ♘fd7 (Black should consider 15...♗d7!?) 16 ♘f2 b4 (16...♘c4 17 ♗xc4 bxc4 18 f4 ♖b8 19 e5! dxe5 20 ♘fe4 ♕b6 21 f5 ± Meulders-Douven, Netherlands 1991) 17 ♘cd1 ♘b6 18 ♗h6 ±.

14	**♗e2**	**♕a5**
15	**0-0!?**	

This is stronger than 15 ♖a3 ♕b4 16 a5 ♘c4 17 ♗xc4 ♕xc4 18 ♘a2

♗b5! and Black's position is already preferable; Krutti-Szalanczi, Kobanya 1992.

After the text move we face a complicated game with chances for both sides.

C3)   8 ♗g5 *(D)*

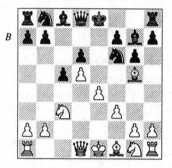

The most popular move. White provokes ...h6, hoping to make use of its weakness.

8 ...   0-0

Black sometimes delays castling for a considerable length of time, for example 8...h6 9 ♗e3 a6 (Black cannot organize himself after 9...♘a6 10 ♕d2 ♘c7 11 ♗d3 ♖b8 12 a4 a6 13 ♖b1 b5 14 b4! cxb4 15 ♖xb4 a5 16 ♗xb5+ ♘xb5 17 ♖xb5 ± Rogers-Danner, Lugano 1989) 10 a4 ♘bd7 11 ♘h3!? (Black's problems are simplified after 11 ♘ge2 ♕e7 12 ♘c1 ♘e5 13 ♗e2 and now both 13...♖b8 14 0-0 0-0 15 h3 g5 16 f4 gxf4 17 ♗xf4 ♘g6 18 ♗h2 b5! Yusupov-Lobron, SWIFT rapid 1992, and 13...g5 14 0-0 0-0 15 ♕d2 ♗d7 T.Georgadze-Psakhis, Vilnius 1981, are satisfactory for Black) 11...♘e5

12 ♘f2 12...g5 (or 12...♗d7 13 ♗e2
g5 14 ♕d2 ♕e7 15 a5 ♖b8 16 ♘a4
♘h5 17 ♘b6 ♗b5 18 0-0 0-0 19 b4!
± Gulko-Kasparov, Frunze 1981)
13 ♗e2 ♕e7 14 h4 ♘h5 15 hxg5
hxg5 16 ♕d2 ♘f4 17 ♖xh8+ ♗xh8
18 ♗xf4 gxf4 19 ♕xf4 ♘g6 20
♕h2 ♗d7 21 g3!? 0-0-0 22 f4 ±
Korchnoi-Lobron, Bad Kissingen
1981.

9   ♕d2

Quite often, especially recently,
White has tried to get away without
playing this queen move. Play might
continue 9 ♘ge2 h6 (or 9...a6 10 a4
♘bd7 11 ♘g3 ♕c7 12 ♗c4! ♘e5 13
♗e2 c4 14 ♗e3 ♘fd7 15 f4 ♘d3+
16 ♗xd3 cxd3 17 0-0 ♕c4 18 ♖c1
± Adorjan-Sax, Hungary 1984) 10
♗e3 (D) and now:

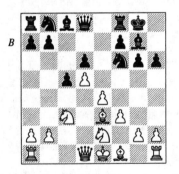

a) White has a pleasant game after the passive 10...b6, for example
11 a4 ♘a6 12 ♕d2 ♔h7 13 ♘b5
♘c7 14 ♘ec3 ♘fe8 15 ♗d3 f5 16 0-
0 fxe4 17 ♗xe4 ♗f5 18 ♗xf5 ♖xf5
19 g4 ♖f7 20 ♘a3 ± Partos-Züger,
Biel 1981.

b) 10...♘bd7 deserves attention,
when Black should attempt to avoid

disturbing the queenside pawns, for
example 11 ♘c1 (or 11 ♘g3 ♘e5 12
♗e2 h5 13 0-0 ♘h7 14 ♕d2 h4 15
♘h1 f5 16 ♘f2 ♕f6 17 f4 ♘f7 18
♗d3 ♗d7 19 a3 ♖fe8 20 ♖fe1 ♖ac8
with an equal position; Vyzhman-
avin-Belov, Moscow 1987) 11...h5
12 ♗e2 ♘h7!? 13 0-0 ♕e7 14 ♘d3
♘e5 15 ♘f2 f5 16 ♕d2 a6 17 a4 g5
18 exf5 ♗xf5 again with equality;
Dolmatov-Khalifman, Kiev 1986.

c) 10...a6 11 a4 ♘bd7 (in reply to
11...h5, 12 ♘f4 looks reasonable, for
example 12...♘bd7 13 ♗e2 ♘e5 14
0-0 ♗d7 15 ♕d2 ♖b8 16 a5 ♘e8 17
♘a4 ♗xa4 18 ♖xa4 with a small advantage; I.Sokolov-Smirin, Elenite
1993) 12 ♘g3 (the most popular
move, but perhaps not the best; 12
♘c1 ♘h7 13 ♗e2 ♖e8 14 ♘d3
♘e5 15 ♘f2 f5 leads to equality, and
in Komljenović-Pigusov, Alicante
1992, the players agreed a draw)
12...h5! (just in time! White has
still not castled and his knight will
now not have the useful h1 square to
retreat to) 13 ♗e2 h4 (the slow
13...♘h7 is weaker: 14 0-0 ♖b8 15
♕d2 ♕e7 16 ♘h1 f5 17 ♘f2 ♘e5 18
♖ae1 ♕f6 19 f4 ♘g4 20 e5! and
White holds the initiative; Cebalo-
Thipsay, Yugoslavia-Asia 1984) 14
♘f1 ♘h7 15 ♘d2 (15 h3 is better for
Black: 15...f5 16 exf5 gxf5 17 ♗f4
♘e5 18 ♘d2 ♘g6 19 ♗e3 ♖e8 20
♘c4 b6 21 ♕d2 ♖a7! Spassov-Be-
lov, Moscow 1985, and only White
can have problems after 15 g4 f5 16
gxf5 gxf5 17 exf5 {or 17 ♖g1 f4 18
♗f2 ♘g5 19 ♘d2 ♘h3 ∓ Danailov-
Marin, Zaragoza 1992} 17...♖xf5 18

♜g1 ♔h8 19 ♕c2 ♕f8 20 f4 ♘df6 21 ♗d3 ♘h5!? I.Sokolov-Ki.Georgiev, Elenite 1993) 15...f5! (but not 15...♗d4?! 16 ♘c4 ♗xe3 17 ♘xe3 ♕g5 18 ♕d2 ♘df6 19 a5 ♜b8 20 ♘c4! ♕xg2 21 0-0-0! ± Psakhis-Ehlvest, Sverdlovsk 1984) 16 exf5 gxf5 17 f4 ♕e7 18 ♗f2 ♜e8 19 ♘f3 h3!? 20 gxh3 ♘df6 21 ♜g1 ♘e4 and the time has come for White to think about defence; Bykhovsky-Gleizerov, USSR 1986.

Returning to the position after 9 ♕d2 *(D)* in the main line:

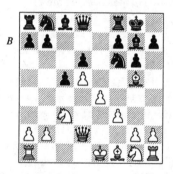

Now Black has two main options:

C31) 9...a6
C32) 9...h6

Other moves have also been tried:

a) 9...♘a6 10 ♘ge2 (10 ♗c4!? is also interesting: 10...♘c7 11 ♘ge2 and after the nervous 11...b5?! 12 ♗xb5! ♘xb5 13 ♘xb5 ♗a6 14 a4 ♕d7 15 ♘ec3 ♜fb8 16 0-0 ♘e8 17 ♗f4 White, in Korchnoi-Shirazi, Lone Pine 1981, achieved a large advantage) 10...♗d7 (or 10...♜e8 11 ♘g3 ♘c7 12 ♗e2 ♕e7 13 0-0 a6 14 ♜ae1!? b5 15 ♗d1 ♕d7 16 ♗h6 ♗b7 17 ♗c2 ♜f8 18 ♕f4 and now White's pressure is very unpleasant; Korchnoi-Garcia Padron, Las Palmas 1981) 11 ♘g3 ♜e8 (things are also unpleasant for Black after 11...♕b6 12 ♗e2 ♜ac8 13 0-0 ♔h8 14 ♜ae1 ♘g8 15 ♔h1 ♕b4 16 a3 ♕d4 17 ♕c1 h6 18 ♗f4 ± Ubilava-Kapengut, USSR 1982) 12 ♗e2 ♜c8 13 ♗xa6!? bxa6 14 0-0 ♜b8 15 ♜ab1 a5 16 h4 h5 17 ♕f4 with a small advantage; Dorfman-Tolnai, Debrecen 1988.

b) 9...♗d7. Now 10 ♘ge2 ♘a6 11 ♘g3 leads to 9...♘a6 and 10 a4 is not bad either, for example 10...♘a6 11 ♗c4 ♘b4 12 ♘ge2 a6 13 a5 ♗b5 14 b3 h6 Ionescu-Wahls, Novi Sad OL 1990, and now 15 ♗e3!? deserves attention.

c) 9...♜e8 (this move rarely has independent significance and we usually come across it in the variations C31 and C32) 10 ♗e2 (or 10 a4 ♘a6 11 ♗b5 ♗d7 12 ♘ge2 ♗xb5 13 axb5 ♘c7 14 0-0 a6 15 ♕d3 ♕d7 = Ionescu-Panno, Dubai OL 1986, whilst 10 ♘ge2 a6 {10...♘a6 is examined under 9...♘a6} 11 a4 brings us to 9...a6) 10...♘a6!? 11 g4!? (11 ♗b5 ♗d7 12 ♘ge2 ♘c7 13 ♗d3 b5 = Ilinsky-Dydyshko, Azov 1991) 11...♘c7 12 h4 b5 13 h5 b4 14 ♘d1 ♕e7 15 ♘f2 a5 16 ♔f1 ♗d7 17 ♔g2 ♘b5 18 ♜e1 ± Fedorowicz-Damljanović, New York 1987.

C31) 9 ... a6
10 a4 *(D)*

It's not worth allowing Black to get active on the queenside: 10 ♘ge2 b5 11 ♘g3 ♘bd7 12 ♗e2 ♖e8 13 0-0 c4 (or 13...♕e7 14 ♗h6 and now 14...♗h8?? is already losing after the deadly reply 15 ♘f5!; Chernin-Yermolinsky, Groningen PCA 1993) 14 ♔h1 ♕c7 15 ♗h6 ♗h8 16 ♖ac1 ♘c5 = Rajković-Cvitan, Yugoslavia tt 1989.

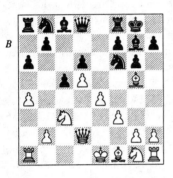

10 ...   ♖e8

Black is waiting for 11 ♘ge2 and only then does he wish to develop the knight. Also possible:

a) 10...♕a5 11 ♖a3 ♕c7 12 ♘ge2 ♘bd7 13 ♘g3 c4 14 ♗e2 ♘e5 15 ♗e3 h5 16 0-0 ♗d7 17 a5 ± Polugaevsky-Nunn, London 1984.

b) 10...h5 11 ♘ge2 ♘bd7 12 ♘c1 ♕c7 13 ♗e2 c4 14 0-0 ♖b8 15 ♗e3 b6 16 ♖b1 b5 17 axb5 axb5 18 b4 ± Kelečević-Stummer, Budapest 1992.

c) 10...♕c7 11 ♗h6 ♘bd7 12 ♗xg7 ♔xg7 13 ♘h3 ♖b8 14 b3 ♕a5 15 ♖b1 b5 16 axb5 axb5 17 ♘f2 ♘e5 18 ♗e2 b4 19 ♘cd1 ± Jakobsen-Mestel, Plovdiv Echt 1983.

d) 10...♘bd7 11 ♘h3 and now:

d1) 11...♖b8 12 ♘f2 (12 ♗e2 allows 12...c4!? 13 ♗xc4 ♘e5 14 ♗e2

♗xh3 15 gxh3 ♕c8) 12...♕c7 13 ♗e2 c4 14 ♖a3!? (14 0-0 b5 15 axb5 axb5 16 b4! cxb3 17 ♘xb5 ♕b6 18 ♗e3 ♘c5 led to great complications in Conquest-Larsen, Hastings 1986) 14...b5 15 axb5 axb5 16 b4 ± Ubilava-Anikaev, USSR 1982.

d2) 11...♖e8 12 ♗e2 ♕a5 13 0-0 h5 14 ♘f2 ♖b8 15 ♔h1 ♕c7 16 ♗e3 ♘h7 17 ♖fc1 ♘e5 18 a5 ♕e7 19 ♘a4 ± Gulko-Suetin, Moscow 1982.

d3) 11...♕a5 and White may now choose:

d31) The consequences of 12 ♖a3 are not clear, for example:

d311) Precise play gives White an advantage after 12...c4 13 ♘f2 (13 ♗xc4 ♘e5) 13...♕c7 14 ♗e2 ♖b8 15 0-0!? (Black has no problems after 15 a5 b5 16 axb6 ♘xb6 17 ♗h6 ♗xh6 18 ♕xh6 ♕c5 19 0-0 ♖e8 with equality; Spassky-Nunn, Toluca IZ 1982) 15...b5 (15...♕c5 16 ♗e3 ♕b4 17 a5 ♘c5 18 ♕c2 ♘fd7 19 ♖b1 ± Georgadze-Bouaziz, Hannover 1983) 16 axb5 axb5 17 b4!.

d312) Black also has an excellent game after 12...♖e8 13 ♘f2 h6 14 ♗e3 (14 ♗xh6 ♗xh6 15 ♕xh6 ♘xd5) 14...♘e5 15 ♗e2 ♕b4 16 ♘a2 ♕xd2+ 17 ♔xd2 b6 18 b4 ± T.Georgadze-Bellón, Benalmadena 1986.

d313) 12...♘e5 13 ♘f2 ♗d7 14 ♗e2 ♕b4 15 0-0 b5 16 axb5 axb5 17 ♖xa8 ♖xa8 18 ♘xb5 ♕xd2 19 ♗xd2 ♗xb5 20 ♗xb5 ♖b8 21 ♗c6 ♘c4 22 ♗c3 ♘h5 = Hjartarson-Westerinen, Brighton 1982.

d32) After 12 ♖a2 c4 13 ♘f2 ♕c7 14 ♗e2, 14...♖b8!? leads to a complex game, but not 14...♘c5?

because of 15 ♗xc4! ♘cxe4 16 ♘fxe4 ♘xe4 17 ♘xe4 ♕xc4 18 ♘f6+ ♔h8 19 b3 ♕xb3 20 0-0 ♗f5 21 g4 ♗d3 22 ♕f2 with an obvious advantage.

d33) 12 ♘f2!? b5 13 ♗e2 b4 14 ♘cd1 ♕c7 (or 14...♘b6 15 ♘e3 ♗d7 16 0-0 ♖fc8 17 ♘c4 ♘xc4 18 ♗xc4 ♕d8 19 b3 ♕f8 20 ♕d3 a5 21 ♖ae1 ± Despotović-Messa, Ivrea 1982) 15 ♖c1 a5 16 b3 ♘b6 17 ♗h6! with an easy and pleasant game for White; Sadler-Mohandessi, Ostend 1992.

11 ♘ge2

11 ♗e2 also deserves attention, for example 11...♕a5 (or 11...♕c7 12 a5 ♘bd7 13 ♘h3 ♖b8 14 0-0 b5 15 axb6 ♖xb6 16 ♘f2 h5 17 ♔h1 ♘h7 18 ♗e3 ♘e5 19 ♖ac1 ♕d8!? with complications; Benjamin-Larsen, Hastings 1987) 12 ♖a3 ♕c7 13 b3 ♘bd7 14 ♘h3 c4 15 b4 ♕b6 16 ♘a2 with chances for both sides; Browne-Rogers, Bath 1983.

11 ... ♘bd7 *(D)*

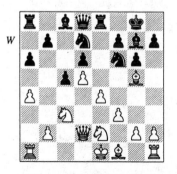

12 ♘g3

Black's problems are solved after:

a) 12 ♘c1 ♖b8 (12...♕a5 is less

convincing: 13 ♖a3 ♘e5 14 ♗e2 ♕b4 15 ♕c2!? with a small advantage, but an incorrect combination by Black quickly ended the game in Chandler-Barczay, Keszthely 1981, viz. 15...♘xd5? 16 ♖b3 ♕a5 17 exd5 c4 18 ♖a3 ♗f5 19 ♕d2 ♘d3+ 20 ♔f1 +−) 13 ♗e2 ♕c7 14 0-0 h5 15 ♗e3 ♘h7 16 ♗f2 ♘e5 17 h3 f5 18 a5 ♕e7 19 ♖a2 ♕f6 ∞ Ubilava-Veličković, Tbilisi 1983.

b) 12 ♘d1 ♘e5 13 ♘ec3 ♕a5 14 ♖a3 h5 15 ♗e2 ♘h7 16 ♗e3 ♗d7 17 0-0 ♕b4 18 ♕c1 f5 19 a5 fxe4 20 ♘xe4 ♘f7 = Botsari-Veroci, Subotica 1991.

12 ... ♕a5

Probably stronger than 12...♖b8 13 ♗e2 ♕c7 14 0-0 c4 15 ♗e3 b5 16 axb5 axb5 17 b4! (17 ♖a7 ♕d8 18 b4 cxb3! 19 ♗xb5 ♖e7 20 ♘ge2 ♘c5 21 ♖xe7 ♕xe7 22 ♘d4 ♗d7 lets the advantage slip away; Chernin-Chekhov, USSR 1984) 17...♘f8 18 ♖a7 ♕d8 19 ♖fa1 ± Seirawan-Hardason, Reykjavik 1986.

12...♕c7 also leads to an advantage for White: 13 ♗e2 c4 14 0-0 ♘c5 (alternatively, 14...b6 15 ♖fc1 ♕c5+ 16 ♔h1 ♘e5 17 ♗e3 ♕b4 18 ♘b1! ± Toth-Gheorghiu, Biel 1983) 15 ♗xc4 ♘fd7 (15...♘cxe4? 16 fxe4 +−) 16 ♖a3 ♘xe4 17 ♘cxe4 ♕xc4 18 ♗e3 ♕c7 19 ♖c1 ♕b8 20 ♗d4 ± Dorfman-Perenyi, Kislovodsk 1982.

13 ♖a3

13 ♗e2 is more often played, but it should not yield an advantage:

a) 13...h5 is not bad: 14 0-0 ♘h7 15 ♗e3 ♕b4 (15...♘e5 is met by 16 h3 ♕b4 17 ♖fc1 h4 18 ♘h1 f5 19

♘f2 ♕a5 20 ♘b1!? with a small advantage) 16 ♖fd1 (or 16 ♘h1 ♘e5 17 ♘f2 ♗d7 18 ♖fc1 b5 19 axb5 axb5 20 ♘xb5 ♖xa1 21 ♖xa1 ♕xd2 22 ♗xd2 ♖b8 was equal in Adorjan-Vukić, Banja Luka 1983) 16...♘e5 17 ♘b1 h4 18 ♘f1 f5 19 ♕xb4 cxb4 20 ♘bd2 ♘f6 = T.Georgadze-Oll, USSR 1983.

b) 13...b5!? 14 0-0 b4 15 ♘d1!? c4!? (15...♘b6 is worse: 16 ♔h1 c4 17 ♕e1 ♖b8 18 ♗d2 ♘xa4 19 ♗xc4 ♘d7 {or 19...♕c7 20 ♖xa4 ♕xc4 21 ♘e3 ♕b3 22 ♖xb4 ♖xb4 23 ♗xb4 ± Dorfman-Chiburdanidze, USSR 1982} 20 ♖a2 ♕c7 21 ♖xa4 ♕xc4 22 ♖xb4 and White has an obvious advantage; Li Zunian-Quinteros, Thessaloniki OL 1984) 16 ♗e3 (another possibility is 16 ♔h1!? ♘e5!? 17 ♕e1 ♗d7 18 ♗d2 ♖ab8 19 ♘e3 ♕c5 20 ♖c1 c3 21 bxc3 b3 22 ♗xa6 ♗xa4 with an interesting position, Vasiukov, but 16 ♗xc4?! is not good: 16...♕c5+ 17 ♘e3 h6 18 ♗xf6 ♗xf6 19 ♖ac1 ♕d4! with an edge for Black) 16...♘b6 17 ♗d4 ♗d7 18 ♘e3 ♖ac8 19 ♖fc1 c3 20 bxc3 bxc3 21 ♖xc3 (21 ♗xc3 ♖xc3! 22 ♕xc3 ♕xc3 23 ♖xc3 ♘fxd5) 21...♘fxd5! (but not 21...♘xa4? 22 ♘c4 ♖xe4 23 ♘xe4 ♗xd4+ 24 ♕xd4 ♖xe4 25 ♘xa5 ♖xd4 26 ♖xc8+ ♗xc8 27 ♘c6 winning for White; Despotović-Lažić, Yugoslavia 1982) 22 ♘xd5 ♘xd5 23 ♖d3 ♕xd2 24 ♖xd2 ♖c2! 25 ♗xg7 ♖xd2 26 ♗h6 ♖b2 27 exd5 ♖exe2 28 ♘xe2 ♖xe2 with equality; Cebalo-Chiburdanidze, Vinkovci 1982.

13   ...   ♖b8

Or 13...h5 14 ♗e2 ♘h7 15 ♗h6 ♗h8 16 ♗e3 h4 17 ♘f1 h3 18 gxh3!? ♗f6 19 ♔f2 ♗h4+ 20 ♔g3 ± Rajković-Barczay, Lillafüred 1989.

14   ♗e2   ♕c7

The queen fall into a dangerous position after 14...♕b4, for example 15 0-0 b5 16 axb5 axb5 17 ♔h1! c4 18 ♗e3 ♘c5 19 ♕c2 ♘fd7 20 ♖b1 ± Lputian-Palatnik, Lvov 1986.

15	0-0	c4
16	♗e3	b5
17	axb5	axb5
18	b4!	♘e5
19	♖a7	♕d8
20	♖a5	

White wields the initiative; Topalov-Reyes, Palma 1992.

C32)   9   ...   h6

Black does not wish to be pinned for long, and he banishes the bishop, not considering the small weakness on the kingside to be dangerous.

10   ♗e3 (D)

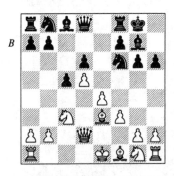

Naturally not 10 ♗xh6?! ♘xe4.

10   ...   a6

Out of the multitude of continuations we will choose the main ones:

a) 10...♔h7 (an old move – these days we don't bother to defend the pawn) 11 ♘ge2 (another interesting try is the sharp 11 h4!?, for example 11...♖e8 12 0-0-0 ♘bd7 13 h5 g5 14 ♘h3 ♕e7 15 ♗xg5!? hxg5 16 ♘xg5+ ♔h8 17 h6 ♗f8 18 ♘b5! with a terrifying attack for White; Lputian-Kolpakov, Moscow 1979) 11...♘a6 12 ♘g3 (again White could have played a bit more sharply: 12 g4!? ♘c7 13 ♘g3 ♗d7 14 g5 hxg5 15 ♗xg5 ♕e8 16 0-0-0 ♖h8 17 h4 ± Efimov-Nun, Hradec Kralove 1984) 12...♘c7 13 ♗e2 ♖b8 14 a4 a6 15 ♖b1 b5 16 axb5 ♘xb5! 17 ♘xb5 axb5 18 b4 c4 19 0-0 ♖a8 20 ♗d4 ± Spasov-Danner, Albena 1983.

b) 10...♘h7 11 ♗d3!? (at least more interesting than the standard 11 ♘ge2, for example 11...♘d7 12 ♘f4 ♘e5 13 ♗e2 ♕h4+ 14 ♗f2 ♕f6 15 0-0 h5 16 ♔h1 h4 17 ♗e3 ♗d7 with equality; Rajković-Atalik, Iraklion 1993) 11...♘d7 12 f4 a6 13 a4 ♕a5 (Priehoda-Mukhitdinov, Moscow 1990) and now 14 ♘f3 gives White a slight plus.

c) 10...♘bd7 11 ♘h3 ♘e5 (the alternative 11...♔h7 is also insufficient for equality, for example 12 ♗e2!? a6 13 a4 ♖b8 14 0-0 ♕e7 15 ♘f2 b6 16 ♖ae1 ♗b7 17 f4 ± Gulko-Ghitescu, Polanica Zdroj 1977) 12 ♘f2 h5 13 ♗e2 a6 14 0-0 ♖b8 15 a4 ♖e8 16 ♖fb1 ♘h7 17 b4 and White's advantage is indisputable; Rogers-Canfell, Melbourne 1992.

d) 10...♘a6 11 ♘ge2 ♘c7 12 a4 a6 13 ♘c1 ♗d7 14 ♗e2 ♘h7 15 ♖b1 ± Spasov-Popov, Bulgaria 1983.

e) 10...h5 11 ♘ge2 ♘bd7 (the alternative 11...♘h7 is also not bad, for example 12 ♘f4 ♘d7 13 ♗e2 ♘e5 14 0-0 ♗d7 15 ♖ab1 ♖c8 16 ♖fc1 a6 17 a4 ♕a5 18 b3 ♖fe8 19 ♔h1 f5 with chances for both sides; Sadler-Fedorowicz, London 1988) 12 ♘c1 (12 ♘f4!?) 12...♘e5 13 ♗e2 ♘h7 14 0-0 (14 h3 f5 15 f4 ♘f7) 14...f5 15 f4 ♘d7!? (other digressions are less successful, for example 15...♘g4 16 ♗xg4 hxg4 17 e5!, or 15...♘f7 16 e5 dxe5 17 ♗xc5 ♖e8 18 ♘d3 e4 19 ♘e1 {stronger than 19 ♘f2 ♘f6 20 ♘fd1 b6 21 ♗d4 ♗b7 22 ♘e3 ♘d6 = Ernst-Tal, Subotica IZ 1987} 19...♘f6 20 ♘c2 ♗d7 21 h3 with a more promising position; Yusupov-Dolmatov, Wijk aan Zee Ct 1991) 16 exf5 gxf5 17 ♗xh5 b5!? 18 ♘xb5 ♘hf6 19 ♗f3 ♘b6 20 ♘e2 ♗a6 21 a4 ♖e8 with some compensation for the sacrificed material in Sadler-Crouch, Hastings 1992/3.

f) 10...♖e8!? *(D)* and now:

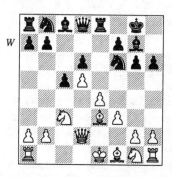

f1) 11 ♗e2 h5 (but not 11...a6? because then 12 ♗xh6 ♘xe4? 13 ♘xe4 ♕h4+ 14 g3 ♕xh6 15 ♕xh6

&xh6 16 ♘f6+ Benjamin-Bouaziz, Szirak IZ 1987, is possible; Black must also watch out for great danger after 11...♔h7 12 h4!? h5 13 g4 hxg4 14 h5 gxh5 15 &g5 ± Seirawan-Scheeren, Wijk aan Zee 1983) 12 a4 ♘a6 13 &b5 &d7 14 ♘ge2 &xb5 15 axb5 ♘b4 16 0-0 ♘d7 17 b3 a6 with an approximately equal game; Sei-rawan-Spraggett, New York 1984.

f2) 11 ♘ge2 and now:

f21) 11...♘a6? is bad because of 12 &xh6 +− Rajković-Vragoteris, Katerini 1993, and the rook's position on e8 is telling in the variation 12...♘xe4? 13 ♘xe4 ♕h4+ 14 g3 ♕xh6 15 ♕xh6 &xh6 16 ♘f6+.

f22) 11...h5 deserves attention, for example 12 ♘f4 ♘bd7 13 &e2 a6 14 ♖c1 b5 15 b3 ♘e5 16 0-0 &d7 (now 16...b4!? is not bad either: 17 ♘d1 a5 18 ♘b2 &a6 but 16...h4?! is less successful: 17 ♘d1 &d7 18 ♘f2 a5 19 ♘4h3 c4 20 bxc4 ♘xc4 21 &xc4 bxc4 22 &d4 with advantage; Sadler-J.Polgar, Hastings 1992) 17 ♘d3 ♘xd3 18 &xd3 (Yusupov-Dol-matov, Wijk aan Zee Ct 1991) and now Black should have continued 18...♕b8!? with an unclear game.

f23) 11...♘bd7 *(D)* with yet another division:

f231) Black is close to equality after 12 ♘g3 h5 13 &e2 h4 14 ♘f1 a6 (or 14...♘h7 15 &h6 &h8 16 ♘e3 a6 17 a4 f5 18 0-0 ♘e5 19 &f4 ♘f7 with mutual chances; Høi-Morten-sen, Vejstrup 1989) 15 ♕c2 (15 a4!?) 15...b5 16 a4 b4 17 ♘d1 ♘h5 18 ♘d2 f5 with complications; Sadler-Gelfand, Oakham 1988.

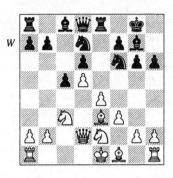

f232) 12 ♘d1 is also interesting: 12...b5 13 ♘g3 h5 (13...a6 14 &xh6 &xh6 15 ♕xh6 ♘xd5 16 ♕d2 ♘b4 17 ♘c3 with advantage) 14 &xb5 ♖b8 15 &e2 h4 16 ♘f1 ♘e5 17 ♖b1! Solozhenkin-Marin, Sitges Hospi-talet 1993, and now Marin suggests 17...♕b6!? with the rough variation 18 b4 &a6 19 b5 h3! 20 g3 &xb5 21 a4? &xe2.

f233) 12 ♘c1 h5:

f2331) 13 ♘d3 ♘h7 14 ♘f2 ♘e5 15 &e2 f5 16 0-0 (16 h3 a6 17 f4 ♘f7 18 exf5 gxf5!? 19 &xh5 ♕h4 20 &xf7+ ♔xf7 21 0-0 b5 22 a3 ♖g8 and Black has enough compensation for the pawn; Timoshchenko-Pigu-sov, Irkutsk 1986) 16...♘f6 17 ♖ae1 fxe4 18 ♘fxe4 &f5 19 ♘g3 &d7 20 h3 ♘h7 with an unclear game in Dragomaretsky-Zlochevsky, Mos-cow 1989.

f2332) 13 &e2 ♘e5 14 0-0 ♘h7 15 f4 (White's attempts to gain an advantage will not be crowned with success after 15 &h6 &h8 16 ♔h1 f5 17 ♘b3 ♘f6 18 &g5 ♘f7 19 &d3 ♘e5 = Sadler-Khalifman, Oviedo 1992, or 15 ♖b1 f5 16 b4 c4! 17 a4 {after 17 &d1 ♘f6 18 &c2 fxe4 19 fxe4 ♘fg4 20 ♗f4 ♖f8 Black already has the initiative; Van der Sterren-Ree, Hilversum 1986} 17...fxe4 18 ♘xe4 ♗f5 19 ♘a2 ♗xe4 20 fxe4 ♘f6 = Cebalo-Tal, Taxco IZ 1985) 15...♘g4 16 ♗xg4 ♗xg4 17 h3 ♗d7 18 ♘1e2 ♖c8 19 f5 b5 ∞ I.Sokolov-Marin, Manila OL 1992.

11 a4 (D)

The weaker 11 ♖c1?! gave Black the initiative after 11...♖e8 12 b3 b5 13 ♗d3 b4!? 14 ♘d1 (14 ♘a4 ♘xd5! 15 exd5 ♗d4 16 ♗e4 ♗xe3 17 ♕xe3 ♔g7) 14...a5 15 ♘e2 a4 in Yusupov-Gelfand, Munich 1993.

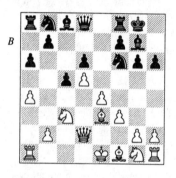

B

11 ... ♖e8

I've already had to write almost a hundred times about the abundance of moves at Black's disposal. Thus you also see:

a) 11...♘h7 and now:

a1) 12 ♗d3!? is interesting, but Black achieves a good game after 12...♘d7 13 ♘h3 ♘e5 14 ♘f2 f5!? (or 14...♘xd3+ 15 ♘xd3 ♗d7 16 0-0 h5 17 ♖ab1 b5 18 axb5 Ionescu-Ardeleanu, Bucharest 1993, and now 18...♗xb5! =) 15 ♗e2 g5 16 exf5 ♗xf5 = Ionescu.

a2) 12 ♘ge2 ♘d7 13 ♘f4 (things are roughly equal after 13 ♘g3 h5 14 ♗e2 h4 15 ♘f1 ♖e8 16 ♖a3 ♖b8 17 ♕c2 ♘e5 18 ♘d2 f5 19 f4 ♘f7 Aksharumova-Cvitan, New York 1987) 13...♘e5 14 ♗e2 ♖b8 15 0-0 ♗d7 (15...♘f6!?) 16 a5 ♘f6 17 g3 b5 18 axb6 ♖xb6 19 ♘g2 ♔h7 20 ♖a2 ♕c7 21 ♕c2 ± Chernin-Zsu.Polgar, Stary Smokovec 1984.

b) 11...♔h7 12 ♘ge2 ♘bd7 13 ♘g3 (both 13 ♘d1 ♖b8 14 ♘ec3 ♕c7 15 a5 ♘g8 16 ♗e2 f5 17 0-0 fxe4 18 ♘xe4 ♘gf6 19 ♘g3 ± Xu Jun-Grosar, Portorož 1987, and 13 ♘c1 ♖b8 14 ♗e2 ♘e8 15 0-0 ♘c7 16 ♔h1 b5 17 axb5 ♘xb5! 18 ♘xb5 axb5 19 ♘b3 ♘b6 20 ♘a5 ♗d7 21 ♗f4 ♕c7 with equality; Gulko-Polugaevsky, Leningrad 1974 are possible) and now:

b1) It is not easy to achieve equality after 13...♕a5 14 ♗e2 ♘e5 (14...b5 15 0-0 b4 16 ♘d1 and c4 simply gapes) 15 0-0 ♗d7 16 ♖fc1 ♕b4 17 a5 ♖fb8 18 ♘a4! ± Psakhis-Zapata, Cienfuegos 1983.

b2) 13...♖e8 is not good either: 14 ♗e2 ♘e5 15 0-0 ♖b8 16 h3! g5 17 f4 gxf4 18 ♖xf4 ♘g6 19 ♖f2 ♖e5 20 ♖af1 ± Pytel-Filipowicz, Polanica Zdroj 1982.

b3) 13...♖b8 14 ♗e2 ♘e5 15 0-0 (it's also worth looking at 15 b3 ♘g8 16 f4 ♘d7 17 0-0 h5 18 e5! dxe5 19 f5 with initiative; Serebrianik-Kraidman, Tel Aviv 1992) 15...♗d7 16 h3 b5 17 f4 ♘c4 18 ♗xc4 bxc4 19 e5 with a small advantage; Dorfman-Keene, Manila 1979.

c) 11...h5 (D) and now:

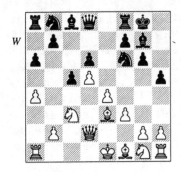

c1) Black has no cause for agitation in the event of 12 ♗h6 ♖e8 13 ♗xg7 ♔xg7 14 ♖b1 ♕a5 15 ♘ge2 ♘bd7 16 ♘c1 ♘e5 17 ♘1e2 ♗d7 = Aksharumova-J.Polgar, Novi Sad OL 1990.

c2) 12 ♗e2 (the battle of nerves continues as White waits for the knight to move to d7) 12...♖e8 (in Yusupov-Dolmatov, Wijk aan Zee Ct 1991, Black could not equalize after 12...♘h7 13 ♗d1 ♘d7 14 ♘ge2 ♖b8 15 a5 b5 16 axb6 ♖xb6 17 0-0 ♘e5 18 b3 f5 19 ♗c2 ±) and now:

c21) White cannot give Black any serious problems after 13 ♗d1 ♘bd7 14 ♘ge2 ♘e5 (14...♕a5 is not bad either: 15 ♖a2 ♖b8 16 0-0 ♕c7 17 a5 b5 18 axb6 ♘xb6 19 b3 ♘fd7 20 ♗c2 ♘e5 = Gheorghiu-Gavrikov, Suhr 1991) 15 b3 ♕a5 16 ♖a2 c4 17 0-0 cxb3 18 ♗xb3 ♘fd7 = Campos-Topalov, Palma 1992.

c22) 13 a5 ♘h7! 14 ♗d1 (14 ♗d3 ♘d7 15 b3 ♘e5 16 ♗c2 b5 17 axb6 ♕xb6 =) 14...♘d7 15 ♘ge2 ♘e5 16 b3; thus far the famous game Seirawan-Kasparov, Skellefteå World Cup 1989, and Black

would have gained an advantage after 16...f5 17 ♗c2 fxe4 18 ♗xe4 c4.

c23) 13 ♖a2!?, which is not seen at the highest levels, deserves attention.

c24) 13 ♗g5 ♕a5 14 ♖a3 ♘h7 15 ♗f4 ♕c7 16 a5 ♘d7 17 ♘h3 ♘e5 18 ♘f2 b5 19 axb6 ♕xb6 and Black has no grounds for complaint at the outcome of the opening; Fedorowicz-Van Wely, Wijk aan Zee 1990.

c3) 12 ♘ge2 ♘bd7 13 ♘f4 (13 ♘c1 ♘e5 14 ♗e2 ♘h7 15 0-0 ♖e8 is examined under 11...♖e8) 13...♘e5 14 ♗e2 b6 (14...♕a5 15 0-0 ♗d7 16 ♖fc1 ♖fc8 =) 15 0-0 ♗d7 16 ♘h3!? c4 (16...♗xh3 17 gxh3 ♕c8 18 f4 ♘ed7 19 ♖ac1 ±) 17 f4 ♘eg4 18 ♗d4 b5 19 e5 dxe5 20 fxe5 ♘h7 21 axb5 (Petursson-Varga, Andorra 1991) and Black should simply have played 21...axb5 22 ♖xa8 ♕xa8 23 e6 fxe6 24 dxe6 ♖xf1+ 25 ♗xf1 ♗xe6 26 ♗xg7 ♔xg7 27 ♘xb5 ♕a1 28 ♘f4 ♗f7 with equality, Varga.

d) 11...♘bd7 and now:

d1) After 12 ♘ge2 it was easy for Black to equalize by avoiding ...♖e8 in Dao-Van Wely, Mesa 1993: 12...♘e5 13 ♘g3 h5 14 ♗e2 h4 15 ♘f1 ♖b8 16 ♕c2 b5!? 17 ♘d2 (17 axb5 axb5 18 ♘xb5 h3!) 17...b4 18 ♘d1 ♘h5 19 f4 ♘g4 =.

d2) 12 ♘h3 and now:

d21) White has an easy game after 12...♘e8 13 ♘f2 ♔h7 14 ♗e2 ♖b8 15 h4!? h5 16 g4 hxg4 17 ♘xg4 with an attack for White; Popov-Loginov, USSR 1986.

d22) After 12...♔h7, both 13 ♘f2 ♕a5 14 ♗e2! b5 15 0-0 b4 16

♘cd1 ♛d8 17 ♖c1 ♘g8 18 b3 ♘e7 19 ♘b2 f5 20 ♘c4 fxe4 21 fxe4 Rajković-Vukić, Yugoslavia 1982, and 13 ♗e2 ♘e5 14 ♘f2 ♛e7 15 0-0 g5 16 a5 ♘h5 17 ♘a4 ♖b8 18 ♘b6 ♘d7 19 ♘c4 ♘e5 20 ♖ac1 ♘xc4 21 ♗xc4 ♘f4 22 ♘d3 Gulko-A.Kuzmin, Moscow 1982, guarantee White supremacy.

d23) Nor did Black manage to equalize after 12...♘e5 13 ♘f2 h5 14 ♗e2 ♖b8 15 0-0 ♗d7 16 h3! b5 17 axb5 ♗xb5 (17...axb5 18 f4 ♘c4 19 ♗xc4 bxc4 20 e5) 18 ♘xb5 axb5 19 b4! ± Raičević-Brenjo, Yugoslavia 1991.

d24) 12...♘h7 (the best chance) 13 ♘f2 h5 14 ♗e2 ♘e5 15 h3 f5 16 exf5 ♗xf5 17 g4 ♗d7 18 f4 ♘f7 19 gxh5 gxh5 20 ♗xh5 ♗f5 and Black has reasonable compensation for the pawn; M.Schmidt-Anka, Biel 1992.

Returning to the position after 11...♖e8 *(D)* in the main line:

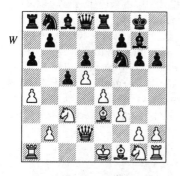

12 ♘ge2

After 12 ♗e2 Black must choose between 12...h5!?, for which see 11...h5, and 12...♘bd7. Not, however, 12...♔h7 13 h4 h5 14 g4! hxg4

15 h5, which gives White a strong attack. After 12...♘bd7 one may continue 13 ♘h3 ♘e5 14 ♘f2 ♔h7 (or 14...h5 15 0-0 ♘h7 16 a5 f5 17 ♘a4 fxe4 18 fxe4 ♗g4 19 ♘b6 ♖b8 20 b4! ♗xe2 21 ♛xe2 cxb4 22 ♖ab1 ± Dokhoian-Damljanović, Sochi 1988) 15 0-0 ♖b8 16 ♖fb1 ♛a5 17 ♛d1 g5 18 ♛c2 ♘fd7 ∞ Topalov-Pedzich, Arnhem jr 1989.

The rare 12 ♗d3 also deserves attention, e.g. 12...h5 13 ♘ge2 ♘bd7 14 b3 ♘e5 15 ♗c2 (stronger than 15 0-0 ♘xd3 16 ♛xd3 ♖b8 17 ♖ab1 ♘d7 18 b4 ♘e5 19 ♛d1 c4 20 ♛d2 b5 = Alterman-Dolmatov, Beersheba 1991) 15...♖b8 16 a5 ♘h7 17 0-0 g5 18 ♔h1 ♛e7 19 ♖ae1 h4 20 h3 ± Ionescu-Musat, Bucharest 1993.

12 ...   ♘bd7

White has a small advantage after 12...♘h7 13 ♘c1 (or 13 ♘f4 ♘d7 14 ♗e2 ♘e5 15 0-0 ♗d7 16 ♖fb1 ♖c8 17 a5 ♘f6! 18 b3 g5 19 ♘d3 ♘xd3 20 ♗xd3 ♘h5 21 ♖a2 f5 = T.Georgadze-Spraggett, Dortmund 1984) 13...f5 14 ♗e2 g5 15 a5 f4 16 ♗f2 ♘d7 17 ♘d3! b5 18 axb6 ♘xb6 19 b3 ♘f8 20 0-0 ♘g6 21 ♖a2 ± Sadler-Berg Hansen, Copenhagen 1992.

13 ♘c1

Black's problems are simplified in the event of 13 ♘d1 ♘e5 14 ♘ec3 ♘h7!? 15 ♗e2 f5 16 0-0 and now both 16...h5 17 ♘f2 ♗d7 18 ♖fb1 ♛f6 19 ♖a3 g5 20 exf5 ♗xf5 21 ♘ce4 ♛g6, Andrianov-Kotronias, Komotini 1993, and 16...♘f7 17 ♘f2 ♗d7 18 ♔h1 ♖c8 19 ♖ae1 ♘f6, Foisor-Cvitan, Tbilisi 1986, are sufficient for equality.

Black has no hint of a problem after 13 ⲵg3 h5 14 ⲹe2 h4 15 ⲵf1 ⲵh7 16 ⲹf2 ⲵe5 17 ⲵe3 ⲵg5 18 0-0 f5 = Novikov-Loginov, Volgodonsk 1983.

13 ...   ⲵe5

13...ⲵh7 is probably just as good as the text move, for example 14 ⲹe2 (14 ⲵd3 ⲵe5 15 ⲵf2 g5 16 ⲹe2 f5 17 exf5 ⲹxf5 18 0-0 ⲵf6 19 f4 gxf4 20 ⲹxf4 ⲵf7 21 ⲹd3 ⲵd7 is equal; Gulko-Loginov, USSR 1983) 14...g5!? (more promising than the alternative 14...ⲵh4+?! 15 g3 ⲵh3 16 ⲵd3 ⲵe5 17 ⲵf2 and 17...ⲵg2 is bad because of 18 0-0-0 ⲵxf3 19 ⲵd3 ⲹd4 20 ⲹf1! and the queen is trapped; Piket-Hulak, Wijk aan Zee 1986, or 14...h5 15 ⲵd3 ⲵe5 16 ⲵf2 ⲹd7 17 0-0 ⲵc8 18 h3 f5 19 f4 ⲵf7 20 exf5 ⲹxf5 21 g4!? hxg4 22 hxg4 ± Korchnoi-Hug, Zurich 1984) 15 ⲵa3 ⲵe7 16 ⲹf2 f5 17 exf5 ⲵe5 18 0-0 ⲹxf5 19 ⲵd1 ⲵf6 20 ⲵe3 ⲹd7 = Vasiukov-A.Kuzmin, Moscow 1986.

14 ⲹe2   ⲵh7

The opening turned out in White's favour in Psakhis-Mestel, Las Palmas IZ 1982, after 14...ⲵh7 15 0-0 ⲹd7 16 ⲵb1 ⲵa5 17 ⲵ1a2! ⲹxa4 18 b4 cxb4 19 ⲵxb4 ⲹb5 20 ⲹxb5 axb5 21 ⲵxb5 with a small advantage.

15 0-0 *(D)*

15 ...   h5

15...g5 16 f4!? (White's chances are also better after 16 ⲵa3 ⲵf8 17 a5 ⲵfg6 18 ⲵa4 f5 19 exf5 ⲹxf5 20 ⲵb6 ⲵb8 21 b4 ± Korchnoi-Ciocaltea, Bucharest 1966) 16...gxf4 17

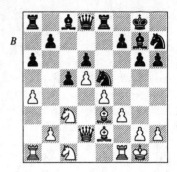

ⲹxf4 ⲵh4 18 ⲵd3 ⲵg5 19 ⲵxe5 ⲹxe5 20 ⲹxe5 dxe5 21 ⲵe3 Yusupov-Ermenkov, Tunis IZ 1985, and Black has no means of organizing himself.

16 ⲵb1

Black has no problems after 16 ⲵh1 f5 17 ⲵ1a2 ⲵf6 18 exf5 ⲹxf5 19 ⲵfe1 ⲵc8 20 ⲵac1 ⲵf7 21 b3 ⲵc7 22 ⲹc4 ⲵce7 with a balanced position in Rajković-Gschnitzer, Bundesliga 1991, whilst after 16 ⲵ1a2 f5 17 b4 cxb4 18 ⲵxb4 f4! 19 ⲹf2 g5 20 a5 ⲵf6 21 ⲵa4 g4 he has already seized control of the game; Czerwonski-Cvitan, Katowice 1992. In Alterman-Gelfand, Riga 1987, White tried a fanciful plan, 16 ⲵa3 f5 17 ⲵ1a2 ⲵf6 18 a5 fxe4 19 ⲵxe4 ⲵxe4 20 fxe4 ⲵg4 21 h3 ⲹxe2 22 ⲵxe2 b5, and handed the initiative to his opponent.

16	...	f5
17	b4	b6
18	ⲵ1a2	ⲵf6
19	bxc5	bxc5
20	ⲵh1	ⲵf8
21	f4!	

White has a small advantage; Rajković-Kofidis, Komotini 1993.

7 Mikenas Attack (A66)

**1 d4 ♘f6 2 c4 c5 3 d5 e6 4 ♘c3 exd5
5 cxd5 d6 6 e4 g6**

7   f4   ♗g7 *(D)*

Black has no serious alternative to the text move, for example:

a) 7...♕e7 8 ♘f3 ♘bd7 (and not 8...♘xe4? 9 ♕a4+; nor does 8...♗g4 9 h3 ♗xf3 10 ♕xf3 ♗g7 11 ♗d3 0-0 12 0-0 ♘bd7 13 ♗d2 bring any relief) 9 e5 dxe5 10 fxe5 ♘xe5 11 ♗b5+ ♘ed7+ (or 11...♗d7 12 0-0-0-0-0 13 ♘xe5 ♕xe5 14 ♗f4 ♕d4+ 15 ♕xd4 cxd4 16 ♖ac1! ± Boleslavsky) 12 ♔f2 ♘g4+ 13 ♔g3 ♘ge5 14 ♘xe5 ♕xe5+ 15 ♗f4 ♕f6 16 ♕e2+ +– *ECO*.

b) 7...♘bd7 8 ♘f3 ♗g7 9 e5 dxe5 10 fxe5 ♘g4 11 e6 fxe6 12 dxe6 ♕e7 13 ♘d5! ♕xe6+ 14 ♗e2 ♕d6 15 ♗g5 ♗d4 16 ♗c4 and White's attack is already practically decisive.

c) 7...a6?! has little to offer: 8 e5 ♘fd7 (8...♕e7?! 9 ♘f3 ♘fd7 10 ♘e4 dxe5 11 d6 ♕d8 12 ♗c4 ♘b6 13 fxe5! +–) 9 ♘f3 ♗g7 10 ♘e4 dxe5 11 ♘d6+ ♔f8 12 ♗e2!? (more convincing than 12 ♘g5 exf4 13 ♘dxf7 ♕e7+ 14 ♗e2 ♘e5 15 ♘xh8 ♕xg5 16 0-0 ♔g8 17 ♗xf4 ♕e7 18 d6 ♕e6 19 ♗xe5 ♗xe5 20 ♘f7 ♗xb2 21 ♗g4 ♕e3+ 22 ♔h1 ♘d7 23 ♕d5 ♗xa1 24 ♗xd7 ♗xd7 25 ♘d8+ ∞ Fedorowicz-Henley, Lone Pine 1977) 12...exf4 13 ♗xf4 ♕f6 14 ♗g3 ♕xb2 15 ♖b1 ± Kapengut.

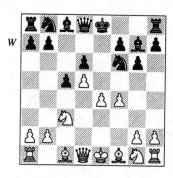

8   e5

With this move White begins the quite dangerous system known as the Mikenas Attack, named after the noted Lithuanian chessplayer who, with the help of his invention, gained victories over the strongest players in the world. These days, however, Black has managed to find an adequate response and White now links his hopes with 8 ♗b5+ (A67) and 8 ♘f3 (A68-69).

Now Black has two main options:
A) 8...dxe5
B) 8...♘fd7

A) 8...dxe5

For many years 8...dxe5 was a theoretical outcast, although it is not easy for White to gain an advantage, or even, quite often, equality.

9   fxe5   ♘fd7

Black cannot get organized after either 9...♘g4 10 e6! or 9...♕e7 10 ♘f3 0-0 (10...♘g4 11 d6) 11 ♗g5 h6 12 ♗xf6 ♗xf6 13 d6 ♕e6 14 ♕d5 ♗xe5 15 ♘xe5 ♖e8 16 0-0-0 ♕xe5 17 ♗c4 ± Mikenas.

10 e6   fxe6

11 dxe6 *(D)*

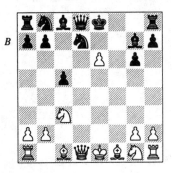

11 ...   ♕e7!

Other moves are less successful:

a) 11...♘f6?! 12 ♕xd8+! (12 ♗c4 ♕xd1+ 13 ♔xd1 ♘c6 14 ♘f3 ♘a5 15 ♗b5+ ♔e7 16 ♖e1 only leads to a small advantage) 12...♔xd8 13 ♗g5 ♗xe6 14 0-0-0+ ♔e7 15 ♖e1 ♔f7 16 ♘h3! ♖e8 17 ♘f4 ♗f5 18 ♗c4+ ♔f8 19 ♖xe8+ ♘xe8 20 ♖f1 and White has very powerful pressure.

b) 11...♕h4+?! 12 g3 ♗xc3+ 13 bxc3 ♕e4+ 14 ♕e2 ♕xe2+ (White is winning after 14...♕xh1? 15 exd7+ ♔xd7 16 ♗h3+) and White has a pleasant choice between 15 ♘xe2 ♘f8 16 ♘f4 ♘xe6 17 ♗c4 ♗xf4 18 ♗xf4 ♗f5 19 0-0 ♘c6 20 ♖ad1 ±, and 15 ♗xe2 ♘f8 (or 15...♘e5 16 ♘f3 ♘xf3+ 17 ♗xf3 ♘c6 18 ♗d5 with an obvious advantage) 16 ♘f3 (16 e7!? also deserves attention:

16...♘e6 17 ♘f3 ♘c6 18 0-0 h6 19 ♗c4 g5 20 ♗a3 b6 21 ♖ae1 ♘c7 22 ♘e5 ♘xe5 23 ♖xe5 ±) 16...♘xe6 17 0-0 (stronger than 17 ♗h6 ♘c6 18 0-0 ♗d7 19 ♘g5 ♘xg5 20 ♗xg5 h6 21 ♗e3 0-0-0 and Black equalized in Mikenas-Polugaevsky, Moscow 1955) 17...0-0 18 ♗h6 ♖e8 19 ♘e5 and not 19...♘d7? because of 20 ♗b5 ♖e7 21 ♖ad1 +− Mikenas.

c) 11...♗xc3+?! (Black is parting with his bishop too lightly) 12 bxc3 ♕e7 13 ♗e2 ♕xe6 (Black loses after 13...♘e5?! 14 ♘f3! ♘xf3+ {14...0-0 15 ♘xe5 ♕h4+ 16 g3 ♕e4 17 ♖f1 ♖xf1+ 18 ♔xf1 ♕h1+ 19 ♔f2 ♕xh2+ 20 ♔f3 ♘c6 21 ♘g4 +− Rastianis-Filipowicz, Warsaw 1977} 15 ♗xf3 ♕xe6+ 16 ♔f2 +−) 14 ♘f3 0-0 0-0 ♘b6 16 ♗h6 ♖e8 17 ♘g5! ♕e3+ 18 ♔h1 ±.

12 ♘d5!?

Black manages to beat off his opponent's onslaught in the event of 12 ♗e2 ♘b6 (12...♘f6 is weaker: 13 ♗f4 ♗xe6 14 ♗d6 ♕d8 15 ♕a4+ ♔f7 16 ♖d1 ♘bd7 17 ♘f3 h6 18 0-0 with a threatening lead in development) 13 ♗f4 ♗xe6 14 ♘f3 ♗c4 (14...♘c6!? 15 ♗d6 ♕d7) 15 0-0 ♗xe2 16 ♘xe2 ♘c6 (16...0-0?! is quite dangerous for Black: 17 ♗d6 ♕e3+ 18 ♔h1 ♖d8 19 ♘f4 Lputian-Magerramov, Riga 1980, and even the objectively best 19...♘c6 20 ♖e1 ♕xf4 21 ♗xf4 ♖xd1 22 ♖axd1 ♗xb2 cannot save Black from suffering in the endgame) 17 ♖e1 0-0 18 ♗d6 ♕e3+ 19 ♔h1 ♖fe8 20 ♘f4 ♕f2 with an unclear game – analysis by Kengis and Lanka.

12 ... ♕xe6+

In such variations, a sidestep is usually tantamount to suicide, for example 12...♕h4+ 13 g3 ♕e4+ 14 ♕e2 ♕xd5 (14...♕xh1 15 exd7+ ♔xd7 16 ♘f3 ♖e8 17 ♗e3 ±) 15 exd7+ ♔xd7 16 ♗g2 ♕f7 (16...♕e5 17 ♗e3 ♕xb2 18 ♖d1+ ♔c7 19 ♗f4+ ♔b6 20 ♕xb2+ ♗xb2 21 ♖b1 +− is of approximately equal worth) 17 ♕b5+ ♘c6 18 ♗f4 ♖e8+ 19 ♘e2 ♗d4 20 0-0-0 +−.

13 ♕e2 ♕xe2+
14 ♗xe2 0-0

14...♗e5 does not promise Black much joy, for instance 15 ♘f3 ♘f6 16 ♗c4 ♘xd5 17 ♗xd5 ♗f6 18 0-0 ♘c6 19 ♗g5 ± Lputian-Norwood, Lvov 1986.

15 ♘c7 ♘c6
16 ♘xa8 ♘b4 (D)

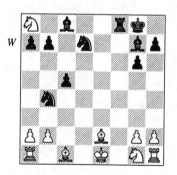

The course of the game has changed dramatically; Black has sacrificed his rook and has seized the initiative at a great cost.

17 ♘f3

Or 17 ♖b1 ♘e5, and 17 ♔d1 ♘e5 18 ♗d2 ♘bd3 also leads to an unclear position.

17 ... ♘c2+
18 ♔d1 ♘xa1
19 ♗c4+ ♔h8
20 ♖e1 a6

20...♘b6 21 ♘xb6 axb6 22 ♖e7 favours White, and 20...♘f6? 21 ♘c7! ♖d8+ 22 ♔d2 ♗h6 (22...♗f5 23 ♘e6 ♗xe6 24 ♖xe6 +−) 23 ♘e6 ♗xe6 24 ♖xe6 gives White a big advantage; Lputian-Magerramov, Beltsy 1979.

21 ♗e6 ♘e5!

and the complications are not unfavourable for Black.

B) 8...♘fd7

9 ♘b5

Black has less problems after:

a) 9 exd6?! 0-0 10 ♘f3 ♘f6 11 ♗e2 ♘e8 12 0-0 ♘xd6 with equality.

b) 9 e6 fxe6 (9...♕e7?! 10 ♗e2 fxe6 11 dxe6 ♗xc3+ 12 bxc3 ♕xe6 13 ♘f3 0-0 14 ♘g5 ♕f6 15 ♘e4 ♕h4+ 16 g3 ♕e7 17 ♘xd6 ♘c6 18 0-0 ♘f6 19 ♗c4+ ♔g7 20 ♖e1 ± Mileika-Sandler, Riga 1980) 10 dxe6 ♘b6 (certainly not 10...♘f8? 11 f5! ♕h4+ 12 g3 ♗xc3+ 13 bxc3 ♕e4+ 14 ♔f2 ♕xf5+ 15 ♘f3 ♕xe6 16 ♗b5+ ♔d8 17 ♖e1 and Black awaits difficult times; De Valliere-Mohn, Corr 1983) 11 ♘e4 0-0 12 ♕xd6 ♕xd6 13 ♘xd6 ♗xe6 14 ♘xb7 ♘a4 with more than sufficient compensation for the pawn.

c) 9 ♘f3 leads to an unclear game: 9...0-0 10 ♗e2 dxe5 11 0-0 a6 (stronger than 11...e4 12 ♘xe4 ♘f6 13 ♘c3 ♗g4 14 h3 ♗xf3 15 ♗xf3

♕b6 16 ♗e3 with a small advantage to White; Nogueiras-Grünfeld, Zagreb IZ 1987) 12 a4 exf4 13 ♗xf4 ♘f6 14 h3 ♘h5 15 ♗h2 Kristiansen-Holm, Denmark 1977.

9 ...   dxe5
10 ♘d6+   ♔e7

Not leaving the knight in peace. White's position is preferable in the event of 10...♔f8 11 ♘f3 h6 (11...exf4 is bad because of 12 ♗xf4 ♘f6 13 ♗c4 ♕e7+ 14 ♘e5! ±, and Black cannot equalize after 11...♕c7 12 ♘xc8 ♕xc8 13 ♗e2 e4 14 ♘g5 ♘f6 15 ♕c2 h6 16 ♘xe4 ♘xe4 17 ♕xe4 ♗d4 18 ♗e3! ♗xb2 19 ♖b1 and the pressure on Black's position is very unpleasant; Armas-Tolnai, Havana 1988) 12 ♗e2 f5 13 fxe5 ♘xe5 14 ♘xc8 ♕xc8 15 0-0 with a small advantage.

11 ♘xc8+

White only has problems after 11 fxe5?! ♘xe5 12 ♘xc8+ ♕xc8 13 d6+ ♔f8 14 ♘f3 ♕e6 15 ♘xe5 ♗xe5 16 ♗e2 ♔g7 17 0-0 ♘c6.

11 ♘b5 leads to complications which are not disadvantageous for Black, for example 11...♖e8! 12 d6+ ♔f8 13 ♘c7 (or 13 ♗e2 ♘c6 14 ♘f3 ♘d4 15 0-0 ♘xe2+ 16 ♕xe2 exf4 17 ♕d1 ♖e4 18 ♘c7 ♖b8 19 ♕d5 ♘f6 20 ♕xc5 b6 21 ♕a3 ♗b7 ∓ Anikaev-Gorelov, Moscow 1981) 13...exf4+ 14 ♗e2 (14 ♘xe8?! is absolutely terrible for White after 14...♕xe8+ {14...♕h4+!? 15 g3!? fxg3 16 ♘f3 g2+ 17 ♘xh4 gxh1♕ with an attack, Kapengut} 15 ♗e2 ♘e5 16 ♗xf4 ♘bc6 ∓ Smirnov-Kapengut, Minsk 1979) 14....♘c6 15 ♘xe8 ♕xe8 16

♘f3 ♘d4 17 ♘xd4 ♗xd4 18 ♗xf4 ♘e5 with enough compensation for the exchange.

11 ...   ♕xc8 (D)

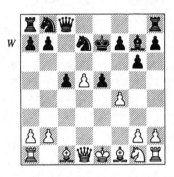

12 ♘f3

The premature 12 d6+?! only eases Black's problems, for example 12...♔f8 13 ♘f3 and now:

a) 13...e4!? is quite possible: 14 ♘g5 h6 15 ♘xf7!? (the cowardly 15 ♘xe4 is also better for Black: 15...♕e8 16 ♕e2 ♘c6 17 ♔f2 ♗d4+ 18 ♔g3 ♔g7 ∓) 15...♔xf7 16 ♗c4+ ♔f8 17 f5 ♗d4!? (only not 17...g5 18 ♕d5 ♘e5 19 f6! ♗xf6 20 0-0 ♔g7 21 ♖xf6 ♔xf6 22 ♗xg5+! and here White is winning) 18 fxg6 ♔g7 19 ♗e6 ♕d8 20 ♕b3 ♕b6 21 ♕g3 ♘f6 ∓ Sulava-Namgilov, Budapest 1990.

b) 13...♘c6 14 ♗e2 (or 14 ♗c4?! ♘b6 15 ♗b3 e4 16 ♘e5 ♘xe5 17 fxe5 c4 18 ♗c2 ♕f5 19 e6 ♕xe6 ∓ Baumach-Polugaevsky, E.Germany 1963) 14...h6 (14...♘d4?! places the initiative in White's hands: 15 0-0 e4 16 ♘e5 f6 17 ♗e3! fxe5 18 fxe5+ ±) 15 fxe5 ♘dxe5 16 0-0 ♘xf3+ 17 ♗xf3 ♗d4+ 18 ♔h1 ♔g7 19 ♗d5

♖f8 20 ♗f4 ♕d8 and Black's position is preferable.

12   ...   ♖e8 *(D)*

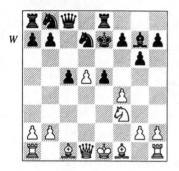

13   fxe5

One cannot recommend 13 ♗e2, as by following Larsen's recommendation 13...♔f8 14 0-0 e4 15 ♘g5 h6 16 f5!? hxg5 17 fxg6 ♘e5 Black can gain an advantage.

13 ♗c4 deserves more attention:

a) 13...♔f8 is another interesting possibility, for example 14 0-0 e4 15 ♘g5 (Black has an obvious advantage after 15 ♘e5 ♘b6 16 ♗b5 ♘8d7 17 ♘xd7+ ♘xd7 18 f5 ♗d4+ 19 ♔h1 a6 20 fxg6 hxg6 21 ♕g4 ♘e5 22 ♕h4 axb5 23 ♗g5 ♘f3! 24 gxf3 e3) 15...♘b6 16 ♗b5 ♖d8 17 ♘xh7+ ♔g8 18 ♘g5 c4! 19 ♕e1!? ♕c5+ 20 ♗e3 ♕xb5 21 f5! ♖xd5 22 fxg6 ♖xg5 23 gxf7+ ♔f8 24 a4 ♕a5 25 ♕h4 ♖f5 26 ♕h7 ♖xf1+ 27 ♖xf1 ♘8d7 28 ♕g8+ ♔e7 29 ♕xg7 ♖f8, Meszaros-Stefanov, Satu Mare 1987, and White should have played 30 ♗g5+!? ♔d6 31 ♗f4+ ♔e7 32 ♗g5+ =.

b) 13...♘b6 14 ♗b5 (14 d6+!? ♔f8 15 ♗b5 ♘c6 16 0-0 ∞) 14...♖d8

15 0-0 ♖xd5 16 ♕e1 ♔f8 17 fxe5 ♘c6 18 ♗xc6 ♕xc6 19 ♕h4 ♔g8 20 ♘g5 h5 21 ♘xf7 ♖f8 22 ♗h6 ♖d4 23 ♕f2 ♕e6 24 ♗xg7 ♖xf7 25 ♗f6 ♘d5 with a small advantage to Black.

13   ...   ♘xe5

You also see 13...♔f8 after which it has not been proven that White has an advantage, for example 14 e6!? fxe6 15 ♗e2 (15 d6?! ♔g8 16 ♗c4 ♘c6 17 0-0 ♘b6 18 ♗b3 ♘d4 19 ♘g5 ♕c6 20 ♕g4 ♘xb3 21 axb3 ♕xd6 with an obvious advantage to Black in Buković-T.Petrosian, Bar 1980) 15...exd5 16 0-0 ♘f6 17 ♘g5 ♕c6 18 ♗b5!? (18 a4 leads to an approximately equal game: 18...c4 19 ♘xh7+ ♔g8 20 ♘xf6+ ♗xf6 21 ♖xf6 ♕xf6 22 ♕xd5+ ♕f7 23 ♕xf7+ ♔xf7 24 ♗xc4+ ♔g7 25 b4 ♘c6 26 ♗b2+ ♔h6 =) 18...♕xb5 19 ♘xh7+ ♔g8 20 ♘xf6+ ♗xf6 21 ♕xd5+ ♔g7 22 ♗g5 ♘d7 23 ♖xf6 ♘xf6 24 ♗xf6+ ♔xf6 25 ♖f1+ ♔g7 26 ♕f7+ and the storm in a teacup ends in perpetual check – Hardicsay.

14   ♗b5   ♘bd7

15   ♘xe5

15 0-0 changes nothing: 15...♔f8! (15...a6? is bad: 16 ♘xe5 ♗xe5 17 d6+! ♔f8 18 ♕d5 ♗d4+ 19 ♔h1 ♘f6 20 ♗h6+ ♔g8 21 ♖xf6! and White is winning) 16 ♘xe5 ♖xe5 – this position can also arise after 15 ♘xe5.

15   ...   ♔f8! *(D)*

15...♗xe5 16 0-0 is worse, since Black cannot get a satisfactory game after either 16...♔f8 17 ♕f3 f5 18 g4 ♗d4+ (or 18...a6 19 gxf5! axb5

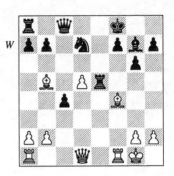

20 fxg6+ ⌯e7 21 ♗f4 with advantage) 19 ⌯h1 ♘e5 20 ♕g2 ♖d8 21 gxf5 ⌯g7 22 ♗g5 ♖d6 23 ♖ae1 ± Rajković-Planinc, Majdanpek 1976, or 16...c4 17 d6+ ⌯f8 18 ♗h6+! (an important improvement) 18...⌯g8 19 ♕d5 ♕c5+ 20 ♕xc5 ♘xc5 21 ♗xe8 ♖xe8 22 ♖ae1 with a clear plus for White – Kapengut.

16 0-0   ♖xe5
17 ♗f4   c4!? (D)

This move may decide the fate of the whole Mikenas Attack; White's position is preferable in the first two lines below:

a) 17...a6 18 ♗xe5 (18 ♗xd7!?) 18...♗xe5 (or 18...♘xe5 19 ♗e2 c4 20 ⌯h1 ♕c5 21 ♕d2 ♖d8 22 ♖fd1 ± Sosonko-Jakobsen, Barcelona 1975) 19 ♗xd7 ♕xd7 20 ♕f3 ⌯g7 21 d6! ±.

b) 17...♖e4 18 ♕f3 f5 19 ♖ae1 ♗d4+ 20 ⌯h1 ♖xe1 21 ♖xe1 ♘f6 22 ♗g5 ♘g4 23 h3 ♘e5 24 ♕g3 ±.

c) 17...♖f5 deserves a great deal of attention, for example 18 ♗d6+ ⌯g8 19 ♖xf5 gxf5 20 ♗xd7 ♕xd7 21 ♗xc5 ♗xb2 22 ♖b1 ♗e5 23 ♕d2 f6 with equality; Curtin-Lobron, Yugoslavia 1980.

18 ♕d4!

An excellent retort allowing White to equalize. His position is unenviable after 18 ♗xe5 ♘xe5 19 ⌯h1 ♕c5 20 ♗a4 ♖d8 ∓, or 18 ♗xd7 ♕c5+ 19 ⌯h1 ♖xd5 20 ♕g4 f5 21 ♕h3 (nor does the following change anything: 21 ♗e6 fxg4 22 ♗d6+ ⌯e8 23 ♗xc5 ♖xc5 24 ♖ae1 ♖e5 25 ♖xe5 ♗xe5 26 ♖e1 ♖d8! ∓ Kapengut) 21...♖xd7 22 ♕xh7 ⌯f7 23 ♖ad1 ♖ad8 24 ♖xd7+ ♖xd7 25 h4 ♕e7 again with an advantage to Black; Yuferov-Kapengut, Minsk 1976.

18 ...   ♖f5

18...♖h5 deserves attention: 19 ♕xc4 ♘b6 20 ♕b4+ ⌯g8 21 ♖ac1 ♕f8 22 ♕b3 ♖d5 23 ♗e3 ♕d6 ∞ Astolfi-S.Kovačević, Cannes 1989.

19 ♕xc4

19 ♗h6? loses to 19...♗xh6 20 ♗xd7 ♗g7! 21 ♕xg7+ ⌯xg7 22 ♗xc8 ♖xf1+ 23 ⌯xf1 ♖xc8 −+ Legky-Shvedchikov, USSR 1978.

19 ...   ♕xc4
20 ♗xc4   ♗xb2
21 ♖ad1   ♘e5

In this endgame it is difficult to imagine any result except a draw.

8 Taimanov's 8 ♗b5+ (A67)

**1 d4 ♘f6 2 c4 c5 3 d5 e6 4 ♘c3 exd5
5 cxd5 d6 6 e4 g6**

    7 f4   **♗g7**
    8 ♗b5+!? *(D)*

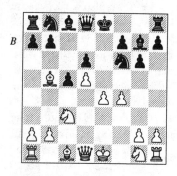

Now we move on to one of the
most dangerous variations for Black
of the Modern Benoni, and, if I am to
be truthful to the end, it is basically
because of this check that I generally
only play 3...c5 after 2...e6 3 ♘f3.

Now we shall investigate two
knight moves in detail:

    A) 8...♘bd7
    B) 8...♘fd7

Of course, the retreat of the knight
from f6 is not an ideal move, as it de-
stroys the harmony in Black's position, but after the other replies Black
has tactical problems.

I should also mention 8...♗d7?! 9
e5 (9 ♗d3 0-0 10 ♘f3 ♗g4 leads to
A68) 9...♘h5 (nor will Black have

much joy after 9...dxe5 10 fxe5 ♕e7
11 ♘f3 {or 11 ♕e2 ♗xb5 12 ♘xb5
♘xd5 13 ♘d6+ ♔f8 14 ♘f3 ♘c6 15
0-0 ♘xe5 16 ♘xe5 ♗xe5 17 ♗h6+
♔g8 18 ♘e4 ±} 11...0-0 12 0-0 ♘g4
13 ♗f4 ♘xe5 14 ♗xe5! ♗xe5 15
♖e1 f6 16 ♗c4 ♔g7 17 d6 and White
has an obvious advantage; Lau-Per-
enyi, Budapest 1981) 10 ♘f3 and
now:

a) 10...0-0 11 ♗xd7 ♕xd7 (or
11...♘xd7 12 g4 ♘xf4 13 ♗xf4
dxe5 14 ♗g5 f6 15 ♗h4 and White
wins) 12 0-0 ♘a6 13 ♖e1 ♖ae8 14 a3
b6 15 b3 ♘c7 16 ♖a2 ♖d8 17 g3
dxe5 18 fxe5 h6 (18...♘xd5? 19 ♘xd5
♕xd5 20 ♖d2 +−) 19 d6 ± Hertneck-
Vlahopoulos, Katerini 1993.

b) 10...dxe5 11 fxe5 0-0 12
♗xd7! ♕xd7 (12...♘xd7 loses: 13
g4 ♘xe5 14 gxh5 ♘xf3+ 15 ♕xf3
♖e8+ 16 ♔d1 ♕h4 17 h6 ♗h8 18
♗f4 +−) 13 0-0 ♕f5 14 ♕a4 ♗xe5
15 ♘xe5 ♕xe5 16 ♗h6 ♖d8 17
♖ae1 ♕d4+ 18 ♕xd4 cxd4 19 ♘b5
♘a6 20 d6! and Black's position is
unenviable.

A) 8...♘bd7

It is significantly more difficult for
White to gain an advantage after this
move than in the lines following
8...♗d7.

    9 e5   **dxe5**

9...♘h5 is also possible: 10 e6 ♕h4+ 11 ♔f1 (11 g3 ♘xg3 12 ♘f3 ♕h3 13 exd7+ ♗xd7 14 ♗xd7+ ♔xd7 15 ♖g1 ♗xc3+ 16 bxc3 ♖he8+ 17 ♘e5+ dxe5 18 hxg3 exf4+ 19 ♔d2 ♕h2+ 20 ♔d3 b5 is totally unclear) 11...♗d4 12 exd7+ ♗xd7 13 ♕e2+ ♔d8 14 ♗xd7 ♔xd7 15 g3 ♘xg3+ 16 hxg3 ♕xh1 17 ♕g2 and White only has a small advantage.

10 fxe5   ♘h5
11 e6 *(D)*

Significantly, you rarely see 11 ♘f3 0-0 12 ♗g5 ♕b6 13 ♕e2 a6 14 ♗a4 (but not 14 ♗c4? ♘xe5 15 ♘xe5 ♖e8 16 0-0 ♖xe5 17 ♕d2 ♕b4 ∓ Cherepkov-Katišonok, Leningrad 1990) 14...♕b4 15 0-0-0! b5 16 ♗c2 with an advantage; Petursson-Müller, Star Fojran 1991.

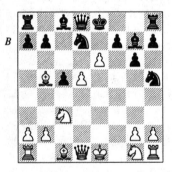

11 ...   ♕h4+

11...fxe6 12 dxe6 0-0 (certainly not 12...♕h4+? 13 g3 ♗xc3+ 14 bxc3 ♕e4+ 15 ♕e2 ♕xh1 16 exd7+ ♔d8 17 ♗g5+ ♔c7 18 0-0-0 +− Mann-Kleinsorgen, Corr 1980) and now:

a) 13 exd7 is weak because of 13...♗xc3+ (but not 13...♕h4+? 14

♔d2 ♗xd7 15 ♗xd7 ♖ad8 {15...♖f2+ 16 ♘ge2 ♗xc3+ 17 ♔xc3 ♕b4+ 18 ♔c2 ♕c4+ 19 ♔b1 +−} 16 ♔c2 ♖f2+ 17 ♔b1 ♗xc3 18 ♕g4! ♗f6 19 ♘h3 and White wins, Aleksandrov-Wojtkiewicz, Wisla Bes 1992) 14 bxc3 ♕h4+ 15 ♔d2 (15 g3 ♕e4+) 15...♗xd7 16 ♗xd7 ♖f2+ 17 ♘e2 ♖d8 18 ♔c2 ♕e4+ 19 ♔b3 ♖xe2 ∓.

b) 13 ♕d5? is also weak because of 13...♕e7 14 ♗xd7 ♗xd7 15 ♕xd7 (15 ♗e3 ♗xc3+ 16 bxc3 ♗c6 17 ♕xc5 ♕xe6 wins for Black; Bert-Poumart, Corr 1985) 15...♗xc3+ 16 bxc3 ♕h4+ and again Black has an advantage.

c) 13 ♘f3! ♗d4!? (White has no problems achieving an advantage after 13...♘df6 14 ♕xd8 ♖xd8 15 e7 ♖d6 16 ♘g5! ♗e6 17 0-0 a6 18 ♘xe6 axb5 19 ♘c7 ♖c8 20 ♘3xb5 ±, or 13...♖xf3 14 ♕xf3 ♗xc3+ {14...♘e5 15 ♕d5 ♕h4+ 16 g3 ♕e7 17 ♗g5 ♕xe6 18 ♕d8+ ♗f8 19 0-0 ♘f7 20 ♖xf7! wins swiftly} 15 bxc3 ♘e5 16 ♕e4 ♕f6 17 e7!? ♕xe7 18 0-0 ♗f5 19 ♕d5+ ♔g7 20 ♗g5! ♕xg5 21 ♕xe5+ ♔h6 22 ♖ae1 ± Kapengut) and now:

c1) Everything is in order for Black after 14 ♘xd4 ♘e5 15 ♕b3 ♔g7 16 ♕d5 ♕h4+ 17 g3 ♕xd4 18 ♕xd4 cxd4 19 e7 ♖g8 20 e8♕ ♖xe8 21 ♗xe8 ♗h3, Martin.

c2) It would appear that Black can support his position after 14 ♕b3!? ♕e7! 15 ♗e3 ♘e5 16 ♘xe5 ♗xe3 17 ♘d5 ♗f2+!? (17...♕h4+ is considerably worse, and after 18 g3 ♗f2+ 19 ♔e2 ♕e4+ 20 ♘e3 ♕xe5

21 e7+ ♗e6 22 exf8♕+ ♖xf8 23
♕xe6+! ♕xe6 24 ♗c4 White gained
the advantage in the game Mestel-
Hodgson, British Ch (Southport)
1983) 18 ♔e2 ♕xe6 19 ♘c7 ♕xb3
20 axb3 ♗d4! 21 ♘xa8 ♗xe5 22
♖xa7 ♗g4+ and Black has enough
compensation for the exchange –
Martin.

c3) 14 ♗c4 deserves close ex-
amination, and now not 14...♕e7 because of 15 ♗g5!.

c4) 14 exd7 ♗xd7 15 ♗g5 ♕e8
(15...♕b6 doesn't help either: 16
♕b3+ ♗e6 17 ♗c4 ♖ae8 18 0-0-0
+–) 15...♕e8+ 16 ♗e2 ♘f4 17 ♗xf4
♖xf4 18 ♘d5 ♖xf3 (the only move)
19 gxf3 ♕e5 20 ♘c3 ♖e8 21 ♕b3+
♔h8 (21...♗e6!?) 22 ♖d1 ♗f5 23
♖d2 and White is winning despite all
Black's tactical tricks; Emanuel Si-
moncini-Caruso, Corr 1985.

12 g3   ♘xg3

13 hxg3

13 ♘f3 gives White nothing:
13...♗xc3+ 14 bxc3 ♕e4+ 15 ♔f2
♘xh1+ 16 ♕xh1 fxe6 17 dxe6 0-0
18 exd7 ♗xd7 19 ♗xd7 ♖f7 20 ♗b5
c4 21 ♗h6 ♕h4+ 22 ♔g2 ♕g4+ 23
♔f2 ♕h4+ = Littlewood-Hartoch,
London 1984.

13 ...   ♕xh1

13...♕xg3+?! is bad because of
14 ♔d2 ♗xc3+ 15 bxc3 ♕g2+ 16
♕e2 ♕xd5+ 17 ♔c2 ♕xe6 18 ♕xe6+
fxe6 19 ♗h6 with a big advantage;
Fecht-Betker, Corr 1989.

14 ♗e3

This move promises White a
small advantage, as does the alternative 14 exd7+ ♗xd7 *(D)* and now:

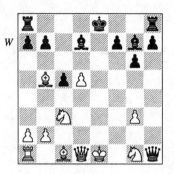

a) 15 ♕e2+ gives Black more
chances for a good game:

a1) 15...♔f8 (not so good) 16
♗e3 ♖e8 (16...♗xc3+ 17 bxc3
♗xb5 18 ♕xb5 ♕xd5 19 ♖d1 ♕e4
20 ♕xc5+ ♔g7 21 ♕d4+ ♕xd4 22
♗xd4+ f6 23 g4! ±) 17 ♔d2!.

a2) 15...♔d8 (a stronger move)
16 ♗g5+! f6 17 0-0-0! ♖e8! (White
is winning after 17...fxg5 18 ♗xd7
♔xd7 19 ♕e6+ ♔d8 20 ♕d6+ ♔c8
21 ♘b5 +–) 18 ♕f1 fxg5 19 ♗xd7
(19 ♕f7? puts the initiative straight
into Black's hands: 19...♗xb5 20
♘xb5 ♗xb2+! 21 ♔xb2 ♕g2+ 22
♔c1 ♕xg3 23 d6 ♕f4+ 24 ♕xf4
gxf4 25 ♘c7 ♔d7 ∓ Savchenko)
19...♔xd7 20 ♕b5+ ♔c7 (20...♔d6?
21 ♕xb7 ♗xc3 22 ♕c6+ ♔e7 23
d6+ and wins; Savchenko-Sandler,
Belgorod 1989) 21 d6+ ♔d8 22
♘d5 ♕g2! 23 ♘c7 ♕xb2+ 24 ♕xb2
♗xb2+ 25 ♔xb2 ♔d7 26 ♘xa8
♖xa8 27 ♘f3 ♖e8 28 ♘xg5 h6 29
♘h7 ♖e2+ 30 ♔c3 ♖f2 31 ♖h1 and
the most likely result is a draw –
analysis by Savchenko.

b) 15 ♗xd7+ ♔xd7 16 ♕g4+ (16
♕a4+ also deserves attention, for
example 16...♔c8 17 ♗e3 ♗xc3+

18 bxc3 ♛xd5 19 ♖d1 ♛c6 20 ♛c4
±) 16...f5 17 ♛a4+ ♚c8 18 ♗e3
♗xc3+! (18...♗h6?! loses: 19 ♗xc5
♛g2 20 ♛c4! ♖e8+ 21 ♘ge2
♛xg3+ 22 ♚d1 ♛g4 23 ♗d4+ ♚d7
24 d6! +− Burgess-Anderson, London 1985) 19 bxc3 ♛xd5 20 ♖d1
♛c6 21 ♛c4!? (21 ♛xc6+ bxc6 22
♗xc5 ♖b8 23 ♖d2 ♖d8 24 ♖e2
♖d3 25 ♗d4 ♚d7 only led to equality in Thorsteins-Ashley, New York
1989) 21...♖e8 22 ♚f2 b5 23 ♛xc5
♛xc5 24 ♗xc5 ♚c7 25 ♘f3 ± Go-
mas-Gallego, Spain 1991.

Returning to the position after 14
♗e3 *(D)* in the main line:

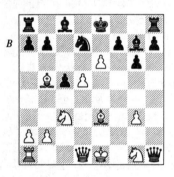

14   ...   0-0

Black could have had huge problems after 14...♗xc3+ 15 bxc3 ♛e4
(15...a6 16 exd7+ ♗xd7 17 ♗xd7+
♚xd7 {Thuesen-de Firmian, Farum
1993} 18 ♛g4+!? f5 19 ♛g5 with an
advantage) 16 ♛f3 ♛xf3 17 ♘xf3!
(promising more than 17 exd7+!?
♗xd7 18 ♗xd7+ ♚xd7 19 ♘xf3 b6
20 ♘e5+ ♚e7 21 a4, with just an
edge for White; Kouatly-Schmitt-
diel, Augsburg 1988) 17...fxe6 18
dxe6 0-0! 19 ♗h6!! (there is only

equality after 19 exd7 ♗xd7 20
♗xd7 ♖xf3 21 ♗xc5 ♖xg3 22
♗e6+ ♚g7 23 ♗d4+ ♚f8 = C.Nik-
olić-Lindermann, Harkany 1987)
19...♖xf3 (or 19...♖e8 20 0-0-0 ♘f6
21 ♗xe8 ♖xe6 22 ♗a4 ♗xa2 23
♘e5 ±) 20 ♖d1! ♖xc3 (both 20...♖f5
21 ♗c4! ♖e5+ 22 ♚f2 ♖h8 23 exd7
♗xd7 24 ♖xd7 ♖g8 25 ♗g7+! ± and
20...♘f8 21 e7 ♗d7 22 exf8♛+
♖axf8 23 ♗c4+ ♚h8 24 ♖xd7 +−
are quite dismal) 21 exd7 ♗xd7 22
♖xd7 a6 Kalinin-Konev, Corr 1991,
and after 23 ♗f1! ♖f8 (23...b5 24
♗g2 +−) 24 ♖g7+ ♚h8 25 ♖xb7
White is winning, Kalinin.

15	exd7	♗xd7
16	♗xd7	♖ae8!?
17	♗xe8	♖xe8
18	♛e2!?	

Probably stronger than 18 ♚d2
♗xc3+! 19 bxc3 ♛xd5+ 20 ♚c2
♛e4+ 21 ♛d3 ♛xe3 ∞ Crouch-Mar-
tin, England 1985.

18	...	♗d4
19	0-0-0	♖xe3
20	♛c2!	

and due to the powerful d5-pawn
we should prefer White.

B) 8...♘fd7

White now has a number of moves,
of which I am absolutely convinced
that 9 a4 is the most dangerous for
Black, but it is worth noting that his
problems are not so easy after other
continuations either. Thus we consider:

    B1) 9 ♘f3
    B2) 9 ♗e2

B3)   9 ♗d3
B4)   9 a4

B1)   9 ♘f3   **a6**
          10 ♗d3

10 ♗e2 b5 11 a4 b4 12 ♘b1 0-0
13 ♘bd2 ♘f6 14 0-0 ♖e8 15 ♗d3
c4! =.

          10 ...   **b5**
          11 0-0   **0-0** *(D)*

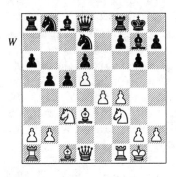

          12 ♔h1

Black has no cause for concern after 12 a4 c4 13 ♗c2 ♕b6+ 14 ♔h1
b4 15 a5 ♕c7 16 ♘e2 ♘c5 17 e5
♗g4 with an equal position, or 12
♘e2 ♘b6 13 ♘g3 ♖e8 14 h3 ♘8d7
15 ♖b1 ♕c7 16 b3 c4; nor is 12 ♕e1
dangerous: 12...♖e8 13 ♕g3 c4 14
♗c2 b4 15 ♘a4 ♘f6 16 f5 ♘xe4 17
♗xe4 ♖xe4 18 ♘g5 ♗xf5 19 ♘xe4
♗xe4 with chances for both sides,
Hartston.

          12 ...   ♖e8

Black also has reasonable chances
to equalize after:

a) 12...b4 13 ♘a4 (13 ♘b1 ♘b6
14 ♘bd2 ♗g4 15 h3 ♗xf3 16 ♘xf3
c4 17 ♗c2 ♘8d7 =) 13...♘b6 14
♘xb6 ♕xb6 15 ♘d2 ♘d7 16 ♘c4

♕c7 17 f5 ♖e8 18 ♗f4 ♘e5 Milov-
Totsky, Moscow 1991.

b) 12...c4 13 ♗c2 b4 14 ♘a4
♘f6 15 ♗e3 ♘bd7 16 ♗d4 ♖e8 17
♖e1 ♗h6 18 g3 a5 Cvitan-Velimirović, Yugoslav Cht 1989.

c) 12...♘b6 deserves attention:
13 f5 ♘8d7!? 14 ♗g5 ♗f6 15 ♗f4
♕e7 16 ♕d2 ♗b7 = Glek-Anikaev,
Minsk 1983.

          13 ♕e1

A pawn attack in the centre is not
very dangerous for Black, e.g. 13 e5
dxe5 14 fxe5 ♘xe5 15 ♗g5 ♕b6 16
♘xe5 ♖xe5 17 ♕f3 ♖a7 18 ♖ae1 f5
19 ♗f4 ♘d7!? with a good game,
Volke-Grünfeld, Saint John 1988,
whilst 13 f5 b4 14 ♘e2 ♘f6 15 ♗g5
♘bd7 16 ♘g3 a5 17 ♕d2 ♗a6 18
♗xa6 ♖xa6 leads to a complicated
game with mutual chances; Volke-
Moiseev, Biel 1993.

          13 ...   b4
          14 ♘d1   ♘f6
          15 ♕h4   a5
          16 ♘f2   ♗a6
          17 ♗xa6   ♖xa6!? =

It is clear that 9 ♘f3 should not
scare Black.

B2)   9 ♗e2!?   **0-0**

The rare move 9...♕h4+!? deserves
attention, with the further possibility
10 g3 ♕e7 11 ♘f3 ♘b6 12 0-0 ♗g4
13 e5 0-0 14 ♘e4 dxe5 15 d6 ♕e8 16
fxe5 ♘8d7 17 ♗f4 ♗xf3 18 ♗xf3
♘xe5 19 ♘xc5 ♘xf3+ 20 ♖xf3 ♕c6
leading to equality; Korzubov-Kap-
engut, Minsk 1985. This variation is
not forced, of course, but the check
itself will be remembered, as we

have already seen it more than once
in this chapter.

10   ♘f3 *(D)*

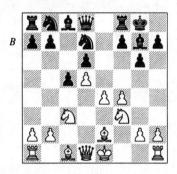

10   ...   ♘a6

Black's attempts to gain equality
after 10...♖e8 have thus far not been
crowned with success, for example
11 0-0 ♘a6 (or 11...♗xc3 12 bxc3
♖xe4 13 ♗d3 ♖e8 14 c4 ♘f8 15
♗b2 with very good compensation;
White has an excellent game after
11...♘f8 12 e5 ♘bd7 13 ♘g5 dxe5
14 f5 ♘f6 15 g4 h6 16 ♘ge4 gxf5 17
gxf5 ♘8h7 18 ♗b5 with enormous
pressure for the pawn; Moskalenko-
Perenyi, Budapest 1988) 12 ♔h1!
♘c7 13 a4 b6 14 f5! ♗a6 (nor does
14...♘e5 bring any relief: 15 ♗g5 f6
16 ♘xe5 ♖xe5 17 ♗f4 ♖e8 18 fxg6
hxg6 19 ♕e1) 15 ♗xa6 ♘xa6 16
♘g5 ♗f6 17 fxg6 hxg6 18 ♕g4 ±
J.Ivanov-Priehoda, Orange 1992,
whilst 10...a6 11 a4 is examined under 9 a4 0-0 10 ♘f3 a6 11 ♗e2.

11   0-0   ♘c7
12   a4

12 ♘d2 deserves attention, for example 12...♖e8 13 ♗f3 ♖b8 14 a4
♗d4+ 15 ♔h1 ♘f6 16 ♖a3! b5 17

axb5 ♘xb5 18 ♘xb5 ♖xb5 19 ♖xa7
♖b4 20 ♖a8 ± Hort-Bellón, Manila
OL 1992.

12   ...   a6

In the game Moskalenko-Mager-
ramov, Rostov 1993, Black could
not equalize after 12...♖e8 13 ♕c2
♘f6 14 ♗d2 ♗g4 15 ♖ae1 ♘a6
(15...a6 16 h3 ♗xf3 17 ♗xf3 b5 18
e5! ±) 16 ♗c4 ♘b4 17 ♕b3 ±.

13   ♗d2

13 ♔h1 ♖b8 14 a5 b5 15 axb6
♘xb6 16 f5 gxf5!? led to an unclear
game in Hollis-Nunn, Oxford 1975,
and Black has no particular difficulties after 13 ♘d2 ♗d4+!? (13...f5?!
14 ♘c4 fxe4 15 ♘xd6 ♗d4+ 16
♔h1 ♘f6 17 ♘xc8 ♖xc8 18 f5! ±
Aleksandrov-Skrobek, Wisla 1992)
14 ♔h1 ♘f6 15 ♗f3 ♖e8.

13	...	♖b8
14	♗e1	b5
15	♗h4	♗f6
16	♗xf6	♘xf6
17	e5	b4
18	exf6	bxc3
19	bxc3	♕xf6
20	♕d2	♖b3
21	♗c4!	

with a small advantage to White;
Moskalenko-Totsky, Moscow 1992.

B3)   9   ♗d3   0-0

9...a6 10 a4 is examined under 9 a4
a6 10 ♗d3.

A reasonable alternative to the
text move would be 9...♕h4+, with
the further possibility of 10 g3 (10
♔f1?! 0-0 11 ♘f3 ♕d8 12 ♔f2 ♕b6
13 ♔g3 f5! 14 exf5 ♘f6 gives Black
the initiative) 10...♕e7 (10...♕d8!?)

11 ♘f3 0-0 12 0-0 ♘b6 *(D)* (White has an easy game after 12...♘f6 13 e5! dxe5 14 fxe5 ♘g4 15 ♗g5 f6 16 ♗c4 ±, or 12...♘a6 13 ♖e1 ♘c7 14 a4 b6 15 ♗f1!? a6 16 e5! ♗b7 17 ♘g5 with a clear advantage; the text move is a good explanation of the idea behind the check – White does not have h3, and it gives Black the chance to exchange his somewhat superfluous bishop).

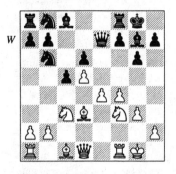

13 ♔g2 (13 ♖e1 ♗g4 14 ♗f1 ♘a6 15 h3 ♗xf3 16 ♕xf3 ♘c7 17 ♗d2 ♕d7 18 a4 ♖ae8 = Kapengut) 13...♗g4 (13...♘a6!? is not bad either, for example 14 ♕e2 ♖e8 15 ♖e1 ♘b4 16 ♗b5 ♗d7 17 ♗xd7 ♕xd7 with a level position; Skembris-Grünfeld, Graz 1981) 14 h3 ♗xf3+ 15 ♕xf3 ♘8d7 (or 15...c4 16 ♗c2 ♘a6 17 a3 ♘c5 18 ♗e3 ♘bd7 19 ♖ad1 ♖ab8 20 ♖fe1 b5 21 e5 b4 with chances for both sides; Lau-Dolmatov) 16 a4 c4 17 ♗c2 ♘c5 18 ♗e3 ♘bd7 19 ♖ad1 a6 = Lukacs-Psakhis, Sarajevo 1981; all the ideas linked with the check on h4 are in need of further investigation.

10 ♘f3 *(D)*

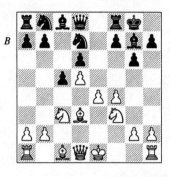

Now we discuss two principal continuations for Black, of roughly equal popularity:

B31) 10...a6
B32) 10...♘a6

Besides these moves, Black may try:

a) 10...b6 11 ♕e2!? (White has the more promising position after 11 a4 ♘a6 12 0-0 ♘c7 ♖e8 15 ♗h4 ± Van Wely-Armas, Sonnevanck 1992, or 11 0-0 ♗a6 12 a4 c4 {12...♗xd3 13 ♕xd3 a6 14 ♔h1 ♖e8 15 ♘d2 ±} 13 ♗c2 ♘c5 14 ♗e3) 11...♖e8 (11...♘f6 12 0-0 ♖e8 13 e5!? ♘bd7 14 ♗c4 dxe5 15 fxe5 ♘g4 16 ♗g5 ± *ECO*) 12 0-0 a6 13 a4 f5 14 ♕c2 fxe4 15 ♘xe4 ♘f6 16 ♘eg5! and by now White's threats are difficult to repulse; Lapenis-Sokolowski, Corr 1980.

b) 10...♘f6!? (for some incomprehensible reason this move is almost never seen in practice) 11 0-0 ♗g4 12 h3 ♗xf3 13 ♕xf3 ♘a6 14 ♖f2!? (or 14 ♗e3 ♘b4 15 ♗b1 ♘d7 16 a3 ♘a6 17 ♗d3 ♖b8 18 ♘b5 ♕b6 19 ♖ab1 ♘c7 = I.Farago-Perenyi, Hungary 1974) 14...♖b8 15

♖e2 ♘c7 16 a4 a6 17 ♗e3 b5 18 axb5 axb5 19 e5 ♘fe8 with an unclear game, Kapengut.

B31) 10 ...   a6
11 a4   ♘f6 *(D)*

White has a clear advantage after 11...♕c7 12 0-0, for example 12...c4 (12...♖e8!?) 13 ♗c2 ♘c5 14 ♗e3 (or 14 h3 ♘bd7 15 ♗e3 ♖b8 16 ♗d4 b5 17 axb5 axb5 18 ♗xg7 ♔xg7 19 ♕d4+ f6 20 ♘d1 ♖e8 21 ♘f2 with a slight plus for White; Ligterink-Lobron, Amsterdam 1983) 14...♗g4 15 ♗d4 (it's not worth losing time with h3, e.g. 15 h3 ♗xf3 16 ♖xf3 ♘bd7 17 a5 ♖fe8 = Furman-Dorfman, Minsk 1976) 15...♗xf3 16 ♖xf3 ♘bd7 (16...♗xd4+ 17 ♕xd4 ♕b6 18 a5! ♕xb2 19 ♖a2 ♕b4 20 e5 ± Szabo-Robatsch, Maribor 1978) 17 ♗xg7 ♔xg7 18 ♕d4+ ♔g8 19 ♕xc4 ♕b6 20 ♖f2, Basin-Kapengut, Minsk 1985. Now 20...♕xb2 is bad because of 21 ♖b1 ♕a3 22 ♖f3 and the queen is in great danger.

Black also has something difficult to think about after 11...♖e8 12 0-0 ♕c7 13 ♕b3!?, for example 13...b6 14 ♗c4 ♗xc3 15 ♕xc3 ♖xe4 16 ♘g5 ♖e7 17 b3! ± Yuneev-Bakalarz, Miedzybrodzie 1991.

12 h3!?

This is probably stronger than the more popular alternative 12 0-0 ♗g4 13 h3 ♗xf3 14 ♕xf3 ♘bd7:

a) Black has no hint of a problem after 15 a5 b5 16 axb6 ♕xb6 17 ♔h1 ♘e8 =.

b) 15 ♔h1 ♕c7 16 ♗e3 ♖ab8 17 a5 b5 18 axb6 ♖xb6 19 ♖xa6 ♖xa6

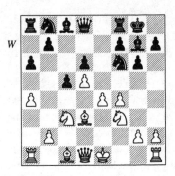

20 ♗xa6 ♖b8 21 ♖f2 ♕a5 22 ♗d3 ♘h5!? gives Black excellent compensation for the pawn; Piskov-Nedev, Star Dojran 1991.

c) 15 ♗e3 is not dangerous either due to 15...♖c8!? (instead 15...♕c7 16 ♗c4 ♘b6 17 b3 ♘fd7 18 ♗f2 ± favours White, as does 15...♖e8 16 ♖ae1 ♖c8 17 ♖e2 c4 18 ♗c2 b5 19 axb5 axb5 20 ♘xb5 ♘c5 21 ♘a7! ♘fxe4 22 ♖xc8 ♕xc8 23 ♗xc5 ♘xc5 24 f5 ± Lapienis-Kasparov, Baku 1978) 16 ♗c4 (16 ♖ae1 c4 17 ♗c2 ♘e8 18 ♕f2 ♕a5 =) 16...♘b6 17 b3 ♘fd7 18 ♗f2 (18 ♗d2!?) 18...g5!? 19 g3 ♕f6 with excellent counterplay – Kapengut.

c) 15 ♗d2!? and now Black should advance his c-pawn, since other attempts to get a good game are not crowned with success:

c1) 15...♘e8 16 a5 ♘c7 17 ♖a2 ♖b8 18 ♔h2 ♖e8 19 ♖b1 b5 20 axb6 ♖xb6 21 b3 ♕b8 22 ♗c4 ± Djurić-Tringov, Sombor 1980.

c2) 15...♖e8 16 ♗c4! ♘b6 (or 16...♘h5 17 g4 ♗d4+ 18 ♔g2 ♘hf6 19 ♖ae1 ♘b6 20 b3 again with advantage to White; Leverett-Wojtkiewicz, Chicago 1989) 17 b3 ♘xc4

18 bxc4 ♘d7 19 ♖ae1 ♕a5 20 ♕d3 with an edge for White.

c3) 15...♕c7 16 ♗c4 ♘b6 17 b3 ♘fd7 18 ♖ae1 ♖ae8 19 ♕d3 ♕d8 20 e5! (20 ♔h1 is worse: 20...♕h4 21 ♖e2 g5! 22 g3 ♕h5 23 ♖g2 ♘xc4 24 bxc4 f5! and Black took the game into his own hands; Farago-Suetin, Dubna 1979) 20...dxe5 21 f5 e4 22 ♘xe4 ♗d4+ (at least freeing the bishop; 22...♘e5 23 ♕g3 ♘xd5 24 ♗xd5 ♕xd5 25 f6 ♗h8 26 ♗h6 ± is unsatisfactory – Pinter) 23 ♔h1 ♘e5 24 ♕c2 ♘bxc4 25 bxc4 ± Pinter-Djurić, Bajmok 1980.

c4) 15...c4!? 16 ♗xc4 ♕b6+ 17 ♖f2 ♕xb2 18 ♖b1 ♕a3 19 ♖xb7 ♘c5 20 ♖b1 ♘fd7 with compensation for the pawn; Lukacs-Szalanczy, Hungary 1982.

12 ...   ♖e8

White's position is better after 12...c4 13 ♗c2 ♘bd7 14 ♗e3, and especially after the insignificant 12...b6?! 13 0-0 ♗b7 14 ♕b3 ♖a7 15 ♗c4 ♘fd7 16 ♗d2 ± Bareev-Ristić, Vrnjačka Banja 1987.

13 0-0   ♘bd7

Or 13...c4 14 ♗c2 ♘bd7 15 ♗e3 ♕c7 16 ♗d4 ♘c5 17 ♖e1 with a slight advantage for White; Shereshevsky-Sarbai, Minsk 1980.

14 ♖e1   ♕c7
15 ♗e3

15 ♘d2!? also deserves attention, for example 15...c4 16 ♘xc4 ♘c5 17 ♗e3 ♘fd7 18 ♖c1 ± F.Portisch-Van der Sterren, Wijk aan Zee 1985, as does 15 ♗c2!?.

15 ...   ♖b8
16 ♖c1

More exact than 16 ♗f2 c4 17 ♗c2 ♘c5 18 e5 ♘fd7 19 ♔h1 b5 ∞ Farago-Grünfeld, Toronto 1984.

16	**...**	**c4**
17	**♗b1**	**b5**
18	**axb5**	**axb5**
19	**♘d4**	**b4**
20	**♘cb5**	**♕c5**
21	**♗f2**	**♗a6**
22	**b3**	**c3**
23	**♗d3**	

and here White's advantage is not in doubt; Farago-Grünfeld, Philadelphia 1986.

B32) 10 ...   ♘a6

This move is linked with organizing counterplay on the queenside.

11 0-0 *(D)*

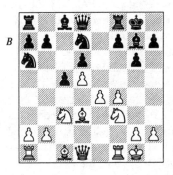

We shall now examine two moves in detail:

B321) 11...♘c7
B322) 11...♖b8

This is how other moves work out:

a) 11...♘b4 and now:

a1) If 12 ♗b1 then after 12...♖b8 (the less exact 12...♖e8 13 ♘d2 ♘f6

14 h3 ♖b8 15 ♕f3 b5 16 a3 ♘a6 17 a4 bxa4 18 ♘c4 ♘b4 19 ♖xa4 ♗a6 20 ♖xa6! ♘xa6 21 e5 ± Boleslavsky, gives White an advantage) 13 a3 ♘a6 Black has no problems after either 14 ♗d3 b5! 15 ♗xb5 (15 ♘xb5 c4!) 15...♗xc3 16 ♗xd7 ♗xb2, or 14 a4 ♘b4 15 ♔h1 a6 16 a5 b5 17 axb6, Spassky-Rashkovsky, Sochi 1973, and now 17...♘xb6 = would have been sufficient.

a2) 12 ♗e2!? and now:

a21) 12...♖e8 13 ♔h1 (13 a3 ♘a6 14 ♘d2 ♘c7 15 ♗f3 ♖b8 16 ♘c4 ±) 13...b6 14 ♘d2 ♘f6 15 a3 ♘a6 16 ♗f3 ♘c7 17 e5 dxe5 18 d6! (18 fxe5 ♘fxd5 19 ♘xd5 ♘xd5 20 ♘c4 ♗e6 21 ♘d6 ♗xe5! 22 ♘xe8 ♕h4 ∓ *ECO*) 18...♕xd6 19 fxe5 ♕xe5 20 ♗xa8 ♘xa8 21 ♘f3 ♕b8 22 ♗g5 ♘g4 23 ♕d2 and White has a small advantage.

a22) 12...b6!? 13 a3 (13 ♘d2 ♖e8 14 ♘c4 ♗d4+ 15 ♔h1 ♘f6 ∞) 13...♘a6 14 ♘d2 ♗d4+ 15 ♔h1 ♘c7 16 ♘c4 ♘f6 17 e5! dxe5 18 d6 ♘e6 19 fxe5 ♘d7 with complications. This variation is not forced, and both Black and White have good chances to roll up the sides.

b) 11...♘b6 is met by 12 h3!?.

c) 11...♖e8 and here:

c1) 12 ♘d2?! is unsuccessful as the kingside remains without the surveillance of its main defender: 12...♘f6 13 ♕f3 (or 13 h3 ♖b8 14 a4 ♘b4 15 ♘c4 b6 ∓) 13...♘g4 14 ♘e2 (14 e5?! dxe5 15 h3 e4 16 ♘dxe4 ♗d4+ 17 ♔h1 f5! 18 hxg4 fxe4 19 ♘xe4 ♕h4+ 20 ♕h3 ♕xg4 and the white pieces are uncomfortably

distributed around the periphery) 14...f5 15 h3 ♘h6 16 ♘g3 ♘c7 with an edge for Black; Wentilbury-Shamkovich, USA 1978.

c2) Nor does Black have any problems after 12 ♔h1 ♘b4 13 ♗e2 b6 14 ♘d2 ♘f6 15 a3 ♘a6 16 ♗f3 ♘c7 =.

c3) 12 ♖e1 ♘c7 (12...♖b8 13 ♔h1 ♘c7 14 e5 dxe5 15 fxe5 ♘xe5 16 ♗g5 ♕d7 17 ♗f4 with compensation, Kapengut) 13 a4 a6 14 e5!? dxe5 15 d6 ♘e6 16 ♘d5! with a powerful initiative.

B321) 11 ...   ♘c7 (D)

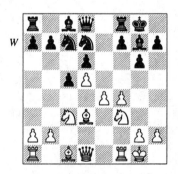

12 a4

12 ♔h1!? a6 13 a4 ♖b8 is examined under 11...♖b8.

Interesting complications begin after 12 ♘d2 ♘f6 (White can also preserve the better chances after 12...♖b8 13 a4 ♘f6 14 ♘c4 b6 15 ♗d2 a6 16 ♗e1 ♗g4 17 ♕c2 b5 18 axb5 axb5 19 ♘a5 c4 20 ♗e2 ± Farago-Honfi, Kecskemet 1979 as well as after 12...b5 13 ♘xb5 ♘xb5 14 ♗xb5 ♖b8 15 ♗d3! ♗xb2 16 ♗xb2 ♖xb2 17 ♘c4 ±) 13 h3 ♘h5!?

(13...♖e8 also deserves attention, for example 14 a4 {but not 14 ♕f3? ♘fxd5! 15 ♘xd5 ♘xd5 16 ♗b5 ♘e3 17 ♗xe8 ♕xe8 18 ♖f2 ♘c2 19 ♖b1 ♗d4 20 ♘c4 ♗xf2+ 21 ♔xf2 d5! with advantage} 14...♘h5!? 15 ♘c4 ♘g3 16 ♖e1 ♗d4+ 17 ♔h2 ♗f2 18 e5! with sufficient compensation, Kapengut) 14 ♕f3 b5!? 15 ♘xb5 ♘xb5 16 ♗xb5 ♗d4+ 17 ♔h1 ♕h4 18 ♔h2 ♖b8 (18...♘xf4?! 19 ♘c4! ±) 19 a4 a6 20 ♗c6 ♖b4! with counter-chances.

12 ... a6 *(D)*

White's chances are better after other moves:

a) 12...♘f6 13 ♗c4! ♗g4 14 h3 ♗xf3 15 ♕xf3 ♘d7 16 ♖a2 a6 17 ♕d3 ♖b8 18 b3 ♕f6 19 e5! dxe5 20 ♘e4 ♕d8 21 d6 ± Timman-Masić, Sombor 1979.

b) 12...♘a6?! 13 ♗e3 ♘b4 14 ♗e2 ♖e8 15 ♗f2 a6 16 ♔h1 ♕c7 17 ♘d2 ♘f6 18 ♗g3 ± Portisch-G.Garcia, Madrid 1973.

c) 12...♖e8 13 ♖e1 (just not 13 ♘d2?! because of 13...♗d4+ 14 ♔h1 ♘f6 15 ♕f3 ♘fxd5!) 13...♘a6 14 h3 ♘b4 15 ♗c4 a6 16 ♗e3 ♖b8 17 ♗f2 b5 18 axb5 axb5 19 ♘xb5 ♘b6 20 ♗f1 ♗xb2 21 ♗h4! ♕d7 22 ♖a7 ♖b7 23 ♖a5 ♗g7 24 e5 ± T.Petrosian-Rodriguez, Las Palmas 1974.

d) The evaluation of the position is not changed by 12...♖b8 13 ♕e1 b6 14 e5! ♖e8 15 ♕g3 ♗a6 16 ♗b5! dxe5 17 fxe5 ♗xb5 18 axb5 ♘xe5 19 ♖xa7 ♘xd5 20 ♗h6! with advantage for White; Lacha-Jerman, Corr 1984.

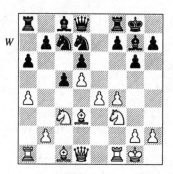

13 ♕e1

13 ♗e3 ♖b8 14 ♗f2 b5 15 ♗h4 ♗f6 leads to equality.

13 ♔h1!? ♖b8 transposes to the line with 11...♖b8.

13 f5!? deserves attention, for example 13...♘e5 14 ♘xe5 ♗xe5 15 ♖f3 and White's initiative can become quite unpleasant for his opponent.

13 ♘d2 often occurs in practice, with the further possibilities:

a) White has an obvious advantage in the event of 13...♖b8 14 ♘c4 ♘f6 15 a5 ♘b5 16 f5! ♗d7 (or 16...♘e8 17 ♘a4 ♘d4 18 ♘ab6 ♘c7 19 ♗f4 ♘cb5 20 ♕g4 ♖e8 21 ♕g3! ± Farago-Planinc, Polanica Zdroj 1979) 17 ♗f4 ♘h5 18 ♗d2 ♖e8 19 ♕g4 ♘f6 20 ♕h4 ± Farago-Rajna, Hungary 1981.

b) 13...♘f6! and now:

b1) After 14 ♘c4 Black must not play 14...♘g4?! because of 15 ♕e1!, but 14...♗g4!? 15 ♕e1 b5 16 axb5 axb5 17 ♖xa8 ♕xa8 18 ♘xd6 c4 19 ♗b1 ♕a6 gives an unclear game.

b2) Black does not experience any particular problems after 14 ♕e1, for example 14...♖b8 15 a5

♗d7 16 ♘c4 ♗b5 17 ♕g3 ♖e8 18 ♖e1 ♘h5 19 ♕f3 ♗xc4 20 ♗xc4 b5 21 axb6 ♖xb6 = Cherepkov-Kapengut, USSR 1980.

b3) 14 h3 ♖b8 (14...♗d7 is not very good: 15 ♘c4 b5 16 ♘xd6 ♘cxd5 17 e5! ♘xc3 18 bxc3 ♘d5 19 ♗xg6 hxg6 20 ♕xd5 with a big advantage for White; Lukacs-Bönsch, Berlin 1982) 15 a5 ♖e8! (15...♗d7 16 ♘c4 {16 e5 ♘fxd5 17 exd6 ♘e3 18 dxc7 ♕xc7 =} 16...♗b5 17 ♕f3 ♗xc4 18 ♗xc4 ♘d7 19 ♗d2 b5 20 axb6 ♘xb6 21 ♗xa6 ♘xa6 22 ♖xa6 ♘c4 23 ♗c1 ♘xb2 = Pieters-Andrijević, Budapest 1988) 16 ♘c4 ♘b5 17 ♖e1 ♘h5 and Black's position is already more promising; Lukacs-Maus, Budapest 1990.

13   ...   ♖b8
14   a5

For many years it was thought that White's threats were irresistible after 14 e5, but recently this point of view has been called into question: 14...♘b6 15 f5!? dxe5 16 fxg6 fxg6! (16...hxg6 17 ♘e4!? gives White the initiative) 17 ♗g5 ♕d6 18 ♕h4 ♘bxd5! (an important improvement compared with 18...♘cxd5? 19 ♖ad1 c4 20 ♘xd5 cxd3 21 ♘e7+ ♚h8 22 ♘xe5!! Gulko-Savon, Lvov 1978) 19 ♗c4 (19 ♖ad1!? ♗e6 20 ♘e4!? deserves attention) 19...♗e6 20 ♖ad1 ♕c6 21 ♗h6 ♘xc3! 22 bxc3 ♗xh6 23 ♘xe5 (23 ♗xe6+ ♘xe6 24 ♕xh6 ♖f5 ∓) 23...♗e3+ 24 ♚h1 ♖xf1+ 25 ♖xf1 ♕d6! and in Seidler-Priepke, Corr 1989, Black repulsed the attack and even stood better.

14   ...   b5
15   axb6   ♘xb6

15...♖xb6 16 e5 ♖e8 17 ♕g3 dxe5 18 f5! ±.

16   f5   ♘d7
17   ♗g5   f6
18   ♗c1   g5
19   ♘d2

with a small advantage to White; Siniavsky-Kapengut, Rostov 1976.

B322)   11   ...   ♖b8!? (D)
A sneaky move, presenting White with the greatest number of problems.

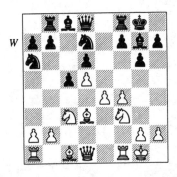

12   ♚h1

Without a doubt the most useful move. Black has no problems after 12 ♖e1 b5! and 13 ♗xb5 is impossible because of 13...♗xc3.

Black equalizes in the event of 12 ♘b5 ♕b6 13 ♚h1 (13 ♗c4 ♘c7 14 a4 ♘xb5 15 axb5 a6 16 ♗d2 ♕c7 =) 13...♘f6 14 a4 ♘b4 15 a5 ♕d8 16 ♘xa7 ♗d7 =.

12 ♗e3 ♘f6 13 ♚h1 ♘c7 14 ♗f2 (14 a4!?) 14...b5 15 ♗h4 b4 16 ♘b1 ♕d7 17 ♘bd2 ♘h5! Rodriguez-Bouaziz, Riga IZ 1979, is fine for Black.

After 12 ♘d2 Black must chose between 12...b5!? 13 a4 (13 ♘xb5 c4! 14 ♘xc4!? ♖xb5 15 ♘xd6 ♖b4 16 a3 ♖d4! 17 ♘b5 ♖xe4 18 ♗xe4 ♕b6+ 19 ♔h1 ♕xb5 20 ♗d3 ♕b6 with a small advantage) 13...bxa4 14 ♖xa4 ♘b4 15 ♘c4 ♗a6 =, and 12...♘f6!? 13 h3 (or 13 ♕f3 ♘g4 14 h3 ♗d4+ 15 ♔h1 ♘b4 16 ♗b1 ♕h4 with an attack) 13...♘h5!? 14 a4 ♘b4 15 ♘c4 f5 =.

12	...	♘c7
13	a4	a6

13...♘f6 gives White additional possibilities: 14 ♗c4! a6 15 e5 ♘fe8 16 ♕e2 with an advantage.

14 a5 (D)

If 14 ♕e2 then 14...♘f6!? 15 a5 b5 16 axb6 ♖xb6 17 ♘d2 ♖e8 18 ♘c4 ♖b4 19 ♗d2 ♘b5 gives Black a comfortable enough position; Pinter-Danner, Lucerne OL 1982.

Black can also look to the future with optimism after 14 f5 b5 15 axb5 (15 ♗g5 ♘f6 16 e5 dxe5 17 ♘xe5 ♗b7 18 ♘c6 ♖xc6 19 dxc6 c4 20 ♗c2 ♕xd1 21 ♖axd1 ♖b6 = Sotnikov-Totsky, Orel 1992) 15...♘xb5 16 ♗g5 and now:

a) 16...f6?! is relatively weak: 17 ♗f4 ♘e5 18 h3 ♖f7 19 g4 ± Spassky-Savon, Moscow 1971.

b) 16...♕c7 deserves attention, for example 17 ♗xb5 axb5 18 e5! f6! (18...dxe5 19 d6 ♕b7 20 ♘d5 with an attack; Reviakin-Tripolsky, Corr 1988) 19 exd6!? (the game is unclear after 19 exf6 ♘xf6 20 fxg6 hxg6 21 ♘h4 ♘h7! 22 ♕d2 ♗f5 Schrancz-Mi.Tseitlin, Corr 1985) 19...♕xd6 20 ♗h4 gxf5 21 ♗g3 ∞.

c) 16...♗f6! 17 ♘xb5 (17 ♗f4!?) 17...axb5 18 ♕d2 c4 19 ♗c2 b4, Zaichik-Taborov, Tallinn 1976.

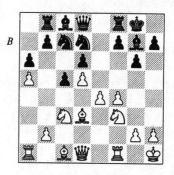

14 ... b5

In Hartston-Nunn, London 1977, 14...♖e8 15 ♗e3 b5 16 axb6 ♖xb6 17 ♖a2 ♘f6 18 ♗f2 ♘b5 19 ♗h4 ♕d7 was roughly equal.

15	axb6	♘xb6
16	f5	gxf5!
17	exf5	♘bxd5
18	♘xd5	♘xd5
19	♗xa6	♘b4
20	♗xc8	♖xc8

with equality; Ehlvest-Dolmatov, Moscow 1981.

B4)   9 a4 (D)

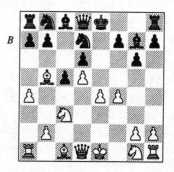

Now we shall look at three continuations in detail:

B41) 9...♕h4+
B42) 9...a6
B43) 9...0-0

Firstly we should note that attempts to manoeuvre the queen's knight before castling run into problems: 9...♘a6 10 ♘f3 ♘c7 (on b4 the knight proves to be isolated from the main battle, for example 10...♘b4 11 0-0 a6?! 12 ♗xd7+! ♗xd7 13 f5! 0-0 14 ♗g5 f6 15 ♗f4 gxf5 16 ♗xd6 ± Kasparov-Nunn, Lucerne OL 1982) 11 0-0!? ♘xb5 (White has a dangerous initiative after 11...a6 12 ♗xd7+ ♗xd7 13 f5 0-0 14 ♗g5 ♗f6 15 ♕d2 ♘e8 16 ♕f4 ♕e7 17 ♕h4 ± Baumbach-Danner, Corr 1985) 12 ♘xb5!? ♘b8 (12...♘b6 13 a5) 13 f5 a6 14 ♘c3 0-0 15 ♗g5 ♕b6 16 ♕d2 with an obvious advantage; Trostianetsky-Sliapkin, Corr 1988.

B41)   9   ...   ♕h4+
10 g3

Black's problems are simpler after 10 ♔f1, for example 10...a6!? 11 ♘f3 ♕d8 12 ♗d3 (or 12 ♗c4 ♘b6 13 ♗e2 ♗g4 14 ♘d2 ♗xe2+ 15 ♕xe2 ♘8d7 16 a5 ♘c8 17 ♘c4 0-0 =) 12...♘f6 13 h3 ♘h5 14 ♔f2 c4! 15 ♗xc4 ♕b6+.

10   ...   ♕e7
10...♕d8 does not equalise: 11 ♘f3 0-0 12 0-0 a6 13 ♗c4! ♘b6 14 ♗e2 ♗g4 15 ♘g5! ♗xe2 16 ♕xe2 ♕e7 17 a5 ♘c8 18 ♗d2 ♘d7 19 ♖ae1 Olafsson-Psakhis, Moscow 1989.

11 ♘f3
11 ♕f3 is not so clear: 11...♘a6 12 ♘ge2 ♘b4 13 0-0 0-0 14 g4 ♘c2 15 ♖a2 ♘d4 16 ♕g2 ♘xb5 17 axb5 ♖e8 with mutual chances; Hort-Hulak, Indonesia 1982.

11   ...   0-0
11...♗xc3+ 12 bxc3 ♕xe4+ 13 ♔f2 0-0 14 ♖e1 ♕f5 15 ♗f1!? ♘f6 16 c4 gives White more than enough compensation.

12 0-0   ♘a6 (D)
Or 12...a6 13 ♗d3 ♖e8 14 ♔g2 ♘f8 15 h3 ♘bd7 16 ♗d2 ♖b8 17 ♖b1 ♕d8 18 ♖e1 with a small advantage for White; Sergienko-Parkanyi, Nagykanizsa 1993.

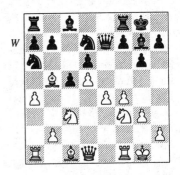

13 ♖e1!?
The game is unclear after 13 e5 dxe5 (13...♘b4?! is weaker: 14 ♘e4 ♘b6 { 14...dxe5 15 d6 ♕e6 16 ♘eg5 ♕f5 17 ♘xe5 ± } 15 ♘xd6 ♘6xd5 16 ♗d2 ♗g4 17 ♕b3 ♖ad8 18 ♗c4 with a large White advantage; Bagirov-Malaniuk, Baku 1983) 14 d6 ♕d8 15 ♘d5 e4 16 ♘g5 (Black has no reason to fear the continuation 16 ♘e5 ♔h8 17 ♘e7 ♘xe5 18 fxe5 ♗xe5 19 ♗f4 ♗g7 Kouatly-Hulak,

Toluca IZ 1982) 16...♗d4+ 17 ♗e3 ♗xe3+ 18 ♘xe3 ♘f6 19 f5.

13 ...   ♘b4

14 e5!?

14 ♕b3 is less dangerous in view of 14...a6 15 ♗f1 b6 16 h3 ♗b7 17 ♗d2 (17 ♗g2? ♘d3 18 ♖e2 b5! 19 axb5 c4 20 ♕c2 axb5 gives Black the initiative; Ree-Lobron, Paris 1983) 17...♖ae8 18 ♖ad1 ♕d8 ∞ Lobron.

White also preserves a small advantage after 14 ♗f1 ♖e8 (or 14...b6 15 ♗c4 ♗b7 16 ♕b3 ♖ae8 17 ♗d2 a6 18 ♖e2 ±) 15 ♘b5!? ♘f6 16 e5 ♘fxd5 17 ♘xd6 ♖d8 18 ♕b3 ♗e6 19 ♗c4 Malaniuk-Yudasin, Moscow 1988.

14 ...   a6

15 ♗f1   dxe5

16 d6   ♕e8

17 fxe5

and Black faces a difficult defence, Tal-Velimirović, Moscow IZ 1982.

B42) 9 ...   a6 *(D)*

Black hasn't dismissed all thoughts of the check, but first he wants to force White to fix a position for the bishop.

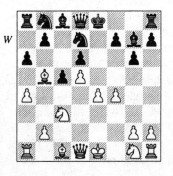

10 ♗e2!?

Black equalizes in the event of 10 ♗d3 ♕h4+!? (White has an advantage after 10...♕b6 11 ♘f3 0-0 12 ♘d2!? ♘f6 13 ♘c4 ♕c7 14 0-0 ♘bd7 15 ♗d2 ♘b6 16 b3! ♘g4 17 ♕f3 f5 18 exf5 gxf5 19 h3 ♘f6 20 ♖ae1 ± Anikaev-Sideif Zade, Dnepropetrovsk 1980) 11 g3 ♕d8 12 ♘f3 0-0 13 0-0 ♘f6 14 ♔g2 (or 14 ♕b3 ♗h3 15 ♖e1 ♘g4 16 ♕xb7 ♘d7 17 a5 ♕e7 and after 18 ♕b3! the game is unclear, but 18 ♗xa6? ♖ab8 19 ♕c7 ♘de5!! loses quickly; Garcia Martinez-Pigusov, Moscow 1987) 14...♗g4 15 h3 ♗xf3+ 16 ♕xf3 ♘bd7 17 ♗e3 ♕a5 18 ♖ae1 ♖ac8 19 ♗g1 ♘e8 20 ♗c2 ♖b8 = Schwarz-Pigusov, Biel 1989.

10 ...   ♕h4+

10...0-0 11 ♘f3 is examined under 9...0-0 10 ♘f3 a6 11 ♗e2.

11 g3   ♕d8

It is difficult for Black to work things out after 11...♕e7 12 ♘f3 0-0 (or 12...♗xc3+?! 13 bxc3 ♕xe4 14 0-0 ♘f6 15 c4 ♗f5 16 ♘h4 ± Kouatly-Tsuboi, Dubai OL 1986) 13 0-0 ♘f6 14 e5 ♘e8 15 e6! fxe6 16 ♗c4 ♘c7 17 ♖e1 b5 18 axb5 ♗xc3 19 bxc3 axb5 20 ♖xa8 ♘xa8 21 ♗xb5 and it is not easy to defend Black's position; Petursson-Fries Nielsen, Næstved 1988.

12 ♘f3   0-0

13 0-0   ♖e8

14 ♔g2

14 ♕c2 ♘f6 15 ♔g2 ♗g4 16 h3 ♗xf3+ 17 ♗xf3 ♘bd7 18 ♖e1 ♖b8 19 a5 h6 20 ♖e2 ♕c7 21 ♗d2 ± Cebalo-Lobron, Reggio Emilia 1985.

14 ♖e1 doesn't look bad either, after which Black should continue 14...♘f8 15 ♗f1 ♗g4 16 h3 ♗xf3 17 ♕xf3 ♘bd7 18 ♗d2 ♖c8 19 b3 ±, since accepting the pawn sacrifice by 14...♗xc3 15 bxc3 ♖xe4 16 c4 ♘f6 17 ♗b2 ♗g4 18 h3! ♗xf3 19 ♗xf3 ♖xe1+ 20 ♕xe1 gives White more than enough compensation; Arkhipov-Sax, Hungary 1984.

Black has a reasonable game in the event of 14 ♘d2 ♗d4+!? 15 ♔g2 ♘f6 16 ♗f3 ♕d7 de Firmian-Grünfeld, Biel 1986.

14 ...   ♘f8
15 e5!

Black's life is not as hard after 15 h3 ♘bd7 16 ♕c2 ♖b8 17 ♗d2 ♘f6 Flear-Kovačević, Paris 1992.

After the text move White also has a clear advantage in the event of 15...♗g4 16 ♘g5! ♗xe2 17 ♕xe2 f6 18 ♘ge4 dxe5 19 f5 ± Savchenko-Pigusov, Ålborg 1992, as well as after 15...dxe5 16 fxe5 ♘bd7 17 ♗g5 ♕b6 18 a5 ♕xb2 19 ♘a4 ±.

B43)   9 ...   0-0 *(D)*

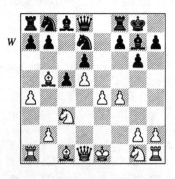

10   ♘f3

10 ♘ge2 is not worth serious attention, as Black easily achieved an advantage after 10...♕h4+ 11 ♔f1 ♕e7 12 ♔f2 ♘f6 13 ♗d3 ♘g4+ 14 ♔f3 ♕h4 in the game Petrović-Minasian, Novi Sad 1988.

10 ...   ♘a6

In Vaiser-Schalkx, Ostend 1992, White easily gained an advantage after 10...♘f6 11 0-0 ♗g4 12 ♖e1!? (12 ♗d2 ♘bd7 13 h3 ♗xf3 14 ♕xf3 a6 15 ♗c4 ♘e8 16 ♖ae1 ♘c7 17 ♕d3 ± Poleksić-Martić, Corr 1989, doesn't look bad either) 12...♘bd7 13 e5 dxe5 14 fxe5 ♘h5 15 ♗xd7! ♕xd7 16 h3 ♗xf3 17 ♕xf3.

Nor can Black manage to equalize after 10...a6 11 ♗e2 (for 11 ♗d3 see 9 ♗d3) and now:

a) Life is not easy for Black after 11...♘f6 12 0-0, for example 12...♖e8 (12...♕c7?! 13 e5 ♘e8 14 e6! fxe6 15 ♗c4 ♕e7 16 dxe6 +− Kasparov-Kuijpers, Dortmund jr Wch 1980; 12...♗g4 13 e5! ♗xf3 14 ♗xf3 dxe5 15 fxe5 ♘fd7 16 e6 ♘e5 17 ♗g4 with an obvious advantage; Semkov-Peev, Sofia 1981) 13 e5!? dxe5 14 fxe5 ♘g4 15 ♗g5 f6 16 exf6 ♗xf6 17 ♗xf6 ♕xf6 18 d6! and White's threats are difficult to repulse; Mestel-Littlewood, Hastings 1982.

b) 11...♕c7 leads to an advantage for White after 12 0-0 c4 13 ♘d2 b5 14 axb5 ♘b6 15 ♔h1 ♘bd7 16 e5! dxe5 17 ♘de4 ♗b7 18 bxa6 ♖xa6 19 ♖xa6 ♗xa6 20 f5 ± Li Zunian-Sax, Biel IZ 1985.

c) 11...♖e8 12 0-0 ♘f8 (Black cannot settle after 12...b6?! 13 h3

♗b7 14 ♗c4 h6 15 ♖e1 ♘f8 16 e5 ±
Littlewood-Vela, Barnsdale 1989, or
12...♗xc3 13 bxc3 ♖xe4 14 ♗d3
♖e8 15 c4 with a strong attack for
the pawn) 13 e5!? (White also preserves a small advantage after 13 h3
♘bd7 14 ♖e1 ♕c7 15 ♗c4 ♘b6 16
♗f1 c4 17 ♗e3 Hort-Tolnai, Dortmund 1989, but the text move is significantly more active) 13...♘bd7 14
♘g5 dxe5 15 f5 ♘f6 16 g4!? b5 17
axb5 c4 (17...e4 18 d6 h6 19 ♘xf7
♔xf7 20 ♗c4+) 18 ♗e3 h6 19 ♘ge4
♘xe4 20 ♘xe4 ♗b7 21 ♗xc4 axb5
22 ♖xa8 ♕xa8 23 ♗b3 with a significant advantage; Petursson-Per-
enyi, Saint John 1988.

11 0-0 *(D)*

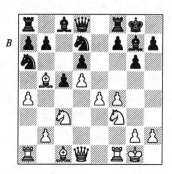

11 ... ♘b4

Where to place the knight is an
eternal problem. Black quite often
plays 11...♘c7:

a) Perhaps the most dangerous
move for Black is 12 ♗d3!?, as examined under 9 ♗d3.

b) 12 ♖e1 ♘xb5 13 axb5 ♖e8 14
h3 a6 15 ♗d2 ♘b6 quickly works in
Black's favour.

c) 12 ♗e2 is not dangerous, for

example 12...a6 13 ♘d2 f5 14 ♘c4
♗d4+ 15 ♔h1 fxe4 16 ♘xe4 ♘f6 17
♘cxd6 ♘xe4 18 ♘xe4 ♘xd5 =
Sjödahl-Atkinson, Arnhem 1989.

d) 12 ♗c4 is possible:

d1) It is difficult for Black to
achieve a good game after 12...a6
13 ♖e1 (13 ♕e1 ♖b8 14 a5 b5 15
axb6 ♘xb6 16 ♗a2 ♗g4 17 ♕g3
♗xf3 18 ♖xf3 ♘b5 = Hölzl-Nunn,
Baden 1980) 13...♖e8 (13...♖b8 14
e5 b5 15 e6!, and 13...b5 14 axb5
♘b6 15 ♗f1 axb5 16 ♖xa8 ♘bxa8
17 ♘xb5 ♘xb5 18 ♗xb5 ♕b6 19
♗c6 also favours White; Skembris-
Bellón, Genoa 1989) 14 e5! dxe5 15
d6 ♘e6 16 fxe5 ♘d4 17 ♗g5! ±
Flear-Qei, Mondorf 1991.

d2) 12...♖e8 13 ♖e1 and now
13...♘b6 is quite possible, for example 14 ♗f1 ♗g4 15 ♗d2 (15 h3?!
♗xf3 16 ♕xf3 ♘bxd5!) 15...♗d4+
16 ♔h1 ♗f2 17 ♖e2 ♗xf3 18 gxf3
♕h4, or 14 ♗b3 ♗g4 15 ♗d2 c4 16
♗a2 a5!? = Malich-Bönsch, Berlin
1979.

d3) 12...♘b6!? 13 ♗a2 (13 ♗b3
changes nothing in principle, but 13
♗e2 ♗g4 14 a5 ♘c8 15 ♘d2 ♗xe2
16 ♕xe2 a6 leads to an equal game)
13...♗g4 14 a5 (14 h3 ♗xf3 15
♕xf3 a6!?) 14...♘d7 15 ♗c4 ♖b8 16
♕d3 ♗xf3 17 ♖xf3 a6! = Kaminik-
Urban, Katowice 1992.

12 ♖e1!

Without any doubt the best move.
White simultaneously frees the f1
square for his bishop and prepares
a pawn breakthrough in the centre.
The latter point also applies to other
moves, but they don't create such big

problems for Black, for example:

a) 12 h3 a6 13 ♗e2 ♖e8 14 ♖e1 f5! 15 exf5 gxf5 16 ♗c4 Hort-Panno, Madrid 1973, and Black could have played 16...♖xe1+ 17 ♘xe1 ♗d4+ 18 ♔h1 ♕f6 19 ♗d2 ♘b6 ∓.

b) 12 f5, which is almost never seen in practice, deserves attention.

c) 12 ♔h1 a6 13 ♗xd7 ♗xd7 14 f5 c4! 15 ♗g5 ♗f6 16 ♕d2 ♘d3 = Basin-Yudasin, Simferopol 1988.

d) 12 ♗e3 a6 (stronger than 12...b6 13 ♗f2!? ♗a6 14 ♗h4 ♗f6 15 ♗xf6 ♕xf6 16 ♗xa6 ♘xa6 17 e5 ±, or 12...♘f6 13 h3 a6 14 ♗c4 ♘xe4 15 ♘xe4 ♖e8 16 ♘e5! b6 17 ♘g5 dxe5 18 fxe5 with a large advantage; Soos-Povah, Birmingham 1977) 13 ♗c4 (13 ♗e2 ♘f6 14 h3 ♖e8 15 e5 dxe5 16 ♗xc5 ♘fxd5! should not frighten Black) 13...♘b6 14 ♗e2 ♗g4 15 a5 ♘d7 16 h3 ♗xf3 17 ♗xf3 ♖e8 with equality.

e) 12 ♗d2 a6 13 ♗e2 (or 13 ♗c4 ♘b6 14 ♗e2 ♗g4!? =) 13...♖e8 14 ♕b3 (after 14 ♗e1!? it is worth looking at 14...♘b6!? 15 a5 ♘d7 16 ♗h4 ♕c7 with an unclear game) 14...♖b8 15 ♔h1 b5 16 axb5 axb5 17 e5!? dxe5 18 fxe5 ♘xe5 19 ♗g5 ♕d7 20 ♖ad1 with complications.

12 ...   **a6** *(D)*

The passive move 12...b6?! unties White's hands: 13 e5! ♕e7 (13...a6 14 e6!) 14 e6 ♘f6 (Bendana-Paz, Corr 1992) 15 f5! ±.

13 ♗f1 *(D)*

13 ♗c4?! gives Black an important tempo, and he can equalize after

13...♘b6 14 ♗e2 ♗g4 15 h3 ♗xf3 16 ♗xf3 ♕h4 17 ♔h2 ♖fe8 18 g3 ♕d8 R.Watson-Nunn, London 1980.

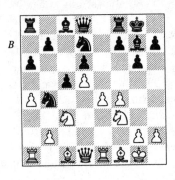

13 ...   **♖e8**
14 h3   **♖b8**

White has a clear advantage after 14...♘f6 15 ♗c4!? ♘d7 16 ♗e3 ♘b6 (16...♗xc3? 17 bxc3 ♖xe4 18 ♘d2 +−) 17 ♗f1 ♗d7 18 ♗f2 ♖c8 19 g4 c4 20 a5 ± T.Horvath-Bönsch, Kesthely 1981, or 14...b6 15 ♕b3 ♗b7 16 ♗d2 ♘f6 17 ♖ad1 ♖b8 18 ♗c1 ♘d7 19 ♗e3 b5 20 axb5 axb5 21 ♗f2 ♗a6 22 e5! ± Lautier-Hamdouchi, Manila OL 1992.

15 ♗e3   **b6**

Or 15...♘f6 16 ♗f2 ♘h5 17 g3 ♘f6 18 ♕d2 ♘d7 19 g4 b6 20 ♖ac1 ♗b7 21 ♗c4 ♗a8 22 ♖cd1 ± Tataev-Blodstein, Voskresensk 1993.

16 ♕d2   **♗b7**
17 ♗f2   **♕e7**
18 ♗c4   **♕f8**
19 ♗g3 ±

Black is restrained and it is difficult for him to organize realistic counterplay.

9 Four Pawns Attack without 9...♖e8 (A68)

1 d4 ♞f6 2 c4 c5 3 d5 e6 4 ♞c3 exd5 5 cxd5 d6

6	e4	g6
7	f4	♝g7
8	♞f3	0-0
9	♝e2	*(D)*

Black has no problems after 9 ♝d3 ♝g4 (9...b5!? is not bad either: 10 e5 dxe5 11 fxe5 ♞g4 with an unclear game) 10 0-0 a6 11 a4 ♞bd7 12 h3 ♝xf3 13 ♕xf3 ♕c7 14 ♝d2 c4 = Ruf-Sher, Moscow 1990.

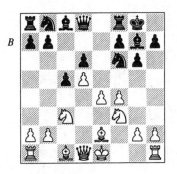

Now there are two main alternatives to 9...♖e8 (which constitutes A69 and so is the subject of the next chapter). They are:

A) 9...b5
B) 9...♝g4

Other moves are either transpositional, or give Black little chance of achieving a playable game:

a) 9...b6?! 10 e5 ♞e8 11 0-0 ♞a6 12 ♝c4 ♞ac7 13 ♖e1 ♖b8 14 a4 a6 15 ♞g5! b5 16 axb5 axb5 17 e6! ± Knežević-Pithart, Olomouc 1975.

b) 9...a6 10 a4!? (10 0-0 leads to an unclear game: 10...b5 11 e5 ♞e8 and now White should play Uhlmann's recommendation 12 ♝e3!?; instead 12 e6 is weaker in view of 12...f5 13 ♞g5 ♝b7 14 ♝f3 ♕e7 15 ♝e3 h6 16 ♞f7 ♞d7 17 ♖e1 ♖xf7! 18 exf7+ ♕xf7 and Black already has an advantage; Monin-Uhlmann, Budapest 1989) 10...♝g4 (10...b6 11 0-0 ♖a7 12 ♞d2 ♖e7 13 ♝f3 ♞e8 14 ♞c4 favours White; Zamanov-Grazman, Moscow 1989) 11 0-0 ♞bd7 12 h3 ♝xf3 13 ♝xf3 leads to 9...♝g4.

c) 9...♞a6 can be met by:

c1) 10 e5!? dxe5 (or 10...♞e8 11 0-0 ♞ac7 12 a4 b6 13 ♖e1 ♝b7 14 ♝c4 ±) 11 fxe5 ♞g4 12 ♝f4 ♖e8 13 e6 fxe6 14 d6 ♝d7 15 ♕d2 (15 h3 ♞f6 16 ♞e5 ♞b4 17 ♝g5 h6! 18 ♝xf6 ♕xf6 19 ♞xd7 ♕h4+ allows Black an advantage) 15...♞b4 16 0-0 with a better game.

c2) 10 0-0 ♞c7 11 ♖e1! is not bad either (Black equalizes after 11 a4 ♖e8 12 ♞d2 ♖b8 13 ♞c4 b6 14 ♝f3 ♝a6 15 ♕b3 ♝xc4 16 ♕xc4 a6 = *ECO*): 11...♖b8 12 e5 dxe5 13 d6

♘e6 14 fxe5 ♘g4 15 ♗c4 ± Videki-
Hertneck, Kecskemet 1990.

A) 9...b5!?

It is significantly more difficult, if
still generally possible, for White to
gain an advantage after this thrust
than after the moves we have just examined. Now a capture on b5 by any
piece does not pose Black any problems, for example 10 ♘xb5 ♘xe4 11
0-0 a6 =, or 10 ♗xb5 ♘xe4 11 ♘xe4
♕a5+ 12 ♔f2 ♕xb5 13 ♘xd6 ♕b6
14 ♘c4 (14 ♘xc8 ♖xc8 15 ♘e5 ♖d8
16 ♖e1 ♘d7 = *ECO*) 14...♕a6 15
♕e2 ♗d7 16 ♗e3 ♗b5 17 ♖hc1 ♖e8
with good compensation. Therefore
White should try:

10 e5

Black must now choose one of
three continuations. We shall take
the traditional move as our main line,
but this may not be Black's most
promising.

10 ...   dxe5

Instead:

a) 10...♘g4!? 11 h3 ♘h6 12
♗xb5 ♘f5 13 0-0 ♕b6 14 ♗c4 ♗a6
15 b3 ♘d7 16 ♘a4 ♕b7 17 ♗xa6
♕xa6 18 ♖e1 ♘b6 19 ♘xb6 ♕xb6
20 ♔h2, Skembris-Vuruna, Vrnjacka
Banja 1989, and now Black should
have played 20...a5!? with compensation.

b) 10...♘fd7!? is a comparatively
new move, employed with success
by the Ukrainian player Frolov.
White's attempts to gain an advantage have thus far not been crowned
with success, for example:

b1) 11 e6 fxe6 12 dxe6 ♘f6 13
♘xb5 d5 14 ♘g5 ♕e7 15 f5 a6 16
♘c3 gxf5 17 ♘xd5 ♘xd5 18 ♕xd5
♗b7 19 ♕c4 ♘c6 ∓ Zakharevich-
Maksimenko, Moscow 1991.

b2) 11 exd6 a6 12 f5 ♘e5 13
fxg6 hxg6 14 0-0 ♗f5 15 ♗f4 ♘bd7
with compensation, Frolov.

b3) 11 ♘xb5 dxe5 12 0-0 e4 13
♘g5 ♘f6 14 ♘c3 ♖e8 15 ♗b5 ♗d7
16 ♗xd7 ♘bxd7 17 ♖e1 ♘b6 18 d6
h6 19 ♘gxe4 ♘xe4 20 ♖xe4 ♗d4+
21 ♔h1 ♘c4 with a good position;
Feldmann-Frolov, Šibenik 1989.

b4) 11 ♗xb5 leads to equality:
11...dxe5 12 0-0 (12 fxe5 ♘xe5 =)
12...♗a6 13 ♗xa6 ♘xa6 14 f5 c4 =
Berkovich-Frolov, Alushta 1992.

10...♘fd7!? may be a stumbling
block in White's attempts to achieve
an advantage.

11 fxe5   ♘g4 (D)

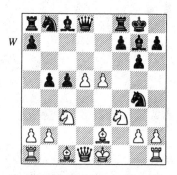

12 ♗g5

This is the only move which lays
any claim to an advantage. Other
moves are harmless:

a) 12 0-0 ♘xe5 13 ♗f4 ♘bd7 14
♗xb5 ♕b6 15 ♘xe5 ♘xe5 16 ♕d2
a6 = is totally inoffensive for Black.

b) 12 ♘xb5 ♘xe5 13 0-0 ♘bd7 14 ♗f4 ♕b6 15 ♔h1 a6 16 ♘c3 ♕xb2 17 ♘a4 ♕a3 18 ♖c1 ♘g4 = is also entirely harmless.

c) Only White will have problems after 12 ♗f4?! b4! (stronger than 12...♘d7 13 e6 fxe6 14 dxe6 ♖xf4 15 ♕d5 ♔h8 16 ♕xa8 ♘b6 17 ♕xa7 ♗xe6 18 0-0 ♘e3 19 ♖f2 b4 Keres-Spassky, Riga Ct 1965, and White would have achieved an advantage after 20 ♘d1!) 13 ♘e4 (or 13 ♘b5 a6 14 ♘d6 ♘xe5 15 ♗xe5 ♗xe5 ∓) 13...♘d7 14 e6 fxe6 15 dxe6 ♖xf4 16 ♕d5 ♔h8 17 ♕xa8 ♘b6 18 ♕c6 ♘e3 19 g3 (19 ♔f2? loses; 19...♗d4 20 ♔g3 ♖g4+ 21 ♔h3 ♕f8 −+) 19...♘c2+ 20 ♔f1 (20 ♔f2? ♕d4+ 21 ♔g2 ♕xe4 22 ♕xe4 ♖xe4 23 ♗d3 ♖xe6 −+ Martin-Botterill, Charlton 1978) 20...♖f5.

12 ... ♕b6

White easily achieves a better game after:

a) 12...♕a5 13 0-0 ♘xe5 14 d6 ♗e6 15 ♘xe5 ♗xe5 16 ♗f3 ♘d7 17 ♗xa8 ♖xa8 18 ♕f3 ♖b8 19 ♖ad1 b4 20 ♘d5, Blokh-Wexler, USSR 1978.

b) 12...f6 13 exf6 ♗xf6 14 ♕d2 (14 ♗xf6 is not bad either: 14...♕xf6 15 ♕d2!? ♖e8 {or 15...a6 16 0-0 ♕e7 17 ♘g5! ♖xf1+ 18 ♖xf1 ♘e3 19 ♖f3 ♘f5 20 g4 ♘d6 21 ♖e3 ♕f8 22 ♘ce4 ± Avshalumov-N.Nikolić, Belgrade 1988} 16 0-0 a6 17 d6 ♘e3 18 ♖fe1 ± Videki-Csuilits, Szekszard 1989) 14...♖e8!? (nor does 14...♗xg5 lead to equality: 15 ♘xg5 ♘a6 16 h3 ♘e5 17 d6 ± Blokh-Krasnov, USSR 1986) 15 0-0 b4 16 ♘d1

♗b7 17 ♘f2 ♗xg5 (17...♕xd5?! loses to the continuation 18 ♕xd5+ ♗xd5 19 ♘xg4 ♗xg5 20 ♘xg5 ♖xe2 21 ♘f6+) 18 ♘xg5 ± Blokh-Kitchev, Corr 1991.

13 0-0 (*D*)

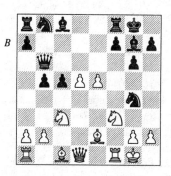

13 ... ♘d7

Black's problems are not solved by any of the following:

a) 13...a6?! 14 d6 c4+ 15 ♔h1 ♗d7 16 ♘d5 ♕b7 17 h3 ♘h6 18 ♘e7+ ♔h8 19 ♘d4 ± Avshalumov-Moracchini, Cannes 1990.

b) 13...♘xe5 14 ♘xe5 ♗xe5 15 ♗e7 ♘d7 16 d6 ♗b7 17 ♘d5 ♕c6 18 ♗f3 again with an advantage; Gorelov-Vasiukov, Moscow 1981.

c) 13...c4+ leads to the same result: 14 ♔h1 ♘xe5 15 ♘xe5 (15 ♗e7 is weaker: 15...♘bd7 16 d6 ♗b7 17 ♘d5 ♗xd5 18 ♕xd5 ♘g4 with a complicated game; Lutikov-Yurtaev, USSR 1977) 15...♗xe5 16 ♗e7 ♖e8 17 d6 ♗b7 (17...♗e6 18 ♘d5 ♕d4 19 ♘c7 ♘d7 20 ♗f3 ♖ac8 21 ♘xe6! fxe6 22 ♗g4 ± Blokh-Bobrov, USSR 1982) 18 ♘d5 ♕d4 19 ♕xd4 ♗xd4 20 ♘c7 ♘d7 21 ♘xb5 ± *ECO*.

| 14 | e6 | fxe6 |
| 15 | dxe6 | c4+ |

White has a minimal advantage in the event of 15...♕xe6 16 ♘xb5 ♖b8!? (but not 16...♗a6? 17 ♘c7 ♗xe2 18 ♘xe6 ♗xd1 19 ♖fxd1 ♖f7 20 ♘d8! +– Sosonko-Hug, Geneva 1977) 17 ♘fd4 ♕d5 18 ♗xg4 ♕xg5 19 ♗e6+.

16	♔h1	♘df6
17	e7	♖e8
18	♕d4!?	

Black can equalize with exact play after 18 a4 ♗b7! 19 ♘d4! ♕c5! (19...♘e5? 20 a5 ♕a6 21 ♘dxb5 ±) 20 ♗xg4 ♕xg5 21 ♗f3 ♗xf3 22 ♕xf3 ♕g4 23 ♕xg4 ♘xg4 24 ♘c6 ♘e5! (an improvement in comparison with Gorelov-Gleizerov, USSR 1986, in which the following occurred: 24...b4 25 ♘d5 ♖ac8 26 ♘cxb4 ±) 25 axb5 ♘xc6 26 bxc6 ♗xc3 27 bxc3 ♖xe7 28 ♖a4 ♖c8 29 ♖xc4 ♖e6 = Gleizerov.

18	...	♗d7
19	♕xb6!	axb6
20	♘d4	h6
21	♗xf6	♘xf6
22	♘dxb5	♖xe7
23	♗xc4+	

with a small advantage to White.

B) 9...♗g4 *(D)*

A logical move, as Black is cramped, and so it is in his interest to exchange some pieces, but recently White, led in the first place by Vaiser, has managed to find the key to this variation.

| 10 | 0-0 |

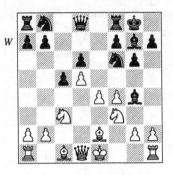

Or:

a) 10 h3 ♗xf3 11 ♗xf3 ♘bd7 12 a4 a6 13 g4 (13 0-0!? is stronger, and is examined under 10 0-0) 13...h6 14 h4 ♘h7 15 ♔f2 c4 16 ♗e3 ♖c8 17 ♗d4 ♘c5 with a better game; D.Gurevich-Gheorghiu, USA 1981.

b) A complicated and interesting game arises after 10 e5!?:

b1) White has an advantage after 10...♘e8?! 11 ♘g5! ♗xe2 (11...♗c8 12 e6 fxe6 13 dxe6 ♘c7 14 0-0 ♘c6 15 f5! ♖xf5 16 ♖xf5 gxf5 17 ♗c4 ± Schön-Szymczak, Naleczow 1988) 12 ♕xe2 ♕e7 13 e6 f5 14 0-0 ♘a6 15 ♗e3 ♘ac7 16 ♖fd1, Kožul-Damljanović, Yugoslavia 1989.

b2) 10...♘fd7 11 e6 fxe6 12 ♘g5 ♗xe2 13 ♘xe2 (13 ♕xe2 leads to roughly the same result: 13...exd5 14 ♕e6+ {14 ♘e6? ♗xc3+ 15 bxc3 ♕f6 with some advantage to Black} 14...♔h8 15 ♘xd5 ♘f6, Sutter-Wojtkiewicz, Bern 1991, and now White should have continued 16 ♘f7+ ♖xf7 17 ♕xf7 ±) 13...exd5 14 ♕xd5+ ♔h8 15 ♘f7+ ♖xf7 16 ♕xf7 ♘c6 17 0-0 and here White has a minimal advantage; Schön-Wojtkiewicz, Naleczow 1988.

b3) 10...dxe5 has unclear consequences: 11 fxe5 ♘fd7 12 ♗g5!? ♕b6 13 0-0 ♗xf3!? (13...♕xb2?! 14 ♘a4 ♕a3 15 ♗c1 ♕b4 16 ♗d2 ♕a3 17 ♖b1! ♘xe5 18 ♘xe5 ♗xe2 19 ♕xe2 ♕xa4 20 ♘xf7! ± Schön-Hellers, Berlin 1988) 14 ♗xf3 ♕xb2 15 ♗d2 ♘xe5 16 ♖b1 ♕a3 17 ♖xb7 ♘bd7 18 d6 and White has enough compensation for the pawn; Schön-Maus, Bundesliga 1989.

b4) 10...♗xf3 11 ♗xf3 dxe5 12 fxe5 ♘fd7 (White's position is more promising after 12...♖e8 13 0-0 ♖xe5 14 ♗f4 ♖e8 {14...♖e7 only strengthens White's initiative: 15 ♕b3 ♘bd7 16 d6 ♖e6 17 ♘d5 ♘xd5 18 ♗xd5 ♗d4+ 19 ♔h1 ± Schön-Cvitan, New York 1987} 15 ♕b3 ♕b6 16 ♖fe1 ♘bd7 17 d6 ♖xe1+ 18 ♖xe1 ♕xb3 19 axb3 ♖b8 20 ♘d5 ♘xd5 21 ♗xd5 with unpleasant threats) 13 e6 ♘e5 14 0-0 (removing the tension from the centre favours Black: 14 exf7+ ♖xf7 15 0-0 ♘bd7 16 ♘e4 ♘xf3+ 17 ♖xf3 ♖xf3 18 ♕xf3 ♘e5 ∓ Knežević-Gligorić, Yugoslavia 1970) 14...♘xf3+ (you also come across 14...fxe6 with the further possibility of 15 ♗e4 ♖xf1+ 16 ♕xf1 ♔h8 17 ♗e3 exd5 18 ♗xd5 with reasonable compensation; Hajenius-Le Quang, Brussels Z 1993) 15 ♖xf3 fxe6 16 ♖xf8+ ♕xf8 17 ♗e3! (17 dxe6?! is bad because of 17...♗d4+ 18 ♔h1 ♘c6 ∓) 17...♘a6 (17...exd5?! 18 ♕xd5+ ♕f7 19 ♕d8+ ♕f8 20 ♕c7 favours White; Schön-Westerinen, Porz 1990) 18 dxe6 ♕e7 19 ♕b3 ♖e8 = Schön-Sherzer, New York 1987.

Now we return to the position after 10 0-0 *(D)* in the main line.

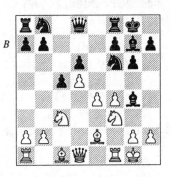

10   ...   ♘bd7
Otherwise:

a) 10...♖e8 11 h3 ♗xf3 12 ♗xf3 ♘bd7 is examined in the notes to 10...♘bd7.

b) The rare move 10...♘fd7!? deserves attention, as White has thus far not found an answer to it, for example 11 ♘g5 ♗xe2 12 ♕xe2 h6 13 ♘f3 ♖e8 14 ♕c2 ♘a6 = Piskov-Neverov, Podolsk 1989 or 11 a4 ♘a6 12 ♘b5 ♕e7 13 h3 ♗xf3 14 ♗xf3 ♘b4 15 e5 dxe5 16 d6 ♕h4 17 ♗xb7 ♖ab8 ∓ Piskov-Itkis, Kastel Stari 1988.

c) 10...♗xf3 11 ♗xf3 ♘bd7 cannot be the best solution; indeed White usually has to waste a tempo on moving the h-pawn in order to get this exchange:

c1) 12 a4 a6 13 ♗e3 ♖e8 14 ♗f2 ♖b8 15 g4 h6 16 h4 b5 17 g5 ♘h7 18 axb5 axb5 19 ♕e2 c4 led to equality in the game Zsu.Polgar-Fedorowicz, New York 1985.

c2) In Doroshkevich-Tal, Erevan 1975, Black seized the initiative after 12 ♔h1 a6 13 ♗e3 (13 a4!? is interesting) 13...♖e8 14 g4 h6 15 g5?! hxg5 16 e5 gxf4! 17 exf6 ♖xe3 18 fxg7 ♘e5.

c3) 12 ♖e1!? ♘e8 (or 12...♖e8 13 ♗e3 a6 14 a4 ♕a5 15 ♕c2 c4 16 ♗f2 ♘c5 17 e5 with initiative for White; Buckley-Hennigan, Guildford 1991) 13 ♖e2 a6 14 ♕e1 ♕e7 15 a4 ♘c7 16 ♗e3 ♖fe8 17 ♖d1 ♕d8 18 ♗f2 ± Vaiser-Mäki, Helsinki 1991.

11 h3

Instead:

a) Only White has problems in the event of 11 ♗e3 ♖e8 12 ♘d2 ♗xe2 13 ♕xe2 b5! 14 ♕f3 b4 15 ♘d1 ♕e7 Kaidanov-Lerner, Norilsk 1987.

b) Black also has no difficulties after 11 ♘d2 ♗xe2 12 ♕xe2 ♖e8 13 ♕f3 a6 (White has a small advantage after 13...♖c8 14 ♔h1 c4 15 g4 ±, but here 15...♘c5?! allows White a real advantage: 16 e5! dxe5 17 fxe5 ♖xe5 18 ♘xc4 ♘cd7 19 ♘xe5 ♘xe5 20 ♕g3 ♘exg4 21 ♗f4 ± Nogueiras-Cvitan, Novi Sad OL 1990; 13...♕e7 14 ♖e1 ♘b6! deserves attention) 14 a4 ♕c7 15 ♘c4 ♘b6 16 ♘xb6 ♕xb6 with an equal position; Sutter-Züger, Switzerland 1992.

c) 11 ♖e1!? is a very reasonable move, and after the correct 11...♖e8 12 h3 ♗xf3 13 ♗xf3 we have reached the position examined in the notes to 11 h3 ♗f3 12 ♗f3 ♖e8 13 ♖e1, whilst after 11...a6?! 12 e5 dxe5 13 fxe5 ♘h5 14 e6 fxe6 15 dxe6 ♗xe6 16 ♘g5 ♗d4+ 17 ♔h1 ♗f7 18 ♘xf7 ♖xf7 19 ♗c4, Kožul-

Damljanović, Belgrade 1989, White has achieved a clear advantage.

11 ... ♗xf3
12 ♗xf3 (D)

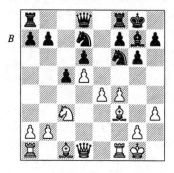

12 ... ♖e8

White's position strikes me as being the more promising after 12...c4 13 ♗e3, for example 13...♕a5 14 ♗d4 (or 14 ♔h1!? ♖fe8 15 ♖e1 – see 12...♖e8) 14...♖fe8 15 b4! (15 g4 meets the standard reaction 15...h6 16 h4 g5!? ∞) 15...♕xb4 16 ♖b1 ♕a5 17 ♖xb7 a6 18 ♘a4!? ♘xe4 19 ♗xg7 ♘dc5 20 ♕d4 ♘xb7 21 ♗h6 f6 22 ♗xe4 ♕xa4 Kouatly-Nunn, Cannes 1992, and 23 f5!? was possible, with initiative.

You also frequently come across 12...a6:

a) Black has plenty of chances for a good game after 13 a4:

a1) 13...c4 14 ♗e3 ♕a5 (the line 14...♖c8 15 ♗d4 ♘c5 16 e5 dxe5 17 fxe5 ♘fd7 18 e6 ♘e5 19 ♗xc5 is unclear; Zsu.Polgar-Nunn, Hamburg 1985) 15 ♕e2 ♖ac8 16 ♔h1 ♖fe8 17 ♕f2 ♘c5 18 ♗xc5 ♕xc5 19 a5 ♖c7 = Berkmortel-Gheorghiu, Bad Wörishofen 1988.

a2) 13...♖b8 is really not too bad either: 14 ♖e1 (14 a5 ♘e8 15 ♕c2 ♘c7 16 ♗d2 b5 17 axb6 ♘xb6 18 ♘e2 ♕d7 = Monin-Sergienko, Budapest 1993) 14...♘e8! 15 a5 ♘c7 16 ♕d3 b5 17 axb6 ♖xb6 18 ♘a4 ♕h4! 19 ♗e3 ♖b4 = Zlochevsky-Schekachev, Moscow 1989

a3) 13...♕a5 14 ♗d2 (14 ♖e1!?) 14...c4 15 ♔h1 ♖fe8 16 ♕c2 ♖ac8 17 ♘d1 ♕d8 18 ♗c3 b5 19 axb5 axb5 with equality; Djukić-Damljanović, Yugoslav Ch 1991.

b) 13 g4!? ♘e8 14 g5 ♘c7 (14...f5 does not lead to equality: 15 exf5 gxf5 16 ♗e3 b5 17 ♕c2 ♘b6 18 ♖ae1 ♘c7 19 b3 ♕d7 20 ♖d1 ♕f7 21 ♗f2 ± Bagaturov-Grigorian, Belgorod 1989) 15 ♗g4 (15 h4 is worth testing, e.g. 15...♘b5 16 ♗d2 ♘d4 17 h5 f6 18 h6 ♗h8 19 ♗g4 with a pleasant game) 15...♘b5! 16 e5 ♘xc3 (16...dxe5 17 f5 ♘d6 18 f6 ♘xf6! 19 gxf6 ♗xf6 also leads to an unclear game) 17 bxc3 dxe5 18 f5! e4! 19 f6 ♘xf6! 20 gxf6 ♗xf6 with mutual chances; Nogueiras-Velimirović, Reggio Emilia 1986.

c) 13 ♖e1!? also deserves attention.

13 ♖e1

White is preparing a pawn break in the centre, as often played by Vaiser, the leading specialist in the Four Pawns Attack, and this may still be an excellent advert. You also see:

a) 13 g4 h6 14 h4 and now:

a1) 14...♘h7 15 g5 hxg5 16 hxg5 a6 (or 16...f6 17 gxf6 ♕xf6 18 ♗e3 ♖e7 19 ♔g2 ± Arencibia-Gonzalez, Cuba 1993) 17 a4 c4 18 ♗e3 ♖c8 19

♗d4 (19 ♗g4 is too adventurous: 19...♗xc3 20 bxc3 ♖xe4 21 ♕f3 ♕e7 22 ♗d4 ♖e8 ∞ Stanković-Paunović, Cetinje 1992) 19...♗xd4+ 20 ♕xd4 ♘c5 21 ♖ad1 ♖c7 22 ♗g2 ± Monin-Purtov, Budapest 1993.

a2) 14...h5!? 15 g5 (15 gxh5 ♘xh5 16 ♗xh5 gxh5 17 ♕xh5 b5! with compensation) 15...♘g4 16 ♗xg4 hxg4 17 ♖e1 (or 17 ♕xg4 ♗xc3 18 bxc3 ♖xe4 19 ♗d2 ♕e7 20 ♖ae1 ♘b6 =) 17...c4 18 ♗e3 ♗xc3 19 bxc3 ♖xe4 20 ♕xg4 ♕e7 = Kouatly-Kindermann, Trnava 1987.

b) 13 a4 (*D*) and now:

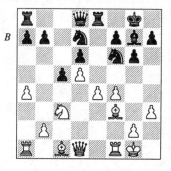

b1) 13...♕a5 is worth testing.

b2) 13...h6 leads to huge complications: 14 ♔h1 ♖c8 15 a5 c4 16 ♖a4 ♘c5!? (stronger than 16...b5?! 17 ♘xb5 ♘c5 18 ♘xa7! ♘xa4 19 ♘xc8 ♕xc8 20 ♕xa4 ♘xe4 21 ♗xe4 ♖xe4 22 a6 ± Piskov-Velimirović, Kastel Stari 1988) 17 ♖xc4 ♕xa5 18 b4 ♕a6 19 ♗e2 b5, Piskov.

b3) White preserves a small advantage after 13...a6 14 a5!? (but not 14 ♔h1?! b5! 15 axb5 axb5 16 ♖xa8 ♕xa8 ∓) 14...c4 (or 14...♖b8 15 ♔h1 b5 16 axb6 ♖xb6 17 ♕d3 ♕c7 18

♖a4 ♖a8 19 ♖d1 ♖a7 20 ♕e2 ♕b8 21 ♖e1! ± Avshalumov-Dumitrache, Baku 1988) 15 ♖a4 b5 16 axb6 ♘xb6 17 ♖a3 ♘fd7 18 ♗e3 f5 19 ♗d4 ± Michaelsen-Southam, Lyngby 1990.

b4) 13...c4!? 14 ♗e3 ♕a5 (Black cannot organize his position after 14...a6?! 15 a5 ♖c8 16 ♖e1 ♘c5 17 ♗xc5! ♖xc5 18 e5 dxe5 19 fxe5 ♘d7 20 e6 ♘e5 21 exf7+ ♘xf7 22 ♖xe8+ ♕xe8 23 d6 with an obvious advantage; Lukov-Grivas, Leningrad 1988) 15 ♗d4 ♖e7!? 16 ♔h1 a6 17 g4 ♖ae8 18 g5 ♘xe4! 19 ♘xe4 ♖xe4 20 ♗xe4 ♖xe4 21 ♗xg7 ♔xg7 with excellent compensation for the exchange; Peev-Velimirović, Sofia 1972.

Now we return to the position after 13 ♖e1 *(D)* in the main line:

B

13 ...   c4

Other moves:

a) Huge complications begin after 13...♕a5 14 ♗e3 b5 (14...♖ac8 is weaker: 15 g4 h6 16 h4 b5 17 g5 hxg5 18 hxg5 ♘h7 19 ♗g4 ♖cd8 20 e5! dxe5 21 f5 and White's attack develops with no problems; Vaiser-

Kindermann, Biel 1991) 15 a3 ♘b6 and now White must play precisely:

a1) 16 ♗f2?! ♘c4 17 ♕c2 (or 17 b3? ♕xc3 18 bxc4 ♘xe4! 19 ♖c1 ♘xf2 20 ♖xe8+ ♖xe8 –+ Kouatly-Barcenilla, Doha 1993) 17...♘d7 18 ♗e2 (after 18 a4 b4 19 ♘b5 a6 20 ♕xc4 axb5 21 ♕xb5 ♕xb5 22 axb5 ♗xb2 White's position is cheerless) 18...♖ab8 19 a4 b4, Kožul-Nunn, Wijk aan Zee 1991, and the variation suggested by Stohl – 20 ♘b5 ♘xb2 21 ♘xd6 b3 22 ♕b1 ♘xa4 23 ♘xe8 ♗xa1 24 ♕xa1 ♖xe8 – does not offer White many chances for salvation.

a2) 16 e5! ♘c4 *(D)* (16...dxe5!? is perhaps stronger: 17 fxe5 ♖xe5 18 ♗xc5 ♖xe1+ 19 ♕xe1 ♘bd7 20 ♗d4 with only a small advantage to White).

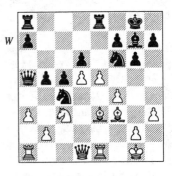

W

17 exf6 ♘xe3 18 ♖xe3 (18 ♕c1? ♗xf6 –+) 18...♖xe3 19 fxg7 ♖ae8 (19...♔xg7!? 20 f5! only strengthens White's attack) 20 f5! gxf5 (nor does Black have an easy life after 20...♔xg7 21 f6+! ♔xf6 22 ♘e4+ ♖8xe4 23 ♗xe4 ♖xe4 24 ♕f3+ ♔e5 25 b4!? with an attack, Glek, or 20...♕d8 21 ♕d2 ♕h4 22 ♘xb5 ± as

in Vaiser-Kruger, San Bernardino 1990) 21 ♕d2! (the error 21 ♘e2 handed the initiative to Black in Glek-Yurtaev, Moscow GMA 1989: 21...♕d8! 22 ♕c2 ♖8e5 23 a4 ♕g5 24 ♔h2 b4) 21...b4 22 ♘e2 c4 23 ♘g3 c3 24 bxc3 bxc3 25 ♕c2 ♕b6 26 ♔h2 ♕b2 27 ♖a2 and White has a distinct advantage; Vaiser-Yrjölä, Helsinki 1991.

b) There is no equality in evidence after 13...a6, for example 14 a4 (14 g4 h6 15 h4 b5 16 g5 hxg5 17 hxg5 ♘h7 18 ♔g2 ♘b6 19 ♖h1 ♖a7 ∞ Kouatly-Al Modiahki, Doha 1993, is interesting) 14...c4 (alternatively, 14...♖b8 15 g4 {15 a5!?} 15...h6 16 h4 ♘h7 17 g5 c4 18 ♗e3 ♖c8 19 ♗g4 ± Yrjölä-Pedzich, Cappelle la Grande 1992) 15 ♗e3 ♕a5 16 ♔h1 ♖e7!? (16...h6 17 ♗d4 ♘c5?! 18 ♗xc5 ♕xc5 19 e5 dxe5 20 fxe5 ♘d7 21 e6 ♘e5 22 exf7+ ♔xf7 23 d6 ± Vaiser-Le Quang, Ostend 1992) 17 ♗d4!? with a small advantage.

c) White has a better game after 13...♖c8:

c1) In Nogueiras-Kasparov, Barcelona World Cup 1989, the World Champion achieved equality after 14 ♗e3 b5!? (14...c4 15 ♔h1 ♘c5 16 ♗xc5 ♖xc5 17 e5) 15 ♘xb5 ♘xe4 16 ♗xe4 ♖xe4 17 ♘xd6 ♖xe3 18 ♖xe3 ♗d4 19 ♕f3 ♖b8 20 ♔h2 ♘f6 21 ♘c4 ♗xe3 22 ♕xe3 ♕xd5.

c2) 14 ♔h1!? a6 15 a4 c4 16 ♗e3 ♘c5 17 ♗xc5 ♖xc5 18 e5 dxe5 19

fxe5 ♘d7 20 e6 ♘e5 21 exf7+ ♔xf7 22 ♘e4 ♖c8 23 ♗g4! ♘xg4 24 ♕xg4 ± Vaiser-Berelovich, Groningen 1993.

14 ♗e3   ♕a5
15 ♔h1

Or 15 ♗d4 ♘c5 16 b4!? cxb3 17 axb3 ♕b4 18 ♘a2 ♕b5 19 ♘c3 ♕b4 with equality; Kouatly-A.Kuzmin, Doha 1993.

15 ...   ♖e7!?

15...♘c5 is weaker because of 16 ♗xc5 ♕xc5 17 e5! dxe5 18 fxe5 ♘d7 19 e6 ♘e5 20 ♘e4 with a big advantage; Glek-Kaminski, Odessa 1989.

16 ♗d4

After 16 ♕d2 Black should continue 16...♖ae8 17 ♗d4 ♘c5 ∞, while 16...♘e8 17 e5! dxe5 18 d6 ♖e6 19 ♗xb7 ♖b8 (19...♖d8 20 ♗d5 ♖xd6 21 ♖ad1 ♘df6 22 fxe5 ♘xd5 23 exd6 ♘xc3 24 d7!, Vera) 20 ♗d5 ♖xd6 21 ♖ad1 ♘f8 22 fxe5 ♗xe5 23 ♗f4 ♗xf4 24 ♕xf4, Vera-Zapata, Santa Clara 1990, is better for White.

16 ...   ♘c5
17 b4!   cxb3
18 axb3   ♕b4
19 ♘a2   ♕b5

19...♕xb3 does not free Black from his problems either: 20 ♗xc5 ♕xd1 21 ♖axd1 dxc5 22 d6 ♖d7 23 e5 with strong pressure.

20 e5   ♘e8
21 ♖e3

and White undoubtedly has the initiative; Glek-Korolev, Corr 1988.

10 Four Pawns Attack: 9...♖e8 (A69)

1 d4 ♘f6 2 c4 c5 3 d5 e6 4 ♘c3 exd5 5 cxd5 d6 6 e4 g6 7 f4 ♗g7 8 ♘f3 0-0

      9 ♗e2   ♖e8 *(D)*

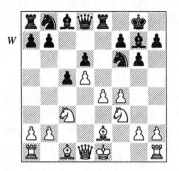

Here White has a limited choice, since 10 ♕c2? fails to 10...♘xe4! 11 ♘xe4 ♗f5 12 ♗d3 ♕e7 13 ♘fd2 ♗xe4 14 ♗xe4 f5 −+.

Thus White has two principal attempts: defend his pawn with his knight, or advance in the centre.

    A) 10 ♘d2
    B) 10 e5

A) 10 ♘d2

Black has a wide choice of continuations at his disposal, allowing him to look hopefully into the future. First of all he must decide where to develop his queen's knight, as both

possibilities deserve attention. If the knight is destined for d7, the next question, which is not easy to answer, is whether to include the moves 10...a6 11 a4. These moves have advantages and disadvantages for both sides. Thus we shall examine three main systems:

    A1) 10...♘a6
    A2) 10...a6
    A3) 10...♘bd7

Other possibilities:

a) 10...c4 11 a4 (11 ♗f3?! gives Black the initiative: 11...♘bd7 12 0-0 b5 13 ♔h1 a6 14 a4 ♖b8 15 axb5 axb5 ∓ Pomar-Fischer, Havana OL 1966, and 11 ♗xc4?! ♘xe4! also favours Black) 11...♘bd7 12 0-0 ♘c5 (for 12...a6 see A22) 13 ♗f3 and the position which has arisen will be examined in note 'd' to White's 12th move in A3.

b) 10...b6 11 0-0 ♗a6 and now White should wait a little before exchanging the bishop:

b1) Black's problems are simplified after 12 ♗xa6 ♘xa6 13 ♖e1 ♕d7 14 ♘f3 ♖ad8 15 ♗d2 ♘b4 16 ♖e2 ♘d3 ∞ Uhlmann-Szabo, Sarajevo 1963.

b2) 12 ♖e1 is reasonable after 12...♗xe2 13 ♕xe2 a6 14 a4 ♖a7 15

♕d3 Iae7 16 ♘f3 b5 17 axb5 axb5 18 ♕xb5 ♘xe4 19 ♘xe4 Ixe4 20 Ixe4 Ixe4 21 ♗d2 ± A.Zaitsev-Kondali, USSR-Yugoslavia 1966.

b3) 12 a4 ♗xe2 13 ♕xe2 a6 (or 13...♘xe4 14 ♘dxe4 f5 15 ♕f3 fxe4 16 ♘xe4 with initiative) 14 ♕f3 Ia7 15 ♘c4 Id7 (15...♕e7 16 Ie1 ♘fd7 17 ♗d2 ±) 16 ♗d2 b5 17 axb5 axb5 18 ♘xb5 ♘xe4 19 ♗a5 ♕e7 20 f5 and Black faced a difficult defence in the game A.Zaitsev-Zhuravliov, USSR 1965.

c) 10...♘g4!? 11 ♗xg4 and now:

c1) 11...♗xc3 12 bxc3 ♕h4+ 13 g3 ♕xg4 14 ♕xg4 ♗xg4 15 ♔f2 f5 16 Ie1 (16 h3 fxe4!) 16...♘d7 17 c4 Ie7 18 Ib1 Iae8! (significantly more precise than 18...b6?! 19 Ib3 Iae8 20 Ibe3 ±) 19 Ixb7 fxe4 with an equal position; Christiansen-Ghitescu, Thessaloniki OL 1984.

c2) 11...♕h4+ 12 g3 ♕xg4 13 ♕xg4 ♗xg4 14 ♘b5 (14 ♔f2!? with the idea of 14...♗d4+ 15 ♔g2 ♘d7 16 ♘b5! is interesting) 14...♘a6 15 ♘xd6 (Black has excellent tactical possibilities after 15 h3 Ixe4+! 16 ♘xe4 ♗f3 17 0-0 ♗xe4 18 ♘c3 ♗d3 19 If3 {19 Id1 c4} 19...♘b4 20 ♗d2 {or 20 ♗e3 ♗xc3 21 bxc3 ♘xd5 ∓} 20...♗d4+ 21 ♔h2 ♗c4 22 Ie1 ♘xa2 and White faces a difficult defence; Panchius-Liberzon, Israel 1984) 15...♘b4! 16 ♘xe8 ♘c2+ 17 ♔f1 ♗h3+ 18 ♔e2 Ixe8 19 Ib1 ♗g4+ 20 ♔d3 (20 ♔f1 ♗h3+ =) 20...♘b4+ 21 ♔c4 ♗e2+ 22 ♔b3 (after 22 ♔xc5? ♘d3+ 23 ♔d6 ♗g4! the white king is face to face with the whole of Black's army)

22...♗d3 23 a3 ♗c2+ 24 ♔c4 ♗d3+ drawing, according to Liberzon.

A1) 10 ... ♘a6
11 0-0 *(D)*

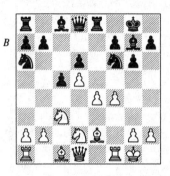

Black has two continuations, both of which guarantee him reasonable chances:

A11) 11...Ib8

A12) 11...♘c7

Instead 11...c4?! is unsatisfactory: 12 e5 dxe5 13 ♘xc4 e4 14 ♗e3 ♘b4 15 d6 ♗e6 16 ♘b5 with a better game; Hvenekilde-T.Horvath, Copenhagen 1983.

A11) 11 ... Ib8!?
A quiet and crafty move. Black is in no hurry to move his knight from a6 to c7, and when he wishes, he can place it on the more active square b4.

12 ♔h1
Other possibilities:

a) 12 a4 ♘c7 (or 12...♘b4!? 13 ♗f3 b6 14 ♘c4 ♗a6 15 ♕b3 Ib7!? with counter-chances) 13 ♔h1 a6 (13...b6 is interesting: 14 ♗f3 ♗a6

15 ♖f2 ♘d7 16 ♘f1 ♗xf1 17 ♖xf1 a6 with equality; Ermenkov-Martinović, Vrnjačka Banja 1978) and now 14 a5 leads us to the variation with 12 ♔h1.

b) 12 ♗f3 ♘b4 (12...♘c7!?) can be met by 13 ♗e2, already inviting a repetition of moves, to which Black could agree, or else he could take a risk and go into an unclear game with 13...c4!? when White should prefer 14 ♕a4!? to 14 ♗xc4? ♘g4 Topalov-Granda, Forli 1988.

c) 12 ♖e1 ♘c7 (Black demonstrated an interesting idea in the game Teichmann-Hartston, London 1984: 12...h5!? 13 h3 ♘c7 14 a4 b6 15 ♖b1 ♗a6 =, and after the error 16 b3? ♘g4! Black easily seized the initiative) 13 a4 b6 and 14 ♗f3 brings us to A12, whilst 14 ♖b1 a6 15 ♕c2 b5 16 axb5 axb5 17 b4 ♘fxd5! 18 exd5 ♗f5 19 ♘ce4 ♘xd5 A.Zaitsev-Vitolinsh, Leningrad 1962, is not unadvantageous for Black.

12   ...   ♘c7

13   a4   a6

White has a small advantage after the pretentious 13...h5 14 f5! a6 15 a5 gxf5 (after 15...♗d7 16 ♘c4, the move 16...♘xe4 is unfavourable for Black: 17 ♘xe4 ♖xe4 18 fxg6 fxg6 19 ♘xd6 ♖d4 20 ♕c2 ±) 16 ♗xh5 ♘b5 (16...fxe4 17 ♘dxe4!) 17 exf5 ♖e5 18 ♗f3 ♖xf5 19 ♘c4 M.Gurevich-Smirin, Moscow 1988.

14   a5   ♗d7

15   ♗f3 *(D)*

Vaiser's idea deserves great attention: 15 e5!? dxe5 16 ♘c4 ♗b5 17 d6 ♘e6 18 fxe5 ♘d7 19 ♗f4 ♘xf4

20 ♖xf4 ♘xe5 21 ♘xb5 axb5 22 ♘b6 Vaiser-Ibragimov, Bern 1992, but we will only know its true value after further practical tests.

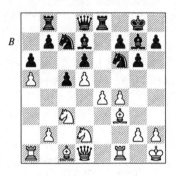

15   ...   ♘b5!?

15...♗b5 also looks quite reasonable: 16 ♖e1 (16 ♘xb5 axb5 17 ♖b1 c4 18 ♖e1 ♘d7 ∓ Nemet-Gheorghiu, Biel 1985, favours Black) 16...♗d3! 17 ♕b3 ♕d7 18 ♘c4 ♗xc4 19 ♕xc4, Arakelian-Ibragimov, Podolsk 1993, and now 19...b5!? 20 axb6 ♖xb6 would have equalized.

16   e5

White cannot organize himself after 16 ♘xb5 ♗xb5 17 ♖e1 c4 18 ♖a3 ♖c8 19 ♘f1 ♘d7 ∓ Toth-de Firmian, Biel 1986.

16   ...   dxe5

17   fxe5   ♖xe5

18   ♘c4   ♖f5

19   ♘e3   ♖f4!

20   ♘e2   ♖h4

21   g3   ♖e4!

22   ♗xe4   ♘xe4

23   ♘c4

Or 23 ♘f4 ♘d4 24 ♔g2 ♕e7 25 ♖e1 h5 with an attack; Ufimtsev-Tal, USSR 1967.

23 ...   ♕e7

24 ♗e3   ♘f6

with an edge for Black; Haba-Smirin, Polanica Zdroj 1989. One gets the impression that White's future attempts will be connected with 15 e5!?.

A12) 11 ...   ♘c7

12 a4 *(D)*

Black has no problems after 12 ♗f3 ♖b8 13 ♘c4 (for 13 a4!? b6 see 12 a4) 13...b5 14 ♘xd6 (White faces difficulties after 14 ♘a5?! ♗d7 15 e5 dxe5 16 fxe5 ♖xe5 17 ♗f4 ♖f5! 18 ♗g3 b4 19 ♘a4 {or 19 ♘c6 ♗xc6 20 dxc6 bxc3 21 ♕xd8+ ♖xd8 ∓ Soos-Matulović, Skopje 1967} 19...♘fxd5 20 ♘xc5 ♗b5 ∓ Zinser-Evans, Venice 1967) 14...♕xd6 15 e5 ♕d8 16 exf6 ♕xf6 = Gligorić.

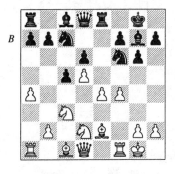

12 ...   b6

12...a6 is also interesting: 13 ♗f3 ♖b8 14 ♘c4 (14 e5 dxe5 15 fxe5 ♘fxd5 16 ♘xd5 ♘xd5 17 ♘c4 ♗e6 18 ♘d6 ♗xe5 is good for Black) 14...b5 15 axb5 axb5 16 ♘a5 ♗d7 17 e5 dxe5 18 d6 e4! 19 dxc7 ♕xc7 20 ♗e2 c4 and, in Nunn's opinion,

Black has quite sufficient compensation for the piece, a view to which I subscribe.

13 ♖e1

Black has an easy game after 13 ♖b1 ♗a6 14 ♗xa6 ♘xa6 15 ♕f3 ♕e7 16 b3 ♘b4 17 ♗b2 ♘c2 (the move 17...a6!?, with the idea of 18 e5? dxe5 19 fxe5 ♘fxd5 20 ♘xd5 ♘xd5 21 ♕xd5 ♖ad8, is also not bad) 18 ♖bc1 ♘d4 19 ♕d3 a6 20 ♖ce1 ♘d7 with equality; K.Grigorian-Suetin, USSR 1975.

Chances are equal in the event of 13 ♔h1 ♗a6 14 ♖e1 (or 14 ♗xa6 ♘xa6 15 ♕f3 ♘b4 16 ♘c4 ♘c2 =) 14...♗xe2 15 ♖xe2 ♘g4 16 h3 ♕h4 17 ♕f1 ♗d4 (17...f5? is weak: 18 ♘f3 ♕h5 19 e5 dxe5 20 fxe5 ♘xe5 21 d6 ± Savon-Beliavsky, Moscow 1973) 18 ♘f3 ♘f2+ 19 ♔h2 ♘g4+ with a draw.

13 ...   ♖b8

The line 13...♗a6!? 14 ♗xa6 (14 ♗f3 ♗d3!?) 14...♘xa6 15 ♘c4 ♘b4 is unclear.

14 ♗f3   ♗a6!?

Or 14...a6 15 ♘c4 b5 16 ♘xd6!? (stronger than 16 axb5 axb5 17 ♘a5 {17 ♘xd6!?} 17...♗d7 18 e5 b4! 19 ♘a4 ♘fxd5 20 ♘c4 ♗xa4 21 ♖xa4 dxe5 22 fxe5 ♘b6 ∓) 16...♕xd6 17 e5 ♕d8 18 d6 (18 exf6 ♖xe1+ 19 ♕xe1 ♗xf6 =) 18...♘e6 19 axb5 axb5 20 exf6 ♗xf6 21 ♘d5 Kožul-Marović, Toronto 1990, and even after the improvement 21...♗b7!? 22 f5!? (22 d7 ♖f8 23 ♘xf6+ ♕xf6 24 ♖a7 ♗xf3 25 ♕xf3 ±) 22...♗xd5! 23 ♕xd5 ♘d4 24 ♗f4 White preserves the better chances, Kožul.

After 14...h5!?, 15 ♘c4 Rogers-Kristiansen, Thessaloniki OL 1984, deserves study, and according to Rogers 15...♘g4!? 16 ♗xg4 ♗xg4 17 ♕d3 ♗c8! leads to an unclear game. Instead, Black has a powerful game after 15 h3 ♘g4! 16 ♘f1 ♗d4+ 17 ♘e3 ♕h4.

15 ♘db1

15 ♘f1 ♗xf1 16 ♖xf1 a6 17 ♔h1 ♘d7 18 ♕c2 b5 = Begovac-Wojtkiewicz, Bern 1991, creates no problems for the opposition, and 15 ♔h1 ♗d3! 16 ♘f1 c4, Garcia Muñoz-Franco, Málaga 1991, gives the initiative to Black.

15 ... ♘d7
16 ♘a3

16 ♗e3 leads to an even game with mutual chances: 16...c4 17 ♗d4 ♗h6!? 18 g3 ♘c5 = Lputian-Cabrilo, Manila IZ 1990.

16 ... c4
17 ♘c2

Or 17 ♘cb5 ♗xb5 18 axb5 c3! 19 ♖b1 cxb2 20 ♗xb2 ♗xb2 21 ♖xb2 ♕f6 22 ♖c2 ♘c5 with a slight plus for Black; Malich-Tringov, Sarajevo 1965.

17 ... ♘c5
18 ♘b4 ♗b7
19 ♗e3 ♘7a6
20 ♘c6 ♗xc6
21 dxc6 ♘d3
22 ♖e2 ♘ab4 ∞

Miles-Emms, Ostend 1992. In the variation with 10...♘a6 White has thus far not had any success.

A2) 10 ... a6
11 a4 ♘bd7

After 11...♘g4 White should probably react with the rare 12 ♘c4!? (Black has reasonable counterplay after 12 ♗xg4 ♕h4+ 13 g3 ♕xg4 14 ♕xg4 ♗xg4 15 ♔f2 ♗d4+ {or 15...f5 16 h3 ♗xc3 17 bxc3 fxe4 18 hxg4 e3+ 19 ♔f3 exd2 20 ♗xd2 ± Yrjölä-Mamombe, Manila OL 1992} 16 ♔g2 ♘d7 17 h3 ♗xc3 18 bxc3 ♗e2 19 ♖e1 ♗d3 leading to an unclear position; Pomar-Szabo, Wijk aan Zee 1967) 12...♗xc3+ 13 bxc3 ♖xe4 14 0-0 f5 15 a5 ♘f6 16 ♘b6 ♖a7 17 ♗f3 with an advantage; Friedstein-Landraf, Corr 1967. The lack of practical tests of 11...♘g4 makes it difficult to give a more precise evaluation.

12 0-0 (D)

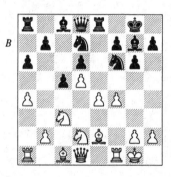

Black generally plays either:
A21) 12...♖b8 (restrained) or
A22) 12...c4 (more forceful).

A21) 12 ... ♖b8
13 ♔h1

13 ♕c2 is best met by 13...b5! 14 axb5 axb5 15 ♗xb5 (or 15 ♘xb5 ♘xd5) 15...♘g4! with initiative for Black; Schinzel-Filipowicz, Poland

1973. Instead White has a small advantage after 13...b6 14 ⬢h1! – this modest king move abruptly curtails the opposition's tactical possibilities, and avoids the unclear game that ensues after 14 ⬛b1 c4! 15 ♘xc4 (15 ⬢h1?! b5 16 axb5 axb5 17 b4 cxb3 18 ⬛xb3 b4 19 ♘b5 ♘c5 20 ⬛xb4 ♘xd5! ∓ Hernandez-Velimirović, Havana 1971) 15...b5 16 axb5 axb5 17 ♘xd6 ♛b6+ 18 ⬢h1 ♛xd6 19 e5.

13 ...   ♛c7 *(D)*

Continuing the waiting tactics. White achieves an advantage after the sharp 13...c4 14 e5! (14 ♗xc4?! ♘c5 15 ♛f3 ♗g4 16 ♛g3 b5 17 axb5 axb5 18 ♗xb5 ♘cxe4 19 ♘dxe4 ♘xe4 20 ♘xe4 ⬛xe4 21 ♛xg4 ⬛xb5 leads to an equal position) 14...dxe5 15 ♘xc4 b5 16 axb5 axb5, and now instead of 17 ♘xe5?! b4 18 ♘b5 (or 18 ♘c6 bxc3 19 ♘xd8 cxb2 20 ♗xb2 ⬛xb2 with more than enough compensation for the queen) 18...♘xe5 19 fxe5 ⬛xe5 20 ♗f4 ♘xd5! with the initiative to Black in Larsen-Ljubojević, Milan 1975, White should have continued 17 ♘d6! ±.

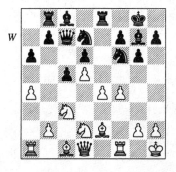

14 ⬛a2!?

White once again has a large and difficult choice:

a) 14 a5 b5 15 axb6 ⬛xb6 16 ♗f3 ⬛b4 =.

b) 14 ♛c2 c4 15 e5! (the c4 pawn is best not taken immediately: 15 ♘xc4 b5 16 axb5 axb5 17 ♘xd6 ♛xd6 18 e5 ♛c5 is unconvincing, and 15 ♗xc4 b5 16 axb5 axb5 17 ♗d3 b4 18 ♘d1 ♛xc2 19 ♗xc2 ♘c5 gives Black superb compensation for the pawn) 15...dxe5 16 ♘xc4 b5 (16...e4?! 17 f5 ±) 17 axb5 axb5, Tukmakov-Arnason, Bor 1983, and White could have gained a small advantage after 18 d6! ♛c6 19 ♘xe5 ♘xe5 20 fxe5 ⬛xe5 21 ♗f4 ♗f5 22 ♗f3! (but not 22 ♛d2 ⬛ee8 23 d7 ♘xd7 24 ♗xb8 ⬛xb8 with compensation) 22...♛b6 23 ♛d2 – Tukmakov.

c) 14 e5!? dxe5 15 ♘c4 ⬛a8 (better than 15...e4?! 16 f5 ± Cserna-Wegner, Berlin 1983) 16 fxe5 ♘xe5 17 ♗f4 ♘fd7 18 ♘e4 ♛d8 19 ♘cd6 ⬛f8 20 ♛b3 ± Cserna.

14 ...   h5

Black does not equalize after either 14...♘f8 15 e5, or 14...b6 15 b3 ♘f8 Izeta-Fernandez, Spain Ch 1987, and the simple 16 ♗d3!? underlines the advantages in White's position. 14...c4?! 15 e5 dxe5 16 ♘xc4 e4 17 f5! leads to a very difficult position; Toth-Nunn, Reggio Emilia 1983/84.

15 h3   ♘h7
16 ♗d3   ♘df8
17 a5 ±

Izeta-Vehi Bach, Spanish Ch 1986.

A22) 12 ...   c4 (D)

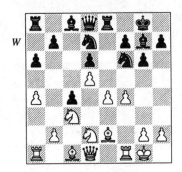

A typical idea in the Four Pawns Attack. By moving the pawn towards certain destruction, Black gains several advantages, in the shape of the excellent c5 square for the knight and the open g1-a7 diagonal for various tactical operations.

13   ♔h1

The most popular and probably the strongest move. Others:

a) 13 ♗xc4?! is met by 13...♘c5 14 ♕f3 (14 ♕c2 ♘g4 15 ♘f3 ♕b6 16 ♔h1 ♗xc3 17 bxc3 ♘xe4 ∓) 14...♘g4!? (or 14...♗g4!?) with initiative.

b) 13 ♘xc4?! ♗xe4 14 ♘xe4 ♖xe4 15 ♗d3 ♖d4 ∓ Cvetković-Suetin, Skopje 1969.

c) 13 e5 dxe5 14 ♘xc4 ♘b6! (14...e4?! 15 ♗e3 clearly cannot satisfy Black, but 14...exf4 deserves attention: 15 ♗xf4 ♘e4 {15...♘c5 16 a5 ♘fe4 17 ♘xe4 ♘xe4 18 ♗f3 with a slight plus for White; Schmidt-L.Karlsson, Vrnjačka Banja 1981} 16 ♗f3 {Black quickly seizes the initiative after 16 ♘xe4 ♖xe4 17 ♗d3 ♖d4 18 ♕f3 ♘f6 19 d6 ♗g4! 20

♕g3 ♗e6 ∓ Wesseln-Luther, Bundesliga 1990} 16...♘b6! 17 ♘xe4 ♘xc4 18 b3!? ♘e5 = Katalymov-Gufeld, Krasnoiarsk 1980) 15 fxe5 and Black has a pleasant choice:

c1) 15...♘fxd5 16 ♘d6 (White has no advantage after 16 ♘xd5 ♘xd5 17 ♘d6 ♖xe5 18 ♘xf7 ♕b6+ 19 ♔h1 ♘e3 20 ♗xe3 ♖xe3 21 ♘g5 ♗e6 =) 16...♘xc3 (16...♗xe5!? 17 ♘xd5 ♕xd6 18 ♘f6+ ♕xf6 19 ♖xf6 ♗xf6 and Black is not at all worse) 17 bxc3 ♖xe5 (but not 17...♗e6?! 18 ♘xe8 ♕xe8 19 ♕d4 ♘d7 20 ♗f4 ± Šahović-Henley, Lone Pine 1978) 18 ♘xf7 ♕xd1 19 ♗xd1 ♖f5 20 ♘h6+ (20 ♗b3 ♖xf1+ 21 ♔xf1 ♗xc3 22 ♖a2 ♖f5 23 ♘d6+ ♔g7 24 ♘xf5+ gxf5 25 ♖f2 ♖e8!? is level; Moutousis-Grabics, Katerini 1993) 20...♗xh6 21 ♗xh6 ♖xf1+ 22 ♔xf1 ♘d5 = Meduna-Anikaev, Moscow 1982.

c2) 15...♘g4!? 16 ♘d6 (16 e6 fxe6 17 ♗xg4 ♘xc4) 16...♗xe5 17 ♘xe8 ♕h4! (avoiding the attractive trap 17...♗xh2+? 18 ♔h1 ♕h4 19 ♗g5! ♕xg5 20 ♗xg4 ♗e5 21 ♕f3 f5 22 ♖ae1, after which White wins; Gligorić-Ničevski, Zagreb 1970) 18 h3 ♕g3 19 ♗xg4 ♕h2+ 20 ♔f2 ♕g3+ 21 ♔g1 ♕h2+ = Taimanov-Tal, Sukhumi 1972.

13   ...   ♘c5

14   e5

14 ♗f3 ♗d7 15 e5 dxe5 16 fxe5 ♖xe5 17 ♘xc4 ♖e8 18 ♗f4 ♘fe4 19 ♘xe4 ♘xe4 = Ehlvest-Szekely, Tallinn 1983.

14   ...   dxe5

15   fxe5

Black has no problems after 15 ♘xc4 exf4 16 ♗xf4 ♘fe4 17 ♘xe4 ♘xe4 18 ♖a3 ♗d7 = Garcia-Tatai, Cuba 1974.

15 ...   ♖xe5
16 ♘xc4 (D)

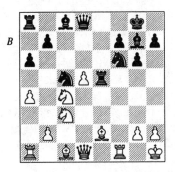

16 ...   ♖xe2!?

This may be the best solution. In practice the following moves have also been tried:

a) 16...♖f5 and now:

a1) 17 ♗f3 ♘g4!? 18 ♗xg4 (better than 18 ♘e3 ♘xh2! {18...♘xe3?! 19 ♗xe3 ±} 19 ♔xh2 ♕h4+ 20 ♔g1 ♖h5! 21 ♗xh5 ♗e5, when Black has a strong attack according to Bykhovsky) 18...♖xf1+ 19 ♕xf1 ♗xg4 20 ♗f4!? or 20 ♗e3 ♖c8 = Bykhovsky-Mi.Tseitlin, USSR 1982.

a2) 17 ♗f4!? is a more promising alternative:

a21) White will meet 17...♘h5!? with 18 ♗e3.

a22) White has an obvious advantage in the continuation 17...g5?! 18 ♗e3 ♖xf1+ 19 ♕xf1 ♘fe4 20 ♘xe4 ♘xe4 21 ♗d3 ♘d6 22 ♗b6 ♕d7 23 ♖e1 Lukacs-L.Karlsson, Helsinki 1983.

a23) 17...♘fe4 also does not lead to equality: 18 ♘xe4 ♘xe4 19 ♕c2 ♘g5 20 a5! ± Farago-Bistrić, Sarajevo 1983.

b) 16...♖e8 17 ♗g5 h6 (17...♗f5 18 d6 ♘ce4 19 ♘xe4 ♖xe4 20 ♘e3 ♗e6 21 ♗f3 ♖b4 22 ♗d5! ± Yrjölä-Teo, Dubai OL 1986) 18 ♗h4 ♘ce4 and now:

b1) White really cannot rely on having such a large advantage after 19 ♘xe4 ♖xe4 20 ♗g3!, although several problems face Black:

b11) 20...♗g4 21 ♗xg4 ♖xc4 (or 21...♖xg4?! 22 ♖xf6 ♖xc4 23 ♖xf7! ♔xf7 24 ♕f1+ wins) 22 ♗f3 with an excellent game for White.

b12) 20...♘xd5?! is even worse: 21 ♖xf7! ♗e6 (the choice is a small one, as both 21...♔xf7 22 ♘d6+, and 21...♖xe2 22 ♖xg7+ ♔xg7 23 ♕xe2 +– are terrible) 22 ♖xb7 ♔h8 23 ♕c2 +– Yrjölä-Vaiser, Sochi 1984.

b13) Yrjölä suggests 20...h5!? ±.

b2) 19 d6!? g5 (one cannot recommend 19...♘xc3 20 bxc3 g5 21 ♗f2 ♘e4 22 ♗b6 ♖xc3 23 ♕d3 ♕d7 24 ♗h5 ♖f8 25 ♗d4! +– Dorfman) 20 ♗e1 ♗e6 21 ♘xe4 ♘xe4 22 ♗a5 with a large advantage for White in Beliavsky-Velimirović, Moscow IZ 1982.

17 ♘xe2

17 ♕xe2 ♗f5 gives Black compensation.

17 ...   ♗g4
18 ♘e5   ♘ce4

18...♗h5 19 ♘f3 ±.

19 ♗f4!

Black has a wonderful game after 19 ♘xg4? ♘xg4 20 ♕e1 ♕b6.

The position after the 19th move was seen in Glek-Tseshkovsky, Budapest 1989, and now by playing 19...♘h5!? followed by 20...♕xd5 Black could have had a reasonable game.

A3) **10 ...** **♘bd7**
       11 0-0 **c4 *(D)***

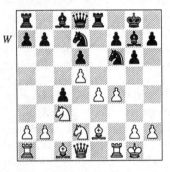

12 ♔h1

White's attempts to gain an advantage with other continuations have not been crowned with success, for example:

a) 12 ♗xc4 ♘c5 13 e5 dxe5 14 fxe5 ♖xe5 15 ♘f3 ♖e8 16 ♔h1 ♘fe4 17 ♘xe4, Kallai-Foisor, Bucharest 1983, and by continuing 17...♘xe4 18 ♕b3 ♘d6 Black could have equalized.

b) 12 ♗f3?! b5.

c) 12 e5 dxe5 13 ♘xc4 ♘b6! 14 fxe5 (or 14 d6 ♘xc4 15 ♗xc4 ♕b6+ 16 ♔h1 e4 ∓) 14...♘fxd5 15 ♘xd5 (White has too many weaknesses after 15 ♘d6 ♘xc3 16 bxc3 ♖f8 17 ♘xf7 {17 ♗f4 ♕e7 ∓} 17...♕xd1 18 ♗xd1 ♗e6! 19 ♘h6+ ♔h8 Kurtenkov-Ghinda, Primorsko 1985)

15...♕xd5 16 ♕xd5 ♘xd5 17 ♗f3 ♗e6!? (17...♘b6!? is not bad either) 18 ♗g5 h6 19 ♗h4 g5 20 ♗g3 ♖e7 = Sines-Ljubojević, Yugoslavia Ch 1982.

d) 12 a4 ♘c5 13 ♗f3 (13 e5 dxe5 14 ♘xc4 exf4!? 15 ♗xf4 ♘ce4 ∞) with the further possibilities of:

d1) 13...♗h6 14 ♕c2 ♘d3 (alternatively, 14...♗xf4 15 ♘xc4 ♗xc1 16 ♖axc1 ±) 15 ♘xc4 ♘xc1 16 ♕xc1 ♗g4 17 ♕d1 ± Nunn.

d2) 13...♕c7 14 e5 dxe5 15 fxe5 ♕xe5 16 ♘xc4 ♕b8 17 ♗e3 b6 18 ♗d4 ± Padevsky-Peev, Varna 1968.

d3) 13...b6!? 14 e5 dxe5 15 fxe5 ♖xe5 16 ♘xc4 and now:

d31) The game is unclear after 16...♖f5 17 d6 ♖b8 18 ♘b5!? (but not 18 ♘e3 ♖e5 19 ♘ed5 ♘xd5 20 ♗xd5 ♘e6 ∓ Ehlvest-Suba, Tallinn 1983) 18...♗e6 19 ♘e3 ♗b3, Zakharevich-Gleizerov, USSR 1987, and now White must sacrifice the queen: 20 ♘xf5! ♗xd1 21 ♘e7+ ♔h8 when 22 ♖xd1 yields compensation (Gleizerov); 22 ♘c6? is worse since 22...♗xf3! 23 ♘xd8 ♗d5 leaves the knight trapped.

d32) 16...♖e8 17 d6 (or 17 ♗g5!? ♗f5 ∞) 17...♗e6! 18 ♗e2 (it's not worth White's while chasing the rook, as after 18 ♗xa8 ♗xc4 19 ♗c6 ♖e6 20 ♖e1 ♖xd6 Black has a better game) was played in Chernin-Granda, Buenos Aires 1992, when, according to Chernin, 18...♘h5! 19 g4 ♕h4 would have led to an equal game.

d4) 13...♗d7!? 14 ♔h1 (14 e5 is of approximately the same value as

the text move, e.g. 14...dxe5 15 fxe5
♖xe5 16 ♘xc4 ♖e8 17 ♗g5 h6 18
♗h4 ♗f5 with equality; Gutman-
Petkevich, USSR 1967) 14...♖c8 15
e5 dxe5 16 fxe5 ♖xe5 17 ♘xc4 ♗f5
∞ C.Hansen-Larsen, Næstved 1985,
and it is important to note that White
cannot play 18 ♘d6?! because of
18...♗xa4!.

12 ...   ♘c5
13 e5

13 ♕c2?! ♘fxe4 14 ♘cxe4 ♗f5
15 ♗f3 ♕e7 16 ♖e1 ♗xe4 17 ♗xe4
f5 is bad, whilst 13 ♗f3 b5!? 14
♘xb5 ♘fxe4 15 ♘xc4 ♗f5 leads to
a game with mutual chances.

13 ...   dxe5 (D)

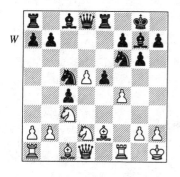

Now White must make a difficult
choice.

14 fxe5

There is another move at White's
disposal, which is of approximately
the same value, viz. 14 ♘xc4 and
now:

a) 14...e4 15 ♗e3 ♘d3 (15...b6?!
16 ♘e5 ♗b7 17 ♗c4 ± Zaltsman-
Wedberg, Reykjavik 1984) 16 ♗xd3
(16 ♘xe4? ♘xb2! ∓) 16...exd3 17
♕xd3 ♗f5 (17...b5 is interesting, but

not sufficient for equality: 18 ♘xb5
♗a6 19 a4 Dlugy-Suba, Tunis IZ
1985, and according to Dlugy Black
should have continued 19...♕xd5!?
20 ♕xd5 ♘xd5 21 ♗d2 ±) 18 ♕d2
♖c8 19 ♘e5 (19 b3?! b5! 20 ♘xb5
♘e4 21 ♕d1 ♗xa1 22 ♕xa1 ♕xd5
23 ♘xa7 ♖cd8, Zaichik-Veličković,
Tbilisi 1983, and Black's position is
preferable) 19...♘e4 (19...b5!? 20
d6 b4 21 ♘b5 has unclear consequences, Dlugy-Fedorowicz, USA
Ch 1984; Dlugy suggests 21...♖c2!
22 ♕xb4 ♖xe5! 23 fxe5 ♘g4 24
♖xf5!? {or 24 ♗f4 ♕a8 25 ♖f3
♘f2+ 26 ♔g1 ♘h3+ 27 ♔h1 ♘f2+
=} 24...gxf5 25 e6 ♕h4 26 ♗f4!
with a wild and wonderful position)
20 ♕d4 (20 ♘xe4 ♗xe4 ∓) 20...f6 21
♘f3 b6 22 ♖ac1 ♗f8! with compensation for the pawn; Meduna-Sax,
Baile Herculane 1982.

b) 14...exf4!? 15 ♗xf4 ♘ce4 16
♗f3 ♘xc3!? (16...♗f5 is not bad
either: 17 ♕b3 ♖c8 18 ♘e3 ♘c5 19
♕a3 ♗d3 20 ♖fd1 a5 = Zaltsman-
Lobron, Reykjavik 1984) 17 bxc3
♘e4 18 ♕b3 b6 19 d6 ♗a6 ∞ Dlugy-
Vaiser, Havana 1985.

14 ...   ♖xe5

14...♘fd7? is unsatisfactory: 15
e6 fxe6 16 ♘xc4 ♘e5 17 d6 ±.

15 ♘xc4   ♖e8!? (D)

Or 15...♖f5:

a) Black can achieve a satisfactory game, if not without a struggle,
after 16 ♗f3:

a1) 16...♘g4 is not so exact. After 17 ♘e3 ♘xe3 18 ♗xe3 b6 White
has a number of ways to seize the initiative:

a11) 19 d6!? ♗a6 20 ♗xc5 ♗xc3 (20...♗xf1? 21 ♗a3 +−) 21 bxc3 ♗xf1 22 ♗a3! ♗b5 (not 22...♗c4?, Piskov-Utemov, Moscow 1989, losing quickly to 23 d7 ♖b8 24 ♗d6 +− Piskov) 23 c4 ♗d7 24 ♗b2 with a strong attack.

a12) 19 ♗d4!? ♗a6 20 ♗xg7 ♔xg7 (20...♗xf1 is bad: 21 ♕d4 ♗a6 22 b4 ♘d7 23 ♗g4 ♖f1+ 24 ♖xf1 ♗xf1 25 ♗xd7 ♕xd7 26 ♘e4 +− Lin Ta) 21 b4! ♘d7 (or 21...♗xf1 22 bxc5 ♗a6 23 c6 ±) 22 ♖e1, Lin Ta-Sun Quinan, China 1987, and Black should have played 22...♘e5! ±.

a13) 19 ♖e1! is very strong, for example 19...♗a6 20 ♗xc5 bxc5 21 d6 ♖b8 22 ♘d5 ± Meduna-Poloch, Ceske Budejovice 1992.

a2) 16...b6!? is best:

a21) 17 ♘e3 ♖e5 18 b4 ♘ce4 19 ♘xe4 ♘xe4 20 ♗b2 ♕h4! (an important improvement in comparison with 20...♖e8? 21 ♗xg7 ♔xg7 22 d6 ±) 21 ♕e1 ♘g3+ 22 ♕xg3 ♕xg3 23 hxg3 ♖xe3 ½-½ Kelečević-Sax, Sarajevo 1982.

a22) 17 d6 ♖b8 (17...♗b7? is significantly worse: 18 ♗xb7 ♖xf1+ 19 ♕xf1 ♘xb7 20 ♗g5 h6 21 ♗h4 g5 22 ♗g3 ♘c5 23 ♖e1 ♘e6 24 ♘b5 ± Haba-Renet, Thessaloniki OL 1988) 18 ♘d5 (or 18 ♘e3 ♖e5 19 ♘ed5 ♘xd5 20 ♘xd5 ♕xd6 21 ♗f4 ♗a6) 18...♘xd5 19 ♗xd5 ♖xf1+ 20 ♕xf1 ♗e6 = Haba.

b) 16 ♗f4!? and now:

b1) 16...g5 favours White: 17 ♗e5! (17 ♗e3?! ♘ce4 18 ♘xe4 ♘xe4 19 ♗f3 ♘f6 =) 17...b5 18 ♘xb5 ♘ce4 19 ♕d4 ♕xd5 20 ♗f3 ♗e6 21 b3 ♘xb5 22 ♗xe4 ♖xf1+ 23 ♖xf1 ♘xe4 24 ♗xg7, Pigusov-Chekhov, Irkutsk 1983, and despite all Black's tactical possibilities, his position is extremely difficult.

b2) 16...♘h5 17 ♗e3:

b21) 17...♗xc3 18 ♖xf5 ♗xf5 19 bxc3 ♘e4 20 ♗xh5 gxh5 21 ♕d4 ♕f6 22 ♖f1 ♕xd4 23 ♗xd4 and Black had an unpleasant position in Alvarez-Yap, Cauto 1985.

b22) 17...b6!? is interesting.

b23) After the exchange of rooks on f1 White has all the chances to increase his opening advantage, for example 17...♖xf1+ 18 ♕xf1 b6 (or 18...♗xc3 19 bxc3 ♘e4 20 ♗xh5 ♕h4 21 ♕f3 gxh5 22 ♗d4 with a clear advantage; Kindermann-Danner, Zurich 1984) 19 ♖d1 ♗a6 20 d6 ♕f6 21 ♘d5 ± Pekarek-Suba, Warsaw Z 1987.

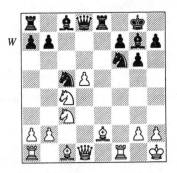

16 ♗g5   h6
17 ♗h4

Or 17 ♗f4 ♘fe4! 18 ♘b5 g5 19 ♗c7 ♕d7 20 a4 ♘a6 21 ♗d6 f5 with an attack; Muse-Kindermann, Bundesliga 1985.

17 ...   ♘ce4!?

It is in Black's interest to relieve the tension in the centre somewhat, as White has unpleasant pressure after 17...b6?! 18 d6 g5 (18...♗b7 19 ♗f3 ♗xf3 20 ♖xf3 g5 21 ♗f2 ±, whilst 18...♗a6 is met with 19 ♘d5!) 19 ♗f2 ♗a6 20 ♗d4 ♖e6 21 ♘e3! with initiative; Cserna-Fedorowicz, Lugano 1984.

White also has an excellent game after 17...♗f5 18 d6 ♕d7 19 ♖c1 ♖e6 20 b4 ♘ce4 21 ♘xe4 ♗xe4 22 ♗f3 ♖ae8 23 a4! ± Gorelov-Petrushin, Aktiubinsk 1985.

18 ♘xe4   ♖xe4
19 ♗g3   ♕xd5

Avoiding the trap 19...♘xd5? 20 ♖xf7! ♗e6 21 ♖xb7 ♕f6 22 ♗f3 ♖xc4 23 ♗xd5 and White wins; Tasić-Murey, Cannes 1992.

20 ♕xd5   ♘xd5
21 ♗f3

Cserna-Gufeld, Pristina 1983. Now 21...♖d4! 22 ♖ad1 ♘b6 would have led to a reasonable game, according to Gufeld.

B) 10 e5 dxe5

10...♘fd7 is very rarely used: 11 exd6 (11 e6 is weaker: 11...fxe6 12 dxe6 ♘b6 with a good game) 11...a6 12 a4 ♘f6 13 0-0 with a small advantage to White.

11 fxe5   ♘g4
12 ♗g5

The most popular move, but far from the only one. Other continuations likewise have their admirers:

a) 12 0-0!? ♘xe5 13 ♗f4 *(D)*:

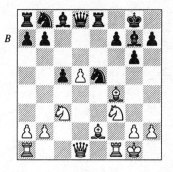

a1) White has a big advantage after 13...♕b6? 14 ♔h1 ♕xb2 15 ♘a4 ♕b4 16 ♗d2 ♕g4 17 ♘xe5 ♕d4 18 ♘xf7 ♕xa1 19 ♘h6+ ♔h8 20 ♕xa1 +− Toth-Popov, Budapest 1965.

a2) White also has strong pressure after 13...♘xf3+ 14 ♗xf3 c4 15 ♕d2 ♗f5 16 ♖ae1.

a3) 13...♗f5 does not lead to equality: 14 ♘xe5 ♗xe5 15 ♕d2 ♘d7 16 ♖ad1 a6 17 ♗xe5 ♘xe5 18 ♕f4 ± Vaiser-Renet, Brussels Z 1993.

a4) 13...♘bd7 14 d6 with two possibilities:

a41) 14...♘xf3+ 15 ♗xf3 ♘e5 16 ♘b5 (16 ♗d5!? ♗e6 17 ♘e4 ♘d7 18 ♗xe6 ♖xe6 19 ♘g5 with compensation) 16...♗f5 (16...♖f8 solves no problems: 17 ♘c7 ♖b8 18 ♖e1 ♘xf3+ 19 ♕xf3 ♕f6 20 ♘e8! ♕d4+ 21 ♗e3 ♕xb2 22 ♖ab1 ♕c3 23 ♘xg7 ± Balogh-Ribli, Hungarian Ch 1972) 17 ♘c7 ♘xf3+ (Szabo suggests 17...♘d3!?) 18 ♕xf3 ♗xb2 19 ♘xe8 ♗xa1 20 ♘c7 ♗d4+ 21 ♗e3 ♖c8 22 ♗xd4 cxd4 23 ♕f4 with a big advantage; Szabo-Zuckerman, Las Vegas 1973.

a42) 14...♕b6!? 15 ♘xe5 ♘xe5 16 ♗xe5 ♗xe5 17 d7 ♗xd7 18 ♕xd7 ♗xc3 19 ♕xf7+ ♔h8 20 bxc3 ♖e2 is unclear – Nunn.

b) 12 ♗f4 ♘xe5 13 ♘xe5 (the stronger 13 0-0!? transposes to variation 'a') 13...♗xe5 14 ♗xe5 ♖xe5 15 0-0 ♘d7 16 ♕d2 ♕g5 with an unclear game.

c) 12 e6 fxe6 and the possibilities are:

c1) 13 d6 ♗d7 (13...♘c6? 14 0-0 ♘d4 15 ♘e4 ♘f5 16 ♗g5 Berković-Shanal, Beersheba 1991) 14 0-0 ♗c6 15 ♘g5 ♘e5 16 ♗e3 b6 17 ♘ge4 ♘bd7 and Black's chances turned out somewhat better in Udovčić-Marović, Zagreb 1964.

c2) 13 ♘g5?! exd5 14 0-0 ♗d4+ 15 ♔h1 ♖f8! 16 ♗f3 ♘c6 with a clear advantage; Pavlović-Ivanović, Yugoslavia 1970.

c3) 13 0-0 exd5 (13...♖f8 is inferior in view of 14 ♗c4 exd5 15 ♘xd5 ♔h8 16 ♗g5 ♕d7 17 h3 b5 18 hxg4 bxc4 19 ♘e5! ♕e8 20 ♖xf8+ ♕xf8 21 ♗e7 ± Sakharov-Nemet, USSR-Yugoslavia 1963, whilst after 13...♗xc3 14 bxc3 exd5 15 ♘g5 White has the initiative) 14 ♘xd5 (Black has an easy game after 14 ♗g5 ♕d6 15 h3 {15 ♘xd5 ♗d4+!} 15...♘f6 16 ♗xf6 ♗xf6 17 ♘xd5 ♔h8 18 ♘xf6 ♕xf6 19 ♗b5 ♘c6 20 ♕c2 ♗f5 = Klompus-Waagmeester, Corr 1990) 14...♗e6 and now:

c31) Black seizes the initiative after 15 ♗c4 ♘c6 (15...♘e5!?) 16 ♗g5 ♘f6 17 ♘e5 ♘xe5 (17...♗xd5? 18 ♗xf6 ♗xf6 19 ♕xd5+ ♕xd5 20 ♗xd5+ ♔g7 21 ♘xc6 bxc6 22 ♗xc6

is clearly better for White) 18 ♗xf6 (18 ♘xf6+ ♗xf6 19 ♗xe6+ ♖xe6 20 ♗xf6 ♕xd1 ∓) 18...♘xc4 19 ♗xd8 ♖axd8 20 ♘e7+ ♔h8 21 ♘xg6+ hxg6 ∓ Nunn.

c32) 15 ♘f4 ♕xd1 16 ♖xd1 ♗f7 17 ♘g5 ♘e5. This complicated position arose in Hodos-Portisch, Lipetsk 1968, and White most likely should have continued 18 ♘xf7!? ♘xf7 19 ♗c4 with enough compensation for the pawn.

Now we return to the position after 12 ♗g5 in the main line:

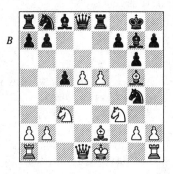

Now Black has two popular moves:

B1) 12...f6
B2) 12...♕b6

Black may also try 12...♕a5!?, a move which is seen very rarely, but which may be better than its reputation: 13 0-0 ♘xe5 14 d6 ♗e6! (White preserves his advantage after both 14...♘bc6 15 ♘d5 ♗e6 16 ♘c7 ♘d7 17 ♔h1 h6 18 ♗h4 ♖ac8 19 ♘xe6! ♖xe6 20 ♗c4 ± Petursson-Thorsteins, Saint John 1988, and 14...♘xf3+ 15 ♗xf3 ♗xc3 16 bxc3

♕xc3 17 ♗d5 ♗e6 18 ♖c1 ♕b4
{18...♕d4+ loses immediately: 19
♕xd4 cxd4 20 ♗xe6 fxe6 21 ♖c7
+–} 19 ♗xe6 ♖xe6 20 d7 ♘c6 21
d8♕+ ♘xd8 22 ♗xd8 ± Lažić-Jo-
vanović, Cetinje 1992) 15 ♘d5
♘bd7 16 ♘c7 ♘xf3+ 17 ♗xf3 c4!?
18 ♗c1 (18 ♗e3?! ♗xb2 19 ♗xb7
♖ab8 20 ♕f3 ♗xa1 21 ♘xe6 fxe6
22 ♕f7+ ♔h8 23 ♖xa1 ♕c3 ∓)
18...♕b6+ (18...c3 19 bxc3 ♗xc3 20
♗h6 ±) 19 ♔h1 ♗e5 20 ♘xa8 ♖xa8
with an unclear game in Kharkova-
Bystriakova, USSR 1989. The variation needs further tests.

**B1)   12   ...   f6
        13 exf6   ♗xf6 (D)**

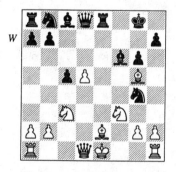

14 ♕d2
Probably the strongest move, and
one which enjoys unstinting popularity amongst theoreticians and
players alike. White even agrees to
exchange queens, hoping for a
strong passage for the pawn, on
which all his hopes are based, and
Black meanwhile cannot manage to
gain reliable equality.

White's other possibilities are:

a) 14 ♗xf6 ♕xf6 15 0-0 (15
♕a4!? ♗d7 16 ♕b3 also deserves attention) 15...♘e3 16 ♕d2 ♘xf1 17
♖xf1 ♗f5 18 ♗c4 ♘d7 19 d6+ ♔g7
20 ♘d5 ♕xd6 21 ♕c3+ ♘f6 22 g4
♗xg4 23 ♘g5 ♗f5 24 ♘xh7 ♖h8!
(24...♔xh7 is weaker: 25 ♘xf6+
♔h6 26 ♕c1+ ♔g7 27 ♖xf5!, with a
strong initiative) 25 ♕xf6+ ♕xf6
26 ♘hxf6 ♖af8 27 ♖xf5 gxf5 28
♘d7 ♖e8 29 ♘xc5 b6 with totally
unclear consequences; L.Grigor-
ian-Kupreichik, USSR 1970.

b) 14 ♗f4!? ♘e3 15 ♗xe3 ♖xe3
16 0-0 ♗g4 17 d6 ♘c6 18 ♘d5 ♖e6
19 ♘xf6+ ♖xf6 20 ♕b3+ ♗e6 21
♕xb7 ♖c8 22 ♖ad1 with a clear advantage to White; Padevsky-Spas-
sov, Bulgaria 1969. 14 ♗f4 needs
further practical tests.

14   ...   ♗f5 (D)
Black's task is not easier after
other moves:

a) 14...♘d7 15 0-0 ♘de5 16 ♗xf6
♕xf6 17 ♘g5 ♕b6 18 ♘ge4 c4+ 19
♔h1 ♗f5 20 d6 ♘d3. Thus continued Peev-Donner, Cienfuegos 1973,
and according to Peev's analysis,
White would have achieved a decisive advantage after 21 d7! ♖e5 22
♗xg4 ♗xe4 23 ♖ae1! ♕d4 24 ♖xe4
♖xe4 25 ♘xe4 ♕xe4 26 ♕g5 ♕d4
27 ♕e7 +–.

b) 14...♘e5 15 0-0-0 ♘xf3 16
♗xf6 ♘xd2 17 ♗xd8 ♖xd8 18 ♖xd2
and White has a small, but quite tangible advantage.

c) 14...♗xg5 15 ♕xg5 and Black
must resolve the difficult question of
whether he should exchange queens
himself on g5, or await the exchange

on d8, despite the fact that White preserves the initiative in both cases.

c1) 15...♘e3 16 ♕xd8 ♖xd8 17 ♔f2 ♘g4+!? (or 17...♘f5 18 ♖ad1 ♘d7 19 ♘e4 b6 20 g4 ♘h6 21 g5 ♘f5 22 ♖he1 ♗b7 23 ♗b5 ± Blokh-Fedorenko, Moscow 1975) 18 ♔g3 ♘e3 19 ♖ae1 ♘f5+ 20 ♔f2 ♘d7 21 ♘e4 with unpleasant pressure by White in Forintos-Enklaar, Wijk aan Zee 1974.

c2) 15...♘e5 16 ♕xd8 (White can consider 16 0-0-0!?) 16...♘xf3+ 17 ♔f2 ♖xd8 18 ♗xf3 ♘d7 19 ♖he1 ♘f6 20 ♖ad1 ± Vaiser-Lević, Vrnjačka Banja 1986.

c3) 15...♗f5 16 h3 ♘e5 17 ♕xd8 ♘xf3+ 18 ♔f2 ♖xd8 19 ♗xf3 ♘a6 20 g4 ♗d7 21 ♖he1 ± Semkov-Striković, Vrnjačka Banja 1987.

c4) 15...♕xg5 16 ♘xg5 and now Black has problems:

c41) 16...♘e3 is insufficient: 17 ♔f2 (17 ♔d2!? ♗f5 18 ♗b5!? is also interesting) 17...♗f5 (or 17...♘f5 18 ♘e6!; in Monin-Balogh, Budapest 1992, Black continued 17...♘c2 18 ♖ac1 ♖f8+ 19 ♗f3 and now the move 19...♘d4!? ± deserved attention) 18 ♘e6 ♗xe6 19 dxe6 ♖xe6 20 ♗f3 ♘c6 21 ♘d5 ±.

c42) 16...♗f5 17 h3 and now:

c421) 17...♘e3 is weak: 18 g4! (18 ♔f2 ♘c2 19 ♖ac1 ♘d4 20 g4 ♘xe2 21 ♘xe2 ♗d7 22 ♖xc5 ♘a6 = Ilić-Striković, Vrnjačka Banja 1987, is not as convincing) 18...h6 (Black has a difficult choice, as 18...♗d7? has even worse consequences: 19 ♔d2 ♖e5 {19...♘g2 20 ♖hf1 h6 21 ♘ge4 ♔g7 22 ♖f2 ♘h4 23 ♖af1 +−}

20 ♘ge4 +− Vaiser-Arizanov, Pula 1988) 19 ♘f3 ♗d7 ± Vaiser.

c422) White has an easy game after 17...♘f6 18 0-0 a6 (18...h6? 19 g4 ♘e4 20 ♘gxe4 ♗xe4 21 ♗b5 ♖e5 22 ♖ae1 +−; 18...♘bd7? loses quickly to 19 g4 ♘e4 20 ♘gxe4 ♗xe4 21 ♗b5 +− Hausner-Jirovsky, Prague 1993) 19 g4 ♘e4 20 ♘cxe4 ♗xe4 21 ♖ae1 ±.

c423) 17...♘e5!? was recommended by Nunn, but it has not yet been tested in practice. White's chances are preferable here as well, but it is without a doubt the least of the evils.

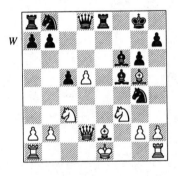

15   0-0

15 ♗f4 ♘d7 16 h3 ♘ge5 is equal, but 15 h3!? deserves attention:

a) An interesting, but very dangerous game for Black arises after 15...♘e5 16 0-0-0 ♘xf3 17 ♗xf6 ♘xd2 18 ♗xd8 ♘e4 19 ♘xe4 ♗xe4 20 ♗h4 ♗xg2 21 ♖he1 ♗xh3 22 d6 ♘d7 (22...♖e4 is better for White: 23 ♗f3! ♖xe1 24 ♖xe1 ♘c6 25 ♗d5+ ♔g7 26 ♖xc6 bxc6 27 ♖e7+ ♔h6 28 ♗f6 ± Goczan-Spiriev, Budapest 1991) 23 ♗c4+ ♔g7 24 ♖e7+

♖xe7 25 dxe7 a6 26 ♗e1! with compensation, Blokh.

b) 15...♗xg5 16 ♕xg5 ♘e5 (or 16...♕xg5 17 ♘xg5 ♘e3 18 ♔f2 ±) 17 ♕xd8 ♘xf3+ 18 ♔f2 ♖xd8 19 ♗xf3 ♘d7 20 ♖he1 with a small advantage to White.

15 ...   ♗xg5

The very moment to hurry into the exchange; White can secure a clear advantage after 15...♘d7:

a) Vaiser-Thipsay, New Delhi 1987, featured 16 h3 ♗xg5 17 ♘xg5 ♘e3 18 ♖xf5 ♘xf5 19 ♗b5, and now Black could have equalized by 19...♘d6! 20 ♘e6 ♕e7 21 ♘c7 ♖ac8 22 ♘xe8 ♖xe8 (Vaiser).

b) White preserves some pressure after 16 ♗b5!? a6 (or 16...♕b6 17 ♗xf6 ♘gxf6 18 ♘g5 ♖e5 19 ♕f4 ♖ae8 20 g4) 17 ♗xd7 ♕xd7 Arencibia-Paneque, Holquin m 1988, and as Arencibia showed, White should have continued 18 h3! ♗xg5 19 ♘xg5 ♘e3 20 ♖f3 ♘c2 21 ♖af1 ♘d4 22 ♖3f2 with initiative.

c) After 16 ♗f4! ♘ge5, Arencibia-Paneque, Holquin m 1988, the line 17 d6 ♘xf3+ (17...c4 18 ♘d5 ♘d3 19 ♗xd3 ♗xd3 20 ♗g5!) 18 ♗xf3 ♗d4+ 19 ♔h1 ♘e5 20 ♗d5+ ♔h8 21 ♘b5 would have given White a clear advantage (Arencibia).

16 ♕xg5   ♘d7

16...♘e3?! is bad: 17 ♕h6! ♕e7 (17...♘xf1 18 ♘g5 ♕e7 19 ♖xf1 ±) 18 ♗b5 ♗d7 19 ♖ae1 ± Peev-Janošević, Niš 1972.

Great complications, which are not unadvantageous for White, arise after 16...♕xg5 17 ♘xg5 ♘e3 18

♗b5! ♖d8 19 ♖fe1! ♘c2 20 ♖e7 a6 (or 20...♘xa1 21 g4!! a6 {21...♗xg4 22 ♘ce4 ♖f8 23 d6 +–} 22 gxf5 gxf5! {22...axb5 23 ♘ce4 ♘d7 24 f6 +–} 23 ♗d3 ♖d7 24 ♖e8+ ♔g7 25 ♗xf5 ±) 21 ♗c4 b5 22 ♖f1! bxc4 23 g4 ♘e3 24 gxf5! +– Crandbourne-Crespo, Corr 1988.

17 h3   ♘e3
18 ♕h6   ♘xf1
19 ♘g5   ♕e7
20 d6   ♕g7!

20...♕e3+ 21 ♔xf1 ♘f8 22 ♖d1 with initiative; Szabo-Timman, Amsterdam 1975.

After 20...♕g7! White must be satisfied with the draw, 21 ♗c4+ ♔h8 22 ♘f7+ ♔g8 = Szabo.

We can most likely come to the conclusion that the move 12...f6 favours White, although achieving an advantage from it demands very precise play.

B2)   12 ...   ♕b6 *(D)*

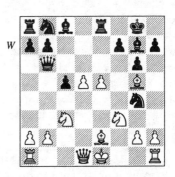

13 0-0

Black has no problems after 13 ♘a4 ♕a5+!? (13...♕b4+ is weaker: 14 ♗d2 ♕e4 15 ♘c3 ♕f5 16 0-0

♗xe5 17 h3 ♘f6 18 ♘g5 ♗d4+ 19 ♔h1 ♕e5 20 ♗f4 ±) 14 ♗d2 ♕d8 with at least an equal game.

However, the little-investigated 13 ♕d2!?, often employed by one of the main connoisseurs of the Four Pawns Attack, Blokh, deserves attention:

a) 13...♘d7?! is unsatisfactory: 14 e6 fxe6 15 dxe6 ♕xe6 (things are even worse for Black after 15...♗xc3 16 bxc3 ♕xe6 17 0-0! ♘df6 {17...♕xe2 18 ♖ae1 ♕xd2 19 ♖xe8+ ♔f7 20 ♖e7+ ♔f8 21 ♘xd2+ +− Blokh} 18 ♖ae1 ♕c6 19 h3 ♘e4 20 ♕f4 h6 21 hxg4 hxg5 22 ♘xg5 ♘xg5 23 ♕xg5 ♔g7 24 ♗c4! +− Blokh) 16 ♘d5 ♗e5 17 ♘xe5 ♕xe5 18 ♗f4 ±.

b) 13...♘xe5 14 0-0-0 ♘a6!? (White has a small advantage after 14...♗f5 15 ♘xe5 ♗xe5 16 ♖he1 ♕b4 17 a3 ♕b3 18 g4 ♗d7 19 ♗f3 Blokh-Schneider, Corr 1989) 15 ♘xe5 ♖xe5 16 ♖he1 (a possible improvement in comparison with Blokh-Lukin, Russian Cht 1992, in which after 16 ♗f4?! ♖e8 17 ♖he1 ♗d7 White should have continued 18 g4!? ∞) 16...♘b4 17 ♗c4 (17 d6? ♖xg5 18 ♕xg5 ♘xa2+! wins for Black) 17...♖xe1 18 ♖xe1 ♗f5 19 d6 with sufficient compensation for the pawn.

13 ...   ♘xe5

One cannot recommend either 13...h6 14 ♗f4!? g5 15 ♗c1 ♘xe5 16 ♘xe5 ♗xe5 17 ♗h5 – analysis by Nunn – or 13...♗f5 14 ♘a4!? (14 e6 is not as convincing: 14...fxe6 15 ♗b5 c4+ 16 ♔h1 ♗d3 with huge

complications; Littlewood-Mordue, British Ch (Eastbourne) 1990) 14...♕a5 15 ♘h4 ♘xe5 (15...♗xe5? is far worse: 16 ♗xg4 {16 ♘xf5!?} 16...♗xg4 17 ♕xg4 ♗d4+ 18 ♔h1 ♕xa4 19 ♘f5! gxf5 20 ♖xf5 h5 21 ♕g3 +− Semkov) 16 ♘xf5 gxf5 17 ♖xf5 ♘bd7 18 ♘c3, Semkov-Apicella, Sofia 1990.

Black quite often tries 13...c4+ 14 ♔h1 ♘d7 (greed is not permissible: 14...♘f2+ 15 ♖xf2 ♕xf2 16 ♘e4 ♕b6 17 ♘d6 ♖f8 18 ♗e7 ♗d7 19 ♘xc4 +−) and now *(D)* White has a choice between two pawn moves:

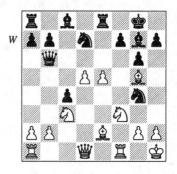

a) 15 d6?! ♘f2+ 16 ♖xf2 ♕xf2 17 ♘d5 (17 ♘e4 ♕b6 18 ♘f6+ ♘xf6 19 ♗xf6 ♗xf6 20 exf6 ♗e6 ∞; 17 ♗xc4?! ♘xe5 18 ♘e4 ♕b6 19 ♘xe5 ♖xe5 20 ♘f6+ ♗xf6 21 ♗xf6 ♖f5 22 ♗e7 ♗d7 ∓ Kouatly-Povah, Ramsgate 1979) 17...♘xe5 18 ♘c7 (18 ♗e3? is weak: 18...♘g4! 19 ♘e7+ ♔h8 20 ♘g5 ♘xe3 21 ♕g1 ♕xg1+ 22 ♔xg1 ♗e6 and Black wins – Nunn) 18...♗d7 ∓.

b) 15 e6 fxe6 16 dxe6 ♘df6 17 h3 (White will not get much joy from the active 17 e7 ♖xe7 18 ♘d5

♘xd5 19 ♕xd5+ ♗e6 20 ♕e4 ♖f7!?
{20...♖c7!? 21 ♖ad1 ♖f8 ∓ Jones-
Povah, British Ch 1979, also deserves attention} 21 ♗xc4 ♗xc4 22
♕xc4 ♘f2+ 23 ♖xf2 ♕xf2 24 ♖f1
♕xb2 25 ♘e5 ♕xe5 26 ♕xf7+ ♔h8
gives Black a slight plus; Semkov-
Murey, Cannes 1989) 17...♕xb2
(17...♘f2+? 18 ♖xf2 ♕xf2 19 ♗xf6
♗xf6 20 ♘e4 ±; 17...♘e3? 18 ♗xe3
♕xe3 19 ♗xc4 ±) and now:

b1) The tempting 18 ♘a4 is re-
futed beautifully by 18...♘f2+!! 19
♖xf2 ♘e4 20 ♖f1 ♘g3+ 21 ♔g1
♕xa1 22 ♕xa1 ♘xe2+ 23 ♔f2
♗xa1 24 ♖xa1 ♗xe6 25 ♖e1 ♖ac8
26 ♖xe2 c3 −+ Kakageldiev-Murey,
Corr 1972 – a fantastic idea; more-
over it is interesting that practically
all of these moves were seen 16
years later in Kouatly-Murey.

b2) 18 ♕c1!? ♕xc1 19 ♖axc1
♘h5 20 ♘e4 ♗xe6 21 hxg4 ♗xg4 ∞
Nunn. The variation is not forced,
but it is interesting.

After 13...♘xe5 *(D)*, White has
two main systems:

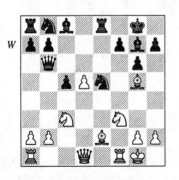

B21) 14 ♘xe5
B22) 14 d6

B21) 14 ♘xe5   ♗xe5
14...♖xe5!? is almost never seen in
practice, but it deserves attention: 15
♕d2 (15 ♗f4 ♕xb2!?) 15...♗f5 16
♗f4 ♘d7!? 17 ♗xe5 ♘xe5 18 ♔h1
c4 with compensation; Ca.Hansen-
Yurtaev, Gausdal 1990.

15 ♗c4
15 ♕d2 is not as dangerous for
Black: 15...♗f5 16 ♖ae1 ♘d7 17
♔h1 and now 17...♗g7!? ∞, but not
17...♘f6? 18 ♗d3 ♗xd3 19 ♕xd3
c4 20 ♕f3 h6 21 ♖xe5 ♖xe5 22
♗xf6 ± Christiansen-Biyiasis, USA
1977.

15 ...   ♗f5 *(D)*
The most popular move, after
which it is not at all easy, although
still generally possible, for White to
gain an advantage.

Other possibilities:

a) 15...♕xb2 16 d6:

a1) 16...♗f5 17 ♖xf5 (17 ♗xf7+
♔xf7 18 ♖xf5+ ♔g7! 19 d7 ♘xd7
20 ♕xd7+ ♔h8 is unclear) 17...gxf5
18 ♗xf7+ ♔f8! (and definitely not
18...♔xf7? 19 ♕h5+ ♔f8 20 ♗h6+
♗g7 21 ♕xf5+ ♔g8 22 ♖f1 +−
Arencibia-Martin del Campo, Bayamo 1989) 19 ♗xe8 ♕xc3 20 ♗e7+
♔xe8 21 ♕h5+ ♔d7 22 ♕xf5+ and
White has a safe draw but could seek
a route to a more pleasing result.

a2) 16...♖f8!? 17 ♗xf7+ (the
move 17 ♘b5?! is interesting, but
not sufficient: 17...♕xa1 18 ♕f3
♕b2 19 ♗xf7+ ♔g7 20 ♗e7 ♗f5 21
♗xf8+ ♔xf7 22 ♕xb7+ ♘d7! 23
♕xd7+ ♔g8 ∓ Vaiser) 17...♔g7
(17...♖xf7? 18 ♕d5 ♗d4+ 19 ♔h1
♗f5 20 ♖ab1 ♕xc3 21 ♖xb7 ♘d7

22 ♖xd7 ♖af8 23 ♖xf7 ♖xf7 24 d7
+−) 18 ♗d5! (again the knight must
not be put on b5 – 18 ♘b5? ♕xa1 19
♗h6+ ♔xh6 20 ♕d2+ ♗f4! 21
♕xf4+ g5 −+ Semkov, and 18 ♕d5?
is also unsatisfactory: 18...♕xc3 19
♖ad1 ♗f5 and Black wins; Semkov-
Marin, Burgas 1990) 18...♕xc3
(18...♗f5 19 ♕c1! ♕xc3 20 ♗h6+
♔h8 21 ♕xc3 ♗xc3 22 ♗xf8 ♘d7
23 ♗e7 ♗xa1 24 ♖xa1 with compensation; 18...♖xf1+?! 19 ♕xf1 ♗f5
20 ♖e1 ♕xc3 21 ♗xb7 ♗xd6 22
♗xa8 ±) 19 ♖xf8 ♔xf8 (19...♕d4+?
is weak, as 20 ♖f2 gives a big advantage) 20 ♕f1+ ♗f5 21 ♖d1! ♘d7 22
g4 ♔g7 23 gxf5 h6! (Black must
play with the utmost accuracy, as
23...♕c2? 24 ♖d2 ♕xf5 25 ♕xf5
gxf5 26 ♗e7 ♗d4+ 27 ♔f1 is bad;
Vaiser-Berthelot, France 1992) 24
♗e7 ♕c2 25 ♕f3 ♕xh2+ 26 ♔f1
gxf5 27 ♕xf5 ♕f4+ 28 ♕xf4 ♗xf4
29 ♗xb7 ♖b8 30 ♗c6 ♘e5 = Elbi-
lia-Berthelot, France 1993.

b) 15...♕b4:

b1) 16 ♕f3 ♗f5 17 ♗b5!? (17
g4? is bad in view of 17...♕xb2! 18
♘e2 ♗d4+, but note that 17...♕xc4?
is wrong: 18 gxf5 f6 19 fxg6 hxg6 20
♗xf6 ♘d7 21 ♗xe5 ♘xe5 22 ♕f6
Szabo-Pietzsch, Salgotarjan 1967)
17...♖f8 18 ♖ae1 f6 19 a3 (Black's
affairs are fully in order after 19
♗h6 ♗xh2+ {19...♕h4 20 ♖xe5}
20 ♔xh2 ♕h4+ 21 ♔g1 ♕xh6 22
♗e7 a6) 19...♗d4+ 20 ♔h1 ♕xb2 21
♗h6. Now White has a big advantage following 21...♕xc3 22 ♗xf8
♕xf3 23 ♖xf3 ♔xf8 24 ♖e8+ ♔f7
25 d6 Matsula-Al.Kharitonov, Kirov

1993, but after 21...♘d7!? Black
preserves reasonable chances, despite the slight material imbalance.

b2) 16 ♕b3 ♗f5 17 d6 ♕xb3 18
axb3 ♗xd6 (18...♗d4+ is worse: 19
♔h1 ♗xc3 20 bxc3 ♗e6 21 ♖ae1
♘d7 22 ♗b5 a6 23 ♗xd7 ♗xd7
♖e7 with a small plus for White;
Forintos-Gudmundsson, Reykjavik
1974) 19 ♘d5 and Black has a reasonable choice:

b21) 19...♘d7 20 ♖xf5 (20 ♗b5
♖e5 21 ♖ad1 ♗c2!) 20...gxf5 21
♗b5 ♗e5! 22 ♗xd7 ♖ed8 23 ♗xd8
♖xd8 24 ♘e7+ (24 ♖d1? ♗d4+ 25
♔f1 ♔f8 −+) 24...♔f8 25 ♗xf5
♔xe7 26 ♖xa7 ♔d6 = Janošević-
Forintos, Vrnjačka Banja 1973.

b22) 19...♘c6!? 20 ♘f6+ ♔g7
21 ♘xe8+ ♖xe8, also with a more or
less balanced position; Nogueiras-
Grünberg, Varna 1982.

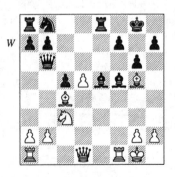

16 ♘b5

White's quest has led him in two
other directions:

a) 16 ♗b5?! ♗d7 (or 16...c4+ 17
♔h1 ♖c8 18 ♕f3 f6 19 ♖ae1! ♕d4
20 ♗f4 ♗xf4 21 ♕xf4 ♕xf4 22
♖xf4 ± Mikenas-Vladimirov, USSR

1963) 17 ♕f3 f5 (17...f6!? deserves attention, for example 18 a4 ♗xb5 19 ♘xb5 ♘d7 20 d6 ♕c6 21 ♗h6 ♕xf3 22 ♖xf3 ♖ad8 23 ♘c7 ♗d4+ with an obvious advantage to Black in Kakageldiev-Zaid, USSR 1973) 18 ♗c4 ♕xb2 19 d6+ ♔h8 20 ♖ac1 ♗c6 21 ♕h3 ♘d7 22 ♘e2 ♗xd6 ∓ Nei-Ciocaltea, Zinnowitz 1966.

b) 16 d6 ♕xd6 (16...♕xb2 leads to 15...♕xb2) 17 ♕xd6 ♗xd6 18 ♘d5 ♗e5 19 ♘e7+ ♖xe7 20 ♗xe7 ♗xb2 21 ♖ae1 ♗d4+ 22 ♔h1 ♘c6 ∓ Mikenas-Damljanović, Sofia 1962.

16 ...   ♘d7 *(D)*

Black can also chose from a number of other possibilities, which may also offer chances of a satisfactory game:

a) 16...♖f8 17 a4 ♕a5 18 ♗e7 ♘d7 was played in Šahović-Dydyshko, USSR 1973, and now White should have continued 19 ♗xf8!?.

b) 16...a6 17 d6 axb5 18 ♗xf7+ ♔xf7 (Black should have drained the cup, as after 18...♔g7 19 ♗xe8 ♗d4+ 20 ♔h1 ♕xd6 21 ♗xb5 ♘c6 22 ♕d2 Vaiser-Kozlov, USSR 1971, White has a winning position) 19 ♖xf5+! gxf5 (19...♔g7 20 d7) 20 ♕h5+ ♔f8 (20...♔e6 does not solve any problems: 21 ♕xe8+ ♔xd6 22 ♖e1 c4+ 23 ♗e3 ♘c6!? 24 ♕xa8 ♗d4 25 ♖d1 ♔c7 26 ♗xd4 ♘xd4 27 ♔h1 ± Wessman-Spasov, Tunja jr Wch 1989) 21 ♗h6+ (21 ♖f1 ♘d7 22 ♕xh7 ♖e6! Nunn) 21...♗g7 22 ♗xg7+ (22 ♖f1? c4+ 23 ♔h1 ♕f2!) 22...♔xg7 23 ♕xe8 c4+ 24 ♔h1 ♕xd6 (24...♕f2 25 d7 ♖xa2 26 ♖e1 ♘c6 27 d8♕ ♘xd8 28 ♖e7+ ♔f6 29

♕f8+ ♔g5 30 ♕g7+ +−) 25 ♖e1 ♖a6 26 ♖e7+ ♔f6 27 ♕f8+ ♔g5 28 ♕g8+ ♕g6 29 ♖g7 ± Nunn.

c) 16...h6 17 ♗xh6 ♕f6 18 ♕d2 is again better for White.

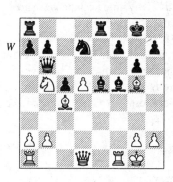

17 a4!?

After 17 d6 with exact play Black can not only repulse his opponent's onslaught, but can also gain an advantage, e.g. 17...♗e6! (17...♗d4+?! 18 ♘xd4 cxd4 19 ♖xf5 gxf5 20 ♕h5 ± Bazon-Negulescu, Corr 1987) 18 ♕b3 (18 ♗xe6 leads to a really depressing result: 18...♖xe6 19 ♘c7 {or 19 ♖xf7 ♕xb5 20 ♕d5 ♔xf7 21 ♖f1+ ♕xf1+ 22 ♔xf1 ♖b8 ∓} 19...♖xd6 20 ♕f3 ♖f8 21 ♗e7 ♕xc7 22 ♗xf8 ♘xf8 −+) 18...♗xd6 19 ♘xd6 ♕xd6 20 ♗xe6 ♖xe6 21 ♕xb7 ♕c6 ∓.

17 ...   f6

17...a5 18 ♖a3!? ♗d4+ 19 ♔h1 ♘e5 20 ♖b3 ♗g4 21 ♕c1 with a promising game; Vaiser-Podvrsnik, Ptuj 1989.

18 a5!?

18 ♗h6 ♗d4+ 19 ♔h1 a5 leads to an unclear position; Kupka-I.Zaitsev, Moscow-Prague 1968.

| 18 | ... | ♕d8 |
| 19 | ♗h6 | ♔h8 |

20 d6 a6 (it's still not too late to go wrong: 20...♗xb2?! 21 ♖a2 ♘e5 22 ♗e2 ♗d4+ 23 ♘xd4 cxd4 24 ♕xd4 and White's chances are preferable; Vaiser-Akopian, Uzhgorod 1988) 21 ♘c7 ♗d4+ 22 ♔h1 ♘e5 and, according to the assessment of perhaps the leading exponent of the Four Pawns Attack, Vaiser, Black has sufficient compensation for the exchange.

B22)   14   d6 *(D)*

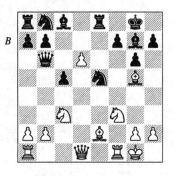

| 14 | ... | ♕xb2 |

Several other moves are possible:

a) 14...♗e6 and now:

a1) After 15 ♗b5 Black should try the untested 15...♘bc6, which offers him reasonable prospects. White has more chances after 15...♘bd7 16 ♗xd7 ♘xd7 17 ♘d5 ♗xd5 (or 17...♗d4+ 18 ♘xd4 ♗xd5 19 ♘f5 ±) 18 ♕xd5 ±.

a2) After 15 ♘d5 ♗xd5 16 ♕xd5 ♘bd7, Blokh's idea is to play 17 ♖ad1!?. Note that 17 ♘xe5 ♘xe5 (17...♖xe5 18 ♕xf7+ ♔h8 19 ♕xd7 ♖xg5 20 ♖ad1 ♖d8 21 ♕f7 ♕c6 22 ♗f3 ♕d7 = Martin-Matulović, Haringey 1989, is also sufficient) 18 d7 ♘xd7 19 ♖xf7 does not work because of 19...♕e6!.

a3) 15 ♘xe5!? ♗xe5 16 ♘d5 ♕xb2 (16...♗xd5? 17 ♕xd5 ♗d4+ 18 ♔h1 ♖f8 is bad because of 19 ♖xf7! +−; White has a clear advantage in the endgame after 16...♗d4+ 17 ♕xd4 cxd4 18 ♘xb6 axb6 19 ♗b5 ♘c6 20 a4 Peev-Vogt, Varna 1973) 17 ♘f6+ ♗xf6 18 ♗xf6 with more than enough compensation.

b) 14...♘bd7 15 ♗b5!? (after 15 ♘d5 Black must sacrifice the queen with 15...♕xd6!? 16 ♘f6+ ♗xf6 17 ♗xf6 ♗xf6, on Nunn's recommendation, with reasonable practical compensation, especially as the mundane 15...♕xb2 16 ♖b1 ♘xf3+ 17 ♗xf3 ♕d4+ 18 ♔h1 ♖b8 19 ♘e7+ ♔h8 20 ♘xc8 favours White) 15...♖e6 16 ♗e7 ♘xf3+ 17 ♕xf3 ♗d4+ 18 ♔h1 ♘e5 19 ♕f4 ♗xc3 20 ♕h6! with a huge initiative.

c) 14...♘xf3+ 15 ♗xf3 ♗d4+ (the move 15...c4+!? deserves practical tests, e.g. 16 ♔h1 ♕xb2 17 ♘d5 ♕xa1 18 ♕xa1 ♗xa1 19 ♖xa1 ♘d7 with an unclear game, whilst 15...♕xb2!? 16 ♘d5 ♕d4+ 17 ♔h1 ♕xa1 18 ♕xa1 ♗xa1 19 ♖xa1 leads to a position which will be examined later) 16 ♔h1 ♕xd6 17 ♗d5 and a seriously unpleasant time awaits Black, no matter how he continues, for example:

c1) 17...♗e6 18 ♗xb7 ♘d7 19 ♗xa8 ♖xa8 20 ♘b5 ♕b6 (20...♕d5 21 ♘xd4 cxd4 22 ♕f3 ♕xf3 23

Ⓧxf3 ♗f5 24 Ⓧf4 d3 25 Ⓧd4 ±) 21
♘xd4 cxd4 22 b3 ♗f5 Knežević-
Trapl, Dečin 1976, and after the
straightforward 23 ♕f3 the position
is very difficult for Black.

c2) 17...Ⓧe6 18 ♕f3 f5 19 Ⓧae1
♗d7 20 ♗xe6+ ♗xe6 21 ♕xb7 +−
also has unpleasant consequences.

d) 14...c4+ 15 ♔h1 ♘d3 16 ♗xd3
cxd3 17 ♕xd3 ♗e6 18 Ⓧac1 ♕a6 19
♕xa6 bxa6 20 Ⓧfd1 ± Peev-Vukić,
Kapfenberg Echt 1970.

15 ♘d5   ♘xf3+

It is not easy for White to find
grounds for hoping for an advantage
after 15...♗f5, for example 16 ♘e7+
(Blokh recommends 16 Ⓧc1!? ∞, as
16 ♘c7 ♘bd7 17 ♘xa8 Ⓧxa8, with
enough compensation for the exchange, creates no problems for the
opposition) 16...Ⓧxe7 17 dxe7 ♘bc6
(D) and now:

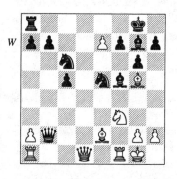

a) 18 ♔h1 Ⓧe8 (18...♘xf3?! is
weak: 19 ♗xf3 ♕xa1 20 ♗xc6!
♕xd1 21 Ⓧxd1 +− Ilić-Sandić, Yugoslavia 1989) 19 Ⓧc1 transposes to
'c3'.

b) 18 ♕e1?! h6 19 ♗h4 g5 20
♗g3 ♕xa1 21 ♕xa1 ♘xf3+ 22 ♗xf3

♗xa1 23 Ⓧxa1 ♘xe7 Rechlis-Badea
Takacs, Haifa 1989. White faces a
tedious struggle for the draw.

c) 18 Ⓧc1 Ⓧe8 and now:

c1) 19 Ⓧxc5? ♘xf3+ 20 ♗xf3
♕d4+ and Black wins.

c2) 19 ♘xe5?! ♕xe5 20 ♗b5
♗e4!? (stronger than 20...♗e6 21
♗xc6 ♕d4+ 22 ♔h1 bxc6 ∞ Vaiser-
Degraeve, Cappelle la Grande 1987)
21 ♗h4 (or 21 ♕b3 ♗d5 22 ♗c4
♗xc4 23 ♕xc4 ♕d4+, and 21 ♕d7
♕d4+ 22 ♕xd4 ♗xd4+ 23 ♔h1
♔g7 24 Ⓧce1 ♗d5 is similarly insufficient) 21...♕b2 22 ♕g4 ♗d4+
23 ♔h1 f5 24 ♗c4+ ♔g7 25 ♕g3
♘xe7 ∓ Barsov-Marin, Budapest
1990.

c3) 19 ♔h1 h6 (19...♘xe7 is also
possible: 20 ♘xe5 ♕xe5 21 ♗c4
♘c6 22 ♕b3 ♗e6 23 ♗xe6 ♕xe6 24
♕xb7 ± Peev-Makropoulos, Greece
1973, but the text move is more
precise) 20 ♗h4 ♘xe7 21 ♘xe5
(21 Ⓧxc5?! ♘7c6 22 Ⓧb5 ♕xa2 23
Ⓧxb7 ♘g4! ∓ Goregliad-Byrne, New
York 1988) 21...♕xe5 22 ♗b5 ♘c6
23 Ⓧe1 Peev-Sikora, Moscow 1977,
and now 23...♕b8 would have led to
an unclear game.

After the quiet developing move
15...♘bc6 prospects are unclear.
White may continue 16 Ⓧb1 (16
♘f6+!? ♗xf6 17 ♗xf6 is very interesting, and 17...♗g4? is bad because
of the elegant 18 ♘xe5! ♗xe2 19
♘g4! ♗xg4 20 ♕xg4 ±) and now:

a) 16...♘xf3+ is bad: 17 ♗xf3
♕d4+ (17...♕e5? is an even less attractive move: 18 ♘f6+ ♗xf6 19
♗xf6 ♕xf6 20 ♗xc6 ♗f5 21 ♗xe8

♖xe8 22 ♖xb7 ± Fang-Van Wely, New York 1993) 18 ♔h1 with a clear advantage to White.

b) 16...♕a2 17 ♘c7 ♗f5 18 ♘xe8 ♖xe8 (18...♗xb1?! 19 ♘xg7 ♗c2 20 ♕e1 ± Vaiser-Belov, USSR 1983; 18...♕xb1? 19 ♕xb1 ♗xb1 20 ♘c7 +− leads to a huge material loss) 19 ♖xb7 ♘d4 20 ♘xd4 cxd4 21 ♗b5 ♕d5! 22 ♗xe8 ♕xb7 with a complex an interesting game.

16   ♗xf3 *(D)*

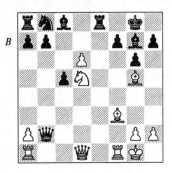

16   ...   ♕d4+!?

It is quite obviously best of all to banish the white monarch to h1 first, and only then to devour the rook, although supporters have also been found for 16...♕xa1, which, it is worth noting, has justly not gained good results. One may continue 17 ♕xa1 (17 ♘e7+ ♔h8 18 ♕xa1 ♗xa1 19 ♖xa1 ♘d7 20 ♖e1 with compensation, Vaiser-Grigoriadis, Odessa 1977, is interesting, but the text move promises more) 17...♗xa1 18 ♖xa1 ♘d7 19 ♗e7 (after the weak 19 ♘c7?! ♖e5 20 ♗d8 ♖b8 21 ♘d5 ♔f8 22 ♗c7 ♖a8 Black avoids danger) 19...♖b8 20 ♘c7 ♖f8 21

♖e1 c4 (21...b5!? deserves attention in analogy with the main variation) 22 ♗xf8 ♔xf8 (22...♘xf8 23 ♖e8 Vaiser-Khodos, USSR 1978, and the game should have ended 23...c3 24 ♗e4 ♗f5 25 ♖xb8 ♗xe4 26 ♘e6! fxe6 27 d7 c2 28 ♖xf8+ ♔g7 29 ♖f1 +−) 23 ♗d5 ♘f6 24 ♗xc4 b5 25 ♗b3 ♗e6 26 ♘xe6+ fxe6 27 ♖xe6 ♔g7 28 ♖e7+ ♔h6 29 ♖xa7 with a large advantage to White.

16...♘c6?! promises Black nothing good either: 17 ♗f6! ♘d4 18 ♖b1 ♕xa2 19 ♗xg7 ♔xg7 20 ♘c7 with a clear plus for White.

17   ♕xd4   ♗xd4+
18   ♔h1   ♗xa1
19   ♖xa1   ♖e5!? *(D)*

The most reliable, but probably not the only way of holding the position together. After huge complications Black maintains equality following 19...♘d7 20 ♗e7 ♖b8 21 ♘c7 ♖f8 22 ♖e1 b5! (22...c4 leads to a position examined in the notes to move 16, when the position of the king on h1 has no significance whatsoever).

Now White must chose from the following moves:

a) 23 ♗c6 b4 24 ♗xf8 ♔xf8 25 ♖e8+ ♔g7 leads to 'c'.

b) 23 ♗d5!? c4 24 ♗xf8 ♘xf8 25 ♖e8 c3 26 ♗b3 ♔g7 27 ♘a6 (27 ♘xb5?! ♖xb5 28 ♖xc8 ♖b6 29 ♖c7 ♘e6 30 d7 ♖d6 and White faces a battle for the draw) 27...♖b6 28 ♖xc8 ♖xa6 29 ♖c7 ♖xd6 30 ♖xf7+ ♔h6 31 ♖xf8 ♖d2 32 ♔g1 ♖b2 33 ♖f2 ♖b1+ with a balanced position − Nuñez.

c) 23 ♗xf8 ♔xf8 (capturing the knight favours White: 23...♘xf8 24 ♖e8 ♔g7 25 ♗c6 c4 26 ♘xb5 ±) 24 ♖e8+ ♔g7 25 ♗c6 b4 with the further possibilities:

c1) 26 ♗xd7?! b3! (the pawn rushes towards its ultimate goal with astounding speed!) 27 axb3 ♖xb3 28 h3 (or 28 h4 ♗xd7 29 ♖e7 ♗f5 30 d7 ♖d3 –+) 28...♗xd7 29 ♖e7 ♗c6 30 d7 ♖xh3+ 31 ♔g1 ♖d3 32 d8♕ ♖xd8 33 ♘e6+ ♔f6 34 ♘xd8 ♔xe7 35 ♘xc6+ ♔d6 36 ♘xa7 c4 and Black wins – Nuñez.

c2) 26 h3 ♘f6 P.Garcia-Nuñez, Ciego de Avila 1989, and after exact play from both players the game should have concluded in a draw: 27 ♖d8! ♗b7 28 ♖xb8 ♗xc6 29 ♘a6 ♘d7 30 ♖c8 ♗b7 31 ♖c7 ♗xa6 32 ♖xd7 ♗c4 33 ♖xa7 ♔f6 34 ♖e7 ♗xa2 35 ♖e5!! ♗e6 36 ♖xc5 ♗a2 37 ♖e5 = (analysis by Nogueiras).

Somehow we seem to have moved unnoticed from analysing an opening variation to a complicated endgame.

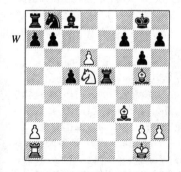

20 ♗f4!?

Only White is in danger after 20 ♘e7+ ♔g7 21 ♘xc8 ♘d7 22 ♗xb7 ♖b8 23 ♗c6 ♖xg5 24 ♗xd7 c4 25 ♘xa7!? (25 h4? is bad: 25...c3! 26 ♗a4 ♖d5 27 ♘xa7 { or 27 d7 c2! 28 ♗xc2 ♖xd7 –+} 27...♖b4 and Black is winning; Dobos-Schlosser, Balatonbereny 1989) 25...c3 (25...♖b7? 26 ♗c6! ♖xa7 27 d7) 26 ♗a4 ♖b2 27 ♖d1 c2 (in Tozer-M.Schlosser, Oakham 1988, the players agreed a draw after 27...♖gxg2 28 d7 ♖xh2+, but I think that Black could have continued the struggle without any risk after 29 ♔g1 ♖bg2+ 30 ♔f1 ♖d2!?) 28 ♗xc2 ♖xc2 29 g3 (29 d7 ♖d5!) 29...♖e5 =.

20 ... ♖xd5!

White can only dream about 20...♖f5? 21 ♘e7+ ♔g7 22 ♘xf5+ gxf5 23 ♖e1 ♘d7 24 ♖e7 ♘b6 25 a4! ♗e6 26 a5 ♘d7 27 a6 with a big advantage.

21	♗xd5	♘c6
22	♗xc6	bxc6
23	♖c1	♗d7
24	♖xc5	♖b8
25	h3	♖b5
26	♖c3	

with even chances.

In *resumé* we may note that the Four Pawns Attack has, perhaps temporarily, survived several crises recently, and I think that future research by White will be linked to 12 0-0!?.

11 Modern Lines after 7 ♘f3 (A70)

1 d4 ♘f6 2 c4 c5 3 d5 e6 4 ♘c3 exd5 5 cxd5 d6 6 e4 g6

    7 ♘f3   ♗g7

For a long time A70 was a theoretical outcast – for example, *ECO* only gives it half a page – but nowadays 2 of every 3 games in the Modern Benoni relates to this chapter. The frequency with which this variation is used is due in the first place, of course, to the cunning move 8 h3!?, which to a certain degree has reduced the popularity of the whole opening.

With the aim of avoiding this dangerous variation, Black sometimes plays 7...a6 8 a4 (8 ♗f4 b5 is A65) 8...♗g4 *(D)* when White has the following possibilities:

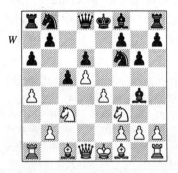

a) Black has no problems after 9 h3 ♗xf3 10 ♕xf3 ♗g7 (or 10...♘bd7

11 ♗e2 ♗g7 12 0-0 0-0 13 ♗f4 ♕e7 14 ♖fe1 ♖ae8 = Topalov-Franco, Elgoibar 1991) 11 ♗d3 (chances are roughly equal after 11 g4 0-0 12 ♗g2 ♘bd7 13 ♕g3 ♘e8 14 0-0 c4! = Douven-Antonio, Thessaloniki OL 1988) 11...♘bd7!? 12 ♕d1 0-0 13 0-0 ♖c8 14 ♖e1 c4 15 ♗f1 ♖e8 16 ♗f4 ♘e5 = Rao-Psakhis, Philadelphia 1992.

b) Black need not be scared by 9 ♗e2 ♗xf3!? (after the pointless 9...♗g7 White seizes the initiative: 10 ♘d2! ♗xe2 11 ♕xe2 ♘bd7 12 ♘c4 ♘b6 13 e5! dxe5 14 ♕xe5+ ♔f8 15 ♘xb6 ♕xb6 16 0-0 ± Benjamin-de Firmian, New York 1993) 10 ♗xf3 ♘bd7 (in Mikhalevsky-Yudasin, Israel 1992, White did not manage to gain an advantage after 10...♗g7 11 0-0 0-0 12 e5!? dxe5 13 ♗g5 ♘bd7 14 a5! h6! 15 ♗h4 ♖b8 16 d6 g5 17 ♗g3 ♘e8 ∞) 11 0-0 ♗g7 12 a5 (or 12 ♗f4 ♕e7 13 e5 dxe5 14 d6 ♕e6 15 ♘d5 ♘xd5 16 ♗xd5 ♕f6 17 ♗g3 ♖b8 18 f4 e4! 19 ♗xe4 0-0 ∞ Callego-Franco, Linares tt 1991) 12...0-0 13 ♖a4 (13 ♗d2 ♕e7 14 ♖e1 ♘e8 15 ♗a3 ♘c7 16 ♖b3 ♖ab8 17 ♗e2 ♖fe8 18 ♗f1 b5 led to equality in Arduman-Wojtkiewicz, Novi Sad OL 1990) 13...♘e8 14 ♗e2 ♘c7 15 ♕c2 ♕e7 16 ♗d2 ♖fb8! with a level position; Pinter-Psakhis, Paris 1990.

c) 9 ♕b3!? ♗xf3 (9...♕c7?! 10 ♘d2! ±) 10 ♕xb7 and now:

c1) White has a small plus after 10...♘bd7 11 gxf3 ♗g7 12 ♕c6! ♕b8 (or 12...0-0 13 ♕xd6 ♘h5 14 f4!?) and now 13 a5! ±, which is stronger than 13 ♗xa6?! 0-0 14 ♕b7 (14 ♗e2 ♖a5!) 14...♘e5 15 ♕xb8 (15 ♔e2 ♕d8!?) 15...♘xf3+ 16 ♔f1 ♖fxb8 17 ♗e2 ♘d4 and Black took over the initiative in the game Douven-Psakhis, Groningen 1993.

c2) 10...♘xe4!? 11 ♕xa8 ♗g7 12 gxf3 ♘xc3 13 ♗e3 0-0 14 ♖a3 ♘b1! with large and unclear complications; Alvarez-Suba, Palma 1992.

Returning to the position after 7...♗g7 *(D)*:

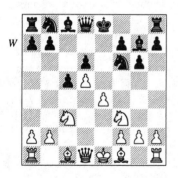

There are three main systems under discussion in this chapter:

A) 8 ♗f4
B) 8 ♕a4+
C) 8 h3

Here are the other options:

a) 8 ♘d2 ♘bd7 (for 8...0-0 9 ♗e2 ♖e8 10 0-0 see A77) 9 ♘c4 ♘b6 10 ♘e3 0-0 11 ♗d3 ♖e8 (White has a small advantage after 11...♘h5 12 0-0 ♕h4 13 g3 ♕e7 14 ♖e1 ♗d7 15 ♘f5!? ± Toth-Lobron, Biel 1992) 12 0-0 ♘bd7 (12...♗d7 13 a4 a6 14 ♗d2 ♖b8 15 a5 ♘c8 16 ♘c4 ♗b5 17 ♖e1 ± Ftačnik-Blodstein, Pardubice 1992) 13 a4 a6 14 f4 c4!? 15 ♗c2 (15 ♘xc4 ♘c5 16 e5 dxe5 17 fxe5 ♘xd5) 15...♘c5 16 ♕f3 ♘b3! with mutual chances, according to Kapengut.

b) 8 ♗b5+ and now:

b1) 8...♗d7 is quite sufficient for equality, for example 9 ♗xd7+ (9 a4 is not dangerous for Black: 9...0-0 10 0-0 ♗g4 11 h3 ♗xf3 12 ♕xf3 ♘bd7 13 ♕d1 a6 14 ♗d3 ♖e8 is equal; Stepak-Gofshtein, Israel Ch 1992) 9...♘bxd7 10 0-0 0-0 11 ♗f4 ♕e7 (or 11...♖e8 12 ♘d2 ♘e5 13 ♕e2 a6 14 a4 ♖c8 15 ♗xe5 ♖xe5 16 f4 ♖e8 17 ♕f3 c4! with equality; Lakić-Andrijević, Yugoslavia Ch 1991) 12 ♘d2 a6 13 a4 (13 ♘c4!? ♘e8 14 ♖e1 b5 15 ♘a5 with an attack, I.Sokolov) 13...♘e8!? (White has a small advantage after 13...♘e5 14 ♔h1 ♖ab8 15 ♗g5! h6 16 ♗h4 g5 17 f4! ± I.Sokolov-Tolnai, Dortmund 1989) 14 ♕c2 ♖b8 15 a5 b5 16 axb6 ♖xb6 17 ♘c4 ♖b4 ∞ Petran-Palkovi, Hungarian Ch 1989.

b2) 8...♘bd7 9 ♗f4 (9 a4 0-0 10 0-0 a6 11 ♗e2 ♖e8 = Forintos-Sax, Hungarian Ch 1981) 9...♕e7 10 0-0 0-0 11 ♖e1 ♘g4 and now both 12 ♗f1 ♘de5 13 ♘xe5 ♘xe5 14 ♕d2 a6 15 ♗g5 f6 16 ♗h4 g5 17 ♗g3 (Gligorić-D.Gurevich, New York 1988) 17...f5!? and 12 ♗g5!? ♗f6

13 ♗xf6 ♘dxf6, Gligorić-Fedoro-
wicz, New York 1988, lead to an
unclear game with mutual chances.

c) 8 ♗d3 *(D)* and now:

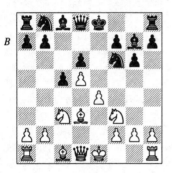

c1) After 8...♗g4 9 ♕a4+ ♘bd7
10 ♘d2 0-0 11 ♕c2 (11 0-0 ♘e5 12
♗b1 g5!? = Smyslov-Tatai, Las Palmas 1973) 11...♘e5 12 h3 ♗d7 (or
12...♘xd3+ 13 ♕xd3 ♗d7 14 ♘c4
♕e7 15 a4 ±) 13 ♗e2 g5 14 a4 ♖e8
15 ♘f1 White has a small advantage.

c2) 8...0-0 9 0-0 (for 9 h3! see 8
h3 0-0 9 ♗d3) 9...♗g4! (to avoid
this, White can also play h3 on move
8 or 9; White has a more promising
position after 9...♘a6 10 h3 ♘c7 11
♖e1 ♖b8 12 a4) 10 h3 ♗xf3 11 ♕xf3
a6 12 a4 ♘bd7:

c21) The position is dead level
after 13 ♗f4 ♕c7 (13...♘e8!? 14
♕g3 ♘e5 also deserves attention) 14
♕e2 ♖fe8 15 ♗h2 ♖ac8 16 ♗c4
♘e5 = Donner-Tal, Zurich 1959.

c22) 13 ♕e2 ♖e8 14 ♗f4 (the
thoughtless 14 f4?! places the initiative in Black's hands after 14...c4! 15
♗c2 {15 ♗xc4 ♘xe4! 16 ♘xe4 f5}
15...♖c8 16 a5 ♘c5 17 ♕f3 ♘fd7 18
♖e1 ♘d3! 19 ♗xd3 cxd3 20 ♕xd3

♘c5 21 ♕c2 ♕h4 ∓ Friedersdorff-
Pekarek, Dortmund 1992) 14...c4!
15 ♗c2 (15 ♗xc4 ♘xe4 16 ♘xe4 f5
=) 15...♘c5 16 ♖fe1 (the pawn is
again unassailable: 16 ♕xc4 ♖c8 17
♕b4 a5! 18 ♕a3 ♘fxe4 19 ♘xe4
♘xe4 20 ♗xe4 ♖xe4 21 ♗xd6 ♖d4
22 ♖ad1 ♕f6 is equal, according to
Polugaevsky) 16...♖c8 = Smyslov-
Polugaevsky, Petropolis IZ 1973.

c23) 13 ♕d1 and now:

c231) White has a more pleasant
position after 13...♘e8 14 ♖e1 ♘c7
15 a5 ♖b8 16 ♗d2 b5 17 axb6 ♘xb6
18 ♕c2! c4 19 ♗f1 ± Tukmakov-
Lukov, Palma GMA 1989.

c232) 13...♕c7 14 ♖e1 c4 15
♗c2! (better than 15 ♗f1?! ♘c5 16
♗xc4 ♘cxe4 17 ♘xe4 ♕xc4 and
now 18 ♘xd6? is bad because of
18...♕b4 and Black wins – Tukmakov) 15...♖ab8 16 a5 ± Tukmakov-
D.Gurevich, Moscow GMA 1989.

c233) 13...♖e8 14 ♖e1 ♖c8 deserves attention, for example 15 ♗e3
(Black should fear neither 15 ♗c4
♘e5 16 ♗f1 c4 17 ♗e3 ♘ed7 18
♕c2 ♘c5 with equality; Kožul-
Damljanović, Cetinje tt 1990, nor 15
♗f4 c4 16 ♗f1 ♘c5 17 ♕c2 ♕c7 18
♖ad1 ♘fd7 19 ♗xc4 ♘xa4 20
♕xa4 ♘b6 21 ♕b4 ♘xc4 22 ♖c1
♕d7! = Tukmakov-Wedberg, New
York 1990, and everything is also
fine for him after 15 a5 c4 16 ♗c2
♖c5!? 17 ♗f4 Novikov-Velimirović,
Kusadasi 1990, and now 17...♘e5!?
with an unclear game, deserves attention) 15...♕a5 16 ♗d2 (or 16
♕d2 ♘e5 17 ♗f1 h5 18 f3 ♘ed7 =
Haik-I.Sokolov, Rilton Cup 1987)

16...c4 17 ♗c2 ♘c5 18 ♔h1 ♕d8 19 ♗g5 b5! 20 axb5 axb5 21 ♘xb5 ♘cxe4 22 ♗xe4 ♖xe4 23 ♕f3 ♕e8! = Kharlov-Semeniuk, Khabarovsk 1990.

c234) 13...♖c8 14 ♖e1 c4 15 ♗f1 ♖e8 16 ♗f4 ♘c5!? 17 ♕c2 ♘b3 18 ♖ad1 ♕c7 = Granda-Hulak, Zagreb IZ 1987.

A) 8 ♗f4 0-0

9 ♘d2 (D)

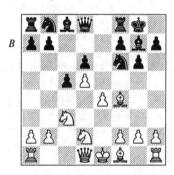

9 ... ♘g4

Or:

a) 9...♕e7 10 ♗e2 ♘bd7 11 0-0 ♘e5 12 ♖e1 a6 13 a4 ♘fd7 14 ♗g3 g5!? 15 ♘f1! with a small advantage; Zsu.Polgar-Winants, Brussels tt 1987.

b) 9...♘e8 10 ♗e2 f5 11 exf5 ♗xf5 12 0-0 ♘d7 13 ♘c4 ♘b6 14 ♘e3 ♗c2!? 15 ♕xc2 ♖xf4 16 g3 ♖f8 17 a4 ± Šahović-de Firmian, Bor 1984.

c) 9...♘a6?! 10 ♗e2 ♖b8 11 ♘c4 ♘e8 12 ♘b5 ♘ac7 (12...f5 13 0-0 fxe4 14 ♗g3 ±) 13 ♘bxd6 ♘xd6 14 ♗xd6 ♖e8 15 ♕d3! b6! (15...b5 16 ♕g3! bxc4 17 ♗xc7 ♕e7 18 ♗xb8 ♕xe4 19 ♕e3 ♕xe3 20 fxe3 ♗xb2 21 ♔f2 +− Yusupov) 16 0-0 with an obvious advantage; Yusupov-Maus, Hamburg 1991.

d) 9...b6 10 a4 ♘a6 (10...♗a6 11 ♗xa6 ♘xa6 12 ♘c4) 11 ♗e2 ♘b4 12 0-0 ♖e8 13 h3 ♗a6 14 ♗xa6 ♘xa6 15 ♕f3 ± Lputian-Vaiser, Berlin 1982.

e) 9...♘h5 10 ♗e3 ♘d7 11 ♗e2 ♘e5 (White has a more promising position after 11...♘hf6 12 0-0 ♕e7 13 ♖e1 ♘e8 14 ♘c4 b6 15 ♕d2, Šahović-Hort, Metz 1984, or 11...♗d4 12 ♘c4 ♗xe3 13 ♘xe3 ♘g7 14 0-0 ♕e7 15 ♕d2 a6 16 a4 f5 17 exf5 gxf5 18 ♖fe1 ♘e5 19 f4 ♘g6 20 ♘c4, Šahović-Velimirović, Budva 1986) 12 f4!? (or 12 0-0 ♕h4 13 ♘f3!? ♘xf3+ 14 ♗xf3 ♖e8 15 ♖e1 a6 16 ♕d2! ± Tukmakov-Lau, Plovdiv Echt 1983) 12...♘g4 13 ♗xg4 ♕h4+ 14 g3 ♕xg4 15 ♕xg4 ♗xg4 16 h3 ♗d7 17 g4 ♗xc3 (17...♘f6 18 ♘c4 ♘e8 19 a4! ±) 18 bxc3 ♘f6 19 ♔f2 ♖fe8 20 ♔f3 ± Reshevsky-Grünfeld, Lugano 1987.

f) 9...♗g4?! 10 f3! ♘h5 (the retreat 10...♗c8 may be relatively best) 11 fxg4! ♘xf4 12 g3 f5 13 gxf5 gxf5 14 ♕c2! fxe4 15 ♘cxe4 ♘g6 16 0-0-0 ♘d7 17 h4 ± Eingorn-J.Horvath, Sochi 1985.

g) 9...♖e8 10 ♗e2 b6 11 0-0 ♗a6 12 h3!? ♕e7 13 ♗b5!? ♘fd7 (or 13...♗xb5 14 ♘xb5 ♘xe4? 15 ♖e1) 14 a4 ± Raičević-Murshed, Subotica 1984.

h) 9...a6 10 a4 ♘g4 (White's position is more pleasant after 10...♘e8

11 ♗e2 ♘d7 12 0-0 ♖b8 13 ♔h1
♘e5 14 ♗g3, as in Vukić-Garcia
Gonzalez, Banja Luka 1979, whilst
10...♘h5 11 ♗e3 ♘d7 {11...♗d4 12
♘c4 ♗xe3 13 ♘xe3 ♘d7 14 g3 ♖b8
15 a5 gives White an edge; Bukić-
Velimirović, Belgrade 1977} 12 ♗e2
is examined under A72) 11 ♗e2 ♘e5
(11...f5 12 ♗xg4 fxg4 13 ♗g3 with a
minimal advantage) 12 0-0 f5 13
exf5 ♗xf5 14 ♗e3 ♕h4 = Szym-
czak-Prudnikova, Naleczow 1989.

10 ♗e2

After the careless 10 ♘c4? Black
quickly gains an advantage by playing 10...♗d4 11 ♗g3 f5! 12 h3 f4!
13 hxg4 fxg3 14 f3 ♗f2+ 15 ♔d2 a6
16 a4 ♕f6 17 ♔c2 ♘d7 ∓ Stanković-
Andrijević, Yugoslav Ch 1991.

10 ... ♘e5

10...f5?! 11 ♗xg4 fxg4 12 ♗g3
favours White.

11 ♗e3!?

White's attempts to gain an advantage are not crowned with success after 11 0-0 f5 12 exf5 (or 12 g3
♘a6 13 ♘f3 ♘xf3+ 14 ♗xf3 g5! 15
♗d2 f4 was level in Lputian-Romanishin, Moscow 1987) 12...♗xf5 13
♗g3 a6 14 a4 ♕c7 15 ♘de4 ♘f7 16
♖c1 ♘d7 17 b4 c4! 18 a5 ♖ac8 19
♘d2 b5! with advantage for Black;
Polugaevsky-Agzamov, Moscow tt
1983, or 11 ♗g3 f5 12 f4 ♘f7 13
0-0 a6 14 a4 fxe4 15 ♘dxe4 ♗f5 16
♗f2 ♖e8 17 ♘d2 h5!? 18 ♘f3 ♘d7
19 ♘h4 ♘h6, as in Eingorn-Pigusov,
Kharkov 1985.

11 ... f5
12 f4 ♘f7
13 0-0 ♘a6

14 exf5!?

14 ♔h1 ♖e8 15 ♗g1 ♘c7 only
leads to equality; Aleksandria-Pigu-
sov, Pula 1988.

14 ... ♗xf5
15 g4 ♗d7
16 ♘de4

White's position is slightly better.

B) 8 ♕a4+ ♗d7

9 ♕b3

9 ♕c2 is not too dangerous for
Black, for example 9...0-0 10 ♗f4
♕e7 11 ♗e2 ♖e8 12 ♘d2 b5 Her-
zog-Klinger, Zug 1985, and Black
should not fear 13 ♘xb5 because
of 13...♘xe4 14 0-0 (14 ♘xe4 ♗xb5
15 ♗xb5 ♕xe4+ 16 ♕xe4 ♖xe4+ 17
♗e3 ♗xb2 18 ♖b1 ♖b4 is also
good for Black) 14...♘xd2 15 ♕xd2
♕xe2 16 ♕xe2 ♖xe2 17 ♘c7 ♘a6!
18 ♘xa6 ♗xb2 with an advantage to
Black, Klinger.

9 ... ♕c7
10 ♗f4 0-0 *(D)*

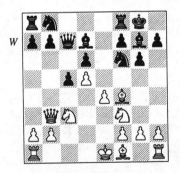

11 ♘d2!?

Undoubtedly the most dangerous
move for Black. Other ideas:

a) 11 e5:

a1) 11...dxe5 (bad) 12 ♗xe5 ♖e8 13 0-0-0! (White has real problems after 13 ♗e2 c4!? 14 ♗xc7 cxb3 15 ♘e5!? {15 axb3 ♘e4 16 ♖c1 ♘a6} 15...b5! {15...♘g4?? 16 ♘xd7 ♘xd7 17 axb3 ± Agdestein-Wedberg, Oslo 1984} 16 ♘d3 ♘a6 17 ♗a5 ♗f5 ∓ Agdestein) 13...♕c8 14 ♗c4 ♗f5 (14...♗g4 doesn't help either: 15 d6 ♗xf3 16 ♗xf6 ♗xd1 17 ♗xf7+ ♔h8 18 ♗xg7+ ♔xg7 19 ♖xd1 ♖f8 20 ♗e6 ♘d7 21 ♘d5 ± Kapengut) 15 ♗xf6! ♗xf6 16 d6 with a big advantage.

a2) 11...♖e8 leads to an interesting game: 12 0-0-0 ♘h5 13 exd6 ♕a5 14 ♗d2 ♘a6 15 a3 ♖ab8 16 ♘b5 ♕b6 with an attack; Ubilava-Basin, Tbilisi 1983, or 12 ♗e2 ♘h5 13 ♗e3 dxe5 14 0-0 ♕b6 ∞ S.Garcia-Kasparov, Baku 1980.

a3) 11...♘h5!? (probably best) 12 exd6 ♖e8+ 13 ♗e3 (but not 13 ♗e2? ♗xc3+! 14 ♕xc3 ♖xe2+ 15 ♔xe2 ♘xf4+ and Black wins – Kasparov) 13...♕a5 14 ♘d2 (14 ♗e2 b5 15 0-0 c4 16 ♕c2 b4 17 ♘e4 ♗f5 with initiative, Hardicsay) 14...f5 15 g3! with chances for both sides.

b) 11 ♗d3 a6 (Black has no grounds for complaint at the outcome of the opening after 11...♘a6!? 12 0-0 ♘h5 13 ♗e3 ♖ab8 14 ♖fe1 ♖fc8!? 15 ♗c4 ♗g4) 12 a4 ♘h5 13 ♗e3 ♗g4 14 ♘d2 ♘d7!? 15 h3 (or 15 f3 ♘e5 16 ♗e2 ♗d7 17 f4 ♘g4 18 ♗xg4 ♗xg4 19 h3 ♗d7 with an unclear game) 15...♘e5 16 ♗f1! ♗d7 17 f4 ♘g3 18 fxe5 ♘xh1 19 exd6 ♕xd6 ∞ Kapengut.

c) 11 ♗e2 *(D)* and now:

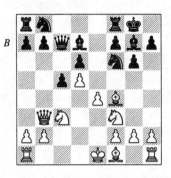

c1) It's not so simple for White to gain an advantage after 11...a6, for example 12 e5!? (after 12 a4 ♘h5 13 ♗e3 ♗g4 14 h3 ♗xf3 15 ♗xf3 ♘d7!? 16 0-0 ♘hf6 a position arises which was examined in the notes to 11...♘h5) 12...♘h5 (if 12...dxe5 13 ♗xe5 ♕c8, 14 ♗xf6! {14 0-0 is not so clear: 14...♗g4 15 h3 ♗xf3 16 ♗xf3 ♘bd7 17 ♗d6 ♖e8 18 a4 ♘e5 19 ♗xe5 ♖xe5 20 ♖ad1 ♖b8 21 d6 b5! 22 axb5 axb5 and Black holds the position; Portisch-Fischer, Palma de Mallorca IZ 1970} 14...♗xf6 15 ♘e4 ♗g7 16 ♖c1 ♗f5 17 ♘d6! ♕d7 18 ♘xf5 ♕xf5 19 0-0 ♘d7 20 ♗d3 ♕f6 21 ♕xb7 with an obvious advantage, Kapengut) 13 exd6 ♕a5!? 14 ♗d2 ♕b4 15 ♕xb4 cxb4 16 ♘d1 a5 17 a3 ♘a6 ∞ Kapengut.

c2) 11...♘h5 12 ♗e3 ♗g4 (after 12...♘a6 13 ♘d2 f5 14 exf5 gxf5 15 ♗xh5 f4 16 0-0 fxe3 17 fxe3 White has a distinct advantage, while 12...a6 13 0-0!? {13 ♘d2 b5 13 0-0 ♖a7!? 15 ♖ac1 ♖b7 16 ♖fe1 ♘f6 17 h3 ♖e8 = Ribli-Ljubojević, Tilburg 1984} 13...b5 14 a4 b4 {14...bxa4!?

15 ♘xa4 ♖a7} 15 ♘b1 ♗g4 16
♘bd2 restricts White to a slight
plus; Sosonko-Vasiukov, Reykjavik
1980) 13 h3 ♗xf3 14 ♗xf3 ♘d7 (after 14...♘f6?! White can make a
breakthrough in the centre by 15 e5!
dxe5 16 d6 ♕xd6 17 ♖d1 ♕e7 18
♕xb7 ♘bd7 19 ♘d5! ♘xd5 20
♖xd5 ± Hjartarson-Sigurjonsson,
Reykjavik 1984) 15 ♗xh5!? (or 15
0-0 ♘hf6 16 ♘b5!? ♕b8 17 ♗f4
♘e8 18 a4 a6 19 ♘a3 ♕c7 20 ♗e2
♖b8 21 ♕c2 with a small advantage;
Gon.Garcia-Velimirović, Moscow
IZ 1982) 15...gxh5 16 ♕c2!? ♖fe8
17 0-0 with a slight advantage for
White; Gaprindashvili-Litinskaya,
Vilnius 1983.

c3) If 11...♗g4, then 12 0-0 a6 13
e5!? is possible, with the initiative.

c4) 11...b5 and it is difficult for
White to gain an advantage:

c41) 12 ♘xb5 ♗xb5 13 ♗xb5
♘xe4 14 0-0 ♘d7 15 ♕a4!? ♘ef6 16
♗xd7 ♘xd7 17 ♕c6!? ♕xc6 18
dxc6 ♘e5 19 ♖ad1 ♖fc8 = Zaichik-
Panczyk, Polanica Zdroj 1984.

c42) 12 e5 ♘h5! 13 exd6 ♕a5 14
♗d2 (Black has the initiative after 14
♗e3 c4 15 ♕d1 b4 16 ♘e4 ♖e8! 17
♘ed2 c3) 14...♖e8 (14...b4 leads to
unclear complications: 15 ♘d1 ♖e8
16 a4 ♗c8 17 ♗e3 ♗a6 18 ♗c4 ♖e4
19 ♘d2 ♗xc4 20 ♘xc4 ♕a6 21 ♖c1
♘f4 Agzamov-Magerramov, Cheliabinsk 1981) 15 ♘d1 ♕b6 with
compensation; Zaid-Gofshtein, Kiev
1977.

c43) 12 ♘d2 c4 13 ♕b4 ♘a6 14
♕xd6 ♕b7, Hardicsay, should not
scare Black.

c44) 12 ♗xb5 ♘xe4 13 ♘xe4
♕a5+ 14 ♗d2 (14 ♘fd2 cannot help
White: 14...♗xb5 15 ♘xd6 ♗a6 16
0-0-0 ♘d7 17 ♘2c4 ♕d8 offers excellent compensation, whilst 14 ♘c3
♗xb5 15 0-0-0 ♗xc3 16 ♕xc3
♕xc3+ 17 bxc3 ♖d8 leads to equality) 14...♕xb5 15 ♕xb5 ♗xb5 16
♘xd6 ♗d3!? 17 0-0-0 (17 ♗c3
♗xc3+ 18 bxc3 ♖d8) 17...♘a6 18
♗e3 c4 and Black is at least equal.

Returning to the position after 11
♘d2 (D):

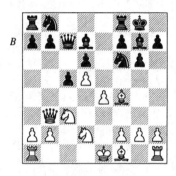

11 ...   ♘h5

White has a significant advantage
after both 11...♖e8 12 ♗e2 b5 13
♗xb5 ♘xe4 14 ♘cxe4 f5 15 0-0
fxe4 16 ♖ae1 Bronstein-Kopylov,
Erevan 1981, and 11...♘g4 12 ♘c4!
♘e5 13 ♘xe5 dxe5 14 ♗e3 (Nunn).

12 ♗e3   f5

In Kasparov-Wahls, Frankfurt
sim 1986, the World Champion ex-
posed the weakness of 12...♗d4?!:
13 ♗e2! ♗xe3 14 fxe3 ♘g7 15 0-0
a6 16 e5! dxe5 17 ♘ce4 b5 18 ♖ac1
c4 19 ♘f6+ ♔h8 20 ♕b4 with a
large advantage.

13 exf5   gxf5

14 ♗e2 ♗e8

White has a large advantage, with no complications, after 14...♘a6 15 ♗xh5 f4 16 0-0 fxe3 17 fxe3 ♗f5 18 e4 ♗d7 19 ♗e2 ±.

On the other hand, enormous complications, also favourable for White, arise after 14...f4?! 15 ♗xc5! *(D):*

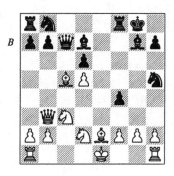

a) 15...♘a6 16 ♗a3 (but not 16 ♗d4 ♗xd4 17 ♗xh5 f3!? 18 ♘xf3 ♘c5 19 ♕c4 ♗xc3+ 20 bxc3?! ♖f4! 21 ♘d4 b5 and Black wields the initiative; Vera-Huerta, Havana 1985) 16...♖ae8 (16...f3 is of approximately equal value, for example 17 ♗xf3 ♖xf3 18 gxf3 ♘f4 19 ♘ce4! ♖c8 20 0-0 ♗e5 21 ♔h1 ± Starck-Enders, E.Germany 1985) 17 ♘ce4 ♘f6 18 ♗xd6! ♕a5 19 ♘c3 ♖xe2+ (19...♘e4?! 20 ♘dxe4 ♖xe4 21 0-0 ♗xc3 22 ♗xa6 ♕xa6 23 ♗xf8 +− Malaniuk-Norwood, Lvov 1986) 20 ♔xe2 ♖e8+ 21 ♔f1 ♗f5 22 ♔g1 and White was winning in Schüssler-Fedorowicz, USA-Nordic 1986.

b) 15...f3 16 ♗xf3 and now:

b1) 16...♕xc5 may be the lesser evil, but 17 ♘de4! (17 ♘ce4? ♖xf3!!

18 ♕xf3 ♕xd5 19 g4 ♕e6 20 gxh5 d5 gives Black an advantage; Perić-Klinger, Lugano 1985) 17...♗xc3+ 18 bxc3 ♖e8 19 0-0 ♕c7 20 ♖fe1 ♖xe4 21 ♖xe4 Bellón-Klinger, Havana 1985, cannot cheer Black up.

b2) 16...♖xf3 17 gxf3! (but not 17 ♘xf3 ♕xc5 18 0-0 ♕b6 19 ♕c2 ♕d8 Legky-Dolmatov, USSR 1983 with an unclear game) 17...♕xc5 18 ♕xb7 ♗xc3 (or 18...♘f4 19 ♕xa8 ♘d3+ 20 ♔e2 ♘f4+ 21 ♔d1 ♗xc3 22 ♕xb8+ ♔f7 23 bxc3 ♗a4+ 24 ♘b3 ♕xd5+ 25 ♔c2 ♕f5+ 26 ♔b2 ♘d3+ 27 ♔a3 ♗xb3 28 ♕xa7+ Korchnoi, and White's attack is repulsed, although his massive material advantage remains) 19 bxc3 ♘f4 (19...♕xc3 20 0-0! cannot save him, and Black loses after both 20...♗h3 21 ♔h1 ♗xf1 22 ♖xf1 ♕xd2 23 ♕c8+ ♔f7 24 ♕e6+ ♔f8 25 ♖g1 +− Van der Sterren-Pokojowczyk, Copenhagen 1984, and 20...♘f4 21 ♔h1 ♗h3 22 ♖g1+ ♗g2+ 23 ♖xg2+ ♘xg2 24 ♖g1 ♕xd2 25 ♖xg2+ +−) and now in Korchnoi-Nunn, London 1984, the master's hand faltered at the moment when he only had to reap the harvest of his brilliant play: 20 ♖g1+? ♔f7 21 ♘e4 ♕xd5 22 ♕xd5+ ♘xd5 23 ♖d1 and Black got off with a little fright. Instead 20 ♕xa8! ♘d3+ 21 ♔e2 ♕xf2+ 22 ♔xd3 ♗f5+ 23 ♔c4 ♕c5+ 24 ♔b3 ♕b5+ 25 ♔a3 wins (Korchnoi).

15 ♘f3

The knight is keeping an eye on e6; Black's problems would be simpler after 15 0-0 a6, when he maintains equality after both 16 ♗xh5

♗xh5 17 ♗f4 ♘d7 18 a4 ♘e5 19
♘c4 ♖ad8 20 a5 ♕f7 Naivelt-Fe-
dorov, Moscow 1985, and 16 ♕d1
♘f6 17 a4 ♘bd7 18 ♘c4 ♘b6 Bur-
ger-Nunn, Brighton 1983, whilst 15
♘c4?! f4 16 ♗d2 ♕e7 17 0-0 b5! 18
♗xh5 bxc4 19 ♕d1 ♘d7 20 ♖e1
♘e5 ∓ Korchnoi-Kuhn, Hamburg
1984.

15 ...   h6

Nor does 15...f4 lead to equality,
for example: 16 ♗d2 ♕e7 17 0-0
♘d7 (17...♗xc3? 18 ♗xc3 ♕xe2 19
♕xb7 ♕a6 20 ♕xa8! ♗d7 21 ♖fe1
♘c6 22 ♕xf8+ ♔xf8 23 dxc6 ♕xc6
24 b4! is good for White; Spraggett-
Norwood, Toronto 1985) 18 ♖fe1
♘e5 19 ♘e4 b5!? 20 ♗c3 ♘xf3+ 21
♗xf3 ♗xc3 22 ♕xc3 ♕d8 23 b4! ±
Sutkus-Sirota, Corr 1987.

16 0-0

Black has quite a satisfactory
game after 16 ♘b5 ♕e7!? (White
has more chances after 16...♗xb5?!
17 ♕xb5 a6 18 ♕d3 ♕e7 19 0-0
♘d7 20 ♖ae1 ± Grünberg-Agzamov,
Potsdam 1985) 17 ♘xd6 ♕xd6 18
♕xb7 ♕b6 19 ♕xa8 ♗d7 20 ♘d2
♘a6 21 ♘c4 Lebredo-Arencibia,
Camaguey 1985, and Black should
have played 21...♖xa8! 22 ♘xb6
axb6 23 ♗xh5 ♘b4 with sufficient
compensation.

	16 ...	a6
	17 a4	♘d7
	18 ♗d3	♕d8
	19 ♖fe1	♖b8
	20 ♕c2	♕f6
	21 a5	

White has a small advantage;
Naumkin-Ulybin, Pinsk 1986.

C) 8 h3!? *(D)*

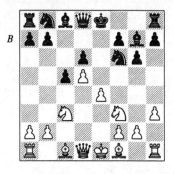

Finally we come to the move
which is the beginning of a plan that
has terrorized Black in recent years.
The strength of this plan lies in its
simplicity. First White stops the
black bishop landing on g4, whilst
developing all his pieces towards the
centre, and, using his spatial advantage, he undertakes to play on any
part of the board. This plan came
into fashion at the end of the 1980s
and since then Black has failed to
find a suitable antidote, in spite of
the fact that the initial terrors have already passed.

| | 8 ... | 0-0 |
| | 9 ♗d3 | |

We shall look principally at three
continuations, which have been subjected to extensive analysis:

C1) 9...♖e8
C2) 9...a6
C3) 9...b5

There has been considerable ex-
perimentation with other moves:

a) 9...b6 10 0-0 ♗a6 11 ♗f4 c4
(or 11...♕e7 12 ♗xa6 ♘xa6 13

♕d3! ♘c7 14 e5! ±) 12 ♗c2 b5 13
a3 ♘h5 Rustemov-Gufeld, Alushta
1993, and White should have continued 14 ♗e3! with a clear advantage.

b) 9...♘bd7 10 0-0 ♘h5 11 ♗g5
(11 ♗e3!? is not bad either, for example 11...♘e5 12 ♘xe5 ♗xe5 13
f4 ♗g7 14 ♕f3 ♘f6 15 ♖ae1 ♘d7
16 e5!? dxe5 17 f5 with initiative;
Tukmakov-Norwood, Reykjavik tt
1990) 11...♗f6 12 ♗h6 ♖e8 (or
12...♗g7 13 ♗xg7 ♘xg7 14 ♕d2 f6
15 ♗e2 ♕e7 16 ♖fe1 ♘e5 17 ♖ab1!
b6 18 b4 ± Fries Nielsen-Maus,
Bundesliga 1989) 13 g4!? ♗g7 14
♗g5 ♘hf6 (14...♗f6 15 ♗e3 ±) 15
♖e1 a6 16 ♕d2 b5 17 ♕f4 ♕e7 18 a3
± Atalik-Cu.Hansen, Thessaloniki
OL 1988.

c) 9...♗d7 *(D)* and now White
should allow Black to play ...b5:

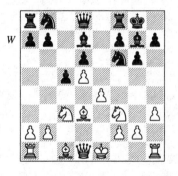

c1) Black equalizes after 10 a4!?
♘a6!? 11 ♗xa6 (or 11 0-0 ♘b4 12
♗c4 ♖e8 13 ♖e1 a6 ∞) 11...bxa6 12
♕d3 ♗c8 13 0-0 ♘d7 14 ♗f4 ♕e7
15 ♖fe1 ♖b8 16 ♕c2 ♖e8 Silva-
Panno, São Paulo Z 1993.

c2) 10 ♗f4 leads to an interesting game, for example 10...♖e8! (the

alternative 10...♕c7 favours White:
11 0-0 c4 12 ♗c2 ♘a6 13 e5! ♘h5
14 exd6 ♕b6 15 ♗e5 ♕xb2 16 ♘e4!
♗xe5 17 ♖b1 ♕xa2 18 ♘xe5 ± Zsu.
Polgar-Blees, Lillafüred 1989) and
now:

c21) If 11 ♗xd6 then Black replies 11...♗xh3!.

c22) 11 ♘d2!? b5 12 0-0 c4 13
♗c2 b4 14 ♘e2 and now D.Gure-
vich recommends 14...♗b5!? ∞ instead of 14...c3 15 bxc3 bxc3 16
♘c4 ♘xe4 17 ♘g3! ± Bronstein-
D.Gurevich, Las Vegas 1993.

c23) 11 0-0 b5 (White has the initiative after 11...c4 12 ♗c2 ♕c7 13
♖e1 ♘a6 14 a3 ♘c5 15 ♕d2 b5 16
e5! Sturua-Hulak, Manila OL 1992)
12 ♗xd6 b4 13 ♘e2 (13 ♘b5 ♘xe4!
∞) 13...♘xe4 14 ♗xe4 ♖xe4 15 ♘g3
♖e8 16 ♗xc5 ♗b5 17 ♖e1 Khalif-
man-Maus, Hamburg 1991, and after
17...♘a6! Black would have equalized, Khalifman.

c3) 10 0-0 b5!? 11 a3!? (chances
are equal after 11 ♘xb5 ♘xe4 12
♘a3 {12 ♕c2?! ♘a6 13 a3 ♕a5 14
♗xe4 ♗xb5 15 ♗d3 c4 ∓ Varga-
Ralkovi, Budapest 1993} 12...♖e8
13 ♖e1 ♘f6 14 ♖xe8+ ♗xe8! 15
♘c4 ♗b5 Golubev-Shabalov, Biel
1992, or 11 ♖e1 c4 12 ♗c2 b4 13
♘e2 ♘a6 14 ♘ed4 ♖c8 15 ♗f4
♕b6, Costa-Shabalov, Suhr 1992)
11...♖e8 (11...♘a6 12 ♖e1 c4 13
♗c2 ♘c5 14 ♗f4 ♕b6 15 e5! dxe5
16 ♘xe5 ♖ad8 17 ♕f3 ± Browne-
D.Gurevich, Philadelphia 1993) 12
♖e1 c4 13 ♗c2 ♘a6 14 ♗e3 and we
have arrived at the position in the
note to Black's 10th move in line C1.

d) 9...♘a6 10 0-0 ♘c7 (10...♘b4 11 ♗c4! ♖e8 12 ♖e1 ♖b8 13 ♗f4 ♘h5 14 ♗h2, San Segundo-Cortes, Zaragoza 1992, and Black's knight turns out to be misplaced, making White's advantage obvious) 11 ♖e1 (White also has a slight advantage after 11 a4 a6 12 ♗g5 h6 13 ♗e3 ♖e8 14 ♕d2 ♔h7 15 ♖ab1 b5 16 axb5 ♘xb5 17 ♘xb5 axb5 18 e5! dxe5 19 ♗xb5, Sarno-Suba, Rome 1990) and Black has a choice *(D)*:

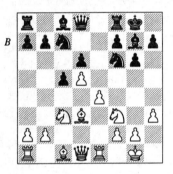

d1) 11...♖e8 12 a4 b6 (for 12...a6 see 11...a6) 13 ♗f4 ♘h5 14 ♗g5 ♗f6!? (14...♕d7 15 ♕d2 ♗b7? 16 g4! ♘f6 17 ♕f4 +– Bönsch-Molnar, Szekszard 1989) 15 ♗e3.

d2) White has an easy game after 11...♘d7 12 ♗f4 ♕e7 13 ♕d2 ♖b8 14 a4 a6 15 ♗f1 f6 16 ♖ab1! ♘e5 17 ♘xe5 fxe5 18 ♗g5 ♕e8 19 b4 ± Magerramov-Garrido, Nîmes 1991.

d3) 11...♖b8 12 a4 b6 (12...♘a6 13 ♗f4 ♘b4 14 ♗c4! b6 15 e5 dxe5 16 ♘xe5 ± Orlov-Bilunov, Podolsk 1989) 12...b6 13 ♗g5!? h6 14 ♗f4 a6 15 ♕d2 g5 16 ♗h2 ♗b7 17 ♖ad1 ♖e8 18 e5! ± Piket-Martinović, Groningen 1989.

d4) 11...a6 12 a4 (Black has no problems after 12 ♗f4?! b5 13 a3 ♗b7 14 ♕d2 ♖e8 15 b4 cxb4 16 axb4 ♖c8 17 ♗h6 ♗h8 18 ♗e3 ♘a8! = Tukmakov-Kovalev, Simferopol 1988) and now Black has two rook moves, leading to roughly similar situations:

d41) 12...♖e8 13 ♗f4 ♖b8 (or 13...b6 14 ♕d2 ♗b7 15 ♖ab1 b5 16 b4 c4 17 ♗c2 ♕d7 18 ♘d4 ± Khuzman-Galego, Benasque 1993, and similarly 13...♘h5 14 ♗h2 ♗h6!? 15 e5 ♗f4 16 ♗xf4 ♘xf4 17 ♗f1 gives an advantage; Goldin-Nun, Sochi 1989) 14 ♖b1!? b5 15 axb5 ♘xb5 16 ♗c4! ♘d4 17 ♕d3 ♕c7 18 ♘d2 ± Abrukh-Gufeld, Moscow Tal mem 1992.

d42) 12...♖b8 13 ♗f1!? (Black is in great difficulties after 13 ♗g5!? h6 14 ♗f4 b5 15 axb5 axb5 16 ♕d2 b4 17 ♘a4 g5 18 ♗h2 ♖e8 19 e5! dxe5 20 d6 ± Makarov-Efimov, USSR 1988) 13...♖e8 (or 13...b5 14 e5 dxe5 15 ♘xe5 ♗b7 16 d6 ♘cd5 17 axb5 ♘xc3 18 bxc3 axb5 19 ♗g5! h6 20 ♗xf6 ♗xf6 21 ♗xb5 ♗xg2 22 ♔xg2 ♖xb5 23 ♕d5! ± Krasenkov-Moskalenko, Moscow 1992) 14 ♗f4!? b5 15 e5 dxe5 16 ♘xe5 ± Browne-Fink, Las Vegas 1993.

This gives the impression that 9...♘a6 leaves Black with more than a few problems.

C1)   9 ...   ♖e8
      10 0-0 *(D)*

Black has greater chances to equalize after 10 ♗g5, for example

10...c4 (10...h6 11 ♗e3 c4 12 ♗c2 b5 13 a3 a5 14 ♘xb5 ♘xe4 15 0-0 ± Ibragimov-Bosboom, Khania 1993) 11 ♗c2 b5 12 a3 ♗d7 (12...♘a6 13 0-0 ♘c5 14 ♖e1 ♕b6 15 ♕d2 a5, Rogozenko-Marin, Bucharest 1993, 16 ♗e3!? ±) 13 0-0 a5 14 ♘d4 ♘a6 15 ♘dxb5 ♗xb5 16 ♘xb5 ♕b6 17 ♘c3 ♕xb2 18 ♗d2 (Rogozenko-Marin, Odorheiu Secuiesc 1993) and 18...♕b8!? 19 ♖b1 ♕d8 20 ♗a4 ♖e7 21 ♗c6 ♖b8 22 ♕c2 ♘c5 would have been unclear.

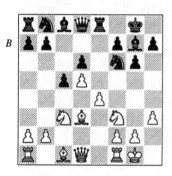

B

10   ...   c4

It is not easy for Black to neutralize his opponent's initiative after the continuation 10...♗d7 11 ♖e1 b5 12 a3!? c4 (12...b4?! 13 axb4 cxb4 14 ♘a2) 13 ♗c2!? (but not 13 ♗f1?! ♘a6 14 ♗f4 ♘c5 ∞ Stajčić-Lobron, Vienna 1991) 13...♘a6 14 ♗e3 ♕c7 15 ♕d2 ♘c5 16 ♗d4 a5 17 e5! Epishin-Izeta, Dos Hermanas 1993.

At this point White must make a choice:

C11) 11 ♗c2
C12) 11 ♗xc4

C11) 11 ♗c2   b5!?

Or:

a) White has a more promising position after 11...♘a6:

a1) 12 ♗e3!? ♗d7 (12...♘b4 13 ♘d2! ♘xc2 14 ♕xc2 ♗d7 15 ♘xc4 ♕e7 16 ♗f4 ♘xe4 17 ♖fe1 ♗xc3 18 bxc3 ♗f5 19 ♘xd6 ♘xd6 20 ♖xe7 ♗xc2 21 ♗xd6 ♖ed8 22 ♗f4 ♖xd5 23 ♖xb7 ± Bagirov-Vasiukov, Moscow 1991) 13 a3!? ♖c8 14 ♗d4 ♘c5 15 e5!? (Black's problems are simpler after 15 ♖e1 ♘h5 16 ♗xg7 ♔xg7 17 e5 ♘f4!? 18 exd6 ♖xe1+ 19 ♕xe1 ♕f6 = J.Horvath-Tolnai, Budapest 1992) 15...dxe5 16 ♘xe5 b5 17 ♕f3 ± Kishnev-Moskalenko, Budapest 1991.

a2) 12 ♖e1 ♘c5 13 ♗f4 b5!? (13...♕b6?! 14 ♖b1 ♘fd7 15 ♘d2 ♕a6 16 a4 ± Dautov-Dinstuhl, Germany 1992) 14 a3 ♕b6 15 ♕d2 a5 16 ♗h6 ♔h8 17 ♗e3! ±.

b) Black's defence is not easy after 11...♗d7 12 ♗f4 ♕b6 13 ♖b1 ♘a6 14 b4! (14 e5 is reasonable, for example 14...dxe5 15 ♘xe5 ♖ac8 16 d6! ♘b8! {16...♗f8? 17 ♘d5!} 17 ♕f3 with strong pressure; Fishbein-Larsen, New York 1990) 14...cxb3 15 ♖xb3 ♕c7 16 ♘d4 ♖ad8 17 ♘db5 ♗xb5 18 ♘xb5 ♕e7 19 ♖e3 ± Azmaiparashvili-Ljubojević, Groningen PCA 1993.

12 a3

White has no hint of an advantage after 12 ♖e1 b4 13 ♘b5 ♕b6 14 ♘xd6 ♕xd6 15 e5 ♕d8 16 ♗g5 ♘bd7 17 ♗a4 h6! = Browne-Wedberg, St Martin 1991.

12 ♘xb5 leads to huge complications after 12...♘xe4 13 ♖e1 (or 13

♗xe4 ♖xe4 14 ♖e1 ♖xe1+ 15 ♕xe1
♘d7 16 ♘xd6 ♘f6 17 ♘xc4 ♕xd5
18 ♘ce5 ♗b7 Lputian-Velimirović,
Yugoslavia tt 1991) and now (D):

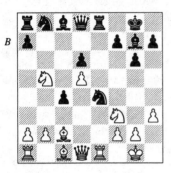

a) 13...♗a6!? 14 a4! ♗xb5 15
axb5 ♘c5 16 ♘d2!? (or 16 ♖xe8+
♕xe8 17 b6 a6 18 ♗f4 ♕b5 19
♗xd6 ♕xb6 20 ♗e5 ♗xe5 21 ♘xe5
♕xb2 22 ♘xc4 ♕f6 = Stohl-Wed-
berg, Gausdal 1991) 16...♖xe1+ 17
♕xe1 c3 18 bxc3 ♗xc3 19 ♖a3 ♗b4
20 ♖e3 ♘bd7 21 ♕e2!? ♘b6 with
chances for both sides, Dreev-Wed-
berg, New York 1991.

b) The other interesting possibility runs 13...♘xf2!? 14 ♖xe8+ (or
14 ♔xf2!? ♖xe1 15 ♕xe1 ♕b6+ 16
♘bd4 ♗xd4+ 17 ♘xd4 ♕xd4+ 18
♕e3 ♕xe3+ 19 ♔xe3 ♘d7 20 ♔d4
♘e5 21 b3 cxb3 22 axb3 Radošević-
Velimirović, Belgrade 1993 and, despite the extra pawn, I would prefer
to be White) 14...♕xe8 15 ♘c7!
♕e7 16 ♕e1 ♕xc7 17 ♕e8+ ♗f8 18
♗h6 ♘xh3+! (18...♘d7 19 ♘g5 +−)
19 gxh3 ♕c5+ 20 ♔h1! (but not 20
♔f1? ♗xh3+ 21 ♔e2 Magerramov-
Totsky, Moscow 1991, and Black
would have won after 21...♕c8! −+)

20...♘d7 21 ♘g5 ♕xd5+ 22 ♗e4
♗b7! 23 ♕xd7 ♗xh6 24 ♗xd5
♗xd5+ with a complicated game.

| 12 | ... | a6 |

White has a small advantage after
12...♗d7 13 ♖e1 ♘a6 14 ♗e3!?
♕b8 15 ♗d4 b4 16 axb4 ♘xb4 17
♗b1 a5 18 ♕d2 ± Gonzalez-Andres,
Capablanca mem 1991, or 12...♘a6
13 ♗g5 ♘c5 (13...b4 14 axb4 ♘xb4
15 ♗b1 a5 16 ♕d2 ±) 14 ♖e1 ♕b6
15 ♕d2 a5 16 e5!? dxe5 17 ♘xe5 ±
Rogozenko-Marin, Bucharest 1993.

13	♖e1	♘bd7
14	♗e3	♗b7
15	♕d2	♖c8
16	♖ad1	♘c5
17	♗g5	♕b6

Chernin-Hulak, Marseille 1990.
White's position is somewhat more
active, but Black cannot complain at
the outcome of the opening either.

C12) | 11 | ♗xc4 | ♘xe4 |
| | 12 | ♘xe4 | ♖xe4 (D) |

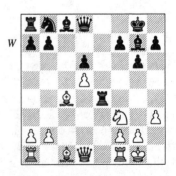

13 ♗g5

After 13 ♗d3 ♖e8 14 ♗g5 the
move 14...♗f6!? transposes back to
the main line, although 14...♕a5!? is

not bad either, e.g. 15 ♖e1 ♗d7 16 ♖xe8+ ♗xe8 17 ♕e1 ♕xe1+ 18 ♖xe1 ♘d7 = Ribli-Gschnitzer, Bundesliga 1991, and in the event of 14...♕b6 White's position is preferable: 15 ♖e1 ♗d7 16 ♖xe8+ ♗xe8 17 ♖c1 ♘d7 18 b3 ♘e5 19 ♗e2 ♘xf3+ 20 ♗xf3 ♗d4 21 ♕d2 ± Epishin-Haist, Baden-Baden 1990.

13 ...   ♗f6!?

13...♕b6 14 ♘d2! ♖e8 15 ♖e1 ♖xe1+ 16 ♕xe1 ♗d7 17 ♘e4 is good for White; Junge-Gschnitzer, Bad Wörishofen 1991.

14 ♗d3   ♖e8
15 ♕d2

It is easier for Black to equalize after 15 ♕a4 ♘d7 16 ♕h4 a6!? (16...♗xg5?! 17 ♘xg5 ♘f6 18 f4! ♔g7 19 f5 with initiative; Gallego-Zelčić, San Sebastian 1991) 17 ♖fe1 ♖xe1+ 18 ♖xe1 b5 19 ♖e4 ♗b7 20 ♖f4 ♔g7! = P.Cramling-Wedberg, Stockholm 1990.

15 ...   ♗xg5

Or 15...♘d7 16 ♖fe1 ♘e5 17 ♗xf6 ♕xf6 18 ♘xe5 dxe5 19 ♕c3 ♕d6 20 ♗b5 ♖e7 21 ♕a3! with an advantage; Wells-Tolnai, Balatonbereny 1992.

16 ♘xg5   h6
17 ♘f3

Norwood suggests the promising sacrificial idea 17 ♘xf7!?.

17 ...   ♔g7
18 ♖fe1   ♖xe1+
19 ♖xe1   ♘d7
20 ♖e4!

With a minimal advantage to White; Bischoff-Cu.Hansen, Hamburg 1991.

C2)   9 ...   a6
10 a4

It is not easy for Black to equalize after 10 0-0, allowing 10...b5 *(D)*, but it seems to me that Black's chances are reasonable:

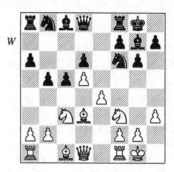

a) After 11 ♖e1 Black should probably continue 11...♖e8 12 ♕c2 (12 ♗f4!?) 12...♘bd7, as after 11...♘bd7 12 a4 b4 (12...c4 13 ♗f1 is good for White) 13 ♘b1 a5 14 ♘bd2 ♘b6 15 ♖a2!? ♗a6 16 ♗xa6 ♖xa6 17 b3 Psakhis-Spraggett, Barcelona European Cup 1993, White's position is more pleasant.

b) You also see 11 a3:

b1) 11...♘bd7 is not bad for Black: 12 ♗f4 ♕e7 (12...c4!? 13 ♗c2 ♕c7 14 ♕d2 ♖e8 15 ♘d4 ♘c5 16 ♖ae1 ♗d7 = Vladimirov-Franco, Marchena 1989) 13 ♖e1 ♘h5 14 ♗h2 ♘e5 15 ♗e2 ♘f6 16 ♘d2 g5! 17 ♖c1 ♘fd7 ∞ Timoshchenko-Pigusov, Sverdlovsk 1987.

b2) In the event of 11...♖e8 12 ♖e1 ♖a7?! 13 ♗e3! White seizes the initiative, for example 13...♘bd7 (or 13...♖ae7 14 e5! dxe5 15 ♗xc5 ♖d7 16 d6 with the initiative) 14 ♖c1

♖a8 15 ♗f4 c4 16 ♗c2 ♘c5 17 ♕d2 ± Sakaev-Lyrberg, Helsinki 1992.

b3) 11...♘h5!? 12 ♗g5 ♕c7 13 ♕d2 ♘d7 14 ♖ac1 ♗b7 15 ♖fe1 ♖ae8 = Levitt-Suba, Dublin 1991.

c) 11 ♗f4:

c1) White's position is preferable after 11...♘e8 12 ♖e1!? ±.

c2) 11...b4 12 ♘a4 ♗d7 13 a3 ♖e8 (13...♗b5 14 axb4 cxb4 15 ♘d4 ±) 14 ♖e1 ♗xa4 15 ♕xa4 bxa3 16 ♖xa3 ♘fd7 17 b4! is also good for White; Zsu.Polgar-Sax, Aruba 1992.

c3) It is significantly more difficult for White to achieve an advantage in the event of 11...♗b7 12 ♖e1 ♕b6 13 ♖c1 ♘bd7 14 b3 ♘h5 15 ♗e3 ♕a5 16 ♕d2 ♖fe8 ∞ Vyzhmanavin-Suba, Copenhagen 1991.

c4) 11...c4!? is also reasonable: 12 ♗c2 ♖e8 (12...♗b7 13 ♕d2 ♕b6 14 b4!? cxb3 15 axb3 ♖c8 16 ♘e2 ♘bd7 17 ♗e3 ♕d8 18 ♘fd4 ± Vyzhmanavin-Emms, Cappelle la Grande 1992) 12...♖e8 13 a3 (13 ♖e1 ♗b7 14 ♕d2 ♕b6 15 b4 cxb3! 16 axb3 ♘bd7 with equality; Foisor-Suba, Romania 1987) 13...♕b6 14 ♗e3 ♕c7 15 ♕d2 ♘bd7 16 ♖ad1 ♘c5 17 ♘d4 ♗d7 18 f3 ♖ab8 = Foisor-Vulević, Gijón rpd 1988.

c5) 11...♖e8 12 ♖e1 (or 12 a3 ♗b7 13 ♖e1 ♕b6 14 ♕d2 ♘bd7 15 ♖e2 c4 16 ♗c2 ♘c5 17 ♖ae1 ♘fd7 18 ♗e3 ♕c7 ∞ Aseev-Magerramov, Rostov 1993) 12...♖a7!? (more interesting and stronger than 12...♕b6 13 a4! c4 14 ♗f1 b4 {14...♗b7 15 axb5 axb5 16 ♖xa8 ♗xa8 17 b4! ♘a6 18 ♗e3 ♕b8 19 ♕b1 ♘g4 20 ♗d2 ± Vyzhmanavin-Stefansson,

Moscow GMA 1989} 15 a5! ♕c7 16 ♘a4 ♘bd7 17 ♕c2 ♗b7 18 ♗xc4 ♖ac8 19 ♘d2 ♗f8 20 ♗e3 ± Vyzhmanavin-Antonio, Beijing 1991) 13 a3 h6!? (13...♖ae7 14 ♖c1!? ♕b6 15 b4! c4 16 ♗e3 ♕b7 17 ♗c2 ± Foisor-Pigusov, Moscow 1987) 14 ♕d2 g5 15 ♗h2 ♕b6 16 e5 dxe5 17 ♘xe5 ♖ae7 with mutual chances; P.Cramling-Gavrikov, Bern 1991.

Now we return to the main line after 10 a4 *(D)*:

10 ...   ♘bd7 *(D)*

Besides this natural move you also see:

a) 10...b6?! 11 0-0 ♘h5 12 ♗g5 ♗f6 13 ♗e3 ♘d7 14 ♕d2 ♘e5 15 ♗e2 ♘xf3+ 16 ♗xf3 ♘g7 17 ♗e2 with advantage to White; Dzhandzhgava-Zaichik, Tbilisi 1991.

b) 10...♕e8?! 11 0-0 ♘fd7 12 ♗f4 ♘e5 13 ♘xe5 ♗xe5 14 ♗h6 ♗g7 15 ♗xg7 ♔xg7 16 f4 ♘d7 17 ♕d2 ± Lobron-Armas, Bundesliga 1990.

c) 10...♘fd7 11 0-0 (or 11 ♗f4 ♕e7 12 0-0 ♘e5 13 ♘xe5 ♗xe5 14 ♗xe5 ♕xe5 15 a5 ♘d7 16 ♕d2 and White is better; Neidhardt-Armas,

French Cht 1991) 11...♘e5 12 ♘xe5 ♗xe5 13 ♗h6 ♖e8 14 ♕d2 ♘d7 15 ♖ae1 ± Nalbandian-Haburdzania, Alma-Ata 1991.

d) 10...♘h5!? 11 ♗g5 (for 11 0-0 ♘d7 see the line 10...♘bd7 11 0-0 ♘h5) 11...♗f6 12 ♗e3 ♘d7 13 ♗e2:

d1) 13...♖e8?! 14 ♘d2! ♗d4?! (14...♘g7!?) 15 ♗xh5 ♗xe3 16 fxe3 ♕h4+ 17 g3! ♕xh5 (17...♕xg3+? loses: 18 ♔e2 ♕g2+ 19 ♔d3 ♘e5+ 20 ♔c2 +– Ivanchuk-Yudasin, Riga Ct (5) 1991) 18 ♕xh5 gxh5 19 ♘c4 ♘e5 20 ♘xd6 ♖d8 ± Yudasin.

d2) 13...♘g7!? is better: 14 ♘d2 (or 14 0-0 ♕e7 15 ♕c2 ♖e8 16 ♘d2 ♗d4 ∞) 14...♗d4 15 ♘c4 ♗xe3 16 ♘xe3 f5 17 exf5 gxf5 with mutual chances, Yudasin.

e) 10...♖e8 11 0-0 c4 (Black cannot coordinate his position after either 11...♘fd7?! 12 ♗f4 ♘e5 13 ♘xe5 ♗xe5 14 ♗xe5 dxe5 15 a5 ♕d6 16 ♘a4 ♘d7 17 ♕c2 ± Xu Jun-Sursock, Novi Sad OL 1990, or 11...b6?! 12 ♖e1 ♖a7 13 ♗f4 ♖ae7 14 ♗h2 ♗b7 15 ♕b3 ♕c7 16 ♘d2 ± Rechlis-Vokac, Ostrava 1991, whilst 11...♘bd7!? transposes back to the main line) 12 ♗c2 (12 ♗xc4 is not bad either: 12...♘xe4 13 ♘xe4 ♖xe4 14 ♗g5 ♗f6 15 ♗d3 ♖e8 16 ♕d2 ♗xg5 17 ♘xg5 with an edge for White; P.Cramling-Antonio, Biel 1991) 12...♘bd7 13 ♗f4 ♕c7 (nor can Black organize himself after 13...♘c5 14 ♖e1 ♘h5 15 ♗h2 ♕b6 16 ♖b1 ♗d7 17 ♘d2 ± Khalifman-Tomczak, Bundesliga 1990) 14 ♖e1 ♘h5 (or 14...♖b8 15 ♕d2 b5? 16 axb5 axb5 17 ♘d4 and White wins;

Murzin-Suetin, Russia 1993) 15 ♗e3 ♖b8 16 ♕d2 b6 17 ♘d4 with a large advantage; Gelfand-Wahls, Arnhem jr 1989.

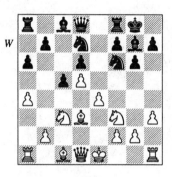

11 0-0 *(D)*

White also has excellent chances for an advantage after 11 ♗f4!? ♕e7 12 0-0, for example:

a) 12...♖b8?! 13 ♖e1 ♘e8 14 ♗f1! b6 15 ♕d2 ♘e5 16 ♘h2 ♘c7 17 ♗g5! f6 18 ♗h4 ♕f7 19 f4 ± Gelfand-Illescas, Amsterdam 1989.

b) 12...♘e8 13 ♖e1 ♘e5 14 ♘xe5 ♗xe5 (14...dxe5!?) 15 ♕d2 ♗xf4 16 ♕xf4 ♕e5 17 ♕e3 g5 18 ♘b1!! ± Khalifman-Luther, Leningrad 1989, doesn't make an impression either.

c) 12...♘h5 13 ♗g5 (13 ♗h2!? deserves close attention, for example 13...♘e5 {13...♘h6 14 ♖e1 f6 15 a5 ♘e5 16 ♘a4 ♗f4 17 ♘b6 ± Piket-Romanishin, Manila OL 1992} 14 ♗e2! ♘xf3+ 15 ♗xf3 with a small advantage) 13...♗f6 14 ♗h6 ♗g7 15 ♗g5 ♗f6 16 ♗e3 ♘e5 (or 16...♖b8 17 ♕d2 ♖e8 18 ♖fe1 ♕d8 19 g4! and White wields the initiative; Zsu. Polgar-de Firmian, New York 1989)

17 ♗e2 ᐃxf3+ 18 ♗xf3 ᐃg7 19 a5 ♗d7 20 ♕d2 ♔h8 21 ♖fe1 ♖ae8 22 ♖ab1 ± Ionov-Szalanczy, Dortmund 1992.

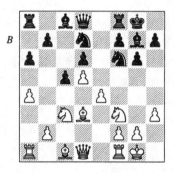

11 ...   ♖e8 (D)

Black has a wide choice of continuations at his disposal, but unfortunately it is difficult for him to get a satisfactory game, for example:

a) 11...♖b8 12 ♗f4 (or 12 ♖e1 ᐃe8 13 ♗g5 f6 14 ♗e3 ᐃe5 15 ᐃxe5 fxe5 16 a5 ᐃc7 17 ᐃa4 ± Priehoda-Kapengut, Morava 1991) 12...ᐃe8 13 ♕d2 ♕e7 14 ♖ac1 ᐃc7 15 b4! b6 (15...cxb4 16 ᐃb5!) 16 ᐃe2 a5 17 bxa5 ± Chernin-Sandić, Belgrade GMA 1988.

b) 11...♕c7 12 ♗g5 (12 ♗f4!? ±) 12...♖b8 13 ♖e1 c4 14 ♗f1 b5!? 15 axb5 axb5 16 b4 cxb3 17 ᐃxb5 ♕b6 18 ♖b1 ᐃc5 with complications; Lukov-Tal, Tbilisi 1988.

c) 11...ᐃe8 12 ♗g5 f6 13 ♗e3 ᐃe5 14 ᐃxe5 fxe5 15 ♗e2! with a small advantage; Campos Moreno-P.Cramling, Barcelona 1989.

d) 11...h6 12 ♖e1 g5!? 13 ᐃe2! g4 14 hxg4 ᐃxg4 15 ᐃg3 ᐃde5 16 ♗e2! f5 17 exf5 ♗xf5 18 ♖f1! with a

distinct advantage for White; Psakhis-Manor, Israel 1992.

e) 11...♕e7 12 ♖e1!? (for 12 ♗f4 see 11 ♗f4 ♕e7 12 0-0) 12...h6 13 ♗f4 ᐃh7 (or 13...g5 14 ♗h2 g4 15 hxg4 ᐃxg4 16 ♗g3 ᐃde5 17 ♗e2 f5 18 exf5 ♗xf5 19 ᐃh4! ±) 14 ♕d2 g5 15 ♗g3 ᐃe5 (Black can scarcely settle after 15...♖d8 16 a5 ᐃhf8 17 ᐃa4 ᐃg6 18 ♖a3 ᐃde5 19 ᐃxe5 ♗xe5 20 ♗xe5 ♕xe5 21 ᐃb6 ♖b8 22 b4 with a clear advantage in Browne-de Firmian, Reno 1993) 16 ᐃxe5 ♗xe5 17 ♗xe5 ♕xe5 18 ᐃb1! ♗d7 19 a5 ♖ab8 20 ᐃa3 with an advantage for White; Chernin-Lobron, Dortmund 1990.

f) 11...ᐃh5:

f1) Black has no problems after 12 g4 ᐃhf6 13 ♗g5 ♕c7 14 ♔g2 ♖b8 15 ♖e1 h5! Baguero-Fedorov, Philadelphia 1992.

f2) 12 ♖e1!? deserves attention, for example 12...ᐃe5 13 ♗e2 ᐃxf3+ 14 ♗xf3 ♕h4 (14...ᐃf6 15 ♗f4 ±) 15 ♗xh5 gxh5 16 ♕d2! Tunik-Cherniak, Smolensk 1991, and Black should have continued 16...f5!? 17 ♕f4 ♕f6 18 a5 ♗d7 19 ♖a3 c4 20 ᐃa4 ♗xa4 21 ♖xa4 c3 22 bxc3 ♕xc3 23 ♗d2 ♕c2 24 ♖b4 fxe4 25 ♕e3, with only a small advantage to White (Tunik).

f3) 12 ♗g5:

f31) White has some advantage after 12...♕c7 13 ♕d2 (or 13 ♖e1 ᐃe5 14 ♗e2 h6 15 ♗e3 ᐃxf3+ 16 ♗xf3 ᐃf6 17 ♕d2 ♔h7 18 ♖ac1 ᐃd7 19 ♗e2 ± P.Cramling-Kofidis, Iraklion 1993) 13...♖e8 14 ♖fe1 ♖b8 15 ♗f1! c4 (nor can Black equalize after 15...♘e5 16 ♘xe5 ♗xe5 17 g4 ♘f6 18 ♔g2 ± Vaganian-Hjartarson, Barcelona World Cup 1989) 16 a5 b5 17 axb6 ♖xb6 18 ♘a4 ♖b8 19 ♘d4 ♘e5 20 ♗e3 ♘f6 21 ♘c3 ± Vaganian.

f32) 12...♗f6 13 ♗e3 (13 ♗h6 ♗g7 14 ♕d2 ♖e8!? 15 ♗g5 ♕c7 16 ♖fe1 ♖b8 17 ♗f1 ♘e5 18 ♘xe5 ♗xe5 19 g4 ♘f6 is less dangerous for Black; San Segundo-Wojtkiewicz, New York 1990) 13...♖e8 (White has an advantage in the event of 13...♘e5 14 ♘xe5 ♗xe5 15 f4! ♗d4 16 ♗xd4 cxd4 17 ♘e2 ♘f6 18 ♕d2 ♖e8 19 ♘g3 ± Dautov-Cherniak, Leningrad 1989) and now:

f321) An approximately level game follows 14 a5 ♖b8 15 ♕c2 (15 ♖e1 b5 16 axb6 ♕xb6 17 ♖b1 ♘e5 18 ♗e2 ♘xf3+ 19 ♗xf3 ♘g7 with an attack, Topalov) 15...♘e5 16 ♗e2 ♘xf3+ (White has an advantage after 16...♘g7?! 17 ♘d2! g5 {the only move} 18 ♘a4 g4 19 hxg4 ♗xg4 20 ♕d1! Topalov-Donchev, Bulgarian Ch 1991) 17 ♗xf3 b5 18 axb6 ♖xb6.

f322) 14 ♕d2 ♗g7!? (14...♖b8 15 ♖ab1 ♕a5 16 g4!? ♘g7 17 ♗f4 ♘e5 18 ♘xe5 ♗xe5 19 ♗xe5 dxe5 20 f4! with advantage; Garcia-Romanishin, Terrasa 1991, whilst 14...♕c7 15 ♖fc1 ♘e5 16 ♗e2 ♘xf3+ 17 ♗xf3 ♘g7 18 a5 ♗e5 19 ♘a4 leads to the same result; Kramnik-Illescas, Madrid m 1993) 15 g4 ♘hf6 16 ♗f4 c4! 17 ♗c2 ♘c5 18 ♖fe1 h5 with reasonable play for Black; Schüssler-Wojtkiewicz, Haifa Echt 1989.

f323) The sharp 14 g4!? has unclear consequences, for example

14...♘g7 15 ♔g2 ♖b8 16 ♕d2 ♕c7 17 ♖ac1 c4 18 ♘e2 b5 19 axb5 axb5 20 b4 h5 Brenninkmeijer-Wojtkiewicz, Kloostertoernooi 1991.

f324) 14 ♖e1 (this move deserves attention) 14...♘e5 15 ♗e2 ♘xf3+ 16 ♗xf3 ♘g7 17 ♕d2 ♗e5 18 ♗f4 ♗d7 19 ♗xe5 ♖xe5 20 ♗d1! ± Dautov-Luther, Leningrad 1989.

f325) 14 ♖b1!? ♗g7 15 ♖e1 ♖b8 16 ♕d2 ♕a5 17 ♕c2!? b5 18 axb5 axb5 19 ♖a1 ♕d8!? (stronger than 19...♕b4 20 ♖a7 ♘e5 21 ♘xe5 ♗xe5 22 ♖b1! ± Khalifman-Suba, London 1991) 20 ♗xb5! ♗xc3 21 ♗xd7 ♗xe1 22 ♗xe8 ♗xf2+ 23 ♗xf2 ♕xe8, with a small advantage to White, but Black preserves chances for a successful defence.

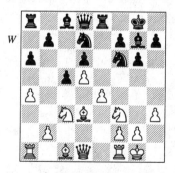

12 ♖e1

12 ♗g5?! does not promise White anything realistic, e.g. 12...h6 13 ♗e3 g5! 14 ♕d2 ♘f8 15 ♖ae1 ♘6d7 16 g3 ♘g6 17 ♔g2 ♖b8 and Black seized the initiative in Wessman-Manor, Tunja jr 1989.

12 ♗f4!? deserves attention:

a) 12...♕c7 13 ♕d2 (for 13 ♖e1!? see 12 ♖e1 ♕c7 13 ♗f4) 13...♘h5

(Black cannot organize himself after 13...c4 14 ♗c2 ♘c5 15 e5! ♘h5 16 ♗e3 ♘d7 {16...dxe5? 17 d6 ♕c6 18 ♗xc5 ♕xc5 19 d7 +–} 17 exd6 ♕xd6 18 ♖fe1 ± Blagojević-Sarlamanov, Yugoslav Ch 1991) 14 ♗h6 ♘e5 15 ♘xe5 ♗xh6 (15...♗xe5 16 g4) 16 ♕xh6 dxe5 17 ♖fc1! ± Salov-Hjartarson, Amsterdam 1989.

b) 12...♕e7 13 ♗h2!? (this prophylactic move guarantees White the better chances, whereas 13 ♕d2 ♘h5 14 ♗g5 ♕f8 15 ♖ae1 ♖b8 16 ♘h2!? h6 17 ♗e3 ♘hf6 18 a5 b5 19 axb6 ♖xb6 20 f4 ♖b4! Psakhis-Minasian, Moscow GMA 1989, leads to an unclear game) 13...♘h5 (Black has an unenviable task after 13...h6 14 ♖e1 ♘h7 15 a5 ♖b8 16 ♕c2 ♘hf8 {16...b5 17 axb6 ♖xb6 18 ♘d2 ♘e5 19 ♗xe5! ♗xe5 20 ♘c4 ±} 17 ♖ad1 b5 18 axb6 ♖xb6 19 ♖a1 with a clear plus; Lutz-Lobron, Baden-Baden 1992) 14 ♘d2 ♕f6 15 ♘c4 ♘f4 16 ♘e2! with a small advantage for White; Rajković-Pavlović, Yugoslavia tt 1991.

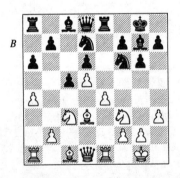

12   ...   ♕e7

Otherwise:

a) After 12...♕c7 the route to an advantage is not difficult; both of the following guarantee White the better game:

a1) 13 ♗c4!? h6 (13...♖b8 14 ♗f4 ♘h5 15 ♗h2 ♘e5 16 ♗e2 ♘xf3+ 17 ♗xf3 ♘f6 18 e5! dxe5 19 d6 ♕d7 20 ♗xe5 ± Klarić-Kljako, Bled 1993) 14 ♗f4 ♘h5 15 ♗h2 ♘e5 16 ♘d2! Dokhoian-Pekarek, Bundesliga 1993.

a2) 13 ♗f4 ♖b8 (13...♘h5 14 ♗h2 ♘e5 15 ♗e2 ♘f6 16 ♘d2 with initiative; P.Cramling-Velimirović, Novi Sad OL 1990) 14 ♖c1!? (14 ♗c4 ♘b6 15 ♗f1 ♘fd7 16 a5 ♘a8 17 ♘d2 Karpov-Timman, Kuala Lumpur Ct 1990, is also reasonable) 14...b6 15 b4! ♘h5 16 ♗h2 ♘e5 17 ♗e2 ♕e7 18 b5! a5 19 ♕d2 Vyzhmanavin-Titkov, Riga 1988.

b) An advantage is not so easy to gain after 12...♘h5, but he can probably get a small advantage:

b1) 13 ♗e3 ♘e5 14 ♗e2 ♘xf3+ 15 ♗xf3 ♘f6 16 ♗f4 ♘d7!? 17 ♗xd6! ♕b6 18 e5! ♘xe5 19 ♗xe5 ♖xe5! (an improvement compared to Zsu.Polgar-Yudasin, Pamplona 1991, in which White achieved an advantage after 19...♗xe5?! 20 a5 ♕d8 21 d6!) 20 ♖xe5 ♗xe5 21 ♕e2 f6! 22 a5 ♕c7 23 ♕c4 ♔g7 24 ♘e4 ♗f5! 25 d6 (or 25 ♘xc5 ♖c8 26 ♘e6+ ♗xe6 27 ♕xc7+ ♖xc7 28 dxe6 =, and similarly 25 ♕xc5 ♖c8!? 26 ♖c1 ♗xe4 27 ♕xc7+ ♗xc7! 28 d6 ♗c6 29 dxc7 ♖xc7 is equal – Yudasin) 25...♗xd6 26 ♘xd6 ♕xd6 27 ♗xb7 ♖a7 = P.Cramling-Yudasin, Dos Hermanas 1992.

b2) 13 ♗f1!? is a noteworthy move: 13...♘e5 14 ♘h2 ♖b8 15 g4 ♘f6 16 f4 ♘ed7 17 ♘f3 gave White a spatial advantage; Kakageldiev-Yurtaev, Bishkek Z 1993.

b3) 13 ♗g5 ♗f6 14 ♗e3 (14 ♗xf6 ♕xf6 15 ♗f1 ♘e5 16 ♘xe5 ♕xe5 17 g3! ± Vyzhmanavin-Tataev, Moscow 1990, is also not bad) 14...♘e5 15 ♗e2 ♘xf3+ 16 ♗xf3 ♘g7 17 ♕d2 ♗d7 18 ♖ab1 (18 ♖a2 h5 19 ♖b1 ♖c8 20 ♘e2 ♗e5 21 b4 c4! 22 ♖c1 f5 with mutual chances; Solozhenkin-G.Kuzmin, St.Petersburg 1993) 18...b5 19 axb5 axb5 20 b4 ♖a3 21 ♖ec1 c4 22 ♗d4 gives White an edge.

13 ♗f4

In Van der Sterren-Vokac, Prague 1992, after 13 ♗e3 h6 14 ♕d2 g5 15 h4 g4 16 ♘h2 ♘e5 17 ♗e2, the move 17...♔h7!? would have given Black a satisfactory game.

13 ...   ♘h5

14 ♗h2!?

If 14 ♗g5 then 14...♕f8 gives Black a reasonable game, e.g. 15 g4 ♘hf6 16 ♗f4 h5! 17 g5 ♘h7 18 h4 f6! with an attack in Lev-Psakhis, Israel 1991, but 14 ♗e3!? deserves attention, e.g. 14...♕f8 (14...♘e5 15 ♗e2 ♘xf3+ 16 ♗xf3 ♘f6 17 a5 ±) 15 ♕d2 h6 16 g4 ♘hf6 17 ♗f4 with an edge for White; Epishin-Minasian, Groningen 1990.

14 ...   ♘e5

After 14...♕f8 White is promised an advantage by the line 15 ♗f1!? b6 (15...♗h6!?) 16 g4! ♘hf6 17 ♘d2 ♖b8 18 f4 h5 19 e5 Khuzman-Davies, Vrnjačka Banja 1991,

whilst 15 ♗e2?! ♗h6! 16 ♘d2 ♘f4 17 ♘c4 ♖b8 18 a5 ♘e5! 19 ♘b6 ♕e7 is at least equal for Black; Psakhis-Minasian, Groningen 1990.

Black cannot solve his problems by means of 14...♗e5 15 ♘xe5 dxe5 16 ♕f3 ♕d6 17 ♗f1 ♖b8 18 a5 ± Novikov-Tolnai, New York 1993.

15 ♗e2   ♗d7

15...♗xf3+ leads to an advantage for White: 16 ♗xf3 ♗e5 (16...♘f6 17 e5!) 17 ♗xh5 ♗xh2+ 18 ♔xh2 ♕e5+ 19 ♔h1!? gxh5 20 ♖f1 ♕g5 21 f4 ± C.Horvath-Goldstern, Leukerbad 1992.

16 a5   ♔h8

17 ♕d2

Lobron-Maus, Hamburg 1991. I prefer White's position.

C3) 9 ...   b5 *(D)*

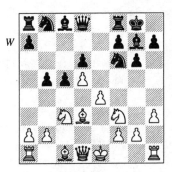

As we have noted more than once, in a quiet period of play the initiative usually belongs to White, and from this comes a desire to change the character of the struggle.

10 ♘xb5

Contemporary theory favours this move. White could also continue:

a) 10 0-0 b4 11 ♘a4 (after 11 ♘b1 ♖e8 12 ♕c2 ♗a6 13 ♖e1 ♗xd3 14 ♕xd3 ♘bd7 15 ♘bd2 ♘b6 16 ♘c4 ♘xc4 17 ♕xc4 ♘d7 Black took the initiative in Stasinos-Wojtkiewicz, Komotini 1993) 11...♗a6 12 ♖e1 ♗xd3 13 ♕xd3 ♘bd7 14 ♗f4 ♘b6 = Zsu.Polgar-Gdanski, Adelaide jr Wch 1988.

b) 10 ♗xb5 ♘xe4 11 ♘xe4 ♕a5+ 12 ♘fd2 ♕xb5 13 ♘xd6 *(D)* and now:

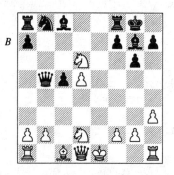

b1) Now not 13...♕d7?! 14 ♘2c4 ♕e7+ 15 ♗e3 ♘d7 16 0-0 ♘b6 17 ♖e1 ± Cvitan-Velimirović, Vršac 1989.

b2) White also has the advantage after 13...♕d3 14 ♘2c4 (14 ♘2e4?! ♕xd1+ 15 ♔xd1 ♗a6 16 ♔c2 ♘d7 17 ♗f4 ♗d4 gives Black compensation; Panchenko-Jurković, Belgorod 1991) 14...♕xd1+ 15 ♔xd1 ♗a6 16 ♔c2 ♘d7 (16...♖d8 is also no good for Black: 17 ♗g5 f6 18 ♗f4 ♗xc4 19 ♘xc4 ♖xd5 20 ♖ad1 ♘c6 21 ♖xd5 ♘b4+ 22 ♔b3 ♘xd5 23 ♗d6 f5 24 ♖d1 ♗d4 25 ♗e5 ± Kramnik) and at this point White may choose between:

b21) Black need not fear 17 ♖d1 ♘b6 18 ♘xb6 axb6 19 ♗g5 ♖a7! 20 ♔b3 (20 ♘e4!? f5 21 ♘c3 h6 22 ♗d2 ♖d8 is equal) 20...♖d7 21 ♘c4 Kramnik-Hall, Oakham 1992, and now 21...♗b7! 22 ♘xb6 ♖d6 23 ♘c4 ♗xd5 would have given Black a good game, Kramnik.

b22) 17 ♗g5!? is interesting, for example 17...♖fb8 18 ♖ad1 ♘e5 19 b3 ♘xc4 20 ♗xc4 ♗xc4 21 bxc4 ♖b2+ 22 ♔d3 ♖xa2 23 d6 ± Atalik-Gdanski, Iraklion 1993.

b23) 17 ♗f4 ♗d4 (17...♘b6 18 ♘xb6 axb6 19 a4! with an obvious advantage to White; Epishin-San Segundo, New York 1990) 18 ♘e3 ♖ab8 19 ♖ab1 with a small advantage.

b3) 13...♕a6 14 ♘2c4 and Black must choose:

b31) 14...♖d8!? 15 ♕e2 (15 ♗f4 ♘d7 16 0-0 ♘b6 17 ♘xb6 axb6 18 ♘xc8 ♕xc8 19 ♕b3 ♗f5 is equal; Estremera-Izeta, Spanish Ch 1991) 15...♗b7 16 ♘xb7 (but not 16 ♕e7? ♖d7 17 ♕e8+ ♗f8 18 ♘xb7 {18 ♗e3 ♖xd6 19 ♘xd6 ♕xd6 20 ♖d1 Varga-Tamas, Balatonbereny 1993, and now 20...♘d7 would have won} 18...♕xc4 −+ Gomez-Izeta, Toledo 1991) 16...♕xb7 17 ♘e3 ♕b4+ 18 ♕d2 Lalić-Marin, Haifa 1989, and now Black should have continued 18...♘c6!? 19 0-0 ♕xd2 20 ♗xd2 ♘e7 = Marin.

b32) 14...♘d7 15 0-0 ♘b6 (the alternative 15...♘e5 does not equalize: 16 ♘xc8 ♖axc8 {or 16...♕xc4 17 ♘e7+ ♔h8 18 ♗e3 ♘d3 19 ♕d2 ♕e4 20 f3 ♕xe7 21 ♕xd3 with a distinct plus for White; Epishin-T.Horvath, Frankfurt 1990} 17 ♘xe5 ♗xe5 18 ♖e1! ♖fe8 19 ♗g5 with an advantage; Bareev-Vera, Novi Sad OL 1990) 16 ♘xb6 and Black has two recaptures:

b321) 16...♕xb6 17 ♘xc8 ♖axc8 18 ♖e1!? (chances are equal after 18 ♖b1 ♕d6 19 ♗e3 ♖fd8 20 ♕a4 ♕xd5 21 ♖fd1 ♗d4 Kožul-Vranesić, Toronto 1990, or 18 ♕c2 ♖fd8 19 ♖d1 ♗d4 20 ♕c4 ♕b7 21 ♗e3 ♕xd5 22 ♕xd5 ♖xd5 23 ♖d2 ♖d6 24 ♔f1 ♖b6! 25 ♗xd4 cxd4 26 b3 ♖a6! Salov-Tal, Skellefteå 1989) 18...♖fe8 (18...♖fd8?! 19 ♗g5! ♖d7 20 ♕a4 ♕d6 21 ♖ad1 ♗d4 22 b4! ±) 19 ♖xe8+ ♖xe8 20 ♗e3 ♗d4!? (or ♕xb2 21 ♖b1 ♕xa2 22 ♗xc5 ±) 21 ♕b3 ♕xb3 22 axb3 ♗xe3 23 fxe3 ♖xe3 with good chances for the draw.

b322) 16...axb6 is possibly no worse than taking with the queen, for example 17 ♕b3 (17 ♖e1!? b5 18 ♘xc8 ♖axc8 19 ♖e2 ♖fe8 20 ♗e3 b4 21 a3 ± Kishnev-Szalanczy, Budapest 1989) 17...♗d7 18 ♗g5! (18 ♗e3 is a less dangerous move for Black: 18...♗a4 19 ♕c4 ♗xb2 20 ♖ab1 ♗g7 ∞ Hsu-Gunawan, Jakarta Z 1993) 18...b5 (White has a clear advantage after 18...f6 19 ♗f4 f5 20 ♖fe1 ♗f6 21 a4! ± Dreev-Shabalov, Tbilisi 1989) 19 ♘e4!? (stronger than 19 ♗e7 f5! ∞) 19...c4 20 ♕b4 f5 21 ♘c3 ♕a5 22 ♗e7 ± Marić-Litinskaya, Malaysia wom IZ 1990.

After White has captured with his knight on b5, Black has tried two moves *(D)*:

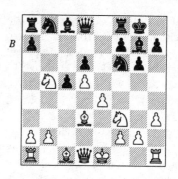

C31) 10...♘xe4?!
C32) 10...♖e8

The former was subjected to a great deal of practical testing, but now looks rather dubious.

C31) 10 ...   ♘xe4?!
11 ♗xe4

White's results have been impressive after this move.

Black's life is significantly easier after 11 0-0?!:

a) 11...a6 12 ♘a3 ♘f6 13 ♘c4 ♖a7!? (White wields the initiative after 13...♗b7 14 ♗f4 ♘e8 15 ♗c2 ♘d7 16 ♘xd6 ♘xd6 17 ♗xd6 ♖e8 18 ♗a4 Dreev-Smirin, USSR Ch (Odessa) 1989, but 13...♖e8!? deserves attention: 14 ♗f4 ♗f8 15 ♗c2! ♗b7 16 ♘e3 ♘bd7 = Petran-Hardicsay, Hungary 1990) 14 ♗f4 (or 14 ♗g5 h6 15 ♗h4 ♖d7 16 ♘e3 ♗b7 17 ♘h2 ♖e7 18 ♕b3 ♕c7 19 ♘hg4 ♘bd7 = Khalifman-de Firmian, Manila IZ 1990) 14...♖d7 15 ♗c2 ♗b7 16 ♘e3 ♕c7 17 ♖b1 ♖dd8 Vyzhmanavin-Yudasin, USSR Ch (Leningrad) 1990.

b) 11...♗a6 is also interesting, and after 12 ♖e1 Black should not play 12...♘f6 13 ♗f4 ♕b6 14 ♘xd6 ♕xb2 15 ♖b1 ♕a3 16 ♗b5! ± Nikolaev-Palkovi, Budapest 1990, but rather 12...♘xf2! 13 ♔xf2 c4 14 ♗xc4 ♗xb5 with an excellent game for Black, according to Kapengut and Gelfand.

11 ... ♖e8

Great problems also await Black after 11...♗a6 12 a4 ♖e8 and now:

a) 13 ♘g5! transposes to 11...♖e8 12 ♘g5! ♗a6 13 a4.

b) 13 ♕c2 ♕e7 14 0-0!? ♕xe4 15 ♖e1 ♕xe1+ 16 ♘xe1 ♖xe1+ 17 ♔h2 ♘d7 18 ♖a3 ± Vyzhmanavin-Neverov, Frunze 1988.

Nor is Black's life made easier by 11...♕a5+ 12 ♘c3 ♖e8 13 0-0 ♗xc3 14 bxc3 (14 ♗xg6!? hxg6 15 bxc3 ♕xc3 16 ♗d2 ♕c4 17 ♖e1 ♗d7 18 ♖xe8+ ♗xe8 19 ♕e1 ♘d7 20 ♕e7 ± H.Olafsson-Johansson, New York 1991, is also interesting) 14...♖xe4 15 ♘g5 ♖e7 16 ♖e1 with an advantage; Bogdanovski-S.Kovačević, Yugoslav Ch 1991.

12 ♘g5! (D)

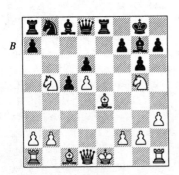

Chernin's move, which has forced Black to avoid 10...♘xe4.

Huge complications arise after 12 ♘d2 ♗a6 13 a4 ♕a5! (13...f5?! 14 0-0 fxe4 15 ♘c4 ♗f8 16 ♗f4 with an advantage; Barbero-Zelčić, Belgrade GMA 1988) 14 ♘xd6 ♘d7! 15 ♕c2! (both 15 g4?! ♖xe4+! 16 ♘6xe4 ♘e5 17 ♖a3 ♘d3+ 18 ♖xd3 ♗xd3 19 f3 f5 20 gxf5 gxf5 21 ♘g3 c4! −+ Kožul-Barlov, Kladovo 1989, and 15 f3? ♗e5 16 ♔f2 ♗xd6 17 ♖e1 c4 −+ Timoshchenko-Shabalov, Barnaul 1988, are weak) 15...f5 16 ♘xe8 (Black gains an advantage after 16 ♔d1 fxe4 17 ♘2c4 ♗xc4 18 ♘xc4 ♕a6 Vera-Neb.Ristić, Bela Crkva 1989) 16...♖xe8 17 ♔d1 fxe4 and now:

a) 18 ♖a3 leads to a double-edged position: 18...♗d3 19 ♖xd3 exd3 20 ♕xd3 ♕xa4+ 21 b3 ♘e5 22 ♕e3! ♕d4 (or 22...♕b5!? 23 ♖e1 ♖d8 24 ♕e4! ∞ Palkovi) 23 ♕xd4 cxd4 24 ♗a3 ♘d3 25 ♖f1 ♘f4 26 d6 ♘d5! with sufficient compensation; Züger-Palkovi, Leibnitz 1990.

b) 18 ♘xe4 ♕b4 (18...♖e5!? is also interesting: 19 ♗d2 ♖xd5 20 ♔c1 ♕c7 21 ♖a3 ♘e5 with an attack for Black; Koczka-Kozlov, Budapest 1991) 19 f3 ♕d4+! (White's has an easier time after 19...♖e5 20 ♗d2!? ♖xd5 21 ♔c1 ♕b8 22 ♖a3 ♘e5 23 ♖b3 ♕f8 24 ♔b1! ± Lokotar-Maidla, Tallinn 1991) 20 ♕d2 ♗d3 21 ♖a3 c4, and it is not easy to give an evaluation to this sharpest of positions.

12 ... h6 (D)

A difficult choice:

a) 12...♗xb2? loses right away to 13 ♗xb2 ♕xg5 14 0-0 ♖xe4 15

♘xd6 ♖b4 (15...♗xh3 16 ♕f3) 16 ♗c3 ♗xh3 17 ♕f3 +–.

b) Black has a bad position after 12...♗a6 13 a4!? (or 13 ♘c3 h6 14 ♘e6! fxe6 15 ♗e3 ± Lorscheid-Lukov, Krumbach 1991) 13...♗xb2 (13...♗f6 14 ♘e6 ♕e7 15 0-0 ♘d7 16 ♖e1 ♗xb5 17 ♘c7 ± Golod-Suetin, Minsk 1993) 14 ♘e6! ♕h4 15 ♘xd6 ♗xa1 16 ♕f3 with a dangerous attack; Hambarzoumian-Peters, Los Angeles 1991.

c) 12...f5 13 0-0 fxe4 14 ♖e1 ♕b6 15 ♘c3 ♘d7 (nor can Black settle after 15...e3 16 fxe3 ♘d7 17 ♘e6 ♗e5 18 ♕f3 ± Kragelj-Goštisa, Bled 1992) 16 ♘cxe4 ♗b7 17 ♗f4 ♘e5 18 ♘e6 ± Alburt-de Firmian, USA Ch 1990.

d) 12...♕a5+ leads to roughly the same result: 13 ♘c3 ♗a6 (for 13...h6 14 ♘e6! see 12...h6 13 ♘e6) and White has a big advantage after either:

d1) 14 ♕f3 ♘d7 (14...f5 15 g4! ♖xe4+!? 16 ♘gxe4 fxe4 17 ♕xe4 ♗xc3+ 18 bxc3 ♕xc3+ 19 ♔d1 ♘d7 {19...♕xa1 20 ♕e8+ ♔g7 21 ♔c2! +–} 20 ♖b1 ♘e5 21 ♖b3 ± Epishin-Bellón, Logroño 1991) 15 ♕xf7+ ♔h8 16 ♕xd7 ♗b5 (16...♗xc3+ 17 ♔d1! +–) 17 ♕xg7+! ♔xg7 18 ♘e6+ ♔g8 19 f3 Dokuchaev-Lukovnikov, Voronezh 1991.

d2) 14 f3!? f5 (14...♗d4 is bad: 15 ♗d2 f5 16 ♘e6! fxe4 17 ♘xe4 ♕b6 18 ♗c3 and White is winning, Rublevsky-Habardzania, Alma-Ata 1991) 15 ♔f2 ♗d4+ 16 ♔g3 ♗e5+ 17 ♗f4 ♕d8! (White has a big advantage after 17...♗xf4+ 18 ♔xf4

Budnikov-Keil, Berlin 1992) 18 h4 ♗xf4+ 19 ♔xf4 ♕f6 20 ♘e6 fxe4+ 21 ♔g3 exf3 22 ♕xf3 ♕e5+ 23 ♕f4 ± Kapengut.

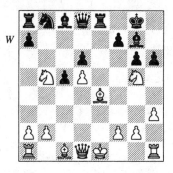

13 ♘e6!   ♕a5+

13...♗xe6 14 dxe6 ♖xe6 15 ♕d5 wins for White.

14 ♘c3   ♗xc3+

14...♗a6 15 ♗d2 fxe6 16 dxe6 ♕b4 17 ♕g4! +– Vragoteris-Radulov, Athens 1991.

15 bxc3   ♕xc3+
16 ♗d2   ♕c4

The black queen is very active and almost all White's light-squared pieces are attacked, but in fact one of them is superfluous!

Black has also tried 16...♕e5 17 0-0 ♗xe6 (17...♕xe4 18 ♘c7 ♖d8 19 ♘xa8 ♕xd5 20 ♗a5 +–) and now 18 ♖e1!? ♗d7 19 ♗xg6 ♕g7 20 ♗d3 a5 21 ♕h5 Buckley-Forbes, British Ch 1991, is good for White, as is 18 dxe6 ♕xe4 19 exf7+ ♔xf7 20 ♖e1 ♕d5 21 ♖xe8 ♔xe8 22 ♗xh6 ♕xd1+ 23 ♖xd1 ♔e7 24 ♗f4 and the only consolation for Black can be found in the fact that he has survived as far as the endgame.

17   ♕f3

17 ♗f3!? fxe6 18 ♗e3 ♗b7 19
♖c1! ♕b4+ 20 ♔f1 Poluliakhov.

17   ...   ♗xe6
18   ♖c1   ♕d4!?

Or 18...♗g4 19 ♖xc4 ♗xf3 20
gxf3 f5 21 ♖g1 ♔h7 22 ♗f4 ± Polu-
liakhov-Glianets, Moscow 1991.

19   0-0!   ♗f5!?

Black loses after 19...♗xh3? 20
♗c3 ♕xe4 21 ♖ce1, but 19...♗g4 20
♕xg4 ♕xd2 21 ♗xg6 ♕g5! 22 ♕a4
♖e7 23 ♗b1 ♘d7 24 ♖c3 ± Golod, is
possible.

20   ♗c3!   ♗xe4

20...♕xe4? 21 ♖ce1 ♕a4 22 ♕f4!
♕d7 23 ♕xh6 f6 24 ♗xf6 +–.

21   ♕f4!   ♕xd5
22   ♕xh6   f6
23   ♗xf6

White has an advantage; Golod-
Kozakov, Bucharest 1992.

C32) 10   ...   ♖e8
11   ♘d2 (D)

Black has no need to worry after
11 ♘c3 ♘xe4! 12 ♘xe4 f5 13 ♗g5
(13 ♘fd2 fxe4 14 ♘xe4 ♗f5 15 f3
♕h4+ with an attack) 13...♕d7! 14
♘fd2 ♗a6 (Stohl recommends the
interesting 14...fxe4 15 ♗c4 {15
♘xe4 ♕f5 16 0-0 ♖xe4 17 ♕d2 ♕e5
18 ♗xe4 ♕xe4 19 ♖fe1 ♕a4 ∓}
15...♗xb2 16 ♖b1 ♗c3 17 ♗b5 ♕f5
18 ♗xe8 ♕xg5 ∞) 15 ♗xa6 ♘xa6 16
0-0 fxe4 17 ♘c4 ♘b4 = Chernin-
Gdanski, Polanica Zdroj 1992.

If 11 ♗g5?! then 11...♕b6 12
♗xf6 ♗xf6 13 ♕b3!? (13 ♕c2 ♘a6
14 a3 ♗d7 15 ♘c3 ♖ab8 16 ♖b1
c4! 17 ♗e2 ♗xc3+ 18 ♕xc3 ♘c5 19

0-0 ♘xe4 20 ♕xc4 ♘g3 –+ Kalini-
chev-Semeniuk, Leningrad tt 1989)
13...♕a5+!? 14 ♘d2 c4 15 ♕xc4
♗a6 16 a4 ♖c8 17 ♕b3 ♘d7 or, alternatively, 11...c4! 12 ♗xc4 ♖xe4+
13 ♗e2 ♕a5+ 14 ♘d2 ♗a6 and
Black can be satisfied.

It is more difficult for Black to
equalize after 11 0-0 ♘xe4 12 ♖e1
(12 ♗xe4 ♖xe4 13 ♖e1 ♖xe1+ 14
♕xe1 ♗b7 15 ♗f4 ♕d7 = San Se-
gundo-Martin del Campo, Antwerp
tt 1992 is less convincing) 12...a6!?
(12...♗a6?! 13 a4 ♘f6 14 ♖xe8+
♘xe8 15 ♗g5 ♗f6 16 ♕d2 ♘d7 17
♗f4 with a small advantage; Epi-
shin-Zelčić, Geneva 1993) 13 ♘a3
♘f6 14 ♖xe8+ ♘xe8 15 ♗g5!?
(Black has more chances to equalize
after 15 ♘c4 ♘d7 16 ♗g5 ♘df6!?)
15...♗f6 (15...♕c7 16 ♕e2!) 16
♕d2 ♗b7 17 ♗c2 ♘d7 18 ♘c4
♗xg5 19 ♘xg5 ♘df6 20 ♘e3 ±
Neverov-Berelovich, Sochi 1993.

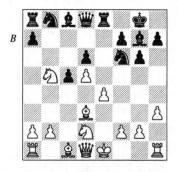

11   ...   ♘xd5

11...♘xe4!? 12 ♗xe4 ♗a6 (or
12...f5 13 0-0 fxe4 14 ♘c4 ♗a6 15
a4 ♗e5 16 ♘xe5 ♖xe5 17 b4! ±
Shipov-Maslej, Katowice 1992) 13

a4 ♕a5!? is analogous to 10....♘xe4 11 ♗xe4 ♖e8 12 ♘d2.

11...♘a6 12 0-0 ♘b4 is bad because of 13 ♗c4 ♘xe4 14 a3!?.

12 ♘c4

12 0-0 only leads to equality: 12...♘f4 13 ♘c4 ♘xd3 14 ♕xd3 ♗a6 15 a4 ♘c6 16 ♕xd6 ♕xd6 17 ♘cxd6 ♖ed8!? 18 ♗e3 ♗xb2 19 ♖ab1 ♗d4 = Mladinović-Radosavljević, Yugoslav Ch 1991.

12 ... ♘b4

13 ♗e2!?

Black has no problems after 13 ♗b1 ♗a6 14 ♘bxd6 ♗xc4 15 ♘xc4 ♕xd1+ 16 ♔xd1 ♘8c6 Sapis-Kizanik, Corr 1991, or 13 0-0 ♗a6 14 ♘cxd6 ♘xd3 15 ♕xd3 ♘c6, Cruz-Martín, Spanish Ch 1991, with good compensation in both cases.

13 ... ♗a6 *(D)*

13...♖xe4, which has not yet been seen in practice, would be interesting to test, for example: 14 ♘cxd6 ♖xe2+ 15 ♕xe2 ♗a6!? (15...a6 is bad because of 16 ♗g5! ♕d7 17 ♘xc8 axb5 18 ♘b6 +− Sapis) 16 ♗g5 ♗xb5 17 ♗xd8 ♗xe2 18 ♔xe2 ♘bc6 19 ♗g5 ♘d4 with some compensation for the exchange, Kapengut.

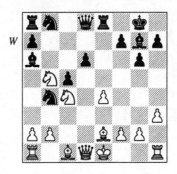

14 ♘bxd6 ♖e6

15 ♗f4 ♘d7

The line 15...♗f8 16 e5 ♗xd6 17 ♘xd6 ♗xe2 18 ♕xe2 ♕xd6 19 exd6 ♘d3+ 20 ♔d2 ♖xe2+ 21 ♔xd3 is advantageous for White.

16 0-0 ♘e5

17 ♗xe5 ♗xe5

18 a3

This was Sapis-Morchat, Corr 1992, and now, according to analysis by Sapis, Black should have played 18...♖xd6! 19 ♘xd6 ♕xd6 20 axb4 ♕xd1 21 ♖fxd1 ♗xe2 22 ♖d2 ♗b5 23 bxc5 a6 with equality.

In these variations Black is held by the scruff of the neck and I wouldn't be surprised if an advantage for White was found somewhere.

12 7 ♘f3 ♝g7 8 ♝g5 (A71)

1 d4 ♘f6 2 c4 c5 3 d5 e6 4 ♘c3 exd5 5 cxd5 d6 6 e4 g6

7 ♘f3 ♝g7

8 ♝g5 *(D)*

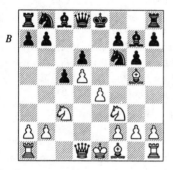

This system enjoyed more than a little popularity at the end of the 1970s and beginning of the 1980s, but nowadays it has practically fallen out of use, and perhaps for no reason, as it has a sting in its tail, and Black's route to equality is far from easy.

8 ... h6

White has an obvious advantage after 8...♝g4 9 ♕a4+! ♝d7 10 ♕b3 ♕c7 11 ♘d2.

After 8...0-0 White plays 9 ♝e2, transposing to A72, or 9 ♘d2!? and now:

a) 9...♘bd7 10 ♝e2 a6 11 a4 ♖e8 12 0-0. This position is examined in the chapter devoted to A74.

b) White has a somewhat better position after 9...h6 10 ♝h4 b6 (or

10...♘a6 11 ♝e2 ♖e8 {11...♘c7 12 a4 ♖b8 13 0-0 b6 14 f4 ♕d7 15 ♘c4 gives White a clear plus; Sorin-Garcia Palermo, Palma 1992} 12 0-0 ♘c7 13 f4 b6 14 a4 ♖b8 15 ♔h1! a6 16 ♘c4 b5 17 axb5 axb5 18 ♘a5 ♝d7 19 e5 dxe5 20 d6 ♘a8 21 fxe5 ♖xe5 22 ♝xb5! with advantage, Kapengut) 11 ♝e2 ♝a6 12 0-0 ♝xe2 13 ♕xe2 a6 14 a4 ♖e8 15 f4 Miles-Robatsch, Biel 1977.

Sometimes Black plays 8...a6, when after 9 a4 h6 10 ♝h4 (10 ♝f4 ♝g4 11 ♝e2 0-0 12 0-0 ♖e8 13 ♕c2 ♕c7 14 ♖fe1 ♘bd7 = Geller-Tal, Tbilisi 1959, is also not dangerous) 10...g5 11 ♝g3 ♘h5 12 ♘d2 ♘xg3 13 hxg3 he achieves a favourable version of the position, as he has exchanged the bishop and not allowed the dangerous check on b5. You also see 9 ♘d2 b5 10 a4 (an interesting position with chances for both sides follows after 10 e5!? dxe5 11 a4 b4 12 ♘ce4 0-0 13 ♝c4 ♘bd7 14 0-0 h6 15 ♝e3 Mikhalevsky-Sarbai, Minsk 1980) 10...b4 11 ♘cb1 0-0 12 ♝d3 ♖e8 13 0-0 ♕c7 14 ♕c2 ♘bd7 and this position is roughly equal.

9 ♝h4

At this point Black has two main systems:

A) 9...g5

B) 9...a6

A) 9...g5

After this move great complications arise, but these are at least equal for White.

10 ♗g3   ♘h5

11 ♗b5+!

This move alone lays claim to an advantage; Black has no problems after 11 ♗d3 0-0 12 0-0 ♘xg3 13 hxg3 ♘d7, or 11 ♘d2 ♘xg3 12 hxg3 a6 13 a4 ♘d7 14 ♘c4 ♘e5! 15 ♘xe5 (15 ♘e3 g4! 16 ♗e2 ♕g5 already gives Black the initiative) 15...♗xe5 with equality.

11 ...   ♔f8

11...♗d7? 12 ♗xd7+ ♕xd7 is bad because of 13 ♘e5! dxe5 (13...♕e7 14 ♕xh5 ♗xe5 15 ♗xe5 ♕xe5 16 h4 ±) 14 ♕xh5 with a big advantage.

12 e5! *(D)*

Not so much strong as practically forced; Black faces no problems at all after 12 ♗e2 ♘xg3 13 hxg3 (nor should Black fear 13 fxg3, for example 13...♘d7 14 0-0 a6 15 a4 ♕e7 16 ♕c2 h5! with initiative) 13...♘d7 14 ♘d2 a6 15 a4 ♕e7 16 ♕c2 (or 16 g4 ♗d4!? 17 ♘c4 {17 0-0? ♘f6 18 ♘c4 h5! with a powerful attack} 17...b6 18 ♕d2 ♖b8 and Black's chances are at least no worse) 16...♗d4 17 ♖f1!? (17 ♘d1?! ♘f6 18 0-0 h5 and again Black has a strong attack, Keene) 17...♔g7 18 0-0-0 b5 with an excellent game.

In Spassky-Daillet, French Cht 1993, after 12 a4 ♘xg3 13 hxg3 ♘d7 14 ♘d2 the simple 14...a6!? 15 ♗e2 ♕e7 promised Black approximately equal chances.

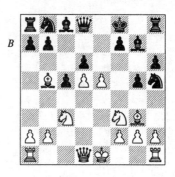

12 ...   a6

You also see:

a) 12...g4 13 ♗h4! (13 0-0!? is not so clear: 13...gxf3! {but not 13...dxe5? 14 ♗h4 ♗f6 15 ♗xf6 ♕xf6 16 ♘d2 ♕g6 17 ♕e2 f6 18 ♘de4 with a big advantage; Hartston-Walbom, Copenhagen 1977} 14 ♕xf3 ♕g5 15 ♗e2 ♗g4 16 ♕xg4 ♕xg4 17 ♗xg4 ♘xg3 18 hxg3 ♗xe5 with mutual chances, Marjanović) 13...♕b6 14 0-0 gxf3 15 e6! with the strongest of attacks.

b) 12...♘xg3 13 fxg3! and Black has a difficult defensive task:

b1) White has an irresistible attack after 13...g4 14 0-0! a6 15 ♗d3 gxf3 (15...c4 16 ♗xc4 b5 17 ♗d3 gxf3 18 ♕xf3 ♖a7 19 e6 ♕g5 20 ♖ac1! with an obvious advantage; Fuller-Kannop, England 1978) 16 ♕xf3 ♕d7 17 e6 ♗d4+ 18 ♔h1 ♕e7 19 ♕xf7+ ♕xf7 20 ♖xf7+ ♔e8 21 ♗g6 ♔d8 22 e7+ ♔d7 23 ♖e1 +– Høi-Van Baarle, Berlin 1980.

b2) The same miserable result awaits Black after 13...dxe5 14 0-0 a6 (14...♔g8?! 15 ♗c4 ♗g4 16 d6 ♗h5 17 ♕d3 ±) 15 ♗d3 b5 (after 15...♔g8 White gets a big advantage from 16 ♘d2!, whilst the psychological attack 16 ♘xe5? does not work after 16...♗xe5 17 ♕h5 ♕f8 18 ♗g6 f6 19 ♖ae1 ♗d4+ 20 ♔h1 ♗d7 and Black is winning; Matera-Rohde, New York 1977) and now:

b21) 16 ♘d2!? c4 (16...♖a7 17 ♕h5 ♔g8 18 ♔h1 c4 19 ♗c2 b4 20 ♘ce4 ♕xd5 21 ♖ad1 ± Shashin-Agzamov, Odessa 1977) 17 ♕h5 f6 18 ♗c2 ♗d7 19 a4! ♗e8 20 ♗g6 and White dominates the board; Miles-Hernandez, Biel 1977.

b22) 16 ♕e2!? c4 17 ♘xe5! ♕b6+ 18 ♔h1 cxd3 19 ♕h5 ♔g8 20 ♕xf7+ ♔h7 21 d6! ♕xd6 22 ♘e4 and White is winning; Dorfman-Shvedchikov, USSR 1978.

b3) 13...a6 14 ♗d3 c4 (14...♕b6 15 ♘d2!) 15 ♗xc4 ♕b6!? (White has a dangerous attack after 15...b5 16 ♗b3 ♕b6 17 ♕e2 g4!? {Black cannot defend his position after 17...dxe5?! 18 0-0-0 b4 19 ♘a4 ♕d6 20 ♘d2! Gulko-Savon, Baku 1977} 18 ♘h4 ♗xe5 19 ♖f1) 16 ♕e2 g4 17 ♘h4 ♗xe5 18 ♖f1 ♔e8 19 0-0-0 ♕c7 20 ♔b1 Visier-Taimanov, Montilla 1977. White's attack is strong, but Black's position is defensible, not least thanks to his mighty dark-squared bishop.

c) White also has the initiative after 12...♗g4!? 13 h3 ♘xg3 14 fxg3 ♗xf3 15 ♕xf3 ♗xe5 16 0-0 ♕e7 17 ♖ae1, Keene.

13 ♗e2

It would be interesting to test 13 ♗d3, e.g. 13...dxe5 14 ♗xe5 g4!? 15 ♗xg7+ ♔xg7 16 ♘g1 ♘f4 17 g3 ♖e8+ 18 ♔f1 ♘xd3 19 ♕xd3 ∞.

13 ...   ♘f4!?

13...♘xg3 14 fxg3 g4 (14...dxe5 15 0-0 ♖a7 16 a4 b6 17 ♕b3 f5 18 ♖ad1!? with powerful play for the pawn) 15 ♘h4 ♗xe5 16 0-0 ♕g5 (the line 16...♖g8?! 17 ♕d3 ♕g5 gives White an important tempo and a strong attack after 18 ♘e4 ♕g7 19 ♔h1 b5 20 ♖f2! Morrison-Ortega, Graz 1978) 17 ♔h1 ♖a7 18 ♕c2 b6 19 ♖f2 with sufficient compensation.

14	♗xf4	gxf4
15	exd6	♗xc3+
16	bxc3	♕xd6
17	0-0	♖g8
18	♘d2	♘d7

With a complex game, in which Black has certain counter-chances; Djurić-Karlsson, Vrnjačka Banja 1981.

B) 9...a6

10	♘d2	b5 *(D)*

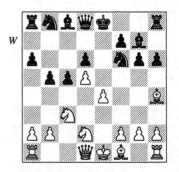

11 ♗e2 *(D)*

White first prepares to complete his development, and only then will he disturb Black on the queenside.

Other ideas:

a) 11 a4 b4 12 ♘cb1 and now:

a1) White's chances are a bit better after 12...g5 13 ♗g3 ♕e7 14 f3 (in Vaganian-Hort, Nikšič 1978, Black equalized after 14 ♗e2 ♘bd7 15 0-0 0-0 16 ♖e1 ♘e5 17 ♕c2 ♘fd7 18 ♘f1 b3! 19 ♕d1 ♖b8) 14...♘h5 (14...♘xd5? 15 ♘c4) 15 ♘c4 ♘xg3 16 hxg3 ♘d7 17 ♘bd2 ♗e5 18 g4 ±.

a2) 12...♕e7 13 f3!? (13 ♗d3 ♘bd7 14 0-0 ♘e5 15 ♗e2 g5 16 ♗g3 ♘fd7 17 ♘b3 a5! with mutual chances) 13...g5 14 ♗f2 0-0 15 ♗e2 ♘bd7 16 ♘c4 ♘h5 17 ♘bd2 ♘f4 18 0-0 with a small advantage.

a3) 12...0-0 13 ♗d3 (Black has no problems in the event of 13 ♗e2 ♖e8 14 f3 g5 15 ♗f2 ♘h5 16 ♘c4 a5! 17 0-0 ♘f4 Lambert-Nunn, London 1977) 13...♖e8 (preparing counterplay on the e-file; Black has a difficult position after 13...g5 14 ♗g3 ♕e7 15 0-0 ♘bd7 16 ♘c4 ♘e8 17 ♘bd2 ♘e5 18 ♗xe5 ♗xe5 19 ♘xe5 ♕xe5 20 ♘c4 Matamoros-Gutierrez, Bayamo 1989) 14 0-0 ♘bd7 (15 ♖e1 ♘bd7 16 ♘c4 ♘b6 17 ♘xb6 ♕xb6 18 ♘d2 ♘g4 19 ♘c4 promises White better chances; Razvaliaev-Kagan, Corr 1980) 15 ♖e1 (Black has an excellent game after 15 f4 ♕c7! 16 ♕f3 c4! 17 ♖c1 c3 18 bxc3 g5 19 fxg5 ♘e5 20 ♕e2 ♘fg4 Kapengut) 15...♘e5 16 ♗f1 g5 17 ♗g3 ♖a7 18 ♖a2 ♖ae7 and Black's position is more promising; Alburt-Tukmakov, USSR 1978.

b) After 11 ♕c2 Black has the choice between:

b1) 11...g5 is weak: 12 ♗g3 ♘h5 13 a4 bxa4 14 ♘c4 ♘xg3 15 hxg3 0-0 16 ♗d3 ♕c7 17 ♕xa4 with an advantage; Lukov-Psakhis, Naleczow 1980.

b2) 11...♘bd7 12 a4 b4 13 ♘d1 0-0 14 ♗e2 ♖e8 15 ♘e3 ♕c7 16 0-0 b3! 17 ♕b1 ♖b8 18 ♗g3 ♘e5 19 h3 g5 ∞ Wolf-Kindermann, Bundesliga 1986.

b3) 11...0-0 12 a4 b4 13 ♘d1 ♖e8 14 ♘e3 b3!? 15 ♕b1 (or 15 ♕d3 ♘bd7 16 f3 ♖b8 17 ♘ec4 ♘b6 with an unclear game; F.Portisch-P.Cramling, Reggio Emilia 1979) 15...g5 16 ♗g3 ♘h5 17 ♗d3 ♘f4 18 0-0 ♘d7! = Spiridonov-Suba, Bajmok 1980.

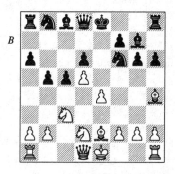

11 ...   0-0

White has a small advantage after 11...b4 12 ♘a4 0-0 13 0-0 ♗d7 14 a3 ♗b5 15 ♖e1 ♘bd7 16 ♗g3 ♘e8 17 ♘c4 Mohr-Wahls, Budapest 1988.

Black may also delay castling in order to organize counterplay on the queenside: 11...♘bd7 12 0-0 c4!? 13 a4 ♖b8 14 axb5 axb5 15 b4! g5 16 ♗g3 ♘e5 17 ♖a5 ♗d7 18 ♕c2 0-0 19 ♖fa1 ♘e8 20 ♘f1 f5! with

chances for both sides; A.Mikhal-
evsky-D.Gurevich, Beersheba 1993.

12 ♕c2 *(D)*

White frees d1 for the knight and
prepares to play 13 a4.

Black has less problems (but they
are not yet all solved) after 12 0-0:

a) White keeps the initiative after
12...g5 13 ♗g3 ♖e8 14 ♕c2 ♖a7
(14...b4 15 ♘a4 ♗d7 16 ♖ae1 ♗b5
17 b3 ± Visier-Outerelo, Albacete
1989) 15 a4 b4 16 ♘d1 ♖ae7 17
♗d3 ♘h5 18 ♘e3 ♘f4 19 ♘ec4
Burger-Barlov, New York 1988.

b) 12...♖e8 13 f4 ♘bd7 14 ♗f3
(the game is also complicated after
14 a4 b4 15 ♘cb1 ♕c7 16 ♗f3 ♖b8
17 ♖e1 c4! 18 ♕c2 c3 ∞ Basin-Psak-
his, Leningrad 1979) 14...♖b8 15
♕c2 c4 (15...♘b6 16 ♖ae1) 16 b4!?
cxb3 17 ♘xb3 ♗b7 18 ♖ac1 ♖c8 19
♕d3 ♘c5 20 ♘xc5 ♖xc5 21 ♘e2
with some advantage (Kapengut).

c) 12...♘bd7 13 ♕c2 (nor should
Black fear 13 ♗g3 ♕e7 14 ♕c2 c4
15 a4 b4 16 ♘d1 ♘c5! 17 ♗f3 ♘h5
18 ♘xc4 ♘xg3 19 hxg3 f5 with excellent compensation for the pawn;
D.Bronstein-Magerramov, Daugav-
pils 1978) and now:

c1) 13...c4 is not at all bad for
Black: 14 f4 (Black already wields
the initiative after 14 b4?! cxb3 15
♘xb3 ♗b7 16 ♖ac1 ♖c8 17 ♕b1
♕b6 18 ♔h1 ♖fe8 Bukić-Cebalo,
Banja Luka 1981, or 14 a4 ♖b8 15
axb5 axb5 16 b4 cxb3! 17 ♕xb3
♘c5 18 ♕b4 ♖e8 Sorin-Vera, Bayamo 1988) 14...♖e8 15 ♖ae1 ♘c5 16
♔h1 ♗d7 = Sigurjonsson-Grünfeld,
Lone Pine 1979.

c2) 13...♖b8!? 14 ♖ae1 c4 15 f4
♖e8 16 ♔h1 ♘c5 17 b4 cxb3 18
♘xb3 ♕c7 with an excellent game;
Vehi-Kasparov, simul 1984.

12 ... ♘bd7

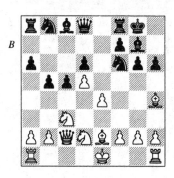

It is also not easy for White to
seize control of the game after
12...♖e8, for example:

a) White has little in the event of
13 a4 b4 14 ♘d1 ♕e7 (14...♖a7!? 15
♘e3 b3) 15 0-0 g5 16 ♗g3 ♘xe4! 17
♘xe4 ♕xe4 18 ♗d3 ♕xd5 19 ♘e3
♕c6 20 ♖fd1 ♗d4 ∞.

b) 13 0-0 and now:

b1) 13...♘bd7!? 14 a4 b4 is examined under 12....♘bd7.

b2) 13...♕e7 arouses interest, for
example 14 ♖ae1 g5 15 ♗g3 ♘bd7
16 a4 b4 17 ♘d1 ♘e5 18 ♘e3 h5!? =
Benjamin-Watson, Lone Pine 1979.

b3) After 13...b4 White gains an
advantage: 14 ♘d1 g5 (or 14...♘bd7
15 f4 ♘b6 16 ♘e3 ♕c7 17 ♗f3 ±)
15 ♗g3 ♘xd5 16 exd5 ♖xe2 17 ♕d3
♖e8 18 ♘c4 ♘d7 19 ♘de3 ♘e5 20
♗xe5! ♗xe5 21 ♘xe5 ♖xe5 22 f4
Timman-Robatsch,Holland-Austria
1978, and White's initiative more
than compensates for the pawn.

b3) 13...♕c7 14 ♖ae1!? (14 a4? b4 15 ♘d1 ♘xd5) 14...♘bd7 15 b3 (after 15 a4 b4 16 ♘d1, Miles-Bouaziz, Dortmund 1979, the standard 16...b3! would have given Black good counterchances) 15...g5 16 ♗g3 ♘e5 17 a4 b4 18 ♘d1 ♘g6 19 ♘e3 ♘f4 with a complicated game.

13 a4

For 13 0-0 see 12 0-0 ♘bd7 13 ♕c2.

13 ... b4

13...bxa4?! only creates additional weaknesses, and White easily achieves a better game after 14 0-0 (14 f3 is not bad either: 14...♘b6 15 ♘xa4 g5 16 ♗f2 ♘xa4 17 ♖xa4 ± Kuligowski-Tringov, Nice 1979) 14...♘b6 15 f4!? ♕c7 16 ♗f3 with a clear advantage for White.

14 ♘d1 ♖e8 (D)

15 ♘e3!?

This is possibly stronger than 15 0-0:

a) White has an advantage after 15...♕e7?! 16 ♘e3 ♘f8 17 ♘ec4 g5 18 ♗g3 ♘xe4 19 ♘xe4 ♕xe4, Timman-G.Garcia, Buenos Aires 1979, 20 ♕xe4 ♖xe4 21 ♖ae1 ±.

b) 15...♕c7 16 ♗c4 g5 17 ♗g3 ♘e5 18 ♘e3 ♘h5 19 ♖ae1 ♗d7 20 ♘f5 ± Keene-Martin, England 1982.

c) 15...♖b8!? deserves attention, e.g. 16 f4 ♕c7 17 ♗f3 a5 18 ♘e3 ♗a6 with an excellent game; A.Rodriguez-Hulak, Toluca IZ 1982.

d) 15...b3!? 16 ♕d3 (or 16 ♕b1 ♕c7 17 ♘c3 ♖b8 18 ♖a3 ♖b4 19 ♗xf6 ♘xf6 20 ♖xb3 ♕b6 with compensation; Wegner-Klinger, Lugano 1984) 16...♖b8 17 f4 ♖b4 18 ♘c4 ♘b6 19 ♘de3 ♘xc4 20 ♘xc4 a5 21 e5 ♗a6! with a sharp game, (analysis by Kapengut).

On the other hand, Black has no hint of difficulties after 15 f3 g5 16 ♗f2 ♘e5 17 ♘e3 ♘g6 18 g3 ♖b8 19 0-0 b3! 20 ♘xb3 g4! Tatai-Hulak, Amsterdam 1977.

15 ... b3!?
16 ♕b1 ♕c7

In Foisor-Pokojowczyk, Polanica Zdroj 1982, White gained an advantage in the complications following 16...♕a5 17 ♘ec4 ♕b4 18 0-0!? (18 ♘xd6? ♘xe4! 19 ♘6xe4 f5 ∓) 18...♘xd5 19 ♘xd6 ♕xd2 20 ♘xe8 ♕xe2 21 ♘xg7 ♘b4 22 ♘e8 ♘c2 23 ♕d1!. A possible improvement for Black could be 21...♘5f6 22 ♖e1 ♕g4 23 ♗xf6 ♘xf6 24 f3 (24 e5? ♗b7) 24...♕g5 ∞.

17 0-0 ♖b8
18 ♗g3 ♘e5
19 ♖a3

Or 19 f4 ♘eg4 ∞.

19 ... ♖b4
20 ♖d1 g5!

Black has fair counterplay; Murshed-Gavrikov, Tbilisi 1983.

13 7 ♘f3 ♗g7 8 ♗e2 0-0 (A72)

**1 d4 ♘f6 2 c4 c5 3 d5 e6 4 ♘c3 exd5
5 cxd5 d6 6 e4 g6**

7	♘f3	♗g7
8	♗e2	0-0 *(D)*

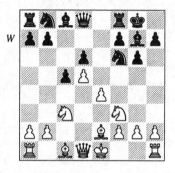

Within the framework of A72, the
only significant moves are:

A) 9 ♗g5
B) 9 ♗f4

In the event of 9 ♘d2 we practically always, after a transposition of
moves, end up outside the bounda-
ries of this chapter, for example 9
♘d2 ♘a6 10 0-0 is A73, whilst 9
♘d2 ♖e8 10 0-0 leads to A77.

A) 9 ♗g5 h6

Correctly considered to be the best
reply.

    10 ♗h4

Black has an excellent game after
10 ♗e3 b5! 11 ♗xb5 (11 e5 ♘g4!)

11...♘xe4 12 ♘xe4 ♕a5+ 13 ♘c3
♗xc3+ 14 bxc3 ♕xb5 15 ♕b3 ♗a6!,
or 10 ♗f4 b5!? (10...g5 11 ♗e3 ♘g4
12 ♗d2 f5! = is not bad either) 11
♘d2 (but not 11 ♘xb5 ♘xe4 12
♘d2 ♖e8 13 ♘c4 ♗a6 14 a4 ♗xb5
15 axb5 ♗xb2! with a large advantage to Black; Kraidman-Pein, Netanya 1984) 11...b4 12 ♘a4 ♖e8 13
f3 ♘h5.

    10 ... g5

10...b5!? also deserves attention,
and in the event of 11 ♗xf6 ♗xf6 12
♗xb5 ♕a5 13 ♖b1!? ♗a6 14 ♗xa6
♕xa6 15 ♕e2 ♖e8 Black has enough
compensation for the pawn; Nadyr-
khanov-Shabalov, Barnaul 1988.

    11 ♗g3 ♘h5 *(D)*

Black will scarcely have any big
problems after 11...b5 12 ♘d2 (the
thoughtless 12 ♗xb5? leaves Black
with a big advantage after 12...♘xe4
13 ♘xe4 ♕a5+ 14 ♘fd2 ♕xb5 15
♘xd6 ♕xb2 16 ♖b1 ♕xa2 17 ♖b3
♗a6 Tošić-Maksimović, Vrnjačka
Banja 1991; nor should he fear 12 e5
dxe5 13 ♗xb5 e4 14 ♘e5 ♘fd7 15
♘c6 ♕b6 ∞) 12...a6 13 0-0 ♖e8 14
♕c2 and now Black should play
14...♖a7!?; the rook is moving to e7,
attacking the pawn on e4 and disturbing White in the execution of his
plans, so Black's position is in no
way worse. Instead 14...♕e7?! is
significantly weaker, e.g. 15 ♖ae1

♘bd7 16 a4 b4 17 ♘d1 ♘e5 18 ♘e3
♘g6 19 ♘ec4 ± Najdorf-Fischer,
Santa Monica 1966, as is 14...♗g4
15 ♗xg4 ♘xg4 16 h3! ♘e5 17 a4 b4
18 ♘d1 with a distinct advantage to
White.

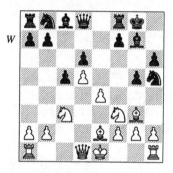

12 ♘d2

After 12 0-0 Black easily achieves
equality after 12...♘xg3 13 hxg3 f5
14 ♘d2 f4 15 gxf4 gxf4 16 ♗g4
♘d7 Johansson-Schmidt, Aabybro
1989, and 12...a6 13 a4 ♘xg3 14
hxg3 ♘d7 15 ♕c2 ♖b8 16 a5 ♕e7
17 ♖fe1 b5 18 axb6 ♖xb6, Martinez-
de Firmian, Las Vegas 1993.

12 ...   ♘xg3
13 hxg3   ♘d7

White has a more promising position in the event of 13...a6 14 a4
♖e8?! 15 ♘c4 ♕c7, Spassky-Stein,
Rostov 1971, 16 f4!, but 13...f5!?
also gives Black excellent chances to
equalize, for example 14 exf5 (or 14
♘c4 ♘a6 15 exf5 ♗xf5 16 0-0 ♕f6
17 g4 ♗g6 18 ♗d3 ♘b4 is level)
14...♗xf5 15 0-0 ♘d7 16 ♘c4 ♘e5
17 ♘e3 (17 ♘xe5 ♗xe5 =) 17...♗g6
18 a4 a6 with approximately equal
chances.

14 ♘c4

14 0-0 ♕e7 15 ♗g4 ♗d4! 16 ♗f5
a6 17 a4 ♘f6 leads to equality,
whilst 14 g4?! gives Black the initiative after the rough variation
14...♘e5 15 f3 a6 16 a4 ♗d7 17 0-0
b5! 18 axb5 axb5 19 ♖xa8 ♕xa8 20
♘xb5 ♗xb5 21 ♗xb5 ♖b8 Kapengut.

14 ...   ♕e7
15 ♕c2

15 ♘b5?! does not win a pawn,
and merely loses time: 15...♘f6 16
f3 ♗d7 17 a4 (17 ♘bxd6? b5) 17...a6
18 ♘c3 b5 and Black has the initiative.

He also has an easy game after 15
g4 ♘e5 16 ♘e3 a6 17 a4 ♗d7 18 a5
b5!? 19 axb6 ♖fb8 =, or 15 0-0 ♘f6
16 ♕c2 ♗d7 17 a4 ♖fe8 18 ♖fe1
♖ad8, again with equality.

15 ...   ♘f6

Also possible: 15...♘e5 16 ♘e3
♖e8! 17 a4 (17 f4?! gxf4 18 gxf4
♘g6 ∓) 17...♖b8 18 f3 a6 =.

16 ♘e3   ♖e8
17 f3   ♘h7

17...g4!? also deserves attention.

18 ...   ♘f8
19 a4   ♘g6
20 ♔f1   ♖b8
21 ♗b5   ♖d8 =

Larsen-Fischer, Santa Monica
1966. 9 ♗g5 obviously represents no
danger for Black.

B) 9 ♗f4 a6

9...b5!? is probably no weaker than
the text move, and after it White has
thus far not managed to prove the

basis for his claims to have an advantage. For example:

a) Black obviously has no problems after 10 ♘xb5?! ♘xe4 11 ♘d2 ♖e8.

b) 10 ♗xd6?! ♕xd6 11 e5 ♕b6 12 exf6 ♗xf6 13 0-0 a6 =.

c) 10 ♗xb5 ♘xe4 11 ♘xe4 ♕a5+ 12 ♕d2 ♕xb5 13 ♘xd6 ♕xb2 14 ♕xb2 ♗xb2 15 ♖b1 ♗c3+ 16 ♗d2 ♗xd2+ 17 ♔xd2 ♖d8 18 ♘xc8 ♖xd5+ 19 ♔c3 ♘c6 = Inkiov-Wojtkiewicz, Stara Zagora Z 1990.

d) After 10 ♕c2 a6 11 0-0 ♖e8 White should already be thinking about maintaining the equilibrium, bearing in mind that 12 ♘d2 b4 13 ♘a4 ♘xd5! 14 ♗xd6!? (14 exd5 ♖xe2 15 ♕d3 ♖e8 16 ♘c4 a5! 17 ♘ab6 ♗f5 ∓) 14...♕xd6 15 ♘c4 ♕f4! 16 exd5 ♗f5 17 ♗d3 ♗xd3 18 ♕xd3 ♘d7 is not unfavourable for Black; Dobrev-Yakovich, Starozagorski Bani 1989.

e) 10 ♘d2:

e1) 10...a6!? 11 0-0 ♖e8 (Black also has quite a decent game after 11...♘e8 12 a3 f5 13 exf5 ♗xf5 14 ♗g3 ♖a7 = Fedorowicz-D.Gurevich, USA 1986) 12 ♗f3 ♗f8 13 ♖e1 ♘bd7 14 a4 ♖b8 15 axb5 axb5 16 b4 ♘e5 17 ♗e2 ♗d7 = Yusupov-Kindermann, Thessaloniki OL 1984.

e2) It is also not easy to gain an advantage after 10...b4 11 ♘b5 ♗a6 12 ♖b1 (12 ♘xd6?! ♗xe2 13 ♕xe2 ♘h5 14 ♕f3 ♗xb2) 12...♘h5!, but not 12...♖e8? 13 ♘xd6 ♗xe2 14 ♕xe2 ♘xd5 15 ♕c4! +− Vukić-Planinc, Novi Sad 1978.

10 a4 *(D)*

10 ...   ♗g4

After 10...♘h5 11 ♗e3 ♘d7 12 ♘d2 ♘e5 (or 12...♘hf6 13 0-0 ♖b8 14 ♕c2 ♘e8 15 ♖fe1 ♘c7 16 ♘c4 ±):

a) 13 g4? f5! 14 gxh5 f4 15 ♗xc5 dxc5 16 ♘f3 ♘xf3+ 17 ♗xf3 ♗d4 was good for Black in Schüssler-Nunn, Dortmund 1979.

b) Black's problems are more difficult after 13 0-0 ♕h4:

b1) 14 f4 is unconvincing, for example 14...♘g4 15 ♗xg4 ♗xg4 16 ♕e1 ♕e7 (16...♖xe1 17 ♖axe1 ♖fe8 18 ♘c4 ±, and now 18...♗xc3?! is bad in view of 19 bxc3 ♖xe4 20 ♘xd6 ±) 17 ♕f2 ♖fe8 18 ♖ae1 b5! (18...♗d7 19 e5! dxe5 20 fxe5 ♗xe5 21 ♘c4 ♗g7 22 ♘b6 ♖ad8 23 ♗xc5 ♕f6 24 ♕xf6 ♘xf6 25 h3! ±) 19 h3 (both 19 f5?! ♗e5 and 19 e5 dxe5 20 ♗xc5 ♕d7 are weaker, and most likely Black should not fear 19 axb5 axb5 20 ♘xb5 ♖eb8 21 ♘a3 ♖xb2!? 22 ♘ac4 ♖c2 ∞; it would then be bad for White to play 23 f5 ♖aa2 24 h3 because of 24...♗xh3! 25 ♘xd6 ♖xd2 ∓) 19...b4 (19...♗d7 20 e5! with initiative) 20 hxg4 bxc3 21 gxh5 cxd2 22 ♗xd2 ♗xb2 (White also maintains the pressure after 22...ᐸd4 23 ᐸe3 ♕xe4 24 ᐸxd4 ♕xd4 25 ♕xd4 cxd4 26 h6) 23 e5!? with a small advantage.

b2) 14 ᐱf3 ᐱxf3+ 15 ᐸxf3 f5!? (this action is forced, as White has a clear advantage after 15...ᐸd7?! 16 ♕d2 ♕e7 17 a5 ♖fe8 18 ᐸxh5 gxh5 19 ᐸh6, or 15...♖b8?! 16 ♕d2 ♕e7 17 ♖fe1 ♖e8 18 ᐸxh5 gxh5 19 ᐸh6 ± Lputian-Pigusov, Nikolaev 1981) 16 g3 (16 exf5 ᐸxf5 17 a5 ᐸe5 18 g3 ♕b4 19 ᐸc1 ᐸd7 is equal; Hort-Grünfeld, Biel 1991) 16...♕e7 17 ᐸxh5!? (playing 17 exf5 is very dangerous for White: 17...ᐸxf5 18 g4? ♕h4 19 gxf5 ᐸe5 20 ♖e1 ♖xf5 with a strong attack) 17...gxh5 18 ♕xh5 fxe4 19 ᐸg5 ♕e8 20 ♕h4 with an edge for White; Lputian-Bönsch, Berlin 1982.

c) White preserves the initiative with 13 f4!? *(D).*

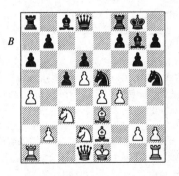

13...ᐱg4 14 ᐸxg4 ♕h4+ 15 g3 ♕xg4 (15...ᐱxg3? 16 ᐸf2) 16 ♕xg4 ᐸxg4 17 h3 ᐸd7 18 g4 ᐸxc3! (18...ᐱf6 19 ᐱc4 ±) 19 bxc3 ᐱf6 20 ♔f2 b5 21 ♔f3 with an edge for White in the endgame; Schüssler-Sosonko, Reykjavik 1980.

11 ᐱd2

For 11 0-0!? see A75.

11	**...**	**ᐸxe2**
12	**♕xe2**	**ᐱh5**
13	**ᐸe3**	**ᐱd7**
14	**g4**	

Black need not fear 14 0-0 ♕h4!? (for 14...♖e8!? see A75; 14...f5 15 exf5 ♖xf5 16 ᐱc4 ᐱe5 17 f4 ᐱxc4 18 ♕xc4 ± Tarjan-Kudrin, USA Ch 1984; 14...ᐸd4!? deserves attention: 15 a5 ♕f6 with mutual chances) 15 g3 ♕h3 16 ᐱf3 ᐱdf6 17 ᐱg5 ♕d7 = Paulsen-Suba, Dortmund 1981.

| **14** | **...** | **ᐱhf6** |
| **15** | **f3!?** | |

Or 15 h3 b5! 16 0-0 b4 17 ᐱd1 ♖e8 18 f3 ᐱb6 with an excellent game; Vukić-Velimirović, Yugoslavia 1981.

15	**...**	**b5**
16	**0-0**	**b4**
17	**ᐱd1**	**a5**
18	**♖a2**	**ᐱb6**

In this complex position, the chances are approximately even; Lputian-Romanishin, Erevan 1986.

14 Classical: Introduction (A73)

**1 d4 ♘f6 2 c4 c5 3 d5 e6 4 ♘c3 exd5
5 cxd5 d6 6 e4 g6**

7	**♘f3**	**♗g7**	
8	**♗e2**	**0-0**	
9	**0-0** *(D)*		

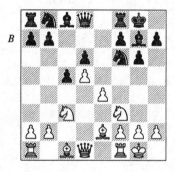

At this point 9...a6 (A74-A75) and 9...♖e8 (A76-A79) are considered to be the main continuations.

In this chapter there are two main alternatives:

A) 9...♗g4
B) 9...♘a6

Besides these you also come across:

a) 9...♘bd7 10 ♘d2 and now:

a1) 10...♖e8!? leads to A77.

a2) White has an obvious advantage after 10...♘b6 11 a4 ♗d7 12 f4 ♖e8 13 ♗f3 ♖b8 14 a5 ♘c8 15 ♘c4 Renman-L.Karlsson, Eksjö 1981.

a3) 10...♘e5 11 f4 (11 a4 g5 12 ♖e1 ♘g6 13 ♘c4 h6 14 f3 b6 15 a5 ±

is less convincing; Tukmakov-Riemers, Antwerp 1992) 11...♘eg4 12 ♘c4 ♖e8 13 h3 is also good for White; I.Farago-Lobron, Amsterdam 1987.

a4) 10...♕e7 11 a4 ♘e5 12 ♖a3 g5 13 ♖e1 g4 14 ♘f1 ♘h5 15 ♘e3 with an edge for White; Bagirov-Timoshchenko, Frunze 1979.

a5) 10...♘e8 with three possibilities for White:

a51) White has a small advantage in the event of 11 a4!? ♘c7 (11...f5 12 exf5 gxf5 13 f4 ♘df6 14 h3 ♘c7 15 ♘c4 b6 16 ♖b1!? ♗b7 17 ♘e3 gives White an edge; Pinter-Bischoff, Dubai OL 1986) 12 ♔h1 b6 13 ♘c4 ♘e5 14 f4!? ♘xc4 15 ♗xc4 ♗a6 16 ♗xa6 ♘xa6 17 f5!.

a52) After 11 ♘c4 ♘e5 12 ♘e3 f5 13 f4 ♘f7 14 exf5 gxf5 15 ♗d3 ♘h6 16 ♗d2 ♗d7 17 a4 ♘c7 18 ♕h5 ♕f6, M.Gurevich-T.Horvath, Balatonbereny 1987, Black is close to equality.

a53) 11 ♔h1!? (an excellent precaution) 11...f5 (or 11...♘c7 12 f4 f5 13 ♘c4 ♘b6 14 e5! with initiative; I.Farago-Renet, Lucerne tt 1985) 12 exf5 gxf5 13 a4 ♘e5 14 f4 ♘g4 15 ♘f3!? and White's advantage is beyond doubt; T.Petrosian-Martinović, Oberwart 1981.

b) 9...b6 10 ♘d2 ♗a6 11 ♖e1 (11 ♗xa6 is less convincing: 11...♘xa6

12 ♘c4 ♖e8!? {12...b5 is met by 13 ♘xb5 ♘xe4 14 ♗f4 ± Polugaevsky-Romanishin, USSR Ch (Moscow) 1983} 13 ♖e1 b5 14 ♘xb5 ♘xe4 15 ♗f4 ♕d7 16 ♘bxd6 ♘xd6 17 ♗xd6 ♗xb2! 18 ♖b1 ♗d4 = Farago-T.Horvath, Hungarian Ch 1984) 11...♖e8 12 h3 ♗xe2 13 ♖xe2 ♘bd7 14 ♘c4 ♘e5 15 ♘xe5 ♖xe5 16 a4 ♖e8 17 ♗f4 and White's position is the more pleasant; Tukmakov-Romanishin, USSR Ch (Moscow) 1983.

c) 9...♘e8 10 ♘d2 f5 (10...♘a6!? transposes to 9....♘a6) 11 exf5 ♗xf5 12 ♘de4!? (Black has no problems after 12 ♗g4 ♘a6 13 ♘de4 ♕d7 14 ♗xf5 ♕xf5 15 ♗e3 b5 16 a3 b4 17 axb4 ♘xb4 = Dlugy-D.Gurevich, New York 1984) 12...♘a6 (stronger than 12...h6 13 ♘g3 ♘d7 14 ♘xf5 gxf5 15 ♗d3 ♘e5 16 ♘e2! ± Guseinov-Blodstein, Kherson 1990) 13 ♗g5 ♘f6 14 ♖e1 (there is only equality after 14 ♘g3 ♗d7 15 ♕d2 ♕b6 16 h3 ♖ae8 17 ♖ae1 ♘c7 18 ♗f3 ♘b5! 19 ♘xb5 ♕xb5 is equal; Fedorowicz-Kudrin, USA Ch 1984) 14...♘c7 15 ♘g3 ♕d7!? 16 a4!? (in Tukmakov-Moskalenko, Riga 1988, the game equalized after 16 ♕d2 b5 17 a3 c4 18 ♘xf5 ♕xf5 19 ♗f3 ♖ae8) 16...♖ae8 17 ♕d2 a6 18 h3 ♔h8 19 ♗f4 with a small advantage to White; Novikov-Nun, Polanica Zdroj 1989.

A) 9...♗g4 (D)

This simple developing move, which activates the c8-bishop, enjoys considerable popularity.

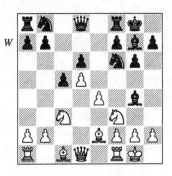

The ...♗g4 idea is often played after the inclusion of 9...a6 10 a4 and then it comes under A75; we very often come across intersecting variations. In principle Black has few feelings for this bishop, as it is hard for it to become active, and exchanging it on a6 creates a weakness on the queenside; it is now not easy for White to prove that he has an advantage.

10 h3

You also see:

a) 10 ♕b3 ♘a6 11 ♕xb7 ♘b4 12 ♕b5 (12 a3 ♖b8 13 ♕xa7 ♖a8 only leads to a draw) 12...♖b8 13 ♕a4 ♖e8 with excellent compensation for the pawn.

b) 10 ♘d2 ♗xe2 11 ♕xe2 and now Black should opt for line 'b3':

b1) 11...♘fd7?! 12 a4 ♘a6 13 ♘b5 ♕e7 14 ♘c4 ♘b6 15 ♘xb6 axb6 16 ♗f4 ± Matanović, is good for White.

b2) 11...♖e8 12 ♘c4 (12 f3 ♘a6 13 ♘c4 ♘c7 14 ♗g5 ♕d7 15 ♘e3 h6 16 ♗h4 ♘h5 = is less convincing) 12...b5 (White has a big advantage after 12...♘xe4? 13 ♘xe4 f5 14 ♘cxd6 ♕xd6 15 ♘xd6 ♖xe2 16

♘xb7) 13 ♘xb5 ♘xe4 14 ♕c2 a6 15 ♘c3 ♘xc3 16 bxc3 ±.

b3) 11...♘bd7! 12 ♘c4 ♘b6 13 ♘e3 (but not 13 f3 ♖e8 14 a4? ♘fxd5! ∓ Menzel-Hort, W.Germany 1986) 13...♕e7 14 f3 and Black has a good game after both 14...♖ae8 15 a4 a6 16 a5 ♘bd7 17 ♖a4 ♘h5!? Efimov-Gavrikov, Geneva 1991, and 14...♘h5!? 15 g4 ♘f4 16 ♕c2 h5 Tatai-Rajković, Budvar 1981.

c) 10 ♗g5 h6 11 ♗h4 ♕b6!? (Kapengut's move is stronger than the standard 11...a6 12 ♘d2 ♗xe2 13 ♕xe2 ♘bd7 14 ♘c4 ♘b6 15 ♘xd6 ♕xd6 16 e5 ♕d8 17 ♘e4 with an advantage to White, Kapengut) 12 ♖b1 ♘bd7 13 ♘d2 ♗xe2 14 ♕xe2 ♖ae8 15 ♖fe1 (after 15 ♘c4 ♕a6 16 ♗g3 ♘xe4 17 ♘xe4 f5, or 15 ♔h1 ♘xe4 16 ♘cxe4 f5 17 ♗g3 fxe4 18 ♖fe1 {18 ♘c4 ♕a6 19 ♖xd6 ♖f5 ∓} 18...e3! 19 fxe3 ♘e5 Peshina-Kapengut, Vilnius 1977, the initiative in Black's hands) 15...♘h5 16 ♕f1 ♘e5 17 ♔h1 (17 f4? ♘g4 18 h3 ♗d4+ 19 ♔h1 ♕d8!!; 17 ♘c4 ♕a6 18 ♘xe5 ♕xf1+ 19 ♖xf1 ♗xe5 20 f3 ♘f4 ∓ Kapengut) 17...♕a6! 18 ♕xa6 bxa6 19 f3 g5 = Y.Zilberman-Kapengut, Sudak 1980.

d) 10 ♗f4 *(D)* and now:

d1) For 10...a6!? 11 a4 see A75.

d2) 10...♘a6 doesn't look at all bad, for example 11 h3 ♗xf3 12 ♗xf3 ♕b6 13 ♖c1 ♖fe8 14 b3 Bagirov-Djurić, Tallinn 1981, and Black could have continued 14...♘d7! 15 ♕d2 ♖ac8 =.

d3) White has a small advantage after 10...♕e7 11 ♘d2 (11 h3 ♗xf3

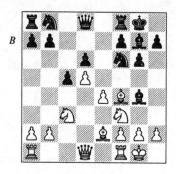

12 ♗xf3 ♘bd7 13 ♖e1 a6 14 a4 c4 15 ♕e2 ♖ac8 = Mitenkov-Blokh, Moscow 1982) 11...♗xe2 12 ♕xe2 ♘h5 13 ♗e3 ♘d7 14 ♔h1 b5!? 15 ♘xb5 ♗xb2 16 ♖ae1 ± Beliavsky-Aseev, USSR Ch (Lvov) 1984.

d4) 10...♘h5 11 ♗g5 ♗f6 12 ♗xf6! ♕xf6 13 ♘d2 ♗xe2 14 ♕xe2 ♘d7 15 g3 ♖ae8 16 ♖ae1 ± Gavrikov-Romanishin, Tallinn 1987.

d5) I much prefer White's position in the event of 10...♗xf3 11 ♗xf3 a6 12 ♖e1! (for 12 a4 see A75) 12...♖e8 (12...b5 13 e5! dxe5 14 d6) 13 ♕d2 ♕c7 14 e5! dxe5 15 d6 ♕b6 16 ♗xe5 ± Ruban-Anastasian, Podolsk 1989.

d6) 10...♖e8:

d61) If 11 ♕c2 then:

d611) 11...a6 12 h3 (for 12 a4 see A75) 12...♗xf3 13 ♗xf3 ♕c7 14 a4 c4 15 a5 ♘bd7 with chances for both sides; Magerramov-Kasparov, Baku 1979.

d612) 11...♘a6 isn't bad: 12 h3 ♗xf3 13 ♗xf3 ♕b6 14 b3 ♘d7 15 a3 ♗d4 =.

d62) After 11 ♘d2 ♗xe2 12 ♕xe2 ♘h5 13 ♗e3 ♘d7 (13...♘a6 14 a3 ♘c7 15 ♖ac1 ♕d7 16 b4! ±

Ruban-Romanishin, Šibenik 1990) 14 g4 ♘hf6 15 h3:

d621) A complex game arises following 15...h5 16 g5 ♘h7 17 f4 ♘b6 18 a4 ♕d7 19 ♔g2 ♗xc3 20 bxc3 ♘xa4 21 c4 a6 Donner-Van der Vliet, Holland 1981.

d622) The trademark Kapengut plan deserves attention: 15...♘b6!? 16 a4 (16 ♖ae1 ♕d7! 17 ♕f3 h5 18 g5 ♘h7 19 ♕g3 ♖ad8 20 ♗f4 ♘a4! ∞ Dydyshko-Kapengut, Minsk 1978) 16...♕d7 17 a5 ♘c8 with chances for both sides, Kapengut.

d63) 11 h3!? ♗xf3 (in Korchnoi-Lutikov, Tbilisi 1959, Black fell into a trap and lost after 11...♘xe4? 12 hxg4 ♗xc3 13 ♗b5! ♗xb2 14 ♗xe8 ♕xe8 15 ♖e1 ♗xa1 {15...f5 16 gxf5 gxf5 17 ♘g5 ♗xa1 18 ♕xa1 ♕g6 19 ♘xe4 fxe4 20 ♖e3 +−} 16 ♕xa1 f5 17 ♗h6 ♕e7 18 ♘g5 ♕e5 19 ♕b1 +−) 12 ♗xf3 a6 (12...b5? 13 ♘xb5 ♘xe4 is bad because of 14 ♕a4 ♗xb2 15 ♘c7! with a decisive advantage) 13 ♖e1 (13 a4!? leads to A75) 13...♗f8 (13...♘fd7!? is interesting: 14 a4 ♘e5 15 ♗e2 ♘bd7 16 ♕d2 ♘b6 or 14 ♗xd6 ♕b6 15 ♗xb8 ♕xb2, Kapengut) 14 e5 dxe5 15 ♗xe5 ♘bd7 16 ♗g3 ♕b6 = Skembris-Fedorov, Pula 1988.

10 ...   **♗xf3**
11 ♗xf3   **♘bd7**

White preserves a small advantage in the event of 11...♘a6 12 ♗f4 ♕e7 13 ♖e1 ♘d7 14 ♕d2 ♘c7 15 ♗e2 a6 16 a4.

12 ♗f4   **♕e7!?**

12...♘e8 13 a4 a6 leads to A75, whilst 13 ♕d2 a6 14 ♗g5 ♘ef6 15

♖ae1 ♖e8 16 ♗d1 b5 17 ♗c2 ♕b6 =, Van der Sterren-Hulak, Lucerne OL 1982, is not dangerous for Black.

13 ♖e1   **a6**

Not 13...♖fe8? 14 ♘b5 ♘e5 15 ♗xe5 ♕xe5 16 ♘c7 ♕xb2 17 ♘xa8 ♖xa8 18 ♖b1 with an advantage; Østenstad-Nielsen, Gausdal 1990.

14 a4

and we have reached a position which will be examined under A75.

B) 9...♘a6

10 ♘d2 *(D)*

A reasonable alternative to the text move would be 10 ♗f4!? (10 ♗g5 is not dangerous for Black, for example, 10...h6 11 ♗h4 g5 12 ♗g3 ♘h5 13 ♘d2 ♘xg3 14 hxg3 ♘c7 15 a4 f5 16 exf5 ♗xf5 17 g4 ♗g6 18 ♘c4 ♗d4 = Lisik-J.Horvath, Budapest 1990) 10...♘c7 (10...♖e8?! 11 ♘d2 ♘c7 12 ♖e1 ♕e7 13 a4 ♘d7 14 ♗g3 h5 15 h3 h4 16 ♗h2 ♗e5 17 f4 ♗d4+ 18 ♔h1 with an obvious advantage; Barlov-Fedorowicz, New York 1985) 11 ♘d2 (White also has a good game after 11 a4, for example 11...♘h5 12 ♗g5 f6 13 ♗e3 f5 14 exf5 ♗xf5 15 ♘g5! ♘f6 16 ♗c4 ♘g4 17 ♘e6 with strong pressure; Karpman-Efimov, Belgorod 1989, or 11 ♖e1 ♘h5 12 ♗g5 f6 13 ♗e3 f5 14 e5 dxe5 15 ♗xc5 ♖e8 16 ♗c4 ± D.Bronstein-Vera, Rome 1990) 11...♘fe8 12 a4 f5 13 exf5 ♗xf5. This position was seen in Plachetka-C.Horvath, Stary Smokovec 1991, and 14 ♗g3 ♗d4 15 ♘c4 would have given White a promising game.

Now 10...♖e8 leads to A78, whilst there are two reasonably popular alternatives:

B1) 10...♘e8
B2) 10...♘c7

Before we investigate these possibilities, here are two rarer moves:

a) 10...♕e7 11 ♖e1!? (11 ♖b1 ♖b8 12 ♖e1 ♘c7 13 a4 b6 14 b4 ♘g4! 15 ♗xg4 ♗xg4 16 ♕b3 cxb4! 17 ♕xb4 ♘a6 = is less dangerous for Black, Polugaevsky-Psakhis, Moscow rpd 1982) 11...♘c7 12 a4 b6 (White has a small advantage in the event of 12...♘d7 13 ♘c4 ♘e5 14 ♗f4 ♗d7 15 ♕d2 ♖fe8 16 ♖ad1 ♘xc4 17 ♗xc4 ♗d4! 18 ♗g3 Podgaets-Psakhis, Sverdlovsk 1984) 13 a5! (a significant improvement over 13 h3 ♖e8 14 ♘c4 ♗a6 15 ♗g5 h6 16 ♗h4 ♕d7 17 ♗f1 ♗xc4 18 ♗xc4 a6 ∞ A.Petrosian-Tal, Lvov 1981) 13...♗d7 14 ♗f3! b5 15 e5 ♖ae8 16 ♘f1! b4 17 exf6 ♕xe1 18 fxg7 ♔xg7 19 ♗d2! ♕xd1 20 ♘xd1 with an advantage; Averkin-Psakhis, Sochi 1982.

b) 10...♖b8 11 a4!? (11 ♘b5 is not dangerous for Black because of

11...♘c7 12 a4 {12 ♘xa7? ♗d7 13 a4 ♖a8} 12...a6 13 ♘xc7 ♕xc7 14 a5 ♗d7 with an equal position; C.Hansen-H.Olafsson, Dortmund 1988) 11...♘b4 12 ♘c4 ♘e8 13 ♗f4 f5 (or 13...a6 14 ♕d2 b6 15 e5 dxe5 16 ♘xe5 ♗b7 17 ♖ad1 ♘d6 18 ♖fe1 ♖c8 19 ♗g4! ± Pinter-C.Hansen, Dortmund 1988) 14 ♕d2 ± M.Gurevich-Szalanczy, Balatonbereny 1987.

B1)   10   ...   ♘e8
    11 ♘c4 (D)

Black has no particular problems after 11 ♔h1 f5 12 exf5 ♗xf5 13 g4 ♗d7 14 ♘de4 ♕a5 15 f4 c4 16 ♘g5 ♘c5 ∞ Schneider-Berelovich, Groningen 1993.

11 ♖e1!? deserves attention, for example 11...♖b8 12 ♔h1 (12 ♗f1 f5 13 ♘f3 fxe4 14 ♘g5 ♘ac7 15 a4 ♘f6 16 ♘gxe4 ♘xe4 17 ♘xe4 ♗f5 18 ♗g5 ♕d7 = Timoshchenko-Romanishin, Belgrade GMA 1988) 12...♗d7 13 f4 b5 14 a4! ♘ac7 15 axb5 ♘xb5 16 ♗xb5 ♗xb5 17 e5 and White's pressure is extremely tangible; Lukacs-Szalanczy, Debrecen 1988.

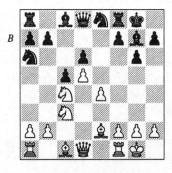

11 ...   **f5**
12 exf5

Undoubtedly the most popular move. Others:

a) 12 ♔h1 ♘ac7 13 a4 ♗xc3 14 bxc3 fxe4 15 ♘d2 ♕e7 16 c4 with compensation for White; Paunović-D.Gurevich, New York 1987.

b) 12 f3 ♖b8 (12...f4 13 ♔h1 ♖b8 14 a4 b6 15 ♘b5 ±) 13 a4 ♘b4 14 ♗e3 f4 15 ♗f2 b6 16 ♕d2 a6 17 ♘a2! ± Kamsky-Madl, Val Thorens 1989.

c) 12 ♗f4!? also deserves attention, for example 12...g5 (12...fxe4 13 ♕d2 ♗xc3 14 bxc3 ♗f5 15 ♗g5 ♕d7 16 h3 with compensation) 13 ♗d2 gives Black problems:

c1) 13...fxe4 14 ♘xe4 h6 15 a4 with a clear plus for White.

c2) 13...f4 14 ♘b5!? ♘ac7 15 a4 ♕e7 16 ♖e1 ♗d7 (16...♘xb5 17 axb5 ♕xe4 18 ♘b6 ♖b8 19 ♘xc8 ♖xc8 20 ♗g4 +−) 17 ♘xc7 ♘xc7 18 ♗c3 ± Lukacs-T.Horvath, Budapest 1989.

c3) 13...♘ac7 14 a4 ♗d4 (14...f4 15 ♗g4 ±) 15 exf5 ♗xf5 16 ♕c1 h6 17 ♘e3 ♘g7 18 ♖a3! with a promising game; I.Farago-Szalanczy, Vienna 1990.

12 ...   **♗xf5**
13 ♗f4 *(D)*

Black faces no problems after any of the alternatives:

a) 13 a4 ♘b4 14 ♘e3 ♗d7 15 ♘c2 ♘xc2 16 ♕xc2 ♗d4 17 ♗f3 ♘g7 = Dlugy-Kudrin, New York 1983.

b) 13 ♘e3 ♗d7 14 ♗d2 ♖b8 15 ♗g4 ♘ac7 16 a4 a6 = Lukasiewicz-Foisor, Cannes 1990.

c) 13 a3 ♖b8 14 ♗f4 ♗d3!? 15 ♗g3 ♗xc4 16 ♗xc4 ♘ac7 17 ♖c1 ♘f6 18 ♗e2 ♕d7 = Chernin-Romanishin, Lvov 1987.

d) He also has no cause for concern after 13 ♗e3 ♖b8!? (it is less difficult to gain an advantage after 13...♘ac7, for example 14 a4 ♕e7!? 15 ♕d2 ♕f7 16 ♖ad1 ♖d8 17 ♖fe1 a6 18 ♘b6 {18 a5 ♘b5 19 ♘xb5 axb5 20 ♘a3 b4 21 ♘c4 ♘c7 =} 18...♘f6 19 ♗g5 ♘a8 20 ♘c4 ♘c7 21 ♕f4 ± Damljanović-Magerramov, Palma de Mallorca GMA 1989) 14 a4 ♘b4 15 ♖c1 b6 16 ♕d2 ♖b7 17 ♗g5 ♗f6!? 18 ♗f4 a6 19 ♘e3 ♗g5 = M.Gurevich-Moskalenko, Belgrade GMA 1988.

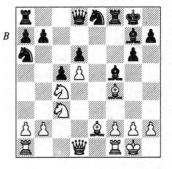

13 ...   **b5**

Of the alternatives, the first two do not manage to equalize, but 'c' and 'd' give Black greater grounds for optimism:

a) 13...♖b8 14 ♗g3 b5 15 ♘e3 ♗d7 16 a4 ♘ac7 17 axb5 ♘xb5 18 ♘xb5 ♗xb5 19 ♗xb5 ♖xb5 20 ♖xa7 ♖xb2 21 ♘c4 ♖b4 22 ♕e2 Browne-D.Gurevich, Palma de Mallorca GMA 1989.

b) 13...♘b4 14 ♕d2 ♕d7 (and not 14...♘c2? 15 g4!) 15 h3 b5 16 ♘e3 ♗d3! 17 ♗g3 ♗xe2 18 ♕xe2 ♖b8 19 a3 ♘a6 20 a4 Toshkov-Romanishin, Jurmala 1987.

c) 13...♗d3!? 14 ♗g3 ♗xc4 15 ♗xc4 ♘ac7 16 ♕d2!? ♕d7 17 ♘e4 b5 18 ♗e2 and now not 18...♗d4?! 19 ♖ad1 ♘xd5 20 ♗xd6! and White wins, Piskov-Yudasin, USSR 1989, but 18...♖d8!?.

d) 13...♘ac7 14 a4 (14 ♕d2!? deserves attention, e.g. 14...b5 15 ♘a5 ♕d7 16 a4 b4 17 ♘b5 with the initiative; Baburin-Pigusov, Voronezh 1988) 14...♗d3!? (14...g5 15 ♗g3 ♗d4 16 ♘e3 ♗g6 17 ♗d3 ♗xd3 18 ♕xd3 favours White; Ftačnik-Kindermann, Altensteig 1987) 15 ♗g3 ♗xc4 16 ♗xc4 ♘f6 17 ♗e2!? ♖e8 (17...a6 is also reasonable: 18 ♕d2 ♖b8 19 ♗f3 b5 20 axb5 axb5 21 b4 cxb4 22 ♘e2 ♘h5! with counterplay; Vilela-Vera, Matanzas 1989) 18 ♗f3 (18 ♕d3 a6 19 ♖ad1 b5! 20 axb5 axb5 21 ♘xb5 ♘xb5 22 ♕xb5 ♘e4 23 ♗f4 ♗d4 ∓ Karpman-Moskalenko, USSR 1988) 18...a6 19 ♕d2 ♕d7 20 ♕f4 ♖e5! 21 ♕c4 ♖ee8 with equality; Baburin-Borovitsky, USSR 1988.

14 ♘e3

14 ♘xb5 ♗d7 15 ♗xd6 ♗xb5 16 ♗xf8 ♗xf8!? 17 ♕b3 ♖b8 18 d6 ♔g7 leads to a complex game with chances for both sides.

14 ... ♗d7

14...b4!? deserves attention, and White must probably content himself with 15 ♗xa6 bxc3 =, as 15 ♘a4 ♗d7!? 16 ♗g3 ♕a5 17 b3 ♗xa1 18

♕xa1 ♗b5 is good for Black; Van Wely-Luther, Arnhem jr 1989.

15 ♗g3 *(D)*

15 ... ♘ac7

15...c4!? is also interesting, as 16 ♖c1 ♘c5 is unclear, whilst 16 a4 b4 17 ♘a2 (17 ♘e4 ♗f5! 18 ♗xc4 ♗xe4 19 ♗xa6 ♗xb2 20 ♖a2 ♗g7 ∓ Baburin-Magerramov, Budapest 1990) 17...♗xb2 18 ♖b1 ♗g7 19 ♗xc4 ♘c5 20 ♘xb4 ♗xa4 21 ♕e2 ♘f6 leads to equality; Polugaevsky-P.Cramling, Haninge 1989.

16 ♕c2!?

White makes no great achievements after 16 ♕d2 b4 17 ♘e4 ♘b5 18 ♖ae1 a5 19 h4 a4 20 ♗c4 ♗f5 21 ♘g5 ♘d4, Ftačnik-Nun, Czechoslovak Cht 1989.

16 ... b4
17 ♘e4 ♗f5!

17...♘b5 18 ♗xb5 ♗xb5 19 ♖fe1 ± is weaker.

18 ♗d3

18 f3?! ♗d4 19 ♗f2 ♗xe4 20 ♕xe4 (20 fxe4? ♖xf2 21 ♔xf2 ♕h4+ 22 g3 ♕xh2+ 23 ♔f3 ♘g7 −+ Perić-Khuzman, Balatonbereny 1988) 20...♘f6 is good for Black.

18	...	♗xe4
19	♗xe4	♘b5
20	♘c4	♘f6

With chances for both sides, Palatnik-Khuzman, Baku 1988. One gets the impression that an improvement is needed for White on the 11th or 12th move.

B2) 10 ...   ♘c7 (D)

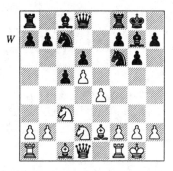

11 a4

Black should not fear 11 f3 ♘d7 (11...a6 12 a4 ♖b8 13 a5 ♗d7 14 ♘c4 ♗b5 ∞) 12 ♔h1 b6 with an unclear game, or 11 ♔h1 ♕e7 12 f3 ♘d7 13 a4 f5 (13...b6!? 14 ♘c4 ♗a6 15 ♗d2 f5 ∞) 14 exf5 gxf5 15 f4 ♘f6 with equality.

11 ...   b6

White preserves his superiority after 11...♖b8 12 ♘c4 (12 f3 a6 13 a5 b5 14 axb6 ♖xb6 15 ♘c4 ♖b8 16 ♗f4 ♘fe8 17 ♕d2 ♘b5 =) 12...♖e8 13 ♕c2 (13 f3!? deserves attention; 13...♗f8 14 ♗g5 h6 15 ♗h4 g5 16 ♗f2 b6 17 ♕d2 ♘h5 18 g3 ♘f6 19 g4! with initiative; Ftačnik-Pekarek, Dortmund 1992) 13...a6 14 ♗f4 ♗f8 15 ♗f3 b5 16 axb5 axb5 17

♘a5 ♗d7 18 ♘c6 Dydyshko-Groszpeter, Minsk 1982.

It is also hard for Black to maintain the equilibrium after 11...♘d7, e.g. 12 ♘c4 ♘e5 13 ♗f4!? (13 ♘e3 is not bad either: 13...f5 14 f4 ♘f7 15 exf5 gxf5 16 ♗d3 ♘h6 17 ♗d2 ♖b8 18 ♖b1 ♗d7 19 ♔h1 a6 20 b4! cxb4 21 ♖xb4 b5 22 axb5 axb5 23 ♖b1 ± Stohl-Dejkalo, Tallinn 1986) 13...♘xc4 14 ♗xc4 a6 (or 14...♖e8 15 ♕d3 h5 16 ♖ae1 a6 17 a5 ♖b8 18 h3 b5 19 axb6 ♖xb6 20 ♘a4 with unpleasant pressure; Wilder-de Firmian, USA Ch 1986) 15 ♕d3 ♖e8 (Rogers-de Firmian, Bor 1984) and 16 ♖ae1! with the idea of 17 ♕g3 would have given White a firm advantage, Rogers.

12 ♘c4

Black has a reasonable game after:

a) 12 ♖b1 ♘fe8 (better than 12...♗a6 13 ♗xa6!? ♘xa6 14 ♘c4 ±) 13 ♖e1 ♖b8 14 ♘c4 f5! =.

b) 12 f3 ♖b8 13 ♘c4 ♗a6 14 ♗d2 ♘h5 15 g4 ♗d4+ 16 ♔h1 ♘g7 17 ♘a3 ♗xe2 18 ♕xe2 a6 De Boer-Riemersma, Busum 1989.

c) 12 ♖e1 ♔h8 (12...♗a6 13 ♗xa6 ♘xa6 14 ♘c4 ♘e8 15 ♗f4 with an initiative for White, Timoshchenko-Grünfeld, Palma GMA 1989) 13 ♖b1 ♘fe8 14 ♘c4 f5! 15 ♗f3 ♗a6 16 ♕b3 ♖b8 = Timoshchenko-Suba, London 1990.

12	...	♗a6
13	f3 (D)	

Besides this you also see:

a) 13 ♘a3 ♗xe2 14 ♕xe2 ♖e8 15 ♕c2 a6 16 ♗f4 b5! =.

b) 13 ♗d2 ♗xc4 (for 13...♖e8 14 f3 see A79) 14 ♗xc4 a6 15 ♕e2 ♖e8 16 f3 ♘d7!? (stronger than 16...♘h5 17 g4! ♗d4+ 18 ♔h1 ♘f6 19 ♕d3 ♘d7 20 f4 with a clear advantage to White; Novikov-Fedorov, Kusadasi 1990) 17 ♖ab1 f5 18 b4 ♗d4+ 19 ♔h1 ♕f6 with equality; Khalifman-Wojtkiewicz, Tallinn 1993.

c) 13 ♖b1 ♕d7 14 ♗d2 (14 b4 cxb4 15 ♖xb4 b5!?) 14...♗xc4 15 ♗xc4 a6 16 b4 b5 17 ♗d3 (or 17 axb5 axb5 18 ♗d3 c4 19 ♗c2 ♖fe8) 17...c4 18 ♗c2 bxa4! 19 ♘xa4 ♖ab8 20 ♘c3 ♘b5 = Tukmakov-Foisor, New York 1988.

d) 13 ♗g5 ♕d7!? (Black is close to equality after 13...♗xc4 14 ♗xc4 a6 15 ♕e2 ♕d7 16 f3 h6 17 ♗d2 ♖fb8 18 ♔h1 ♕e8 19 ♖fe1 ♖b7 Kapengut, or 13...♖b8 14 b3 ♖e8 15 ♕c2 ♕d7 16 ♖ae1 b5 17 axb5 ♘xb5 Lalić-Spraggett, Andorra 1993) 14 b3 (or 14 ♕d2 ♗xc4 15 ♗xc4 a6 16 ♖fe1 {16 ♕d3 ♘g4!} 16...b5 17 ♗f1 ♖fe8 18 f3 h5 = Wiedenkeller-Hulak, Banja Luka 1987) 14...♖fe8 (14...♖ae8!? deserves attention) 15 f3!? (problems start appearing for White after 15 ♕c2?! ♗xc4! 16 bxc4 {16 ♗xc4 a6 17 ♕d3 ♘g4} 16...♘xe4!! 17 ♘xe4 ♕f5 18 ♗d3 ♗xa1 19 ♘xd6 {or 19 ♘f6+ ♕xf6 20 ♗xf6 ♗xf6 ∓} 19...♕xg5 20 ♘xe8 ♘xe8 21 ♖xa1 ♕e5 with a small advantage to White; Dlugy-Suba, New York 1987) 15...♘g4 16 ♕e1 ♘e5 17 ♕d2 f5 18 exf5 ♘xc4 19 ♗xc4 ♕xf5 =.

e) 13 ♗f4 ♗xc4 (after 13...♘h5 the best reply would undoubtedly be 14 ♗d2!?, as 14 ♗xh5 ♗xc4 15 ♗e2 ♗xe2 16 ♕xe2 f5 17 e5 dxe5 18 ♗xe5 ♘xd5! 19 ♖ad1 ♘xc3 20 ♕c4+ ♘d5 21 ♖xd5 ♕e8 22 ♖d8+ ♕f7 23 ♖d7! ♗xe5! 24 ♖xf7 ♖xf7 Wilder-Suba, London 1989, leads to approximate equality) 14 ♗xc4 a6 15 ♖e1 ♖e8 (15...♘h5 is also not bad, for example 16 ♗d2 ♖b8 17 ♗e2 ♘f6 18 ♖b1 b5 19 axb5 ♘xb5! with equality; Neverov-Kuschch, Smolensk 1991) 16 ♕d3 ♘g4 17 ♕g3 ♘e5 18 ♗f1 ♕d7 19 h3 b5 20 ♗d2 Barlov-Suba, Saint John 1988, and a good move now would be 20...f5! ∞.

f) 13 ♔h1 ♖b8 14 ♗g5 (14 f3 ♕d7 15 ♖b1 ♗xc4 16 ♗xc4 a6 17 b4 b5 18 ♗d3 c4 19 ♗c2 bxa4! 20 ♗xa4 ♘b5 = Schmidt-Wojtkiewicz, Polish Ch 1992) 14...♗xc4!? (14...h6 15 ♗h4 ♗xc4 16 ♗xc4 a6 17 ♗d3 ♕d7 {17...b5 18 axb5 axb5 19 f4 c4 20 ♗b1 b4 21 ♘e2 ♕d7 22 ♘d4 ± Shneider} 18 f4 ♖fe8 19 ♗c2! ± Schneider-Ciemniak, Groningen 1992) 15 ♗xc4 a6 16 ♕d3 (16 ♗d3!?) 16...♕e8 = Wojtkiewicz.

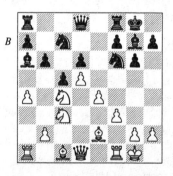

13   ...   ♖b8

For 13...♖e8!? see A79.

13...♕d7 is also quite common:

a) It's easy for Black to gain equality in the event of 14 ♘a3 ♗xe2 15 ♕xe2 ♖fe8 16 ♕c2 ♕e7 17 ♗d2 ♘d7 =.

b) 14 ♗g5!? is interesting, with the aim after 14...h6 of simply playing 15 ♗d2 and the h6 pawn does nothing for Black's position, rather than 15 ♗h4 ♔h7 16 ♖e1 ♖fe8 17 ♕d2 ♗xc4 18 ♗xc4 a6 19 ♕d3 ♘h5!? 20 ♗f2 ♘f4 21 ♕f1 g5 ∞ Thomson-Foisor, Thessaloniki OL 1988. Instead 14...♔h8 15 ♕d2 ♗xc4 16 ♗xc4 a6 17 ♕d3 ♘g8 18 ♖fe1 f5 19 exf5 ♖xf5 20 ♗h4 ± was Pares-Suba, Roses 1992.

c) 14 ♗d2 ♗xc4 15 ♗xc4 a6 16 ♕e2 ♖fb8 17 ♖fb1 ♕e7 18 ♔h1 ♘d7 19 f4 ♖e8 20 ♖e1 ♗d4 21 ♖ab1 ± Schmidt-Panczyk, Czestochowa 1992.

14 ♗d2   ♗xc4
15 ♗xc4   a6

16 ♕e2   ♕c8
17 ♖ab1   ♘d7
18 f4!   ♖e8

18...♕b7!? 19 e5 dxe5 20 d6 ♘e6 21 ♗xa6 ♘d4 deserves attention.

19 e5   dxe5
20 f5!

20 d6 ♘e6.

20 ...   b5!
21 axb5   axb5
22 ♘xb5   ♘xb5
23 ♗xb5   e4
24 ♗e3

Black's house is in order after 24 ♗c3 ♗d4+ 25 ♔h1 e3.

24 ...   ♗d4
25 ♗c6   ♖b4!?

A little stronger than 25...♖e7?! 26 ♗xd4 cxd4 27 f6 ♖e5 28 ♕d2 ± Polugaevsky-Hulak, Moscow GMA 1990, or 25...♖b3? 26 ♗xd4 cxd4 27 fxg6 hxg6 28 ♕f2!.

26 ♔h1   ♖e5

With chances for both sides; Polugaevsky-Psakhis, Sochi 1988.

15 Classical: 9...a6 without 10...♗g4 (A74)

1 d4 ♘f6 2 c4 c5 3 d5 e6 4 ♘c3 exd5 5 cxd5 d6 6 e4 g6

7	♘f3	♗g7
8	♗e2	0-0
9	0-0	a6 *(D)*

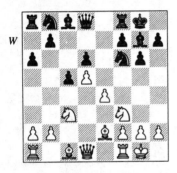

10 a4

Chances are approximately even after 10 e5 dxe5 11 ♘xe5 ♘bd7 12 ♘xd7 ♗xd7 13 ♗g5 ♖c8 14 a4 ♖e8 15 ♖c1 ♕a5 Dorfman-Dolmatov, Moscow 1981.

10 ...   ♘bd7

10...b6?! is too sluggish, and White has the opportunity to distribute his pieces undisturbed, for example 11 ♗f4 ♖a7 12 ♘d2 ♖e7 13 ♗f3 ♘e8 14 ♘c4 with an advantage; Smyslov-Ragozin, Gagra 1953.

10...♗g4 is significantly stronger, and is examined under A75.

11 ♗f4

You also see:

a) 11 ♗g5 and now:

a1) 11...♖e8 12 ♘d2:

a11) 12...♕c7:

a111) 13 ♕c2 is not convincing: 13...♖b8 14 ♔h1 (14 a5 b5 15 axb6 ♖xb6 16 ♘c4 ♖b4 17 ♗f4 ♗f8 18 f3 ♘b6 19 b3 ± Ikonnikov-Emelianov, Budapest 1991) 14...b6 (the standard 14...c4?! is no good at this point: 15 ♗xc4 b5 16 axb5 axb5 17 ♗d3 ♘e5 18 ♘d1! with an advantage) 15 f4 c4!? 16 ♗xc4 ♘g4! 17 ♕d3 ♕c5 18 ♘d1 b5 with counterplay.

a112) 13 f4!? ♖b8 14 ♔h1 (a precise move; 14 ♕c2?! c4! 15 ♔h1 {15 ♗xc4 b5 16 axb5 axb5 17 ♗d3 b4 18 ♘a4 ♕xc2 19 ♗xc2 ♘g4 with more than enough compensation} 15...b5!? 16 axb5 axb5 allows Black to breathe easily) 14...c4 15 ♗xc4 ♘c5 16 ♗xf6! ♗xf6 17 e5! ±.

a12) White also has a preferable position after 12...h6 13 ♗h4 ♕c7 (13...g5 14 ♗g3 ♘e5 15 f4! gxf4 16 ♗xf4 ♕e7 17 ♔h1 ♘g6 18 ♗g3 ♘d7 19 ♘c4 ♘de5 20 ♘e3 ♗f6 21 ♘f5 ♗xf5 22 ♖xf5 ♗g7 23 h3 ± Vukić-Martinović, Borovo 1982) 14 ♕c2 (Black's problems are simpler after 14 f4 c4!? 15 ♕c2 ♘c5, and incidentally 15 ♗xc4?! is no good because of 15...♕b6+ 16 ♗f2 ♕xb2

17 ♗d4 ♘xd5!) 14...♖b8 (14...g5 is good for White: 15 ♗g3 ♘e5 16 ♗xe5! ♖xe5 17 ♘c4 ♖e8 18 f4 with a big advantage) 15 h3 (the hasty 15 f4 allowed Black to achieve a wonderful game in Babu-D'Amore, Manila OL 1992, after 15...c4! 16 ♗xc4 b5 17 axb5 axb5 18 ♗d3 b4 19 ♘d1 ♕xc2 20 ♗xc2 ♘c5) 15...g5 16 ♗g3 ♘e5 17 f4!? gxf4 18 ♗xf4 ♘fd7 19 ♘f3 ♘g6 20 ♗g3 with a small but tangible advantage.

a2) 11...♕e7!? 12 ♘d2 h6 13 ♗h4 g5 14 ♗g3 ♘e5 and now:

a21) Black has no problems after 15 ♗xe5!? ♕xe5 16 ♘c4 ♕e7 17 e5 ♘e8!? 18 exd6 ♘xd6 19 ♖e1 ♗d4 Kapengut.

a22) After 15 ♕c2 one may continue 15...♗d7 (White preserves the initiative after 15...♘fd7 16 ♘d1 ♘g6 17 ♗g4 ♗d4 {or 17...♘de5 18 ♗xc8 ♖axc8 19 ♘e3 h5 20 ♘f5 ♕f6 21 ♖a3 with initiative; Vera-Velasquez, Mexico 1980} 18 ♘c4 ♘ge5 19 ♘de3!) 16 a5 ♖ae8 17 ♘d1 ♘g6 18 ♘e3 ♘f4 19 ♗f3 h5 with chances for both sides; Am.Rodriguez-Ortega, Bayamo 1982.

a23) 15 ♖e1 ♘fd7 (or 15...♖b8 16 ♗f1 ♘fd7 17 ♖b1 ♘g6 18 ♘c4 ♘de5 19 ♘e3 ♕f6 20 b4 ± Grivas-Doghri, Manila OL 1982) 16 ♘f1 ♘g6 17 ♗g4 ♘de5 18 ♗xc8 ♖axc8 19 ♘e3 and in view of the weakness of f5, White's position is preferable; Averbakh-Tal, Portorož IZ 1958.

b) 11 ♘d2 and here:

b1) For 11...♖e8!? see A77.

b2) It is difficult for Black to equalize after 11...♖b8 12 ♘c4 (12 ♔h1 is not bad either, e.g. 12...♕c7 13 f4 ♘e8 14 ♘f3 c4 15 e5! dxe5 16 fxe5 ♘xe5 17 ♗f4 with excellent compensation for the pawn; I.Farago-Damljanović, Belgrade 1984) 12...♘b6 13 ♘e3 ♖e8 14 a5 with a small advantage.

b3) In the event of 11...♘e8 12 ♘c4 ♘e5 (12...♘b6 13 ♘e3 ♗d7 14 ♗d3 ♖b8 15 f4 ♘c8 16 a5 ♘a7 17 ♕e2 ± Marin-Stefanov, Romania 1988) 13 ♘e3 f5 14 f4 ♘f7 15 exf5 gxf5 16 ♗d2 (16 ♔h1 is also interesting: 16...♘h6 17 g3 b6 18 h3!? ♖a7 19 ♖g1 with reasonable possibilities for an attack; Inkiov-Pekarek, Warsaw Z 1987) 16...b6 17 ♖b1 ♖a7 18 ♗d3 ♘h6 19 ♘e2! ♔h8 20 ♗c3 Novikov-Kolev, Odessa 1989, and White's position is preferable.

b4) 11...♕e7 12 ♖e1 ♖b8 (or 12...g5 13 ♘c4 h6 14 ♗f1 ♘e5 15 ♘b6 ♖b8 16 ♖a3 ± Yuferov-Mochalov, USSR 1988) 13 f4 (White played too academically in Mochalov-Kapengut, Minsk 1976: 13 h3 ♘e8 14 ♗f1 ♘c7 15 ♘c4 ♘e5 16 ♘e3 g5 and Black managed to rebuild and could look hopefully into the future) 13...b6 14 ♗f3 b5 15 axb5 axb5 16 ♖a5 with an advantage; T.Petrosian-Kapengut, Moscow 1972.

11   ...   ♕e7

Also possible is 11...♘e8 12 ♖e1 ♖b8 13 ♕d2 b6 14 ♗f1 ♕e7 15 ♖ad1 ± Lein-Hébert, Montreal 1986.

12 ♘d2   ♘e5

White maintains an advantage after both 12...♘e8 13 ♘c4 ♖b8 14

a5 ♘e5 15 ♘xe5 ♗xe5 16 ♗xe5
♕xe5 17 f4, as in Šahović-Djukić,
Bor 1983, and 12...♖b8 13 h3 ♘e8
14 ♗h2 (14 ♖e1 g5! 15 ♗g3 ♗e5 16
♘f1 ♘g7 = Belotti-Schneider, Budapest 1987) 14...♘c7 15 ♘c4 ♘e5
16 ♘b6.

13 h3 *(D)*

Black has a good game after 13
♖e1 ♖b8 14 h3 ♘e8 15 ♗e3 g5! 16
♘f1 f5 ∞, whilst 13 ♗xe5?! ♕xe5 14
♘c4 ♕e7 15 e5 dxe5 16 ♘b6 ♖b8 17
d6 ♕d8 18 a5 ♗e6 Silman-Arda-
man, New York 1987, already puts
the initiative in his hands.

13 ♗g3 deserves attention, for example 13...g5!? 14 ♖e1 (14 f4 gxf4
15 ♗xf4 ♘g6 16 ♗g3 ♘d7 17 ♗g4
♗d4+ 18 ♔h1 ♘de5 =) 14...♖b8 15
♕b3 ♘fd7 16 ♘d1! (16 ♘f1 b5 17
axb5 c4!) 16...b5 17 axb5 axb5 18
♘e3 with a slight plus for White;
Kožul-Renet, Marseille 1989.

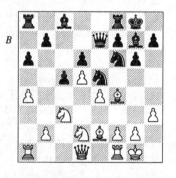

13   ...   ♘fd7

13...♘e8!? is interesting, and after, for example, 14 ♗h2 g5 15 f4
gxf4 16 ♗xf4 ♘g6 17 ♗h2 ♗d4+ 18

♔h1 ♘g7 White's advantage still
has to be proved.

14 ♗g3

14 ♕c2 is less clear: 14...f5 15
exf5 gxf5 16 ♖ae1 ♕f6 and Black's
position is not at all bad.

With the text move White is preparing 15 f4, and in practice it forces
Black to make serious weaknesses
on the kingside.

14   ...   g5
15 f4!?

Often the most straightforward
play is the most correct. Black has
fewer problems after 15 ♕c2 ♖e8 16
♖a3 (or 16 ♖ae1 ♘f8 17 ♘d1 ♘fg6
18 ♘e3 ♘f4 19 ♗xf4 gxf4 20 ♘f5
♕f6 21 g3 ♗h6 ∞ Mirallès-Renet,
Cannes 1987, and White also has no
advantage after 16 a5 ♘f8 17 f4
gxf4 18 ♗xf4 ♘fg6 19 ♗h2 ♖b8 20
♖a3 b5 21 axb6 ♖xb6 = Lalić-Spraggett, Zagreb 1993) 16...♘f8 17 ♘c4
♘xc4 18 ♗xc4 ♘g6 with equality;
Burger-Spraggett, New York 1983.

15   ...   gxf4
16 ♗xf4   ♘g6
17 ♗h2   ♘de5
18 ♔h1   f5

White has an overwhelming position after 18...♗d7 19 ♕c2 ♕h4 20
♖f5! ♗xf5 21 exf5 ♘h8 22 ♘de4
Dusart-Schuller, Corr 1988, and the
extra exchange provides little comfort for Black.

19 exf5   ♗xf5
20 ♘de4

White has a small advantage;
Naumkin-Aseev, USSR 1986.

16 Classical: 9...a6 10 a4 ♗g4 (A75)

1 d4 ♘f6 2 c4 c5 3 d5 e6 4 ♘c3 exd5 5 cxd5 d6 6 e4 g6 7 ♘f3 ♗g7 8 ♗e2 0-0

	9	0-0	a6
	10	a4	♗g4!? *(D)*

W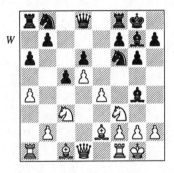

My favourite weapon against the Classical System. By exchanging the knight on f3, Black reduces White's attacking potential, and gains the possibility of positioning his own pieces harmoniously, whilst the absence of the light-squared bishop is not too noticeable. Frequently, in order to avoid this system, White plays the knight to d2 on move 7, 8 or 9.

We shall consider four main replies for White in detail:

A) 11 ♗g5
B) 11 h3
C) 11 ♘d2
D) 11 ♗f4

Of these the fourth has the greatest significance.

Instead 11 ♖e1 has no independent significance and usually, after a transposition of moves, we end up in the tracks of one of the more popular variations. 11...♘bd7 12 ♕c2 (or 12 ♗f4 ♖e8!? 13 ♘d2 ♗xe2 14 ♕xe2 ♘h5 15 ♗e3 ♕h4 =) 12...♖e8 13 ♗d2 ♕c7 14 ♖ad1 ♖ab8 (14...c4!?) 15 b3 ♗xf3 16 gxf3 c4!? 17 bxc4 ♘e5 with a good game for Black; Nei-Tal, Tallinn 1971.

A) 11 ♗g5 h6

The most popular reply to the bishop thrust. You also see:

a) 11...♘bd7 (this natural move may not be best, as White manages to arrange his forces in comfort) 12 ♘d2 ♗xe2 13 ♕xe2 ♖e8 (the line 13...♕c7!? 14 f4 ♖ae8 deserves attention) 14 f4 ♕c7 15 ♖ae1 (15 ♕f3 is also not bad, e.g. 15...c4 16 ♔h1 ♖ab8 17 ♖ae1 b5 18 axb5 axb5 19 e5 dxe5 20 f5! ♖f8 21 ♘de4 ♖b6 22 ♖d1 ±) 15...b5 (White also has the initiative after 15...h6 16 ♗xf6 ♗xf6 17 e5! dxe5 18 f5 e4, Spassky-Balashov, Moscow 1971, and now White should have continued 19

♘dxe4 ♔g7 20 ♕f3 with an attack)
16 axb5 axb5 17 ♕xb5 ♖eb8!? (or
17...♖ab8 18 ♕c6!? ♕a7 19 ♖a1
with an advantage) 18 ♕d3 (18 ♕c6
♕a7) ♖xb2 19 ♘c4 ♖b3 20 ♗xf6!
♗xf6 21 e5 dxe5 22 d6 ♕a7 (22...e4
23 ♕xe4! ±) 23 ♕c2 ♕b7 24 fxe5
♘xe5 25 ♘e4! ± Pinter-Martin Gonzalez, Rome 1983.

b) 11...♗xf3 12 ♗xf3 ♘bd7 13
♕d2 (Black also has no particular
problems after 13 ♗e2 ♖e8 14 ♕c2
♕a5!? 15 b3 {15 ♖fe1 ♖ac8 16 f4?!
c4 17 ♗h4 ♘c5 18 ♗f1 ♕b4 19 h3
♘d3! gives Black the initiative; For-
intos-Bönsch, Cuba 1979} 15...♖e7
16 ♗d2 ♖ae8 17 ♔h1 ♕c7 =)
13...♖e8 (or 13...c4 14 ♗e2 ♕c7 15
♔h1 ♘c5 16 ♕e3 ♖fe8 = Ståhlberg-
Spassky, Gothenburg IZ 1955) 14 a5
c4 15 ♖a4 ♘c5!? (stronger than
15...♕c7 16 ♕f4 h5 17 ♗e2 ♘h7 18
♗h6 ± C.Hansen-Agdestein, Gjøvik 1985) 16 ♖xc4 ♘b3 17 ♕f4
♘xa5 18 ♖b4 ♖c8 with a roughly
equal position, C.Hansen.

12   ♗h4   ♗xf3

It's essential to exchange the
knight, as once again White has an
advantage in the event of 12...♘bd7
13 ♘d2 ♗xe2 14 ♕xe2 ♖e8 15 f4!
♕c7 16 ♕f3 c4 17 ♔h1 ♖ab8 18
♗f2!? b5 19 axb5 axb5 20 ♖a6
Schmidt-de Firmian, Smederevska
Palanka 1981.

13   ♗xf3   ♘bd7
14   ♗e2   ♖e8
15   ♕c2

15 f4 ♕b6 16 ♕c2 ♕b4 17 ♗f3
c4 18 ♖ae1 b5, with equality, does
not scare Black.

15 ...   ♕a5!
16 ♔h1   ♖ac8
17 f3   c4
18 ♗e1   ♕c7 =

Beliavsky-Suba, Tunis IZ 1985.
11 ♗g5 does not pose any serious
danger for Black.

B) 11 h3

This move is of course not bad, but
as Black usually exchanges on f3
anyway, it is perhaps not worth losing a tempo.

11   ...   ♗xf3
12   ♗xf3   ♘bd7 (D)

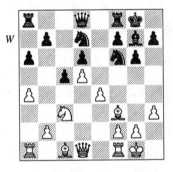

13   ♗f4

Black's position has only one
weakness – the d6 pawn – and White
is quick to take aim at it.

Black's problems are simpler after:

a) 13 ♖e1 ♖b8 14 ♗e2 ♘e8 15
♗f1 ♘c7 16 ♗f4 ♘e5 17 a5 b6 18
axb6 ♖xb6 is level; Bradbury-Pigu-
sov, Cappelle la Grande 1992.

b) 13 ♕c2 ♖e8 14 ♗d2 (14 a5
♕c7 15 ♖a4 ♖e7 16 ♗g5 h6 17 ♗e3
♖ae8 18 b3 ♘h7 with a balanced

position; Larsen-Christiansen, Mar del Plata 1981) 14...♕c7 15 a5 (or 15 b3 c4!? 16 b4 ♖e7 17 ♖fe1 ♖ae8 18 ♖ac1 h6 19 a5 ♕b8 = T.Petrosian-Ivkov, Santa Monica 1966) 15...♖e7 16 ♖a4 ♖ae8 17 b3 (nor does Black have any problems after 17 g3 c4 18 ♗g2 ♖c8 Kapengut) 17...c4!? 18 ♘d1 ♘e5 19 bxc4 ♘ed7! 20 ♘c3 ♘c5 21 ♖a3 ♘fxe4 22 ♘xe4 ♘xe4 is equal.

13 ...   ♕c7

White has a small advantage after 13...♘e8 14 ♗e2 ♕e7 (or 14...♕c7 15 ♖c1 ♖b8 16 b3 ♘ef6 17 ♕c2 ♖fe8 18 ♗h2 ± Smyslov-Filip, Vienna tt 1957) 15 ♕c2 ♘c7 16 ♖fe1 ♖ab8 17 ♗f1 ♖fe8 18 ♕d2 ♗d4 19 ♔h1 Polugaevsky-Vilela, Buenos Aires OL 1978.

However, 13...♕e7!? deserves attention, for example:

a) Black need not fear either 14 ♕c2 ♖ab8 15 a5 ♘e8 16 ♖fe1 ♘c7 17 ♗e2 ♗d4! 18 ♗f1 b5 19 axb6 ♖xb6 is equal; Razuvaev-Tseshkovsky, USSR 1978.

b) 14 ♕d2 c4!? 15 ♖ae1 ♘e5 16 ♗e2 ♖ac8 17 ♗g5 b5! 18 axb5 axb5 19 ♗xf6 (19 ♘xb5 ♘xe4 20 ♗xe7 ♘xd2 21 ♗xf8 ♔xf8 22 ♘xd6 ♖d8 =) 19...♕xf6 20 f4 ♘d3! = C.Hansen-Luther, Uzhgorod 1988.

c) 14 ♖e1 ♖fe8 15 ♕c2 (or 15 a5 ♖ac8 16 ♖a4 h5 17 ♗e2 ♘h7 18 ♗f1 ♕f6 19 ♗h2 ♗h6!? = Komljenović-Suba, Seville 1993) 15...h5 16 b3 ♘h7 17 ♗d2 ♗d4 with a good game for Black; Velikov-Ivanović, Belgrade 1988.

14   ♕c2 (D)

Vaganian-Tal, USSR Ch (Leningrad) 1971 continued 14 ♕d2 ♖fe8 15 a5 ♖ac8 16 g4 ♖e7 17 ♖fe1 ♘e8 18 ♗g2 ♖b8 19 ♗g5 and Black could have played 19...♖e5!? 20 ♗f4 (20 f4 ♖xg5!? ∞) 20...♖e7 with equality.

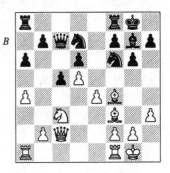

14 ...   ♖fe8

After 14...c4!? 15 ♗e2 (15 ♖ac1?! ♘c5 16 ♘e2 b5 17 axb5 axb5 18 b4 cxb3 19 ♕xb3 ♕b6 ∓ Malich-Nunn, Budapest 1978) 15...♖fe8 16 a5 we return to the main line.

15 a5

Black has an excellent game after 15 b3 c4! 16 b4 ♖e7 17 ♖fe1 ♖ae8, or 15 ♗e2 ♖e7 16 ♖fe1 ♖ae8 17 ♗f1 ♘e5 18 ♖ad1 c4 = Podgaets-Zaid, Kharkov 1980.

15 ...   c4
16 ♖a4   ♘e5!?

The line 16...b5 17 axb6 ♘xb6 18 ♖a5 ♘fd7 19 ♗e3 ♘e5 20 ♗e2 ♘d3!? 21 ♗xd3 cxd3 22 ♕xd3 ♘c4 23 ♖a2 ♘xb2 = deserves attention.

17 ♗xe5

Or 17 ♗e2 ♘fd7 18 ♗xe5 ♘xe5 19 f4 ♘d3 20 ♗xd3 cxd3 21 ♕xd3 b5 22 ♖aa1 ♖ac8 = Kasparov.

| 17 | ... | ♖xe5 |
| 18 | ♖d1!? | |

After 18 ♘b1 ♖ae8! 19 ♘a3 ♘xe4, Portisch-Kasparov, Tilburg 1981, Black seizes the initiative.

18	...	♘d7
19	♖d4	b5
20	axb6	♘xb6

with a complex game, Kasparov.

C) 11 ♘d2 ♗xe2

| 12 | ♕xe2 | ♘bd7 |

12...♖e8? is an error because of 13 ♘c4! ♗f8 (or 13...♕e7 14 ♗f4 ♘xe4 15 ♖fe1 ♗xc3 16 bxc3 ♕d8 17 ♖ab1 ±) 14 ♗g5 ♘bd7 15 a5 ± Namgilov-Psakhis, Rostov 1977.

| 13 | ♘c4 | |

13 f4 ♖e8 14 ♕f3 ♕c7 15 g4 (15 a5 c4 16 ♖a4 b5 17 axb6 ♘xb6 =) 15...c4 16 g5 ♘h5 leads to a roughly even position; Peev-Tringov, Plovdiv 1980.

| 13 | ... | ♘b6 |
| 14 | ♘e3 | |

Black has no problems after 14 ♘xb6 ♕xb6 15 ♗e3 ♖fe8 16 f3 ♖ab8, or 14 ♘a3 ♖e8 15 ♕c2 ♘h5! 16 a5 ♘d7 17 ♘c4 ♘e5 18 ♘b6 ♖b8 19 ♖a3 ♕h4 Lputian-Suba, Debrecen Echt 1992.

14	...	♕e7
15	a5	♘bd7
16	♘c4	♘e5
17	♘b6	

Or 17 ♘xe5 ♕xe5 18 f4 (18 ♖a4 ♖ae8 19 ♕f3 ♘d7 20 ♗f4 ♕e7 21 ♕g3 ♘e5 is level; Renaze-Magerramov, Chartres 1990) 18...♕e7 19 ♗d2 ♖fe8 20 ♖ae1 ♘d7 =.

17	...	♖ae8
18	♗g5	h6
19	♗h4	

19 ♗d2 is effectively met by 19...♘fd7!, when 20 f4? is no good because of 20...♘xb6 21 fe ♘c8 22 ed ♘d6 with an advantage to Black.

| 19 | ... | g5 |

19...♕c7 20 f4 ♘ed7 21 ♘c4 is not bad either, Kovacs-Ničevski, Dečin 1978, when the continuation 21...♘xe4!? 22 ♘xe4 f5 23 ♘cxd6 ♕xd6 24 ♘xd6 ♖xe2 would have led to equality.

20	♗g3	♘fd7
21	f4	gxf4
22	♘xd7	♘xd7
23	♖xf4	

with an unclear game.

D) 11 ♗f4 *(D)*

This move is considered fundamental in official theory.

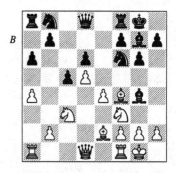

We shall look at three moves in detail:

D1) 11...♕e7
D2) 11...♖e8
D3) 11...♗xf3

11...♘h5 is a rarer move: 12 ♗g5 (more active than 12 ♗e3 ♘d7 13 h3 ♗xf3 14 ♗xf3 ♘hf6 15 a5 ♕c7 16 ♕c2 ♖fb8 17 ♖a2 ♖e8!? 18 ♗e2 ♖e7 = Gon.Garcia-Tal, Moscow IZ 1982) 12...♗f6 (White has a small advantage in the event of 12...♕b6 13 ♕d2 {or 13 ♕c2 ♘d7 14 h3 ♗xf3 15 ♗xf3 h6 16 ♗d2 ♘hf6 17 ♗e2 ♖fe8 18 b3 ± Magerramov-Kasparov, Baku 1979} 13...♘d7 14 a5 ♕c7 15 h3 ♗xf3 16 ♗xf3 ♘hf6 17 ♕f4!? b5 18 axb6 ♕xb6 19 ♖a2 Zaid-Kasparov, Moscow tt 1977) 13 ♗e3 (13 ♗h6 ♖e8 14 ♘d2 ♗xe2 15 ♕xe2 ♘d7 16 ♔h1 ♗d4 17 g4 ♘hf6 ∞ Salov-Romanishin, Irkutsk 1986) 13...♘d7 (in Beliavsky-Romanishin, Wijk aan Zee 1985 White got the better of the game after 13...♗xf3 14 ♗xf3 ♘g7 15 ♗g4 ♖e8 16 ♕c2 ♘d7 17 a5 ♘e5 18 ♗e2 ♖b8 19 ♘b1!) 14 a5 b5 15 axb6 ♕xb6 16 ♖a2 ♗xf3 17 ♗xf3 ♘g7 18 ♘a4 ♕b7 19 ♕c2 ♖fb8 and Black was close to equality in Spraggett-Romanishin, Wijk aan Zee 1985.

D1) 11 ...   ♕e7
12 ♘d2

Black has a reasonable game in the event of 12 ♖e1 ♘bd7 13 h3 ♗xf3 14 ♗xf3 ♘e8 15 ♕d2 ♘c7 16 ♗e2 ♖fb8!?.

12 ...   ♗xe2
13 ♕xe2   ♘bd7

This rare move strikes me as being more promising than 13...♘h5 14 ♗e3 ♘d7 when:

a) The sharp 15 g4 gives Black good equalizing chances: 15...♘hf6

(15...f5 16 exf5 gxf5 17 gxh5 ♗xc3 18 bxc3 f4 19 ♔h1 ± Sturua-Pigusov, Vilnius 1984) 16 f3 (or 16 h3 ♘e8 17 a5 ♘c7 18 ♘a4 b5 19 axb6 ♘xb6 20 ♖a2 ♖ae8 = Lakić-Cebalo, Banja Luka 1981) 16...♘e8 17 ♔h1 ♘c7 18 ♘c4 (18 a5!?) 18...b5!? 19 ♘a5 b4 20 ♘d1 (20 ♘c6 ♕e8 21 ♘d1 ♘e5 22 ♘xe5 ♕xe5 does not frighten Black either) 20...f5 21 gxf5 gxf5 22 ♖g1 ♔h8 and Black's position is no worse; Bönsch-Psakhis, Trnava 1988.

b) 15 a5!? *(D)*:

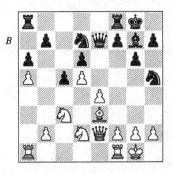

b1) 15...♖ab8 16 ♖a4 ♘hf6 17 ♗g5 ♖fe8 18 f4 ± Gligorić-Rajković, Yugoslavia 1982.

b2) 15...♖fb8 16 ♖fe1 b5 17 axb6 ♖xb6 18 ♘c4 ♖bb8 19 g4!? ♘hf6 20 ♗f4 ♘e8 21 ♗g3 ± Gavrilov-Blokh, Moscow 1982.

b3) 15...♗e5 deserves attention, for example 16 g3 (16 f4?! ♗xc3 17 bxc3 ♘hf6 18 ♗f2 ♘xd5) 16...♖ae8 17 ♗h6 ♗g7 18 ♗xg7 ♘xg7 19 ♖fe1 f5 = H.Olafsson-Tal, Reykjavik 1987.

b4) 15...♗d4 16 ♖a4! ♕f6 17 ♕d3 ♘e5 18 ♗xd4 ♘xd3 19 ♗xf6

♘xf6 20 ♘c4 ♖ad8 21 ♖d1 ♘b4 22
♖d2! ♘e8 23 ♖a1 and now after both
23...f6!? 24 f4 ♘c7 25 ♖ad1 ♔g7 26
e5 Ghitescu-Stoica, Romanian Ch
1983, and 23...♘c7 24 ♖e1 ♔g7 25
b3, Kasparov-Suba, Lucerne OL
1982, White wields the initiative.

14 ♘c4

Or 14 a5 ♖ae8 15 ♖a4 ♘e5 16 h3
♘fd7 17 ♗h2 g5 ∞.

14 ...   ♘e8

15 ♗g3

Black also has no cause for concern after 15 ♖fe1 ♖b8 16 a5 ♗d4!?,
with a double-edged position.

15 ...   ♗d4!

16 ♖fe1   h5 =

Ruban-Kapengut, USSR 1985.

D2)   11 ...   ♖e8 (D)

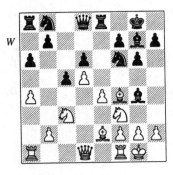

12 ♘d2

In Uhlmann-Fischer, Palma de
Mallorca IZ 1970, White fell into an
elementary trap and had a lost position after 12 h3? ♘xe4 13 ♘xe4 (13
hxg4 ♗xc3) 13...♖xe4 14 ♗g5 ♕e8
15 ♗d3 ♗xf3 16 ♕xf3 ♖b4 17 ♖ae1
♗e5 −+. White has no chances for an
advantage after 12 ♕c2, for example

12...♕c7 (12...♕e7 is less convincing: 13 ♖ae1 ♘bd7 14 h3 ♗xf3 15
♗xf3 ♖ab8 16 ♗e2 ♔h8 17 ♕d2
♕f8 18 ♗c4 ± Schüssler-Lobron,
Bochum 1981) 13 ♖fe1 ♘bd7 14 a5
♖ab8 15 h3 ♗xf3 16 ♗xf3 b5 17
axb6 ♖xb6 18 ♖a2 ♖eb8 19 ♗e2 a5!
= Tal-Stein, Moscow 1971.

12 ...   ♗xe2

13 ♕xe2   ♘h5

13...♘bd7? is weak because of 14
♘c4 (but not 14 ♗xd6 ♘b6 15 e5
♘fxd5 16 ♘xd5 ♘xd5 with an unclear game; Jasnikowski-Panczyk,
Polish Ch 1991).

14 ♗e3   ♘d7

The initiative remains in White's
hands after 14...♗d4 15 ♘c4 ♗xe3
16 ♕xe3 b6 17 f4 Gligorić-Petryk,
Vienna 1982.

Now White has two main continuations:

D21)   15 a5

D22)   15 g4!?

After neither move is Black's defence at all easy, and so both deserve
a good deal of attention.

Other moves are less troublesome:

a) There is no danger for Black in
15 ♖ae1 b5 16 axb5 axb5 17 ♘xb5
(17 ♕xb5 ♖b8 18 ♕d3 ♖xb2 19
♘c4 ♘e5 20 ♘xe5 ♗xe5) 17...♕b8
18 ♖b1 ♖a4 and 15 f4 f5 16 ♘c4
♘df6 17 exf5 gxf5 18 ♖f3 ♘g4
Bönsch-Wojtkiewicz, Stara Zagora
Z 1990.

b) 15 ♔h1 leads to an unclear
game, for example 15...♘e5 16 ♖g1
♘f6 17 g4 ♕c8 18 g5 ♘fg4 19 f4

♘xe3 20 ♕xe3 ♘d7 21 ♕d3 ♕c7 Bellón-Kindermann, Zurich 1985.

D21) 15 a5   ♗d4 *(D)*

Alternatively:

a) 15...♖b8 16 ♖a4! ♕f6 17 g3 ♕e7 18 ♖c1 ♘e5 19 f4 ♘d7 20 ♗f2!? ±.

b) 15...♕c7 16 g4!? (Black has a reasonable game after 16 h3 f5! 17 exf5 ♘g3! 18 fxg3 ♖xe3 19 ♕g4 ♗d4 20 ♔h1 ♘e5, or 16 ♖a4 ♗d4!? 17 ♖fa1 ♗xe3 18 ♕xe3 ♖e7 Khenkin) 16...♘hf6 17 h3!? (Black's has fewer problems after 17 f3 b5! 18 axb6 ♘xb6 19 ♔h1 {19 ♖xa6? ♖xa6 20 ♕xa6 ♘bxd5} 19...♕b7 20 ♖a2 ♘fd7 21 ♖fa1 ♗d4 L.Bronstein-Tringov, Buenos Aires OL 1978) 17...h6 18 f4 with initiative.

c) 15...♗e5!? 16 f4 ♗d4 17 ♖a4 ♕f6 (not 17...b5 18 axb6 ♘xb6 19 ♖xd4!) 18 g3 b5 19 axb6 ♘xb6 20 ♖a3 ♗xe3+ 21 ♕xe3 ♕d4 22 ♕xd4 cxd4 23 ♘e2 ♘f6 =. This variation demands practical tests.

d) 15...♖c8 16 g4 ♘hf6 17 f3 ♘e5 18 ♔h1 h6 19 g5! ♘h5 (19...hxg5 20 ♗xg5 ♕d7 21 f4 ♘eg4 22 h3 ♘h6 23 ♕f3 with an advantage) 20 f4 ♘d7 21 gxh6 ♗xh6 22 ♘c4 ♕e7 23 ♖ae1 ♗g7 24 ♕f3 ± Browne-de Firmian, USA Ch 1985.

e) 15...♕h4:

e1) 16 ♘c4 ♘f4 (16...♗xc3? 17 bxc3 ♖xe4 18 ♘xd6 ♖e5 19 ♕f3 ± Van der Vliet-Grooten, Amsterdam 1983) 17 ♗xf4 (17 ♕f3?! is weaker because of 17...♘e5! 18 ♘xe5 ♗xe5 19 g3 ♕h5 20 ♕xh5 ♘xh5 = Beliavsky-Kasparov, USSR Ch (Minsk)

1979) 17...♕xf4 18 g3 ♕f6 19 f4 ♕e7 20 ♖ae1 ± Plaskett-Pritchett, England 1983.

e2) 16 ♖a4!? ♘e5 17 f3! ♖ab8!? with a slight plus for White – Naumkin (but not 17...♘f4 18 ♗xf4 ♕xf4 19 g3 ♕f6 20 f4 ♘d7 21 e5! dxe5 22 ♘de4 ♕d8 23 f5! ± Naumkin-Minasian, Moscow 1992).

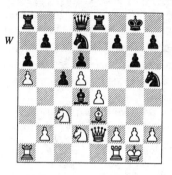

16 ♖a4

After 16 g4 ♘hf6 17 f3 Black gets a good game following:

a) 17...b5!? 18 axb6 ♘xb6 19 ♘d1:

a1) 19...h5!? 20 h3 (not 20 g5?! ♘fxd5!) transposes to 'b'.

a2) 19...♘bxd5 is also interesting: 20 exd5 ♘xd5 21 ♘c4 f5 (21...♕g5 22 f4! ♘xf4 23 ♕f3) 22 f4 fxg4 23 ♖a3 with complications; Korchnoi-Nunn, London 1980.

b) 17...h5!? 18 h3 b5!? 19 axb6 ♘xb6 20 ♘d1 ♘bxd5 (alternatively, 20...hxg4 21 hxg4 ♘bxd5 22 exd5 ♘xd5 with compensation; Čabrilo-Schmidt, Vrnjačka Banja 1981) 21 exd5 ♘xd5 22 ♘c4 (22 ♖a3 ♖b8 23 ♘e4 ♘xe3 24 ♘xe3 ♖xb2) 22...♖b8 23 ♖a3 ♖b4 Rajković-de Firmian,

Vršac 1983, with a strong initiative for the piece.

16 ...   ♕f6

White has an advantage after 16...♘g7?! 17 ♗xd4 cxd4 18 ♖xd4 ♕xa5 19 ♘c4 ♕c7 20 ♘e3 b5 21 ♕d2 ♘c5 22 ♘g4! Ruban-S.Garcia, Santa Clara 1991.

16...♗xe3 deserves attention: 17 ♕xe3 f5!? 18 f4 b5 (or 18...♘hf6 19 ♕d3 b5 20 axb6 ♘xb6 21 ♖aa1 fxe4 22 ♘dxe4 ♘bxd5 23 ♘xd5 ♘xe4 24 f5 with excellent compensation for the pawn, C.Hansen) 19 axb6 ♘xb6 20 ♖aa1 ♕f6 = Ubilava-Anikaev, Minsk 1983.

17 ♕d3   ♘e5

17...♗xe3 gives White the initiative: 18 ♕xe3 b5 19 axb6 ♘xb6 20 ♖a2 ♘f4 21 ♕f3 ± Grün-Cebalo, Plovdiv 1983.

18 ♗xd4   ♘xd3
19 ♗xf6   ♘xf6
20 ♖b1   ♖ad8
21 ♘d1   ♘b4
22 f3   ♘h5 =

Karpman-Shabalov, Minsk 1990.

D22) 15 g4!?   ♘hf6
16 f3 *(D)*

Or:

a) Black has a pleasant game after 16 a5 h5!? 17 h3 hxg4 18 hxg4 ♘e5 19 f3 ♖c8, or 16 f4 h5 17 h3 hxg4 18 hxg4 ♘b6!? 19 ♔g2 (19 a5 ♘fxd5!) 19...♕e7 20 ♖ae1 ♕d7 21 g5 ♕g4+ 22 ♕xg4 ♘xg4 23 ♗g1 ♗xc3 24 bxc3 ♘xa4 25 ♔f3 f5 F.Portisch-Lobron, Dortmund 1980.

b) It is difficult for Black to equalize after 16 h3:

b1) 16...h5?! 17 g5 ♘h7 18 f4 ♗d4 19 ♔h1 ±.

b2) 16...♕c7 17 ♗f4 ♘b6 18 ♕d3 ♘fd7 19 a5 ♘c8 20 ♘c4 ♘e5 21 ♗xe5 ♗xe5 22 ♘xe5 (22 ♘a4 ♗d4 23 ♖ab1 ♕e7 was level in Tukmakov-Semeniuk, Tashkent 1977) 22...♖xe5 23 f4 with an obvious advantage.

b3) 16...♖b8!? 17 ♗f4 (Black has a simpler game after 17 a5 ♕c7 18 ♔g2 b5 19 axb6 ♖xb6 20 ♖xa6 ♖eb8 21 ♖xb6 ♕xb6 22 ♘c4 ♕a6 with compensation; Basin-Bystrov, Minsk 1987) 17...♘e5 18 ♗g3 b5!? 19 axb5 axb5 20 ♘xb5 ♕d7 21 ♘a3 ♖xb2 22 ♗xe5! ♖xd2 23 ♕xd2 ♘xe4 24 ♕c2 ♖xe5 25 ♖ae1 f5 with some compensation, but White's chances are preferable, Kapengut.

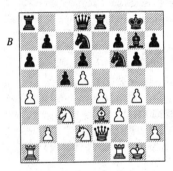

16 ...   h6

The alternatives do not equalize:

a) 16...b5?! 17 axb5 axb5 18 ♖xa8 ♕xa8 19 ♕xb5 ♘e5 20 ♔g2 h5!? 21 g5 ♘fd7 22 ♕e2 ♖b8 23 ♘d1 with an advantage to White; Schmidt-Foisor, Warsaw 1983.

b) 16...h5?! 17 g5 ♘h7 18 f4 ♖b8 19 ♔h1 ♘b6 20 a5 ♘c8 21 ♕d3 f6

22 h4 with a clear plus for White; Van der Sterren-Witt, Baden-Baden 1980.

c) 16...♕c7 17 a5 b5 18 axb6 ♘xb6 19 ♔h1! ♕b7 20 ♖a3 ♘fd7 21 ♘b3! ± Schmidt-Foisor, Warsaw 1983.

d) 16...♖c8 17 ♔h1 h6 18 g5! hxg5 19 ♗xg5 ♕e7 20 f4 ♕f8 21 ♗xf6 ♘xf6 22 e5 with an attack, Kožul-Vlahović, Novy Bečej 1986.

17 ♔h1   ♘e5

White has an easy game after 17...b6?! 18 ♖g1 ♕e7 19 g5 hxg5 20 ♗xg5 ♕f8 21 ♘c4 ♘h5 22 ♕g2 ♖ab8 23 ♕h3 K.Grigorian-Pimonov, Moscow 1981, but 17...♕c7!? deserves attention, for example 18 a5 b5 19 axb6 ♘xb6 20 ♖a3 (20 ♖xa6? ♖xa6 21 ♕xa6 ♘bxd5!) 20...a5 21 ♖fa1 h5 22 g5 ♘fd7 23 ♖1a2 a4 24 ♔g2 ♖a5 = Vukić-Suba, Tuzla 1981.

18 g5

Black has fewer problems after 18 ♖g1 b5! 19 g5 hxg5 20 ♗xg5 c4 21 axb5 axb5 22 ♖xa8 ♕xa8 23 ♘xb5 ♕b8 24 ♘a3 ♕xb2 25 ♘axc4 ♘xc4 26 ♕xc4 ♘h5 with sufficient compensation for the pawn; Portisch-Kasparov, Moscow 1981.

18 ...   hxg5
19 ♗xg5   ♘ed7

Black succumbs to a powerful attack after 19...♕c7?! 20 ♗xf6! ♗xf6 21 f4 ♘d7 22 ♕g2!.

20 ♕g2   b5!?
21 axb5   axb5
22 ♖xa8   ♕xa8
23 ♘xb5   ♕b8
24 ♘a3   ♕xb2

25 ♘ac4   ♕b8
26 ♖b1   ♕c7
27 f4 ±

Kapengut.

D3) 11 ...   ♗xf3

In recent years this move has acquired great popularity.

12 ♗xf3 (D)

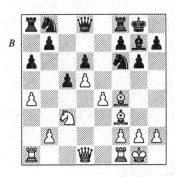

12 ...   ♕e7 (D)

I think that e7 is the best place for the queen in this variation. White's chances are preferable after other moves:

a) 12...♖e8 13 ♖e1 ♕c7 14 e5! dxe5 15 d6 ♕b6 16 a5! ♕b4 17 ♖a4 ♕xb2 18 ♗d2 ± Gligorić-Cvitan, Yugoslav Ch 1982.

b) 12...♕c7 13 ♖e1 (13 a5 ♘bd7 14 ♖a4 ♖fe8 15 ♕c2 h5! 16 ♘b1!? b5 17 axb6 ♘xb6 18 ♖a2 ♕e7 19 ♘d2 ♘fd7 20 ♖fa1 ♗d4! ∞ Skembris-Psakhis, Novi Sad OL 1982; 21 ♖xa6?! ♖xa6 22 ♖xa6 does not work because of 22...g5 23 ♗e3 ♗xe3 24 fxe3 g4 25 ♗e2 ♘xd5!) 13...♘bd7 14 ♕d2 ♘e8 15 ♗g4! ♘e5 16 ♗e2 f5 17 exf5 gxf5 18 a5 ± Naumkin-Ruban, Norilsk 1987.

c) 12...♘e8 13 ♕d2 (Black has a simpler game after 13 ♕c2 ♘d7 14 ♗e2 ♕e7 15 a5 ♘c7 16 ♖fe1 ♖ab8 17 ♖a4 b5 18 axb6 ♖xb6 19 ♖ea1 ♖fb8 20 ♗c1 ♘b5!? 21 ♖xa6 ♘d4 with compensation for Black; Velikov-Ermenkov, Albena 1983, but 13 ♗e2!? deserves attention, e.g. 13...♘d7 14 ♗g3 f5 15 exf5 gxf5 16 ♗f4! ♘e5 17 a5 with a small advantage; Hjartarson-Lobron, Reykjavik 1984) 13...♘d7!? (or 13...♕e7 14 ♗g5!? ♕e5 15 ♖fe1 ♘d7 16 ♖ad1 ♘c7 17 ♗g4! ♘b6 18 ♕c1 with initiative; Gligorić-Barlov, Yugoslav Ch 1982) 14 ♗g5 (14 ♗h6?! ♖c8 15 b3 ♗xh6 16 ♕xh6 ♕a5 = Wagner-Lobron, Bad Wörishofen 1989) 14...♗f6 15 h4!? (more interesting than 15 ♗xf6 ♘exf6 16 ♗e2 ♖e8 17 f3 ♖c8 18 a5 c4 19 ♕d4 ♖c5! 20 ♗xc4 ♖xa5 with equality; Gligorić-Hulak, Subotica 1984) 15...♘g7 16 ♗g4 ♗e7 17 ♗h3 c4 18 ♕d4! with initiative; Röder-Lobron, Vienna 1991.

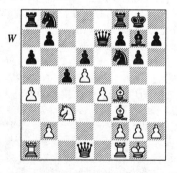

13 ♖e1

The following continuations have also had practical tests:

a) 13 ♕c2 ♘bd7 14 ♖ae1 (neither 14 b3 ♖ab8 15 a5 ♖fe8 16 ♖fe1 h6!? 17 h3 g5 18 ♗d2 ♘e5 19 ♗e2 ♘g6 = Ksienski-Psakhis, Naleczow 1980, nor 14 a5 ♘e5 15 ♗e2 ♘fd7 16 ♗e3 g5!? 17 ♕d2 g4 18 ♔h1 ♔h8 19 f4 gxf3 20 gxf3 f5 Lukacs-Groszpeter, Kecskemet 1983, creates problems for Black) 14...c4 15 ♗e2 ♖ac8 16 ♗g5 h6 17 ♗h4 g5 18 ♗g3 ♖fe8 with more or less equal chances; Agzamov-Psakhis, Baku 1979.

b) 13 ♕d2 ♘bd7 14 a5 (White has no advantage in the event of 14 ♖ae1 c4!? {14...♘e8 15 ♗g5! ♗f6 16 h4 ♘c7 17 ♗e2 ♖ab8 18 f4 with initiative; Rashkovsky-Kharitonov, Sochi 1979} 15 ♗d1 ♖ab8 16 ♗c2 b5 17 axb5 axb5 18 ♗h6 ♗xh6 19 ♕xh6 b4 20 ♘d1 ♕d8 = Torre-Dolmatov, Manila 1982) 14...h5!? (an important move, which has not yet been seen in any publications; Black also has a reasonable game in the event of 14...♖ab8 15 ♗e2 ♘e8!? 16 ♖a4 ♘c7) 15 h3 ♖ac8!? (15...♖ab8 16 ♖a2 ♘h7 17 ♖e1 ♖fe8 18 ♗e2 ♗d4! 19 ♖a4 ♘hf6 = Ruban-Emms, Hastings 1991) 16 ♖fe1 c4 17 ♘a4!? (17 ♖a4 ♘e5 18 ♗e2 ♘fd7 19 ♗xe5 ♘xe5 20 f4 ♗h6! with an unclear position) 17...♘e5 18 ♗xe5 ♕xe5 19 ♘b6 c3! 20 bxc3 ♖xc3 = Gaprindashvili-Madl, Smederevska Palanka 1987.

c) 13 e5 (the most principled move, but not one which Black should fear, as with exact play he can even gain the initiative) 13...dxe5 14 d6 ♕e6 and now:

c1) White is promised little after 15 ♗g5 ♘bd7!? (not 15...♘c6?! 16 ♗xf6! ♗xf6 17 ♗xc6 bxc6 18 ♘e4 ♖fd8 19 ♕e2 with advantage; Alburt-Kudrin, USA Ch 1983) 16 ♗xb7 ♖a7 (16...♖ab8 is also not bad: 17 ♗xa6 ♖xb2 18 ♗b5 ♖b4 or 17 ♗d5 ♘xd5 18 ♘xd5 ♖xb2 19 ♗e7 ♖c8! 20 ♘c7 ♕c4! ∞ Fedorowicz-Psakhis, Chicago 1983) 17 ♗f3 h6 18 ♗e3 ♖b8 Nogueiras-Foisor, Tbilisi 1983, and Black's position is at least no worse.

c2) 15 ♖e1 ♘bd7 16 ♗xb7 ♖a7!? (again 16...♖ab8 is not bad: 17 ♗xa6 ♖xb2 18 ♗b5 and now 18...♘g4! with counterplay; is better than 18...♖d8 19 ♖c1! ♕f5 20 ♗e3 e4 21 ♗xd7! ♖xd7 22 h3 c4 23 ♖e2 ± Hjartarson-de Firmian, Reykjavik 1984) 17 ♗c6!? (17 ♗f3 gives Black the initiative after 17...♖b8! 18 ♘d5 ♕xd6 19 ♗g5! ♘xd5 20 ♗xd5 ♕f8 ∓ Browne-D.Gurevich, New York 1984) 17...♖c8 (17...♖b8 deserves attention: 18 ♗g3 ♖b4! 19 ♘d5 ♖d4 20 ♘e7+ ♔f8 21 ♘c8! ♖xd1 22 ♖axd1 ♕b3 23 ♘xa7 ♕b6 24 ♗xd7 ♘xd7 25 ♘c8 ♕c6 26 ♘e7 ♕xa4 ∓ Huss-Kindermann, Beersheba 1985 or 18 ♕d2 ♖b6 19 ♘d5 ♘xd5 20 ♗xd5 ♕e8 21 ♗e3 ♕b8 22 ♖ab1 a5 with mutual chances; C.Hansen-Grünfeld, Thessaloniki OL 1984) 18 ♘d5 ♘xd5 19 ♗xd5 ♕f6 20 ♗e3 ♗f8! Browne.

13   ...   ♘bd7 *(D)*
14 a5

A logical move. White fixes the weakness of b6 and prepares to move the knight there. Black faces

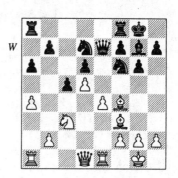

no problems after 14 ♗g5 h6 15 ♗h4 ♘e5 16 ♗e2 g5 17 ♗g3 ♘fd7 18 ♕c2 ♘g6 = Christiansen-Perenyi, Saint John 1988, or 14 h3 ♘e8 15 ♕d2 ♘c7 16 ♗e2 ♖fe8 17 ♗f1 ♗d4!? ∞.

The only serious alternative to the text move is perhaps 14 ♕d2!?:

a) 14...c4 15 ♕e2 ♖ac8 16 ♕e3 Fedorowicz-D.Gurevich, New York 1983, and now 16...♘c5!? deserves attention, with an unclear game.

b) 14...♖ac8 15 ♗e2 c4 16 ♗f1 ♘g4 17 h3 ♘ge5 18 ♗g5 f6 (not 18...♗f6? 19 ♗h6 ♗g7 20 ♗xg7 ♔xg7 21 f4 +−) 19 ♗e3 ♘c5 20 ♗xc5 ♖xc5 21 f4 ♘f7 22 g3 with an advantage; Bönsch-Perenyi, Leipzig 1988.

c) 14...♘e8 15 ♗g5! ♗f6 16 ♗h6 ♗g7 17 ♗xg7 ♔xg7 18 ♗e2 f6 19 f4 ♘c7 20 ♖ad1 and White's position is again preferable; Browne-Wedberg, New York 1988.

d) 14...♖ab8 15 ♗e2!? (playing 15 ♖ab1 lets Black solve his problems: 15...c4! 16 a5 ♖fc8 17 ♘a4 ♘e8 18 ♗e3 ♘c7 19 ♖bc1 ♘b5 20 ♗g4 c3! 21 bxc3 ♖c4 22 ♗xd7 ♖xa4 with reasonable compensation for the pawn; Kallai-Hardicsay, Hungary 1985) and now Black can play 15...&fc8!?, when for 16 a5 &e8 see 14 a5. Nor is it easy for White to gain an advantage after 15...&e8, for example 16 &f1!? (16 &g5 &f6 17 h4 &xg5 {stronger than 17...&e5 18 &ad1 &c7 19 &c1! &xg5 20 hxg5 &g7 21 f4 with initiative; Gavrikov-Cebalo, Vršac 1985} 18 hxg5 f6!?) 16...&c7 17 &h1 &fc8 18 &g3 &d4!? with quite a decent position.

e) 14...&fe8 15 h3 c4 (or 15...h5 16 &e2 &h7 17 &g3 &d4 = Mascarinas-Antonio, Bacolod 1991) 16 &e2 &ac8 17 &f1 &e5 18 &h6 &xh6 19 &xh6 &c7 is equal; Gligorić-Suba, Vršac 1983.

f) 14...h5!? 15 h3 (Black has no hint of a problem after 15 &h6 &e5 16 &e2 &xh6 17 &xh6 &fg4 18 &xg4 {18 &f4 f5!} 18...hxg4 Šahović-Vera, Aosta 1989) 15...c4 16 &e2 &ac8 17 a5 (17 &f1 &fe8 18 &h2 &h7 = Gual-P.Cramling, Barcelona 1989) 17...&fe8 18 &f1 &h7 19 &a4 f5! 20 &xc4 (20 &xc4 b5 21 axb6 &xb6 22 &xa6 &xc3! 23 bxc3 &xa4 24 &xc8 &xc8 25 exf5 &f7 26 fxg6 &xg6 27 &e6 &b1+ 28 &h2 &xc3 leads to unclear complications) 20...&xc4 21 &xc4 g5 22 &h2 f4 Van der Sterren-Psakhis, Tallinn 1987, and Black has quite enough compensation for the pawn.

Now we return to the main line after 14 a5 (D):

14   ...   h5!?

This move instantly solves several problems, freeing h7 for the knight, from where it can spring onto g5,

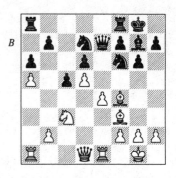

and, very importantly, taking control of g4. You also come across:

a) 14...&e5?! 15 &e2 &fb8 (or 15...&fe8 16 &a4 ±) 16 &c2 b5 17 axb6 &xb6 18 &a2 &e8 19 &e3 g5 20 &ea1 &c7 21 &d2! with a clear advantage for White, W.Schmidt-Abramović, Niš 1983.

b) 14...&fb8 15 &a4 &e8 (15...b5 16 axb6 &xb6 17 &xc5!? dxc5 18 &xb8 &xb8 19 e5 is unsatisfactory for Black) 16 &e3 &ab8 17 &b1 &e5 18 &e2 &c7 19 b4 cxb4 20 &b6 with an edge for White; Baburin-Goldstern, Leukerbad 1992.

c) 14...&fd8 15 &a4 &ab8 16 &b1 &e5 17 &xe5 &xe5 18 b4 ± Browne-D.Gurevich, Estes Park 1984.

d) 14...h6 15 &a4 &h7 16 &g4! (if only the pawn had been on h5!) 16...&e5 17 &b6 &ad8 18 &b1 &fe8 19 g3 h5 20 &h3 ± Wojtkiewicz-Veličković, Komotini 1993.

e) 14...&e8 15 &d2 (15 &a4!? also deserves attention: 15...&c7 16 &g4! &e5 17 &b6 &ad8 18 &h3 &a8 19 &xe5! &xe5 20 &c4 with advantage; Ehlvest-Minasian, New York 1993) 15...&b8 (or 15...&c7 16

♗g5! ♗f6 17 ♗xf6 ♕xf6 18 ♗g4 ♘e5 19 ♗e2 g5 20 ♖a3! and White's position is the more promising, Browne-D.Gurevich, USA Ch 1984) 16 ♗e2 ♘c7 17 ♗g5 ♗f6 18 ♗xf6 ♘xf6 19 ♗c4! b5 20 axb6 ♖xb6 21 f4 with initiative; Christiansen-Kudrin, USA Ch 1984.

f) 14...♖ac8!? 15 ♕d2 (in Litinskaya-Madl, Thessaloniki OL 1988, the game equalized after 15 ♘a4 c4 16 ♖c1 h5! 17 h3 ♘h7 18 ♕d2 ♕f6 =) 15...h5 16 h3 c4 17 ♘a4 ♘e5 18 ♗xe5 ♕xe5 19 ♘b6 c3! = Wagner-Tolnai, Balatonbereny 1988.

g) 14...♖ab8:

g1) After 15 ♕d2 Black usually replies 15...♖fc8 (White has a small advantage after 15...♘e8 16 ♗e2 ♘c7 17 ♗g5! f6 {17...♗f6!?} 18 ♗e3 b5 19 axb6 ♖xb6 20 ♖a2 ♖fb8 21 ♕c2 Gaprindashvili-Armas, Berlin 1988, but 15...h5!? deserves attention) 16 ♗e2 ♘e8 (16...h5 is not bad here either, for example 17 ♗g5 ♕f8 18 h3 ♘e8 19 f4 ♗d4+ 20 ♔h1 ♘ef6 21 ♖a4 ♖e8 with mutual chances; Pavlović-S.Kovačević, Yugoslav Ch 1991) 17 ♗g5 (Black has no problems in the event of 17 ♗g4 b5 18 axb6 ♖xb6 19 e5 dxe5 20 ♗xd7 ♕xd7 21 ♗xe5 ♗xe5 22 ♖xe5 ♘d6 with equality; Naumkin-Nun, Namestovo 1987) 17...♕f8 18 g3 ♘c7 19 ♗e3 b5 = Šahović-Cebalo, Yugoslavia 1986.

g2) 15 ♘a4:

g21) White keeps his initiative after 15...♘e8 16 ♖b1 ♘c7 17 b4 cxb4 18 ♖xb4 ♘b5 19 ♕d2 ♖fc8 20 ♗g4 Browne-Cebalo, Taxco IZ 1985.

g22) White's advantage is tangible after 15...♖fe8 16 ♕d2 ♘e5 17 ♗xe5! ♕xe5 18 ♘b6 ♕e7 19 e5! Browne-Kudrin, USA Ch 1984.

g23) As usual 15...h5!? deserves attention, e.g. 16 h3 ♘e5 17 ♘b6 (17 ♗xe5!?) 17...♘fd7 18 ♘xd7 ♘xd7 = Teo-Kindermann, Dubai OL 1986.

g24) 15...♘e5 16 ♗xe5 ♕xe5 17 ♖b1 ♘d7 18 b4 ♕d4 with equality; Browne-D.Gurevich, USA Ch 1985.

h) 14...♖fe8 *(D)*:

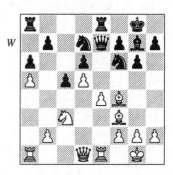

h1) 15 h3 h5 16 ♖b1 (16 ♗g5 ♕f8 17 ♕d2 ♔h7 18 ♗d1 b5 19 axb6 ♘xb6 20 ♗c2 ♘fd7 21 ♖a2 ♖eb8 22 ♕e2 ♕h8!? = Portisch-Tolnai, Hungarian Ch 1991; the black queen occupies a somewhat extravagant, but reasonable position) 16...♘h7 17 ♕d2 ♕f6 18 ♘a4 g5 19 ♗g3 ♕g6 with an interesting game; Piket-Spraggett, Oviedo rpd 1992.

h2) 15 ♕d2 and now:

h21) 15...♖ac8 16 ♗e2!? (interesting possibilities appear for Black in the event of 16 ♘a4 h5 17 ♖ac1 ♘h7 18 h3 ♕f6 19 ♖c4 {19 b3?! g5!? 20 ♗e3 ♕g6 = Paulsen-Foisor, Berlin 1987} 19...g5 20 ♗h2 ♕g6

21 ♗d1! ♗d4 22 ♗c2 ♘e5 Browne-Foisor, New York 1988) 16...♕f8 17 ♖a4 h6 18 ♗e3 ♖c7 19 f3 Gavrikov-Foisor, Nîmes 1991, and White has a small but stable advantage.

h22) 15...h5!? 16 h3 (Black need not fear the variation 16 ♘a4 ♘e5 17 ♘b6 ♖ad8 18 ♗g5 ♘ed7!? 19 ♘c4 ♘e5 Browne-Stefansson, New York 1988) 16...♘h7!? 17 ♖a3 ♕f6! 18 ♘a4 g5 19 ♗h2 ♕g6 20 ♗d1! ♗d4 21 ♗c2 ♘e5 with mutual chances; Hjartarson-Suba, Manila OL 1992.

15   ♘a4!?

Interesting complications occurred in Gligorić-Psakhis, Sarajevo 1986: 15 g3 ♖ab8 (15...♘e8!?) 16 ♘a4 ♘e8 (White is well prepared for 16...b5, viz. 17 axb6 ♘xb6 18 e5! with initiative) 17 ♖c1 ♕d8! (again 17...b5? 18 axb6 ♘xb6 19 ♘xc5! g5 20 ♘xa6 doesn't work; 17...♘c7? is also bad due to 18 ♘xc5! ♘xc5 19 ♖xc5 dxc5 20 d6 with a decisive advantage) 18 ♕d2 (18 ♗d2 ♗d4! ∞) 18...b5 19 axb6 ♘xb6 20 ♘xc5!? dxc5 21 ♗xb8 ♕xb8 22 ♖xc5 ♘d6 and the position which arises is not easy to evaluate.

White also has nothing after 15 e5 dxe5 16 d6 ♕e6 17 ♗xb7 ♖a7 (or 17...♖ab8 18 ♗xa6 with a minimal advantage) 18 ♗f3 ♖b8! 19 ♕d2 (19 ♗e3?! is weaker: 19...♗f8! 20 ♖e2 ♗xd6 21 ♖d2 ♗f8 ∓ Tukmakov-Psakhis, Sochi 1987) 19...♗f8 20 ♖ad1 ♕xd6 21 ♕xd6 ♗xd6 22 ♖xd6 exf4 with an unclear game, Tukmakov.

15   ...   ♘h7 *(D)*

Also possible: 15...♘e8 16 ♖c1 ♕d8!? (or 16...g5 17 ♗d2 g4 18 ♗e2 ♕xe4 19 ♗xa6 ♕xd5 20 ♗b5 ♘ef6 21 ♗c3 Magerramov-Moiseev, USSR 1986, and White has sufficient compensation for the pawn) 17 ♗d2 ♗d4 18 b4 ♕f6 ∞ Moiseev.

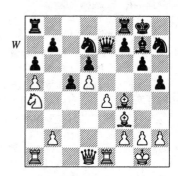

16   ♗d2   ♘g5
17   g3   ♘xf3+

with an equal position; Beliavsky-Psakhis, USSR Ch (Minsk) 1987.

In the majority of variations Black experiences no difficulties, and this explains the popularity of 10...♗g4.

17 Classical: 9 0-0 ♖e8 10 ♕c2 (A76)

1 d4 ♘f6 2 c4 c5 3 d5 e6 4 ♘c3 exd5 5 cxd5 d6 6 e4 g6 7 ♘f3 ♗g7 8 ♗e2 0-0 9 0-0 ♖e8

10 ♕c2 *(D)*

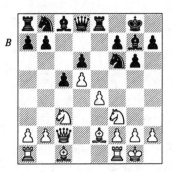

10 ♘d2!? (A77) is significantly stronger than the text move, which has practically fallen out of use recently, as achieving equality after it does not create huge problems for Black.

10 ... ♘a6!?

Probably the strongest move, as it forces White to avoid using this variation.

a) White has a better game after 10...b6?! 11 ♖e1 ♘a6 12 ♗b5 ♖e7 13 ♗f4.

b) 10...a6 11 a4 ♘bd7 is quite possible, for example 12 ♗f4 ♕e7 13 ♘d2 (13 ♖fe1!? h6 14 h3 g5 15 ♗d2 ♘e5 16 ♘xe5 ♕xe5 17 ♖ab1

b6 18 b4 with a minimal advantage; Azmaiparashvili-Sideif Zade, Dnepropetrovsk 1980) 13...♘e5 14 h3 ♘h5 (14...h6 15 ♖ad1 g5 is weaker because of the response 16 ♗xe5! ♕xe5 17 ♘c4 ♕e7 18 e5 dxe5 19 d6 ♕d8 20 a5 ± Makogonov–Sideif-Zade, Baku 1975) 15 ♗h2 f5 16 ♖ae1 ♕h4 17 f4 ♘g4 18 ♘f3 ♗d4+ 19 ♘xd4 cxd4 ∞ Kapengut.

c) 10...♗g4 11 ♖e1 a6 12 a4 ♘bd7 13 ♗f4 ♕c7 14 a5 ♗xf3!? 15 ♗xf3 ♖e7 also deserves attention.

11 ♖e1

Others:

a) Black is completely in order after 11 ♗g5 h6 (or 11...♘c7 12 ♘d2 ♖b8 13 a4 b6 14 ♘c4 ♗a6 ∞) 12 ♗h4 ♘b4 13 ♕b1 g5 14 ♗g3 ♘h5 (here the combination analogous to Tal's famous one does not work: 14...♘xe4? 15 ♘xe4 ♗f5 16 ♘fd2 ♘xd5 because of 17 ♗b5! ♖e7 18 ♘f6+ winning for White) 15 a3 ♘xg3 16 fxg3 ♗a6 17 ♘d2 ♘c7 18 ♘c4 ♖f8 19 ♔h1 b5!? = (Kapengut).

b) After 11 a3 Black has several ways to get a reasonable game:

b1) 11...♗g4 arouses interest: 12 ♗f4 c4!? (12...♘h5?! 13 ♗g5 f6 14 ♗d2 f5 15 h3 fxe4 16 hxg4 exf3 17 ♗xf3 ♘f6 18 g5 ± Hort-Ničevski, Skopje 1968 is poor, but Ničevski's

suggestion is interesting:12...♕e7!?
13 ♗b5 ♗xf3 14 ♗xe8 ♗xe4 15
♘xe4 ♕xe4 16 ♕xe4 ♘xe4 17 ♗a4
c4 18 ♗c2 ♘ac5 with excellent compensation) 13 ♗xc4 ♗xf3 14 gxf3
♘h5 15 ♗g3 ♗e5 again with a good
game for the pawn; Reshevsky-Ni-
čevski, Skopje 1976.

b2) 11...♘c7 12 ♖e1 (Black has
no problems in the event of 12 ♘d2
a6 13 a4 ♖b8 14 a5 ♗d7 15 ♘c4
♘b5 16 ♘xb5 ♗xb5 = Vuković-
Matulović, Yugoslavia 1960, or 12
♖d1?! ♗g4 13 ♗g5 h6 14 ♗h4 g5
15 ♗g3 ♘h5 16 h3 ♘xg3 17 fxg3
♗d7 18 a4 ♕e7 19 ♗d3 ♘a6 ∓
Klasup-Tal, Riga 1959) 12...b5!?
(12...♖b8 13 ♗f4 b5 14 b4 ♘xe4!?
15 ♘xe4 ♗f5 16 ♘fd2 ♘xd5 17
♗xd6 ♗xa1 18 ♖xa1 ♕xd6 19
♘xd6 ♗xc2 20 ♘xe8 ♖xe8 21
♗xb5 ♖d8 22 ♘f1 cxb4 23 axb4
♘xb4 24 ♖xa7 and the mutual destruction has led to a dead drawn position; Veksler-Shestoperov, Omsk
1973) 13 ♗xb5 ♘xb5 14 ♘xb5
♘xd5 15 ♖d1 ♗a6 16 ♘xd6 ♕xd6
17 ♖xd5 ♕e7 Boleslavsky, with excellent play for the pawn.

c) After 11 ♗f4 (D):

c1) 11...♘h5 12 ♗g5 f6 13 ♗e3
f5 14 ♗g5 ♘f6 15 ♗b5 ♗d7 16
♗xd7 ♕xd7 17 exf5 gxf5 18 ♗xf6
♗xf6 19 ♘e2 ♘b4 20 ♕d2 ±,
Gliksman-Janošević, Sarajevo 1969.

c2) 11...♗g4 deserves attention,
e.g. 12 h3 ♗xf3 13 ♗xf3 ♕b6 14 b3
(after 14 a3 c4! 15 ♘a4 ♕c7 16 ♘c3
♕d7 17 ♗e2 ♖ac8, as in Donner-
Nunn, Anglo-Dutch match 1977, the
initiative passes to Black) 14...♘d7

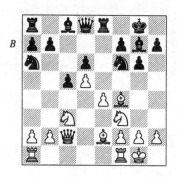

15 a3 ♖ac8! 16 ♖ac1 ♘b4 17 ♕d2
♘a6 =.

c3) 11...♘b4 is possible. After 12
♕b1 Black may reply:

c31) 12...♗g4!? 13 a3 ♘a6 14
♖e1 c4!? 15 ♗xc4 (15 h3? ♗xf3 16
♗xf3 ♘c5 17 ♖e2 ♘b3 ∓) 15...♗xf3
16 gxf3 ♘h5 17 ♗g3 ♗e5 18 ♗b5
♖f8 with sufficient compensation.

c32) 12...♘h5 13 ♗g5 f6 14 ♗e3
(Black should not fear 14 ♗h4 ♘f4
15 ♗c4 ♗g4 16 ♘d2 ♕c8 17 ♗g3
♗h6, or 14 ♗d2 f5 15 ♘g5 f4! 16
♘e6 {16 ♗xh5? ♕xg5} 16...♗xe6
17 dxe6 ♗e5 18 ♘d5 ♘c6 with an
interesting game) 14...f5 15 a3 (15
♗b5?! fxe4 16 ♖xe8 exf3 17 ♗b5
fxg2 18 ♖d1 ♗f5 ∓ Čirić, or 15 ♗g5
♘f6 16 ♗b5 ♗d7 {16...fxe4!? 17
♘xe4 ♗f5} 17 exf5 ♗xb5 18 ♘xb5
♕d7 = Cvetković-Minić, Yugoslavia
1972) 15...fxe4 (15...f4?! 16 ♗xc5!?
♘xd5 17 ♘xd5 dxc5 18 ♖d1 ±
R.Marić) 16 ♘g5 (or 16 ♘xe4 ♗f5;
16 axb4 exf3 17 ♗xf3 cxb4 =)
16...♘d3 17 ♗xh5 (17 ♘gxe4 ♘xb2!
18 ♖a2 ♗f5 ∓ Čirić) 17...gxh5 18
♘cxe4 (capturing with the other
knight changes things a little: 18
♘gxe4 c4 19 ♕d1 {19 ♗g5?! ♕b6

20 ♘f6+ ♗xf6 21 ♗xf6 ♖f8 ∓ Portisch} 19...♗f5 with an edge for Black) 18...c4! 19 ♕d1 (or 19 ♕c2?! h6 20 ♕xc4 ♘e5 21 ♕c2 hxg5 22 ♘xg5 ♕f6 23 ♕h7+ ♔f8 24 ♕xh5 ♕g6 ∓ Ree-Tringov, Titovo Užice 1967) 19...♗g4 20 ♕d2 h6 21 ♘e6 ♗xe6 22 dxe6 ♖xe6 with a more promising position for Black, Tatai-Bouaziz, Siegen OL 1970.

11 ...   ♗g4

Others:

a) 11...♘b4 12 ♕b3 (for 12 ♕b1 ♗g4 13 ♗f4 see note 'a' to Black's 12th) 12...♗g4 13 ♗g5 (13 a3 is not dangerous: 13...♗xf3 14 gxf3 ♘a6 15 ♕xb7 ♘c7 16 ♗g5 h6 17 ♗h4 g5 18 ♗g3 ♘h5 with standard compensation for the pawn) 13...h6 14 ♗h4 g5 15 ♗g3 ♗xf3 16 ♗xf3 ♘d3!? 17 ♖e3 ♘e5 18 ♗xe5 ♖xe5 19 ♕xb7 ♖b8 20 ♕xa7 ♖xb2 21 h3 ±.

b) 11...♘c7 12 ♗f4 (12 ♗f1?! ♗g4 =) 12...♘h5 13 ♗g5 f6 14 ♗h4 ♘f4 15 ♗c4 ♕d7!? (15...a6 16 a4 g5 17 ♗g3 ♘g6 18 a5 ± Portisch-Janošević, Skopje 1968) 16 ♗g3 ♘h5! 17 a4 ♘xg3 18 hxg3 a6 19 a5 ♖b8 leads to equality, Kapengut.

12 ♗f4 (D)

Black is fine after 12 a3 c4! 13 ♗e3 ♖c8 14 ♖ad1 ♘c5, whilst 12 ♗g5 h6 13 ♗h4 ♗xf3 14 ♗xf3 c4! 15 ♗e2 ♖c8 gives him the initiative; Kluger-Matulović, Sombor 1968.

12 ...   c4!

An excellent move, freeing Black from all his problems. Other moves are less convincing:

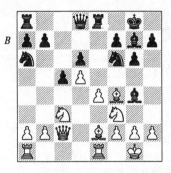

a) 12...♘b4 13 ♕b1 ♘h5 14 ♗g5 ♗f6 (or 14...f6 15 ♗d2! f5 16 h3 fxe4 17 hxg4 exf3 18 ♗xf3 ♖xe1+ 19 ♕xe1 ♘f6 20 g5 ± Filip-Janošević, Wijk aan Zee 1970) 15 ♗e3 c4 16 a3 ♗xf3 17 axb4 ♗xe2 18 ♖xe2 a6 19 g4! ♘g7 20 ♕c2 ± Nemet-Doda, Štip 1978.

b) 12...♘h5 13 ♗g5 ♗f6 14 ♗e3 (14 ♗d2?! c4! 15 ♗xc4 ♗xf3 16 gxf3 ♗e5 ∓ Bukić) 14...c4 (in the game Nemet-Rogulj, Yugoslavia 1979, Black obtained a bad position after 14...♘b4 15 ♕d2 c4?! 16 ♗xc4 ♗xf3 17 gxf3 ♘a6 18 ♘e2! ±) 15 ♘d2! ♗xe2 16 ♖xe2 ♘b4 17 ♕b1 ±.

13 ♗xc4   ♗xf3
14 gxf3   ♘h5
15 ♗g3   ♗e5
16 ♗f1

Or 16 ♗xa6 bxa6 17 ♘e2 ♕f6 18 f4 ♘xf4 19 ♘xf4 ♗xf4 with an unclear position; Nemet-Gobet, Biel 1983.

16 ...   ♕f6

Nemet-Rogulj, Karlovac 1979. Black has excellent compensation for the pawn.

18 Classical with 9 0-0 ♖e8 10 ♘d2 (A77)

1 d4 ♘f6 2 c4 c5 3 d5 e6 4 ♘c3 exd5 5 cxd5 d6 6 e4 g6 7 ♘f3 ♗g7 8 ♗e2 0-0 9 0-0 ♖e8 10 ♘d2 *(D)*

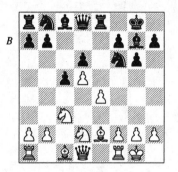

We have ascertained that 10 ♕c2 is not dangerous for Black. He is presented with much greater difficulties after the natural move 10 ♘d2, which is the subject of the final three chapters of this book. White prepares now to defend the e4-pawn permanently by moving the pawn to f3. The knight is already prepared to move to c4, and it is far more difficult in this variation for Black to create counterplay.

10 ... ♘bd7 *(D)*

10...♘a6 is considered under sections A78 and A79.

The passive 10...♗d7?! allows White seizes the initiative without problems, for example 11 a4 ♘a6 12

f3 ♘b4 (12...♘h5!?) 13 ♘c4 ♕c7 14 ♗f4 ♗f8 15 g4! ± Polugaevsky-Wedberg, Haninge 1988.

Black plays 10...b6 (or 10...a6 11 a4 b6 – see 'c31') noticeably more often:

a) 11 f4!? is not bad: 11...♗a6 12 a4 ♗xe2 13 ♕xe2 a6 14 ♘c4 ♖a7 15 ♕f3 with a small advantage.

b) 11 f3 ♘h5!? (11...♗a6 12 ♗xa6 ♘xa6 13 ♘c4 ♕d7 14 a4 ♘c7 15 ♗f4 ♗f8 16 g4 ±) 12 ♘c4 ♗d4+ 13 ♔h1 ♗a6 14 g4 ♘g7 15 ♗f4 ♗xc4 16 ♗xc4 a6 17 a4 g5! ∞ Tatai-Mariotti, Rome 1977.

c) 11 a4 with three options for Black:

c1) 11...♘a6 does not lead to equality: 12 f3 ♘b4 13 ♘c4 ♗a6 (13...a6 14 ♗f4 ♗f8 15 g4! ±) 14 ♘b5!? ♗xb5 15 axb5 ♘h5 16 g4! Lalić-Delmont, Belfort 1989.

c2) 11...♗a6 12 ♗b5!? (12 ♗xa6 ♘xa6 13 f3 is not bad either, but 13 ♖e1 ♘d7 14 a5?! ♘e5 15 axb6 ♕xb6 = Schmidt-Romanishin, Indonesia 1983, is less convincing) 12...♗xb5 13 axb5 ♘bd7 14 ♕c2 ±.

c3) 11...a6:

c31) 12 f4!? leads to an interesting game with possibilities for both sides, e.g. 12...♖a7 (12...♘bd7 13 ♗f3 ♖b8 14 ♘c4 ♕c7 15 ♕b3 ±) 13

♗f3 ♖ae7 14 ♘c4 (if 14 ♖e1 then 14...b5!? is possible: 15 axb5 axb5 16 ♘xb5 ♗a6 17 ♘c3 ♗d3 with compensation) 14...♘xe4!? 15 ♘xe4 ♖xe4 16 ♗xe4 ♖xe4 17 ♕b3 ♗g4 18 ♗e3 ♗e2 19 ♕c2 ♖xc4 20 ♕xe2 ♖e4, Kapengut, with reasonable compensation for the exchange.

c32) 12 ♕c2 ♘bd7 13 f4!? (after 13 ♘c4 ♘e5 14 ♘xe5 ♖xe5 15 ♗f4 ♖e8 16 h3 ♖a7 17 ♖ae1 ♖ae7 the position is equal, whilst 13 ♖a3 is examined via the move-order 10...♘bd7 11 a4 a6 12 ♖a3 b6 13 ♕c2) 13...♖b8 14 ♔h1 (accuracy is demanded of White: 14 ♖b1?! c4! 15 ♔h1 {15 ♗xc4 b5 16 axb5 axb5 17 ♘xb5 ♖xb5 18 ♗xb5 ♕b6+} 15...b5 16 axb5 axb5 and Black is already better) 14...♕c7 15 ♗c4!? ♘g4 16 ♕d3 ♗d4 17 ♘d1 and White's position is preferable.

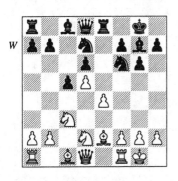

Now we shall focus on:
A) 11 ♕c2
B) 11 h3
C) 11 a4

Other ideas:
a) 11 f4!? transposes to A69.

b) 11 ♔h1 ♘e5 12 f4 (12 h3 g5 is equal) 12...♘eg4 13 ♖f3 (13 ♘c4? ♘xe4! and not 14 ♗xg4? ♗xg4 15 ♕xg4 because of 15...♘f2+ and Black wins) 13...♘h5 14 ♕e1 f5, Zaltsman-Lobron, New York 1983, and Black has the initiative.

c) 11 f3 a6 12 a4 (12 ♘c4 ♘b6 13 ♘e3 ♘h5!? 14 f4 ♗xc3!? 15 bxc3 ♘f6 is not dangerous for Black, Gligorić) and now:

c1) 12...♕c7 deserves attention, for example 13 ♕b3 (13 ♘c4 ♘b6 14 ♘a3 ♗d7 15 ♕b3 ♘xa4!? 16 ♘xa4 b5 17 ♘c3 b4 =) 13...♘e5 14 a5 ♖b8 15 ♘d1 ♘h5 = Tukmakov-Tal, USSR Ch (Moscow) 1969.

c2) 12...♘e5 13 ♔h1 (Black has an easy game after 13 ♕c2 ♘h5! 14 f4 ♘g4 15 ♘f3 f5! 16 exf5 ♗xf5 17 ♗d3 ♗xd3 18 ♕xd3 c4 19 ♕c2 b5! ∓ Peev-Mi.Tseitlin, Pamporovo 1977, or 13 ♘c4 ♘xc4 14 ♗xc4 ♘d7 15 a5 ♘e5 16 ♗e2 b5 17 axb6 ♕xb6 = Cuellar-G.Garcia, Bogota 1979) 13...♖b8 14 ♘c4 (Black also should not fear 14 ♖a3 ♗d7 15 ♖b3 ♕c7 16 ♘c4 ♘xc4 17 ♗xc4 I.Farago-Velimirović, Banja Luka 1981, as now he could continue 17...♗xa4!? 18 ♘xa4 b5 19 ♗e2 bxa4 20 ♖xb8 ♕xb8 21 ♕xa4 ♘xd5! =) 14...♘xc4 15 ♗xc4 ♘d7 16 ♗e3 f5 17 ♕d2 ♘e5 18 ♗e2 ♘f7 = J.Benjamin-Nunn, England 1979.

d) 11 ♖e1 ♘e5 12 ♘f1 (for 12 a4 see 11 a4 ♘e5) 12...a6 13 a4 h5 14 h3 (14 f4 ♘eg4) 14...♖b8 15 ♕c2 ♘h7 16 f4 ♘d7 17 ♘e3 ♕h4 was unclear in Bouaziz-Plaskett, Bahrain 1990.

A) 11 ♕c2 ♘e5!? (D)

Black also has reasonable counter-chances after other continuations:

a) 11...♘b6!? can give Black interesting play:

a1) 12 a4 ♘fxd5! 13 exd5 ♗xc3 14 bxc3 (14 ♗b5?! ♗xd2 15 ♗xe8 ♗xc1 16 ♗xf7+ ♔xf7 17 ♕xc1 ♘xd5 ∓) 14...♖xe2 15 c4 ♕f6!? 16 ♗b2 ♗f517 ♕b3 ♕e7 18 ♕c3 f6 is unclear.

a2) 12 ♖e1 ♘g4! 13 ♘f1 f5 ∞.

a3) 12 ♕b3!? ♗g4 13 ♗b5 ♗d7 14 a4 ♖b8 15 ♗e2 a6 16 ♖e1 ♕c7 was unclear in Dydyshko-Kopionkin, Katowice 1992.

a4) 12 ♗b5 ♗d7 13 a4 ♗xb5 14 ♘xb5 (14 axb5!?) 14...a6 15 ♘c3 ♘fd7 16 a5 ♘c8, as in Polugaevsky-Mecking, Lucerne Ct 1977, is equal.

b) 11...a6 12 ♘c4 (for 12 a4!? see 11 a4 a6) 12...♘b6 13 ♘e3 ♖b8 14 a4 ♕e7 15 f3 ♘fd7 16 ♖e1 ♘a8 17 a5 ♘c7 = Goldin-Arbakov, Moscow 1981.

c) 11...♘h5 (an interesting idea, which became fashionable after Spassky-Fischer, Reykjavik Wch (3) 1972) 12 ♗xh5 gxh5 and now:

c1) 13 b3 ♘e5 14 ♗b2 ♗d7 15 ♖ae1 ♕h4 16 ♘d1 (16 ♖e3!? deserves attention, but 16 f4?! is no good because of 16...♘g4 17 ♘f3 ♗d4+ 18 ♔h1 ♘f2+ 19 ♖xf2 ♕xf2 20 ♕b1!? {20 ♕c1?! ♗h3! 21 ♖g1 ♔f8 ∓ Polugaevsky-Nunn, Skara Echt 1980} 20...♗f5 21 ♖f1 ♗xe4 22 ♘xe4 ♕xb2 23 ♕d3 with a small advantage to Black) 16...♕f4 17 ♗c1 (17 g3?? ♕xd2 −+ loses, and

17 ♘e3 b5! 18 a4 a6 19 f3 ♘d3! 20 ♕xd3 ♗xb2 favours Black; Rajna-Flesch, Pecs 1980) 17...♗h6 18 ♘b2 ♔h8! 19 f3 (19 ♘dc4? ♘f3+! −+) 19...♖g8, Kapengut, and Black has a very active game.

c2) 13 ♘c4 ♘e5 14 ♘e3 (14 ♘xe5 ♗xe5 15 f4 ♗d4+ 16 ♔h1 ♗d7 ∞) and Black faces an important decision:

c21) White gains some advantage after 14...♕h4 15 ♘e2!? (15 ♗d2?! ♘g4 16 ♘xg4 hxg4 17 ♗f4?! ♕f6 18 g3?! {18 ♗g3!?} 18...♗d7 19 a4 b6 ∓ Spassky-Fischer, Reykjavik Wch (3) 1972) 15...♘g4 16 ♘xg4 hxg4 17 ♘g3 ♗e5 18 ♗d2 ±.

c22) 14...♘g4!? has not been seen since in practice, and deserves attention.

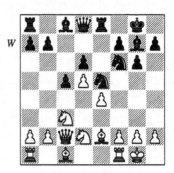

12 b3

12 a4!? is probably stronger, and will be examined under 11 a4 ♘e5 12 ♕c2. On the other hand, 12 f4 is weak: 12...♘eg4 13 ♘f3 ♘h5 14 h3 ♘h6 15 ♔h2 f5 16 e5 dxe5 17 fxe5 ♘g4+! 18 hxg4 fxg4 19 ♗g5 ♗xe5+ with an advantage to Black.

12 ...   ♘fg4!?

White's chances are better after 12...♕e7 13 ♗b2 ♗d7 14 ℤae1 g5 15 ♗b5 ②h5 16 ♗xd7 ♕xd7 17 ②d1 ± Ftačnik-Tisdall, Århus 1983, but 12...g5!?, which is standard in such positions, deserves attention, for example 13 ♗b2 ②g6 14 ℤae1 ②f4 15 ♗b5 ℤf8 16 a4 a6 17 ♗c4 ②g4 18 ②e2!? ②e5 = Lein-Plaskett, Hastings 1982.

13	h3	②h6
14	f4	

14 ♗b2 is met by 14...f5.

14	...	②eg4!
15	②f3	

And not 15 hxg4? ♗d4+ 16 ♔f2 ♕h4.

15	...	♕a5
16	♗d2	

The complications after 16 e5 ♗f5 17 ♕d2 (17 ♗d3 ♗xd3 18 ♕xd3 dxe5! 19 hxg4 e4) 17...dxe5 18 hxg4 exf4 19 ♗b2 ②xg4, as in Panczyk-Kindermann, Polanica Zdroj 1984, favour Black.

16	...	②e3
17	♗xe3	♕xc3
18	♕xc3	♗xc3
19	ℤac1	♗b2
20	ℤc2	ℤxe4
21	♗xc5	dxc5
22	ℤxb2	ℤxf4

and Black has a wonderful game.

B) 11 h3!?

White plans to answer the knight move to e5 by playing f4.

11	...	g5

For 11...a6 12 a4, see line C11.

12	②c4	

Or 12 a4 ②e5 13 ②f3 ②xf3+ (13...g4 also deserves attention: 14 ②xe5 ℤxe5 15 ♗f4 ℤe8 with an unclear game; Toth-Kindermann, Biel 1986) 14 ♗xf3 and now:

a) 14...②d7?! is weak: 15 ♗g4! ②e5 16 ♗xc8 ℤxc8 17 ♕h5 ± Henley-Grünfeld, Lone Pine 1981.

b) 14...②e5 15 ♗e2 ②xe4 16 f4 ②xc3 17 bxc3 gxf4 18 ♗xf4 ℤe8 (White also has the initiative in the event of 18...♕h4?! 19 ♗d3 ♗d7 20 ♕f3 ℤf8 21 ♗xe5 ♗xe5 22 ℤab1 Van der Sterren-Grünfeld, Amsterdam 1982) 19 ♗d3 f5 20 ♕h5 ℤf8 21 ℤae1 c4!? 22 ♗xc4 ♗d7 23 ♗g5 ± McCambridge-Fedorowicz, New York 1984.

c) 14...h5 15 ℤb1 (Beliavsky-Gavrikov, USSR 1978) and after 15...②d7!? the game is unclear.

12	...	②xe4
13	②xe4	ℤxe4
14	♗d3	

Black also has reasonable chances to equalize after 14 ②xd6 ℤd4 15 ♕c2 ℤxd5!? (White has a small advantage after 15...②b6 16 ②xc8 ℤxc8 17 ♗e3 ℤb4 {17...ℤxd5 18 ♗f3 ℤd7? 19 ♗g4} 18 ♗g4! ℤxb2 {or 18...ℤc7 19 ℤad1 ♗d4 20 b3 ②xd5 21 ♗d2 ℤb6 22 ♗a5 Podgaets-Zheliandinov, USSR 1977} 19 ♕c1 ℤc7 20 ♗xg5 ♕xd5 21 ℤd1 ♗d4 22 ♗e3 ②c4 23 ♗xd4 cxd4 24 ♗f3 Lahav-Psakhis, Tel Aviv 1990) 16 ②xc8 ②e5 17 ♕b3 ℤxc8 18 ♕xb7 ℤc7 19 ♕b3 ②d3 ∞ Kapengut.

14	...	ℤh4

The exchange sacrifice 14...ℤd4

15 ♗e3 ‖xc4 16 ♗xc4 ♗xb2 is insufficient: 17 ‖b1 ♗g7 18 f4! ♕e7 19 ♕d3 Raičević-Dizdarević, Yugoslavia tt 1989.

15   ♘xd6   ♘e5
16   ♘f5

The game Langeweg-Psakhis, Sarajevo 1981, ended unexpectedly quickly: 16 ♘xc8? ‖d4 17 ♕e2 ‖xd3 18 f4 gxf4 −+.

16   ...   ♘xd3!

Much stronger than 16...♗xf5 17 ♗xf5 ♕f6 18 ♕c2 g4 19 hxg4 ♘xg4 20 ♗f4 ♘e5 21 ♗g3 ‖h5 22 ♗h3 ♘f3+ 23 gxf3 ‖xh3 24 ♔g2 ‖h5 25 ‖h1 ± Rumiantsev-Peshina, Vilnius 1979.

17   ♕xd3

Black need not fear 17 ♘xh4?! ♕xd5 18 ♘f3 h6, with compensation.

17   ...   c4
18   ♕g3

18 ♕c2 is met by 18...♗xf5 19 ♕xf5 ‖d4.

18	**...**	**♗xf5**
19	**♗xg5**	**‖g4!**
20	**hxg4**	**♕xg5**
21	**gxf5**	**♕xg3**
22	**fxg3**	**♗xb2**

The chances are roughly even.

C) 11 a4 *(D)*

The most popular move; White secures the c4-square in anticipation of the knight's arrival there, and prepares active play on the queenside.

Black has investigated two moves intensively, both in theory and in practice:

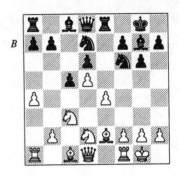

C1) 11...a6
C2) 11...♘e5

First we should investigate the possibilities after 11...g5:

a) It is not easy for White to find an advantage after 12 h3 h6 13 f4 gxf4 14 ‖xf4 ♘e5 15 ‖a3 ♘g6 16 ‖f1 b6 17 ♗b5 ‖e7 18 ♕f3 a6 19 ♗e2 ‖b8, Magerramov-Kasparov, Baku 1979.

b) 12 ♘c4!? ♘xe4 13 ♘xe4 ‖xe4 14 ♘xd6 (14 ♗d3 ‖h4!? 15 g3 ‖d4 16 ♗e3 ‖xc4! 17 ♗xc4 ♗xb2 18 ‖b1 ♗g7 19 f4 gxf4 20 ♗xf4 ♕f6! 21 ♔h1 b6 22 ♕h5 ♕d4 gives Black the initiative; I.Farago-Suba, Belgrade 1984) 14...‖d4 15 ♕c2! (a stronger move than 15 ♕b3?! ♘b6 16 a5 ♘xd5 17 ♘xc8 ‖xc8 18 ♕xb7 ‖c7 19 ♕b3 c4 20 ♕g3 h6 ∓ Bonchev-Mi.Tseitlin, Pamporovo 1977) 15...‖xd5!? (15...♘b6 16 ♘xc8 ‖xc8 17 ♗e3 ‖b4 18 a5 ♘xd5 19 ‖ad1 ♗d4 20 ♗c4 Hernandez-Stoica, Polanica Zdroj 1983, favours White) 16 ♘xc8 ♘e5 with an unclear game.

c) 12 ‖e1!? ♘f8 13 ♗b5 ‖e7 14 a5!? (Black has a good game in the event of 14 ♘f3 g4 15 ♘h4 a6 16 ♗c4 ♕e8 17 ♕d3 ♘h5!? 18 ♗g5 ♖e5 19 f4 ♖xg5 20 fxg5 ♘f4 Tukmakov-Suba, Las Palmas IZ 1982, but 14 ♘f1 arouses interest, for example 14...a6 15 ♗d3 h6 16 ♘e3 ♘g6 17 ♘c4 ♘g4 18 ♗e2!? ♘4e5 19 ♘xe5 ♗xe5 20 ♗g4 ± Pinter) 14...a6 15 ♗d3 h6 16 ♘c4 ♘g6 17 ♘a4! ♖b8 18 ♘ab6 ♖e8 19 ♗d2 with a small advantage; Pinter-Suba, Warsaw Z 1987.

C1) 11 ...   a6

There are now three main lines:

C11) 12 h3
C12) 12 ♖a3
C13) 12 ♕c2

Other moves deserve attention too:

a) 12 f4 transposes to A69.

b) 12 a5 b5 13 axb6 ♘xb6 14 f3 (14 ♖a3 c4!? 15 ♖e1 ♕c7 16 ♕c2 ♗d7 17 ♘f1 ♗b5 = Panno-Ljubojević, San Paulo 1979) 14...♘h5 15 f4 ♘f6 16 ♗f3 ♖b8 17 ♘b3 ♘c4! 18 ♖a4 (18 ♗e2 ♘g4!) 18...♘b6 = Matveeva-Prudnikova, USSR 1991.

c) 12 ♖e1 and now:

c1) White is slightly better after 12...b6 13 f4 ♖b8 14 ♗c4!? ♘h5 15 ♘f3 Zlotnik-Sulipa, Groningen 1991.

c2) 12...♖b8 13 a5 ♘e5 14 ♘f1 h5 15 f3!? ♘fd7 16 ♘e3 ±.

c3) 12...♕c7 deserves attention: 13 h3 (13 ♕c2 ♖b8 14 ♘c4 ♘b6 15 ♘e3 ♗d7 16 ♗d2 ♘c8 17 a5 ♘a7 = Grooten-Short, Lugano 1983) and now 13...♖b8!? gives an unclear game, but not 13...g5?! 14 ♘c4 h6

because of 15 f4! ♘xe4 16 ♗d3 ♗d4+ 17 ♔h2 ♗xc3 18 bxc3 ♘df6 19 fxg5 hxg5 20 ♕f3 ± Hübner-Garcia Padron, Las Palmas 1986.

c4) 12...♘e5:

c41) Black is fine in the event of 13 ♘f1 ♖b8!? 14 f4 ♘ed7 15 ♘d2 (15 ♗c4 is met by 15...b5 16 axb5 axb5 17 ♗xb5 ♘xe4!, but it would be interesting to try 15 a5!?) 15...c4! 16 e5 (16 ♗xc4 ♘c5) 16...dxe5 17 ♘xc4 b5 18 axb5 axb5 19 ♘xe5 b4 20 ♘a4 ♘xe5 21 fxe5 ♖xd5 Van der Sterren-Chandler, Amsterdam 1983.

c42) 13 ♕c2 ♖b8 14 a5 g5!? is no problem for Black.

c43) The thoughtless 13 f4?! allows Black to gain a big advantage: 13...♘eg4 14 ♗f3 h5 15 ♘c4 ♘xe4! 16 ♖xe4 (16 ♘xe4 ♗d4+ 17 ♗e3 ♘xe3 18 ♘xe3 ♗f5 ∓) 16...♗d4+ 17 ♖xd4 cxd4 18 ♘e4 ♕h4 19 ♘cxd6 ♕xh2+ 20 ♔f1 ♗f5! Gheorghiu-Liu Wenzhe, Lucerne OL 1982.

c44) 13 h3 g5 14 ♘f1 h6 15 ♘e3 ♘g6 16 ♗d3 ♘e5!? (stronger than 16...♘f4?! 17 ♘c4! ♘xd3 18 ♕xd3 ♘d7 19 f4 ± Ivanchuk-de Firmian, Biel 1989) 17 ♗c2 g4 with an unclear game – Ivanchuk.

C11) 12 h3   g5!?

The most direct. Other ideas:

a) 12...♘f8?! is too passive: 13 ♕c2 ♘6d7 14 b3 ±.

b) White also achieves an advantage after 12...♖b8, provided he advances his a-pawn immediately:

b1) Black has good chances for a favourable result in the event of 13 ♕c2 ♕c7 14 b3 (14 f4 c4! 15 ♗xc4

b5 16 axb5 axb5 17 ♗d3 b4 18 ♘d1
♘c5 Tosić-Pavlović, Vrnjačka Banja
1991, is not unadvantageous for
Black) 14...c4!? 15 bxc4 b5 16 axb5
axb5 17 ♖a2 (Black already has an
advantage after 17 ♖b1?! b4 18 ♘d1
♘c5 19 ♗f3 ♗d7 Radojčić-Velimi-
rović, Yugoslavia 1982) 17...bxc4
(but not 17...b4 18 ♘b5 ♕b6 19
♕b1! ♘c5 20 ♕xb4 ± Radojčić-
Velimirović, Yugoslavia 1982) 18
♘xc4 ♘c5 19 e5 (19 f3 ♘h5 with
compensation) 19...♗f5 20 exd6
♕b7 21 ♕d1, Kapengut, with an unclear game.

b2) 13 a5! ♕c7 14 ♖a3! (stronger
than 14 ♕c2 b5 15 axb6 ♘xb6 16
♘b3! c4!? 17 ♘a5 ♗d7 18 ♗e3 ♗b5
19 ♖a2 ♘fd7 =) 14....b5 15 axb6
♖xb6 16 ♕c2 ♘e5 (16...♖b4!?) 17
f4 ♘ed7 18 ♔h1 ♖b4 19 b3! (White
has no reason to hurry with 19
♗xa6 ♗xa6 20 ♖xa6 ♘b6, when
Black has compensation for the
pawn) 19...♘b6 20 ♗b2 ♕e7 21
♖aa1 ♘g4 22 ♗xg4 ♗xg4 23 ♘a2
T.Petrosian-Quinteros, Lone Pine
1976, with an obvious advantage.

c) Black can use a little cunning:
12...♕c7!? 13 ♕c2 and only now
13...♖b8!? with a transposition to
12...♖b8 13 ♕c2 ♕c7 (line 'b1'
above).

13 ♘c4

Or 13 ♕c2 ♘e5 14 ♖a3 (14 ♘c4
♘xc4 15 ♗xc4 ♘h5! 16 ♗d2 ♗e5
=) 14...♖b8 (14...♕e7 is also not bad
e.g. 15 ♘f3 ♘xf3+ 16 ♗xf3 h6 17
♘e2 ♗d7 18 ♘g3 b5 =) 15 ♖e1 g4!?
16 hxg4 ♘fxg4 17 ♘f1 ♕h4 18 ♘d1
♘g6 ∞ Kozlov-Gofshtein, USSR

1978; Black also has no cause for
concern after 13 ♖a3 ♘e5 14 ♘f3
♘xf3+ 15 ♗xf3 h6 16 ♕c2 b6 17
♘e2 ♗d7 18 ♘g3 b5 19 axb5 axb5
20 ♖xa8 ♕xa8 21 b3 c4!? Tisdall-
Arnason, Brighton 1981.

13 ... ♘xe4
14 ♘xe4 ♖xe4
15 ♘xd6

After 15 ♗d3 the manoeuvre we
have already seen – 15...♖h4 16
♘xd6 ♘e5 17 ♘f5 ♘xd3 18 ♕xd3
c4 19 ♕g3 ♗xf5 20 ♗xg5 ♖g4! 21
hxg4 ♕xg5 22 gxf5 ♕xg3 23 fxg3
♗xb2 24 ♖ab1 c3 Bukić-Wedberg,
Bajmok 1980 – leads to equality.

15 ... ♖d4
16 ♕c2 ♘b6!?

Instead 16...♖xd5 17 ♘xc8 ♖xc8
18 ♗f3 ♖d4 19 ♗xb7 ♖b8 20 ♗xa6
Bronstein-Yndesdal, Gausdal 1990
favours White. After the text move
Black has a promising position.

C12) 12 ♖a3!? *(D)*

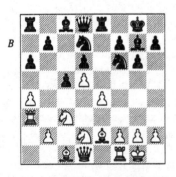

12 ... ♘e5

a) White has a pleasant position
after 12...g5 13 ♘c4 ♘xe4 14 ♘xe4
♖xe4 15 ♘xd6 ♖d4 16 ♕c2.

b) 12...≖b8 13 a5 ≖e7 14 ≤c4 ≤e5!? 15 ≤b6 ≤ed7 is less clear.

c) 12...b6 13 f4 (13 ≖c2 ≖b8 14 ≤c4 ≤e5 15 ≤xe5 ≖xe5 16 h3 ≜e7 17 ≜d3 ≖c7 18 ≖e2 ≜b7! = Burger-Tisdall, Brighton 1981) 13...≖b8 14 ⊈h1 h5 15 ≤c4 ≤xe4 16 ≤xe4 ≖xe4 17 ≤xd6 ≖d4 18 ≖d3 ≤f6 with a level position; A.Petrosian-G.Garcia, Jurmala 1983.

13 ≖e1   ≤h5!?

Black cannot organize himself after 13...g5 14 ≤f1 (14 a5 is less clear: 14...≤g6 15 ≜f1 ≤g4 16 ≜e2 ≤4e5 17 ≖c2, Anikaev-K.Grigorian, Frunze 1979, 17...≤f4! 18 ≜f1 ≖f6 =) and now:

a) 14...g4 has sad consequences: 15 ≜g5! (15 ≖c2 ≖b8 16 a5 b5 17 axb6 ≖xb6 18 ≤g3 h5 = is significantly weaker; Garcia Palermo-Henley, Lone Pine 1977) 15...h6 16 ≜h4 ≜d7 17 ≤g3 ≖c8 18 a5! (an important improvement in comparison with Browne-Nunn, London 1980, in which Black achieved a reasonable game after 18 ≖d2 ⊈h7 19 ≤d1 b5 20 ≤e3 c4) 18...≤g6 19 ≜xf6 ≜xf6 20 ≤a4 ≜d8 21 ≤b6 ≜xb6 22 axb6 ≤e5 23 f4! gxf3 24 gxf3 and White has the advantage; Khasanov-Psakhis, Alma-Ata 1980.

b) 14...h6 15 ≤g3 ≖b8 (or 15...≤g6 16 ≜d2 ≤d7 17 ≤f5 ≤de5 18 ≤xg7 ⊈xg7 19 ≖c2 b6 20 ≤d1!? with the initiative; Pinter-Aquilar, Manila OL 1992) 16 ≖c2 ≖c7 17 a5 ≤g6 18 ≜d2 ≜d7 19 ≤a4 ≤f4 20 ≤b6 with an edge for White; Rago-zin-Baev, USSR 1986.

14 ≤f1

14 ≜xh5 gxh5 15 ≖c2 ≤g4 is not dangerous for Black, and 16 h3?! is bad because of 16...≤xf2!.

14 ...   ≖h4
15 g3   ≖h3!
16 ≤e3   ≤f6 =

Lerner-Agzamov, Tashkent 1980.

C13) 12 ≖c2   ≤e5

Other moves:

a) White has an obvious advantage after 12...≤h5 13 ≜xh5 gxh5 14 ≤d1 ≤e5 15 ≤e3 ≖h4 16 ≖a3 ≜d7 17 f4 ≤g4 18 ≤xg4 hxg4 19 ≤c4 ≖e7 20 e5!.

b) 12...≖b8 13 ≖a3 (13 ≤c4 ≤b6 14 ≤a3 ≜d7 15 ≜g5 h6 =) and now:

b1) 13...b6 14 ⊈h1 ≤e5 15 b3 ≖f8 16 ≜b2 ≤h5 17 ≜xh5 gxh5 18 ≤d1 f5 19 f4 ≤g4 20 ≜xg7 ⊈xg7 21 ≖c3+ leads to a clear advantage for White; Timman-G.Garcia, Rio de Janeiro IZ 1979.

b2) White faces more complex problems after 13...≖c7 14 a5 ≤e5 (White has an easy game in the event of 14...b5 15 axb6 ≖xb6 16 ≤c4 ≖b4 17 ≜f4 ≜f8 18 f3 ≤b6 19 b3 ± Pinter-Gobet, Rome 1986, or 14...≖a8?! 15 b3 b5 16 axb6 ≤xb6 17 ≜b2 ≤h5?! 18 ≜xh5 gxh5 19 ≤d1 ± T.Petrosian-Lutikov, Moscow 1981) 15 f4 ≤eg4 16 ≤c4 ≤h5 17 ⊈h1 (in Toth-Nunn, Geneva 1979, Black seized the initiative after 17 e5 dxe5 18 d6 ≖d8 19 ≤d5 exf4 20 ≤xf4 ≜f5 21 ≖d1 ≤xf4 22 ≜xg4 ≜xg4 23 ≖xg4 ≤e2+ 24 ⊈h1 f5 25 ≖f3 ≖e4) 17...≖d8 18 ≜xg4 ≜xg4 19 e5 ≖h4 20 ≤e4 dxe5 with an unclear game – Nunn.

b3) After 13...♘e5, 14 a5 takes us back to the main line, whilst 14 ♔h1 ♘h5 15 ♗xh5 gxh5 16 ♘e2 h4 17 ♘f4 ♘g6 18 ♘c4 (18 ♘h5 ♗d4 19 ♘f3 ♗g4 20 ♘xd4 cxd4 21 ♘f4 ⩲c8) 18...b5 19 axb5 axb5 20 ♘a5 ♗d7 leads to a complex game with mutual chances.

13   ⩲a3

Others cause Black no problems:

a) Only White will have difficulties after 13 f4?! ♘eg4 14 ♘f3 (14 ♘c4 ♘xe4 15 ♘xe4 ♗d4+ 16 ♘f2 ♗f5 17 ♕d2 ♕h4 18 ♗xg4 ♗xg4) 14...♘h5 (14...♘xe4 is also not bad: 15 ♘xe4 ♗f5 16 ♗d3 c4 17 ♕xc4 ⩲c8 18 ♕b4 ♗xe4 19 ♗xe4 a5 20 ♕xb7 ⩲xe4 with initiative for Black; Baumbach-Maliutin, Corr 1981) 15 h3 f5! 16 e5 dxe5 17 hxg4 fxg4 18 ♘xe5 ♕h4 19 ♘e4 ⩲xe5! 20 fxe5 ♗xe5 21 ⩲d1 ♗h2+ 22 ♔f1 ♘g3+ 23 ♘xg3 ♗xg3 24 ♕xc5 ♗d7 ∓ ECO.

b) Black has a comfortable game after 13 ♔h1 ♘h5!? 14 ♗xh5 gxh5 15 ♘d1 ♕h4 16 ⩲a3 ♗g4 17 f3 ♗d7 Goodman-Kraidman, London 1978.

c) 13 ♘c4 ♘xc4 14 ♗xc4 ♘g4 15 ♗f4 g5! 16 ♗d2 ♗e5 is fine for Black; Diker-Kindermann, Beersheba 1986.

d) 13 b3 ♘fg4!? (or 13...g5 14 ♗b2 ⩲b8 15 ♔h1 ♘g6 16 ⩲ae1 ♘g4 17 g3 h5! with an attack; Dydyshko-Dolmatov, Minsk 1982) 14 ♗b2 (14 h3 ♘h6 15 f4 ♘eg4! 16 ♘f3 ♕a5! 17 ♗d2 ♘e3 18 ♗xe3 ♕xc3 19 ♕xc3 ♗xc3 with an advantage to Black) 14...♕h4 15 ♗xg4 ♘xg4 16 ♘f3 ♕h5 =.

13 ...	♕e7

13...b6!? 14 b3 ⩲a7 15 ♘c4 ⩲ae7 = Kojder-Suba, Bucharest 1980, is not bad either.

14 a5	⩲b8
15 ♘a4	

15 ⩲b3 ♕c7 16 ⩲b6 ♘ed7.

15 ...	♗d7
16 f4	♗xa4
17 ♕xa4	♘ed7
18 ♗f3	c4
19 ♕c2	⩲bc8

Both sides have chances; Bukić-Velimirović, Borovo 1981.

C2)   11   ...   ♘e5 (D)

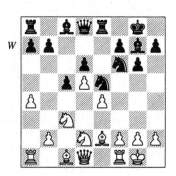

Four moves deserve detailed consideration:

C21) 12 ♘db1?!
C22) 12 ♕c2
C23) 12 ⩲e1
C24) 12 ⩲a3

Other moves can be dealt with briefly:

a) 12 f4?! ♘eg4 13 ⩲f3 ♘h5 14 ♕e1 f5 15 h3 ♗d4+ ∓.

b) 12 ♔h1?! ♘fg4 13 ♘f3 ♘xf3 14 ♗xf3 ♕h4 15 ♗xg4 ♗xg4 16

♕c2 ♗d7 17 f3 f5 with an advantage to Black; Cooper-Lobron, Lucerne OL 1982.

c) 12 ♗b5 ♗d7 13 f4 ♘eg4 14 ♗xd7 ♕xd7 15 ♖e1 ♘h5 16 ♘f3 f5 = Soffer-Wedberg, Berlin 1988.

d) 12 h3 g5 – see 11 h3 g5 12 a4 ♘e5.

C21) 12 ♘db1   h5!

This strong move has forced White to abandon this variation. Black suffered more than a few disasters before he found the correct solution, for example:

a) 12...c4?! 13 ♘a3 a6 14 ♗f4 ♘fd7 (or 14...b5 15 axb5 axb5 16 ♘axb5 ♗a6 17 ♕c2 ♕d7 18 ♗xe5 ♖xe5 19 ♗xc4 ± I.Farago-Danner, Albena 1983) 15 ♗e3 ♕c7 16 ♖c1 ♘c5 17 ♗xc4! ♘xc4 18 ♘xc4 ♗xc3 19 ♗xc5! dxc5 20 ♖xc3 ♖xe4 21 d6 ± Lukacs.

b) 12...a6 13 ♘a3 h6 14 f4 ♘ed7 15 ♕c2 ♖b8 16 ♔h1 ♘f8 17 ♗d2 ± Barlov-Hulak, Budvar 1986.

c) 12...♘ed7 13 ♕c2 ♘b8 14 f3 ♘a6 15 ♗e3 h6 16 ♕d2 g5 17 ♘a3 ± Lukacs-Schneider, Lienz 1984.

d) 12...♘fg4 (more popular, but fails to equalize) 13 h3 ♘h6 14 f4 ♘eg4!? (14...♘d7 15 g4! f5 16 exf5 gxf5 17 g5 ♘f7 18 h4 h6 19 ♔g2! ♘f8 20 ♗d3 Lukacs-Wedberg, Gausdal 1987, with the initiative to White) and now White should play 15 ♕e1!? ± (Lukacs), rather than 15 ♗xg4? ♗xg4 16 hxg4 ♗d4+ 17 ♖f2 ♕h4 18 ♕f3 ♘xg4 19 ♘d1 ♖xe4 –+ or 15 hxg4 ♗d4+ 16 ♖f2 ♕h4 17 ♕e1 ♗xg4 18 ♘d2 ♗e2 19 ♘xe2

♘g4 20 ♘xd4 cxd4! 21 ♘f3 ♕xf2+ 22 ♕xf2 ♘xf2 23 ♔xf2 ♖xe4 = Vera-Andres, Havana 1987.

e) 12...h6 leads to great complications: 13 f4 ♘ed7 14 ♗f3 c4 15 ♘a3 (or 15 ♗e3 ♘xe4 16 ♘xe4 f5 17 ♘xd6 ♖xe3 18 ♘xc4 ♖e8 19 ♘c3 ♘b6 20 ♘e5 {20 ♘a3 ♕d6 and Black has sufficient compensation} 20...♘d7! {20...♗xe5 21 fxe5 ♖xe5 22 ♕d4 ±} 21 ♘xg6!? ♕b6+ 22 ♔h1 ♕xb2 {22...♕xg6? 23 ♗h5} 23 ♘b5 ♕xa1 24 ♕xa1 ♗xa1 25 ♖xa1 ♖e3 ∞ Lukacs) 15...♘c5 16 e5 dxe5 17 fxe5 ♖xe5 18 ♘xc4 ♖f5!? (stronger than 18...♖e8 19 ♗e3 ♘fe4 20 ♘xe4 ♘xe4 21 ♖c1 ♘d6 22 ♗d4 ± Ftačnik) 19 ♗e3 b6 20 g4 ♘xg4 21 ♗xg4 ♖xf1+ 22 ♔xf1 ♗xg4 23 ♕xg4 ♗xc3 24 bxc3 ♕xd5 with an unclear game – Ftačnik.

13 h3   ♘h7
14 f4   ♘g4!
15 ♕e1   ♗d4+!

The cowardly retreat 15...♘h6?! gives White an advantage after 16 f5! gxf5 17 ♗xh5; Traito-Agapov, USSR 1987.

16 ♔h1   ♘gf6
17 ♗f3   ♗f5

Agapov. Even in purely visual terms, Black is the more active.

C22) 12 ♕c2   g5 (D)

Instead:

a) 12...♕e7 (a rare move, which has not yet had enough practical tests) 13 b3 ♗d7 14 ♗b2 a6!? 15 a5 (15 ♖ae1!?) 15...g5 16 ♖fe1 (16 ♖ae1 ♕d8!) 16...g4 Foisor-Kindermann, Warsaw 1983, is unclear.

b) 12...♘fg4 (an interesting manoeuvre, but not sufficient for a playable game) 13 h3 ♘h6 14 f4 ♘d7 (14...♘eg4 15 ♘f3) 15 ♘f3 f5 16 ♘g5 ♘f8 17 e5!? dxe5 18 ♗c4 I.Farago-Lyrberg, Budapest 1993, and White has the initiative.

c) A complex position which is good for White arises after 12...♘h5 13 ♗xh5 gxh5 14 ♘d1! (Black has no problems in the event of 14 f4 ♘g4 15 ♘f3 f5! 16 e5 dxe5 17 fxe5 ♘xe5 18 ♗f4 ♘g6 19 ♗g5 ♕d6) and now:

c1) 14...b6 15 ♖a3! (15 ♘e3 ♗a6 16 ♘ec4 ♘xc4 17 ♘xc4 ♗xc4 18 ♕xc4 ♗d4 = is weaker) 15...♗a6 (White has a dangerous attack after 15...f5 16 exf5 ♗a6 17 ♘e4! ♗xf1 18 ♔xf1 ♘f7 19 ♖g3 ♔h8 20 f6 ♗f8 21 ♗d2) 16 ♖h3 (a standard exchange sacrifice; 16 ♘e3 ♗xf1 17 ♘dxf1 ♔h8 18 ♘f5 h4 19 ♗f4 is also sufficient for a plus) 16...♗xf1 17 ♘xf1 T.Petrosian-Rashkovsky, USSR Ch (Moscow) 1986; Black has no counterplay and the disintegration of his kingside pawn structure means that he cannot count on a pleasant result.

c2) 14...♕h4 15 ♖a3 (Black's problems are significantly eased by 15 ♘e3 ♘g4 16 ♘xg4 hxg4 17 ♘c4 g3 18 fxg3 ♕xe4 19 ♕xe4 ♖xe4 20 ♘xd6 ♗d4+ 21 ♔h1 ♖e2 22 ♘xf7 ♗d7 with compensation) 15...♗d7 16 h3!? (an interesting idea appeared in Yailian-Oll, USSR 1986: 16 ♖g3!? ♔h8 17 b3! ♗h6 18 ♗b2 f6, and now 19 ♘c4!? deserved attention, e.g. 19...♘xc4 20 bxc4 ♗f4 21

♘c3 ♗xg3 22 fxg3 with a strong attack for the exchange) 16...b5 17 axb5 ♗xb5 18 ♖e1 f5 19 ♘e3 (19 exf5 ♗d3 20 ♖xd3 ♘xd3 21 ♖xe8+ ♖xe8 22 ♕xd3 ♖e1+ 23 ♘f1 ♕d4! =) 19...f4 (nor can Black sort himself out after 19...fxe4 20 ♘f5 ♗d3 21 ♕d1 ♕f6 22 ♘xg7 ♔xg7 23 ♘xe4 ♗xe4 24 ♖xe4) 20 ♘f5 with an obvious advantage to White; Dlugy-Wedberg, New York 1988.

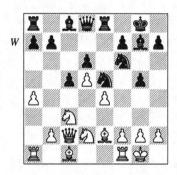

13   ♘c4

Other moves:

a) 13 ♖a3!? transposes to 12 ♖a3 g5 13 ♕c2.

b) 13 ♘f3 ♘xf3+ 14 ♗xf3 ♘d7 (the renowned game Gligorić-Fischer, Palma de Mallorca IZ 1970, continued 14...h6 15 ♗d2 a6 16 ♗e2 ♕e7 17 ♖ae1 ♕e5 18 ♔h1 ♕d4 and now White could have played 19 f4!? g4 20 e5 ♘xd5 21 ♘xd5 ♕xd5 22 ♗c4 with the initiative) 15 ♗g4 ♘e5 16 ♗xc8 ♖xc8 17 ♘e2 c4 =.

c) 13 ♘d1!? ♘g6 (more than a few difficulties await Black after 13...♘fg4 14 ♖a3 ♘g6 15 ♘c4 ♘4e5 16 ♘de3 ♘f4 17 ♘xe5 ♘xe2+ 18 ♕xe2 ♗xe5 19 ♘c4 ± Nesis-Mertel,

Corr 1988, or 13...g4 14 ♘e3 ♘h5 15 f4! gxf3 16 ♘xf3 ♘f4 17 ♘xe5 ♗xe5 18 ♘g4 ±) 14 ♘e3 a6 (or 14...♔h8 15 ♖b1 ♘f4 16 ♗b5 ♖g8 17 b4 a6 18 ♗d3 cxb4 19 ♖xb4 ± Littke-Arduman, Philadelphia 1992) 15 ♖e1 g4 16 ♖b1 ♕e7 17 b4 ±.

d) 13 b3 g4 (it is quite likely that the pawn is better off staying put, and that Black should instead continue 13...♕e7 14 ♗b2 ♖b8 15 ♖ae1 ♗d7 16 ♗b5 ♘h5 ±) 14 ♗b2 ♘h5 (14...♕e7 also favours White: 15 ♖ae1 ♘h5 16 g3!? ♗d7 17 ♘d1 ♕g5 18 f4! gxf3 19 ♘xf3 ♘xf3+ 20 ♗xf3 ♘f4 21 ♗c1! ♘h3+ 22 ♔h1 ♕g6 23 ♕e2 ± Gligorić-Grünfeld, Skara Echt 1980) 15 g3 (it is best not to allow the knight on to f4; 15 ♘c4 ♘xc4 16 ♗xc4 ♘f4 17 ♘d1 ♗e5 18 ♗xe5 ♖xe5 19 ♘e3 ♕e7 =) 15...♖f8 (the overly optimistic 15...f5 leads to a bad position after 16 exf5 ♕g5 17 ♘ce4! ♕xf5 18 f4! gxf3 19 ♗xf3 ♕g6 20 ♗xh5 ♕xh5 21 ♘xd6) 16 ♖ae1 f5 17 f4 gxf3 18 ♘xf3 ♘g4 19 ♗d3 and White has the initiative.

13   ...   ♘xc4
14 ♗xc4   ♘g4 *(D)*

It's not so easy for White to gain an advantage after 14...♘h5, for example 15 ♘e2 (Black has no problems in the event of 15 ♖a3 ♗e5 16 ♘e2 ♕f6 17 ♔h1, F.Portisch-Danner, Reggio Emilia 1979, 17...♔h8!? 18 g3 ♖g8 =, or 15 g3 ♗h3 16 ♖e1 ♗e5 17 ♕d1 ♘g7 = Flear-Plaskett, Lewisham 1983) 15...♕e7 16 f3 ♗e5 17 g3 g4! 18 ♖a3 gxf3 19 ♖axf3 f6 20 ♗b5 ♖f8 Schmidt-Stoica, Bagneux 1982, but after 21 b3!? White's

position is nevertheless more promising.

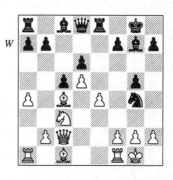

15   ♘e2   ♕e7!?

White has a dangerous attack after 15...a6 16 ♖a3 ♕e7 17 ♖g3 h6 (17...♕xe4 18 ♗d3 ♕xd5 19 ♗xh7+ ♔h8 20 ♘c3 ±) 18 f4! ♕xe4 19 ♗d3 ♕b4 20 fxg5 hxg5 21 ♗xg5.

15...♕f6 deserves attention, for example 16 ♘g3 ♕g6 17 ♗e2 and now rather than the inferior 17...♗e5 18 ♗xg4 ♗xg4 19 f4 gxf4 20 ♗xf4 ± Nickoloff-Hulak, New York 1989, 17...♗d4!? gives chances for both sides.

16   ♘g3

Black need not fear 16 ♗b5 ♕xe4 17 ♕xe4 ♖xe4 18 f3 ♖e2! 19 ♗xe2 ♗d4+ 20 ♔h1 ♘f2+ 21 ♖xf2 ♗xf2 22 ♗xg5 ♗d4 =, and 16 f3 ♘e5 17 ♗b5 ♖f8 18 ♘g3 a6 19 ♗e2 ♘g6 ∞ Orso-Sapi, Hungarian Ch 1977.

16   ...   ♗d4
17 h3   ♕e5
18 ♖a3   ♘f6
19 ♖f3

Foisor-Suba, Romania 1984. According to Foisor's analysis, Black should have continued 19...♘xe4!?

20 ♘xe4 ♕xe4 21 ♗d3 ♕xd5 22 ♗xh7+ ♔g7 23 ♖g3 g4 24 hxg4 ♕e5 25 ♗e3, when White's advantage is not so large.

This analysis creates the impression that 12 ♕c2 presents Black with awkward problems, which he has yet to solve completely.

C23) 12 ♖e1 g5

White is better after 12...♘h5 13 ♘f1 (but not 13 ♘f3 ♗g4 14 ♗d2 ♗xf3 15 ♗xf3 ♘f6 16 ♗e2 c4 17 ♗e3 ♕a5 L.Popov-Wedberg, Berlin 1988, with an excellent game for Black) 13...f5 14 ♗xh5! (14 h3 creates no particular problems for Black: 14...♕h4 15 exf5 ♗xf5 16 ♘b5 {16 g4 ♖f8! 17 gxf5 ♖xf5 18 ♘e3 ♘f4 with an attack} 16...♖f8 Karpeshov-Vaiser, USSR 1983, or 14 exf5 ♗xf5 15 ♗e3 ♘f6 16 ♘g3 ♘fg4 17 ♘xf5 gxf5, Karpeshov-Razuvaev, USSR 1983) 14...gxh5 15 ♘g3 fxe4 16 ♘cxe4 h6 17 h3 ± Fominykh-Moiseev, Hartberg 1991.

Nor does Black equalize after 12...♘fg4 13 h3! (13 ♘f1 f5 14 h3 ♘h6 15 ♘g3 ♖f8!? {15...a6 16 ♗e3 ♕h4 17 ♕d2 ♘ef7 = Seirawan-Ljubojević, Indonesia 1983} 16 exf5 ♘xf5 17 ♘xf5 ♗xf5 18 ♗e3 ♕h4, Skalkotas-Soulu, Kavala Z 1985, is not worse for Black) 13...♘xf2 14 ♔xf2 ♕h4+ 15 ♔g1 ♗xh3 16 ♘f1 ♘g4 17 g3! (17 ♗xg4 ♗xg4 18 ♕d2 ♗d4+ 19 ♖e3 f5 gives Black the initiative; Dydyshko-Agapov, USSR 1983) 17...♕h5 18 ♗xg4 ♗xg4 19 ♕c2 f5 20 ♘h2 fxe4 21 ♘xg4 ♕xg4 22 ♘xe4 ♕f3 Vladimirov-Agapov,

USSR 1984, and now 23 ♖a3! ♗d4+ 24 ♔h2 ♕h5+ 25 ♔g2 ♕xd5 26 ♖f3 would have given a small advantage.

13 ♘f1 h6

White has an advantage after 13...g4 14 ♘g3 a6 15 ♗d2 ♖b8 16 ♕c2 c4 17 b4! Pinter-Lawton, Balatonbereny 1983.

14 ♗b5

14 ♕c2 ♘g6 15 ♘g3 ♘f4 16 ♗d2 a6 17 a5 h5 Karolyi-Vaiser, Frunze 1987, gives chances for both sides.

14	**...**	**♖e7**
15	**♘g3**	**♘g6**
16	**♗d2**	**♘g4**
17	**h3**	**♘4e5**

The position is complicated; Ftačnik-Womacka, Bundesliga 1990.

C24) 12 ♖a3 (D)

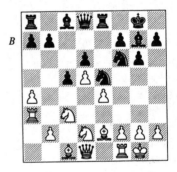

A manoeuvre typical of this variation. The rook takes up an active position and is ready for action on the kingside.

12 ... g5

Practically forced. White has a big advantage after 12...♗d7 13 ♕c2 (13 f4!? is also possible: 13...♘eg4 14 ♘c4 ♘xe4 15 ♗xg4 ♗d4+ 16 ♘e3!

♘f6 17 ♗xd7 ♖xe3 18 ♗xe3 ♗xe3+ 19 ♔h1 ♕xd7 20 ♘b5 with an advantage) 13...♖c8 14 f4 ♘eg4 15 ♘c4 ♕e7 16 h3 b5 (unfortunately 16...♘xe4 17 ♘xe4 ♕xe4 18 ♕xe4 ♖xe4 does not work because of 19 ♗xg4 ♗xg4 20 ♘xd6 ♗d4+ 21 ♔h1 ♗e2 22 ♖e1 ♗f2 23 ♘xe4 ♗xe1 24 ♖e3 Ljubojević, and White is winning) 17 axb5 +− T.Petrosian-Ljubojević, Milan 1975. 12...h5 13 ♕c2 h4 14 f4 ♘eg4 15 ♘c4 ♘h5 16 ♗xg4 ♗xg4 17 ♘b5 ♗f8 18 e5 ± leads to roughly the same result; Lukacs-Vallo, Debrecen Echt 1992.

13 ♕c2 *(D)*

Chances are approximately even after 13 ♘f3 ♘xf3+ 14 ♗xf3 h6 15 h3 ♕e7 16 ♘e2 g4!? 17 hxg4 ♘xg4 18 ♘g3 h5! Rajković-L.Karlsson, Vrnjacka Banja 1981.

Black also has no problems in the event of 13 ♖e1 ♘g6 14 ♗b5 ♖e7!? (14...♖f8 is not bad either: 15 ♘e2 ♘g4 16 ♘f3 h6 17 ♘g3 ♘4e5 18 ♘f5 ♘xf3+ 19 ♕xf3 ♘e5 = G.Garcia-Andres, Cuba 1989, or 15 ♘f1 a6 16 ♗e2 ♘f4 17 ♘g3 ♖e8 18 a5 ♖b8 ∞ A.Petrosian-Gavrikov, Lvov 1984) 15 ♘f1 a6 16 ♗c4 h6 17 ♘g3 ♗d7 18 ♗d2 ♕c7 19 ♕c2 ♖ae8 = Stempin-Suba, Prague Z 1985.

13 ... g4

Otherwise:

a) A difficult defensive task awaits Black after 13...♘fd7 14 ♘d1 ♘f8 15 ♗b5 (15 f3 ♘fg6 16 g3 ♗h3 17 ♖e1 ♖c8 18 ♘f2 ♗d7 19 ♘f1 c4 20 ♗e3 ± is also not bad; T.Petrosian-Rajković, Vršac 1981) 15...♖e7 16 ♘e3 ♘fg6 17 ♘f5 ♖c7 18 ♘xg7

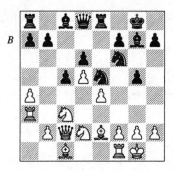

♔xg7 19 ♘c4! h6 20 ♘xe5 ♘xe5 21 f4, Ehlvest-Arduman, Saint John 1988.

b) 13...♘g6 14 ♘c4 ♘f4 15 ♗f3 ♕e7 16 ♗xf4 gxf4 17 ♕d2 ♗h6 18 ♘b5 ♖d8 19 ♖e1 ± Rajković-Hulak, Budvar 1981.

c) White also has the initiative after 13...♔h8 14 ♘c4 ♘fg4 15 ♘xe5 ♘xe5 16 f4 gxf4 17 ♗xf4 a6 18 ♕d2 ♗f6 19 ♔h1 Timoshchenko-Lobron, Moscow GMA 1989.

d) 13...♘fg4 14 ♘d1 ♘g6 15 ♗xg4!? ♗xg4 16 ♘e3 ♗d7 17 ♘dc4 ♕e7 18 f3 again with the initiative; Portisch-Winants, Brussels 1988.

e) 13...a6 is more popular:

e1) Black need not fear 14 ♔h1 b6!? 15 f4 gxf4 16 ♖xf4 ♖b8 17 ♘d1 ♘g6 18 ♖f2 ♕e7 19 ♗f3 b5 ∓ Peshina-T.Petrosian, Vilnius 1978.

e2) 14 a5:

e21) 14...♘fg4!? is interesting.

e22) 14...♖b8 15 ♘d1 (15 ♘c4 ♘xc4 16 ♗xc4 ♘g4 17 ♘e2 ♘e5 18 b3 g4 = Huss-Veličković, Luxembourg 1981) 15...♘g6 (15...b5 16 axb6 ♖xb6 17 ♘e3 ♘g6 18 ♘dc4 ♖b4 19 f3 ♘f4 20 ♗d1 ± Miles-Winants, Brussels 1986) 16 ♘e3 ♕e7

17 f3 ♖f8 18 ♘dc4 ♘e8 19 ♔h1
♗d4 20 ♖b3 ± Miles-S.Kovačević,
Mendrisio 1985.

e23) 14...g4!? 15 ♘d1 ♘h5 16
g3 ♘f6! 17 ♘e3 ♕e7 with good
counterplay; K.Grigorian-Psakhis,
Erevan 1986.

e3) 14 ♘d1 ♘g6 (nor is Black's
happiness complete after 14...♖b8
15 a5 ♘g6 16 ♘e3 ♘f4 17 ♗d1 h5
18 ♘ec4 h4 19 ♖b3 ± Portisch-
Suba, Tunis IZ 1985, or 14...b6 15
♕b1!? ♘g6 16 ♘e3 ♖a7 17 f3 ♖ae7
18 b4 ± Novikov-Savchenko, Kherson 1989) 15 ♘e3 ♘f4 16 ♗d1 b6
17 f3 ♖b8 18 g3 ♘g6 19 ♘dc4 h6 20
♗d2 ♘e5 21 ♘xe5 ♖xe5 22 b4 ±
Spraggett-Barlov, New York 1987.

14   ♘d1!? *(D)*

The knight is going to f5. After
other continuations Black does not
experience any particular difficulties:

a) 14 ♘c4 ♘h5 15 ♘xe5 (or 15
♘e3 ♘f4 16 ♗b5 ♖f8 =) 15...♗xe5
16 g3 ♕f6 (16...♘g7 17 ♗d3 a6 18
♘d1 ♗d7 19 a5 ♗b5 20 ♘e3 ♕d7 =
is not bad either; Vilela-Vera, Havana 1987) 17 ♘d1 ♕g6 = Ionescu-
Stefanov, Romania 1979.

b) 14 b3 ♘h5 15 ♘c4 ♕f6! 16
♘b5 ♘f3+!? (16...♘xc4 17 bxc4
♖e7 18 g3! quickly helps White) 17
♔h1 (it is not easy for White to repulse his opponent's unexpected attack after 17 ♗xf3 gxf3 18 ♘bxd6
♕g6 19 g3 ♗d4 20 ♔h1 ♗h3)
17...♘xh2 18 ♔xh2 ♕h4+ 19 ♔g1 g3
20 fxg3 ♘xg3 Sonntag-Thormann,

Berlin 1988, with huge complications.

c) Black's chances are at least no
worse after 14 ♖e1 ♘h5 15 ♘f1 ♕f6
16 ♘d1 ♕g6 17 ♗b5 ♖f8 18 ♘de3
a6; Zaltsman-Grünfeld, Lone Pine
1981.

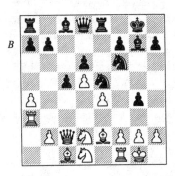

14   ...   ♘g6!?

14...♘h5 is justified after 15 g3
♘f6!?, or 15 ♘e3 ♘f4 16 ♗d1 b6 17
♘dc4 ♘xc4 18 ♘xc4 ♘g6, Antu-
nac-Grünfeld, New York 1981, but in
the event of 15 f4!? gxf3 16 ♘xf3
♘g6!? 17 ♘g5 ♘f6 (Kouatly-Renet,
Marseille 1988) 18 ♖af3! White's
initiative is very strong, all the more
so as 18...♗g4? does not help because of 19 ♖xf6 ♗xe2 20 ♖xg6
♗xf1 21 ♖xg7+ ♔xg7 22 ♔xf1.

15	♘e3	♕e7
16	♗b5	♖f8
17	a5	♖b8
18	♖d1	h6
19	♖b3	♘h7

Averkin-Pigusov, USSR 1985,
with an interesting game in which
both sides have possibilities.

19 The Old Classical: 10 ♘d2 ♘a6 (A78)

1 d4 ♘f6 2 c4 c5 3 d5 e6 4 ♘c3 exd5 5 cxd5 d6 6 e4 g6 7 ♘f3 ♗g7 8 ♗e2 0-0 9 0-0 ♖e8

    10 ♘d2   **♘a6** *(D)*

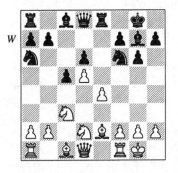

The text move was very popular in the 1960s and 1970s, but nowadays it is far rarer than 10...♘bd7.

    11 ♖e1

The undoubtedly stronger 11 f3 comes under A79. You also see:

a) 11 f4 – see A69.

b) 11 g4 ♘c7 12 f3 ♖b8 13 a4 a6 (13...b6!?) 14 a5 ♗d7 15 ♘c4 ♗b5 with equality.

c) 11 ♗xa6?! bxa6 12 f3 (12 ♖e1 ♘g4!? 13 h3 ♘e5 14 ♕e2 f5!) 12...♗d7 13 a4 ♘h5 14 ♘c4 ♖b8 ∓.

d) 11 a4 ♘b4 12 ♖e1 b6 13 ♖a3 ♕e7 14 ♘c4 ♗a6 15 ♗f1 ♗xc4 16 ♗xc4 a6 = Temirbaev-Ruban, Uzhgorod 1988.

e) 11 ♔h1 ♘c7 12 a4 ♖b8 (after 12...♕e7 13 ♖e1 b6 White can seize the initiative by 14 ♘c4 ♗a6 15 e5 ♘g4 16 ♗xg4 ♗xc4 17 ♗f4 Tukmakov-Schmittdiel, Lugano 1985) 13 f3 a6 14 ♘c4 (Black is also quite comfortable after 14 a5 ♗d7!? {14...b5 15 axb6 ♖xb6 16 ♘c4 ♖b4 17 ♗d2 ± Vilela-Estevez, Havana 1983} 15 ♘c4 ♗b5) 14...b5 15 axb5 axb5 16 ♘a5 ♗d7 17 ♘c6 ♗xc6 18 dxc6 b4 19 ♘a4! (19 ♘d5?! ♘fxd5 20 exd5 ♘xd5! ∓ Shneider-Agzamov, USSR 1982) 19...♘e6 with chances for both sides.

f) 11 ♖b1 and now:

f1) Black can continue his plan with 11...♘c7, for example 12 a4 (12 f3 a6 13 a4 ♖b8 14 a5 ♗d7 15 ♘c4 ♗b5 = Vaidya-Agzamov, Calcutta 1986) 12...b6 (12...a6 13 a5 ♗d7 14 b4 ± Miles-Plaskett, British Ch 1988; White has managed to make use of the position of the rook on b1) 13 ♖e1 ♖b8 is examined in the notes to 11 ♖e1 ♘c7 12 a4 b6.

f2) 11...♗d7 12 ♖e1 ♘c7 (Black achieved a comfortable game in the famous encounter Gligorić-Tal, Belgrade 1959, after 12...♖b8 13 b3 {13 ♗xa6?! bxa6 14 a4 ♖b4 15 ♕c2 ♘g4 gives Black the initiative} 13...b5 14 ♗b2 ♘c7 15 ♕c2 ♕e7 16

♘d1 ♗h6! 17 f3 ♘h5) 13 a4 a6 is equal. Black need not fear 14 b4 cxb4 15 ♖xb4 because of 15...♘g4! 16 ♗xg4 (16 ♖xb7? ♘xf2! 17 ♔xf2 ♗d4+ 18 ♔g3 {18 ♔f1 ♕h4 −+} 18...♕g5+ 19 ♔g4 ♗e5+ with a decisive advantage) 16...♗xc3 =.

11   ...   ♘c7

In my opinion 11...♖b8 is not bad either, but it has yet to be seen in practice, for example:

a) 12 ♕c2 ♘g4! 13 ♘f1 f5 14 ♗xg4 (14 ♘g3?! ♘b4 15 ♕d1 ♘xf2! 16 ♔xf2 ♗d4+ 17 ♔f1 ♕h4 18 ♗f3 b6 with an attack) 14...fxg4 with an excellent game.

b) 12 a4 ♘b4 13 h3 a6 14 a5 ♘d7 15 ♘c4 ♘e5 =.

c) 12 h3 ♘c7 13 a4 a6 14 a5 ♗d7 15 ♗d3 (15 ♗f3 ♗b5) 15...♘b5 16 ♘c4 ♘xc3 17 bxc3 ♗b5 18 ♗g5 h6 = Kapengut.

12   a4 *(D)*

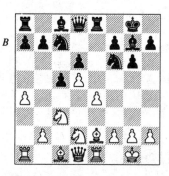

In reply to 12 ♕c2 the simplest route to equality is 12...b5!? 13 ♘xb5 ♘fxd5 = Boleslavsky.

12   ...   a6 *(D)*

12...b6 has also passed tests successfully:

a) 13 ♗f1 ♘g4! 14 ♘f3 f5 15 ♗g5 ♕d7 =.

b) 13 ♕c2 and now:

b1) White preserves a small advantage after 13...♘g4 14 ♗xg4! (14 h3? ♘xf2! 15 ♔xf2 ♕h4+ 16 ♔f1 ♗d4 17 ♘d1 ♕xh3! 18 ♗f3 ♕h2 19 ♘e3 f5 −+ Gurgenidze-Tal, Moscow 1957) 14...♗xg4 15 ♘c4 ♕f6 16 ♗e3 ♗d7 17 ♕d2 ±.

b2) 13...♘a6!? deserves attention, e.g. 14 ♗b5 (14 ♗xa6 ♗xa6 15 f3 ♘h5 =) 14...♘b4 15 ♕d1 ♗d7 16 ♘c4 ♘g4!? 17 ♗f4 ♗d4 18 ♗g3 f5 Lokvenc-Tal, Miskolc 1963, with mutual chances.

b3) 13...♖b8 14 ♘c4 (chances are even in the event of 14 ♘b5 a6 15 ♘xc7 {15 ♘a7 ♗b7 16 ♘c6 ♗xc6 17 dxc6 d5! with initiative for Black} 15...♕xc7 16 ♖a2 b5 Birbrager-Tal, Kharkov 1953) 14...♗a6 15 ♗f4 (or 15 ♖b1 ♗xc4 16 ♗xc4 a6 17 b4 b5 18 axb5 axb5 19 ♗e2 cxb4! 20 ♖xb4 ♘a6 21 ♖xb5 ♖c8 with excellent compensation for the pawn − Hort) 15...♗xc4 16 ♗xc4 and Black has three good continuations:

b31) 16...a6 17 ♕d3 b5 18 axb5 axb5 19 ♘xb5 ♘xb5 20 ♗xb5 ♖xe4 21 ♖xe4 ♘xe4 22 ♕xe4 ♖xb5 23 ♗xd6 ♗xb2 = Kapengut.

b32) 16...♘h5 17 ♗e3 a6 18 ♗e2 ♘f6 (it is, of course, not worth weakening the pawn structure on the kingside: 18...b5?! 19 axb5 axb5 20 ♗xh5 gxh5 21 ♘e2! h4 22 ♘f4 ± Reshevsky-Tarjan, USA Ch 1977) 19 ♖ab1 ♕e7 =.

b33) 16...♘g4!? 17 ♘b5 (or 17 ♗e2 ♘e5 18 ♗d2 a6 with equality)

17...♘xb5 18 ♗xb5 ♗d4 19 ♗g3 h5 and Black has good counterplay.

c) 13 h3!? ♖b8 (13...♘d7 14 ♘c4 ♘e5 15 ♘e3 ±) 14 ♗f1 (Black has no problems after 14 ♗d3 a6 15 ♘c4 b5 16 axb5 axb5 17 ♘a5 ♗d7, but 14 ♗b5!? deserves attention, e.g. 14...♗d7 15 ♘c4 a6 16 ♗xd7 ♕xd7 17 ♗f4 ♗f8 18 e5 ± or 14...♖e7 15 ♗c6 ♗d7 16 ♘f3! ♗xc6 17 dxc6 ♕e8 18 ♗f4 with initiative) 14...a6 15 ♘f3!? b5 (White has a clear advantage after 15...♘d7 16 ♗f4 ♘e5 17 ♘xe5 ♗xe5 18 ♗xe5 ♖xe5 19 f4) 16 e5 (16 ♕c2 b4 17 ♘b1 b3!? Hertneck-Wahls, Berlin 1986, is not unadvantageous for Black) 16...dxe5 17 d6 (17 ♘xe5 ♗b7) 17...♘e6 18 axb5 ♘d4 19 bxa6 ♕xd6 20 a7 (the position is quite unusual; it is rare for a white pawn to have such a brilliant career in the middlegame, but the active position of the black pieces allows him to look to the future with optimism) 20...♖a8 21 ♘xd4 cxd4 22 ♕f3 ♗d7 Semeniuk-Poliuschuk, Corr 1977, with unclear complications.

d) 13 ♖b1:

d1) 13...♗a6 14 ♗xa6 ♘xa6 15 ♘c4 ♘b4 16 ♗g5 with a slight plus for White; Ghitescu-Armas, Romanian Ch 1987.

d2) 13...h5 14 f3 ♘d7 (14...a6 15 b4 ♘g4 {15...cxb4 16 ♖xb4 ♘g4 17 ♘db1 ±} 16 fxg4 ♗xc3 17 bxc5 bxc5 18 gxh5 with a big advantage)

15 ♘c4 ♘e5 (15...♗d4+ 16 ♗e3 ♗xe3+ 17 ♘xe3 f5 18 ♘c4 ±) 16 ♗e3 ♖b8 17 ♕d2 ♘xc4 18 ♗xc4 ± Ftačnik-Suba, New York 1987.

d3) 13...♖b8!? 14 ♘c4 (or 14 h3 a6 15 ♕c2 b5 16 axb5 ♘xb5!? 17 ♘xb5 axb5 = Boudhiba-Wang Zili, Lucerne Wcht 1989) 14...♗a6 with roughly equal chances.

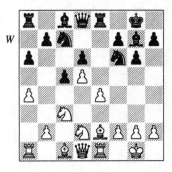

13 ♕c2

Black has no cause for concern after 13 ♗f1 ♘g4!? 14 ♘f3 (14 h3?! allows Black to play a combination we already know: 14...♘xf2 15 ♔xf2 ♗d4+ with an attack) 14...♘e5 =, or 13 f4 ♖b8 14 a5 ♗d7 15 ♗f3 ♗b5, again with equality.

13	...	♖b8
14	a5	♗d7
15	♘c4	♘b5
16	♗g5	♘d4
17	♕d1	♗b5

Black's pieces are harmoniously developed and the chances are approximately even.

20 Old Classical: 10 ♘d2 ♘a6 11 f3 (A79)

1 d4 ♘f6 2 c4 c5 3 d5 e6 4 ♘c3 exd5 5 cxd5 d6 6 e4 g6 7 ♘f3 ♗g7 8 ♗e2 0-0 9 0-0 ♖e8 10 ♘d2 ♘a6

11 f3 *(D)*

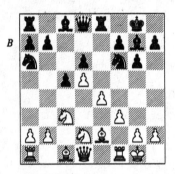

It is far more difficult for Black to achieve winning chances now than in the previous chapter.

11 ...   ♘c7

Others are certainly no more promising:

a) 11...♘h5?! 12 ♘c4 f5 13 g4!? fxg4 14 fxg4 ♘f6 15 e5 dxe5 16 ♗g5 h6 17 ♗xf6 ♗xf6 18 ♘e4 with a big advantage to White.

b) 11...♖b8 12 a4 ♘b4 13 ♘c4 a6 14 a5 ♘h5?! 15 g4! ♘f6 16 ♗f4 with a distinct advantage for White.

c) White also has a preferable position in the event of 11...♘d7:

c1) 12 ♘b5 ♘b6 13 a4 ♕e7 14 ♘c4 ♘xc4 15 ♗xc4 ♘b8! 16 ♗f4

♖d8 17 ♕d2 a6 18 ♘a3 ♘d7 leads to equality; Birbrager-Tal, Moscow 1966.

c2) 12 ♔h1!? also deserves attention, e.g. 12...♘c7 13 a4 is considered under 11 f3 ♘c7 12 a4 ♘d7 13 ♔h1, whilst 12...f5 13 exf5 gxf5 14 ♘c4 ♘e5 15 ♘xe5 ♗xe5 16 f4 ♗g7 17 ♗h5 ♖e7 18 ♗d2 is not unfavourable for White; Moura-Nederkoorn, Corr 1987.

c3) 12 ♘c4 ♘e5 13 ♘e3 (after 13 ♗f4 ♘xc4 14 ♗xc4 ♘c7 15 ♕d2 a6 16 a4 ♖b8, 17 ♕d3!? gives White a small advantage, whilst 17 a5 b5 18 axb6 ♖xb6 leads to equality, as in Bertok-Tal, Bled 1961) 13...f5 (13...♘c7?! 14 f4 ♘d7 15 e5! dxe5 16 f5 ♘f6 17 d6 ±) 14 exf5 gxf5 15 f4 with a small advantage.

12 a4

Black has a reasonable game in the event of 12 ♔h1 ♕e7!? (or 12...a6 13 a4 ♖b8 14 a5 ♗d7 15 ♘c4 ♗b5 16 ♗g5 ♗xc4 17 ♗xc4 h6 18 ♗e3 b5 19 axb6 ♖xb6 20 ♕d2 ♔h7 21 ♖a2 ♘d7 = Ree-Portisch, Amsterdam 1981) 13 ♘c4 (13 a4 allows Black to play a standard tactical blow: 13...♘fxd5! 14 ♘xd5 ♘xd5 15 ♘c4 ♗d4) 13...b5 14 ♘a5 ♗d7 15 ♘c6 (unclear complications arise after 15 ♘b7 b4 {15...♖ab8 16

♘xc5} 16 ♗f4 ♗c8! 17 ♘xd6 bxc3 Dydyshko-Kapengut, Minsk 1984, and White should have continued 18 ♘xe8!? ♘cxe8 19 bxc3 ♘h5 20 ♗d2 f5 ∞) 15...♗xc6 16 dxc6 a6 with chances for both sides; Dydyshko-Kapengut, Minsk 1982.

12 ... b6

White has a big advantage after 12...♘h5?! 13 ♘c4 ♗d4+ 14 ♔h1 ♕f6 15 ♕d2! ♗d7 16 g4.

12...♘d7 *(D)* deserves attention:

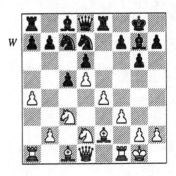

This indicates Black's desire to develop activity on the kingside. Play may continue:

a) Obviously 13 ♘b5?! ♘xb5 14 axb5 ♘b6 15 ♗d3 ♗d7 16 ♖a3 ♕e7 is not dangerous for Black.

b) Nor should Black fear 13 f4:

b1) 13...♗d4+ is weak: 14 ♔h1 ♘f6 15 ♗f3 h5 16 f5! ±.

b2) The active 13...f5!? is interesting, for example 14 exf5!? (14 ♘c4 ♗d4+ 15 ♔h1 ♕f6 16 exf5 gxf5 17 ♖a3 b6 =) 14...gxf5 15 ♘f3 ♘f6 16 ♗d3 ♘g4 17 h3 ♘e3 18 ♗xe3 ♖xe3 19 ♕c2 ♕f6 20 ♖ae1 ♖xe1 21 ♖xe1 ♗d7 = Baburin-de Firmian, Farum Poland 1993.

b3) 13...♘f6 14 ♗f3 b6 (White can only dream about 14...a6?! 15 ♘c4 b5 16 ♘xd6! ♕xd6 17 e5 ♕b6 18 d6) 15 ♘c4 (or 15 ♔h1 ♗a6 16 ♖e1 ♕e7 17 ♘b3 ♖ad8!? {a significant improvement over Beliavsky-Rogulj, Tallinn 1977, where White gained a big advantage after 17...c4? 18 ♘d4 ♘fxd5 19 ♘xd5 ♘xd5 20 ♘c6 ♕e6 21 e5! ±} 18 a5 ♗c4 with counterplay) 15...♗a6 16 ♕b3 (16 ♕d3 ♖b8 17 ♖b1 b5! 18 axb5 ♘xb5 19 ♘xb5 ♗xb5 20 ♗d2 ♘xe4 21 ♗xe4 ♗d4+ 22 ♔h1 ♗xc4 23 ♕xc4 ♖xe4 is not unfavourable for Black; Furman-Tal, Tbilisi 1959) 16...♗xc4 17 ♕xc4 ♖b8 =.

c) 13 ♔h1:

c1) The optimum solution for Black is probably 13...b6, transposing to 12...b6 13 ♔h1 ♘d7, as after the moves that follow, White's advantage is evident.

c2) 13...h5?! 14 f4 ♘f6 15 f5! gxf5 16 ♗xh5 ♖e5 (16...fxe4 17 ♘dxe4! +−) 17 ♘c4 ♖xe4 18 ♘xe4 ♘xe4 19 ♗f3 +−.

c3) 13...f5 14 exf5 gxf5 15 ♘c4 ♘e5 16 ♘xe5!? ♗xe5 17 f4 ♗g7 18 ♗h5 ♖f8 19 ♖f3 ♘e8 20 ♗xe8! ♕xe8 21 ♖g3 ♗d7 22 ♗d2 ±.

c4) 13...♕e7 also helps White: 14 ♘c4 f5 15 ♗f4 ♘e5 16 ♘xe5 ♗xe5 17 ♗xe5 ♕xe5 18 f4 ♕d4 19 e5! (19 ♗f3 b6 20 ♕c2 ♕e3! 21 ♕c1 ♕xc1 22 ♖axc1 ♗a6 =) 19...dxe5 20 d6 ♘e6 21 fxe5 ♗d7 22 ♗b5! ♗xb5 23 ♘xb5 ♕xe5 24 ♖e1 ±.

d) 13 ♘c4 ♘e5 14 ♘e3 (Black has no problems after 14 ♗f4 ♘xc4 15 ♗xc4 a6 16 ♕d3 f5!? =) and now:

d1) 14...b6 deserves attention, e.g. 15 ♖e1 (15 ♔h1!?) 15...♖b8 16 f4 ♘d7 17 ♘c4 ♗d4+! (in the game Kraidman-Fischer, Netanya 1968, Black played the weaker 17...♘f6?! 18 ♗f3 ♗a6 19 ♘a3 ♘d7 20 ♘ab5 ♗xb5 21 axb5 ±) 18 ♔h1 ♘f6 19 ♗f3 ♗a6 with reasonable counterplay.

d2) 14...f5 executes Black's plan:

d21) 15 exf5 gxf5 16 f4 ♘f7 (from h6 the knight will defend the pawn securely; White maintains an edge after 16...♘g6 17 ♔h1 {17 ♗d3 ♕f6 18 ♕c2 ♖f8 19 ♗d2 ♗d7 20 ♖ae1 ♖ae8 21 ♔h1 a6 22 a5 ♘b5 = Spassky-Quinteros, Buenos Aires 1979} 17...♕f6 {or 17...b6 18 ♗d3 ♖f8 19 ♗d2 ♘a6 20 ♕b1! with initiative} 18 ♗d3 ♗d7 19 ♕c2 ♖f8 20 ♗d2 b6 21 ♖f3 ♖ae8 22 ♖af1 ♔h8 23 ♖h3) 17 ♗d3 and now:

d211) 17...♕f6 is probably the weaker option: 18 ♕c2 ♘h6 19 ♖f3 ♗d7 20 ♗d2 ♖e7 21 ♖b1 (Black's has fewer problems after 21 ♘cd1?! ♖ae8 {but not 21...♘e8?! 22 ♖g3 ♕d4 23 ♘f2 ♔h8 24 ♗c3 ♕xf4 25 ♘h3 ♕h4 26 ♖f1 ± Bukić-Tal, Budvar 1967} 22 ♗c3 ♕h4 23 ♖g3 ♕xf4 24 ♘f2 ♔h8 25 ♘h3 ♕h4) 21...♘a6 22 ♗xa6! bxa6 23 h3 ♖ae8 24 ♘e2 ±.

d212) 17...♗d4!? 18 ♖f3 ♕f6 19 ♔h1 ♗d7 20 ♗d2 ♘h6 21 ♕c2 ♖e7 is level. It is quite probable that White could improve his play somewhere, but in any case Black is not short of counterchances.

d22) An innocent transposition of moves had huge consequences in Toth-Matulović, Hungary 1972, after 15 f4 ♘f7 16 exf5 ♘h6! 17 fxg6? (this was the time to stop; 17 ♔h1 ♘xf5 18 ♘xf5 ♗xf5 19 ♗f3 would have led to an even game) 17...♗d4 18 gxh7+ ♔h8 19 ♖f3 ♘g4 20 ♕d3 ♕h4 21 h3 ♘xe3 22 ♖xe3 (22 ♗xe3 ♖xe3 23 ♖xe3 ♕xf4 24 ♘d1 ♖xd5 −+) 22...♕xf4 23 ♘d1 ♘xd5 and Black was winning – a beautiful idea.

After 12...b6, White has two serious options:

A) 13 ♔h1

B) 13 ♘c4

Besides these natural moves, White may try:

a) 13 ♗b5?! ♘xb5 14 axb5 ♘d7 15 ♘c4 ♘e5 16 ♘e3 ♕h4 (or 16...f5!? 17 exf5 ♗xf5 18 ♘xf5 gxf5 19 ♕c2 ♕d7 ∓ Sarosi-Tolnai, Kecskemet 1987) 17 g3 ♕h3 and Black has an excellent game.

b) 13 ♘b5 a6 14 ♘xc7 ♕xc7 15 ♘c4 ♘d7! =.

c) 13 a5?! b5! (refuting White's plan; 13...♖b8 14 axb6 axb6 15 ♘b5 ♘h5 16 ♘xc7 ♕xc7 17 g4 ♘f6 18 ♗b5 ♗d7 19 ♕b3 h5! also gives Black a reasonable game) 14 ♘xb5 ♘fxd5! 15 exd5 (or 15 ♘xc7 ♕xc7 16 ♘c4 d5 17 exd5 ♗d4+ 18 ♔h1 ♘xd5 with an advantage) 15...♗a6 16 ♘c3 ♗xc3 17 ♗xa6 ♗d4+ 18 ♔h1 ♘xa6 ∓.

d) 13 ♕c2 ♖b8 14 ♘c4 ♗a6 15 ♗g5. Now 15...♕d7!? gives Black a reasonable position, but not 15...h6 16 ♗h4 ♕d7?, as now 17 ♘xd6! is possible: 17...♕xd6 18 ♗g3 ♕d7

(18...♖e5 19 f4) 19 d6 ♘e6 20 ♗xa6 +– Yailian-Peshina, Belgorod 1989.

e) 13 ♖b1 ♘h5 (White has a small advantage in the event of 13...♖b8 14 ♘c4 ♗a6 15 ♗g5 ♕d7 16 b4 ♗xc4 17 ♗xc4 a6 18 b5!) 14 ♘c4 f5 15 f4 ♗d4+ 16 ♔h1 ♗a6! with possibilities for both sides.

A) 13 ♔h1

This is the only serious alternative to bringing the knight to c4 immediately.

13 ...   ♖b8

a) 13...♗a6?! 14 ♗xa6 ♘xa6 15 ♘c4 ♘c7 16 ♗f4 ♗f8 17 ♗g5 with a distinct White advantage; T.Petrosian-Hernandez, Banja Luka 1979.

b) 13...h6?! 14 ♘c4 ♗a6 15 ♗e3 ♗xc4 16 ♗xc4 a6 17 ♕d2 ♔h7 18 ♗d3! ♕d7 19 ♖ab1 b5 20 b4 c4 21 ♗c2 ♕e7 22 ♗b6 ♖ab8 23 a5 ♖bc8 24 f4 ± Simić-Kelečević, Pernik 1981.

c) 13...♘h5 14 ♘c4 ♗a6 15 ♗d2 ♕h4 16 ♕e1! ♕e7 17 g4 ♘f6 18 ♕g3 ± Bangiev-Rajna, Budapest 1989.

d) 13...♕d7 14 ♘c4 ♗a6 15 ♗g5 ♗xc4 (or 15...h6 16 ♗d2 ♗xc4 17 ♗xc4 a6 18 ♕e2 ♕e7 19 ♖ae1 ♘d7 20 f4 ±) 16 ♗xc4 a6 17 ♕e2 ♕c8 18 ♗f4 ♗f8 19 ♖ab1, and White has the initiative; Zaltsman-Hulak, New York 1989.

e) 13...♘d7 is more popular: 14 ♘c4 ♘e5 15 ♘e3 ♖b8 (15...f5 16 exf5 gxf5 17 f4 ♘f7 18 ♗d3 ♘h6 19 ♕c2 ♖f8 20 ♗d2 a6 21 ♖f3 ♖b8 22 ♖g3 with initiative for White; Dydyshko-Lukov, Polanica Zdroj 1983)

16 ♗d2 (complications follow 16 f4 ♘d7 17 e5!? dxe5 18 f5 e4 {18...♖f8 19 ♘g4 ♘f6 20 ♗g5 ± Benjamin-Buzbuchi, New York 1985} 19 d6 ♘a6 20 ♘ed5 ♘b4) 16...a6 17 f4 (or 17 ♖b1 b5 18 b4!? c4 {18...cxb4 19 ♖xb4 a5 20 ♖xb5! with compensation} 19 axb5 axb5 20 ♖a1 f5 21 exf5 gxf5 22 f4 ♘f7 ∞ Adorjan) 17...♘d7 18 ♘c4 and the advantage is on White's side after both 18...♘f6 19 ♗f3 h5 20 ♘xd6! ♕xd6 21 e5 ♕d8 22 d6 ♘e6 23 exf6 ♗xf6 24 f5!, and 18...♘f8 19 ♗f3 b5 20 axb5 ♘xb5!? 21 ♘xb5 axb5 22 ♘a5 ♖a8 23 ♘c6 ♖xa1 24 ♕xa1.

14 ♘c4

After other continuations Black has nothing to fear:

a) 14 ♘b3?! a6 15 ♗g5 h6 16 ♗h4 g5 17 ♗f2 ♘h5 18 ♖e1 ♘f4 19 ♗f1 f5 20 ♘c1 b5 ∓ Taimanov-Gheorghiu, Leningrad 1977.

b) 14 ♘b5?! a6 15 ♘a7 ♗b7 16 ♘c4 ♕e7 17 ♗g5 (alternatively, 17 ♘xb6 ♘cxd5!) 17...♘cxd5! 18 exd5 ♕e2 19 ♘xd6 ♕xd1 20 ♖axd1 ♘xd5 21 ♘xe8 ♖xe8 with an advantage to Black.

c) 14 ♘db1 a6 15 ♘a3 ♕e7 16 ♗g5 h6 17 ♗h4 g5 18 ♗f2 ♘d7 19 ♕d2 ♘e5 20 ♖ae1 ♗d7 =.

d) Black has an advantage after 14 ♖b1 a6 15 ♘c4 (15 ♕c2 b5 16 axb5 axb5 17 b4 cxb4 18 ♖xb4 ♘fxd5! 19 exd5 ♗xc3 20 ♕xc3 ♘xd5 21 ♕d4 ♘xb4 22 ♗b2 ♖e5 23 ♕xb4 ♖xe2 24 ♘e4 ♖xb2 ∓ *ECO*) 15...b5 16 axb5 axb5 17 ♘a5 ♗d7 18 ♘c6 ♗xc6 19 dxc6 ♖b6 20 b4 c4.

e) Black can equalize after 14 ♗b5!? ♖f8 (Black's position is too passive after 14...♘xb5 15 axb5 ♕e7 {15...♖b7!? 16 ♘c4 ♖d7} 16 ♘c4 ♖d8 17 ♖e1 ♘e8 18 ♗f4 ♗e5 19 ♕d2 Pinter-Badii, French Cht 1993) 15 ♗c6 a6 16 ♖b1 b5 17 b4 c4 18 ♗b2 ♗d7 = Ogaard-Tisdall, Norway 1987.

14   ...   ♗a6
15   ♗g5

Black has no difficulties after 15 ♖b1 ♗xc4 16 ♗xc4 ♘d7 17 ♕c2 a6 18 b4 b5 Sygulski-Lukov, Polanica Zdroj 1983.

15   ...   h6

It is too soon to exchange on c4: 15...♗xc4?! 16 ♗xc4 a6 17 ♕d3 ♕c8 18 ♗f4 ♗f8 19 ♖ab1 ♘d7 20 b4 cxb4 (20...b5 21 axb5 cxb4 22 ♖xb4 a5 23 ♖bb1 +−) 21 ♖xb4 ♘c5 22 ♕d2 a5 23 ♖bb1 Neverov-Woda, Poznan 1985, with a big advantage to White.

White's position is also more promising in the event of 15...♕d7:

1) After 16 ♖b1?! Black equalizes easily: 16...♗xc4 17 ♗xc4 a6 18 b4 b5 19 ♗d3 (19 axb5 ♘xb5!) 19...c4 20 ♗c2 bxa4 21 ♗xa4 ♘b5 with a balanced position.

2) White has a more pleasant game after 16 ♕d2 ♗xc4 17 ♗xc4 a6 18 ♗d3 b5 19 axb5 axb5 20 b4! c4 21 ♗c2 ♖a8 22 ♖xa8 ♖xa8 23 ♗e3 ♖a3 24 ♘e2 ♕e8 25 ♗d4.

3) 16 b3 ♘h5 17 ♖c1 (17 ♕d2 is insufficient for an advantage: 17...f6 18 ♗h4 f5, and 19 g4? is no good because of 19...fxg4 20 fxg4 ♗xc3 21 ♕xc3 ♖xe4; the same applies to 17

♗d2 ♘f4!? 18 ♗xf4 ♗xc4 19 bxc4 ♗xc3 20 ♖a3 ♗d4 = Burger-Quinteros, New York 1983) 17...f6 (or 17...♗d4 18 g4 ♘g7 19 ♗f4 ♗xc4 20 bxc4 ♖e7 21 ♗d3 ♖be8 22 ♘e2 ♗e5 23 ♗d2 ± Ivanchuk-Manor, Adelaide jr Wch 1988) 18 ♗d2!? (an improvement in comparison with Portisch-Nunn, London 1982, in which Black achieved a good game after 18 ♗e3 f5 19 g4 {19 f4 ♗xc4 20 bxc4 ♘f6} 19...♗xc4 20 bxc4 fxg4 21 fxg4 ♘f6 22 ♗f3 ♕e7 23 ♗g5 h6 24 ♗h4 g5 25 ♗e1 ♖f8) 18...f5 19 exf5 gxf5 20 ♖e1 f4 21 ♗d3 ± Ivanchuk-Wahls, Adelaide jr Wch 1988.

16   ♗e3

Black cannot complain at the outcome of the opening after 16 ♗h4 ♕d7 17 b3 (or 17 ♕d2 ♗xc4 18 ♗xc4 a6 19 ♗d3 b5 20 axb5 axb5 21 ♖a7 b4 22 ♘d1 ♖a8 =) 17...♘h5 18 ♖c1 ♘f4 19 ♗g3 ♘xe2 20 ♘xe2 ♗xc4 21 bxc4 a6 22 ♘c3 b5 =, or 16 ♗d2 ♗xc4 17 ♗xc4 a6 18 ♕e2 ♕c8 19 ♗f4 (19 ♖ab1?! ♘d7 20 b4 cxb4 21 ♖xb4 b5! 22 axb5 ♗xc3! 23 ♗xc3 axb5 ∓) 19...♗f8 20 ♖fd1 ♕b7 with a reasonable game.

16   ...   ♕e7!

Only this strong move, discovered by Kapengut, allows Black to look to the future with optimism; White's position is more promising after the alternatives:

a) 16...♕d7 17 ♕d2 ♗xc4 18 ♗xc4 ♔h7 19 ♖ab1 a6 20 b4 b5 21 ♗d3 c4 22 ♗c2 bxa4!? 23 ♗xa4 ♘b5 24 ♗d4 ± Polugaevsky-Martin, Seville 1987.

b) 16...♗xc4 17 ♗xc4 a6 18 ♕d3 ♕c8 (the pawn sacrifice 18...b5?! does not save Black from difficulties: 19 axb5 axb5 20 ♘xb5 ♘xb5 21 ♗xb5 ♖e7 22 ♗d2! ♖eb7 23 ♖a5 ♘h5 24 b3 ♘f4 25 ♕c4 ± Schmidt-Filipowicz, Poland 1980) 19 ♗f4! ♖d8 20 ♖ab1 ♗f8 21 b4 ♘d7 22 ♕d2 ♔h7 23 ♗e2 ♘e8 24 b5 a5 25 ♗g3 with a big advantage, because Black has absolutely no counterplay; Polugaevsky-Bouaziz, Riga IZ 1979.

17	♕d2	♔h7
18	♖fe1	

Chances are approximately even after 18 e5!? ♗xc4 19 exd6 ♕xd6 20 ♗xc4 ♘d7.

18	...	♘d7
19	♖ab1	

19 f4!?.

19	...	♗xc4
20	♗xc4	a6
21	♗f1	b5
22	axb5	♘xb5
23	♘d1	♖b6 =

Veremeichik-Kapengut, Minsk 1982.

B) 13 ♘c4!? *(D)*

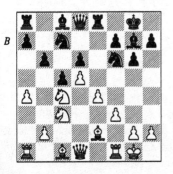

13	...	♗a6
14	♗g5 *(D)*	

This is the only move that lays claim to an advantage.

a) Black has not even the slightest difficulty after 14 ♖a3?! ♕d7 15 ♖b3 ♖ab8 16 ♘b5 ♗xb5 17 axb5 a6!?.

b) 14 ♘e3 ♗xe2 15 ♕xe2 a6 is absolutely OK for Black.

c) 14 ♗f4?! ♘h5! 15 ♗e3 (15 ♗xd6? ♗xc4 16 ♗xc7 ♗xe2) 15...f5 16 ♘d2 f4 17 ♗f2 ♗c8 18 ♘c4 ♖b8 19 ♕c2 a6 =.

d) 14 ♘a3? fails to 14...♘fxd5! 15 ♗xa6 ♘xc3 16 ♕d3 ♘xa4 17 ♗b5 c4! – Janošević.

e) After the move 14 ♗e3, both 14...♗xc4!? 15 ♗xc4 a6 16 ♖e1 (16 ♕d3 ♘d7 17 f4 f5! ∞) 16...♘d7 17 ♗f1 ♖b8 18 ♕c2 b5 19 axb5 axb5 =, and 14...♖b8 15 ♕d2 ♗xc4 16 ♗xc4 a6 17 ♖ab1 (17 ♕d3 b5 18 axb5 axb5 19 ♘xb5 ♘fxd5! 20 ♗xd5 ♘xd5 ∞) 17...♘d7 18 b4 f5 19 ♗g5 ♗f6 20 ♗xf6 ♕xf6 21 exf5 gxf5 22 ♔h1 ♕h4 equalize (Kapengut).

f) Black need not fear 14 ♖b1 ♗xc4 (14...♘h5?! 15 g4 ♘f6 16 ♗f4 ♗xc4 17 ♗xc4 a6 18 ♕d2 h5 19 h3 ♕d7 20 ♕d3 ♖ab8 21 b4 is good for White; Chetverik-Sergienko, Matra 1993) 15 ♗xc4 ♘d7 16 ♘b5 ♘xb5 17 ♗xb5 (17 axb5 f5!? 18 exf5 ♕h4 ∞) 17...♖f8 with equality.

14	...	h6

White has a clear advantage after 14...♗xc4 15 ♗xc4 a6 16 ♕d3, or 14...♖b8?! 15 b3 h6 16 ♗d2.

Black quite often tries 14...♕d7:

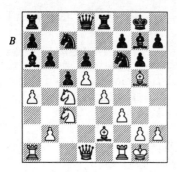

a) 15 ♔h1 is considered under 13 ♔h1 ♕d7.

b) Unclear complications arise after 15 b3 ♘g4 16 ♕d2 ♗d4+ 17 ♔h1 ♘f2+ 18 ♖xf2 ♗xf2 19 ♗f6 ♗d4 20 e5 ♖xe5 (only he with iron nerves can embark upon 20...♗xc3 21 ♕h6 ♘e6 22 ♘xd6 ♕xd6 23 dxe6 {23 exd6 loses beautifully: 23...♗xf6 24 ♗xa6 ♗xa1 25 d7 ♘c7! 26 dxe8♕+ ♖xe8 27 ♕c1 and now 27...♗b2! −+} 23...♕f8 24 exf7+ ♕xf7 25 ♗xa6 ♗xe5 26 ♗c4 ♗xf6 27 ♗xf7+ ♔xf7 ∞ Hug-Anka, Lenk 1991) 21 ♘xe5 (21 ♕h6 ♘e8) 21...♗xe5 (or 21...dxe5!? 22 ♗xa6 ♕f5 23 d6 ♗xc3 24 ♕xc3 ♘d5 25 ♕xe5 ♕xf6 ∞ Huss-Mascariñas, Switzerland 1991) 22 ♗xe5 dxe5 23 ♗xa6 ♘xa6 24 ♕e2 ♘b4 25 ♕xe5 ♖e8 = Karpman-Andrijević, Pancevo 1989.

c) If 15 ♖b1 then 15...h6!? 16 ♗d2 (16 ♗h4?! ♗xc4 17 ♗xc4 ♖ab8 is equal) 16...b5 17 axb5 ♘xb5 18 ♘xb5 ♗xb5 19 ♘e3 a5 equalizes, as does 15...♗xc4 16 ♗xc4 a6 17 b4 b5 18 ♗d3 (18 axb5 axb5 19 ♗d3 ♖a3!? 20 ♘e2 ♖ea8) 18...c4 19 ♗c2 bxa4! (the capture is forced;

otherwise White would play 20 a5 and his hands would be free to play on the kingside) 20 ♗xa4 (20 ♘xa4!?) 20...♘b5 21 ♕d2 (21 ♔h1?! ♕b7 22 ♗xb5 axb5 23 ♗e3 ♘g4! 24 ♗d4 ♘e3! 25 ♗xe3 ♗xc3 Beliavsky-Portisch, Szirak IZ 1987, and the initiative is already firmly in Black's hands) 21...♕b7 22 ♗xb5 axb5 =.

d) 15 ♖e1!? also deserves attention White is not hindering Black's active play on the queenside, and has freed f1 for his bishop in good time: 15...♖ab8 (or 15...h6 16 ♗h4 ♖ab8 17 ♕d2 ♗xc4 18 ♗xc4 g5 19 ♗f2 a6 20 ♗f1 ♘h5 21 ♘d1 ± G.Garcia-Gutierrez, Havana 1988) 16 ♕d2 ♗xc4 17 ♗xc4 a6 18 ♗f1 h5 19 ♔h1 ♖b7 20 e5! with an advantage; Vera-Ionescu, Albena 1989.

e) 15 ♕d2 ♗xc4 (15...♖ab8?! 16 b3 ♘h5 17 g4! ♗d4+ 18 ♔h1 ♘g7 19 ♗e3 ±) 16 ♗xc4 a6 17 ♕d3 ♘h5 (after 17...♖eb8 White begins to play successfully in the centre: 18 f4!? ♘g4 19 e5 dxe5 20 f5 ±; he also has an advantage after 17...h6 18 ♗e3 ♕c8 19 ♗f4! ♗f8 20 ♖fb1 ♕b7 21 b4 cxb4 22 ♖xb4 Birbrager-Tal, USSR 1955) 18 g4 ♗d4+ 19 ♔h1 ♘g7 20 ♖ab1!? with an edge for White; Dlugy-de Firmian, USA Ch 1988.

15 ♗h4

15 ♗d2 (15 ♗f4 ♘h5!) 15...♗xc4 16 ♗xc4 a6 17 ♔h1 ♘d7 18 ♖b1 ♖b8 19 ♕e2 ♕c8!, when 20 b4?! is no good because of 20...b5 21 axb5 cxb4 22 ♖xb4 ♗xc3! 23 ♗xc3 axb5, is quite inoffensive for Black.

15 ♗e3 deserves attention:

a) White has a clear advantage after 15...♖b8 16 ♕d2 (the less traditional 16 ♖e1!? is interesting, for example 16...♕d7 17 ♕d2 ♔h7 18 e5 dxe5 19 d6 ♘a8 20 ♘xe5 ♖xe5 21 ♗xa6 with an advantage; Gaprindashvili-Kapengut, Reggio Emilia 1992) 16...♔h7 17 b3!? ♕e7 18 ♖fe1!? with the initiative.

b) 15...♕e7?! 16 ♕d2 ♔h7 (the line 16...g5 17 h4 gxh4 18 ♗xh6 ♘h5 19 ♗xg7 ♔xg7 20 ♘e3, Chekhov-Psakhis, Lvov 1984, also favours White) 17 ♖ae1 ♘d7 18 ♗f2 ♗xc4 19 ♗xc4 ♘e5 20 ♗e2 ± Dydyshko-Kapengut, Minsk 1982.

c) 15...♕d7 16 ♕d2 ♔h7 17 b3! ♗xc4 18 bxc4 ♘a6 19 ♖ae1 ♘b4 20 ♗d1 ± Novikov-Hernandez, Manzanillo 1987.

d) 15...♘h5!? deserves some attention. In Portisch-Rajna, Hungary 1980, White did not manage to gain an advantage: 16 ♕d2 (16 g4 ♘f6 17 ♗f4 ♗xc4 18 ♗xc4 a6) 16...g5 17 g4 ♘f6 18 ♗f2 ♗xc4 19 ♗xc4 ♘d7 20 ♘d1 ♕f6 21 ♗e2 a6 with an unclear game.

e) 15...♗xc4 16 ♗xc4 a6 17 ♕d2 ♔h7 18 ♖ab1 (18 ♖ae1 ♖b8 19 ♗d3 b5 20 axb5 ♘xb5!? 21 ♘xb5 axb5 =) and Black has a choice:

e1) 18...♖b8 19 b4 (19 ♕d3!? is interesting, and 19...b5?! 20 axb5 axb5 21 ♘xb5 ♘fxd5 22 ♗xd5 ♘xd5 23 ♕xd5 ♖xb5 24 ♕xf7 leads to an advantage for White) 19...b5 and now:

e11) 20 ♗e2 c4 (20...cxb4 21 ♖xb4 a5 simply forces White to sacrifice the exchange for fantastic compensation: 22 ♖xb5! ♘xb5 23 ♗xb5 ♖e7 24 ♘e2) 21 ♗d4 (21 a5 ♖e7 22 ♗d1 ♕h8! 23 ♘e2 ♖f8 24 ♗f4 ♘ce8 25 ♗c2 ♘d7 Lukacs-J.Horvath, Budapest 1987; Black has arranged his pieces successfully and his chances are in no way worse) 21...♖e7 22 a5 ♕h8! 23 ♖bd1 ♘ce8 24 ♖fe1 (24 g3 ♘d7 25 ♗xg7 ♘xg7 26 f4 f5 27 ♗f3 fxe4 28 ♘xe4 ♘f5 was level in Glek-Ivanchuk, USSR 1987) 24...♘d7 25 ♗xg7 ♘xg7 26 f4 f5 Ivanchuk-Manor, Groningen 1986, and Black has a playable game.

e12) 20 axb5 axb5 21 ♗e2 c4 22 ♖a1 ♖a8 23 ♗d4 with a small advantage.

e2) 18...♕d7 19 b4 b5 20 ♗e2 (20 ♗d3? ♘fxd5!; 20 axb5 axb5 21 ♗e2 c4 22 ♗d4 ♕e7 23 ♗d1 ♖a3 24 ♗c2 ♘d7 25 ♖a1 ♖ea8 26 ♖xa3 ♗xd4+ 27 ♕xd4 ♖xa3 28 f4 ♕f6!? = Zaltsman-Dzindzichashvili, Lone Pine 1980) 20...c4 (again 20...cxb4?! 21 ♖xb4 a5 is no good because of 22 ♖xb5 +−) 21 a5 (after 21 ♖be1!? it would be interesting to test 21...a5!?, all the more so as 21...♕e7 22 ♗d4! ♖ab8 23 a5 ♕f8 24 ♗d1 ♕h8 25 f4 ♘d7 26 ♗xg7 ♕xg7 27 ♗c2 is good for White; C.Hansen-Paavilainen, Pohja 1985) with a division:

e21) White has a big advantage after 21...♕e7 22 ♗d4 ♕f8 23 ♗d1! ♘d7 (23...♕h8 24 ♘e2! ±) 24 ♗xg7 ♕xg7 25 ♗c2 ♖e7 26 ♖be1 ♘e8 27 f4 ±.

e22) White also wields the initiative in the event of 21...♖e7 22 ♗d1

(22 ♖be1 ♕e8 23 ♗d4 ♕h8! 24 ♖d1 ♘ce8 25 ♕c2 ♘d7 26 ♗xg7 ♘xg7 27 f4 f5! =) 22...♕e8 23 ♗f4 (23 ♗c2 ♕h8! 24 ♖bd1 ♘g4! 25 ♗d4 ♗xd4+ 26 ♕xd4 ♕xd4+ 27 ♖xd4 ♘e3 28 ♖c1 f5 = Petran-Horvath, Szirak 1985) 23...♖d8 24 g4 ♕h8 25 ♘e2 ♘ce8 26 ♗e3 ♘d7 27 ♘d4 with the initiative; Van der Sterren-Fernandez, Lucerne OL 1982.

e23) 21...♘g8 22 ♗d1!? (or 22 ♗d4 ♗xd4+ 23 ♕xd4 f5 24 ♗d1 ♕g7 =) 22...f5 23 ♗c2 fxe4 24 fxe4 ♗e5 25 ♖f3 ♕g7 26 ♘e2 ♘f6 = Ogaard-Nunn, Gjøvik 1984.

e3) 18...♘d7!? 19 ♔h1 (Black has a good game in the event of 19 b4?! f5! 20 bxc5 bxc5 21 ♔h1 {21 exf5?? ♖xe3} 21...♕f6 22 ♖b7 ♖ec8 23 ♖c1 ♘e5 I.Farago-Toshkov, Albena 1984) 19...♖b8 20 b4 b5 21 axb5 (a standard manoeuvre equalizes for Black after 21 ♗d3 c4 22 ♗c2 bxa4 23 ♗xa4 ♘b5 24 ♗xb5 axb5 25 ♗d4 ♘e5 26 ♖a1 ♘d3 = Farago-Karolyi, Budapest 1985) 21...axb5 22 ♗d3 c4 23 ♗c2 ♖a8 24 f4 Stertenbrink-Karoly, Corr 1985, and now 24...f5!? 25 ♗d4 (25 exf5?! ♗xc3 26 fxg6+ ♔g8 27 ♕xc3 ♘xd5) 25...♗xd4 26 ♕xd4 ♕f6 would have promised Black a reasonable game.

15 ...   ♕d7 (D)

White has the initiative after 15...♗xc4 16 ♗xc4 g5 17 ♗f2 a6 18 ♖e1 ♘d7 19 ♗f1 ♖b8 (19...♘e5 20 ♘e2!? ♘c4 21 ♘g3 ♘xb2 22 ♕c2 b5 23 axb5 axb5 24 ♖xa8 ♕xa8 25 ♘f5 ± Beliavsky-Rogulj, Tallinn 1977) 20 ♖c1.

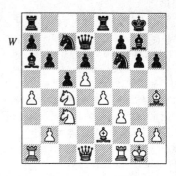

16 ♗f2!?

The unfortunate 16 g4? loses after 16...♘xg4! 17 fxg4 ♗xc3 18 bxc3 ♖xe4 19 h3 ♗xc4 20 ♗xc4 ♖xc4 21 ♕d2 ♖xg4+! −+ I.Farago-Lim, Kikinda 1978.

Black has a good game in the event of 16 ♖b1 ♗xc4!? 17 ♗xc4 a6 and 18 b4 is not very good because of 18...♘g4!, or 16 ♕d2 ♗xc4 17 ♗xc4 a6 18 ♕d3 (18 ♗xf6 ♗xf6 19 ♕xh6 b5 with good compensation for the pawn) 18...♘h5 19 ♖fd1 g5 20 ♗f2 ♘f4 21 ♕f1 ♘g6 ∞ Boleslavsky.

16 ...   ♗xc4

16...♖ab8 does not lead to equality either: 17 ♖e1! ♗xc4 18 ♗xc4 a6 19 ♗f1 ♖ec8 (19...b5? 20 axb5 axb5 21 ♖a7 c4 22 e5!) 20 g3 b5 21 axb5 axb5 22 ♖a7 b4 23 ♘a4 Vera-P.Cramling, Las Palmas 1988, with an advantage.

17	**♗xc4**	**a6**
18	**♕d3**	**♘h5**
19	**g3**	**♖f8**
20	**♔g2**	

G.Garcia-Abreu, Havana 1988. White's position is more active and more promising.

Index of Variations

1 d4 ♘f6 2 c4 c5 3 d5 e6